Chicano School Failure and Success

This new edition of the best-selling and award-winning *Chicano School Failure and Success* has been updated and expanded to provide state-of-the-art coverage of the Chicano school experience. The contributors include experts in the fields of anthropology, psychology, educational history and policy, special education, and child and family studies, reflecting the wide and complex range of issues affecting Chicano students. The book is in five parts:

- *Part I:* A comprehensive review of schooling conditions and outcomes; the educational implications of a rapidly growing Chicano population; segregation, desegregation and integration; issues arising from the high dropout rate of Chicano students.
- *Part II:* Language, public policy and schooling issues for English language learners; the effectiveness of bilingual education in the U.S.A.
- *Part III:* Chicano/Latino ethnography of education; the relationship between Chicano families and schools.
- *Part IV:* Select testing issues that impact on Chicano students; the role of special education in the history of Chicano schooling.
- *Part V:* Analysis of systemic factors contributing to the success or failure of Chicano education; a synthesis of ideas to help promote success.

This is a timely new edition that will be of great interest to academics, researchers, and students in the areas of education, sociology, and anthropology.

Richard R. Valencia is Professor of Educational Psychology at The University of Texas at Austin. He has previously worked at Stanford University and the University of California, Santa Barbara, and has published widely, particularly on the issues of test validity and bias, and Chicano education.

Chicano School Failure and Success

Past, Present, and Future
2nd edition

Richard R. Valencia

London and New York

First edition published 1991 by Falmer Press
2nd edition published 2002 by RoutledgeFalmer
11 New Fetter Lane, London EC4P 4EE

Simultaneously published in the USA and Canada
by RoutledgeFalmer
29 West 35th Street, New York, NY 10001

RoutledgeFalmer is an imprint of the Taylor and Francis Group

© and 2002 Selection and editorial matter, Richard R. Valencia;
individual chapters, the contributors.

Typeset in Galliard by BC Typesetting, Bristol
Printed and bound in Great Britain by
TJ International Ltd, Padstow, Cornwall

British Library Cataloging in Publication Data
A catalogue record for this book is available from the British Library

Library of Congress Cataloging in Publication Data
Chicano school failure and success: past, present and future/[edited by]
Richard R. Valencia.–2nd ed.
    p.   cm.
    "Contributors of this second edition offer updated, comprehensive,
state-of-the-art coverages of their respective chapters"–Introd.
    Includes bibliographical references and index.
    1. Mexican American students.   2. School failure–United States.
    I. Valencia, Richard R.

LC2683.C47   2002
373.1′2913089′68–dc21   2002021959

ISBN 0–415–25773–5 (hbk)
ISBN 0–415–25774–3 (pbk)

This book is dedicated to the memory of my dear mother, Veronica, who taught me how to read and helped put me on the path to acquire knowledge.

Richard R. Valencia

Contents

Tables and figures

Tables

Figures

Contributors

Alfredo J. Artiles is Associate Professor at Vanderbilt University. Dr. Artiles' main affiliation is with Peabody College; he also holds a joint appointment in the Departments of Special Education and Teaching and Learning. His work focuses on the representation of students of color in special education and teacher learning about diversity. Recent work (with R. Rueda, J. Salazar, and I. Higareda) includes "Factors associated with English learner representation in special education: Emerging evidence from urban school districts in California" (in D. Losen and G. Orfield [Eds.], *Minority Issues in Special Education in the Public Schools*, Harvard Publishing Group, in press).

Rubén Donato is Associate Professor and Chair of Educational Foundations, Policy and Practice in the School of Education at the University of Colorado at Boulder. His research focus is on the history of American education and Mexican American educational history. Dr. Donato is the author of *The Other Struggle for Equal Schools: Mexican Americans During the Civil Rights Era* (State University of New York Press, 1997). A recent publication is "Hispano education and the implications of autonomy: Four school systems in Southern Colorado, 1920–1964." *Harvard Educational Review*, 1999, *69*, 117–149.

Douglas E. Foley is Professor of Education and Anthropology at The University of Texas at Austin. His research interests are race and ethnicity in American education, ethnic social movements, and immigration. Dr. Foley is the author of *From Peones to Políticos: Class and Ethnicity in a South Texas Town, 1900–1989* (University of Texas Press, 1989); *Learning Capitalist Culture: Deep in the Heart of Tejas* (University of Pennsylvania Press, 1990); and *The Heartland Chronicles* (University of Pennsylvania Press, 1995). A more recent publication is his co-edited book (with B. Levinson and D. Holland), *The Cultural Production of the Educated Person: Critical Ethnographies of Schooling Practices* (State University of New York Press, 1996).

Eugene E. García is Professor of Education at the University of California, Berkeley. He has published extensively in the area of language teaching and bilingual development. He served as a Senior Officer and Director of the Office of Bilingual Education and Minority Languages Affairs in the U.S. Department of Education from 1993–1995. Dr. García is currently conducting research in the areas of effective schooling for linguistically and culturally diverse student populations. His most recent book is *Hispanic Education in the United States: Raíces y Alas* (Rowen and Littlefield, 2001).

Michael D. Guerrero is Assistant Professor of Curriculum and Instruction at The University of Texas at Austin. His research examines issues such as the academic Spanish language proficiency of bilingual education teachers, Spanish literacy development of children, and language testing. A recent publication is "The unified validity of the Four Skills Exam: Applying Messick's framework." *Language Testing*, 2000, *17*, 397–421.

Ignacio Higareda is a doctoral candidate in Education at the University of Southern California. His research interests focus on sociocultural influences on academic achievement for English language learners. He has worked on research projects involving symbolic representation of objects in hearing and deaf preschoolers' collaborative play, and is investigating the impact of paraeducators' strategies and funds of knowledge during instruction with language minority students.

Martha Menchaca is Professor of Anthropology at The University of Texas at Austin. Her research interests are in the field of historical and legal anthropology. She is the author of *The Mexican Outsiders: A Community History of Marginalization and Discrimination in California* (University of Texas Press, 1995), which won two coveted awards (*CHOICE* "Outstanding Academic Book," 1995; Gustavus Meyers Award, 1996). Dr. Menchaca's most recent book is *Recovering History, Constructing Race: The Indian, Black, and White Roots of Mexican Americans* (University of Texas Press, 2001).

Robert P. Moreno is Associate Professor of Child and Family Studies at Syracuse University. His research examines familial and cultural influences on children's learning and academic achievement among Latinos and low-income families. He is a recent recipient of the National Academy of Education/Spencer Fellowship for his work on effective everyday instruction of Mexican American mothers with their preschool children. A recent publication is "Teaching practices of Mexican American mothers with everyday and school related tasks." *Merrill Palmer Quarterly*, 2000, *15*, 613–631.

Arthur Pearl is Professor Emeritus of Education, University of California, Santa Cruz. His primary research focus is on structural determinants of "disadvantaged/at risk," and implementing democratic education into classroom practices. One of his many publications is "Cultural and accumulated environmental deficit models" (in R.R. Valencia [Ed.], *The Evolution of Deficit Thinking: Educational Thought and Practice*, pp. 132–159, Falmer Press, 1997). Dr. Pearl's most recent book (with T. Knight) is *The Democratic Classroom: Theory to Guide Educational Practice* (Hampton Press, 1999).

Gloria M. Rodríguez is Assistant Professor of Educational Leadership at the California State University, Hayward. In addition to Chicano/Latino education issues, Dr. Rodríguez is also a specialist in school finance with a focus on equity issues. Her current research focuses on local school leaders' conceptualizations of equity in resource allocation in Texas and California. She serves on the Board of Directors for the American Education Finance Association. A recent publication is "Education finance developments in the United States: The influence of 'deficit model' views of low-income children and communities of color on school finance formulas and policy" (in *In Search of a More Equitable and Efficient Education System: The State of the States and Provinces*, pp. 159–163, American Educational Research Association, Fiscal Issues, Policy, and Education Finance Special Interest Group, Monograph, August, 2001).

Robert Rueda is a Professor in the Division of Learning and Instruction at the Rossier School of Education at the University of Southern California. His research focuses on the sociocultural basis of learning and instruction with a focus on academic achievement (especially reading) and the acquisition and uses of literacy with English language learners in at-risk contexts and students with mild learning handicaps. A recent publication (with

A. Arzubiaga and L. Monzo) is "Family matters related to the reading engagement of Latino children." *Journal of Latinos and Education* (in press).

Russell W. Rumberger is Professor, Gevirtz Graduate School of Education at the University of California, Santa Barbara, and Director of the University of California Linguistic Minority Research Institute. His research focuses on the education of disadvantaged students in such areas as school dropouts, student mobility, and school segregation. His research has appeared in such journals as *Economics of Education Review*, *Sociology of Education*, and *American Educational Research Journal*. A recent publication by Dr. Rumberger is "The distribution of dropout and turnover rates among urban and suburban high schools." *Sociology of Education*, 2000, *73*, 39–67.

Jesús Salazar is a doctoral student at the University of Southern Cali fornia School of Education. His research interests include studying early literacy development and identifying effective English language learner programs. He has been working 15 years with the Program Evaluation and Research Branch at the Los Angeles Unified School District (LAUSD). He is responsible for evaluating the achievement outcomes and English proficiency gains of LAUSD's 315,000 English language learners.

Moises F. Salinas is Assistant Professor of Psychology at Central Connecticut State University. His research focuses on the effects of stereotypes on academic performance, and reducing the performance gap between minorities and non-minorities. Dr. Salinas is currently completing a book about education, stereotypes, and affirmative action. A recent publication (with J. Aronson, C.M. Steele, and M.J. Lustina) is "The effect of stereotype threat on the standardized test performance of college students" (in E. Aronson [Ed.], *Readings About the Social Animal* [8th ed.], pp. 415–430, Worth Publishers, 1999).

Bruno J. Villarreal is a doctoral candidate in the Department of Educational Psychology at The University of Texas at Austin. His research interests are on factors that contribute to the successful identification and placement of English language learners in programs for the gifted/talented. He is currently working as a research assistant on a language test development project for bilingual Latino children.

Sofia Villenas is Assistant Professor of Education, Culture and Society at the University of Utah. In working with Latina mothers in North Carolina, her research centers on investigating Latino home and community education within the dynamics of racial/cultural community politics. She is co-editor (with L. Parker and D. Deyhle) of *Race Is . . . Race Isn't: Critical Race Theory and Qualitative Studies in Education* (Westview Press, 1999).

Ann-Marie Wiese is Assistant Professor of Education at the University of California, Santa Cruz. She has published in the area of bilingual education policy, and has most recently completed her dissertation at the University of California, Berkeley, focusing on the local implementation of bilingual education policy in three elementary teachers' classrooms. A recent publication (with E.E. García) is "The bilingual education act: Language minority students and U.S. federal educational policy." *International Journal of Bilingual Education and Bilingualism*, 2001, *4*, 229–248.

Foreword

The United States of America, the most powerful country in the world, with an amazing array of research universities, is experiencing a historic change in its population with the emergence of a group, Chicanos/other Latinos, currently 35.3 million strong based on 2000 U.S. Census data, and growing at a dramatic rate. If this group were a nation unto itself, it would rank 34th among the world's 50 most populous countries. Yet Chicanos/other Latinos are, for the most part, terribly isolated and in trouble, both in education and in access to decent jobs. Although Chicanos/other Latinos have been recognized as the nation's largest minority in the 2000 U.S. Census, they face a threatened future, and society faces serious risks. Chicanos—the subject of this book—comprise, by far, the largest share of the Latino population, experience particularly acute educational problems, and are concentrated in states (e.g. California and Texas) that have witnessed some of the most negative policy changes in recent years.

It seems reasonable to think that there would be an urgent mobilization of research and many constructive policy initiatives to help develop the potential of this huge and growing community and to avoid the creation of an isolated, locked-out, and socially distressed population—issues so obviously significant to the nation's future—but that has not been so. There has been little constructive work in the conservative era of the last quarter century. In fact, many of the policies intended to produce educational opportunity—bilingual education, desegregation, affirmative action in college admissions, expansion of the minority teaching force, multiethnic curriculum, and other policies are under attack or abandoned in the states where the Chicano/other Latino population is most concentrated. Scholarship has been far too limited. The dropout crisis has not been addressed, and testing reforms threaten to make a bad situation worse.

For years, I have relied on the first edition of *Chicano School Failure and Success* to introduce my students to a deeply important set of issues, and a remarkable group of Chicano/Latino as well as White scholars. It has had a deep impact. The arrival of a new, expanded, and updated version reporting many more research findings, theories of educational change, and recommendations for policy changes is a major event. This is a book that will help researchers, teachers and educational leaders, policymakers, and students across the country understand educational questions of great consequence to the nation's future.

Dr. Gary Orfield,
Harvard Graduate School of Education,
Harvard University

Acknowledgments

This book represents the contributions of a number of individuals. I gratefully thank Anna Clarkson of RoutledgeFalmer for her support throughout this project. Appreciation is also extended to the fine staff at RoutledgeFalmer who assisted in the book's production. To my contributors—Marta, Rubén, Russ, Gloria, Gene, Ann-Marie, Michael, Sofia, Doug, Robert (Moreno), Bruno, Moises, Robert (Rueda), Alfredo, Jesús, Ignacio, and Art—*muchísimas gracias* for your outstanding work. I also want to thank the Center for Mexican American Studies at The University of Texas at Austin for providing me with a research grant to undertake work on this book. Very special appreciation goes to Bruno Villarreal, my research assistant, who performed outstanding work in locating valuable scholarly sources and in typing (in part and in whole) the chapter contributions I have provided to this volume.

To my dear wife, Marta, I extend my deep affection and gratitude for your great support while I worked on the book. And, as always, I thank Carlos and Juan, my twin boys, who were so patient and supportive while Daddy did his writing. You're the best sons a father could have.

Note on the editor

Richard R. Valencia is Professor of Educational Psychology and Faculty Associate at the Center for Mexican American Studies at The University of Texas at Austin. His area of scholarly specialization is racial/ethnic minority education, with a particular focus on Mexican Americans (educational history; testing/assessment issues; social thought; demographic trends; educational litigation; factors of intellectual/academic test performance; educational policy). He is the author/editor of several books, including the first edition of *Chicano School Failure and Success* (Falmer Press, 1991), which won an "Outstanding Academic Book" award (selected by *CHOICE*, 1993). He is also the editor of *The Evolution of Deficit Thinking: Educational Thought and Practice* (Falmer Press, 1997). His most recent book (with L.A. Suzuki) is *Intelligence Testing and Minority Students: Foundations, Performance Factors, and Assessment Issues* (Sage, 2001). Dr. Valencia's recent honors include the 2001 Distinguished Career Contribution Award, awarded by the American Educational Research Association (Committee for Scholars of Color in Education), and the 2001 Distinguished Faculty Award bestowed by the Texas Association of Chicanos in Higher Education.

Introduction

It has been over a decade since the publication of the first edition of *Chicano School Failure and Success*. Much has transpired in the educational arena in the last ten-plus years affecting Chicano students.[1] Some of these developments have been positive, some negative. Regarding the former, there have been important scholarly publications on Chicano schooling that have enhanced our knowledge base (e.g., Donato, 1997; García, 2001; Moreno, 1999; San Miguel and Valencia, 1998; Valenzuela, 1999). Another significant development was the 2002 launching of the *Journal of Latinos and Education*, a long overdue scholarly venture.

With respect to negative developments, there have been a number of issues that do not bode well for Chicano students—for example, the growing anti-bilingual education and anti-affirmative action movements (San Miguel and Valencia, 1998), the demise of school desegregation (Orfield, 2001), the expansion of high-stakes testing (Valencia and Bernal, 2000), and the resurgence of deficit thinking (Valencia, 1997). In the 1998 issue of the *Harvard Educational Review*, San Miguel and Valencia asserted that due to a trilogy of oppressive Propositions passed in California and the adverse effects of the *Hopwood* case in Texas, "Mexican Americans [in California and Texas] face an educational crisis of unprecedented magnitude in the history of racial/ethnic minority education" (p. 354).

With both the positive and negative developments in mind, the contributors of this second edition offer updated, comprehensive, state-of-the-art coverages of their respective chapters. As was the focus of the first edition, the second edition explores—from various perspectives—the school failure and success of Chicano students, with particular emphasis on elementary and secondary education. By its very nature, school failure among Chicanos is a complex and multidimensional construct. Thus, to understand the factors and processes of such low academic achievement (and academic enhancement as well), it is necessary to study the educational problems, research findings, and policy/reform implications through various windows and perspectives. As seen in the present volume, the contributors' research specializations range widely—cultural anthropology, bilingual education, educational history, special education, educational psychology, educational policy, child and family studies, tests and measurement, educational anthropology, school dropouts, and the political economy of education. Given the broad nature of schooling problems experienced by Chicano students, it is necessary to cast a wide scholarly net to capture the complexities of the issues and the resultant research findings and policy implications. I believe that understanding the educational plight and improvement of schooling for Chicanos benefits greatly from having such interdisciplinary teams.

The content and structure of the second edition deviates somewhat from the first edition of *Chicano School Failure and Success*. First, in several chapters, there is a much closer examination of schooling in the Southwest region of the U.S. (Arizona, California, Colorado,

New Mexico, and Texas), home to 75 percent of the nation's Mexican American population. Second, the population growth of the Chicano people and the resultant educational implications are more fully examined. The attendant question here is: As the Chicano population dramatically grows, will its educational status commensurately increase, or will the Chicano people's quest for educational equality remain elusive? Third, there are several chapters covering new material. These include sustained coverage of the Chicano/Latino population growth (Chapter 2), Chicano/Latino critical ethnography of education (Chapter 7), and Chicano parental involvement in their children's schooling (Chapter 8). Furthermore, I can assure the reader that the remaining chapters are thorough updates of material covered in the first edition. As editor of this volume, I sought to produce a book that was intended to be authoritative, comprehensive in scope, and would serve as a valuable reference text. I believe that this goal has been met. This is evidenced by the solid analyses and syntheses of the respective chapters and by the sheer number of references (1,340 compared to 976 references in the first edition). Fourth, the contributor list has undergone considerable change, thus allowing fresh perspectives. Of the 12 authors who contributed to the first edition, eight provide chapters for the second edition; there are ten new contributors. In sum, my team of contributors consists of senior scholars of national reputation, junior scholars whose stars are rising, and several outstanding Ph.D. candidates. I feel that I have assembled a team of colleagues who are among the most accomplished and promising scholars in writings and research on the Chicano schooling experience.

The book consists of five parts. In Part I, "Current realities of the Chicano schooling experience," there are four chapters. Chapter 1 ("The plight of Chicano students: an overview of schooling conditions and outcomes"), written by Richard Valencia, examines 15 schooling conditions and outcomes germane to Chicano students (e.g., segregation; school financing; teacher–student interactions; high-stakes testing). This chapter provides a foundation for the remainder of the book. Chapter 2 ("The explosive growth of the Chicano/Latino population: educational implications"), also written by Valencia, discusses the extraordinary growth of the Mexican American people, as well as other Latino groups. Based on 2000 U.S. Census data, the Chicano/Latino sector experienced the greatest increase from 1990 to 2000 (in both percentage rate and absolute numbers) of any other racial/ethnic group in the country. Also, Chicanos/Latinos eclipsed African Americans in the 2000 Census to become the nation's largest minority group. Valencia provides rich data on the remarkable growth of Chicanos/Latinos and concludes the chapter by discussing a number of implications of such growth for education. In Chapter 3 ("Segregation, desegregation, and integration of Chicano students: old and new realities"), Richard Valencia, Martha Menchaca, and Rubén Donato provide a comprehensive update of the isolation of Chicano students. The authors cover the history of school segregation, early desegregation litigation, the prevalence of segregation and its adverse effects on Chicanos, contemporary issues (with a focus on resegregation), and suggestions for integration. One of the most disturbing trends discussed by Valencia *et al.* is that Chicano students are presently maintaining a pattern of hypersegregation that was first reported in the first edition of this book. Chapter 4 ("Chicano dropouts: an update of research and policy issues") is written by Russell Rumberger and Gloria Rodríguez. The authors cover one of the most significant schooling outcomes faced by many Chicano students—their extremely high dropout rate from secondary education. Rumberger and Rodríguez approach the problem of Chicano dropouts by exploring four facets: extent of the problem via incidence data; correlates of dropping out from an individual and institutional perspective; individual and social consequences of leaving school before graduation; solutions to the Chicano dropout problem.

Part II, "Language perspectives on Chicano student achievement," consists of two chapters. Chapter 5 ("Language, public policy, and schooling: a focus on Chicano English language learners") is written by Eugene García and Ann-Marie Wiese. The authors provide a discussion of federal and state policy issues regarding language instruction of Chicano English language learners. A major goal in this chapter is to provide the reader with a further understanding of how such policies attempt to either disadvantage or enhance the education of Chicano students. García and Wiese discuss federal executive, legislative, and court articulations, and state articulations and recent initiatives as well (e.g., the highly controversial Proposition 227 in California that brought an end to bilingual education). A recommended set of guidelines related to policy issues germane to Chicano English language learners and bilingual students is presented. Michael Guerrero offers Chapter 6 ("Research in bilingual education: moving beyond the effectiveness debate"). Guerrero presents an overview of research conducted during the 1990s regarding the effectiveness of bilingual education in the U.S. A number of major investigations are described and critiqued. In addition, Guerrero distills these findings and offers conclusions regarding the effectiveness of bilingual education. Recommendations are offered for improving program evaluations and for moving beyond the effectiveness debate in order to continue learning how to best meet the needs of Chicano and other English language learner children and youths.

Part III, "Cultural and familial perspectives on Chicano student achievement," contains two chapters. Chapter 7 ("Chicano/Latino critical ethnography of education: cultural productions from *la frontera*") is written by Sofia Villenas and Douglas Foley. The authors begin by situating the conceptual and methodological developments of Chicano/Latino ethnography of education within the construct of "critical ethnography" and the dominant paradigms explaining the educational achievement gap. They then move to explore how Chicano/Latino ethnography, influenced by the material and symbolic presence of *la frontera*, has produced complex and dynamic portraits of families and communities. These portraits highlight how Latino youths are socialized differently in their families and communities, how they participate in diverse cultural and linguistic worlds enacting multiple identities, and how they achieve differently in schools. The authors also examine ethnographic findings that indict schools for failing Latino children. Villenas and Foley close by discussing future directions in understanding Chicano/Latino student agency and cultural production through borderlands, postnational, and Diaspora lens. In Chapter 8 ("Chicano families and schools: myths, knowledge, and future directions for understanding"), Robert Moreno and Richard Valencia provide a compre hensive coverage of the relationship between Chicano families and the schools, with a particular emphasis on Mexican American parental involvement in their children's education. Moreno and Valencia organize their chapter around a brief overview of parental involvement research, a thorough discussion and rebuke of the long-standing myth that Mexican Americans do not value education, and a coverage of the research findings on what we know about Chicano parental involvement. A major point that Moreno and Valencia underscore throughout the chapter is that Chicano parental involvement is positively associated with Chicano academic achievement. The authors close by discussing future research directions for a better understanding of the relationship between Chicano families and the schools.

Part IV, "Educational testing and special education issues germane to Chicano students," has two chapters. Chapter 9 ("Educational testing and Chicano students: issues, consequences, and prospects for reform") is offered by Richard Valencia, Bruno Villarreal, and Moises Salinas. The authors begin by discussing the functions of testing, then follow by examining a number of testing issues (historical role of intelligence tests in the stratification of learning opportunities for Chicanos; a comprehensive literature review of research investigations on cultural bias in intelligence tests in which Chicanos served as participants; cognitive assessment of Mexican American English language learners; underrepresentation of Chicanos in gifted/talented programs; adverse impact of high-stakes testing on Chicano students). Valencia *et al.* conclude their chapter by presenting a number of research and policy oriented ideas how educational testing might be improved to help promote Chicano school success. Chapter 10 ("An analysis of special education as a response to the diminished academic achievement of Chicano/Latino students: an update") is written by Robert Rueda, Alfredo Artiles, Jesús Salazar, and Ignacio Higareda. The authors present a historical overview of the role special education has played in the education of Chicano/Latino students in the last 20 years, with an emphasis on what has transpired over the last ten-plus years since the publication of the first edition of *Chicano School Failure and Success*. Rueda *et al.* discuss a number of new issues and developments pertinent to Chicano/Latino students (e.g., recent litigation; changes in special education legislation; teacher preparation and professional development; changing theoretical views of teaching and learning; assessment and diagnosis concerns). The authors close by providing an outline of alternatives to the current special education system/structure and identifying the challenges to be faced by the field, as changes are considered and implemented.

Part V, "The big picture and Chicano school failure and success," consists of two chapters. Arthur Pearl offers Chapter 11 ("The big picture: systemic and institutional factors in Chicano school failure and success"). The author provides a comprehensive analysis of systemic and institutional factors that contribute to school failure among Chicano students. Foundations forming this chapter are discussions of: what "systemic" means; historical legacies of educational inclusion and exclusion; the grim reality that Chicanos continue to lag behind in education. Pearl also covers new developments since the first edition (e.g., current right-wing onslaught; postmodernism [a critique]; the growing standards/accountability movement at the national level). The author critiques those efforts that have been advanced to ameliorate Chicano school failure (e.g., compensatory education), and argues for a democratization of the institution of education. "Democratic education," Pearl argues, is needed to ensure Chicano school success. Specific and workable principles/practices of democratic education are presented. Editor Richard Valencia concludes the volume by presenting Chapter 12 ("Conclusions: towards Chicano school success"). Here, Valencia offers some final thoughts on the promotion of Chicano school success. The focus is on a synthesis of ideas presented by the various contri butors. The author zeroes in on six specific areas: keeping Chicanos in school; the academic and social contexts of schooling; the Chicano English language learner and bilingual education; Chicano parental involvement; the assessment context of schooling; democratic education. Valencia concludes by asserting that it is critical to embrace the Chicano community in any discussions of promoting Chicano school success.

Note

1 The term "Chicano," a group within the diverse Latino population, refers to Mexican-origin people either born in the U.S. or Mexico. Throughout this volume, Chicano is used interchangeably with the term "Mexican American." Likewise, "Latino" and "Hispanic" are used interchangeably. The term "Chicano/Latino"—which refers to a combination of Chicanos and other Latinos—is frequently used in this volume. Finally, when the term "Latino" is used singularly, it refers to Chicanos and other Latinos, unless otherwise stated.

References

Donato, R. (1997). *The other struggle for equal schools: Mexican Americans during the civil rights era.* Albany: State University of New York Press.

García, E.E. (2001). *Hispanic education in the United States: Raíces y alas.* Lanham, MD: Rowen & Littlefield.

Moreno, J.F. (Ed.). (1999). *The elusive quest for equality: 150 years of Chicano/Chicana education.* Cambridge, MA: Harvard Educational Review.

Orfield, G. (2001). *Schools more separate: Consequences of a decade of research.* The Civil Rights Project, Harvard University. Cambridge, MA: Harvard University. Available online at: http://www.law.harvard.edu/groups/civilrights/publications/schoolsseparate.pdf

San Miguel, G., Jr., and Valencia, R.R. (1998). From the Treaty of Guadalupe Hidalgo to *Hopwood*: The educational plight and struggle of Mexican Americans in the Southwest. *Harvard Educational Review, 68*, 353–412.

Valencia, R.R. (Ed.). (1997). *The evolution of deficit thinking: Educational thought and practice.* The Stanford Series on Education and Public Policy. London: Falmer Press.

Valencia, R.R., and Bernal, E.M. (Eds.). (2000). The Texas Assessment of Academic Skills (TAAS) case: Perspectives of plaintiffs' experts [Special issue]. *Hispanic Journal of Behavioral Sciences, 22* (4).

Valenzuela, A. (1999). *Subtractive schooling: U.S.-Mexican youth and the politics of caring.* Albany: State University of New York Press.

Part I

Current realities of the Chicano schooling experience

1 The plight of Chicano students: an overview of schooling conditions and outcomes

Richard R. Valencia

> School failure among Chicanos is not a new situation. On the contrary, it is an old and stubborn condition. It refuses to relent. It continues even in the face of opposition. Imagine having a toothache that never goes away, and you can get a sense of the persistent nature of the poor academic performance of a substantial portion of the Chicano school population. In short, Chicano school failure is deeply rooted in history.
>
> (Valencia, 1991a, p. 4)

The historical rooting of Chicano school failure has been clearly documented (e.g., Donato, 1997; González, 1990; Moreno, 1999; San Miguel and Valencia, 1998; Valencia, 1991b). In addition to historical expressions, it also manifests in various ways in the contemporary period. In my view, such school failure has largely been shaped by *educational inequality*, a form of oppression.[1] This is why Chicano school failure has been so difficult to combat. Chesler (1976) in an essay on theories of racism—which, I assert, can be generalized to the study of other forms of oppression—asserts that there are three forms of evidence from which theorists can draw to identify the existence of oppression. These evidential bases are: (a) personal attitudes or cultural values—as seen in symbol systems and ideology; (b) institutional processes—as seen in mechanisms that lead to differential advantages and privileges; (c) effects or outcomes—as seen in unequal attainments among groups. Within this framework, Chicano students—the target group of this book—are prime examples of pupils affected by the pernicious ideologies, institutional practices, and outcomes of educational inequality. How some people have viewed the educability of Chicano students (i.e., through the ideological lens of "deficit thinking"), how the schools have been structured to disallow Chicanos from learning (via unequal schooling arrangements), and the resultant differential schooling outcomes attained by Chicano and White students (e.g., differences in high school graduation rates) are all important subject matters for the present volume. I need to underscore, however, that "how" Chicano students can achieve "school success" is also a very important topic of this book.

In this introductory chapter, two aspects of the unequal schooling experiences of Chicano students will be discussed. First, I unpack the important construct of "Chicano school failure." Second, there is an overview of 15 conditions and outcomes that characterize the schooling for a substantial number of Chicano students.

Chicano school failure

Although the term "school failure" with respect to racial/ethnic minority students has been used by other scholars (e.g., Boykin, 1983; Erikson, 1987; García, 2001; Ginsburg, 1986;

McDermott, 1997; Nieto, 1996), the notion itself is in need of further theoretical development and refinement. Its heuristic value and potential in theory generation about the many schooling problems experienced by Chicano students appear to be vast. How might one conceptualize school failure, a construct, among Chicano students?[2] I offer this broad, working definition: School failure among Chicano students refers to their *persistently, pervasively, and disproportionately, low academic achievement*. Next, we turn to a brief discussion of each of the italicized terms.

Persistence

When Chicanos did eventually gain wider access to public schooling at the turn of the twentieth century (Cameron, 1976; San Miguel and Valencia, 1998), major problems emerged and strenuously persisted for decades (e.g., segregation; poor academic achievement). Numerous studies reporting achievement test data and other indices of achievement since the 1920s (e.g., Drake, 1927; Manuel, 1930) and through the 1930s (e.g., McLennan, 1936; Reynolds, 1933), 1940s (e.g., Cromack, 1949; McLean, 1950), 1950s (e.g., Clark, 1956), 1960s (e.g., Barrett, 1966), 1970s (e.g., U.S. Commission on Civil Rights, 1971a, 1971b), 1980s (e.g., Brown and Haycock, 1985), 1990s (Campbell *et al.*, 1997; Texas Education Agency, 1998), and the present (Campbell *et al.*, 2000; Texas Education Agency, 2000a) all confirm that many Chicano students have not achieved as well in school compared to their White peers (either by using direct Chicano/White comparisons or White normative data comparisons).

Pervasiveness

Chicano school failure is not confined to one single location. Wherever Chicano communities exist, school failure appears to be widespread among Chicano student enrollments—especially in schools with high percentages of students of low-socioeconomic background. There are at least two evidential ways of looking at the pervasive character of such low academic achievement. First, one can analyze it from a geographical vantage point. Whether one views the academic performance data described in national (e.g., Campbell *et al.*, 1997, 2000; Coleman *et al.*, 1966), regional (e.g., U.S. Commission on Civil Rights, 1971b), state (e.g., Brown and Haycock, 1985; Campbell *et al.*, 2000; Texas Education Agency, 2000a), or numerous local reports, the results are alarmingly consistent: Chicano students, on the whole, tend to exhibit low academic achievement compared to their White peers. Second, one can study such data using a cross-sectional approach (i.e., comparing various grade levels at one point in time; for example, see Brown and Haycock, 1985; Campbell *et al.*, 2000; Texas Education Agency, 2000a). Again, Chicano academic performance—on the average—is characterized by poor achievement. In sum, the pandemic branches of Chicano school failure are clearly tied to their persistent taproots.

Disproportionality

The modifying term, "disproportionately," is an important qualifier in that Chicano school failure, which contains its explicit meaning of low achievement, also has a second denotation—comparative performance. In the context of examining the school achievement of Chicano students, their academic performance is frequently compared to White students. Here, the common procedure is to use the aggregated performance (e.g., reading achievement as measured on a standardized test) of White grade-level peers as a referent and then to compare the aggregated performance of Chicano students to this grade level. When this is done, the common result is one of *asymmetry*. That is, when the Chicano distribution of achievement test scores, represented as interval data, is juxtaposed to the curve of the White grouped scores, the Chicano distribution is often positively skewed. Simply put, there is a disproportionately greater percentage of Chicano students, compared to their White peers, reading below the middle of the distribution. Conversely, compared to White students, there is a disproportionately lower percentage of Chicano students reading above the middle of the distribution.

In addition to examining the notion of disproportionality of achievement scores from a perspective of asymmetry, once can also look at *disparity*. For example, when a comparison is made between the percentage of Chicano secondary school dropouts to White dropouts (i.e., represented as dichotomous data—dropout/non-dropout), the common pattern shows disparity, where the Chicano rate of dropouts in secondary schools is higher than one would predict when compared to the percentage of Chicano students in the general secondary school population.

Before we leave the term, disproportionality, a caveat is in order. Although the difference between Chicano and White students in academic achievement is large, there is considerable variability in Chicano academic development and performance (see Laosa and Henderson [1991] for a discussion of some predictors that help to explain such variability; see Valencia and Suzuki [2001] for a discussion of correlates of the intellectual performance of Chicanos). Some Chicano students do read at or above grade level. Many Chicano students graduate from high school. In short, there are noticeable within-group differences, and thus the issue of disproportionality is not confined only to between-group (i.e., White/Chicano) differences. We must not forget that within-group differences in achievement typically exceed between-group differences. That is, the vast proportion of the variability in academic achievement (and intellectual ability) lies *within* racial/ethnic and socioeconomic groups, not *between* them (Loehlin *et al.*, 1975; Valencia and Suzuki, 2001). Notwithstanding the reality that some Chicano students do not have academic problems, it is important to underscore, however, that given the current schooling outcomes experienced by many Chicano students as measured by most achievement indicators, the available evidence indicates that the low academic achievement is the norm for a substantial portion of the Chicano school population in the nation's public elementary and secondary schools (see Campbell *et al.*, 2000).

Low academic achievement

Here, I need to provide a justification for the usage of "low academic achievement." Let us begin by examining the term "achievement." Achievement (academic) is a concept, an "abstraction formed from the observation of certain behaviors of children . . . associated with the 'learning' of school tasks—reading words, doing arithmetic problems . . . and so on" (Kerlinger, 1986, p. 27). According to major reports and studies (e.g., California Superintendents' Council on Hispanic Affairs, 1985; U.S. Commission on Civil Rights, 1971b), two of the most significant academic achievement indicators, particularly in the schooling of Chicano students, are (a) test performance in the content areas (especially reading) and (b) secondary school holding power (i.e., the "school systems' effectiveness in its ability to hold its students until they have completed the full course of study" [U.S. Commission on Civil Rights, 1971b, p. 8]).[3]

I have deliberately chosen the term "low academic achievement" rather than the often used notion of "underachievement."[4] It is tempting to want to use the construct of under-achievement as it connotes that the typical group performance of low test scores and high dropout rates among Chicano students are not truly reflective of what they are capable of achieving. Although there is likely a great deal of credence to the belief that the depressed academic achievement of Chicanos does not reflect what they can do, an attempt to interpret this discrepancy as "underachievement" presents several conceptual problems.

First, the converse notion of underachievement (that is, "overachievement") appears to be "a logical impossibility" (Anastasi, 1984, p. 131) because the term implies that a person is performing above his/her capacity (as measured by an intelligence test). Second, the terms underachievement/overachievement are meaningless if not looked at from a measurement perspective (Anastasi, 1984; Jensen, 1980). Anastasi (citing Thorndike, 1963) has noted: "Actually, the question of underachievement and overachievement can be more properly for-mulated as overprediction and underprediction from the first to the second test" (p. 131). These intraindividual differences from one measure to another merely inform us "that no two tests are perfectly correlated" (see Anastasi, 1984, p. 131). Third, the concept of under-achievement is typically used in describing the special education category of learning dis-abilities. A commonly accepted characteristic of learning disabilities is a marked discrepancy between measured intelligence and school achievement.[5] The discrepancy model is particu-larly troubling in trying to describe the test behavior of normal Chicanos (i.e., non-special education students), in that research studies have found some Chicano students perform well within the normal range on intelligence tests, but perform far below the norm on achievement tests (see, e.g., Valencia and Rankin, 1988). Given all the confusion and issues associated with the term underachievement, I have selected the term "low academic achieve-ment"—a more meaningful construct—for inclusion in my definition of Chicano school failure.[6] Now that we have configured the notion of school failure, we move next to a description of 15 conditions and outcomes that characterize the schooling experiences of many Chicanos.

Schooling conditions and outcomes: an overview

In the first edition of *Chicano School Failure and Success*, I provided a discussion of 11 schooling conditions and outcomes that have characterized experiences for a sizeable pro-portion of the Chicano public school population (Valencia, 1991a). In this second edition, I have added four more conditions and outcomes (i.e., grade retention; teacher certification; gifted/talented education; high-stakes testing). The reader should keep in mind that the following overview of these 15 schooling conditions and outcomes—many having both historical and contemporary expressions—contains broad-based general statements. The ensuing discussion is meant to capture the schooling reality for a substantial segment of the Chicano student population, not every Chicano student.

Segregation

By the early 1930s, the blueprint for the future of Chicano education had been formed. "Forced and widespread school segregation and inferior schooling of Mexican American children became the norm—although there were no legal statutes that mandated such racial/ethnic isolation" (San Miguel and Valencia, 1998, p. 370). School segregation of Chicanos throughout the Southwest became the crucible in which Chicano school failure originated and festered. Given the strong connections between segregation, inferior schooling, and poor academic outcomes for many Chicano students (e.g., substandard performance on achievement tests), it is not surprising that segregation has been a significant topic of study in the field of Mexican American education (e.g., Álvarez, 1988; Donato, 1997; Donato *et al.*, 1991; González, 1990; Menchaca and Valencia, 1990; San Miguel, 1987; San Miguel and Valencia, 1998; U.S. Commission on Civil Rights, 1971a).

In the first edition of *Chicano School Failure and Success*, I (on p. 7) quoted Menchaca and Valencia (1990), noting: "The segregation of school-age Latinos, of which two-thirds are Chicano, has increased to such an extent that they now have the dubious distinction of being the most highly segregated group of America's children" (p. 222).[7] Gary Orfield and his associates, who have studied segregation trends for some time now, have recently reported continued hypersegregation of Chicanos and other Latino students (e.g., see Orfield *et al.*, 1997; Orfield and Yun, 1999). Orfield *et al.* (1997) commented:

> Latino students, who will soon be the largest minority group in American public schools, were granted the right to desegregated education by the Supreme Court in 1973, but new data show they now are significantly more segregated than black students, with clear evidence of increasing isolation across the nation. Part of this trend is caused by the very rapid growth in the number of Latino students in several major states. Regardless of the reasons, Latino students now experience more isolation from whites and more concentration in high poverty schools than any other group of students.
>
> (p. 5)

Suffice it to say, the continuing and growing segregation of Chicano students does not bode well for their prospects in obtaining equal educational opportunity. In the present book, Valencia *et al.* (Chapter 3) provide a comprehensive analysis of this critical issue by examining the segregation, desegregation, and integration of Chicano students in the context of past, present, and future trends.

Language/cultural exclusion

Given that the Chicano people are a conquered people—stemming from the Mexican American War of 1846–1848 and the pursuant Treaty of Guadalupe Hidalgo in 1848—it is not surprising, then, that Chicano students have experienced persistent and pervasive language suppression and cultural exclusion. Following the Treaty, it was common throughout the Southwest for Chicano students in public schools to endure Americanization programs, severe restriction on the use of Spanish as a curricular vehicle, and the exclusion of Mexican culture as an area of curricular study (San Miguel and Valencia, 1998).[8] These policies and laws were intended to ensure the dominance of the English language and Anglo culture.

Not only was Spanish excluded from the curriculum as a means of instruction, some schools in the five Southwestern states (Arizona, California, Colorado, New Mexico, and Texas) institutionalized "No Spanish" rules regarding conversational use of Spanish between students in classes and schoolgrounds. In Texas, for example, 41 percent and 66 percent of all elementary schools surveyed discouraged the use of Spanish on schoolgrounds and in classrooms, respectively (U.S. Commission on Civil Rights, 1972a).[9] The enforcement of the "No Spanish" rule was institutionalized in some cases. Punishment included, for example, corporal punishment, fining students, and "Spanish detention classes" (U.S. Commission on Civil Rights, 1972a). At the 1968 U.S. Commission on Civil Rights hearing in San Antonio, Texas, a violation slip for Spanish detention used in an El Paso school was exhibited. Figure 1.1 is a reproduction of the slip.

VIOLATION SLIP — SPANISH DETENTION

_____ was speaking

(Student's name and classification)

Spanish during school hours. This pupil must report to Spanish

Detention in the Cafeteria on the assigned day. (The teacher

reporting should place the date on this slip.)

_____   _____

(Dates to report)   (Teacher reporting)

Return this slip to Mr. _____

or Mr. _____ before 3:30 p.m.

9/66

Figure 1.1 Reproduction of violation slip used to place child in Spanish detention class, Texas: 1968. Source: U.S. Commission in Civil Rights (1972a, p. 19).

Another adverse schooling condition related to language exclusion faced by Chicano students is the limited use of bilingual education. Historically, this issue was brought to the nation's attention about three decades ago when the U.S. Commission on Civil Rights (1972a) Mexican American Education Study (MAES) found that 6.5 percent of the public schools in the Southwest offered bilingual education; 2.7 percent of the Chicano student population was being served in these programs. In three states (Arizona, Colorado, and New Mexico), bilingual education reached less than 1 percent of the Chicano student population. In sum, about one in forty Chicano students in the five Southwestern states were being served in bilingual education classes, although about one in two first graders were likely in need of such services due to their mother tongue being Spanish (U.S. Commission on Civil Rights, 1972a).

Although the percentage of Mexican American English language learners (ELLs) in bilingual education has increased over the years, there continues to be a substantial proportion of ELLs who are not served (see, e.g., Olsen, 1988; Macías, 1993; also see San Miguel and Valencia, 1998). Even more alarming, however, is the dismantling of bilingual education, as evidenced by the recent passing of Proposition 227 in California and Proposition 203 in Arizona (see García and Wiese [Chapter 5] and Guerrero [Chapter 6], present book).

In addition to language exclusion, Chicano students have also been subject to cultural exclusion in the school curricula. In the early 1970s, the MAES reported, in detail, the extent of such cultural exclusion (U.S. Commission on Civil Rights, 1972a). It was found that only 4.3 percent of the elementary schools surveyed in the five Southwestern states offered Mexican American "units" in their social studies curriculum; only 4.7 percent of these schools offered Mexican history units. At the secondary level, only 7.3 percent of the schools provided Mexican American history in their curriculum, and only 5.8 percent provided Mexican history. The report noted: "In spite of the rich bicultural history of the Southwest, the schools offer little opportunity for Mexican Americans to learn something about their roots—who they are and where they came from and what their people have achieved" (p. 30).

Since the publication of the MAES report on cultural exclusion of Chicanos in the school curricula (U.S. Commission on Civil Rights, 1972a), other studies have documented such neglect. For example, Revett (1986) in her master's thesis examined the treatment of Mexico and Mexican Americans in 14 U.S. history textbooks copyrighted in the 1950s and used in grades 8 through 11 in Texas public schools. For a comparison set, she reviewed ten such books that were under adoption in 1985–1986. Revett was interested in whether the intervening years—particularly the civil rights movement—between the 1950s and 1980s would reflect more pluralistic perceptions of Mexican Americans in the latter textbooks. Here major conclusions were:

> Textbooks of the 1950s generally omitted it, or gave token attention to Hispanic culture in the U.S. Accounts relating to Mexico and Mexican Americans were concentrated in early Spanish conquest of Native American cultures, explorations and colonies, the Texas and California issues, the War with Mexico, and 20th century relations with Latin America. Stories were usually one-sided and led to distortions of the facts.
>
> In comparison, those U.S. history textbooks under current adoption in Texas at least attempted to include the Hispanic culture, its influence and long-standing presence in American history. By far, Blacks and women received the most frequent discussion. Mexico and Mexican Americans did feature in many accounts of U.S. history. These tended to be in passages related to the Southwest, or to the Spanish-speaking population in the country. Their roles in recent history and contemporary society were included to a lesser degree.
>
> It is the nature of these discussions that has merited concern and question. The textbook treatment of Mexico and Mexican Americans was found to still contain omissions and distortion. They were of such a nature, as to foster stereotyping. This was seen particularly in accounts of the western settlement, Texas and California, the War with Mexico, and in more contemporary issues, such as living conditions and civil rights.
>
> (pp. 97–98)

Another germane study on the cultural exclusion of Chicanos is that of Escamilla (1996) who discussed an investigation she and others conducted in the late 1980s (Escamilla, 1987). The study, which took place in southern Arizona, involved over 3,000 sophomores attending 10 high schools in a large urban district. The school district, located only 65 miles from the Mexican border, had an enrollment of 40 percent Mexican American. Escamilla (1996) observed: "One might assume that, in such a location both Mexican American and White teenagers would have a thorough knowledge of Mexican American culture and history" (p. 6).

In this survey by Escamilla and associates (reported in Escamilla, 1996), two open-ended questions were asked to the respondents:

1 "Name two contributions that the United States has given to the world," and,
2 "Name two contributions that Mexican Americans have given to the United States or to the world" (p. 7).

Escamilla (1996, p. 7) reported the finding as follows:

> First, 80 percent of the students, no matter what their ethnicity, were able to readily identify two contributions that they felt the United States had given to the world. Their answers ranged from television to the atomic bomb to democracy. Not surprisingly, the three most common answers were popular culture answers—rock and roll, blue jeans, and Coca-Cola.
>
> Sadly, however, only 20 percent of the students in the study could identify two contributions that Hispanics had given the United States or the world. The students were evenly divided by ethnicity; that is, no ethnic group knew any more about Hispanic contributions than any other ethnic group. This study, again, took place in a city whose predominate architecture reflects Hispanic contributions, where popular rock star Linda Ronstadt was born and raised, and where street names, school names, and the very name of the state are in Spanish. In spite of being surrounded by Hispanic historical and cultural influences, high-school students in this area had great difficulty identifying (and identifying *with*) cultural contributions of Hispanics. Even more telling, I feel, is that not one student in the survey identified a Hispanic contribution as being an *American* contribution to the world (question #1).

Escamilla (1996) concluded that neither Mexican Americans nor students of other racial/ethnic groups had a good understanding of the history, culture, or contributions of the Mexican American people. Furthermore, she noted, there is a need "to explore new ways of incorporating the history and culture of Mexican Americans into our school curricula (social studies as well as other subjects)" (p. 7). This call for the cultural inclusion of Chicanos (and other people of color) has been voiced by numerous other scholars (see, e.g., Banks, 1994, Banks and McGee Banks, 2001; Bennett, 1999; Gollnick and Chinn, 1994; Grant, 1992; Nieto, 1996). Rodolfo Anaya (1992), educator and writer, has referred to the exclusion of Chicano culture from the school curricula as "the censorship of neglect" (p. 19). He voiced:

> Our community stretches from California to Texas, and into the Northwest and Midwest. But not one iota of our social reality, much less our aesthetic reality, is represented in the literature read in the schools. . . . Chicano literature, in a country that has over fifteen-million Mexican Americans, is still virtually unknown in the classroom. . . . Where is our freedom to teach? Who trained us, or brainwashed us, to the point that we cannot see fifteen-million people? The teachers of this country cannot see, I mean that literally, the children of fifteen-million people. That is how strong the censorship of neglect has been. That is why I say we have not been free to teach.
>
> (p. 19)

The language/cultural exclusion issue looms large for Chicano students, as well as for other disenfranchised and neglected students of color (see, e.g., Ovando and McLaren, 2000a). The available literature asserts that multicultural education—if properly conceptualized and implemented—"can have a substantive and positive impact on the educational experiences of most students" (Nieto, 1996, p. 2; also, see, e.g., Banks and McGee Banks, 2001). Furthermore, "culture and language help to define the very soul of a people, and to insist on wiping them out is both an unusually cruel strategy and, in the end, a counterproductive one" (Nieto, 1996, p. 4).

Finally, we need to keep in mind that bilingual education and multiculturalism are fiercely contested political, moral, and pedagogical issues (see Ovando and McLaren's [2000a] volume, *The Politics of Multiculturalism and Bilingual Education: Students and Teachers Caught in the Cross Fire*). As such, political remedies are necessary in this battle of cultural politics. Ovando and McLaren (2000b) commented: "multicultural education, as defined by Banks (1992), affirms the importance of reflection and action (praxis), creating an empowering school culture for minority students by completely restructuring the organization and culture of the school" (p. xxi).

Academic achievement

As we have previously discussed in our conceptualization of Chicano school failure, Chicano students—compared to their White peers—achieve, on the average, at lower levels on various achievement tests. Regarding the persistent nature of Latino low academic achievement, let us examine the 1927 master's thesis written by Drake.[10] His thesis, entitled *A Comparative Study of the Mentality and Achievement of Mexican and White Children*, is one of the first comparative studies of academic achievement of Mexican American and White students. The participants in Drake's study were Mexican American and White seventh- and eighth-grade students attending a public school in Tucson, Arizona. Table 1.1 presents comparative descriptive statistics for this investigation undertaken three-fourths of a century ago. For the Mexican American sample, I present, on the bottom half of Table 1.1, characteristics that describe the group's performance on the Stanford Achievement Test. As one can observe, the Mexican American students' performance, compared to that of their White peers, can be characterized as having a depressed mean, restriction in variability, and a positively skewed distribution. We must also underscore that the Mexican American group demonstrated overlap, meaning that some Mexican American students in Drake's study performed higher than their White peers on the Stanford Achievement Test (i.e., 15.4 percent of the Mexican American students exceeded the median score for the White students). It is important to emphasize that these four characteristics of Mexican American test performance seen in this 1927 study would become a recurring pattern for Mexican American students for decades to come. In addition to the feature of a depressed mean, restricted variability, and positive skew

Table 1.1 Descriptive statistics for Stanford Achievement Test (Form A) for Mexican and White students

Descriptive statistic	Race/ethnicity	
	Mexican (n = 95)	White (n = 108)
Mode (most frequent interval)	60–64	65–69
Range	44 (max. = 79; min. = 35)	54 (max. = 94; min. = 40)
Median	60.5	68.9
Mean	60.2	69.4
Standard deviation	8.9	10.2

Characteristics of Mexican American achievement performance
- Mean: depressed
- Variability: restricted
- Skew: positive
- Overlap: present

Source: Adapted from Drake (1927, Tables IV and V).

in scores—which signal trouble—we also need to be mindful of the overlap feature. To not be aware of, or to ignore, overlap is a disservice to Chicano students as it leads to a stereotype that all Chicano students are low achievers.

The MAES report on reading achievement (U.S. Commission on Civil Rights, 1971b) also provided data on the enduring and pervasive poor academic performance of most Chicano students in the five Southwestern states. At grades 4, 8, and 12 the *majority* of Chicano students in the Southwest were reading *below* grade level; African American students even had higher rates of reading below grade level compared to their Chicano peers. By sharp contrast, about one-fourth to one-third of White students performed below grade level (see U.S. Commission on Civil Rights, 1971b, p. 25, Figure 7).

Still yet, the most recent data from the National Assessment of Educational Progress (NAEP)—an ongoing monitor of student achievement dubbed our nation's "report card"— show that Chicano/other Latino students, compared to their White peers, consistently perform at lower levels (Campbell *et al.*, 2000). Students—at age 9, 13, and 17 years—are compared on reading, mathematics, and science scores. Although the difference in average scores between Chicano/other Latino students and White students has diminished over time in the three subject areas for the three age groups, the gaps remain substantial. As an example, I present data on science achievement scores for age 13 years. Figure 1.2 shows that in the baseline year, 1977, the average science scale score difference between Hispanic 13-year-olds and their White peers was 43 scale points. The next year of comparison, 1982, the average difference diminished to 32 points. For a decade, from 1986 to 1996, the gap remained fairly constant (33 to 34 points). Then, for the most recent year (1999) in which data are reported, the average score difference between Hispanic and White students increased to 39 points. Regarding White–Black average science scale score differences for 13-year-olds, gaps (reported between 1970 and 1999) were also persistent and substantial—and greater than the White–Hispanic gaps (Campbell *et al.*, 2000).

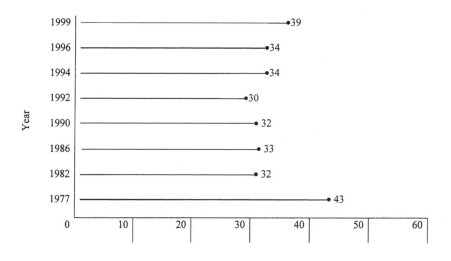

Score difference

Figure 1.2 Trends in differences between White and Hispanic students' average science scores across
     years (White minus Hispanic) for age 13 years.

Source: Adapted from Campbell *et al.* (2000, p. 40, Figure 2.5).

A further example of the persistence of the White–Chicano gap in academic achievement is seen in the highly segregated Texas public schools. I illustrate this enduring racial/ethnic difference in achievement by examining percent passing all tests (reading, mathematics, writing) on the state-mandated Texas Assessment of Academic Skills (TAAS) test. As a case in point, let us examine grade 4 students. Table 1.2 shows the TAAS pass rates for White and Hispanic students from 1994 to 2000. For a more comprehensive racial/ethnic comparison, I also include African American pass rates. The data in Table 1.2 show that *all* racial/ethnic groups demonstrated substantial gains in pass rates from 1994–2000, with Hispanic and African American students having the largest gains. Notwithstanding the TAAS test score gap reductions observed in Table 1.2, observable gaps in measured academic achievement between White–Hispanic and White–African American students clearly persist in Texas schools (see Texas Education Agency [2000a] for data on other grade levels).

Although TAAS test score gaps between White and Chicano/other Latino and White and African American students have decreased in Texas, have such gap reductions occurred at the national level? Barton's (2001) report, *Raising Achievement and Reducing Gaps: Reporting Progress Toward Goals for Academic Achievement* (submitted to the National Education Goals Panel), found that most states failed to significantly reduce the average NAEP achievement scores between students in the top 25 percent and bottom 25 percent of the distributions of White and racial/ethnic minority students (Black and Hispanic combined). Specifically, Barton reported:

- From 1992 to 1996, only *two* of the participating states (Georgia and Massachusetts) succeeded in reducing the gap in 4th grade math NAEP scores between White and minority students.
- From 1990 to 1996, *none* of the participating states succeeded in reducing the gap in 8th grade math NAEP scores between White and minority students.
- From 1992 to 1998, only *one* of the participating states (Delaware) was able to reduce the gap in 4th grade NAEP reading scores between White and minority students.

On a final note about NAEP performance, there is another alarming finding from recent data analyses. NAEP reading achievement is divided into four levels: "Below Basic," "Basic," "Proficient," and "Advanced." Donahue *et al.* (2001) reported that Black, Hispanic, and American Indian students—compared to their White peers—were far more likely to

Table 1.2 Grade 4 percent passing all TAAS tests taken, racial/ethnic comparisons: 1994–2000

Race/ethnicity	*Year*							*Gain in percentage points*
	1994	*1995*	*1996*	*1997*	*1998*	*1999*	*2000*	*(1994–2000)*
White	63	72	72	77	81	85	88	25
Hispanic	41	51	53	58	67	73	74	33
African American	32	39	45	50	59	62	64	34

Source: Adapted from Texas Education Agency (2000a, p. 6, Table 1.5).

Note
TAAS refers to Texas Assessment of Academic Skills. All TAAS tests taken refer to: reading, mathematics, and writing.

perform at the Below Basic level, and were far less likely to perform at the Advanced level on the 4th grade reading test. For example, in 2000, 27 percent and 11 percent of White students performed at the Below Basic and Advanced levels, respectively (Donahue *et al.*, 2001, p. 30, Figure 2.4). For Hispanic students, 58 percent and 3 percent of them performed at the Below Basic and Advanced levels, respectively (Donahue *et al.*, 2001, p. 31, Figure 2.4). Such strikingly disparate racial/ethnic patterns in NAEP data have been holding fairly stable since 1992.

Grade retention

In the first edition of *Chicano School Failure and Success*, I did not include "grade retention" as a schooling outcome experienced by some Chicano students. For two reasons, I have decided to include it in the second edition. First, although being retained at one's grade generally affects only a small proportion of Chicano students, the consequences of being retained can be quite negative for their educational progress (e.g., increasing the probability of dropping out). Second, grade retention is now intertwined with standards-based school reform via high-stakes testing. The current movement of anti-social promotion policy, in which high-stakes testing plays a crucial role in controlling promotion to the next grade, will have adverse impact on Chicano students by increasing their school failure (Valencia, 2000a). This significant issue will be further explicated by Valencia, Villarreal, and Salinas in Chapter 9 of the present volume.

Grade retention, a euphemism for "flunking," is a long-standing educational practice and concern in the U.S.[11] In *Laggards in Our Schools*, Ayres (1909) reported that a little over 16 percent of the nation's students were "repeating" class. His conclusion was that "slow progress" was the major reason why repeaters were being retained; late entrance to school was a small factor.

The rationale behind retention is that an extra year at the same grade will serve as a powerful remedy for the student who is experiencing school failure (e.g., reading significantly below grade level). This commonplace remedial strategy for school failure has been widely researched in the literature regarding its efficacy. The existing literature on grade retention shows, quite strongly, that this policy has not fulfilled its promise. House (1989) noted: "the practice of retaining students in education is absolutely contrary to the best research evidence" (p. 204). Conclusions such as the following are frequently voiced: "reviews of the literature . . . show little to no academic achievement benefits from retention. . . . On average, retained children are worse off than their promoted counterparts on both personal adjustment and academic outcomes" (Holmes, 1989, pp. 17, 27). Roderick (1994) commented: "This literature [the impact of retention on school performance] almost unanimously concludes that retention is not as effective as promotion in improving school performance" (p. 732).[12]

The literature on the issue of grade retention–promotion, both in empirical studies and expository writings, is voluminous. The interested reader who wants to learn more about the issues surrounding retention–promotion may want to consult the more well-known literature reviews on the topic (e.g., Holmes, 1989; Holmes and Matthews, 1984; Jackson, 1975; Shepard, 1989; Shepard and Smith, 1990). Also, there is a prominent book on grade retention by Shepard and Smith (1989), *Flunking Grades: Research and Policies on Retention*. A number of empirical studies and literature reviews have reported that students who are retained, compared to matched students who were promoted, typically fall behind in their academic achievement (e.g., reading; mathematics), make fewer or no gains, and seldom or never catch up.[13] Furthermore, there are ample and consistent findings from the literature

Table 1.3 Grade promotion and failure percentages by race/ethnicity in Austin public schools: 1942–1943

School level	Anglo–American		Spanish-name	
	Promotion (%)	Failure (%)	Promotion (%)	Failure (%)
Elementary	94	6	76	24
Junior high	92	8	88	12
Senior high	80	20	70	30

Source: Adapted from McLean (1950, p. 41, Figure 15).

that strongly link grade retention of students with an increased likelihood that they will drop out of school.[14]

There are considerable historical and current data showing striking racial/ethnic differences in grade retention rates in the Southwest, with Chicano students having higher rates compared to White students. In the case of Chicano students in Texas, for example, a number of investigations from decades past reported that Chicano students, compared to their White peers, were more frequently overage for their grade level (e.g., Coan, 1936) and were more frequently retained (e.g., Calderón, 1950; McLean, 1950). As a case in point, McLean—more than a half-century ago—undertook a longitudinal investigation of Austin, Texas public schools. As part of his study, McLean reported grade "promotions" and "failures" for "Anglo-American" (i.e., White) and "Spanish-name" (i.e., Mexican American) students at the elementary, junior high, and high school levels. His findings are shown in Table 1.3. McLean's data show that Chicano students in the Austin public schools were, in comparison to their White peers, four times more likely to be retained at the elementary school level, and 1.5 times more likely to be retained at the junior high and high school levels.[15]

Historically, the most comprehensive investigation of racial/ethnic differences in grade retention in the Southwest was the landmark MAES conducted by the U.S. Commission on Civil Rights three decades ago. In report no. 2 of the MAES (U.S. Commission on Civil Rights, 1971b), data are presented for grade repetition by race/ethnicity (White; Mexican American; Black) for the five Southwestern states. Regarding retention rates of White and Mexican American students, two major points can be gleaned from these revealing historical data reported over 30 years ago. First, Mexican American students, in comparison to their White peers, experienced higher rates of first- and fourth-grade repetition in each of the five states in the Southwest. For the aggregated data for all five states, Mexican American first graders and fourth graders were retained, respectively, at rates 2.7 times and 2.2 times greater than their White peers. Second, of the five Southwestern states, Texas showed the highest retention rates (first and fourth grades) for Mexican American students. For example, 22.3 percent of Mexican American first graders were retained—3.1 times the White percentage of 7.3 percent; Colorado had the lowest retention rates (first and fourth grades) for Mexican American students. Regarding Mexican American students, the focal group of the MAES, the U.S. Commission on Civil Rights (1971b) drew this conclusion about the connection between grade repetition and academic achievement:

There appears to be a strong relationship between grade repetition and low student achievement. *Thus, the State of Texas, which has the highest proportion of grade repetition in the first and fourth grades, also has 74 percent, the highest proportion of Mexican American eighth graders reading below grade level.*

(p. 36)

Regarding current grade retention information by race/ethnicity, such data are scattered (for national data on the overrepresentation of Hispanic students among the retained, see Meisels and Liaw, 1993). Yet, there is one document—the *2000 Comprehensive Biennial Report on Texas Public Schools* (Texas Education Agency, 2000a)—that contains rich data. For the five academic years studied (1994–1995 to 1998–1999), the number of retained students in K-12 totaled nearly three-fourths of a million (741,741) at an aggregated retention rate of 4.3 percent (my calculations from p. 48, Table 4.1 in Texas Education Agency, 2000a). The average yearly number of retained students was 148,348. It is important to keep in mind, however, that the average retention rate of 4.3 percent (for the five-year period) is for the aggregate—all racial/ethnic groups combined. When the data are disaggregated by race/ethnicity, however, a distinct pattern is observed (Texas Education Agency, 1998, 2000a). Figure 1.3 shows average grade retention percentages by race/ethnicity for academic years 1994–1995 through 1998–1999. These data in the *2000 Biennial Report* show that overall retention rates (K-12) range from 2.3 percent to 2.9 percent for White students, 5.6 percent to 6.4 percent for African American students, 5.6 percent to 6.5 percent for Hispanic (i.e., overwhelmingly Mexican American students), and 2.3 percent to 2.5 percent for other minority students (i.e., predominantly Asian Americans and American Indians). This comparative analysis informs us that Mexican American/other Latino and African American K-12 students were about *2.2 times more likely than their White peers to be retained during the 1994–1999 period*. As we have discussed, these current higher retention rates experienced by Chicano and African American students, in comparison to their White peers in Texas and elsewhere in the Southwest, are not recent developments. They appear to

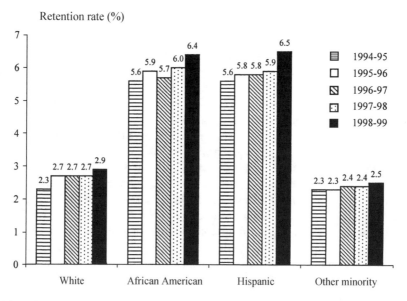

Figure 1.3 K-12 retention rates by race/ethnicity: 1994–1995 to 1998–1999.

Source: Texas Education Agency (2000a, p. 50, Figure 4.2).

be part of a continuous pattern of higher rates, as evidenced by data observed in reports 30 to 50 years ago. The extant literature on the relation between grade retention and diminished academic achievement informs us that being retained is a contributor to Chicano school failure. Later, in Chapter 9, Valencia *et al.* discuss how pending high-stakes testing at various promotional gates (e.g., grade 3) in Texas will exacerbate such school failure.

School holding power

This term was used by the U.S. Commission on Civil Rights (1971b) in its MAES. Rather than using the term "dropout," the Commission chose to use "school holding power"—which was defined as "A basic measure of a school system's effectiveness . . . to hold its students until they have completed the full course of study" [i.e., kindergarten through grade twelve] (p. 8). By placing the onus on the school for keeping students in school, the Commission advocated an anti-deficit thinking perspective.

The issue of very high dropout rates among Chicano youths has been a long-standing concern (see, e.g., Buckner, 1935; Cromack, 1949; Wilson, 1953; also see, San Miguel and Valencia, 1998). In a master's thesis (*A Study of Pupil Elimination and Failure Among Mexicans*) written 67 years ago, Buckner (1935) interviewed 160 "Mexican" students (80 boys; 80 girls) who had dropped out from Los Angeles County area public schools. Buckner provides rich data on age of dropping out, reasons for leaving schools, familial background of students, occupational status of dropouts, reentry desires of the ex-students, efforts by schools to prolong school longevity of Mexican students, and so on. In an atypically sensitive insight to the plight of Mexican students, Buckner voices this about his study's purpose:[16]

> It is hoped that a much clearer insight will be given of the Mexican trying to adjust himself to "our" schools; that a more sympathetic attitude on the part of the public school for and toward the Mexican school population will result.
>
> (p. 1)

Finally, commenting on the consequences of dropping out, Buckner's words of more than six decades past still carry some merit today:

> The cost of failure in school and the stupendous cost of caring for indigents after leaving school places a responsibility upon the educator of America to better prepare Mexican pupils for a more complex society, to become better American citizens and to become economically substantial. Permitting gross negligence toward meeting the problem of elimination and failure and the failure to study the problem will not solve it.
>
> (p. 7)

The scandalously high dropout rate among Chicano youths first received national attention more than 30 years ago with the publication of report no. 2 of the MAES (U.S. Commission on Civil Rights, 1971b).[17] With respect to comparative school holding power rates for White and Mexican American students within the five Southwestern states, the MAES reported rates of 86 percent and 60 percent, respectively. When disaggregated by state, Arizona showed the highest Mexican American school holding power rate (81 percent), and Texas, as expected, the lowest (53 percent). The school holding power rates for the other Southwestern states were: California, 64 percent; Colorado, 67 percent; and New Mexico, 71 percent. The MAES did not offer a discussion of possible reasons for the differences in school holding power among the five states. As to why Texas had the lowest school holding power rate, San Miguel and Valencia (1998) suggest that this was largely due to Texas having a longer and more pronounced history of inferior education regarding Mexican Americans.

Although completion rates for both Whites and Mexican Americans have risen, current data on school holding power or dropouts rates show that the gap strongly persists. National trend analyses from 1975 to 1995 for persons 25 to 29 years of age reveal that the Latino high school completion rate, as well as the rate for Whites, has increased (Carter and Wilson, 1997). The White-Latino gap, however, has remained relatively constant, on the average, about 30 percentage points over the 20-year period. For instance, in 1975 the White and Latino high school completion rates were, respectively, 65 percent and 38 percent—a gap of 27 percentage points. In 1995, the White and Latino rates were, respectively, 83 percent and 53 percent, a gap of 30 percentage points. Given that Mexican Americans have the *lowest* high school graduation rate of any Latino subgroup (Chapa and Valencia, 1993, p. 173, Table 6), this White-Latino gap is likely to be larger for a White/Mexican American comparison.

Even more contemporary data show that public schools have poor school holding power in relation to Chicano students. For example, in Texas, data from 1998–1999 show that Chicano (and other Latino) students comprised 36.0 percent of all students in the 7th–12th grade total enrollment, yet were 52.2 percent of all 7th–12th grade dropouts. By contrast, Whites comprised 47.0 percent of the 7th–12th grade cohort, and only 25.4 percent of the dropouts (Texas Education Agency, 2000a, p. 23, Table 4.1).

Recent data at the national level show that the five Southwestern states fare quite poorly in their "cohort survival rate," which is defined as the "ratio of fall 9th grade enrollment divided by regular high school graduates 4 years later" (Rubanova and Mortenson, 2001, sheet 22). The median cohort survival rate in 1998–1999 (based on the 50 states and the District of Columbia) was 71.8 percent (Connecticut, rank 26). All five Southwestern states had cohort survival rates *below* the median. These rates (in descending order) and ranks are as follows:

State	Rate (%)	Rank (out of 51)
Colorado	70.4	30
California	68.3	33
Texas	60.6	38
Arizona	60.2	39
New Mexico	59.4	42

Rubanova and Mortenson also provided national cohort survival rates for each consecutive year from 1981 to 1999. For these 19 yearly data points, Colorado had rates at or above the median for 14 years. By contrast, the other Southwestern states—Arizona, California, New Mexico, and Texas—all had cohort survival rates below the median for each of the 19 yearly data points.

Suffice it to say, there is widespread interest and activity in trying to understand and cope with the Chicano dropout problem. Rumberger and Rodríguez (Chapter 4, present book) provide a comprehensive analysis of (a) the incidence of the dropout problem, (b) causes and explanations for Chicano dropouts, (c) consequences of dropping out, and (d) addressing the problem of Chicano dropouts.

School financing

Since the beginning of public education in the Southwest, Chicano students have been shortchanged in the funding of their schools. Reynolds (1933) in a regional study (*The Education of Spanish-Speaking Children in Five Southwestern States*) sponsored by the Office of Education of the Department of the Interior reported: "Teaching materials adequate in amount and of the right kind for Mexican children are conspicuously absent" (p. 13). A great deal of these historical financing inequities can be attributed to the rise of segregation between 1930 and 1960 (San Miguel and Valencia, 1998). The financial neglect of Chicano segregated schools during this period has been amply documented (see, e.g., Calderón, 1950; Gilbert, 1947; see also, San Miguel and Valencia, 1998).[18] Mexican American education from 1930 to 1960 was not only characterized by the rise of school segregation, but also by the inferior nature of such schooling during the pre- and postwar years. For example, in 1934 the League of Latin American Citizens (LULAC) issued a report on the condition of schools in the West Side barrio of San Antonio (San Miguel, 1987), which noted that the teacher–student ratio in the West Side schools was 1:46, while the ratio in the Anglo schools was 1:36. The report also stated that the per pupil expenditures were $24.50 and $35.96, respectively, for the Mexican American and Anglo schools. Conditions deteriorated in San Antonio to such a degree that community activist Eluterio Escobar described (in 1947) the temporary wooden classroom buildings as "fire traps" (García, 1979).

Over the years, school finance equity litigation has taken on national prominence, and Chicanos have been the torchbearers. As Hertert (1994) observed:

> Since the first legal challenge was filed almost thirty years ago, courts in thirty-six states have considered plaintiff's allegations that their state's method of financing public education violated certain constitutional requirements. In some states the matter was settled swiftly and decisively. In others, successive challenges were mounted, and in at least one state, Texas, the time required to settle its case is approaching the incredible. Federal district courts, state courts, and the United States Supreme Court have all considered the question.
>
> (p. 1)

Of the numerous school finance lawsuits, two of the most significant and well known cases have been brought forth by Chicano plaintiffs—*Serrano v. Priest* (1969) in California and *Rodríguez v. San Antonio Independent School District* (1971) in Texas. Regarding the importance of *Serrano*, Hertert (1994) has noted that the case was highly influential in that litigative strategy by plaintiffs shifted away from an early definition of equity (referred to as "children's equity" by Hertert) in which "plaintiffs sought equal spending per pupil or distributions based on educational need" (p. 1). As Hertert discusses, this litigative approach proved unsuccessful in the courts. As a result, the plaintiff's requests shifted to a new definition of equity, "equity as equal access to a tax base." Here, plaintiffs moved to the conception of "equity as defined as equal access, with the focus on the district's ability to raise funds rather than on the monies spent on children" (p. 1). *Serrano* was significant in that the lawsuit resulted in a new and acceptable standard for the court (the California Supreme Court ruled that the plaintiffs' complaint was legally sufficient).

The *Rodríguez* (1971) case of Texas is also considered one of the most important school finance equity cases in educational history.[19] *Rodríguez* spanned a quarter of a century before being resolved. It is unique in that it is the first, and only, case of school finance equity to be adjudicated before the United States Supreme Court. Hertert (1994) offered this historical note:

> The second influential case of this period, *Rodríguez v. San Antonio Independent School District* (1971) became the first—and only—school finance equity proceeding for which the United States Supreme Court has issued an opinion. Filed in federal district court, this suit claimed, as had others, that the state financing system discriminated against the plaintiffs in terms of fewer education resources and a lower quality of education. Further, they claimed that the finance system fostered racial discrimination.
>
> The district court postponed its decision for some two years in the hope that the Texas Legislature would remedy the disparities inherent in the state's financing system. In 1971, unimpressed with the legislature's actions or lack thereof, the court ruled the system unconstitutional, basing its reasoning on *Serrano*. Texas appealed to the United States Supreme Court and, in the spring of 1973, the Court in a five to four decision reversed the lower court's ruling, and thus limited the possibility of successfully basing legal challenges on the equal protection clause of the federal Constitution.
>
> (p. 10)

Notwithstanding the U.S. Supreme Court's decision in 1973, the *Rodríguez* case remained quite alive. Reestablished on May 23, 1984 as *Edgewood*, 13 public school districts sued the State of Texas, alleging that their pupils were not receiving equitable educational funds. At that time, the most affluent districts in Texas were spending $2,000 to $10,000 more in the education of each of their pupils, compared to the poorest districts (Brooks, 1994). After vigorous litigation by both plaintiffs and defendants, the Texas Supreme Court ruled in a 9–0 decision on October 2, 1989 that the state's public school system of financing was unconstitutional (Graves, 1989). The court's mandate to state legislators was blunt: Prepare a new, comprehensive funding plan by May, 1990. Appeal after appeal occurred after the Legislature passed three different laws to no avail. Even property-poor school districts challenged the most recent funding law, claiming the new strategy actually takes money from them (Graves, 1993). In what seemed to be an endless case, State District Judge Scott McCown of Austin upheld the new law "but he ordered lawmakers to devise an equitable way of paying for classrooms and equipment by Sept. 1, 1995" (Brooks, 1994, p. A6). Immediately, a fourth appeal was filed and the case was to be heard by the Texas Supreme Court. Finally, in 1995, the Court—in a 5–4 ruling—upheld the latest plan, Senate Bill (SB) 7 to provide a constitutionally acceptable school finance system.

Although there have been gains in providing a more equitable school finance system in Texas via Senate Bill (SB) 7, the crisis is not over. Two issues are noteworthy. First, there is the subject of "Chapter 41" schools. Under the changes in the school finance law in Texas, districts that become property wealthy, or super rich—as defined by a formula in which wealth per student equals at least $295,000 per student—are required to share their wealth with poorer districts. As of the 2000–2001 school year, there were 84 Chapter 41 districts (8.1 percent of the 1,041 total districts; Texas Education Agency, 2000b). During the 2000–2001 academic year, these 84 districts shared $522 million of their property-tax revenues (Parrott, 2001). Based on a demographic analysis I conducted, 61 (72.6 percent) of the 84 districts are majority White, and 21 (25.0 percent) are majority minority.[20] It is with some of these latter districts where the irony rests. For example, in the Austin Independent School District (AISD)—the largest, by far, of the Chapter 41 districts ($N = 77,723$ students)—65.2 percent of the K-12 enrollment in 1999–2000 was minority (including

45.8 percent Chicano/other Latino, 16.7 percent African American, and 2.8 percent other). AISD was required, under state law, to surrender $34.1 million in property taxes in the 2000–2001 school year (Spencer, 2001). Under the wealth-sharing formula, AISD relinquished $94.6 million in the 2001–2002 school year (Spencer, 2001). This is a sad state of affairs, as AISD is a highly segregated school district with a large number of Chicano and African American students who, as a group, do not academically perform at par with their White peers (see Chapter 3 by Valencia *et al.*, present book).

On a final note regarding Chapter 41 districts, four of the 84 property-wealthy districts filed suit in April, 2001. The plaintiffs call the funding plan "an unconstitutional statewide property tax" (Parrott, 2001, p. B1) and are asking for relief. Parrott reported that, "Nearly three dozen [other Chapter 41] districts were expected to file documents in support of the four lead plaintiffs" (p. B1). Plaintiffs argue that due to sharing their wealth, they simply have less money with which to fund, for example, some ongoing curriculum projects, to hire new teachers and teachers' aides, and to reduce class size (Reston, 2001a). José Cárdenas, a well known scholar of Mexican American education in Texas and lifelong activist for educational equity, "used one word to describe his reaction to the new round of lawsuits by wealthy districts who are once again challenging the state's [school funding] system: 'disgust'" (Reston, 2001b, p. A1). In her interview with Cárdenas, reporter Reston wrote:

> After more than a 30–year struggle and five major lawsuits, Texas finally has a system that approaches equity, Cárdenas says, and the same wealthy school districts that he has been fighting for decades are still trying to tear it down.
>
> (2001b, p. A13)

On July 11, 2001, Travis County Judge Scott McCown dismissed the plaintiffs' lawsuit, ruling that it was premature for property-wealthy districts to bring suit because only a small percentage of districts in the state had reached the level of wealth that triggered the state's share-the-wealth law. It appears that the financial concerns raised by the property-wealthy districts will be a top priority for legislation when the Legislature convenes in 2003 (Reston, 2001c).

In addition to the Chapter 41 district issue, a second major issue regarding school finance equity in Texas involves a serious limitation in the 1995 Texas Supreme Court approved SB 7. Although the law provides for funding of maintenance and operations, it does not include a separate provision for funding *school facilities* (e.g., new school construction) (Dawn and McLaughlin, 1996). Such funding needs are very prevalent in Texas public elementary, middle, and high schools. In a statewide survey, Dawn and McLaughlin found "strong evidence that school districts are increasingly unable to provide facilities through local taxation efforts. . . . This knowledge is particularly true for school districts in regions with limited taxable property wealth" (pp. 1–2).

Dawn and McLaughlin (1996) estimated that $4.76 billion in facilities needs, covering 38 percent of Texas schoolchildren and youths (primarily in low-wealth districts) are needed. New school construction due to student enrollment growth, plant modernization needs, and financing underfunded state mandates was among the priority needs. Not surprisingly, many of these low-wealth districts are found along the Texas–Mexico border and in the Rio Grande Valley—a region where a substantial proportion of Mexican American students attend school. Regarding Brownsville Independent School District (BISD), as a case in point, in the 1999–2000 school year it enrolled 40,195 students (97.3 percent Mexican American/other Latino students; Texas Education Agency, 2000c). In describing the sad state of affairs in the BISD, Dawn and McLaughlin reported:

Brownsville is Texas' southernmost city, just across the border from Matamoros in the Mexican state of Tamaulipas. This urban school district is experiencing steady growth and many of the schools are overcrowded.

. . . With 525 portable buildings, Brownsville ISD has more portables than any other district in the state, including an elementary campus that consists entirely of portable buildings. The portables are moved from campus to campus as the attendance and growth patterns shift and change. Yet this large number of portables does not provide much relief from the overcrowded situations on many campuses as evidenced by its history of waiver requests, which include 58 requests for 25 campuses in three years.

Because waiver requests apply only to kindergarten through fourth grade classrooms, the waiver history does not reveal the extent of overcrowding problems. One of the existing middle school campuses that was built for 1,200 students is currently serving over 1,700 students, and another middle school campus serving about 1,300 students is operating at capacity.

One of the high school campuses that was built for 1,500 students now serves at least 2,200. This school is so overcrowded that lunch must be served in hallways and outdoor areas. The lunch lines are so long that students are often still in line when the lunch period ends. The principal at this school says that they have an open campus policy for lunch because they could not possibly serve all of the students on campus. This leads to problems with attendance because many students do not return to campus after they leave for lunch. This campus also has over 60 portables in its parking lot, most of which are over 20 years old and in relatively poor condition.

In lieu of new construction, Brownsville ISD also uses a year-round, multi-track school calendar to help alleviate overcrowding problems. Year-round schedules reduce the number of children on campus at any given time which makes it easier for students to move around and improves safety, but it is more expensive to operate schools year-round because of personnel costs and additional wear and tear on facilities. Because administrator burn-out is a problem in schools that operate on a year-round schedule, Brownsville has chosen to hire additional personnel in an effort to ease the administrative load. The increased personnel and operation costs of year-round school further limit the ability of the school district to devote funds to construction of new facilities.

(Appendix, pp. 1–3)

Now that we have entered the new decade, the nation's eyes will continue to be on Texas— our country's second most populous state, and home to approximately 5.1 million Chicanos (33 percent of the nation's total Chicano population of 20.6 million; U.S. Department of Commerce, Bureau of the Census, 2000). Notwithstanding some improvement in school financing reform, problems still exist—namely the oxymoronic nature of some Chapter 41 districts (e.g., AISD), and the severe problem in financing public school facilities. Regarding facilities, the resultant need for new school construction in Texas brought on by overcrowding will likely develop into a larger issue in light of the dramatic growth in the Chicano population (see Chapter 2, present volume). If the Texas Legislature does not act promptly in helping property-poor districts (primarily Chicano) resolve their school facilities financing problems, then Texas will continue with its two-tiered structure of public education—one kind for the economically advantaged, one kind for the poor.

Teacher–student interactions

Although it is small in quantity, there is evidence that teachers tend to treat Chicano students, compared to White students, less favorably (e.g., less praise) and hold lower expectations for Chicanos' academic success. Here, I am discussing both (a) interaction patterns between teacher and student, *and* (b) teacher expectations of Chicano students. I cluster both under "interactions" for ease of communication.

It is difficult to pinpoint the exact motivational bases for such biased teacher behavior, but one can draw inferences. It is probable that there are two kinds of forces at work. First, there are "perceived" personality or behavioral traits of Mexican American students that may influence unfavorable teacher–student interactions. There is evidence, some historical, that White educators hold negative stereotypes of Mexican Americans. For example, in her master's thesis, Meguire (1938) offered a primer for teachers of Mexican American students. She has a chapter, entitled "How to deal with racial traits." In the section, "Overcome the undesirable traits," she notes: "Those familiar with Mexican people list such traits as irresponsibility, imitativeness, thriftlessness, sex-consciousness, individualism,[21] and procrastination as being among the ones which hold them on the low plane at which most of them in the United States exist" (p. 52).[22]

A second likely factor that has shaped unfavorable teacher–student interactions is related to "educability." Here, I am conceptualizing educability as a belief one holds that the quality and quantity of schooling for an individual student is dictated by one's perceptions and/or measurement of that individual student's abilities and other background characteristics (Valencia, 1997b; also, see Valencia and Aburto, 1991a). There is much historical evidence that Chicano students' educability has been viewed as limited (Valencia, 1997b). To some extent, such negative perceptions of their educability have been molded by beliefs that a Chicano student's mental capacity is presumed deficient. As early as the second decade of the 20th century, such views by psychologists were voiced. Lewis Terman, father of the intelligence testing movement in the U.S., wrote in 1916 that the observed mental "dullness" of Mexicans, Indians, and Negroes of the Southwest "seems to be racial, or at least inherent in the family stocks from which they came" (p. 91). Regarding the educability of Mexican and other children of color, Terman opined: "*They cannot master abstractions* [italics added], but they can often be made efficient workers, able to look out for themselves. . . . Children of this group should be segregated in special classes and be given instruction which is concrete and practical" (p. 92). Terman's racist pronouncement likely helped spur the widespread belief that Mexican American children were not cut out for "book study" or "brain work," and thus should be trained for "hand work" (Stanley, 1920; see González [1990, 1999] for historical discussions of the industrial education of Mexican American children).

The practice of some White teachers treating Mexican American students less favorably than White students is related, in part, to teachers' perceptions of (alleged) diminished educability among the former students. Observe the findings from a study conducted more than six decades ago. Summers (1939) cited the findings by West (1936):

> He [West] found that Anglo-American teachers were more strongly inclined than were the Spanish-American [i.e., Mexican American] teachers to claim superiority for pupils of their own race. On the average the Anglo-Americans appeared to claim superiority in the traits by more than twice as great a percentage as the Spanish-Americans conceded the traits to the Anglos.

(pp. 4–5)

Regarding historical research findings of unfavorable teacher–Chicano student inter-actions, the literature is sparse, but informative. For example, Parsons (1965) found a great deal of racial/ethnic cleavage in a small farming community in California. Regarding school-ing, Parsons observed that social relationships and interactions between students and students, and teachers and students, mirrored the larger social structure of the community—one of White dominance. Teachers routinely demonstrated preference for Whites over Mexican Americans by selecting the former students for leadership roles. Mexican Americans were also negatively stereotyped by teachers (e.g., perceived to be lazy; not bright).

In the most comprehensive and frequently cited study to date of teacher–student inter-actions involving White teachers and Chicano students, the U.S. Commission on Civil Rights (1973) MAES report no. 5 (*Teachers and Students: Differences in Teacher Interaction with Mexican American and Anglo Students*) found significant differences in the quality and quantity of teacher–student interactions along lines of students' racial/ethnic background. Based on systematic observations and evaluations of teacher–student interactions in over 400 classes in New Mexico, California, and Texas, the Commission staff found—among other results—that Mexican American students, compared to Whites, received significantly less praise and encouragement from White teachers. Furthermore, teachers were found to spend significantly less time in asking questions of Mexican Americans, and they provided signifi-cantly more non-criticizing talk to White pupils than to Mexican Americans. These and other findings of teacher–student disparities in interaction patterns led the U.S. Civil Rights Commission to conclude:

> The basic finding of this report is that the schools of the Southwest are failing to involve Mexican American children as active participants in the classroom to the same extent as Anglo children. . . . The classroom is the setting in which a child's schooling takes place and the interaction between teacher and students is the heart of the educational process . . . all elements of this interaction, taken together, create a climate of learning which directly affects educational opportunity. Consequently, the discovered disparities in teacher behavior toward Mexican Americans and Anglos are likely to hinder seriously the educational opportunities and achievement of Chicano pupils. These findings raise disturbing questions concerning the ability of our schools to meet the educational needs of all students adequately.
>
> (p. 43)

Subsequent investigations have provided some confirmation of the earlier research that observed White teachers treat Chicano students less favorably than their White peers (see, e.g., Buriel, 1983; Cazden, 1988; Foley, 1990; Ortiz, 1988).[23] With respect to teacher expectancies, it has been found that White students are expected to outperform, academi-cally, their Mexican American peers (Prieto and Zucker, 1978; Zucker, 1979; Zucker and Prieto, 1978; all cited in Dusek and Joseph, 1983). Finally, there have been studies designed to assess Chicano and other Latino students' perceptions of their teachers (e.g., Delgado-Gaitán, 1986; Katz, 1999; Levy *et al.*, 1997). Katz, for example, reported that Mexican American and Latino middle school students "named teachers' discrimination against them as Latinos as the primary cause of their disengagement from school, [thus] refusing to invest in learning from these teachers" (p. 809).

In sum, it appears that some teachers in U.S. schools continue to respond more favorably and positively to White students than they do to Chicano students. This has serious implica-tions for improving teacher training (see Valencia *et al.*, Chapter 3, present book). Further-more, it is vital that our vision of schooling embraces philosophies and practices consonant with a democratic educational process in which useful knowledge, students' rights, and equal participation and encouragement are promoted (see, Pearl, Chapter 11, current volume).

Teacher certification

I include this schooling condition in the second edition of *Chicano School Failure and Success* in the light of a renewed interest in teacher quality, and the emergence of new data showing that teacher certification is associated with Chicano school achievement.[24]

Attention toward the preparation and quality of the nation's public school teachers has waxed and waned for decades. Once again, the limelight is on them. The recent American Federation of Teachers (AFT, 2000) task force report on K-16 teacher education called for "an urgent national commitment to bring higher quality, greater resources and more coherence to the way higher education screens and prepares teacher education candidates" (p. 7). The AFT report specifically recommended reshaping teacher preparation in ten significant ways (e.g., instituting higher entry criteria; having a national entry test; strengthening the clinical experience; instituting a rigorous exit/license test). In another recent national report on teacher quality (Finn *et al.*, 1999) released by the Thomas B. Fordham Foundation, 49 states were given "grades" based on four select criteria (e.g., accountability; subject mastery). The report concluded: "The news is not good. Overall, the states earn a 'D+' for their teacher quality policies" (p. iii). Texas, which earned an "A," was one of nine states that received an overall "A" or "B" grade. The report noted, however, that "Texas' greatest weakness is its vexing out-of-field teaching rate—some 49 percent" (p. 38).

Recent data confirm the criticism raised by Finn *et al.* (1999) that Texas has a problem with some of its teachers teaching subjects in which they are not certified. Triesman (1999) analyzed trends in Texas teacher certification data (1996–1997 school year) provided in a report by the State Board for Educator Certification (SBEC, 1998). His analysis examined, in part (a) number of students taught by noncertified teachers, (b) the type of schools in which certified teachers work, and (c) the relation between teacher certification and TAAS performance.[25] I can summarize Triesman's major findings in these three areas. First, the percentages of students taught by noncertified teachers ranged from 16.5 percent (pre-K to grade 6 level) to 22.2 percent (grade 9 to 12).[26] In all (i.e., pre-K to grade 12), over 3 million students (20.8 percent) of the total 14.7 million enrollment had noncertified teachers. The fact that one in five of public school students are being taught by noncertified teachers does not bode well for Texas. A related issue is that rookie teachers are more likely to be placed in high-enrollment minority schools, which is troubling given that the students who have the greatest needs are taught by the teachers with the least experience (see, e.g., Kurtz [1999] for a news report of the rookie teacher issue in the Austin Independent School District, a district that had twice as many teachers with no experience in low-SES schools, compared to schools with greater economic advantagement).

Second, Triesman (1999) also gathered SBEC data on *where* noncertified teachers held positions. This was done *indirectly* by identifying the percentage of *certified* teachers. The distribution of these certified teachers was examined by inspecting: (a) the percentage of economically disadvantaged students in schools; (b) the percentage of White students in schools; and (c) school type (e.g., rural; urban; suburban). The analyses were provided for elementary, middle school, and high school teachers (1996–1997 school year).[27] Triesman's study of the SBEC data informs us that noncertified teachers disproportionately teach in low-socioeconomic status (SES), urban, high enrollment minority schools in Texas.[28] Although one cannot conclude unequivocally that a noncertified teacher is less qualified to teach than his/her certified peer, the question of qualifications remains a specter. All students

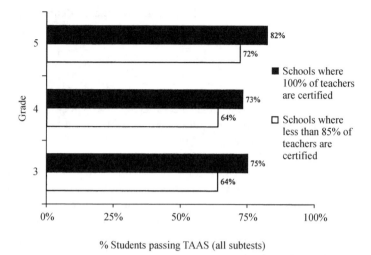

Figure 1.4 Relation between teacher certification and students' TAAS performance.

Source: Adapted from Triesman (1999).

and parents, regardless of race/ethnicity and SES, deserve teachers who have state credentials that document they have (a) taken course work in the subject areas they teach, (b) acquired knowledge of teaching methodology, and (c) passed a state teacher examination for licensure.

The third major aspect of Triesman's (1999) analysis of SBEC data was concerned with the relation between teacher certification status and TAAS performance. This association was examined for grades 3, 4, and 5 for (a) all students, (b) disaggregated by race/ethnicity, and (c) for economically disadvantaged students.[29] Figure 1.4 shows the finding for all students. The data suggest a link between teacher certification and students' TAAS performance (1997 scores). Comparisons are made between schools where 100 percent of the teachers are certified and schools where 85 percent or less of the teachers are certified. The differences in pass rates at grades 3, 4, and 5 are 12, 9 and 10 points, respectively. Students who attend schools that have 85 percent or less of the teachers noncertified, compared to students who attend schools that have 100 percent of the teachers certified, have a lower probability of passing all TAAS subtests. Although I do not present the data here, this pattern is observed for all three racial/ethnic groups. The magnitude of the difference in pass rates, however, varies across groups. At grade 3, Hispanic students show the largest difference (9 points), Whites the smallest (6 points). At grade 5, Whites show the largest difference (7 points), and African Americans the smallest (4 points). At grade 5, African Americans have the highest (13 points), Whites the smallest (4 points).

In conclusion, the data provided by Triesman (1999) demonstrate two major associations. First, noncertified teachers are more likely to teach in high-enrollment minority schools than in high-enrollment White schools. Second, noncertified teachers are more likely to be found in schools with lower TAAS scores. Given these findings, we can conclude that there is a connection between teacher certification status and students' TAAS performance. For Chicano and African American students, this linkage works against them. There are data from other investigations that have also drawn conclusions about the association between teacher qualifications and students' test scores. For example, Goldhaber and Brewer (1997), using data from the National Educational Longitudinal Study of 1988, found that "several teacher characteristics (in particular, teachers' math specific preparation) do appear to matter—that is, they are statistically significant and influence student achievement [i.e., 10th-grade math test scores] in the expected direction" (p. 506).

Curriculum differentiation

Curriculum differentiation, which I define as the *"sorting of students into instructional groups based on perceived and/or measured educability"* (Valencia, 1997c, p. 71), first came into widespread practice in the 1920s with the advent of mass intelligence and achievement testing (see, e.g., Chapman, 1988; Valencia, 1997c).[30] The historical justification for curriculum differentiation was grounded in the belief that too many differences in ability level among students in the same classroom created ineffectual climates for teaching and learning. The argument went: The presence of "slow" learners and "fast" learners learning together resulted in frustration for the former and boredom for the latter. As such, it was asserted, having classes with an excessive variability in mental ability made for a pedagogical disadvantage. The solution? Curriculum differentiation. The sorting tools? Intelligence and achievement tests. The anticipated results? Efficiency (Valencia, 1997c).

Regarding Chicano students and curriculum differentiation, historical analysis informs us that whether Mexican Americans were enrolled in (a) "Mexican" schools, (b) self-contained and separate classrooms in racially/ethnically mixed schools, or (c) mixed classrooms in mixed schools, they were presented an inferior, differentiated schooling that led to "the unwritten tradition of tracking Mexican children into vocational and slow learner classes [that] became institutionalized almost everywhere" (González, 1990, p. 23).[31]

More than a quarter century ago, the MAES report on ability grouping revealed that curriculum differentiation continued to prevail into the contemporary period (U.S. Commission on Civil Rights, 1974). Drawing from survey data of 1,100 schools in the Southwest, the Commission found clear evidence of unfavorable curriculum differentiation *vis-à-vis* Mexican American students. The majority of Whites and Mexican Americans were placed in the medium-ability group level, and enrolled in average classes or provided average level instruction. The MAES suggested that medium-ability groups and average classes were of a standard curricular type. Mexican American students, however, were overrepresented (more than twofold) in low ability classes/instruction and underrepresented (by about twofold) in high ability classes/instruction.

Since the publication of the MAES study in 1974 (U.S. Commission on Civil Rights, 1974) there have been considerable research and writings that demonstrate curriculum differentiation—particularly tracking—has had a negative impact on Chicano/other Latino and African American students by denying them equal educational opportunity (e.g., Oakes, 1985, 1990, 1995; Oakes *et al.*, 1992; Page and Valli, 1990; Wheelock, 1992). In particular, Chicano and other students of color have been disproportionately excluded from acquiring "high-status" knowledge, the knowledge deemed to be a prerequisite for college admission and academic success in higher education (Oakes, 1985).[32]

Notwithstanding the great interest in curriculum differentiation and its connection to stratified schooling, it has only been in the last decade that researchers have studied this important issue using *national* student-level data (see, e.g., Braddock, 1990; Braddock and Dawkins, 1993; Hallinan and Kubitschek, 1999; Rees *et al.*, 1996). For example, Braddock and Dawkins analyzed data from the base year and follow-up of the National Educational Longitudinal Study of 1988 (National Center for Education Statistics, 1992); their focus was on 8th graders. Regarding "Latino" (which I assume includes Chicanos and other Latinos) and White comparisons, Braddock and Dawkins reported, in part, the following enrollment data across high- and low-ability groups by subject:

	English classes		Math classes	
	High	*Low*	*High*	*Low*
White	32%	14%	35%	15%
Latino	18%	29%	18%	25%

Similar patterns were observed for Anglo–African American and Anglo–American Indian comparisons.[33]

Curriculum differentiation and the resultant denial of equal educational opportunity for Chicano and other minority students are historically rooted and contemporarily pervasive. In speaking of the harm that accrues to these students, Oakes (1995) has noted that it takes at least three forms: "(a) unjustifiable disproportionate and segregative assignment to low-track classes and exclusion from accelerated classes; (b) inferior opportunities to learn; and (c) lower achievement" (p. 689). In the final chapter of this book ("Conclusions: towards Chicano school success"), I will offer some thoughts on how to approach the "detracking" of our schools.

College enrollment

In light of the low academic achievement of many Chicano students, their high dropout rate from secondary schools, their unmet language needs, and their limited access in secondary schools to high-status knowledge due to unfavorable curriculum differentiation, it is not at all surprising then that they enroll in disproportionately low numbers in higher education. This underrepresentation in college has been long-standing. As noted by San Miguel and Valencia (1998), in the 1920s, 1930s, and up to the mid-1940s, a Chicano presence in higher education was rare. For example, more than 70 years ago, Manuel (1930) surveyed institutions of higher education in Texas. He reported that of the 38,538 students who were enrolled in colleges and universities in Texas, only 188 (0.49 percent) were classified as "Mexican." Of these 188 students, 34 (18.1 percent) claimed residence in Mexico.

At the end of World War II, however, Mexican American enrollment in college increased as some Mexican American veterans took advantage of the G.I. Bill of Rights that provided them with low-interest loans to attend college (Morín, 1963). Notwithstanding this postwar increase of Chicano students in higher education, they remained severely underenrolled in college relative to their presence in the college-age population and in comparison to their White peers. Based on 1950 U.S. Census data, Barrett (1966) noted that only 2.2 percent of the "Spanish-speaking" people (overwhelmingly Mexican American) in Texas had completed "college or more" (p. 181, Table 9B), although they comprised 13.4 percent of the Texas population. This disparity (underrepresentation), which I calculated, is 83.6 percent. Similarly low underrepresentation rates in college completion also existed for the Spanish-speaking populations in the other Southwestern states of Arizona, California, Colorado, and New Mexico (compare Tables 1C and 9B in Barrett [1966], pp. 161 and 181, respectively).

Even 20 years later, following the reporting of the 1950 Census data, Chicano presence in higher education was dismal. The MAES in its report no. 2—*The Unfinished Education: Outcomes for Minorities in the Five Southwestern States* (U.S. Commission of Civil Rights, 1971b)—found that for the five Southwestern states, combined, 49 percent of White students entered college, and 24 percent completed. By sharp contrast, 23 percent of Mexican

American students entered college, with only 5 percent finishing and earning bachelors' degrees.

Many other studies over the years, including U.S. Census data, confirm that the low college enrollment and completion rates for Chicanos reported by the MAES study of 30 years past stubbornly persist (e.g., Carter and Wilson, 1997; Keller *et al.*, 1991; Olivas, 1986; Pérez and De La Rosa Salazar, 1993). For example, Carter and Wilson presented a national trend analysis (1975 to 1995) of college completion rates by race/ethnicity of persons 25 to 29 years of age. The Chicano and other Latino completion rate in 1975 was about 6 percent, rising to 9 percent in 1995. By contrast, the White completion rate was 15 percent in 1975 and 24 percent in 1995—thus pointing to a sharp increase in the White/Latino gap (from 9 percentage points in 1975 to 15 percentage points in 1995). These data were not disaggregated by Latino subgroup. If they had been, the White/ Mexican American completion gap would likely be larger—given that Mexican Americans have the *lowest* college completion rate of the various Latino subgroups (Chapa and Valencia, 1993, p. 173, Table 6).

There are a number of reasons why Chicanos, as a whole, do not enroll in higher education in the percentage one would expect based on their proportion of the college-age population (Mingle, 1987; O'Brien, 1993; Orum, 1986). In my view, the most revealing factor is their dismal enrollment in college preparatory courses. Although dated, Orum's (1986) report is informative. She found that 75 percent of Chicanos and other Latino high school seniors from a national study (U.S. Department of Education, 1980), had not completed high school curricula of a college preparatory nature. Furthermore, about 33 percent of these high school graduates had received a "D" or "F" grade-point average in one or more key academic subjects.

More recent data show that Chicano/other Latino high school students—compared to their White peers—continue to enroll in and complete college preparatory courses in significantly less numbers. Data from Texas' public high schools provides a definitive picture of this persistent pattern. For this analysis, I examined Texas Education Agency data (Texas Education Agency, 2000c) for the 1999–2000 school year. The data set was the ten largest independent school districts (ISDs)—Arlington ISD, Austin ISD, Cypress-Fairbanks ISD, Dallas ISD, El Paso ISD, Fort Bend ISD, Fort Worth ISD, Houston ISD, Northside ISD, and San Antonio ISD. For the high schools in these districts, district level data (1998–1999 school year) were available for (a) percentage of students completing and receiving credit for at least one advanced course in grades 9–12, and (b) percentage of students completing the "Recommended High School Program" (RHSP) or "Distinguished Achievement Program" (DAP; scrutiny of the requirements for these two programs—compared to the "Minimum Graduation Plan"—indicates that they are college preparatory programs). All data were presented by race/ethnicity (class of 1999 graduates). In *all* ten districts, White students had higher percentages, compared to Chicanos/other Latinos, in completing advanced courses, and in *nine of the ten* districts in which data were available, White students had higher percentages in comparison to Chicanos/other Latinos in completing the RHSP or DAP. For instance, in Fort Worth ISD, 23.4 percent of Whites—compared to 9.7 percent of Chicanos/other Latinos—completed advanced courses, and 20.4 percent of Whites— compared to 5.5 percent of Chicanos/other Latinos—completed the RHSP or DAP.

How does such curricular stratification occur? If one is to conceive curriculum differentiation as an "allocation mechanism that sorts students into college preparatory (academic) or noncollege preparatory (vocational or general education) programs" (Braddock and Dawkins, 1993, p. 329), then one can address the above question as follows: Matriculating or not matriculating to college is highly associated with the degree of access a Chicano student has in acquiring high-status knowledge, the type of knowledge (e.g., critical thinking skills; intellectual risk-taking; scientific inquiry) that is a necessary for admission to, and success in, higher education.

Evidence abounds that Chicano students, in comparison to their White peers, do not, in fact, have equal access to high-status knowledge. Braddock and Dawkins (1993), in their analysis of the National Educational Longitudinal Study of 1988, reported that Latino 10th-graders—compared to their White peers—were significantly overrepresented in the "vocational" track at a rate of 60 percent higher. In the "academic" (i.e., college preparatory) track, Latino 10th-graders were significantly underrepresented, compared to White students, at a rate of 77 percent lower.

One would think that the active recruitment of Chicanos to higher education is a top priority of the public at large, and college officials. Two developments in California in the 1990s, however, have made it more difficult to recruit and enroll Chicanos.[34] In November 1996, Proposition 209—(the self-labeled "Civil Rights Initiative")—was passed by 54 percent of those who voted (Epstein, 1997). Prior to passage of this referendum, in 1995, the Regents of the University of California adopted a new admissions policy (SP 1) that ended affirmative action in the University of California system (Pachón *et al.*, 1997). Proposition 209 went much further, however, prohibiting local and state agencies from granting "preferential treatment" to racial/ethnic minorities and women in the areas of state contracting, employment, and education (Epstein). The ironically labeled Civil Rights Initiative brought an end to affirmative action in public higher education throughout California.

The impact of SP 1 and Proposition 209 on Chicano and other Latino student access to the University of California (UC) system is still emerging. The analyses presented by Pachón *et al.* (1997) show that in the UC system, Latino freshman enrollment rates increased from 1985 to 1989, were relatively stable through 1995, and declined from 1995 through 1998.[35] More recent data show that Chicano/other Latino UC undergraduate admits have continued to decline through 1999 (University of California, 2001). Even more dramatic enrollment decreases have occurred at law schools in the UC system, including Berkeley, Davis, and Los Angeles, where Chicano/Latino enrollments dropped by 50 percent between 1994 and 1997 (from 14.6 percent to 7.2 percent), while White enrollments in these law schools increased from 54.5 percent to 73.5 percent during the same period (Pachón *et al.*, 1997). These decreases are clear signs of the negative effects SP 1 and Proposition 209 are having on Chicano/Latino access to one of the premiere public university systems in the nation.

A similar blow to affirmative action occurred in Texas in the early 1990s. In 1992, Cheryl Hopwood, a White woman, was denied admission to The University of Texas School of Law. Hopwood, along with three other White plaintiffs who were also denied admission, filed suit against the university, claiming reverse discrimination as a result of the use of race in the law school's admission process. In 1994, U.S. District Judge Sam Sparks of Austin ruled in *Hopwood v. State of Texas* (1996) that although The University of Texas School of Law violated Hopwood's (and three other white plaintiffs') constitutional rights to equal protection under the Fourteenth Amendment, it did not have to ban its affirmative action policies. The plaintiffs appealed to the Fifth Circuit Court of Appeals, and to the shock and dismay of affirmative action proponents, the appellate court, in March 1996, reversed Judge Sparks' ruling (Phillips, 1996). Thus, the appellate courts' decision in *Hopwood* made illegal the use of race/ethnicity and gender (i.e., affirmative action) in undergraduate and graduate admissions in institutions of higher education within the jurisdiction of the Fifth Circuit Court of Appeals, which includes Texas, Louisiana, and Mississippi.

The effects of the *Hopwood* decision on Chicano (and African American) student enrollment in Texas higher education were immediately felt. Chapa (1997) reported that the admission of enrollment of Chicanos declined at The University of Texas at the undergraduate level and among first-year law and medical students. In an attempt to reverse declines of minority admissions at the undergraduate level in Texas public universities, House Bill (HB) 588 (authored by Mexican American State Representative Irma Rangel) and its Senate companion, SB 177 (authored by Mexican American State Senator Gonzalo Barrientos) were passed into law. Coined as the "Top Ten Percent Plan," high school students who graduate in the top 10 percent of their classes will be automatically admitted to one of Texas' premier institutions, such as UT or Texas A&M. "The intended effect of the automatic admissions policy, which does not allow standardized test scores or other criteria to be used in admissions, is for ethnic and racial minorities who attend [high] schools with high concentrations of minorities to be admitted" (Chapa, 1997, p. 11). The Top Ten Percent Plan went into effect in Fall 1998. It appears the plan has had some positive results. Chapa (2001), citing Walker (2000), notes that the Fall 1999 Latino freshman class at The University of Texas was comparable to the pre-*Hopwood* level. Chapa does note, however, that Texas A&M, another flagship university, had in 1999 far less minority students than was the case before *Hopwood*.

The recent attacks on affirmative action in California and Texas—the home states of about 74 percent of the nation's Chicano people (see Chapter 2, this volume)—have created a civil rights crisis in higher education. This arrives at a time when the Chicano/other Latino college-age population is growing at an unprecedented rate (Carnevale and Fry, 2000). Attempts to recruit and enroll these students in higher education in the current era of anti-affirmative action will be a major challenge. It appears, however, that the "percent plans"—as discussed above—hold some promise in attaining greater racial/ethnic diversity at the undergraduate level.

On a final note, it needs to be emphasized that the number of Chicano/other Latino undergraduates will rise nationally as a whole, and in all 50 states, in both absolute numbers of students and in percentage terms. Using U.S. Census Bureau projections of national growth and estimated growth for all 50 states (and the District of Columbia), Carnevale and Fry (2000, p. 9, Figure 2) have projected that Latino undergraduates (public and private colleges) will demonstrate the largest percentage point increase in undergraduate (UG) enrollment share, compared to the other racial/ethnic groups, for the 1995 to 2015 time period. These projections are:

Group	Net gain in percentage point change in share of UG enrollment from 1995 to 2015
Latino	+4.8%
Asian	+3.0%
African American	+0.4%
White	−7.8%

Although Latino college students are projected to have the largest percentage point change in share of the undergraduate enrollment from 1995 to 2015, a caveat is in order. White students will continue to comprise the strong majority of the nation's undergraduate college enrollment, as well as having the largest excess in student enrollment (about 400,000) in 2015, in relation to the overall population share of 18- to 24-year-olds (Carnevale and Fry,

2000, p. 10, Figure 3). Regarding racial/ethnic minority groups, Carnevale and Fry note that while minority college enrollment in undergraduate education is on the rise, "the playing field still will not be level in 2015. Among minority groups, only Asian youth will be attending college in numbers at or above their share of the 18- to 24-year-old U.S. population" (p. 10). Latino students will incur the largest deficit in student enrollment (approximately 550,000) in relation to the overall 18- to 24-year-old U.S. population share. The deficit for African American students will likely be in excess of about 250,000 (see Carnevale and Fry, 2000, p. 10, Figure 3).

Special education

In addition to Chicano students being influenced by the currents of the educational mainstream, they are also—albeit in considerably smaller numbers—participants in the educational tributary referred to as "special education." Students in special education (e.g., students with mild mental retardation; specific learning disability) perform below the norm to such an extent that special intervention is necessary. Approximately 12 percent ($n = 5.6$ million) of the nation's 46 million elementary and secondary public school students in 1998 were served in special education (U.S. Department of Education, Office for Civil Rights, 2001).

How have Chicanos fared historically in the special education system? Are they over-represented in certain special education categories? How responsive has special education been in meeting the low academic achievement of Chicano students, especially ELLs? Since the time Rueda (1991) wrote his special education chapter for the first edition of *Chicano School Failure and Success*, what major developments have occurred in the 1990s that helped shape the current context of special education and its relation to Chicano students? Rueda *et al.* in Chapter 10 of the present book provide comprehensive coverage of these and other important questions. More specifically, Rueda *et al.* discuss a number of new issues and developments pertinent to Chicano students (e.g., changes in special education legislation; political initiatives; teacher preparation and professional development; school reform; assessment and diagnosis concerns; changing theoretical views of teaching and learning). The authors outline alternatives to the current education system/structure and identify the challenge to be faced as changes are considered and implemented.

Gifted/talented education

In the first edition of the present book, I did not include "gifted/talented education" as a schooling condition. I do so, however, in this second edition. As evidenced by the growing number of scholarly article citations and published books, the study of gifted/talented students (hereafter referred to as "gifted" students) and their education has now become a distinct scholarly domain in education and psychology (see Valencia and Suzuki, 2001, p. 209). Notwithstanding the growth in the study of gifted students, an examination of the literature informs us that "there is a large amount of information about gifted White students (particularly of middle- and upper-socioeconomic status . . . backgrounds). Regarding gifted minority students, however, a similar claim cannot be made" (Valencia and Suzuki, 2001, p. 209). The scant amount of literature on gifted minorities has spurred a renewed interest in the field, with a focus on the various racial/ethnic minority groups: African American (e.g., Woods and Achey, 1990), Mexican American (e.g., Tallent-Runnels and Martin, 1992), Asian American (e.g., Plucker, 1996), and American Indian (e.g., Romero, 1994).

In Chapter 9 of the present volume, Valencia *et al.* provide a brief section on gifted Chicano students. The issue the authors highlight is the nagging underrepresentation of Chicano and other Latino students in programs for the gifted. Table 1.4 presents data from the U.S. Department of Education, Office for Civil Rights (2001) 1998 national survey (K-12 grades) on the incidence of gifted students by race/ethnicity. In Table 1.4, I provide incidence data for "Hispanic" and White students for the five Southwestern states. I also present disparities (over- and underrepresentations) that I calculated. The data in Table 1.4 show highly discernible patterns across race/ethnicity. For Hispanics (overwhelmingly Chicanos), they are *underrepresented* in each of the Southwestern states, ranging from a high rate (54.2 percent) in Arizona to a low rate (30.6 percent) in Colorado. Regarding White students, they are *overrepresented* in all five states, ranging from a high rate (84.7 percent) in New Mexico to a low rate (9.1 percent) in Colorado. What is so disturbing about the underrepresentation of Chicano and other Latino students in gifted programs is that the pattern is not merely confined to the five Southwestern states. Chicanos/Latinos are underrepresented in such programs in *49 of 50* states (Louisiana being the exception) plus the District of Columbia (U.S. Department of Education, Office for Civil Rights, 2001).

In addition to the underrepresentation issue of Chicano students in gifted programs, Valencia *et al.* in Chapter 9 of the present book also offer a brief discussion on some of the bright spots in the existing literature on gifted Chicano and other minority students. A number of studies have identified, through discourse and empirical findings, specific practices that can lead to an increase in the percentage of gifted Chicano students, including ELLs.

Chicano teaching force

Another major problem facing Chicano school-age students is the low percentage of teachers of their own ethnic group. Ample data inform us that there is a large disparity (underrepresentation) of Chicano teachers in comparison to the Chicano school-age population. Why is this an issue? Valencia and Aburto (1991b) have developed a rationale for the value of having Chicano and other Latino teachers. They discuss three points. First, there is the notion of "shared identity" between teacher and learner. Drawing from the essay by Jackson (1986), in which he discusses the idea of shared identity, Valencia and Aburto (1991b) have asserted that given the common cultural heritage Latino teachers and students often share: "it appears that other factors being equal, Latino teachers are likely to have some advantage teaching and enhancing the learning of Latino students, with whom they share similar backgrounds" (p. 172).[36]

Second, Valencia and Aburto (1991b) discussed the importance of role models, which they argue, is a logical pedagogical extension of shared identity. One feature of role modeling is "model–client similarity." There is some research that similarity in model–learner attributes is associated with improvement in learning outcomes (e.g., Rosenthal and Bandura, 1978), and this generality can be extended to modeling in the school setting, in which research has shown teachers can and actually do serve as role models (e.g., Barton and Osborne, 1978; Brophy and Puttham, 1979). Thus, one can justifiably assert that Chicano and other minority students would educationally profit more directly from a teacher role model when there is a racial/ethnic match between teacher and learner (Graham, 1987).

A third facet of a rationale for having Chicano and other Latino teachers is multicultural education. Given the dramatic increase in the Latino school-age population, and the growth of the overall racial/ethnic minority K-12 sector, the need for a culturally pluralistic curricu-

Table 1.4 Disparity analysis of gifted and talented enrollment in five Southwestern states: 1998

State	Hispanic			White		
	Enrollment[a] (%)	Gifted/talented[b] (%)	Disparity[c] (%)	Enrollment[a] (%)	Gifted/talented[b] (%)	Disparity[c] (%)
Arizona	32.27	14.78	−54.20	54.83	73.39	+33.85
California	41.33	20.93	−49.36	37.71	54.42	+44.31
Colorado	19.65	13.63	−30.64	70.50	76.94	+9.14
New Mexico	47.85	22.73	−52.50	37.33	68.96	+84.73
Texas	37.83	26.43	−30.14	44.47	58.20	+30.88

Source: U.S. Department of Education, Office for Civil Rights (2001).

Notes
[a] Percentage Enrollment = percentage of racial/ethnic group in total K-12 enrollment.
[b] Percentage Gifted/Talented = percentage of racial/ethnic group in gifted/talented category.
[c] In the percentage disparity category, a plus sign (+) indicates overrepresentation and a minus sign (−) indicates under-representation.

lum is critical for minority, as well as for White students. Valencia and Aburto (1991b) noted that a growing numbers of scholars (e.g., Gay, 1988; Suzuki, 1984) contend:

> that the rationale for multicultural education rests on two firm foundations—valuative and ideological. The valuative foundation refers to the need to develop knowledge and to foster appreciation of ethnic and cultural diversity. The ideological aspect refers to the need to equalize educational opportunities—that is, the importance of linking multicultural education goals of excellence and equity for diverse learners.
>
> (Valencia and Aburto, 1991b, p. 173)

Although multicultural curriculum, as do all curricula, has standard components (e.g., rationale, goals and objectives, and means of evaluation; see Gay, 1988), the prime mover of the curriculum is the teacher. On the role of the teacher, Valencia and Aburto (1991b) commented:

> Given what we discussed earlier on the presumption of shared identity and role models, we would say that, as a whole, Latino teachers would have some advantage over White teachers in the delivery of multicultural education. Latinos, by their backgrounds and experiences, are: more likely to have had interactions with other Latinos in general, more able to empathize with Latino students, and more likely to share a common cultural heritage. In contrast, White teachers—as a whole—are more likely to have certain disadvantages in teaching multicultural education.
>
> (p. 174)

How grave is the Chicano teacher underrepresentation? To address this, let us turn to some data from California and Texas. Table 1.5 presents information on the underrepresentation of Chicano and other Latino teachers in the K-12 public school systems of both states. The data reveal that Chicano and other Latino teachers are severely *underrepresented* in California (70.1 percent) and Texas (58.1 percent). In comparison, White teachers are clearly *overrepresented* in both states—California (104.3 percent) and Texas (71.5 percent). Regarding California, it appears that the underrepresentation percentage has held fairly stable over the last decade and a half, while the White overrepresentation percentage has actually increased (compare recent data with older data presented in Valencia and Aburto, 1991b, p. 182).

Notwithstanding the overall shortage of Chicano teachers, a particularly critical need area is in bilingual education. As a case in point, let us examine this serious problem in Texas. In 1997–1998 (the most recent period in which I was able to obtain data), there were 9,616 teachers who held the bilingual education teaching certificate (State Board of Educator Certification, 1999). As of April, 2001, there were 284,223 ELLs (early childhood, pre-K, K, and grades 1–6) enrolled in bilingual education (computer printout provided by Texas Education Agency [TEA] Office of Bilingual Education; data source is the Public Education Information Management System). Based on a demand calculation of 22:1 (i.e., student to teacher ratio of 22 to 1, a TEA average minimum for elementary grades), I estimate a shortage of 3,303 bilingual teachers in Texas schools.

What obstacles do aspiring Chicano teachers face in becoming educators and how can Chicano (and other Latino) access to the teaching profession be improved? One major obstacle appears to be the very low percentage of Chicano students in college pursuing teaching careers (Valencia and Aburto, 1991b). This specific issue is related, of course, to the previous concern we discussed—i.e., the general problem of disproportionately low

Table 1.5 Disparity analysis of teachers by race/ethnicity in California and Texas K-12 schools: 1999–2000

State	Latino students		Latino teachers			White students		White teachers		
	No.	Total enrollment (%)	No.	Total teaching force (%)	Disparity percentage[a]	No.	Total enrollment (%)	No.	Total teaching force (%)	Disparity percentage[a]
California[b]	2,513,453	42.2	36,719	12.6	−70.1	2,195,706	36.9	220,250	75.4	+104.3
Texas[c]	1,578,967	39.6	44,555	16.6	−58.1	1,721,969	43.1	197,998	73.9	+71.5

Notes
[a] In the percentage disparity category, a plus sign (+) indicates overrepresentation and a minus sign (−) indicates underrepresentation.
[b] Data are from California Department of Education (2001).
[c] Data are from Texas Education Agency (2000c).

college enrollment of Chicano students. A second significant hurdle to improved Chicano teacher education is their disproportionately high failure rate on competency tests used for admissions to teacher education programs and eventual teacher certification (see, Valencia and Aburto, 1991b; Valencia and Guadarrama, 1996). With respect to the second part of the above question, "How can Chicano (and other Latino) access to the teaching profession be improved?," there are numerous possible strategies. In their review of the literature, Valencia and Aburto (1991c) identified at least 16 elements of collegiate outreach and intake strategies that have been, or can be, used to increase the number of Chicano and other minority teachers (e.g., early identification and recruitment of minority high school students; test-taking skills development; partnership cultivation between two-year and four-year collegiate institutions). Valencia and Aburto (1991c) also discussed ways in which teacher competency testing can be improved to increase Latino access to teaching.

In the final analysis, without an adequate supply of Chicano teachers, much is lost. This issue is disturbing and threatening to our society, which is ever increasing in its cultural and linguistic diversity. The severe shortage of Chicano and other minority teachers is solvable, where, given the political will, educators, researchers, and policymakers working together could rectify the problem (Valencia and Guadarrama, 1996). The comments (Valencia, 1991a) I shared in the first edition of *Chicano School Failure and Success* regarding the Chicano teacher shortage are worth repeating:

> The growing shortage of Chicano public school teachers is a concern for all in that it works against the need to have a multicultural teaching force at a time when our school system is becoming more and more culturally diverse. Chicano teachers are needed to serve as role models for Chicano students, to deliver bilingual education, and to help promote racial/ethnic understanding and respect among all students . . . for our country to dive into the twenty-first century without Chicano and other minority teachers is unpardonable. As such, we need to get on with the business of identifying and implementing strategies that will increase the percentage of Chicano teachers.
>
> (p. 14)

High-stakes testing

In the first edition of *Chicano School Failure and Success*, I did not list high-stakes testing as a schooling condition. Aburto and I (Valencia and Aburto, 1991a) did offer, however, a discussion in our testing chapter about the emergent data on this issue. At this time, high-stakes testing is a fully blown controversy in which Chicano and other minority students are major players.

Exactly what is high-stakes testing and how is it linked to standards-based school reform? Valencia and Bernal (2000a, p. 405) commented, as such:

> Standards-based school reform is rapidly sweeping across the terrain of U.S. public school education, kindergarten through twelfth grade (K-12). Large-scale criterion-referenced and norm-referenced achievement tests have become major barometers of students' academic achievement and progress. The national limelight is particularly on the use of "high-stakes testing," which holds important educational and personal consequences for students and sometimes their parents, teachers, administrators, schools, and districts. High-stakes tests are increasingly being used to make decisions about grade promotion, curriculum differentiation (e.g., tracking), and the awarding of a high school diploma. Heubert and Hauser (1999)—editors of *High-stakes: Tests for Tracking,*

Promotion, and Graduation—noted: "These policies enjoy widespread public support and are increasingly seen as a means of raising academic standards, holding educators and students accountable for meeting those standards, and boosting public confidence in the schools."

(p. 1)

In their testing chapter for this second edition, Valencia *et al.* (Chapter 9) include a discussion of how high-stakes testing is adversely impacting many Chicano students. As a case in point, the authors focus on Texas—particularly on a recent court case in which Chicano and African American student plaintiffs brought suit against the Texas Education Agency *et al.*, claiming discrimination in that they were being denied a high school diploma due to failure to pass a high school exit-level test (see Valencia and Bernal, 2000b, 2000c). Bernal and Valencia (2000) also discuss the pending Senate Bill (SB) 4 in Texas, a law that will go into effect in the 2002–2003 school year. SB 4 will authorize the use of high-takes testing to control promotion from grades 3, 5, and 8. Valencia *et al.* in Chapter 9 assert that the new law will exacerbate school failure for Chicano and African American students by increasing their retention rates (also see Valencia, 2000a). In addition to presenting a discussion of the adverse impact high-stakes testing has on minority students, Valencia *et al.* also offer some insights for realizing nondiscriminatory assessment.

School stress

Stress is typically defined as "any influence that interferes with . . . normal functioning . . . and produces some internal strain or tension" (Barker, 1987, p. 159; quoted in Icard *et al.*, 1999, p. 20). Stress can be positive (e.g., physically and mentally preparing in ways that will improve performance in a competitive athletic event) or negative (e.g., experiencing test anxiety that results in debilitative performance), the latter being "distress." Here, I use the term "stress" in the negative sense (for discussions on the construct of stress, see e.g., Attar *et al.*, 1994; Icard *et al.*, 1999; Mirowsky and Ross, 1989; Saldaña, 1994). Furthermore, here the focus is on stress among schoolchildren, which "derives from situations associated with parental, sibling, peer, and school relationships" (Icard *et al.*, 1999, p. 21).

In light of all the previously discussed unfavorable schooling conditions and outcomes faced by many Chicano students, it is not surprising that some of these students encounter stressful events and experiences that adversely affect their academic performance. The research on Chicano students and school stress is meager, but informative. Furthermore, such research has a basis in history. Over six decades ago, Kurth (1941) wrote a master's thesis on *A Study of Four Racial Groups in a Pasadena Junior High School*. Kurth noted that the purpose of her study "was to draw conclusions from whatever differences or similarities might be found that would be significant in the school adjustment and broader social adjustment of the members of these groups, especially of the non-White races" (p. 6). The author sought the attitudes of students (e.g., about themselves; toward school); the participating school was McKinley Junior High in Pasadena, California. In 1941, the time of the study, the total enrollment of the school was 1,328 students. The percentages of the four "racial" groups were: "White" (78 percent), "Mexican" (12.5 percent), "Negro" (5.6 percent), and "Oriental" (3.9 percent).

Although the questions posed to the students by Kurth (1941) were not directly developed to address school stress (nor did Kurth use the term "stress") one can imply that some of the questions did indeed tap into perceptions of school stress. For example, Kurth asked (question no. 48, an attitude about themselves item): "Do you find it difficult to overcome the feeling that you are inferior to others?" She reported that Mexican boys and girls (approximately $n = 20$ for each group) answered in the affirmative more frequently than the White boys and girls. Mexican boys and girls responded affirmatively ("often/sometimes") 52 percent and 56 percent of the time, respectively. In comparison, White boys and girls responded affirmatively 40 percent and 42 percent of the time, respectively. Another example is one of Kurth's question (no. 25) that dealt with attitudes toward school: "Is your work often so hard that you often stop trying?" Again, the Mexican boys (66 percent) and girls (61 percent) responded in the affirmative ("often/sometimes") more frequently than did the White boys (30 percent) and girls (47 percent). As noted earlier, Kurth's intention was not to study stress (her use of terms was "adjustment"). In any event, it would be fairly safe to conclude that most of her findings revealed Mexican students were not as well adjusted to school as were their White peers. It is highly suggestive that schooling for Mexican Americans was more stressful. Regarding minority (i.e., "non-White") students as a whole (Mexican, Negro, and Oriental), Kurth's concluding statements offer an insight to this probable existence of school stress among the students:

> All non-white children were bothered by feelings of inferiority and insecurity. They registered uneasiness in class discussions and reluctance to participate in class activities. It was apparent that most personal and social adjustments of these children were poor. Many non-white children felt that people were unfair to them and that frequently they felt there was no use trying to do anything. Many of them said they did not have as many friends as they wished they had.
>
> (p. 122)[37]

A small number of studies spanning the last 25 years plus have found that Chicano school-age students experience considerably high and harmful levels of stress (e.g., Alva and de Los Reyes, 1999; Attar *et al.*, 1994; Gerard and Miller, 1975; Icard *et al.*, 1999; Phillips, 1978). High stress levels have also been observed with Chicano college students (e.g., Muñoz, 1986; Saldaña, 1994). Regarding school-age youths, let us examine the investigation by Alva and de Los Reyes, as a case in point. The sample consisted of 171 9th-grade Latino students (males and females) from a predominantly Latino public high school in Los Angeles. Although the authors do not provide ample detail regarding the sample composition, it appears that at least one-half of the sample was Chicano. Based on four instruments that were designed to measure stress, anxiety, depressive symptomatology, and perceived competence (all viewed as possible predictor variables of academic achievement), Alva and de Los Reyes reported statistically significant relations "between psychosocial stress and an increase in internal symptomatology and a decrease in academic achievement among Hispanic adolescents" (p. 353).

As to why some Chicano and other minority students experience debilitating stress in school, one major factor—an "environmental stressor"—that has been of theoretical interest is racial/ethnic prejudice in the school setting. Goughis (1986) has commented that theoretically such "stress is likely to adversely affect [minority] students' daily academic performance by reducing their willingness to persist at academic tasks and interfering with the cognitive processes in learning" (p. 147). More recently, Clark *et al.* (1999) have developed a comprehensive biopsychosocial model in which White racism serves as a significant stressor for African Americans. This model appears to have some utility in understanding racism as a stressor for Latinos and other populations of color. Furthermore, Canino and Spurlock (2000) have discussed a number of social stressors (including prejudice and discrimination) that negatively affect culturally diverse children and adolescents.

Further research will inform us about how stressors tend to lower Chicano academic achievement. There is ample scholarly work available now, however, to help us be proactive in designing psychologically healthy learning environments for Chicano students and other students of color (see, e.g., Banks and McGee Banks, 2001; Nieto, 1996; Ovando and McLaren, 2000a; Pearl, Chapter 11, this volume).

The general profile I just painted of 15 schooling conditions and outcomes faced by many Chicano students is indeed disturbing. Yet, as we shall see in the chapters ahead, the authors are optimistic that Chicano school success can be realized. Many suggestions for promoting healthier and more equitable schooling experiences for Chicano students are offered. There is the need, however, to mount this formidable challenge in a timely fashion. Given the tremendous current and future growth rate of the Chicano population, now is the time for informed action. Lest, the educational progress of Chicanos will stagnate as their population swells (see Chapa and Valencia, 1993). In the next chapter, we examine these growth projections and changing demographic patterns, and the implications for the schooling of Chicanos.

Notes

1 García and Noble (1988) have drawn a sharp distinction between the concepts of "equity" and "equality." Equity, they assert, refers to the legal right of students having access to the same schools, textbooks, classes, and general educational resources. The landmark *Brown* decision (*Brown v. Board of Education of Topeka*, 1954) was the cornerstone of educational equity. The concept of equality, García and Noble assert, moves beyond the basic civil rights addressed by equity. Equality considers the reality that students (e.g., English language learners) may require different educational needs because of different educational characteristics. Thus, providing all students with equal educational opportunities may not necessarily result in equal outcomes. A good example of educational equality is bilingual education.

   Although the equity/equality framework discussed by García and Noble (1988) has merit, I prefer to use the term "equality" (and its converse "inequality") in a global sense because of its widespread use and ease of communicative import when discussing the plight of Chicano students. The referents "equality" and "inequality"—when referring to the overall educational plight and struggle of Chicanos—have been commonly used in the literature (e.g., Donato, 1997; Moreno, 1999; San Miguel, 1987; San Miguel and Valencia, 1998; Valencia, 1991a).

2 Here, I follow the logic of Kerlinger (1986) who describes the distinctions between a concept and a construct. "A *concept* expresses an abstraction formed by generalizations from particulars" (p. 26), and although a construct is a concept, a construct has an added meaning ". . . of having been deliberately and consciously invented or adopted for a special scientific purpose" (p. 27). Furthermore, Kerlinger notes that constructs can be of the *constitutive* and *operational* type. A constitutive definition defines a construct by using other constructs, and is particularly valuable in theory construction. An operational definition describes, with some precision, how a particular construct will be observed and measured. In the present analysis, our use of Chicano school failure is largely along constitutive lines, yet it can be refined in an operational sense.

3 The "dropout rate," which is the converse of school holding power, is simply estimated by subtracting the school holding power (a percentage) from 100 percent.

4 Underachievement refers to a discrepancy between measured aptitude (i.e., intelligence) and achievement (see, e.g., Kubiszyn and Borich, 1987). When one's obtained aptitude score is higher than one's obtained achievement score, a student is typically labeled as an "underachiever." Conversely, an "overachiever" is a student whose aptitude score is lower than his/her obtained achievement score. It appears, however, that the underachievement/ overachievement constructs are losing some currency. These notions are gradually being replaced by the term "aptitude-achievement discrepancies" (Kubiszyn and Borich, 1996).

5 For a critique of the discrepancy formula in identifying learning disabilities in children, see Aaron (1997).

6 The problems attached to the term underachievement (as well as overachievement) are so grave that they have led Cronbach, a highly noted tests and measurement expert, to conclude: "The terminology of over- and underachievement should be abandoned" (1984, p. 255).

7 Also, see Orfield and Montfort (1992) and Orum (1986).

8 The exclusion of Spanish in schools was in violation of the Treaty of Guadalupe Hidalgo (Article 9), which guaranteed Mexican Americans all the rights of citizens—including the right to maintain their language (see Miller, 1937; San Miguel and Valencia, 1998).

9 The other states of the Southwest were less restrictive on the "No Spanish" rule (see U.S. Commission on Civil Rights, 1972a, Figure 7, p. 16).

10 The following paragraph is excerpted, with minor modifications, from Valencia (1997a, pp. 24–25).

11 The remainder of this discussion on grade retention is excerpted, with minor modifications, from Valencia (2000a, pp. 2–3, 7–9, and 11–15).

12 Although there is a strong consensus in the literature that retention is mostly ineffective in enhancing or sustaining the achievement of low-performing students, there are a few scholars who are cautious in drawing this conclusion. Jimerson *et al.* (1997) observed: "while evidence supporting retention has been in short supply, the issue is not fully resolved" (p. 6).

13 See, e.g., Gredler (1984); Holmes (1983, 1989); Holmes and Matthews (1984); Jimerson *et al.* (1997); Mantzicopoulos and Morrison (1992); Meisels and Liaw (1993); Reynolds (1992); Rose *et al.* (1983); Shepard and Smith (1987).

14 See, e.g., Byrnes (1989); Cairns *et al.* (1989); Dawson (1991); Deridder (1988); Ekstrom *et al.* (1986); Fernández *et al.* (1989); Grissom and Shepard (1989); Hirano-Nakanishi (1986); Lloyd (1978); Neill and Medina (1989); Roderick (1994); Wehlage and Rutter (1986).

15 McLean (1950) also reported similar trends in racial/ethnic grade retention differences for academic years 1943–1944, 1944–1945, 1945–1946, 1946–1947, and 1947–1948.

16 I refer to Buckner's insight as being "atypically sensitive" in that most of the published research of the 1920s and 1930s on the education of Mexican American students was condescending, filled with negative stereotypes, and some, even racist.

17 The remainder of this paragraph plus the following paragraph are excerpted, with minor modifications, from San Miguel and Valencia (1998, p. 382).

18 The following three sentences are excerpted, with minor modifications, from San Miguel and Valencia (1998, p. 371).

19 See the U.S. Commission on Civil Rights (1972b) report, *Mexican American Education Study, Report 4: Mexican American Education in Texas: A Function of Wealth* for background on the school finance inequities issue in Texas.

20 Two districts (2.4 percent) of the total *n* of 84 are 50 percent White and 50 percent racial/ethnic minority.

21 Meguire (1938) sees "individualism" among Mexicans as negative in that "It manifests itself . . . in the lack of cooperative enterprises by the Mexican people . . . Mexican boys and girls seem to have no conception of team-work as understood by American youngsters" (p. 55). This is certainly an interesting observation by Meguire given that later empirical research would suggest that Mexican American children tend to be *more* cooperative than their White peers (e.g., Padilla and Ruiz, 1973).

22 In all due fairness to Meguire (1938) she also has a section on "Develop the desirable traits." Although some of the "traits" are stereotypic (e.g., Mexicans' "love of color and beauty"), they—as a whole—cast the Mexican in positive light.

23 See Losey (1995) for an overview and critique of research studies on Mexican American students and classroom interactions.

24 The remainder of this section is excerpted, with minor modifications, from Valencia (2000b, pp. 451–454).

25 Triesman did point out that his investigation was not a "formal" study (i.e., peer-reviewed and published) (personal communication, April 22, 1999). For a newspaper story on these data, see Brooks (1999a).

26 These data are for the aggregate. Triesman (1999) also provided analyses by individual subject area (e.g., language arts, mathematics, and science at the high school level).

27 Data were provided for the aggregate, as well as for individual classifications (e.g., self-contained classrooms and special education classes at the elementary school level; core subject areas [e.g. social studies, mathematics, and English] at the middle and high school levels).

28 It is important to note that this conclusion is based on a snapshot of aggregated data. For a richer analysis, individual school districts need to be examined. A case in point is an analysis conducted by the *Austin American-Statesman* (Brooks, 1999b) of the AISD and surrounding districts. In the AISD, the statewide pattern was observed in which noncertified teachers were disproportionately located in low-SES, minority schools. For example, at the elementary level, 18 of 66 schools were identified as having noncertified teachers. Of these, 10 (55 percent) are located in East Austin (overwhelming minority neighborhoods); 26 (39 percent) of the district's elementary schools are located in East Austin. In sum, East Austin has 39 percent of the district's total elementary schools and 55 percent of the elementary schools in which noncertified teachers are found—an overrepresentation. Triesman was quoted in this newspaper article as saying, "In districts like Austin, which are ethnically and economically diverse, advantaged schools—which tend to be White and affluent—are able to hijack the best teachers" (Brooks, 1999b, p. A1).

29 Triesman (1999) controlled for average length of teacher experience in one analysis and let it vary in another analysis. I report data from the former.

30 One useful framework for describing contemporary curriculum differentiation is presented by Slavin (1997). "Within-class ability grouping" refers to student groupings (e.g., in mathematics) of similar levels in elementary school classes. "Tracking" refers to curricular assignments in high school (e.g., college preparatory; general). Finally, "between-class ability grouping" is in reference to student groupings by ability in separate classes in junior high school and middle schools.

31 The next paragraph is excerpted, with minor modifications, from San Miguel and Valencia (1998, pp. 382–383).

32 Oakes (1985) speaks of "low-status" and "high-status" knowledge. The former type refers to non-challenging, rote learning. By contrast, high-status knowledge involves abstract thinking, creativity, and the like.

33 Rees *et al.* (1996) also analyzed the National Educational Longitudinal Study data base (1988), but focused on the 10th-grade sample. They reported data for mathematics, English, science, and social studies. As did Braddock and Dawkins (1993), Rees *et al.* also found that Latinos and African American students—compared to their White peers—were less likely to be enrolled in upper-track classes and more likely to be enrolled in lower-track classes.

34 The remainder of this section is excerpted, with minor modifications, from San Miguel and Valencia (1998, pp. 391, 392, and 412).

35 UC Berkeley released its fall 1998 admissions data in late March 1998 (Burdman, 1998). It appears that the combined impact of Proposition 209 and SP 1 on minority admissions was devastating. Admissions officials reported that the number of African American, Chicano/Latino, and Native American freshman admits fell from 1,678 in 1997 to 610 in 1998—a 64 percent decline. The decline for Mexican American students was 61 percent, drops for African Americans and Native Americans were 70 percent and 63 percent, respectively. On other campuses, reports varied considerably. For example, UC Riverside reported a 42 percent increase in Mexican American freshmen, while UC San Diego reported a 40 percent drop in Mexican American freshmen admittees (Burdman, 1998).

36 Valencia and Aburto (1991b) do, however, make this caveat: "In no way do we mean to imply that *only* Latino teachers can and should teach Latino students, nor are we implying that *only* White teachers can and should teach White students" (p. 172).

37 It is difficult to draw clear conclusions regarding the relation between race/ethnicity, personal adjustments, and academic achievement in Kurth's study, as there appears to be interactions between race/ethnicity and sex. For example, Mexican boys, tended to have better grades than White boys (not girls), but Mexican girls had considerably lower grades than Mexican boys and White boys and girls. Oriental boys and girls, another "non-White" group, had, by far, the highest grades of any racial/ethnic group (see Kurth, 1941, p. 35, Table IV).

References

Aaron, P.G. (1997). The impending demise of the discrepancy formula. *Review of Educational Research, 67,* 461–502.

Alva, S.A. and de Los Reyes, R. (1999). Psychosocial stress, internalized symptoms, and the academic achievement of Hispanic students. *Journal of Adolescent Research, 14,* 343–358.

Álvarez, R., Jr. (1988). National politics and local responses: The nation's first successful desegregation court case. In H.T. Trueba and C. Delgado-Gaitán (Eds.), *School and society: Learning content through culture* (pp. 37–52). New York: Praeger.

American Federation of Teachers. (2000). *Building a profession: Strengthening teacher preparation and induction.* Report of the K-16 Teacher Education Task Force. Washington, DC: Author.

Anastasi, A. (1984). Aptitude and achievement tests: The curious case of the indestructible strawperson. In B.S. Plake (Ed.), *Social and technical issues in testing: Implications for test construction and usage* (pp.129–140). Hillsdale, NJ: Erlbaum.

Anaya, R. (1992). The censorship of neglect. *English Journal, 81,* 18–20.

Attar, B.K., Guerra, N.G. and Tolan, P.H. (1994). Neighborhood disadvantage, stressful life events, and adjustment in urban elementary-school children. *Journal of Clinical Child Psychology, 23,* 391–400.

Ayres, L.P. (1909). *Laggards in our schools: A study of retardation and elimination in city school systems.* New York: Russell Sage.

Banks, J.A. (1992). Multicultural education: Nature, challenges, and opportunities. In C. Díaz (Ed.), *Multicultural education for the 21st century* (pp. 23–37). Washington, DC: National Education Association.

Banks, J.A. (1994). *An introduction to multicultural education.* Boston: Allyn & Bacon.

Banks, J.A. and McGee Banks, C.A. (2001). *Multicultural education: Issues and perspectives.* New York: Wiley.

Barker, R.L. (1987). *The social work dictionary.* Washington, DC: National Association of Social Workers.

Barrett, D.N. (1966). Demographic characteristics. In J. Samora (Ed.), *La Raza: Forgotten Americans* (pp. 159–199). Notre Dame, IN: University of Notre Dame Press.

Barton, E.J. and Osborne, J.G. (1978). The development of classroom sharing by a teacher using positive practice. *Behavior Modification, 2,* 231–249.

Barton, P.E. (2001). *Raising achievement and reducing gaps: Reporting progress toward goals for academic achievement.* A Report to the National Education Goals Panel. Washington, DC: National Education Goals Panel.

Bennett, C.I. (1999). *Comprehensive multicultural education: Theory and practice* (4th ed.). Boston: Allyn & Bacon.

Bernal, E.M. and Valencia, R.R. (2000). The TAAS case: A recapitulation and beyond. *Hispanic Journal of Behavioral Sciences, 22,* 540–556.

Boykin, A.W. (1983). The academic performance of Afro-American children. In J. Spence (Ed.), *Achievement and achievement motives: Psychological and sociological approaches* (pp. 321–371). San Francisco: W.H. Freeman.

Braddock, J.H. (1990). Tracking in the middle grades: National patterns of grouping for instruction. *Phi Delta Kappan, 71,* 445–449.

Braddock, J.H. and Dawkins, M.P. (1993). Ability grouping, aspirations, and attainments: Evidence from the National Educational Longitudinal Study of 1988. *Journal of Negro Education, 62,* 324–336.

Brooks, A.P. (1994). School funding goes to high court. *Austin American-Statesman,* May 22, pp. A1, A6.

Brooks, A.P. (1999a). Teacher credentials, TAAS scores linked. *Austin American-Statesman,* April 11, pp. A1, A12–13.

Brooks, A.P. (1999b). A question of school equity: Certified teacher shortage worse in Austin's low-income areas. *Austin American-Statesman,* May 9, pp. A1, A14–15.

Brophy, J.E. and Puttham, J.G. (1979). Classroom management in the elementary grades. In D. Duke (Ed.), *The seventy-eighth yearbook of the National Society for the Study of Education* (pp. 186–216). Chicago: The National Society for the Study of Education.

Brown, P.R. and Haycock, K. (1985). *Excellence for whom?* Oakland, CA: The Achievement Council.

Brown v. Board of Education of Topeka, 347 U.S. 483 at 494 (1954).

Buckner, H.A. (1935). *A study of pupil elimination and failure among Mexicans.* Unpublished master's thesis, University of Southern California, Los Angeles.

Burdman, P. (1998). UC Berkeley to see drop in minorities. *San Francisco Chronicle,* March 31, p. A1.

Buriel, R. (1983). Teacher student interactions and their relationship to student achievement: A comparison of Mexican American and Anglo-American children. *Journal of Educational Psychology, 75,* 889–897.

Byrnes, D.A. (1989). Attitudes of students, parents and educators toward repeating a grade. In L.A. Shepard and M.L. Smith (Eds.), *Flunking grades: Research and policies on retention* (pp. 108–131). London: Falmer Press.

Cairns, R.B., Cairns, B.D., and Neckerman, H.J. (1989). Early school dropout: Configuration and determinants. *Child Development, 60,* 1437–1452.

Calderón, C.I. (1950). *The education of Spanish-speaking children in Edcouch-Elsa, Texas.* Unpublished master's thesis, The University of Texas at Austin.

California Department of Education. (2001). *Number of teachers in California public schools by ethnic designation and gender, 2000–01.* Sacramento, CA: Author. Available online at: http://data1.cde.ca.gov/dataquest/

California Superintendents' Council on Hispanic Affairs. (1985). *Response to the first term report.* Sacramento, CA: State Department of Education.

Cameron, J.W. (1976). *The history of Mexican public education in Los Angeles, 1910–1930.* Unpublished doctoral dissertation, University of Southern California, Los Angeles.

Campbell, J.R., Hombo, C.M. and Mazzeo, J. (2000). *NAEP 1999 trends in academic progress: Three decades of student performance.* National Center for Education Statistics. Washington, DC: U.S. Department of Education, Office of Educational Research and Improvement.

Campbell, J.R., Voelkl, K.E. and Donahue, P.L. (1997). *Report in brief, NAEP 1996 trends in academic progress.* Princeton, NJ: Educational Testing Service.

Canino, I.A. and Spurlock, J. (2000). *Culturally diverse children and adolescents: Assessment, diagnosis, and treatment* (2nd ed.). New York: Guilford Press.

Carnevale, A.P and Fry, R.A. (2000). *Crossing the great divide: Can we achieve equity when generation Y goes to college?* Princeton, NJ: Educational Testing Service.

Carter, D.J. and Wilson, R. (1997). *Minorities in higher education.* Washington, DC: American Council on Higher Education.

Cazden, C. (1988). *Classroom discourse: The language of teaching and learning.* Portsmouth, NH: Heinemann.

Chapa, J. (1997). *The Hopwood decision in Texas as an attack on Latino access to selective higher education programs.* Paper presented at the Harvard University Civil Rights Project, Research Conference on the Latino Civil Rights Crisis, Los Angeles, CA and Washington, DC, December.

Chapa, J. (2001). *Affirmative action, X% plans, and Latino access to higher education in the twenty-first century.* Paper presented at the UT/UC Latino Educational Advancement Roundtable, The University of Texas at Austin, January.

Chapa, J. and Valencia, R.R. (1993). Latino population growth, demographic characteristics, and educational stagnation: An example of recent trends. *Hispanic Journal of Behavioral Sciences, 15,* 165–187.

Chapman, P.D. (1988). *Schools as sorters: Lewis M. Terman, applied psychology, and the intelligence testing movement, 1890–1930.* New York: New York University Press.

Chesler, M.A. (1976). Contemporary sociological theories of racism. In P.A. Katz (Ed.), *Towards the elimination of racism* (pp. 21–71). New York: Pergamon Press.

Clark, G. (1956). *A study of the achievement of the Spanish-speaking child.* Unpublished master's thesis, The University of Texas at Austin.

Clark, R., Anderson, N.B., Clark, V.R. and Williams, D.R. (1999). Racism as a stressor for African Americans: A biopsychosocial model. *American Psychologist, 54,* 805–816.

Coan, B.E. (1936). *A comparative study of the American and Mexican children of the "Big Bend" area for 1935–1936.* Unpublished master's thesis, The University of Texas at Austin.

Coleman, J.S., Campbell, E.Q., Hobson, C.J., McPartland, J., Mood, A.M., Weinfeld, F.D. and York, R.L. (1966). *Equality of educational opportunity.* Washington, DC: Government Printing Office.

Cromack, I.W. (1949). *Latin-Americans: A minority group in the Austin public schools.* Unpublished master's thesis, The University of Texas at Austin.

Cronbach, L.J. (1984). *Essentials of psychological testing* (4th ed.). New York: Harper & Row.

Dawn, L. and McLaughlin, M. (1996). *Financing public school facilities in Texas.* Austin, TX: Texas Center for Educational Research.

Dawson, D.A. (1991). Family structure and children's health and well-being: Data from the 1998 National Health Interview Survey on children's health. *Journal of Marriage and the Family, 53*, 573–584.

Delgado-Gaitán, C. (1986). Teacher attitudes on diversity affecting student socio-academic responses: An ethnographic interview. *Journal of Adolescent Research, 1*, 103–114.

Deridder, L.M. (1988). School dropout prevention begins in the elementary years. *Education, 108*, 488–492.

Donahue, P.L., Finnegan, R.J., Lutkus, A.D., Allen, N.L. and Campbell, J.R. (2001). *The nation's report card: Fourth-grade reading 2000* (NCES 2001–499). Washington, DC: U.S. Department of Education, Office of Educational Research and Improvement, National Center for Education Statistics.

Donato, R. (1997). *The other struggle for equal schools: Mexican Americans during the civil rights era.* Albany: State University of New York Press.

Donato, R., Menchaca, M. and Valencia, R.R. (1991). Segregation, desegregation, and integration of Chicano students: Problems and prospects. In R.R. Valencia (Ed.), *Chicano school failure and success: Research and policy agendas for the 1990s* (pp. 27–63). The Stanford Series on Education and Public Policy. London: Falmer Press.

Drake, R.H. (1927). *A comparative study of the mentality and achievement of Mexican and White children.* Unpublished master's thesis, University of Southern California, Los Angeles.

Dusek, J.B. and Joseph, G. (1983). The bases of teacher expectations. *Journal of Educational Psychology, 75*, 327–346.

Ekstrom, R.B., Goertz, M.E., Pollack, J.M. and Rock, D.A. (1986). Who drops out of high school and why? Findings from a national study. *Teachers College Record, 87*, 356–373.

Epstein, A. (1997). Affirmative action ban stands. *Austin American-Statesman*, November 4, pp. A1, A12.

Erikson, F. (1987). Transformation and school success: The politics and culture of educational thought. *Anthropology and Education Quarterly, 18*, 335–356.

Escamilla, K. (1987). *Do they really know their culture?* Paper presented at the annual conference of the Arizona Association for Bilingual Education, Flagstaff, AZ, February.

Escamilla, K. (1996). *Incorporating Mexican American history and culture into the social studies curriculum* (ERIC Document Reproduction Service No. ED 393 645).

Fernández, R.M., Paulsen, R. and Hirano-Nakanishi, M. (1989). Dropping out among Hispanic youth. *Social Science Research, 18*, 21–52.

Finn, C.E., Jr., Kanstoroom, M. and Petrilli, M.J. (1999). *The quest for better teachers: Grading the states.* Washington, DC: Thomas B. Fordham Foundation.

Foley, D.E. (1990). *Learning capitalist culture: Deep in the heart of Tejas.* Philadelphia: University of Pennsylvania Press.

García, E.E. (2001). *Hispanic education in the United States: Raíces y alas.* Lanham, MD: Rowen & Littlefield.

García, H.D.C. and Noble, M. (1988). *Equity, equality, excellence, and empowerment: Their significance for language minority children.* Paper presented at the meeting of the American Educational Research Association, New Orleans, LA, February.

García, M.T. (1979). *Mexican Americans: Leadership, ideology, and identity, 1930–1960.* New Haven, CT: Yale University Press.

Gay, G. (1988). Designing relevant curricula for diverse learners. *Education and Urban Society, 20*, 327–340.

Gerard, H.B. and Miller, N. (1975). *School desegregation: A long-term study.* New York: Plenum.

Gilbert, E.H. (1947). *Some legal aspects of the education of Spanish-speaking children in Texas.* Unpublished master's thesis, The University of Texas at Austin.

Ginsburg, H.P. (1986). The myth of the deprived child: New thoughts on poor children. In U. Neisser (Ed.), *The school achievement of minority children: New perspectives* (pp. 169–189). HIllsdale, NJ: Erlbaum.

Goldhaber, D.D. and Brewer, D.J. (1997). Why don't schools and teachers seem to matter? *Journal of Human Resources, 32*, 505–523.

Gollnick, D.M. and Chinn, P.C. (1994). *Multicultural education in a pluralistic society* (4th ed.). New York: Maxwell Macmillan International.

González, G.G. (1990). *Chicano education in the era of segregation.* Philadelphia: Balch Institute Press.

González, G.G. (1999). Segregation and the education of Mexican children, 1900–1940. In J.F. Moreno (Ed.), *The elusive quest for equality: 150 years of Chicano/Chicana education* (pp. 53–76). Cambridge, MA: Harvard Educational Review.

Goughis, R.A. (1986). The effects of prejudice and stress on the academic performance of black-Americans. In U. Neisser (Ed.), *The school achievement of minority children: New perspectives* (pp. 145–167). Hillsdale, NJ: Erlbaum.

Graham, P.A. (1987). Black teachers: A drastically scarce resource. *Phi Delta Kappan, 68*, 598–605.

Grant, C.A. (Ed.). (1992). *Research and multicultural education: From the margins to the mainstream.* Bristol, PA: Falmer Press.

Graves, D. (1989). School finance woes echo across nation. *Austin American-Statesman*, October 7, pp. A1, A15.

Graves, D. (1993). 75 property-poor districts challenge funding law. *Austin American-Statesman*, June 12, pp. A1, A11.

Gredler, G.R. (1984). Transition classes: A viable alternative for the at-risk child? *Psychology in the Schools, 21*, 463–470.

Grissom, J.B. and Shepard, L.A. (1989). Repeating and dropping out of school. In L.A. Shepard and M.L. Smith (Eds.), *Flunking grades: Research and policies on retention* (pp. 34–63). London: Falmer Press.

Hallinan, M.T. and Kubitschek, W.N. (1999). Curriculum differentiation and high school achievement. *Social Psychology of Education, 3*, 41–62.

Hertert, L. (1994). *School finance litigation: A history of the changing definition of equity.* Paper presented at the meeting of the American Educational Research Association, New Orleans, LA, April.

Heubert, J.P. and Hauser, R.M. (Eds.). (1999). *High stakes: Testing for tracking, promotion, and graduation.* Committee on Appropriate Test Use, Board on Testing and Assessment, Commission on Behavioral and Social Sciences and Education, National Research Council. Washington, DC: National Academy Press.

Hirano-Nakanishi, M. (1986). The extent and prevalence of pre-high school attrition and delayed education for Hispanics. *Hispanic Journal of Behavioral Sciences, 8*, 61–76.

Holmes, C.T. (1983). The fourth r: Retention. *Journal of Research and Development in Education, 17*, 1–6.

Holmes, C.T. (1989). Grade level retention effects: A meta-analysis of research studies. In L.A. Shepard and M.L. Smith (Eds.), *Flunking grades: Research and policies on retention* (pp. 16–33). London: Falmer Press.

Holmes, C.T. and Matthews, K.M. (1984). The effects of nonpromotion on elementary and junior high school pupils: A meta-analysis. *Review of Educational Research, 54*, 225–236.

Hopwood v. State of Texas, 78 F. 3d 932, 5th Cir. (1996).

House, E.R. (1989). Policy implications for retention research. In L.A. Shepard and M.L. Smith (Eds.), *Flunking grades: Research and policies on retention* (pp. 202–213). London: Falmer Press.

Icard, L.D., Longres, J.F. and Spencer, M. (1999). Racial minority stress and distress among children and adolescents. *Journal of Social Science Research, 25*, 19–40.

Jackson, G.B. (1975). The research evidence on the effects of grade retention. *Review of Educational Research, 45*, 613–635.

Jackson, P.W. (1986). *The practice of teaching.* New York: Teachers College Press.

Jensen, A.R. (1980). *Bias in mental testing.* New York: Free Press

Jimerson, S., Carlson, E., Rotert, M., Egeland, B. and Sroufe, L.A. (1997). A prospective, longitudinal study of the correlates and consequences of early grade retention. *Journal of School Psychology, 35*, 3–25.

Katz, S.R. (1999). Teaching in tensions: Latino immigrant youth, their teachers, and the structures of schooling. *Teachers College Record, 100*, 809–840.

Keller, G.D., Deneen, J.R. and Magallán, R.J. (1991). *Assessment and access: Hispanics in higher education.* Albany: State University of New York Press.

Kerlinger, F.D. (1986). *Foundations of behavioral research* (3rd ed.). New York: Holt, Rinehart, & Winston.

Kubiszyn, T. and Borich, G. (1987). *Educational testing and measurement: Classroom application and practice* (2nd ed.). Glenview, IL: Scott, Foreman.

Kubiszyn, T. and Borich, G. (1996). *Educational testing and measurement: Classroom application and practice* (5th ed.). New York: HarperCollins.

Kurth, M. (1941). *A study of four racial groups in a Pasadena junior high school.* Unpublished master's thesis, University of Southern California, Los Angeles.

Kurtz, M. (1999). Poorer students get rookie teachers. *Austin American-Statesman*, October 27, pp. A1, A15.

Laosa, L.M. and Henderson, R.W. (1991). Cognitive socialization and competence: The academic development of Chicanos. In R.R. Valencia (Ed.), *Chicano School Failure and Success: Research and policy agendas for the 1990s* (pp. 164–199). The Stanford Series on Education and Public Policy. London: Falmer Press.

Levy, J., Wubbels, T., Brekelsman, M. and Morganfield, B. (1997). Language and cultural factors in students' perceptions of teacher communication style. *International Journal of Intercultural Relations, 21*, 29–56.

Lloyd, D.N. (1978). Prediction of school failure from third-grade data. *Educational and Psychological Measurement, 38*, 1193–1200.

Loehlin, J.C., Lindzey, G. and Spuhler, J.N. (1975). *Race differences in intelligence.* San Francisco: Freeman.

Losey, K.M. (1995). Mexican American students and classroom interaction: An overview and critique. *Review of Educational Research, 65*, 283–318.

Macías, R.F. (1993). Language and ethnic classification of language minorities: Chicano and Latino students in the 1990s. *Hispanic Journal of Behavioral Sciences, 15*, 230–257.

Mantzicopoulos, P. and Morrison, D. (1992). Kindergarten retention: Academic and behavioral outcomes through the end of second grade. *American Educational Research Journal, 29*, 182–198.

Manuel, H.T. (1930). *The education of Mexican and Spanish-speaking children in Texas.* Austin: University of Texas Press.

McDermott, R.P. (1997). Achieving school failure 1972–1997. In G.D. Spindler (Ed.), *Educational and cultural process: Anthropological approaches* (3rd ed., pp. 110–135). Prospect Heights, IL: Waveland Press.

McLean, R.J. (1950). *A comparative study of Anglo-American and Spanish-name children in the Austin public schools over a seven-year period.* Unpublished master's thesis, The University of Texas at Austin.

McLennan, L. (1936). *A comparison of the Spanish-speaking and English-speaking children in nine schools over a five-year period.* Unpublished master's thesis, The University of Texas at Austin.

Meguire, K.H. (1938). *Educating the Mexican child in the elementary school.* Unpublished master's thesis, University of Southern California, Los Angeles.

Meisels, S.J. and Liaw, F-R. (1993). Failure in schools: Do retained students catch up? *Journal of Educational Research, 87*, 69–77.

Menchaca, M. and Valencia, R.R. (1990). Anglo-Saxon ideologies and their impact on the segregation of Mexican students in California, the 1920s–1930s. *Anthropology and Education Quarterly, 21*, 222–249.

Miller, H. (1937). *Treaties and other international acts of the United States of America* (Vol. 5). Washington, DC: Government Printing Office.

Mingle, J.R. (1987). *Focus on minorities: Trends in higher education participation and success.* Denver, CO: A joint publication of the Education Commission of the States and Higher Education Executive Officers.

Mirowsky, J., II, and Ross, C.E. (1989). *Social causes of psychological distress.* New York: Aldine de Gruyter.

Moreno, J.F. (1999). *The elusive quest for equality: 150 years of Chicano/Chicana education.* Cambridge, MA: Harvard Educational Review.

Morín, R. (1963). *Among the valiant: Mexican Americans in WWII and Korea.* Los Angeles: Borden.

Muñoz, D.G. (1986). Identifying areas of stress for Chicano undergraduates. In M.A. Olivas (Ed.), *Latino college students* (pp. 131–156). New York: Teachers College Press.

National Center for Educational Statistics. (1992). *First follow-up: Student component data file user's manual.* Washington DC: Author.

Neill, M.D. and Medina, N.J. (1989). Standardized testing: Harmful to educational health. *Phi Delta Kappan, 70*, 688–697.

Nieto, S. (1996). *Affirming diversity: The sociopolitical context of multicultural education* (2nd ed.). White Plains, NY: Longman.

Oakes, J. (1985). *Keeping track: How schools structure inequality.* New Haven, CT: Yale University Press.

Oakes, J. (1990). *Multiplying inequalities: The effects of race, social class, and tracking on opportunities to learn mathematics and science*. Santa Monica, CA: The Rand Corporation.

Oakes, J. (1995). Two cities' tracking and within-school segregation. *Teachers College Record, 96*, 681–690.

Oakes, J., Gamoran, A. and Page, R. (1992). Curriculum differentiation: Opportunities, outcomes, and meanings. In P. Jackson (Ed.), *Handbook of research on education* (pp. 570–608). New York: Macmillan.

O'Brien, E.M. (1993). *Latinos in higher education* (Research Briefs, Vol. 4, No. 4). Washington, DC: Division of Policy Analysis and Research, American Council on Education.

Olivas, M.A. (Ed.). (1986). *Latino college students*. New York: Teachers College Press.

Olsen, L. (1988). *Crossing the schoolhouse border: Immigrant students and the California public schools*. Boston: California Tomorrow.

Orfield, G., Bachmeier, M.D., James, D.R. and Eitle, T. (1997). Deepening segregation in American public schools: A special report from the Harvard Project on School Segregation. *Equity and Excellence in Education, 30*, 5–22.

Orfield, G. and Montfort, F. (1992). *Status of school desegregation in the 1980s: The next generation*. Report to the National School Boards Association. Alexandria, VA: Council of Urban Boards of Education.

Orfield, G. and Yun, J.T. (1999). *Resegregation in American schools*. The Civil Rights Project, Harvard University. Cambridge, MA: Harvard University. Available online at: http://www.law.harvard.edu/groups/civilrights

Ortiz, F.I. (1988). Hispanic-American children's experiences in classrooms: A comparison between Hispanic and non-Hispanic children. In L. Weis (Ed.), *Class, race, and gender in American education* (pp. 63–86). New York: State University of New York Press.

Orum, L.S. (1986). *The education of Hispanics: Status and implications*. Washington, DC: National Council of La Raza.

Ovando, C.J. and McLaren, P. (Eds.). (2000a). *The politics of multiculturalism and bilingual education: Students and teachers caught in the cross fire*. Boston: McGraw-Hill.

Ovando, C.J. and McLaren, P. (2000b). Editors' preface. In C.J. Ovando, and P. McLaren (Eds.), *The politics of multiculturalism and bilingual education: Students and teachers caught in the cross fire* (pp. xvii–xxiv). Boston: McGraw-Hill.

Pachón, H.P., Mejía, A.F. and Bergman, E. (1997). *California Latinos and collegiate education: The continuing crisis*. Paper presented at the Harvard Civil Rights Project, Research Conference on the Latino Civil Rights Crisis, Los Angeles, CA and Washington, DC, December.

Padilla, A.M. and Ruiz, R.A. (1973). *Latino mental health: A review of literature*. Rockville, MD: National Institute of Mental Health.

Page, R. and Valli, L. (Eds.). (1990). *Curriculum differentiation: Interpretive studies in U.S. schools*. Albany, NY: State University of New York Press.

Parrott, S. (2001). Districts sue over "Robin Hood." *San Antonio Express-News*, April 10, pp. B1, B7.

Parsons, T.W. (1965). *Ethnic cleavage in a California school*. Unpublished doctoral dissertation, Stanford University, Stanford, CA.

Pérez, S.M. and De La Rosa Salazar, D. (1993). Economic, labor force, and social implications of Latino educational and population trends. *Hispanic Journal of Behavioral Sciences, 15*, 188–229.

Phillips, B.N. (1978). *School stress and anxiety: Theory, research, and intervention*. New York: Human Sciences Press.

Phillips, J. (1996). College officials reel over UT ruling. *Austin American-Statesman*, March 21, pp. A1, A18.

Plucker, J.A. (1996). Gifted Asian-American students: Identification, curricula, and counseling concerns. *Journal for the Education of the Gifted, 19*, 315–343.

Prieto, A. and Zucker, S. (1980). The effects of race on teachers' perceptions of education placement of behaviorally disordered children. *Resources in Education, 15*, ED 188427.

Rees, D.I., Argys, L.M. and Brewer, D.J. (1996). Tracking in the United States: Statistics from the NELS. *Economics of Education Review, 15*, 83–89.

Reston, M. (2001a). School finance system facing a new lawsuit. *Austin American-Statesman*, April 10, pp. A1, A8.

Reston, M. (2001b). Texas schoolrooms linked to courtrooms for 30 years. *Austin American-Statesman*, April 15, pp. A1, A13.

Reston, M. (2001c). Judge rules for school finance plan. *Austin American-Statesman*, July 12, pp. A1, A10.

Revett, K.H. (1986). *Mexico and Mexican Americans in U.S. history textbooks*. Unpublished master's thesis, The University of Texas at Austin.

Reynolds, A. (1933). *The education of Spanish-speaking children in five Southwestern states* (Bulletin 1933, No. 11). Washington, DC: Government Printing Office.

Reynolds, A.J. (1992). Grade retention and school adjustment. *Educational Evaluation and Policy Analysis, 14*, 101–112.

Roderick, M. (1994). Grade retention and school dropout: Investigating the association. *American Educational Research Journal, 31*, 729–759.

Rodríguez v. San Antonio Independent School District, 337 F. Supp. 280 (W.D. Tex. 1971)

Romero, M.E. (1994). Identifying giftedness among Keresan Pueblo Indians: The Keres study. *Journal of American Indian Education, 34*, 35–58.

Rose, J.C., Medway, F.J., Cantrell, V.L. and Marus, S.H. (1983). A fresh look at the retention–promotion controversy. *Journal of School Psychology, 21*, 201–211.

Rosenthal, T.L. and Bandura, A. (1978). Psychological modeling: Theory and practice. In S.L. Garfield and A.E. Bergin (Eds.), *Handbook of psychotherapy and behavior change: An empirical analysis* (2nd ed., pp. 621–658). New York: Wiley.

Rubanova, N. and Mortenson, T. (2001). *Public high school graduate rates by state: 1981 to 1999*. Postsecondary Education Opportunity: Oskaloosa, IA. Available online at: http://www.postsecondary. org/Spreadsheets.htm

Rueda, R. (1991). An analysis of special education as a response to the diminished academic achievement of Chicano students. In R.R. Valencia (Ed.), *Chicano School Failure and Success: Research and policy agendas for the 1990s* (pp. 252–270). The Stanford Series on Education and Public Policy. London: Falmer Press.

Saldaña, D.H. (1994). Acculturative stress: Minority status and distress. *Hispanic Journal of Behavioral Sciences, 16*, 116–128.

San Miguel, G., Jr. (1987). *"Let them all take heed": Mexican Americans and the campaign for educational equality in Texas, 1910–1981*. Austin: University of Texas Press.

San Miguel, G., Jr. and Valencia, R.R. (1998). From the Treaty of Guadalupe Hidalgo to *Hopwood*: The educational plight and struggle of Mexican Americans in the Southwest. *Harvard Educational Review, 68*, 353–412.

Serrano v. Priest, General Civil No. 938254 (Super. Ct. for Los Angeles County, CA, decided Jan 8, 1969), 487 P.2d. 1241, f Cal. 3d 584 (1971).

Shepard, L.A. (1989). A review of the research on grade retention. In L.A. Shepard and M.L. Smith (Eds.), *Flunking grades: Research and policies on retention* (pp. 64–78). London: Falmer Press.

Shepard, L.A. and Smith, M.L. (1987). Effects of kindergarten retention at the end of first grade. *Psychology in the Schools, 24*, 346–357.

Shepard, L.A. and Smith, M.L. (Eds.). (1989). *Flunking grades: Research and policies on retention*. London: Falmer Press.

Shepard, L.A. and Smith, M.L. (1990). Synthesis of research on grade retention. *Educational Leadership, 47*, 84–88.

Slavin, R.E. (1997). *Educational psychology: Theory and practice* (5th ed.). Boston: Allyn & Bacon.

Spencer, J. (2001). Austin schools get red-inked budget proposal. *Austin American-Statesman*, June 6, pp. B1, B5.

Stanley, G. (1920). Special schools for Mexicans. *The Survey, 44*, 714–715.

State Board for Educator Certification. (1998). *Who is teaching in Texas public schools?* Austin, TX: Author.

State Board for Educator Certification. (1999). *Who is teaching in Texas public schools?* Austin, TX: Author. Available online at: http://www.sbec.state.tx.us

Summers, H. (1939). *An evaluation of certain procedures in the teaching of the non-English-speaking Mexican child*. Unpublished master's thesis, University of California at Los Angeles.

Suzuki, B.H. (1984). Curriculum transformation for multicultural education. *Education and Urban Society, 16*, 294–322.

Tallent-Runnels, M.K. and Martin, M.R. (1992). Identifying Hispanic gifted children using the Screening Assessment for Gifted Elementary Students. *Psychological Reports, 70*, 939–942.

Terman, L.M. (1916). *The measurement of intelligence: An explanation of and a complete guide for the use of the Stanford revision and extension of the Binet-Simon intelligence scale.* Boston: Houghton Mifflin.

Texas Education Agency. (1998). *1998 comprehensive biennial report on Texas public schools.* Austin, TX: Author.

Texas Education Agency. (2000a). *2000 comprehensive biennial report on Texas public schools.* Austin, TX: Author.

Texas Education Agency. (2000b). *List of Chapter 41 districts, 2000–2001.* Austin, TX: Author. Available online at: http://www.tea.state.tx.us/school.finance

Texas Education Agency. (2000c). *Academic Excellence Indicator System.* Austin, TX: Author.

Thorndike, R.L. (1963). *The concepts of over- and under-achievement.* New York: Teachers College Press.

Triesman, U. (1999). (Texas teacher certification analyses). Unpublished raw (tabular) data. Charles A. Dana Center for Educational Innovation. The University of Texas at Austin.

Trower, T.A. (2000). Austin schools consider May vote on taxes. *Austin American-Statesman,* February 9, pp. B1, B7.

University of California. (2001). Table VIIj: Enrollment by campus, ethnicity, gender, and level. *Statistical Summary of Students and Staff.* Oakland, CA: Office of the President, University of California, Information Resources and Communications.

U.S. Commission on Civil Rights. (1971a). *Mexican American education study, report 1: Ethnic isolation of Mexican Americans in the public schools of the Southwest.* Washington, DC: Government Printing Office.

U.S. Commission on Civil Rights. (1971b). *Mexican American education study, report 2: The unfinished education. Outcomes for minorities in the five southwestern states.* Washington, DC: Government Printing Office.

U.S. Commission on Civil Rights. (1972a). *Mexican American education study, report 3: The excluded student. Educational practices affecting Mexican Americans in the Southwest.* Washington, DC: Government Printing Office.

U.S. Commission on Civil Rights. (1972b). *Mexican American education study, report 4: Mexican American education in Texas: A function of wealth.* Washington, DC: Government Printing Office.

U.S. Commission on Civil Rights. (1973). *Mexican American education study, report 5: Teachers and students: Differences in teacher interaction with Mexican American and Anglo students.* Washington, DC: Government Printing Office.

U.S. Commission on Civil Rights. (1974). *Mexican American education study, report 6: Toward quality education for Mexican Americans.* Washington, DC: Government Printing Office.

U.S. Department of Commerce, Bureau of the Census. (2000). *Profile of general demographic characteristics for Texas: 2000.* Washington, DC: Author. Available online at: http://www.census.gov/Press-Release/www/2001/tables/dp_tx_2000.pdf

U.S. Department of Education. (1980). *High school and beyond.* Washington, DC: National Center for Education Statistics, Office of Education Research and Improvement.

U.S. Department of Education, Office for Civil Rights. (2001). *Fall 1998 elementary and secondary school civil rights compliance report.* Washington, DC: Author.

Valencia, R.R. (1991a). The plight of Chicano students: An overview of schooling conditions and outcomes. In R.R. Valencia (Ed.), *Chicano school failure and success: Research and policy agendas for the 1990s* (pp. 3–26). The Stanford Series on Education and Public Policy. London: Falmer Press.

Valencia, R.R. (Ed.). (1991b). *Chicano school failure and success: Research and policy agendas for the 1990s.* The Stanford Series on Education and Public Policy. London: Falmer Press.

Valencia, R.R. (1997a). Latinos and education: An overview of sociodemographic characteristics and schooling conditions. In M. Yepes-Baraya (Ed.), *ETS Invitational Conference on Latino Education Issues: Conference Proceedings* (pp. 13–37). Princeton, NJ: Educational Testing Service.

Valencia, R.R. (Ed.). (1997b). *The evolution of deficit thinking: Educational thought and practice.* The Stanford Series on Education and Public Policy. London: Falmer Press.

Valencia, R.R. (1997c). Genetic pathology model of deficit thinking. In R.R. Valencia (Ed.), *The evolution of deficit thinking: Educational thought and practice* (pp. 41–112). The Stanford Series on Education and Public Policy. London: Falmer Press.

Valencia, R.R. (2000a). *Legislated school reform via high-stakes testing: The case of pending anti-social promotion legislation in Texas and its likely impact on racial/ethnic minority students.* Commissioned paper for the National Academy of Sciences Committee on Educational Excellence and Testing

Equity. Paper presented at the National Academy of Sciences workshop on School Completion in Standards-Based Reform, Washington, DC, July.

Valencia, R.R. (2000b). Inequalities and the schooling of minority students in Texas: Historical and contemporary conditions. *Hispanic Journal of Behavioral Sciences, 22*, 445–459.

Valencia, R.R. and Aburto, S. (1991a). The uses and abuses of educational testing: Chicanos as a case in point. In R.R. Valencia (Ed.), *Chicano school failure and success: Research and policy agendas for the 1990s* (pp. 203–251). The Stanford Series on Education and Public Policy. London: Falmer Press.

Valencia, R.R. and Aburto, S. (1991b). Competency testing and Latino student access to the teaching profession: An overview of issues. In G.D. Keller, J. Deneen, and R. Magallán (Eds.), *Assessment and access: Hispanics in higher education* (pp. 169–196). Albany: State University of New York Press.

Valencia, R.R. and Aburto, S. (1991c). Research directions and practical strategies in teacher testing and assessment: Implications for improving Latino access to teaching. In G.D. Keller, J. Deneen, and R. Magallán (Eds.), *Assessment and access: Hispanics in higher education* (pp. 197–234). Albany: State University of New York Press.

Valencia, R.R. and Bernal, E.M. (2000a). Guest editors' introduction. *Hispanic Journal of Behavioral Sciences, 22*, 405–409.

Valencia, R.R. and Bernal, E.M. (Eds.). (2000b). The Texas Assessment of Academic Skills (TAAS) case: Perspectives of plaintiffs' experts [Special issue]. *Hispanic Journal of Behavioral Sciences, 22* (4).

Valencia, R.R. and Bernal, E.M. (2000c). An overview of conflicting opinions in the TAAS case. *Hispanic Journal of Behavioral Sciences, 22*, 423–444.

Valencia, R.R. and Guadarrama, I.N. (1996). High-stakes testing and its impact on racial and ethnic minority students. In L.A. Suzuki, P.J. Meller, and J.G. Ponterotto (Eds.), *Multicultural assessment: Clinical, psychological, and educational applications* (pp. 561–610). San Francisco: Jossey-Bass.

Valencia, R.R. and Rankin, R.J. (1988). Evidence of bias in predictive validity on the Kaufman Assessment Battery for Children in samples of Anglo and Mexican American children. *Psychology in the Schools, 25*, 257–263.

Valencia, R.R. and Suzuki, L.A. (2001). *Intelligence testing and minority students: Foundations, performance factors, and assessment issues.* Thousand Oaks, CA: Sage.

Walker, B. (2000). *The implementation and results of HB 588 at The University of Texas at Austin, report number 2.* (Updated December 16, 2000). Available online at: http://www.utexas.edu/student/research/reports/admissions/HB5882000329.html

Wehlage, C.G. and Rutter, R.A. (1986). Dropping out: How much do schools contribute to the problem? *Teachers College Record, 87*, 374–392.

West, G.A. (1936). Racial attitudes among teachers in the Southwest. *Journal of Social Psychology, 31*, 331–337.

Wheelock, A. (1992). *Crossing the tracks: How "untracking" can save America's schools.* New York: New Press.

Wilson, J.H. (1953). *Secondary school dropouts with special reference to Spanish speaking youth in Texas.* Unpublished master's thesis, The University of Texas at Austin.

Woods, S.B. and Achey, V.H. (1990). Successful identification of gifted racial/ethnic group students without changing classification requirements. *Roeper Review, 13*, 21–36.

Zucker, S. (1979). Racial determinants of teachers' perceptions of placement of the educable mentally retarded. *Resources in Education, 14*, ED 171051.

Zucker, S. and Prieto, A. (1978). Teacher bias in special class placement. *Resources in Education, 13*, ED 153389.

2 The explosive growth of the Chicano/Latino population: educational implications

Richard R. Valencia

Beginning in the late 1970s, the steadily increasing growth rate of the Chicano population captured the interest of demographers. This "rediscovering" of the Chicano people was also seen in the media (journalism and films). Lengthy news stories on Chicanos began to appear in national magazines. The articles ranged, for example, from the general ("Chicanos on the Move," *National Geographic*, June, 1980) to the specific ("A Year with the Gangs of East Los Angeles," *Ms.*, July, 1978). A controversial movie (*Boulevard Nights*) that glorified Chicano gangs was viewed by millions of moviegoers in 1979. In 1981, *Zoot Suit*—a powerful movie about oppression against Chicanos in the early 1940s—was released.

Accompanying the national attention that Chicanos and other Latinos received in the late 1970s and early 1980s was the often-stated claim that the 1980s would be the "decade of the Hispanic." There were expectations within and outside the larger Latino community that Chicanos and other Latinos would benefit from their growing presence. Gains were anticipated along educational, economic, political, and general "quality of life" aspects. Contrary to the expected gains during the "decade of the Hispanic," the 1980s left many Latinos—particularly Chicanos and Puerto Ricans—worse off. In a report by the National Council of La Raza, *The Decade of the Hispanic: A Sobering Economic Retrospective* (Miranda and Quiroz, 1989), seven trends were identified that characterized Latinos' economic situation during the 1980s compared to the 1970s (e.g., higher rates of poverty; stagnated income levels). Miranda and Quiroz's major conclusion was: "By any standard, Hispanics lost ground economically during the 1980s" (p. 27). Among several immediate policy interventions, "improving educational opportunities" was targeted by the National Council of La Raza.

Although the 1980s did not materialize as the "decade of the Hispanic," the demographic limelight was once again on the Latino community when the 1990 U.S. Census data were made available. The total U.S. population increased by over 22 million people—a nearly 10 percent increase—from 1980 to 1990 (U.S. Department of Commerce, Bureau of the Census, 2000a, 2000b).[1] The national non-Hispanic White population only grew by 4.0 percent. In sharp contrast, all racial/ethnic minority populations outstripped the White rate: Asian/Pacific Islanders grew by 95.6 percent, Hispanics (the U.S. Census designation) by 53.0 percent, American Indians, Eskimos, and Aleuts by 35.3 percent, and Blacks by 11.8 percent. While it was true that the Asian/Pacific Islander population had the highest growth *rate* of any racial/ethnic minority group, Hispanics demonstrated—by far—the greatest growth in *absolute numbers*. The Hispanic population growth from 1980 to 1990 of 7.8 million people exceeded the *combined* growth (7.0 million people) of the Asian/Pacific Islander, American Indian/Eskimo/Aleut, and Black groups. The Hispanic absolute growth of 7.8 million even exceeded the absolute growth of Whites ($n = 7.2$ million).

In this chapter, I focus on the explosive growth of the Chicano/Latino population by examining recent U.S. Census data and other demographic sources.[2] This discussion is organized around the following topics: (a) racial/ethnic group increases in the U.S.: 1990 to 2000; (b) the size and location of the Mexican American population; (c) racial/ethnic group growth projections: 2000 to 2100; (d) racial/ethnic group public school enrollments: national and Southwest; (e) Chicano/Latino growth: educational implications.

Racial/ethnic group increases in the U.S.: 1990 to 2000

As shown in Table 2.1, the general U.S. population in 2000 numbered 281.4 million people—an increase of 32.7 million (13.2 percent) from 1990 (U.S. Department of Commerce, Bureau of the Census, 2000b). Racial/ethnic minority groups outpaced, by far, the 1990–2000 growth rate of the White population, which was only 3.4 percent. The Chicano/Latino population had the greatest growth increase (57.9 percent), with Asian/Pacific Islanders a close second (50.4 percent), followed by the African American (16.2 percent) and American Indian/Alaska Native (15.3 percent) populations. Regarding growth in absolute numbers, the Chicano/Latino population had the largest increase (nearly 13 million people)—*1.5 times* larger than all other racial/ethnic minority groups *combined* (8.5 million), and *double* the increase of the White population (6.4 million). Of the total U.S. population increase of 32.7 million, Chicanos/Latinos accounted for the largest share (39.6 percent). In addition to the tremendous growth of the Chicano/ Latino population, the U.S. Census of 2000 revealed a landmark demographic development: *The Chicano/Latino population of 35.3 million eclipsed the African American population of 33.9 million to become the nation's largest racial/ethnic minority group.*

It is important to underscore that the Latino population is a heterogeneous group regarding national origin. Table 2.2 presents data to this effect. Of the 35.3 million Latinos enumerated in the 2000 U.S. Census, the Mexican-origin population at 20.6 million was, by far, the largest group, accounting for 58.5 percent of all Latinos. Puerto Ricans numbered 3.4 million (9.7 percent), and Cuban Americans numbered 1.2 million (3.5 percent) (U.S. Department of Commerce, Bureau of the Census, 2000b). Note, however, that the group labeled "Other Latino" in Table 2.2 is the *second* largest (10 million), comprising 28.4 percent of the total Latino population. "Other Latino" consists of people from Central America (e.g., Salvadorans; Guatemalans; Hondurans), South America (e.g., Colombians; Ecuadorians; Peruvians), Spain, and the Dominican Republic (Guzmán, 2001).[3] Regarding within-Latino population proportionate distributions of total Latinos for 1990 and 2000, U.S. Census data revealed the following (Guzmán):

- Mexican Americans (58.5 percent in 2000, down from 60.4 percent in 1990).
- Puerto Ricans (9.6 percent in 2000, down from 12.2 percent in 1990).
- Cuban American (3.5 percent in 2000, down from 4.7 percent in 1990).
- Other Latino (28.4 percent in 2000, up from 22.8 percent in 1990).

Finally, with respect to within-Latino population growth rates from 1990 to 2000, the groups/rates in descending order were (Guzmán):

- Other Latino (96.9 percent, from 5.1 million to 10.0 million).
- Mexican American (52.9 percent, from 13.5 million to 20.6 million).
- Puerto Rican (24.9 percent, from 2.7 million to 3.4 million).
- Cuban American (18.9 percent, from 1.0 million to 1.2 million).

Table 2.1 U.S. population increases by race/ethnicity: 1999 to 2000

Racial/ethnic group	1990[a]		2000[a]		Increase[b]		
	N	Total population (%)	N	Total population (%)	N	Own group (%)	Total population (%)
Total	248,710	100.0	281,422	100.0	32,712	13.2	100.0
White	188,128	75.6	194,553	69.1	6,425	3.4	19.6
Hispanic	22,354	9.0	35,306	12.6	12,952	57.9	39.6
Black	29,216	11.8	33,948	12.1	4,732	16.2	14.5
Asian/Pacific Islander	6,968	2.8	10,477	3.7	3,509	50.4	10.7
American Indian and Alaska Native	1,794	0.7	2,069	0.7	275	15.3	0.8
Some other race	na	na	468	0.2	na	na	na
Two or more races	na	na	4,602	1.6	na	na	na

Source: U.S. Department of Commerce, Bureau of the Census (2000b).

Notes

All Ns are in thousands (rounded): "White," "Black," "Asian/Pacific Islander," "American Indian and Alaska Native," are "non-Hispanic"; "Hispanic" can be of any race; "na" refers to not available.

[a] Due to rounding errors, the total count for the various racial/ethnic groups does not exactly equal the total N.

[b] Due to nonavailable increase data for the "Some other race" and "Two or more races" categories, the total count for the various racial/ethnic groups does not equal the total N.

Table 2.2 Latino population by subgroup: 2000

Total Latino and subgroup	N	Total (%)
Total	35,305,818	100.0
Mexican origin	20,640,711	58.5
Puerto Rican	3,406,178	9.7
Cuban	1,241,685	3.5
Other Latino	10,017,244	28.4

Source: U.S. Department of Commerce, Bureau of the Census (2000b).

The size and location of the Mexican American population

Here, I turn our attention to the target population of the present book—the Mexican American people, who account for about six of every ten Latinos in the U.S. Although Mexican Americans are a nationally situated group, they overwhelmingly reside in the five Southwestern states (Arizona, California, Colorado, New Mexico, and Texas). As shown in Table 2.3, 8.5 million (41.0 percent) of our nation's 20.6 million Mexican Americans reside in the most populous state, California. Texas, the country's second most populous state, is home to 5.1 million (24.6 percent) Mexican Americans. Together, about two of every three of the nation's 20.6 million Mexican Americans reside in California and Texas (similarly, about one of every two of the nation's 35.3 million Latinos live in these two states; see Guzmán, 2001, p. 4, Table 2). In the states of Arizona, Colorado, and New Mexico resides 1.9 million (9.0 percent) of the total Mexican American population. In sum, 75 percent of the country's 20.6 million Mexican American people live in the five Southwestern states.

Notwithstanding their highly visible and immense presence in the Southwest, it is important to emphasize that Mexican Americans also reside in the other 45 states and the District of Columbia (see Guzmán, 2001, p. 4, Table 2). Other states (in descending order) that have a population of over 100,000 Mexican Americans are:

Table 2.3 Mexican American population in the five Southwestern states: 2000

State	N	Total U.S. Mexican American population (%)	Cumulative (%)
Total U.S. Mexican American population	20,640,711		
California	8,455,926	41.0	41.0
Texas	5,071,963	24.6	65.6
Arizona	1,065,578	5.2	70.8
Colorado	450,760	2.2	73.0
New Mexico	330,049	1.6	74.6
Total Southwest	15,374,276		

Source: U.S. Department of Commerce, Bureau of the Census (2000c, 2000d, 2000e, 2000f, 2000g).

- Illinois (1,114,390)
- Florida (363,925)
- Washington (329,934)
- Nevada (285,764)
- Georgia (275,288)
- New York (260,889)
- North Carolina (246,545)
- Michigan (220,769)

- Oregon (214,662)
- Indiana (153,042)
- Kansas (148,270)
- Utah (136,416)
- Oklahoma (132,813)
- Wisconsin (126,719)
- New Jersey (102,929).

Racial/ethnic group growth projections: 2000 to 2100

I introduced this chapter by discussing demographers' interests over the last 20 plus years in the rapidly growing Chicano/Latino population. Given the continuing dramatic growth of Chicanos/Latinos—as solidly documented by the 2000 U.S. Census—it is not surprising that demographers also have interest in *long-term* population projections for Chicanos/Latinos, as well as for other racial/ethnic groups. Table 2.4 presents U.S. population growth projections, by race/ethnicity, for the next 100 years (U.S. Department of Commerce, Bureau of the Census, 2000h). The projections suggest that the White population, which

Table 2.4 U.S. population growth projections by race/ethnicity, national level: 2000 to 2100

Year		Total	White	Hispanic	Black	Asian/ Pacific Islander	American Indian and Alaska Native
2000	N	281,422	194,553	35,306	33,948	10,477	2,069
	%	100	69.1	12.6	12.1	3.7	0.7
2010	N	299,861	201,956	43,687	37,482	14,435	2,299
	%	100	67.3	14.6	12.5	4.8	0.8
2020	N	324,926	207,145	55,156	41,548	18,527	2,549
	%	100	63.8	17.0	12.8	5.7	0.8
2030	N	351,070	210,983	68,167	45,567	23,563	2,787
	%	100	60.1	19.4	13.0	6.7	0.8
2040	N	377,349	212,474	82,691	49,617	29,542	3,023
	%	100	56.3	21.9	13.1	7.8	0.8
2050	N	403,686	212,990	98,228	53,466	35,759	3,241
	%	100	52.8	24.3	13.2	8.9	0.8
2060	N	432,010	214,190	114,796	57,297	42,277	3,448
	%	100	49.6	26.6	13.3	9.8	0.8
2070	N	463,639	217,028	132,492	61,286	49,179	3,652
	%	100	46.8	28.6	13.2	10.6	0.8
2080	N	497,829	220,954	151,154	65,452	56,416	3,852
	%	100	44.4	30.4	13.1	11.3	0.8
2090	N	533,605	225,300	170,514	69,795	63,948	4,045
	%	100	42.2	32.0	13.1	12.0	0.8
2100	N	570,954	230,236	190,330	74,360	71,789	4,237
	%	100	40.3	33.3	13.0	12.6	0.7

Source: Data for the year 2000 are from U.S. Department of Commerce, Bureau of the Census (2000b); all other data (for years 2010 to 2100) are from U.S. Department of Commerce, Bureau of the Census (2000h).

Note
All Ns are in thousands (rounded); "%" refers to percent of total; "White," "Black," "Asian/Pacific Islander," and "American Indian and Alaska Native" are "non-Hispanic;" "Hispanic" can be of any race.

accounted for 69.1 percent of the general U.S. population in 2000, will gradually decrease in proportion over the next ten decades. By 2060, Whites are expected to lose majority status, and by 2100, they will only account for about four of every ten people in the U.S. population. By sharp contrast, Chicanos/Latinos and Asian/Pacific Islanders are projected to comprise greater and greater shares of the U.S. population as a whole. The Chicano/Latino population, which comprised 12.6 percent of the total U.S. population in 2000, is projected to constitute 33.3 percent of the general population in 2100, a remarkable increase. Likewise, the Asian/Pacific Islander population, which made up 3.7 percent of the total population in 2000, is projected to comprise 12.6 percent of the general population in 2100, also a dramatic increase in proportion. Although the African American and American Indian/ Alaska Native populations will grow in absolute numbers, their respective proportions of the whole are projected to remain relatively constant. For example, African Americans, who constituted 12.1 percent of the general population in 2000, are projected to comprise 13 percent of the total U.S. population in 2100.

The data for increases in absolute numbers and percentages presented in Table 2.5 further illustrate the prodigious projected growth in the Chicano/Latino and Asian/Pacific Islander populations, as well as the smaller, but significant, increases in the African American and American Indian/Alaska Native populations. For the U.S. population as a whole, it is projected to double in size—from 281.4 million in 2000 to 571 million in 2100. Likewise, the African American and American Indian/Alaska Native populations are expected to double in size from 2000 to 2100. By comparison, the projections shown in Table 2.5 suggest that the Chicano/Latino population will grow in extraordinary numbers—a 155 million increase from 35.3 million in 2000 to 190.3 million in 2100, which is a remarkable increase of 439.1 percent. Similarly, the Asian/Pacific Islander population is projected to grow in enormous numbers—a 61.3 million increase from 10.5 million in 2000 to 71.8 million in 2100, an immense increase of 585.2 percent. Although the White population is projected to increase by 35.7 million people, that is, 194.6 million in 2000 to 230.2 million in 2100, the percentage increase is only 18.3 percent, which is considerably smaller than those projected increases for populations of color.

Table 2.5 U.S. population projected increases by race/ethnicity, national level: 2000 to 2100

Population	Projected increase	
	N	*%*
National	289,532	102.9
White	35,683	18.3
Hispanic	155,024	439.1
Black	40,412	119.0
Asian/Pacific Islander	61,312	585.2
American Indian and Alaska Native	2,168	104.8

Source: Author's calculations from data provided in U.S. Department of Commerce, Bureau of the Census (2000h).

Note
All *N*s are in thousands (rounded); "White," "Black," "Asian/Pacific Islander," and "American Indian and Alaska Native" are "non-Hispanic;" "Hispanic" can be of any race.

Racial/ethnic group public school enrollments: national and Southwest

Based on the U.S. Census survey of 2000, there were 46.8 million children and youths enrolled in U.S. public schools in kindergarten through grade 12 (U.S. Department of Commerce, Bureau of the Census, 2000i). These data—disaggregated by kindergarten/elementary/high school enrollments and by race/ethnicity—are presented in Table 2.6.

For total kindergarten to grade 12 (K-12) enrollment, White students accounted for 61.5 percent ($n = 28.7$ million) of the public school students, while the Chicano/Latino and African American total student enrollments were very similar in size—16.5 percent (7.7 million) and 17.1 percent (8.0 million), respectively. Asian/Pacific islander students comprised 4.3 percent (2.0 million) of the total enrollment.

The current public school enrollment proportions by race/ethnicity reflect the demographic pattern seen in the general U.S. population—that is, a decline among Whites and increases in racial/ethnic minorities. These shifts in the school-age population can readily be seen by examining data over a 30-year period (1968–1998; Orfield, 2001). Table 2.7 shows K-12 public school enrollment changes, by race/ethnicity, from 1968 to 1998. Indeed, the transformations that have transpired in the U.S. public school population from 1968 to 1998 are quite profound. Referring to these data in Table 2.7—which were generated by Orfield and associates—Orfield remarked:

> The nation's schools have changed in amazing ways since the civil rights era. The number of black and Latino students in the nation's public schools is up 5.8 million, while the number of white students has declined by 5.6 million. The schools reflect the transformation of the U.S. population in an era of low birth rates and massive immigration. Latino students, a group that was just 2 million in 1968 has grown to 6.9 million, an extraordinary growth of *245%* in just thirty years. In 1968 there were more than three times as many blacks as Latinos in our schools, but in 1998 there were seven Latino students for every eight blacks, and soon there will be more Latino than black students. This is an extraordinary switch. The decline of white students by 5.6 million during these 30 years has a massive impact on the college-going population and the

Table 2.6 Kindergarten, elementary, and high school public school enrollments by race/ethnicity, national level: 2000

Group	Total enrollment[a] (N = 46,760)		Kindergarten enrollment (N = 3,173)		Elementary enrollment[b] (N = 29,347)		High school enrollment[c] (N = 14,120)	
	n	*%*	*n*	*%*	*n*	*%*	*n*	*%*
White	28,733	61.5	1,846	58.2	17,740	60.5	9,147	64.8
Hispanic	7,719	16.5	639	20.1	5,000	17.0	2,080	14.7
Black	7,979	17.1	547	17.2	5,127	17.5	2,305	16.3
Asian/Pacific Islander	1,995	4.3	124	3.9	1,252	4.3	619	4.4

Source: Adapted from U.S. Department of Commerce, Bureau of the Census (2000i).

Note

All *N*s and *n*s are in thousands (rounded); "%" refers to percent of total; "White," "Black," and "Asian/Pacific Islander" are "non-Hispanic;" "Hispanic" can be of any race; U.S. Census Bureau did not present enrollment data for American Indian/Alaska Native.
[a] Total enrollment = sum of kindergarten, elementary, and high school enrollments. [b] Elementary refers to grades 1–8. [c] High school refers to grades 9–12.

Table 2.7 K-12 public school enrollment changes by race/ethnicity: 1968 to 1998

Race/ ethnicity	Year and N					Change (1968–1998)	
	1968	1980	1994	1996	1998	N	%
White	34.70	29.16	28.46	29.11	28.93	−5.77	−16.6
Hispanic	2.00	3.18	5.57	6.38	6.90	+4.90	+245.0
Black	6.28	6.42	7.13	7.69	7.91	+1.63	+26.0

Source: Adapted from Orfield (2001, p. 19, Table 1). With permission of author.

Note
Ns are in millions.

future work force. Our schools will be the first major institutions to experience non-white majorities.

(p. 18)

Given that 75 percent of the nation's Mexican American people reside in the five Southwestern states (see previous Table 2.3), it is informative to examine the racial/ethnic makeup of the K-12 public school enrollment in the Southwest. Table 2.8 presents such data for the Southwest (2000–2001 school year). Although these data are not disaggregated by subgroup for the Latino population, Chicanos account for at least 75 percent of the total 4.9 million Latino students in the public schools of the Southwest.[4] The data in Table 2.8 clearly illustrate the large presence of Chicano/Latino school children and youths in the public schools in the Southwest. Of the total 12 million plus students, Chicanos/ Latinos number nearly 5 million (40.4 percent). Given their high birth rate coupled with the continuing growth via immigration among Chicanos/Latinos in the Southwest, they will become the majority group in the region in the very near future. As of the 2000–2001 school year, Chicano/Latino students had plurality in California, and were approaching plurality in Texas. Together, 4.3 million (87.8 percent) of the total 5 million Southwestern Chicano/Latino students are enrolled in California and Texas schools. The majority (53.8 percent) of Southwestern Chicano/Latino students attend schools in California. In 1999–2000 (the most recent data available), Chicano/Latino students in New Mexico were on the verge of becoming the majority group. Finally, Chicanos/Latinos clearly constitute the largest racial/ethnic minority group in Southwestern schools. For example, for every four Chicano/Latino students, there is one African American student.

For a closer examination of Southwestern public school enrollments, by race/ethnicity, I identified the ten largest school districts. Enrollment data, for the 2000–2001 school year, are provided in Table 2.9. These districts' enrollments vary greatly in size, from the mammoth Los Angeles (California) Unified School District (rank number 1; 721,346 students), to the considerably smaller Austin (Texas) Independent School District (rank number 10; 77,862 students). In 2000–2001, these ten largest districts enrolled 1.7 million students (14.4 percent of the total Southwestern enrollment of 12 million). Not unexpectedly, the strong majority (*n* = 8) of the top ten districts are located in California (*n* = 4) and Texas (*n* = 4). Two major points can be gleaned from the data in Table 2.9. First, Chicano/Latino presence is clearly observed in the total student enrollment of the ten districts with a solid majority (55.9 percent). As well, Chicano/Latino students currently have majority status in several of the ten districts and will soon be the majority group in most of

Table 2.8 K-12 public school enrollments by race/ethnicity in the Southwest: 2000–2001

State	N for total state enrollment	White		Hispanic		Black		Asian/Pacific Islander		American Indian	
		n	*Total (%)*	*n*	*Total (%)*	*n*	*Total (%)*	*n*	*Total (%)*	*n*	*Total (%)*
California[a]	6,050,895	2,171,861	35.9	2,613,480	43.2	510,779	8.4	667,630	11.0	51,926	0.9
Texas[b]	4,071,433	1,713,436	42.1	1,650,560	40.5	586,712	14.4	108,605	2.7	12,120	0.3
Arizona[c]	847,762	466,597	55.0	268,098	31.6	38,421	4.5	16,171	1.9	58,475	6.9
Colorado[d]	724,508	494,308	68.2	159,600	22.0	40,967	5.7	20,932	2.9	8,701	1.2
New Mexico[e]	330,463	117,975	35.7	162,918	49.3	7,601	2.3	3,305	1.0	36,351	11.0
Total Southwest	12,025,061	4,964,177	41.3	4,854,656	40.4	1,184,480	9.9	816,643	6.8	167,573	1.4

Sources: [a]California Department of Education (2001a); [b]Texas Education Agency (2001a); [c]Arizona Department of Education (2000); [d] Colorado Department of Education (2001a); [e]New Mexico Department of Education (2001a).

Note
The grade spans for Arizona, Colorado, and New Mexico are from pre-kindergarten to grade 12; the grade span for Texas is Early Childhood Education to grade 12. The most recent data available for Arizona are from the 1998–1999 school year; the most recent data available for New Mexico are from the 1999–2000 school year.

Table 2.9 K-12 public school enrollments by race/ethnicity in the ten largest districts in the Southwest: 2000–2001

School district	N for total district enrollment	White		Hispanic		African American		Asian/Pacific Islander		American Indian	
		n	Total (%)	n	Total (%)	n	Total (%)	n	Total (%)	n	Total (%)
Los Angeles (CA) USD[a]	721,346	71,178	9.9	510,367	70.8	92,096	12.8	45,632	6.3	2,073	0.3
Houston (TX) ISD[b]	208,672	20,286	9.7	112,889	54.1	65,706	31.5	5,923	2.8	113	0.1
Dallas (TX) ISD[b]	161,670	12,386	7.7	87,056	53.9	56,869	35.2	2,176	1.4	589	0.4
San Diego (CA) USD[a]	141,804	38,291	27.0	54,613	38.5	22,906	16.2	25,172	17.8	822	0.6
Long Beach (CA) USD[a]	93,694	16,678	17.8	42,559	45.4	18,431	19.7	15,697	16.8	320	0.3
Jefferson (CO) CPS[c]	87,703	72,320	82.5	10,589	12.1	1,235	1.4	2,824	3.2	735	0.8
Albuquerque (NM) PS[d]	85,276	33,343	39.1	42,212	49.5	3,241	3.8	1,620	1.9	3,923	4.6
Fort Worth (TX) ISD[b]	79,764	16,560	20.8	35,573	44.6	24,059	30.2	1,577	2.0	182	0.2
Fresno (CA) USD[a]	79,007	15,978	20.2	38,881	49.2	9,155	11.6	14,328	18.1	665	0.8
Austin (TX) ISD[b]	77,862	25,359	32.6	36,570	47.0	11,970	15.4	1,901	2.4	212	0.3
Total	1,736,798	322,379	18.6	971,309	55.9	305,668	17.6	116,850	6.7	9,634	0.6

Source: [a]California Department of Education (2001b); [b]Texas Education Agency (2001b); [c]Colorado Department of Education (2001b); [d]New Mexico Department of Education (2001b).

Note
CA = California; CO = Colorado; NM = New Mexico; TX = Texas. USD = Unified School District; ISD = Independent School District; CPS = County Public Schools; PS = Public Schools. The grade spans for Colorado and New Mexico districts are from pre-kindergarten to grade 12; the grade span for California districts is kindergarten to grade 12; the grade span for Texas districts is Early Childhood Education to grade 12.

the others. Chicano/Latino students are the majority in three districts (Los Angeles USD, Houston ISD, and Dallas ISD) and were on the verge of becoming the majority (based on 2000–2001 enrollment data) in two other districts (Albuquerque PS, and Fresno USD). In three other districts (Long Beach USD, Fort Worth ISD, and Austin ISD) the percentages of Chicano/Latino students in 2000–2001 ranged from 44.6 percent to 47.0 percent, suggesting that these districts are on their way to becoming majority Chicano/Latino.

A second observation one can make regarding the data in Table 2.9 is that the percentages of White students are relatively small in most of the ten largest districts of the Southwest. Of the total enrollment of 1.7 million students in the ten districts, Whites account for only 18.6 percent. In each of the three largest districts (Los Angeles USD, Houston ISD, and Dallas ISD)—which enroll 62.9 percent of all students in the ten largest districts—White students are less than 10 percent of the enrollments. The isolation of White students, as a group, from students of color in the ten largest school districts in the Southwest speaks to the persistent and continuing segregation in American public schools (see Valencia *et al.*, Chapter 3, present volume). Furthermore, one must be cognizant that even when enrollments at the district level appear fairly multi-racial/ethnic in makeup (see, e.g., Austin ISD, Table 2.9), segregation among individual schools can and does prevail (see Valencia *et al.*, Chapter 3, Table 3.4, current book, for a discussion of pervasive segregation in the Austin ISD).

Chicano/Latino growth: educational implications

For sure, there are a number of educational implications that spring forth from the dramatic current and future growth of the Chicano/Latino people, and the commensurate increase in the Chicano/Latino student population. Here, I focus our discussion on issues related to (a) segregation, (b) school financing, (c) the teaching force, (d) English language learners, (e) testing/assessment, (f) higher education, and (g) geographical location of the Mexican American people. This is not an exhaustive list of educational implications, but they are issues that are particularly central to consequences stemming from the explosive growth of the Chicano/Latino population. The bases of the following implications have been introduced in Chapter 1 of the current volume.

Segregation

As I have introduced in Chapter 1 and is elaborated on by Martha Menchaca, Rubén Donato, and myself in the next chapter, Chicano and other Latino students have been experiencing increasing racial/ethnic isolation in U.S. public schools. In light of the demise of school desegregation and the future growth in the Chicano/Latino student sector, these students will continue to experience hypersegregation. Given that segregation of Chicano/Latino students is statistically associated with indices of school failure (particularly achievement test scores and the dropout rate; see Valencia *et al.*, Chapter 3, current book), the growing isolation of Chicano/Latino students will become an issue of even greater concern in the years ahead. Pessimistically speaking, the adverse effects of Chicanos/Latinos attending segregated schools will likely intensify. We must, however, be optimistic and proactive. Valencia *et al.* (Chapter 3, present book) and Orfield (2001) offer a number of policy issues that can lead to more stable and promising interethnic/interracial education.

School financing

As the Chicano/Latino school population swells, the need for greater school funding and more equitable means of school financing will become major challenges for policymakers, state educational bureaucracies, and local school boards. A particularly pressing problem is the current and future necessity to build new schools in those communities in which the Chicano/Latino population is growing at great rates. In Chapter 1, I discuss this issue of new school construction using Texas as a case in point. Although Texas has made some strides in developing a more equitable system of school financing, a major flaw in the present law is that there is no separate provision for funds for new school construction. The Mexican American student population is substantially increasing—particularly along the Texas–Mexico border, but the school districts there are overwhelmingly property poor and thus are strapped to raise money to build new schools. Without financial relief from the Texas Legislature, Chicano children and youths in property poor districts will continue to enroll in overcrowded and underfunded schools for years to come.

Teaching force

In Chapter 1, I discussed the major issue of the severe shortage of Chicano and other Latino K-12 teachers, using California and Texas as examples. If the limited production of Mexican American K-12 teachers continues unabated, then the underrepresentational disparity of such teachers will increase as the Mexican American student population continues its rapid growth. As such, factors of shared identity between Chicano teachers and students, role-modeling, and the delivery of multicultural education will become even more salient in discussions of promoting Chicano school success. Once again, proactivism is imperative. In Chapter 1, I mention the writing of Valencia and Aburto (1991) who identified numerous strategies that can be employed to increase the number of Chicano and other minority teachers.

English language learners (ELLs)

A highly significant, but often overlooked and underserved segment of the Mexican American school-age population is the ELL population. Commensurate with the immense growth of the general Mexican American student sector, the ELL population is also increasing in great numbers (see., e.g., García, 2001; Macías, 1993; Ruiz-de-Velasco *et al.*, 2000). Presently and in the years ahead, the Mexican American ELL population will need even greater attention in areas dealing with, for example, the shortage of bilingual teachers (see Valencia, Chapter 1, present book), linguistic segregation (see Valencia *et al.*, Chapter 3, present book), the demise of bilingual education in some states (e.g., California; see García and Wiese, Chapter 5, present book), and the technical limitations of cognitive measures (see Valencia *et al.*, Chapter 9, present book).

Testing and assessment

One of the major long-standing problems faced by Mexican American children and youths—English speakers and ELLs alike—lies in the area of testing and assessment (see Valencia, *et al.*, Chapter 9, and Rueda *et al.*, Chapter 10, present book). These concerns have centered around test abuse (e.g., inappropriate placement of students in special education; curriculum differentiation), exclusion (underidentification of the gifted), cultural bias in tests, and poor or unknown psychometric properties of achievement and intelligence tests and language assessment measures. Exacerbating these problems has been the scarcity of trained bilingual/ bicultural testing personnel. Furthermore, a more recent testing issue adversely affecting many Mexican American students is high-stakes testing, in which state-mandated tests have determinative weight in allowing school administrators to make profound decisions about students' futures (e.g., whether a student should be awarded or denied a high school diploma based on performance on an exit-level test; see Valencia *et al.*, Chapter 9). Suffice it to say, if all these above testing/assessment issues are not expediently addressed, then many more Mexican American students will be adversely impacted as their population swells (see Valencia *et al.*, Chapter 9 for suggestions on how educational testing and assessment can be improved for Chicano students).

Higher education

In Chapter 1, present volume, I discussed the unprecedented growth of the Chicano/Latino college-age population. Projections by Carnevale and Fry (2000) suggest that Chicano/ Latino undergraduates—compared to other racial/ethnic groups—will experience the greatest percentage point increase in enrollment share from 1995 to 2015. This increase will be so dramatic that "Hispanic undergraduates will outnumber African American under-graduates for the first time in the year 2006 . . . and Hispanics are projected to be . . . the country's largest college-going minority—accounting for about one in six undergraduates in 2015" (Carnevale and Fry, 2000, p. 23). Regarding the total overall increase in under-graduate enrollment from 1995 to 2015, greater than half of the growth will take place in just five states—including three Southwestern states (California, Texas, and Arizona), and Florida and New York. Yet, compared to their overall population share of college-age youths, Chicano/Latino undergraduates will likely incur the largest deficit in student enroll-ment. Although White students will experience the smallest enrollment share (a decline), they will still remain the strong majority of undergraduates and incur the largest excess in student enrollment in comparison to their overall population share of 18- to 24-year-olds.

Although the Chicano/Latino undergraduate enrollment is projected to soar in absolute numbers from 1995 to 2015, it is important to underscore that in the report by Carnevale and Fry (2000), the authors did *not* discuss the impact of the dismantling of affirmative action in higher education (e.g., the *Hopwood* case in Texas, and Proposition 209 in Cali-fornia; see San Miguel and Valencia, 1998). Thus, if race/ethnicity continues to be disallowed as a factor in the admission process in a number of locations (particularly California and Texas, the homes of a vast proportion of Chicano/Latino college-age youths), then the pro-jected increases of Chicano/Latino undergraduates computed by Carnevale and Fry may be overestimations. In any event, the Chicano/Latino college-age population will continue to escalate in the years ahead. The identification of acceptable and workable means to increase diversity in the post-affirmative action era in the short- and long-term futures will present formidable challenges. Therefore, as urged by Carnevale and Fry, policymakers need to ensure that closing the college enrollment gap for White and Latino/African American students becomes a national priority.

Geographical location of the Mexican American people

A demographic reality is that the Mexican American population is quite geographically con-centrated. Based on the 2000 U.S. Census, about 75 percent ($n = 15.4$ million) of the nation's total Mexican American population of 20.6 million people resides in the five Southwestern states of California, Texas, Arizona, Colorado, and New Mexico (see Table 2.3, present chapter). California is home to a substantial proportion (41 percent, $n = 8.5$ million people) of the total U.S. Mexican American population, with Texas also having a sizable percentage (25 percent; $n = 5.1$ million Mexican Americans) of the total. The high concentration of the Mexican American people in the Southwest—particularly in California and Texas, which together contain two of every three Mexican Americans in the U.S.—deserves our attention for several reasons. First, such geographical concentration of the Mexican American population, hence Mexican American school-age children and youths, suggests that specific school districts in these states (e.g., Los Angeles USD in California with over a half million Chicano/Latino students in 2000–2001; see Table 2.9, current chapter) may be fruitful grounds for research projects. Second, from a policy perspective, the large presence of Chicano/Latino students in Texas, for example (41 percent or 1.7 million students of the state's total K-12 enrollment in 2000–2001; see Table 2.8, present chapter), indicates where interventions leading to improved schooling may have great numerical impact. Third, given the very large number of Chicano/Latino K-12 students in California and Texas combined ($n = 4.3$ million students; see Table 2.8, present chapter), it appears prudent for researchers and policymakers to keep abreast of educational developments in these two states, particularly for policies that adversely impact Chicano/Latino students (e.g., the oppressive trilogy of propositions passed in California from 1994 to 1998—see San Miguel and Valencia, 1998; the high-stakes testing movement in Texas and its negative impact on Chicano/Latino and other minority students—see Valencia and Bernal, 2000).

Although Mexican American students in the Southwest certainly merit our attention in light of their vast presence, I am not suggesting at all that we should ignore the existence of Mexican American communities, families, and students who live outside the five Southwestern states. A simple arithmetical calculation based on the data presented in Table 2.3 (current chapter) shows that 25.4 percent ($n = 5.2$ million) of the nation's total Mexican American population of 20.6 million resides *outside* the Southwest—i.e., in the other 45 states and the District of Columbia (see Guzmán, 2001, p. 4, Table 2 for a state-by-state breakdown). As I discussed earlier, there are 15 states outside the Southwest with populations of more than 100,000 Mexican American people. Of these states, Illinois has the largest number of Mexican Americans with 1,114,390 people (based on 2000 U.S. Census), and ranks number three in the nation in Mexican American population—larger, in fact, than Arizona, a Southwestern state with 1,065,578 Mexican Americans. In a number of areas outside the Southwest, the presence of Mexican Americans has been long established (e.g., Chicago, Illinois).

There is, however, another aspect of the demographic reality of Mexican American presence outside the Southwest of which we should be aware. In progress, there is a relatively new development—the increasing number of Latinos (mostly Mexican origin and Central American) in U.S. locales that have not traditionally been homes to Mexican Americans and other Latinos.[5] This Latino newcomer movement to these areas is called the "New Latino Diaspora." The settlement of these Latinos, who are in search of employment, is described and discussed in the new book, *Education in the New Latino Diaspora: Policy and the Politics of Identity* (Wortham *et al.*, 2001). Using ethnographic case studies, the various contributors of this edited volume explore the New Latino Diaspora occurring in communities in Georgia, North Carolina, Maine, Colorado (near resort communities), rural Illinois, and Indiana. This book by Wortham *et al.* focuses, in part, on the schools as an institutional setting in which the Latino newcomers adopt identities and simultaneously have identities forced upon them. I urge the reader to pay heed to those scholars who are writing about the New Latino Diaspora. The editors of *Education in the New Latino Diaspora* inform us:

The emergent patterns in the New Latino Diaspora seem inauspiciously familiar. . . . Preliminary data on schooling in the New Latino Diaspora—high school completion rates, representation in higher school tracks, etc.—are not encouraging. New Latino Diaspora students are often placed in less-preferred spaces—sometimes literally in closets. And they are often taught by less credentialed teachers, who are themselves stigmatized by peers through an academic "caste-system" that looks down on bilingual/ESL education (Grey, 1991).

(Hamann *et al.*, 2001, p. 2)

On a final note about demographic trends, population growth, and the future is the vital point that we must be mindful about the interdependence of Chicanos/Latinos and the rest of society, particularly the White sector. This linkage was clearly articulated in the 1988 signal work, *The Burden of Support: Young Latinos in an Aging Society*, by Hayes-Bautista *et al.* In their study of California's changing population, these authors pointed out that the aging of the "Baby-Boom Anglos" will result in a more than tripling of the 65-and-over population around 2030. The young, vastly undereducated Chicano/Latino population will likewise triple in size. Therefore, the "burden of support" for the elderly (e.g., regarding the cost of health care; income support through Social Security payments) will fall primarily on the shoulders of the income earning, taxpaying Chicano/Latino workers. Hayes-Bautista *et al.* argued, in 1988, that if the current working-age generation in California invests in improving schooling for Chicano/Latino youths, this will assist in providing a stronger economic foundation for its own security in the future. More recently, a similar argument has been laid out by Murdock *et al.* (1997) in *The Texas Challenge: Population Change and the Future of Texas*. These authors have made the following case regarding the explosive growth of Chicanos/Latinos and other minority groups and the implications for Texas' future:

The implications of the growth of minority populations in Texas depend on how quickly and completely minorities become full participants in the Texas economy. The analysis of the alternative futures noted above clearly indicates that if minorities "catch up" with Anglos, the result will be increased wealth for Texas, reduced public service demands, and increased tax revenue. If minorities do not obtain greater equity, Texas could become a society with increased socioeconomic inequity, a pattern also occurring in other parts of the United States (Karoly, 1992). . . .

For the public sector, a continuation of Anglo-minority differentials indicates both rapid growth in public service needs and reduced public resources to meet such needs. As shown in the service data provided throughout this volume, the continuation of the status quo will produce a sobering future for Texas.

For both the private and public sectors of Texas, the need to improve the socio-economic resources of minorities is of utmost importance. With more than 87 percent of the net increase in the population [overwhelmingly due to Chicanos/Latinos] and two-thirds of the net increase in the labor force projected to be due to minority populations, it is clear that the future of Texas is directly tied to its minority populations. How well minorities do in the economy and how well they can compete with other workers in the global economy is of importance to all Texans. With education being the traditional route to improvement in economic mobility, educational attainment is likely to be of critical importance if we are to change the future for minorities and the future of Texas. Texas must invest in the socioeconomic improvement of its minority populations because the state's future is increasingly dependent upon them.

(pp. 221–222)

In sum, the reduction of inequality between Chicanos/Latinos and the more privileged sectors of society is, as Miranda and Quiroz (1989) so strongly voiced, "an economic imperative" (p. 28). Improving the educational status of Chicanos and other undereducated Latinos *now* has tremendous positive implications for the good of the *future* of our nation.

Notes

1 The 1980 to 1990 population growth in rates and absolute numbers reported in this paragraph are based on my calculations of 1980 and 1990 U.S. Census data (U.S. Department of Commerce, Bureau of the Census, 2000a, 2000b).

2 Deep appreciation is extended to my research assistant, Bruno Villarreal, who assisted me in identifying pertinent demographic data.

3 Together, these groups comprise 11.1 percent of the total Latino population of 35.3 million. There is also another group, "all other Hispanic," that accounts for 17.3 percent of the Latino population; these are individuals who did not give a detailed answer to the national-origin question in the U.S. Census survey (Guzmán, 2001). In that such a sizable portion of the Latinos surveyed in the Census did not provide a detailed answer for their national origin, it is likely that counts for all the other Latino groups were underidentified, particularly Mexican-origin people.

4 This estimate I offer is based on U.S. Census data provided in Guzmán (2001, p. 4, Table 2). There were 20,432,826 Latinos enumerated in the five Southwestern states. Of these, 15,374,276 (75.2 percent) were identified as Mexican origin.

5 Two states, for examples, that have not historically been homes to very many Latinos, and are now experiencing extraordinary growth among Mexican Americans and other Latinos, are North Carolina and Georgia. Based on my calculations from the data presented by Guzmán (2001, p. 4, Table 2) North Carolina increased its Latino population by 394 percent—from 76,726 in 1990 to 378,963 in 2000. Georgia's Latino population increased 141 percent—from 180,922 in 1990 to 435,227 in 2000. These 1990 to 2000 growth rates in North Carolina and Georgia are considerably larger than in those states with long-standing Latino populations. For example, the 1990 to 2000 Latino growth rates in Texas and California were 54 percent and 43 percent, respectively. On a final note, the presence of Mexican-origin people in the new settlement areas is substantial. Based on 2000 U.S. Census data, Mexican Americans in North Carolina and Georgia, for example, accounted for 65 percent and 63 percent, respectively, of the total Latino populations in these states (my calculations from data presented in Guzmán, 2001, p. 4, Table 2).

References

Arizona Department of Education. (2000). *Arizona enrollment figures, state of Arizona: October 1, 1998 enrollment, SY99*. Phoenix, AZ: Author. Available online at: http://www.ade.state.az.us/researchpolicy/azenroll/sy99.asp

California Department of Education. (2001a). *Statewide enrollment in California public schools by ethnic group, 2000–01*. Sacramento, CA: Author. Report available online using Dataquest search engine at: http://data1.cde.ca.gov/dataquest/

California Department of Education. (2001b). *Enrollment in California public schools by ethnic group, 2000–01*. Sacramento, CA: Author. Report available online using Dataquest search engine at: http://data1.cde.ca.gov/dataquest/OthEnrPg2.asp

Carnevale, A.P. and Fry, R.A. (2000). *Crossing the great divide: Can we achieve equity when generation Y goes to college?* Princeton, NJ: Educational Testing Service.

Colorado Department of Education. (2001a). *State level membership trends by ethnic/racial and gender fall 1996 through fall 2000*. Denver, CO: Author. Available online at: http://www.cde.state.co.us/cdereval/download/pdf/Fall2000StateMbrEthnicityTrends.pdf

Colorado Department of Education. (2001b). *Fall 2000 membership by county, district, and ethnic/racial group*. Denver, CO: Author. Available online at: http://www.cde.state.co.us/cdereval/download/pdf/2000PMbyCountyDistEth.pdf

García, E.E. (2001). *Hispanic education in the United States: Raíces y alas*. Lanham, MD: Rowen & Littlefield.

Grey, M.A. (1991). The context for marginal secondary ESL programs: Contributing factors and the need for further research. *The Journal of Educational Issues of Language Minority Students*, 9, 75–89.

Guzmán, B. (2001). *The Hispanic population: Census 2000 brief.* Washington, DC: U.S. Department of Commerce, Economics and Statistics Administration, U.S. Census Bureau. Available online at: http://www.census.gov/prod/2001pubs/c2kbr01–3.pdf

Hamann, E.T., Wortham, S. and Murillo, E.G., Jr. (2001). Education and policy in the New Latino Diaspora. In S. Wortham, E.G. Murillo, Jr. and E.T. Hamann (Eds.), *Education in the New Latino Diaspora: Policy and the politics of identity* (pp. 1–16). Westport, CT: Ablex Publishing.

Hayes-Bautista, D.E., Schink, W.O. and Chapa, J. (1988). *The burden of support: Young Latinos in an aging society.* Stanford, CA: Stanford University Press.

Karoly, L.A. (1992). *The trend of inequality among families, individuals, and workers in the United States.* Santa Monica, CA: Rand.

Macías, R.F. (1993). Language and ethnic classification of language minorities: Chicano and Latino students in the 1990s. *Hispanic Journal of Behavioral Sciences*, 15, 230–257.

Miranda, L. and Quiroz, J.T. (1989). *The decade of the Hispanic: A sobering economic retrospective.* Washington, DC: National Council of La Raza.

Murdock, S.H., Hoque, Md.N., Michael, M., White, S. and Pecotte, B. (1997). *The Texas challenge: Population change and the future of Texas.* College Station, TX: Texas A&M University Press.

New Mexico Department of Education. (2001a). *New Mexico facts about education: 1995/2000.* Santa Fe, NM: Author. Available online at: http://www.sde.state.nm.us/divisions/ais/datacollection/facts9900.pdf

New Mexico Department of Education. (2001b). *Percent of student enrollment ethnic category by district: School year 2000–2001.* Santa Fe, NM: Author. Available online at: http://www.sde.state.nm.us/divisions/ais/datacollection/ethnicenrollment.pdf

Orfield, G. (2001). *Schools more separate: Consequences of a decade of research.* The Civil Rights Project, Harvard University. Cambridge, MA: Harvard University. Available online at: http://www.law.harvard.edu/groups/civilrights/publications/schoolsseparate.pdf

Ruiz-de-Velasco, J., Fix, M. and Clewell, B.C. (2000). *Overlooked and underserved: Immigrant students in U.S. secondary schools.* Washington, DC: Urban Institute.

San Miguel, G. Jr. and Valencia, R.R. (1998). From the Treaty of Guadalupe Hidalgo to *Hopwood*: The educational plight and struggle of Mexican Americans in the Southwest. *Harvard Educational Review*, 68, 353–412.

Texas Education Agency. (2001a). *2000–2001 student enrollment: Statewide totals.* Austin, TX: Author. Available online using PEIMS search engine at: http://www.tea.state.tx.us/adhocrpt/adste01.html

Texas Education Agency. (2001b). *2000–2001 student enrollment: Statewide district totals.* Austin, TX: Author. Available online using PEIMS search engine at: http://www.tea.state.tx.us/adhocrpt/adste01.html

U.S. Department of Commerce, Bureau of the Census. (2000a). *Statistical abstract of the United States.* Washington, DC: Author.

U.S. Department of Commerce, Bureau of the Census. (2000b). *Profile of general demographic characteristics for the United States: 2000.* Washington, DC: Author. Available online at: http://www.census.gov/prod/cen2000/dp1/2kh00.pdf

U.S. Department of Commerce, Bureau of the Census. (2000c). *Profile of general demographic characteristics for Arizona: 2000.* Washington, DC: Author. Available online at: http://www.census.gov/Press-Release/www/2001/tables/dp_az_2000.pdf

U.S. Department of Commerce, Bureau of the Census. (2000d). *Profile of general demographic characteristics for California: 2000.* Washington, DC: Author. Available online at: http://www.census.gov/Press-Release/www/2001/tables/dp_ca_2000.pdf

U.S. Department of Commerce, Bureau of the Census. (2000e). *Profile of general demographic characteristics for Colorado: 2000.* Washington, DC: Author. Available online at: http://www.census.gov/Press-Release/www/2001/tables/dp_co_2000.pdf

U.S. Department of Commerce, Bureau of the Census. (2000f). *Profile of general demographic characteristics for New Mexico: 2000.* Washington, DC: Author. Available online at: http://www.census.gov/Press-Release/www/2001/tables/dp_nm_2000.pdf

U.S. Department of Commerce, Bureau of the Census. (2000g). *Profile of general demographic characteristics for Texas: 2000*. Washington, DC: Author. Available online at: http://www.census.gov/Press-Release/www/2001/tables/dp_tx_2000.pdf

U.S. Department of Commerce, Bureau of the Census. (2000h). *Projections of the resident population by age, sex, race, and Hispanic origin: 1999 to 2100*. Washington, DC: Author. Available online at: http://www.census.gov/population/www/projections/natdet-D1A.html

U.S. Department of Commerce, Bureau of the Census. (2000i). *Educational attainment of the population 15 years and over, by age, sex, race, and Hispanic origin: March 2000*. Washington, DC: Author. Available online at: http://www.census.gov/population/www/socdemo/education/p20–536.html

Valencia, R.R. and Aburto, S. (1991). Research directions and practical strategies in teacher testing and assessment: Implications for improving Latino access to teaching. In G.D. Keller, J. Deneen, and R. Magallán (Eds.), *Assessment and access: Hispanics in higher education* (pp. 197–234). Albany: State University of New York Press.

Valencia, R.R. and Bernal, E.M. (Eds.). (2000). The Texas Assessment of Academic Skills (TAAS) case: Perspectives of plaintiffs' experts [Special issue]. *Hispanic Journal of Behavioral Sciences, 22*(4).

Wortham, S., Murillo, E.G., Jr. and Hamann, E.T. (Eds.). (2001). *Education in the New Latino Diaspora: Policy and the politics of identity*. Westport, CT: Ablex Publishing.

3 Segregation, desegregation, and integration of Chicano students: old and new realities

Richard R. Valencia, Martha Menchaca, and Rubén Donato

Segregation has been, and continues to be, a reality for a substantial number of Chicano children and youths in elementary and secondary public schools. In that segregation practices and conditions are not conducive for optimal learning, it is not surprising that school segregation is inextricably linked to Chicano school failure. As noted by Valencia (Chapter 1, this volume), the segregation of Chicano students constitutes a major obstacle in their schooling experience, meaning that such racial/ethnic isolation can be considered a key institutional process in denying Chicanos equal educational opportunities.

This chapter offers a comprehensive update of what we presented in the first edition of *Chicano School Failure and Success* (Donato *et al.*, 1991). Our current chapter is organized around four sections. First, there is the "Introduction" in which we cover: (a) prevalence of segregation, and (b) adverse effects of segregation. Second, we present "Racism and Chicano school segregation: a historical perspective." This section includes: (a) racism and the structural foundation of segregation; (b) the rooting of Chicano school segregation; (c) early Chicano desegregation litigation. Third, we offer a section on "Contemporary issues in Chicano segregation." Here, we present discussions on: (a) community studies of Chicano segregation: a silent problem; (b) language segregation: old problems, new issues; (c) academic resegregation. Fourth, we present a section on "Towards integration," in which we discuss: (a) community case studies of historical segregation; (b) residential segregation; (c) busing; (d) Chicano/African American coalitions; (e) Chicano school board membership; (f) two-way bilingual education; (g) "critical theory" in teacher education.

Introduction

The forced separation of Chicano children and youths from their White peers in public schools has its roots in the post-1848 decades following the Treaty of Guadalupe Hidalgo. Subsequently, racial/ethnic isolation of schoolchildren became a normative practice in the Southwest—despite states having no legal statutes to segregate Chicano students from White students (San Miguel and Valencia, 1998). What follows is a capsulation of the historical and contemporary prevalence of Chicano school segregation and the adverse effects of such segregation on Chicano academic achievement.

Prevalence of segregation[1]

Local officials such as city council and school board members established schools for Mexican-origin children in the post-1848 period, but given that they were more interested in first providing White children with school facilities, the Mexican schools were few in number. Local and state political leaders' lack of commitment to public schooling, racial prejudice, and political differences among Anglos and Mexicans accounted for this practice (Atkins, 1978; Friedman, 1978; Hendrick, 1977; Weinberg, 1977).

After the 1870s, the number of schools for Mexican-origin children increased dramatically due to popular demand, legal mandates, increasing financial ability, and a greater acceptance of the ideal of common schooling by local and state political leaders (Atkins, 1978; Eby, 1925; Ferris, 1962). This educational access occurred, however, in the context of increasing societal discrimination and a general subordination of Mexican Americans. Out of this relationship between society and education there emerged a pattern of institutional discrimination that was reflected in the establishment of segregated schools for Mexican-origin children. In New Mexico, for instance, officials began to establish segregated schools in 1872. By the 1880s, over 50 percent of the territory's school-age population, most of whom were Mexican children, were enrolled in these segregated schools (Chaves, 1892).

Despite the influx of Mexican immigrant students, California officials did not build any additional schools for Mexican children until the turn of the century. Those that existed continued to be segregated and, in some cases, were inferior to the Anglo schools (California Superintendent of Public Instruction, 1869).[2]

In Texas, officials established segregated schools for Mexican working-class children in the rural areas during the 1880s and in the urban areas in the 1890s. The need to maintain a cheap labor source in the ranches probably accounted for the earlier presence of Mexican schools in the rural areas (Friedman, 1978; Weinberg, 1977). In the early 1900s, segregated schools were established by large-scale growers as a means of preventing the Mexican students from attending White schools. One of the first Mexican schools was established at the turn of the century in Central Texas (Seguin), and afterwards the process of constructing separate Mexican schools became a common practice throughout the state (Rangel and Alcala, 1972).

The segregation of Mexican American students in the Southwest continued to rise into the 1890s and spilled over to the 20th century. By the beginning of the 1930s, the educational template for Chicano students—one of forced, widespread segregation and inferior schooling—was formed. In California and Texas, the Mexican American population increased dramatically, and local school boards instituted practices that led to the further segregation of Mexican American students from their White peers. By 1931, 85 percent of California schools surveyed by Leis (1931) reported segregating Mexican American students either in separate schools or separate classrooms (also, see Hendrick, 1977). Leis, with the cooperation of the County Superintendent of San Bernardino, surveyed 13 school districts in California. These districts had nearly 88,000 students enrolled—25 percent of whom were Mexican American. Leis reported that 11 (85 percent) of the 13 districts surveyed stated that they segregated Mexican American students for the first several grades. Reasons given for the separation of White and Mexican American children was "entirely or partly . . . for educational purposes" (p. 25). More specifically, Leis reported that generally

> segregation ends in the fourth, fifth, or sixth grade because the language handicap has practically disappeared and social adaptation has fitted the Mexican child to go into the grades with the white children if he remains in school. Excessive dropping out at these levels is a large factor in discontinuing segregation.
>
> (1931, p. 66)

The school segregation of Mexican students was also widespread in Texas and coincided with a period of dramatic growth in the immigrant population (Montejano, 1987). As in

California, segregated schools were a direct outgrowth of residential segregation, increasing Mexican immigration, and in particular, racial discrimination. Moreover, in the late 1920s school segregation became more intense and it coincided with the growth of the Mexican immigrant population (Montejano, 1987). In the areas where the newcomers were concentrated, such as the lower Rio Grande Valley, the school segregation of Mexican students radically increased. Reconstructing the educational histories of local communities in the lower Rio Grande Valley, Montejano concluded that Mexican immigration and residential and school segregation were inextricably part of the same process:

> The towns of Edinburg, Harlingen, and San Benito segregated their Mexican school children through the fourth and fifth grades. And along the dense string of newcomer towns of Highway 83—the "longest mile" of McAllen, Mercedes, Mission, Pharr-San Juan, and Weslaco—Mexican school segregation was an unbroken policy. On the Gulf Coast plains, Raymondville, Kingsville, Robstown, Kenedy, and Taft were among the new towns where segregation was practiced. And in the Winter Garden area, Mexicans were segregated through the fifth grade in Crystal City, Carrizo Springs, Palm, Valley Wells, Asherton, and Frio Town.
>
> (p. 168)

By 1930, 90 percent of the schools in Texas were racially segregated (Rangel and Alcala, 1972).

With the increase in the Mexican-origin population and the escalating barrioization of Chicano communities, school segregation from the 1930s to the 1970s became fairly entrenched for many Chicano students throughout the Southwest. In 1971, the Mexican American Education Study (MAES) report on the racial/ethnic isolation of Mexican American elementary and secondary students in the five Southwestern states (Arizona, California, Colorado, New Mexico, and Texas) confirmed that the historical segregation of Mexican American students persisted into the contemporary period (U.S. Commission on Civil Rights, 1971). In 1968, one in two Mexican American students attended schools in which they comprised the predominant racial/ethnic group (i.e., 50 to 100 percent Mexican American enrollment); one in five Mexican American students attended schools that were 80 to 100 percent Mexican American.

Later studies showed that Mexican American student segregation intensified from the MAES 1968 baseline date. For example, Orfield (1988a) compared Latino student segregation regionally and nationally from 1968 to 1984 (also, see Orfield, 1988b).[3] The data in Table 3.1 show that for this 16-year period, Orfield's analysis of national data revealed that the percentage of Latinos enrolled in predominantly White schools dropped by 36 percent. For Latino students enrolled in 90 to 100 percent minority schools, Latino enrollment increased 35 percent. For the West, Latino enrollment in predominantly White schools declined by 45 percent; in 90 to 100 percent minority schools, Latino enrollment soared by 92 percent.

Orfield and associates have continued to study school segregation trends (see, e.g., Orfield, 2001; Orfield *et al.*, 1997; Orfield and Yun, 1999). Regarding Chicanos/other Latinos, these students presently maintain a pattern of hypersegregation that was reported in the first edition of the present volume (Donato *et al.*, 1991, p. 28; Valencia, 1991, p. 7). In their recent study, Orfield and Yun found that one of the most important trends "is the continuation of a long and relentless march toward even more severe segregation for Latino students as they become our largest minority" (p. 11). Orfield and Yun also noted: "Latino

Table 3.1 Latino segregation by region: 1968–1984

Region	Latino students in predominantly White schools (%)		Change (%)	Latino students in 90–100% minority schools (%)		Change (%)
	1968	1984		1968	1984	
West	58	32	−44.8	12	23	+91.7
South	30	25	−16.7	34	37	+8.8
Northeast	25	22	−12.0	44	47	+6.8
Midwest	68	46	−32.4	7	24	+242.9
U.S.	45	29	−35.6	23	31	+34.8

Source: Adapted from Orfield (1988a). With permission of author.

students are significantly more segregated than African Americans and segregation has been rapidly growing in the states where they have the largest enrollments" (p. 21).

The most recent reports by Orfield and associates—Orfield (2001), and Orfield and Yun (1999)—contain rich data on Latino segregation trends. Here we glean three of the authors' major findings.

National trends

In the 1968–1969 school year, 45 percent of Latino students attended majority White schools. The next generation of Latino students has significantly less contact with White students. In the 1998–1999 school year—three decades later—only 25 percent of Latinos were enrolled in majority White schools (see Orfield, 2001, p. 33, Table 9).

Another manner of viewing national trends in school segregation is to examine changes over time of the presence of Latinos and African Americans in predominantly and intensely segregated schools. Orfield (2001) has done just such. These data are presented in Table 3.2.

Table 3.2 Percentage of Latino and African American students in predominantly and intensely segregated minority schools: 1968–1998

Time period	Predominantly Latino/African American school (50–100% minority)		Intensely Latino/African American school (90–100% minority)	
	Latino	African American	Latino	African American
1968–1969	54.8	76.6	23.1	64.3
1972–1973	56.6	63.6	23.3	38.7
1980–1981	68.1	62.9	28.8	33.2
1986–1987	71.5	63.3	32.2	32.5
1991–1992	73.4	66.0	34.0	33.9
1994–1995	74.0	67.1	34.8	33.6
1996–1997	74.8	68.8	35.4	35.0
1998–1999	75.6	70.2	36.6	36.5

Source: Adapted from Orfield (2001, p. 33, Table 9). With permission of author.

Two major points can be gleaned from these data:

- Whereas African American presence in intensely segregated schools (90 to 100 percent minority) has dropped from 64.3 percent in 1968–1969 to 36.5 percent in 1998–1999 (decline of 27.8 percentage points), Latino percentage in intensely segregated schools actually *increased* 13.5 percentage points during the same period (from 23.1 to 36.6 percent).

- Regarding presence in predominantly segregated (50 to 100 percent) minority schools in the 1968–1969 to 1998–1999 time period, African Americans declined by 6.4 percentage points (from 76.6 to 70.2 percent). By sharp contrast, Latino presence *increased* 20.8 percentage points. In 1968–1969, more than half (54.8 percent) of Latino students attended predominantly minority schools across the nation. By 1998–1999, however, three-fourths (75.6 percent) of Latinos were enrolled in such schools. Orfield noted: "By this measure Latinos have been substantially more segregated than black students since 1980, although black resegregation gradually narrowed the gap in the 1990s" (p. 34).

In sum, these national trends clearly point to hypersegregation of Chicano/Latino students. Unfortunately, such patterns often go overlooked. As Orfield (2001) commented: "The more dramatic and largely ignored [segregation] trends are those affecting Latinos" (p. 34).

Regional trends

In the 1998–1999 school year, the Northeast was the most segregated region for Latino students (79 percent attended 50 to 100 percent minority schools); the Midwest was the least segregated (56 percent). The South and West regions were slightly behind the Northeast in Latino student segregation. In the West, where the vast majority of Chicano/other Latino students attend school, 78 percent were enrolled in 50 to 100 percent minority schools, and 35 percent of these students were enrolled in 90 to 100 percent minority schools (see Orfield, 2001, p. 46, Table 18).

State trends (Southwest)

Orfield and Yun (1999) noted: "The scope of the changes in Latino segregation has not been widely recognized because Latinos are concentrated in the Southwest, where they play a very large and historic role in the society" (p. 22). As such, we focus on the five Southwestern states from the data Orfield (2001) presents in his Table 19 (p. 47).[4] Table 3.3, shows the changes in the percentages of White students attended by a typical Latino student, from 1970 to 1998. The five Southwestern states are listed alphabetically.

The data presented in Table 3.3 show that in all five Southwestern states, Latino students attended schools with higher percentages of White students in 1970 than they did in 1998. For example, in California in 1970 Latino students were enrolled in schools with an average 54 percent White enrollment. In 1998, however, Latinos attended schools where the average White enrollment had sharply declined to 22 percent. Table 3.3 also shows data from the Orfield (2001) report that suggest segregation/desegregation trends in the Southwestern states. Drawing from the slightly earlier report of 1999, Orfield and Yun explained the trends as follows:

Table 3.3 Changes in the percentage of White students in Southwestern states attended by a typical Latino student: 1970–1998

State	1970	1980	1998	Change 1970–1980	Change 1980–1998	Change 1970–1998
Arizona	45.5	43.5	34.8	−2.0	−8.7	−10.7
California	54.4	35.9	22.3	−18.5	−13.6	−32.1
Colorado	56.8	59.0	49.0	2.2	−10.0	−7.8
New Mexico	36.9	32.6	28.9	−4.3	−3.7	−8.0
Texas	31.1	35.1	23.5	4.0	−11.6	−7.6

Source: Adapted from Orfield (2001, p. 47, Table 19). With permission of author.

Texas and Colorado Latinos actually had an increase in integration from 1970 to 1980, probably from busing orders, but Texas was one of the first states to end its urban desegregation plans and Latinos were more segregated in 1996 than they had been 26 years earlier. Colorado Latinos were far more integrated than those on the other Southwestern states through 1996, but since then the federal court has ended desegregation in Denver and state law forbids busing for desegregation without a federal court order.

(p. 22)

National, regional, and Southwestern reports certainly provide data on the prevalence of Chicano student segregation. It is also important, however, not to forget segregation at the local district level. As a case in point, we present a profile of one school district—the Austin Independent School District (AISD), which is 1 of 1,041 districts in Texas.[5] In the 1998–1999 school year, AISD had a total of over 78,000 students in its 92 elementary, middle, and high schools. The percentage breakdowns by race/ethnicity were: Hispanic (43.9 percent), White (36.0 percent), Black (17.3 percent), Asian/Pacific Islander (2.5 percent), and American Indian (0.3 percent) (Texas Education Agency, 2000a). Similar to many other racially/ethnically diverse school districts in Texas, AISD is highly segregated. To quantify the extent of this racial/ethnic isolation, Valencia (2000) divided the AISD into three school levels—elementary, middle, and high—and then calculated the number of racially/ethnically "balanced" and "imbalanced" schools. The rule of thumb Valencia used to determine balance/imbalance was the "±15%" rule (see, e.g., U.S. Commission on Civil Rights, 1971). One takes the percentage of the *combined* total enrollment of minority students in a school district, and then adds 15 percentage points to obtain the *upper limit* of the band and also subtracts 15 percentage points to obtain the *lower limit* of the band. Individual schools that fall *within* the band's upper and lower limits in combined minority percentage are deemed racially/ethnically "balanced." Schools that fall *outside* the lower or upper limits are considered "imbalanced." Table 3.4 presents the results of Valencia's analysis for the AISD elementary, middle, and high schools levels—which Valencia viewed as independent units for the sake of illustration, although all together they constitute one school district. The data show that at the elementary level ($N = 67$ schools), 76 percent of the schools ($n = 51$) are imbalanced (61 percent being predominantly minority, 39 percent being predominantly White), and only 24 percent of the schools ($n = 16$) are deemed balanced using the (±15% rule.[6] Of the 31 predominantly minority schools, 24 are majority Chicano/other Latino, five are majority African American, and two are neither majority Chicano/other Latino or African American. Table 3.3 also shows similar segregation patterns for the middle and high school levels. One can only conclude that AISD is a highly segregated school

Table 3.4 Segregation in Austin Independent School District: 1998–1999

School level		Segregation status (racial/ethnic mix) of schools				Race/ethnicity of imbalanced schools			
		Balanced		Imbalanced		Predominantly White		Predominantly minority	
		n	%	n	%	n	%	n	%
Elementary									
Total schools	67	16	23.9	51	76.1	20	39.2	31	60.8
Total enrollment	42,356								
White enrollment	14,038 (33.1%)								
Minority enrollment	28,318 (66.9%)								
Middle									
Total schools	15	7	46.7	8	53.3	3	37.5	5	62.5
Total enrollment	16,023								
White enrollment	5,988 (37.4%)								
Minority enrollment	10,035 (62.6%)								
High									
Total school	10	2	20.0	8	80.0	4	50.0	4	50.0
Total enrollment	19,697								
White enrollment	8,105 (41.1%)								
Minority enrollment	11,592 (58.9%)								

Source: Valencia (2000, p. 449, Table 1). Data source is Texas Education Agency (2000a).

district. The degree of segregation in AISD is typical of Texas' K-12 public schools. In the 1993–1994 school year, close to two in three (64 percent) of all Chicano/other Latino students in the state attended schools in which 70 percent or more of the students were racial/ethnic minorities. About one in two (49 percent) of all African American students were enrolled in such schools. By sharp contrast, about one in fourteen (7 percent) of all White students were enrolled in these 70 percent or greater minority schools (Brooks and South, 1995). This pervasive pattern of school segregation in Texas schools continues to the present.

Adverse effects of segregation

Historically, the context for learning in Chicano segregated schools has been extremely poor. González (1990) described these early conditions (1930s) as such:

> Inadequate resources, poor equipment, and unfit building construction made Mexican schools vastly inferior to Anglo schools. In addition, school districts paid teachers at Mexican schools less than teachers at Anglo schools, and many times a promotion for a teacher at a Mexican school meant moving to the Anglo school. Quite often, however, teachers in Mexican schools were either beginners or had been 'banished' as incompetent.
>
> (p. 22)

There are a number of accounts from decades past that document the considerably poor conditions endured by Chicano students in segregated schools. For example, Menchaca and Valencia (1990) contrasted the Mexican and Anglo schools built in the mid-1920s in Santa Paula, California. The Mexican school enrolled nearly 1,000 students in a schoolhouse with eight classrooms (grades K-8) and contained two bathrooms and one administrative office. On the other hand, the Anglo school enrolled less than 700 students and contained 21 classrooms, a cafeteria, a training shop, and several administrative offices. In short, the Mexican school—compared to the Anglo school—had a much higher student per classroom ratio and inferior facilities. Fifteen miles away from Santa Paula, in the coastal city of Oxnard, Chicano students fared no better in segregated schools. McCurdy (1975) in a *Los Angeles Times* article reported how several past school superintendents described the deplorable schooling conditions Chicano children experienced in the 1930s.[7]

> One school was described as "literally no more than a chicken coop. It had a dirt floor, single thickness walls, very run down, some stench from the toilet facility." Another school had a floor made from "just black asphalt of the type you would see placed on street pavement," a former superintendent said. "In the classroom, there was a single light bulb, not a large one. . . . It may have been a 100-watt bulb, screwed into an outlet in the center of the ceiling", he said. "It was one of the least desirable learning environments that one could devise."
>
> (p. 3)

The inferior conditions in Mexican American schools were further documented by Calderón (1950) in his master's thesis, which consisted of case studies of two Mexican American schools and one Anglo school in Edcouch-Elsa, Texas (lower Rio Grande Valley).[8] Calderón reported that average class sizes in the Mexican American schools were in the high 30s and low 40s, while the average size in the Anglo school was 33. Regarding promotion practices, he noted that the Mexican American "children were compelled to spend two years in the first grade without regard to the ability of the student to do the work" (p. 20). The Anglo school had a band, cafeteria, and students had regular access to dental and medical services, whereas the Mexican American schools did not have such access to these facilities and services. Additionally, Calderón noted that Anglo and Mexican American children traveled to school together, but the latter students "were traditionally seated in the rear of the bus" (p. 40). Calderón's thesis is particularly insightful as his report contains contrasting, highly detailed photographs of facility conditions at the schools. The Anglo school had inside lavatories, with walls separating the commodes, and tile floors. Water fountains, electrically cooled, were also located inside the school building. Classroom light bulbs were shielded, thus providing diffuse lighting. By sharp contrast, the Mexican American schools had lavatories outside the building, no separating stalls, and bare concrete floors. Drinking fountains with non-cooled water were also located outside. Finally, bare light bulbs hung from the ceilings.

Another example of the early inferior schooling conditions in the Southwest that Mexican American students faced comes from the study by Maddux (1932) who described schooling conditions for Mexican American children in separate classrooms in Weld County, Colorado. Mexican children often attended "rooms . . . located in basements [of schools] with bad lighting and poor ventilation. The Mexican room in [the town of] Kersey is in the basement under the gymnasium," said Maddux. "When the gymnasium is in use the noise is deafening. . . . [In this school] the small children have to sit on cigar boxes" (pp. 34–35).

It is not surprising that during the 1930–1960 time period, segregated and inferior schooling conditions for Mexican Americans would frequently lead to poor academic performance, progress, and attainment.[9] In a comprehensive report, titled *The Education of Spanish-Speaking Children in Five Southwestern States*, Reynolds (1933) quoted an Arizona study as follows: "In general, the type of Mexican child taken into the Arizona school tends to be backward in rate of mental development, lags a year behind other pupils, shows a heavy failure percentage, and an early elimination from school" (p. 38). An example of such school failure was the finding that for every "100 Mexican children in grade 1 there are 7 in grade 8, while for 100 non-Mexican children in grade 1 there are 52 in grade 8" (p. 39).

The above study by Reynolds (1933) was sponsored by the Office of Education of the U.S. Department of the Interior. Though ambitious in scope, the study provided scattered information about schooling conditions of "Mexican" (i.e., Mexican American) students attending schools in the five Southwestern states. Major findings were:

1   Mexican American children frequently attended segregated schools, and such isolation, it was noted, was based on "instructional" reasons (usually to learn English). Reynolds noted: "In the opinion of the many experienced teachers and supervisors the fourth or fifth is the grade at which separate instruction form Mexican pupils should end" (p. 11). Reynolds also commented: "Practically, however, so few Mexican pupils reach the upper elementary grades that the opinion has not to date received much of a test" (p. 11).

2   "Teaching materials adequate in amount and of the right kind for Mexican children are conspicuously absent" (p. 13).

3   "Teachers, even experienced ones, reported they were ill-equipped to teach the Mexican American students (particularly Spanish-speakers), and received 'little supervisory guidance'" (p. 22).

4   The percentage of Mexican American teachers was extremely small; based on a survey of seven selected counties in the five states, "the total number of teachers . . . is 2,320. This number includes 26 [1.1 percent] Mexicans" (p. 23).

5 Mexican American pupils "are not attending school to anything like the extent to which English-speaking [i.e., White] pupils living in the same sections attend" (p. 37).

6 The percentage of Mexican American students who were pedagogically retarded (overage for their grade) was very high.

In sum, there is considerable historical evidence that Chicano students experienced massive schooling inequalities.[10] This segregated and inferior schooling led to school failure for many of these students (e.g., poor academic achievement; early exiting from the schooling process). It is not surprising that the Chicano community mounted a campaign for educational equality, a topic we cover later in this chapter (also, see: Donato, 1997; San Miguel, 1987; San Miguel and Valencia, 1998; Valencia and Black, 2002).

Suffice it to say, the inadequate educational conditions experienced by Chicano students in the past were detrimental to promoting an optimal learning environment. Although the current facilities in Chicano segregated schools may not be as deplorable as in the past, the legacy of inferiority certainly continues. A major contributing factor to the maintenance of inferior conditions—as manifested in limited resources for Chicano segregated schools—is school financing inequities (see Valencia, Chapter 1, this volume).

Notwithstanding the extreme importance of attaining equity in school financing for Chicano schools (e.g., more funds to build new schools; money to purchase computers), there remains the stubborn relation between school segregation of Chicanos and lowered academic achievement. The studies we discuss next clearly point to the reality that school segregation of Chicanos leads to limited equal educational opportunities, and these limitations, in turn, manifest in poor academic achievement. For example, Jaeger (1987) examined the relation between achievement test scores and percent Black and Latino high school students in metropolitan Los Angeles (1984–1985 school year). The observed correlations were very strong: mathematics (-0.89), reading (-0.90), and writing (-0.85). That is, as minority enrollment increased, achievement decreased. Jaeger reported that the correlations between school enrollment percentage of White students and achievement test scores were likewise of very high magnitudes (0.80s), but of the opposite direction (i.e., as White enrollment in the high schools increased, test scores also increased). Finally, Jaeger disaggregated the data and found that when only the percentage of Latino students in the high schools was correlated with achievement, the relations were not as strong for the Black/Latino aggregate, but still quite substantial (mathematics, -0.53, reading, -0.58, and writing, -0.53).

Espinosa and Ochoa (1986) have also provided supporting evidence for the connection between Chicano segregation and diminished achievement in California—a state in which Chicano school segregation has also increased in the last 30 years. Using a large statewide sample (4,268 public elementary schools and 791 public high schools), Espinosa and Ochoa correlated California Assessment Program (CAP) scores (average of math and reading achievement) with percent of Latino students in grades 3, 6, and 12. The relation between Latino concentration and CAP achievement was strongly defined (e.g., at grade 12 the observed r was -0.49).

In another investigation, Valencia (1984a) also found a substantial relation between minority concentration in schools and academic achievement. The setting for the study was the Phoenix Union High School District (PUHSD) No. 210. Valencia—as part of his work as an expert witness in a school closure trial in the PUHSD—calculated the correlation between the percentage of Black/Latino enrollment with mean stanines of the Comprehensive Tests of Basic Skills for grades 9 through 12 in the District's 11 high schools. Table 3.5 lists the ranking of the 11 schools by minority student enrollment accompanied by each

Table 3.5 Rank correlation analysis between percentage of minority student body enrollment and academic achievement

School	Minority student enrollment (%)	Minority enrollment rank	Achievement rank (1 is lowest, 11 is highest)[a]
Union	94.2	1	1
South	87.7	2	2
Hayden	75.0	3	3
North	64.4	4	4
East	56.7	5	5
West	25.7	6	7
Maryvale	19.5	7	8
Browne	18.0	8	6
Alhambra	13.2	9	9
Central	9.4	10	11
Camelback	7.8	11	10

Source: Adapted from Valencia (1984a, p. 25, Table 6).

Note
[a] Achievement based on Fall, 1978 mean stanines of the Comprehensive Tests of Basic Skills for grades 9–12. $r_S = 0.96$ (significant < 0.01).

school's respective rank (lowest to highest) on achievement. The statistical analysis (Spearman rank correlation coefficient) computed by Valencia revealed that the association between Black/Latino percentage of the various high schools with their respective test scores was very strong ($r_S = 0.96$)—once again underscoring the ubiquitous connection between school segregation and low academic performance.

Orfield (1988a) reported that the Black/Latino percentage of schools was very negatively associated ($r = -0.92$) with average college admissions test scores. When the analyses were disaggregated by ethnicity, the correlations for Latino high school students were -0.40 (percent Latino with graduation rate) and -0.43 (percent Latino with college entrance scores).

Still yet another example of empirical research investigating the relation between Chicano (and other minority student) segregation and achievement test scores is the study by Valencia (2000). He correlated failure rates on the Texas Assessment of Academic Skills (TAAS— all test sections, all students; 1998–1999 school year) with the percentage of combined minority student enrollment in the 67 elementary schools in the Austin Independent School District (AISD; see previous discussion on "Prevalence of segregation" for a description of the racial/ethnic distribution of the AISD). The cornerstone of Texas' accountability system is the TAAS test, which is administered annually in grades 3 to 8, and 10, and consists of reading, mathematics, and writing. Figure 3.1 graphically presents Valencia's results via a scatterplot of the correlational analysis. It can be clearly seen that as the percentage of minority enrollment increases in the schools, there is a tendency for the percentage of students who fail TAAS to increase. The observed Pearson product-moment correlation of 0.87 suggests a very strong relation between the two variables.[11] Though Valencia did not graphically present the correlational analyses for the middle and high schools in the AISD, he reported that the correlation coefficients were also robust—0.84 for the 15 middle schools and 0.96 for the ten high schools (see Table 3.3 of the present chapter for racial/ethnic distributions of the middle and high schools, and for segregation patterns).

On a final note, there is evidence that the relation between school segregation and schooling problems is not confined to test score outcomes. For example, Orfield (1988a) found

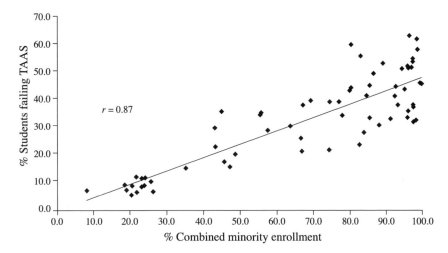

Figure 3.1 Scatterplot of correlation between percentage of students failing all tests on TAAS and percentage of combined minority enrollment in Austin Independent School District elementary
schools ($N = 67$).

Source: Valencia (2000, p. 450, Figure 1). Data source is Texas Education Agency (2000a).

that the correlation between the percentage of Black/Latino students and graduation rate in
metropolitan Chicago high schools was a staggering −0.83. Furthermore, a correlation of
−0.47 was observed between percent minority high school students and percent of students
taking the college entrance examinations.

In a more recent study demonstrating that minority school segregation is linked to higher
dropout rates, Valencia (2001) examined the high schools in the AISD. Of the ten high
schools, campus graduation rates ("% graduated") for the class of 1999 were available for
eight schools (Texas Education Agency, 2000a). Valencia correlated percentage of combined
Hispanic and African American students (grades 9–12) with campus graduation percentage.
The observed r was −0.89, suggesting a very strong negative correlation between percent
minority enrollment and rate of graduation in the AISD's high schools. An example of this
relation is illustrated by examining two extreme schools (of the eight). Johnston High School,
a predominantly Chicano/other Latino and African American school (combined 84.1 percent;
15.3 percent White), had a campus graduation rate of 67.7 percent. By sharp contrast,
Anderson High School (predominantly White [67.3 percent]; 27.6 percent combined
Chicano/other Latino and African American) had a campus graduation rate of 90.6 percent.
What this above r of −0.89 means is that Chicano/other Latino and African American
students who attend the more highly segregated high schools in the AISD have a lower
probability of graduating from high school, and subsequently matriculating to four-year
colleges.

Valencia (2001)—in his investigation of the AISD high schools—also investigated an
indirect indicator of student success in college—"TAAS/TASP equivalency." The TAAS,
which we described previously, is Texas' mandated testing program. The TASP (Texas
Academic Skills Program), on the other hand,

is a test of reading, writing, and mathematics, required of all persons entering undergraduate programs at Texas public institutions of higher education for the first time.
This indicator [the TAAS/TASP equivalency] shows the percent of [high school]

graduates who did well enough on the exit-level TAAS [administered in grade 10] to have a 75 percent chance of passing the Texas Academic Skills Program . . . test.

(Texas Education Agency, 2000b, p. 34)[12]

Valencia correlated the percentage of combined Hispanic and African American students with the TAAS/TASP equivalency (a percentage) for the ten high schools in the AISD. The observed r was a strong −0.79. This relation suggests that Chicano/other Latino and African American students, as a group, who attend the more highly segregated minority high schools in the AISD have a lower probability of doing well on the TAAS/TASP equivalency indicator. Thus, these students—on the average—have a smaller chance of passing the TASP compared to their White peers, who—on the average—have a higher TAAS/TASP equivalency. For example, Reagan High School (92.9 percent combined Chicano/other Latino and African American enrollment) had a campus TAAS/TASP equivalency of only 39.1 percent, which means that only four in ten Reagan graduates did well enough on the TAAS to have a 75 percent chance of passing TASP. Strikingly different is Anderson High School (27.6 percent combined Chicano/other Latino and African American), which had a campus TAAS/TASP equivalency of 70.9 percent. This means that about seven in ten Anderson students scored well enough on TAAS to have a 75 percent chance of passing TASP. Similar test score discrepancies are clearly seen statewide in Texas' highly segregated high schools. The most recent data show the following TAAS/TASP equivalencies, which are for the aggregate (state) and disaggregation (race/ethnicity) (Texas Education Agency, 2000a, p. 42):

Group	TAAS/TASP Equivalency (%): Class of 1999
State	53.5
Asian/Pacific Islander	67.4
White	65.5
Native American	56.7
Hispanic	37.7
African American	34.9

The implication of these data does not fare well for Texas' public high schools. The *vast majority* of Latinos and African American students who *graduate* from high school do not perform well enough on TAAS to even have a 75 percent chance of passing the TASP. It is important to reiterate that there is a statistical connection between school segregation and TAAS/TASP equivalency at the campus level. As racial/ethnic isolation of Chicano/other Latino and African American students increases at the high school level, there is a tendency for the TAAS/TASP equivalency indicator to decrease. Furthermore, when Chicano/other Latino and African American students enroll in four-year public universities, their TASP pass rates are considerably lower than their White peers. Although such data are not available by race/ethnicity, examining TASP pass rates at traditionally White (e.g., The University of Texas at Austin; 63.6 percent White), Hispanic (e.g., The University of Texas, Pan American; 83.5 percent Hispanic), and African American universities (e.g., Prairie View A&M University; 87.8 percent African American) suggest that different racial/ethnic patterns exist (Texas Higher Education Coordinating Board, 2001). The TASP pass rates for UT Austin, UT Pan American, and Prairie View A&M in the 1998–1999 school year were 71.2 percent, 32.3 percent, and 20.4 percent, respectively.

In conclusion, there is a great deal of historical and contemporary evidence that the school segregation of Chicano students in our nation's public elementary and secondary schools is connected to school failure, hence inequality. Findings from various studies and reports inform us that segregated Chicano schools tend to be schools characterized by a disproportionately high percentage of low-income students, low funding, high dropout rates, low achievement test scores, few college preparatory courses, and low matriculation rates to college. There is no doubt that the isolation of Chicano students in schools that suffer from inequities in facilities, resources, and curricula offerings is far from desirable. The desegregation of Chicano schools and the subsequent integration of Chicano/other minority and White students in equitable learning contexts is a commendable goal. Later, we share our thoughts and ideas how such integration could be realized. But first, it is necessary to understand the historical roots of segregation. Our proposition is that in order to move toward the goal of desegregation and integration of Chicano students, one must have a good grasp of the events and forces that helped shape the educational isolation of Chicanos.

Racism and Chicano school segregation in the Southwest: a historical perspective

In this section we offer our perspective on the historical development of Chicano school segregation. We do so by discussing three major aspects: racism and the structural foundations of segregation, the rooting of Chicano school segregation, and a brief overview of early Chicano school desegregation litigation.

Racism and the structural foundations of segregation

There is ample evidence that the ideological foundations of school segregation date back to the 19th century racial belief that White groups should not socially interact with biologically inferior colored races (Konvitz, 1946; Menchaca, 1987, 1997; Menchaca and Valencia, 1990). During the 19th century, White supremacy ideologies helped to promote the belief that racial minority groups were inherently inferior and helped to provide the rationale to segregate the "colored races" (Comas, 1961; Jackson, 1986). Racism was institutionalized within the academic, religious, and governmental spheres and it culminated in the passage of *de jure* segregation (Menchaca and Valencia, 1990). Within the academic sphere, historians were at the forefront in proselytizing a White superiority ideology and argued in favor of eugenics to ensure that the White races would remain pure (Feagin, 1989; Gossett, 1953, 1977). Historians also favored the social segregation of the colored races as being the most practical method of preventing racial intermingling. The religious sphere was also included in the racist ideologies of the era, in which some churches practiced segregation. The belief that the Anglo-Saxons were "God's chosen people" provided the rationale to support the view that God did not intend the races to mix because he had "not created all the races equal." Within the Protestant Church, White supremacist pastors interpreted the doctrine as God's plan to rid the world of the "colored" races and thus make room for the superior White races. For example, the genocide of the American Indian was figuratively interpreted to be the result of God's predestined will to improve the racial makeup of the world (Gossett, 1953, 1977; Newcombe, 1985). In many congregations, racism was manifested in the total exclusion of racial minority groups. "Colored people" were expected to attend services in their own churches, and in more tolerant congregations racial minorities were allowed to attend church but were expected to sit apart from the White congregation (Cadena, 1987; Glazer and Moynihan, 1963; Menchaca, 1989, 1995; Menchaca and Valencia, 1990).

White supremacist views also surfaced in the governmental sphere and culminated in the legislation of segregationist laws. The passage of "separate but equal legislation" in the 19th century reflected the government's endorsement of the widespread racial ideologies of the period (Feagin, 1989; Hendrick, 1977; Wollenberg, 1978). At the federal level, the passage of *Plessy v. Ferguson* in 1896 was a blatant example of the government's approval of the rationale that the colored races should not mix with Whites. Though *Plessy* was passed with the specific intention of segregating Blacks, the case was used to justify all forms of social segregation. At the local level, city governments used the legislation to segregate other racial minority groups by arguing that the spirit of the law applied to all "coloreds" (Hyman and Wiecek, 1982; Konvitz, 1946; Menchaca, 2001). Moreover, *Plessy v. Ferguson* represented a symbolic action on part of the federal legislators to enact an undisputable law that gave the states the right to practice segregation.

By the early 1900s, most states practiced some form of social segregation and had institutionalized school segregation as the main vehicle to maintain a segregated society (Feagin, 1989). The rationale being that if the children of the White and "colored" races were socialized not to intermingle, the groups would not marry, and thus the purity of each race would be retained (Konvitz, 1946). Racial minorities questioned the extension of segregationist legislation to the educational domain and therefore took their plight to the U.S. Supreme Court. In several U.S. Supreme Court cases, however, the court asserted the states' rights to segregate the "colored races" and ruled against anti-segregationist practices. For example, in 1927 the U.S. Supreme Court ruled in *Gung Lum v. Rice* that the separation of the colored races in the schools was within the discretion of the State and not in conflict with the 14th amendment (Konvitz, 1946). Over a decade later, the rule of separate but equal facilities in educational institutions was reasserted in the U.S. Supreme Court decision of 1938 in *Gaines v. Canada*. Although the federal courts did not legislate a mandate that "all colored children must be segregated," they supported the states' rights to institute school segregation if desired by the legislators.

Paradoxically, although Chicanos were not specifically mentioned in the "separate but equal legislation" there is ample evidence that they were often treated as "colored" and were consequently segregated in most social spheres. Historically, the rationale used to socially segregate Mexicans was based on the racial perspective that Mexicans were "Indian," or at best "half-breed savages" who were not suited to interact with Whites (Menchaca and Valencia, 1990; Paredes, 1978; Surace, 1982). Although the ratification of the Treaty of Guadalupe Hidalgo had guaranteed Mexicans the political privileges enjoyed by Whites (Griswold del Castillo, 1990), state legislators in the latter half of the 19th century and early 1900s attempted to violate the agreement (Menchaca, 2001). Legislators sought to limit the Mexicans' political and social rights based on the rationale that Mexicans were Indians. They argued that because Indians by law were prohibited from voting, residing in White neighborhoods, and attending schools with White children, these laws also applied to Mexicans (Heizer and Amquist, 1971). For example, in California the state constitution prohibited Mexicans who were Indian, Black, and mestizo (White/Indian) from voting, and only extended that privilege to "White-looking Mexican" males (California State Constitution of 1849, Article II, Section 1; Menchaca, 2001; Padilla, 1979). In the area of naturalization the federal government also attempted to deny Mexican immigrants their right to apply for citizenship on the basis that they were Indian (Hull, 1985; *In re Rodriguez*, 1897; Kansas, 1941; Konvitz, 1946; *People v. De La Guerra*, 1870).

Racial discrimination against the "Indianism" of Mexicans was also manifested in the form of residential segregation. This exclusionary practice eventually provided the underlying structure for the school segregation of Mexican students, and thus it is important to examine the structural relation between residential and school segregation. By 1870, the residential segregation of the Mexican was firmly entrenched in the multiethnic structure of the Southwest, and such housing patterns were viewed by Anglo Americans to be the natural division between the inferior "half-breed Mexican" and the "superior" White race (Acuña, 1988; Camarillo, 1984a). Using 19th century archival records, historian Alberto Camarillo attributed the early stages of Mexican residential segregation to Anglo American racial prejudice. Camarillo stated, "The old Mexican pueblos were viewed by most Americans as 'foreign,' 'backward,' and undesirable locations in which to live" (p. 224). For example, in California the residential segregation of the Mexican began as early as 1850 and the process was completed by 1870. In San Francisco, San Jose, Santa Barbara, Los Angeles, San Diego, Santa Cruz, and Monterey, Anglo American settlers restructured the old pueblos by constructing new subdivisions in the towns and prohibited Mexicans from moving into Anglo neighborhoods. Throughout California the residential segregation of the Mexican was enforced by the use of racial harassment and violence, and in many cities by the use of housing covenant restrictions prohibiting Mexicans from residing in the White zones (Hendrick, 1977).

Social historian David Montejano (1987) also reported that a similar process of residential segregation became widespread and provided the foundation for school segregation in Texas. Throughout the state, Mexicans were segregated in separate sections of the cities, and in many Anglo American farm communities, local *de jure* laws were used to prevent Mexicans from establishing residence. Residential segregation was planned by the ranchers and town developers and maintained through local laws and real estate policies. For example, in Weslaco, Texas, Mexicans were only allowed to buy property in designated areas near the Missouri Pacific Railroad tracks, and municipal ordinances required that Mexican neighborhoods and businesses only be established in those areas.

By the early 1900s, the intensification of Mexican residential segregation became more complex in Texas, California, and other parts of the Southwest. Contributing factors were the industrial and urban development of the Southwest. It is very clear, however, that the growth of such residential segregation accompanied school segregation and was strongly linked to Anglo American racial prejudice. Later, we will discuss the need for policymakers to explore strategies that might lead to residential integration—a major solution to eliminate school segregation.

The rooting of Chicano school segregation

We noted how the increasing Mexican immigration to the United States in the 1920s became a period when racism turned into a strong ideological force that pushed forward the growth of all forms of segregation, especially in housing and schools (Camarillo, 1984a, 1984b; Montejano, 1987). As the Mexican population increased in the Southwest, Anglo Americans responded by demanding residential and school segregation (San Miguel and Valencia, 1998; Wollenberg, 1978). In addition to housing and schools, however, it also became common to segregate Mexicans in swimming pools, theaters, restaurants, and other public facilities (Kibbe, 1946; Menchaca, 1995). In California, the segregation of Mexicans became such a priority during the 1920s and 1930s that government officials attempted to classify Mexican students as Indians in order to segregate them on the basis that they were "colored." On January 23, 1927, the Attorney General of California stated that Mexicans could be treated as Indians, thereby placing them under the mandate of *de jure* segregation (Hendrick, 1977). In 1930, the California Attorney General once again issued an opinion on the racial background of the Mexican students. According to Attorney General Webb, Mexicans were Indians and therefore should not be treated as White. Webb stated, "It is well known that the greater portion of the population of Mexico are Indians and were [*sic*] such Indians migrate to the United States, they are subject to the laws applicable generally to other Indians" (cited in Weinberg, 1977, p. 166). Webb's opinion was used by school boards to classify Mexicans as Indians and therefore attempted to segregate them on the basis that they were not White. Finally, in 1935, the California legislature passed a law to segregate officially Mexican students on the basis that they were Indian. Without explicitly mentioning Mexicans, the 1935 school code prescribed that schools segregate Mexicans who descended from Indians. The California school code of 1935 stated:

> The governing board of the School district shall have power to establish separate schools for Indian children, excepting children of Indians who are the wards of the U.S. government and children of all other Indians who are the descendents of the original American Indians of the U.S., and for children of Chinese, Japanese, or Mongolian parentage.
>
> (cited in Hendrick, 1977, p. 57)

Although the school code did not mention Mexicans by name, it was explicit that the state's intention was to segregate dark-skinned Mexican students. Thus, Mexican children became the principal target of the discriminatory school code without being identified, and American Indians, though named directly, were released from legally mandated segregation.

Language was a second rationale used to segregate Mexican students. Allegedly, Mexican students were not permitted to attend classes with their Anglo American peers because they needed special instruction in English (González, 1990; Menchaca and Valencia, 1990; San Miguel, 1986, 1987; San Miguel and Valencia, 1998). The pedagogical rationale was that the limited- or non-English-speaking Mexican children would impede the academic progress of the Anglo children. The racial overtones of these practices were blatantly seen when Mexican American students, who did *not* speak Spanish, were also forced to attend the Mexican schools (Álvarez, 1986; Menchaca, 1987). The need to acculturate Mexican students in special Americanization classes was a third major excuse used to justify segregation (San Miguel and Valencia, 1998). Mexican students were characterized as dirty, dull, unchristian, and lacking any social etiquette. Therefore, the educational belief was that Mexicans needed special classes where they would learn to emulate their Anglo American counterparts (García, 1979; González, 1990).

The results of IQ tests were also used, in part, to segregate Mexican students and provided the alleged scientific rationale (González, 1990; Valencia, 1997a). Lewis Terman, Professor of Education at Stanford University, and other researchers presented many findings from "race psychology" studies of intelligence testing research supporting the view that Blacks, Indians, and Mexican Americans were intellectually inferior to Whites (Blum, 1978; Valencia, 1997a). Regarding Mexican American children, Garth's (1925, 1930) race psychology reviews showed that these children were frequent participants in intelligence testing research (Valencia, 1997a).[13] Based on Valencia's (1997a) analysis, and drawing from Sánchez (1932), there are eight such studies published between 1920–1929 in which Mexican American children were participants (Garretson, 1928; Garth, 1923, 1928; Goodenough, 1926; Koch and Simmons, 1926; Paschal and Sullivan, 1925; Sheldon, 1924; Young, 1922). The point of most interest is that in all eight studies the author(s) concluded that the lower intelligence test performance of the Mexican American children—compared directly to their White peers or White normative data—was due to heredity. In some cases, the hereditarian conclusions of inferior genetic constitution of Mexican American children were made explicit (e.g., Garretson, 1928; Young, 1922) or were suggestive (such as, Goodenough, 1926).

Historically, IQ tests had practical purposes and significant social functions (Valencia, 1997a). Such tests (along with achievement tests) were widely used in the schools to sort students into homogeneous groups. This general practice is referred to as "curriculum differentiation," which Valencia (1997a) defines as "the sorting of students into instructional groups based on perceived and/or measured educability" (p. 71). A good case in point is what transpired in the Los Angeles public schools in the 1920s.[14] González (1974a, 1974b, 1990) found the institutionalization of mass intelligence testing, homogeneous groupings, curriculum differentiation, and counseling programs in Los Angeles schools were used in ways that effectively stratified students along racial/ethnic and socioeconomic status (SES) lines. Mexican American elementary school children were frequently placed in classes for "slow learners" and the "mentally retarded." González also found that vocational education in Los Angeles public junior and senior high schools was designed to prepare poor students of color for manually oriented occupations (skilled, semiskilled, or unskilled).

Early Chicano desegregation litigation

The Mexican community in the Southwest did not idly stand by while its children were being segregated in inferior facilities.[15] The legal struggle for school desegregation was initiated in Texas and California in the early 1930s. The *Independent School District v. Salvatierra* (1930, 1931) case, which was brought about by Mexican American parents in Del Rio, Texas, was significant for several reasons (San Miguel, 1987). First, the constitution of the State of Texas, adopted in 1875 and ratified in 1876, allowed for the segregation of White and "colored" children—colored meaning only "Negro."[16] Thus, *Salvatierra* was a landmark case in determining the constitutionality of separating Mexican American children on racial grounds. Second, the findings of the court would serve as the basis for future legal challenges of segregation of Mexican American students. Third, the counsel for the plaintiffs in *Salvatierra* were lawyers of the League of United Latin American Citizens (LULAC), the newly established Mexican American advocacy organization, which had its first opportunity to flex its muscles in this important test case.

The District Court ruled in *Salvatierra* that the school district illegally segregated Mexican American students on the basis of race (Rangel and Alcala, 1972), although they were considered to be members of the White race—a strong point argued by plaintiffs' lawyers.[17] The court granted an injunction that restrained the district from segregating the Mexican American children, but the school board appealed the injunction (Álvarez, 1986). The District Court's judgment, however, was overturned by the Texas Court of Civil Appeals on the basis that the school district did not intentionally, arbitrarily segregate the Mexican American children by race, and given that the children had special language needs (i.e., to learn English), the school district had the authority to segregate Mexican American students on educational grounds. This latter ruling would serve as a major obstacle in desegregation rulings for years to come. The Texas Court of Civil Appeals decision in *Salvatierra* was appealed by LULAC to the U.S. Supreme Court, but the case was dismissed for lack of jurisdiction (Balderrama, 1982; cited in Álvarez, 1986).

In *Álvarez v. Lemon Grove* (1931), the school board of the Lemon Grove School District (Lemon Grove, California, near San Diego) sought to build a separate grammar school for the Mexican American children, claiming overcrowding at the existing school where both Anglo and Mexican American students attended (Álvarez, 1986). Mexican American parents organized a protest, forming the *Comité de Vecinos de Lemon Grove* (The Lemon Grove Neighborhood Committee). The parents instructed their children not to attend the so-called new school, which the children called *La Caballeriza* (the stable). Judge Claude

Chambers, Superior Court of California in San Diego, ruled in favor of the plaintiffs on the basis that separate facilities for Mexican American students were not conducive towards their Americanization and retarded the English language development of the Spanish-speaking children. Judge Chambers also found that the school board had no legal right to segregate Mexican American children, as California law had no such provisions.[18] Although the *Álvarez* case was deemed the nation's first successful desegregation court case, "it was isolated as a local event and had no precedent-setting ruling affecting either the State of California or other situations of school segregation in the Southwest" (Álvarez, 1986, p. 131). Nevertheless, *Álvarez* is noted as the first successful legal challenge to school segregation in the country (Álvarez, 1986; González, 1990).

The *Méndez v. Westminister* (1946, 1947) case in California, which preceded the 1954 *Brown v. Board of Education of Topeka* by nearly a decade, was the *first* federal court decision in the area of school segregation and marked the end to *de jure* segregation in California (González, 1990). In this class action lawsuit, Gonzalo Méndez *et al.* claimed their children were denied access to a White school simply because they were Mexican (i.e., in appearance; Spanish surname). The historical importance of this landmark case rested on the judge's ruling regarding a new interpretation of the Fourteenth Amendment (i.e., a break from the prevailing *Plessy v. Ferguson* [1896] doctrine of "separate but equal"), as well as his decision on the legality of segregating Mexican Americans on linguistic grounds. The court concluded that the school board had segregated Mexican American children on the basis of their "Latinized" appearance and had gerrymandered the school district in order to ensure that Mexican American students attend segregated schools. The court concluded this was an illegal action, as there was no constitutional or congressional mandate that authorized school boards in California to segregate Mexican American students. Judge Paul McCormick stated that the Fourteenth Amendment had guaranteed Mexican Americans equal rights in the United States. Particularly significant about Judge McCormick's ruling is that it differed substantially from the rulings in *Salvatierra* and *Delgado* regarding the nature of segregation:

> McCormick contended that no evidence existed that showed segregation aided in the development of English proficiency, that on the contrary, evidence demonstrated that segregation retarded language and cultural assimilation. Consequently, the segregation of Mexican children *had no legal or educational justification* [italics added].
>
> (González, 1990, p. 153)

According to González (1990), Judge McCormick departed from the prevailing separate but equal doctrine of *Plessy*:

> In so stating, the Judge broke with *Plessy* and clearly defined a distinction between physical equality (facilities) and social equality. In this case, separate but equal facilities were unconstitutional because they created a social inequality. Thus, rather that acting as a protection for the practice of segregation, the Fourteenth Amendment served to repeal segregation.
>
> (p. 153)

Although the *Méndez* case helped to end *de jure* segregation in California, the school segregation of Mexican American students remained widespread (Hendrick, 1977) and, in fact, increased over the following decades. Moreover, as González (1990) has noted when speaking of *Méndez* and its aftermath: "Eventually, de jure segregation in schools ended throughout the Southwest, but not before an educational policy reinforcing socioeconomic inequality severely victimized generations of Mexican children" (p. 29).

In 1948, the centennial of the Treaty of Guadalupe Hidalgo, *Delgado et al. v. Bastrop Independent School District of Bastrop County et al.* was litigated in the U.S. District Court for the Western Division of Texas, and was backed by a cadre of powerful Mexican American individuals and organizations.[19] Minerva Delgado and 20 other plaintiffs sued several school districts in Central Texas, claiming that "school officials . . . were segregating Spanish-speaking [Mexican American] children contrary to the [Texas] Constitution" (San Miguel, 1987, p. 123). It appears that the catalyst for bringing forth *Delgado* was the momentous victory in *Méndez* (González, 1990; San Miguel, 1987), as the plaintiffs believed that *Delgado* would do for Texas what *Méndez* did for California—bring an end to school segregation. Judge Ben Rice ruled that segregation of the Mexican American students was discriminatory and illegal, and violated the students' constitutional rights as guaranteed by the Fourteenth Amendment (see San Miguel, 1987). A major setback for the plaintiffs, however, was the ruling that the school district could segregate first-grade Mexican American students who had English-language deficiencies. Such segregation was to be on the same campus attended by all other students.

Initially viewed by plaintiffs as the decision that could bring an end to segregation in Texas, these hopes were never realized (San Miguel, 1987). In what Allsup (1979) described as a clash of White obstinacy and Mexican American determination, school districts throughout Texas failed to comply with the *Delgado* decision. This was made easy, in part, by the State Board of Education and its creation of a complex bureaucratic system of grievances and redress and the noncompliance of the *Delgado* proviso through evasive schemes designed at the local level. San Miguel (1987) has noted:

> The mid and late 1950s can probably be called the *era of subterfuge* [italics added], since it was during this period that a multitude of practices—for example, freedom of choice plans, selected student transfer and transportation plans, and classification systems based on language or scholastic ability—were utilized by local school districts to maintain segregated schools.
>
> (p. 134)

In conclusion, the early history of Chicano school segregation is a troubled one, filled with numerous events of forced isolation. History informs us that racism was a driving force in the relation between school segregation and subsequent Chicano school failure. But, Chicano communities were resolute in their struggle for educational equality. *Salvatierra*, *Álvarez*, *Méndez*, *Delgado*, and other early desegregation lawsuits are testimony to the Chicano's campaign for desegregated schools and equal educational opportunity. Notwithstanding these legal accomplishments, one can argue that to some degree these were pyrrhic victories: That is, although Chicanos won the battle against *de jure* segregation, their isolation in segregated schools continued. We now turn to an analysis of a modern form of school segregation in desegregated schools—resegregation.

Contemporary issues in Chicano school segregation: resegregation

Thus far, we have examined the inequalities Chicanos experienced over time in American public schools. Given the Mexican American community's resoluteness in bringing an end to the segregation of "Mexican schools," school desegregation in the Southwest slowly began to unfold. However, given society's neglect of Chicano school segregation—and the lack of appreciation of its magnitude—desegregation over the past decades touched only a small number of Chicano students and contained a number of pitfalls. In this section, we examine these problems by analyzing the reality of resegregation—that is, the process of Chicanos being further segregated in racially/ethnically isolated schools, *and* Chicanos being segregated within desegregated settings. We discuss three aspects of current school desegregation and resegregation. First, we briefly look at Chicano segregation as a silent problem; second, language segregation as an old problem but with new issues brought forth; and third, the implications of academic resegregation.

Chicano school segregation: a silent problem

In 1954, the U.S. Supreme Court decision in *Brown v. Board of Education* stated that public schools could not place students in separate facilities based on race, religion, or national origin. Racially segregated schools were deemed "inherently unequal" and practices fostering them were unconstitutional (*Brown*, 1954). The impact of *Brown* was so dramatic that many social scientists believed the case helped launch the modern civil rights movement. Indeed, school desegregation became one of the most controversial issues in American educational history (Welch and Light, 1987). The problem with *Brown*, however, was the court's failure to establish a deadline for dismantling segregated public schools. This omission gave segregationists time to pressure federal officials to delay its enforcement. On May 31, 1955, the U.S. Supreme Court judges passed *Brown II* and delegated the responsibility of determining the pace of integration to federal judges (Solomone, 1986). This created the mechanism to retain segregated school systems, as most judges throughout the United States did not favor immediate and total desegregation.

At the national level, local school boards manipulated school assignments to prevent desegregation. Some schools allowed racial/ethnic minority students to attend White schools, but failed to place Whites in minority schools. In the South, the courts allowed parents the "freedom of choice" to send their children to specific schools. In this way, a desegregation plan was laid out on paper—but without actually desegregating schools (Moye, 1999). Once parents were given the choice to send their children to White or minority schools, the federal mandate was allegedly met, even though racial mixing had not been done. This was a mockery of *Brown* throughout the South because employers and White parents placed pressure on Black parents not to send their children to White schools. In Texas, White voters and the state government blatantly defied *Brown*. In 1956, a referendum on interposition (state sovereignty) was approved by the voters (see Houston, 2000). It upheld the state's right to protect itself from unjust federal action. The referendum, for example, prohibited integrated schools in Texas. To support majority rule, legislators introduced 12 school segregation house bills, of which two passed and became law. In 1957, House Bill 65 allowed communities to hold elections to determine if school districts shall have a dual school system of integrated and segregated schools. Furthermore, House Bill 231 allowed school boards to determine pupil assignments, thus determining which schools would remain exclusively White and which would be racially/ethnically mixed. The latter bill became the safety valve for anti-desegregationist legislators, who wanted to comply with federal law, but without mixing White students. Many school boards began desegregating Black schools by busing Mexican students (*Cisneros v. Corpus Christi Independent School District*, 1970; Houston, 2000). By 1965, at the national level, only the District of Columbia had desegregated completely (Solomone, 1986).

In the initial stages of school desegregation, scholars focused on the American South. But as the policy gathered momentum, scholars started to look to the east, midwest, and the western part of the United States (Crain, 1968; Edwards and Wirt, 1967; Kirp, 1982; Rist, 1979). Given the attention school desegregation received, most Americans saw the process as a Black/White issue (Donato, 1997). While Chicanos had always been actively involved in several court cases for desegregated schooling throughout the Southwest (see previous discussion; San Miguel and Valencia, 1998), their efforts were not publicized and recognized at the national level (Orfield, 2001). It was not until the early 1970s that the courts truly recognized the right of Chicano/Latino students to desegregated education (Orfield and Yun, 1999; San Miguel and Valencia, 1998), and it was not until the 1970s and 1980s that researchers began to speak directly to Chicano segregation in schools. As Orfield *et al.* (1987) noted, "School segregation has been widely understood as a problem for blacks. There is little public discussion of the fact, however, that black students are now less likely to attend schools with less than half whites than are Hispanics" (p. 24).

The two most important cases in the post-*Brown* era concerning the desegregation of Chicano children were *Cisneros v. Corpus Christi Independent School District* in Texas (1970) and *Keyes v. School District No. 1* (1973, 1975) in Denver, Colorado.[20] A landmark case in the history of desegregation lawsuits initiated by Mexican Americans, *Cisneros* set off a flood of similar cases (Salinas, 1971). Prior to *Cisneros*, some school districts in the Southwest were desegregating their schools by pairing African American and Mexican American students, given that the latter group was considered "other White." In *Cisneros*, the judge ruled that Mexican Americans were an ethnically identifiable minority group, and thus were entitled to the protection of the *Brown* (1954) decision (see, e.g., Salinas, 1971; San Miguel, 1987). As such, the court found, the mixing of African Americans and Mexican Americans for purposes of desegregation did not produce a unitary school system. This case demonstrated how Mexican Americans thought it was necessary to be identified as a separate class or an identifiable minority group in order to benefit from *Brown*. Because the court ruled that Mexican Americans were indeed an identifiable ethnic minority group, they were found to be unconstitutionally segregated in Texas public schools. As San Miguel (1987) noted, Mexican Americans wanted to discard "the 'other white' legal strategy used . . . during the 1940s and 1950s to eliminate segregation and substitute the equal protection argument used in black desegregation cases" (p. 178; also, see Note 17 in present chapter).

In *Ross v. Eckels* (1970), a desegregation case in Houston, Texas, in which Mexican American students were similarly paired with African Americans, the Fifth Circuit Court of Appeals held that Mexican Americans were *not* an identifiable minority group for purposes of desegregation. Ironically, the *Cisneros* and *Ross* rulings were made by the same court. This confusion was finally settled in *Keyes* by the U.S. Supreme Court. In *Keyes*, which involved a desegregation case in Denver, Colorado, the court was compelled to make a decision on "how to treat Mexican American children in the desegregation process" (San Miguel, 1987, p. 180). The court decided that Mexican Americans were an identifiable minority group, and thus could not be paired with African Americans in the desegregation process. Yet, despite the importance of *Cisneros* and *Keyes*, the educational isolation of most Chicano students continued in both segregated and desegregated public schools. This isolation, as we have earlier discussed, now exhibits patterns of hypersegregation. Chicano/Latino students in 1998–1999 were considerably more segregated in predominantly minority schools than they were in 1968–1969—a whole generation ago (Orfield, 2001).

Language segregation: old problem and new issues

After Chicanos gained "minority status" in the early 1970s, a number of legal cases emerged, changing the nature of schooling for them in the United States. As we noted earlier, language segregation of Chicano English language learners (ELLs) had always been an issue. Since the early 20th century, educators segregated Chicano children because of their (alleged) inability to speak English. In the previously discussed *Salvatierra*, *Álvarez*, *Méndez*, and *Delgado* cases, defendants all ventured, to some degree, to use the argument that Chicanos needed to be in separate schools or classrooms (apart from mainstream students) until they learned English.

In the 1970s, however, a major legal case brought attention to the education of ELLs in the United States. Brought forth by the Chinese American community in San Francisco, the *Lau v. Nichols* (1974) decision held that public schools needed to provide an education that was comprehensible to students who could not speak English. Because English was the *only* vehicle of instruction, ELLs were being denied access to a meaningful educational experience. The U.S. Supreme Court recognized that in order for ELLs to participate in schools, they first had to understand the English language. This was seen as an educational contradiction and thus made "a mockery of public education" (*Lau*, 1974). It was after the *Lau* decision that educators began to wrestle with alternative ways to serve ELLs in the United States.

Although *Lau* did not prescribe specific remedies or pedagogical strategies for ELLs, this ruling paved the way for new reforms. In California, for example, Assembly Bill 1329 was passed in 1976. The Bill required bilingual education in schools that had specific numbers of ELLs (California State Department of Education, 1976 [AB-1329]; 1982 [AB-507]). This passage spurred interest in equity for ELLs and provoked many influential policymakers throughout the nation to respond to the educational needs of this student population. Other states followed suit and passed bilingual education policies (Crawford, 1989).

Meeting the needs of ELLs, however, became challenging for many educators. Early on, researchers began to notice the conflicting implications from the joint applications of the Supreme Court's ruling of *Lau* and *Brown* (Cárdenas, 1975). Although it was recognized that bilingual education and desegregation were both essential approaches in promoting better opportunities for Chicano ELLs, the issue was much more complicated than it appeared. For example, Zerkel (1977) pointed out that bilingual education and desegregation had different, if not opposite, meanings. Desegregation, he argued, typically meant "scattering Black students to provide instruction in 'racially balanced' settings. Bilingual education, on the other hand, usually meant the clustering of Spanish-speaking students so they could receive instruction through their native language" (p. 181). Even if bilingual education and desegregation were not completely conflicting remedies, Zerkel argued, "they were not fully compatible" (p. 181). He further asserted that bilingual education and desegregation were at conflict because the two mandates competed with each other in school systems with limited resources.

Most educators were familiar with the school desegregation debate. How to factor in the ELLs within the desegregation process, however, was confusing, counterintuitive, and political. After the landmark *Lau* case, Cárdenas (1975) pointed out that some school districts were pitting bilingual education against school desegregation. He claimed that some Chicano ELLs were enrolled in either segregated bilingual education or were integrated without the benefits of bilingual education. In many cases, educators were taking an either/ or approach. That is, some school systems were circumventing the implementation of bilingual education by scattering ELLs throughout their districts; others were using bilingual education as an opportunity to segregate them (Cárdenas, 1975). While some educators understood that Chicano ELLs needed to be educated in integrated classroom settings, limited resources and other problems drove educators to ask the following questions: Was it better for Chicano ELLs to forgo their curricular and pedagogical needs in integrated classrooms? Or was it better for them to be in segregated classrooms where their curricular and pedagogical needs were going to be met?

By the early 1980s, this issue became noteworthy for a number of educators (Arias and Bray, 1983). Astute researchers began to point out that bilingual education and desegregation did not necessarily have to conflict with one another. Stephen and Feagin (1980) pointed out, for example, that successful desegregation plans should "include . . . provisions that preserve existing bilingual programs" (p. 323). In 1983, the California State Department of Education sponsored a conference to discuss the issue. Presenters from various institutions and interests (U.S. Department of Education, the Office for Civil Rights, and the California State Department of Education; scholars and legal experts) came together to discuss bilingual education and desegregation. In most cases, researchers, policymakers, and practitioners argued that "integration and bilingual education, [were] in effect, looking at two different but valid definitions of equality" (California State Department of Education, 1983, p. 7). Most presenters at the 1983 conference believed that "integrated education and bilingual education [were] partners in the social enterprise" (p. 15). There seemed to be a consensus that schools could provide quality education to ELLs in integrated classroom settings. Bilingual education and desegregation were seen as two important components of equal educational opportunities for ELLs.

Bilingual education became highly political in the late 1980s. Ironically, critics began to blame the increasing segregation of Chicano ELLs on bilingual education. One critic, for example, noted that, "for the sake of bilingual education, some thirty-five years after *Brown v. Board of Education,* we have resegregated the classroom along ethnic and linguistic lines" (Bikales, 1989). While there was an increasing segregation trend, the notion that bilingual education was the culprit was called into question because, at the time, only a small percentage of Chicano ELLs were being served in bilingual classes. A study conducted by Baratz (1986) found that "68% of eighth-grade and 82% of eleventh-grade language minority students received neither bilingual or English-as-a-second language instruction" (cited in Valdivieso, 1986, p. 191). To imply that bilingual education was responsible for ethnic segregation was inaccurate because most ELLs were *not* being served in bilingual education classes. Olsen (1988) found that 75 percent of ELLs in California public schools received little, if any, instructional support in their native language (also, see Macías, 1993; Valencia, Chapter 1, present book). To charge bilingual education as the cause for ethnic segregation distorts a more complicated issue.

By the late 1990s, an anti-bilingual education sentiment in California reached its peak. With the passage of California's Proposition 227 in 1998, many public schools were forbidden to use native language instruction to educate ELLs (see García and Wiese, Chapter 5, current book). The proposition called for transitional programs of structured English immersion that was not to last more than one year. Ironically, most studies on Proposition 227 generally examined school district response to the new law, how it impacted the nature and organization of instruction, how it influenced teacher training programs, and how bilingual teacher recruitment was going to be affected (Gándara *et al.,* 2000). Very little was mentioned about how the proposition was going to influence earlier concerns—that is, the potential conflict between bilingual education and desegregation. If one considers the potential impact of Proposition 227 on Chicano ELLs, one could reasonably conclude that language segregation will no longer be an issue because bilingual education is, for the most part, forbidden in the state. With this in mind, Chicano ELLs ought to be easily integrated in mainstream classes. We do not believe that Proposition 227 will have an effect on the segregation of Chicano students because their numbers in bilingual classes were small in the first place. As Gándara *et al.* noted, only "29% of English learners were in a primary language program prior to 227, and only 12% assigned to one after the implementation of 227" (Abstract). How California's proposition will affect Chicano ELLs, however, is for future researchers to investigate.

On a final note, there are *national* data pointing to the continued segregation of Chicano/Latino and other ELL students by language status. Based on 1993–1994 survey data, Ruiz-de-Velasco *et al.* (2000) found:

> Nearly half of all LEP [limited-English-proficient] [immigrant] students attend schools that are at least 31 percent LEP. . . . The segregation of LEP from other students is particularly pronounced in elementary schools; 53.3 percent of LEP primary school students versus 31.3 percent of LEP secondary school students attend schools in which 30 percent or more of the students are LEP. . . . Nationwide, almost two-thirds of students attend schools where less than 1 percent of students are LEP. . . . These findings suggest that many immigrant children are attending schools that are not just ethnically segregated but *linguistically* isolated.
>
> (pp. 3, 14)

Academic resegregation

Another form of segregation in desegregated schools is referred to as "academic" or "intellectual" resegregation. This type of segregation "generally takes place when schools that have been racially desegregated go to a system of academic tracking or ability grouping" (Hughes *et al.*, 1980, p. 14). It is widely acknowledged that racial/ethnic minority students, on the average, achieve at lower levels than their White peers (Valencia, Chapter 1, present volume). Thus, under circumstances when minority and White students attend the same schools, there is likely to be a stratified and hierarchical structure in the delivery of instruction (see Valencia, Chapter 1, present volume).

Aside from the broad issue of ability grouping, and tracking, is there evidence that Chicano students experience academic resegregation in desegregated schools? There is some research that provides indirect and direct confirmation that academic resegregation occurs. For example, Valencia (1984a) examined potential curriculum differentiation (i.e., *indirect* evidence) in a Phoenix, Arizona high school that was likely to undergo considerable racial/ethnic mixing in light of a school closure court case (*Castro et al. v. Phoenix Union High School District #210 et al.*, 1982).[21] The anticipated enrollment of Central High School— a 90 percent White, high-achieving, high-SES background school was to increase in size by 57 percent in the 1982–1983 school year (a jump from 2,044 to 3,200 students). This dramatic 1,000 plus increase in enrollment would be predominantly Chicano and African American students from two high schools that were being proposed for closure (Phoenix Union, 94 percent minority; East, 56 percent minority). In the *Castro* case, Chicano and African American plaintiffs sued in order to keep their schools open. Valencia (1984a)— an expert witness for the plaintiffs—predicted that academic resegregation would occur at Central High School, the host school. This hypothesis was given considerable credence based on Valencia's analysis of 1982–1983 resegregation statistics in which preregistration course-by-course enrollments were listed by ethnicity. In court, Valencia testified that because of the very sharp differences in average academic performance between the high-achieving Central High White students and the incoming, low-achieving Chicano and Black students, there would be serious academic resegregation at Central High. To provide some support for this claim of resegregation along lines of achievement, Valencia did a comprehensive analysis of the preregistration data and prepared exhibits for the court (see Donato *et al.* [1991], p. 48, for a capsule discussion of the analysis). Valencia's analysis showed that minority students were overrepresented in the basic, non-college preparatory courses and were underrepresented in the advanced, college preparatory courses. White students' enrollment patterns were the opposite.

Although the Phoenix situation was not a desegregation case *per se,* it had all the ingredients of one (e.g., the typical one-way transfer of minorities to a White host school; mixing of low-achieving minorities with high-achieving White students). Thus, one can draw inferences from this case to understand more fully the potentialities of academic segregation within a desegregated setting. As Valencia (1984a) concluded, there was sufficient predictive evidence that Central High School would undergo considerable curricular stratification between White and Chicano/Black students. Such a separation—as in other instances of academic resegregation—would likely result in the raising of barriers to equal educational opportunity for minority students. The bottom line, as Valencia underscores, is "that resegregation on intellectual grounds is just as invidious as segregation on racial grounds" (p. 94). The lesson we learn from academic resegregation is that desegregation planners and educators must work with commitment and vigor to avoid widespread curriculum differentiation. Integration, in its truest sense, has as a cornerstone the goal of equity, in which all students in a desegregated school should have equal access to knowledge.

There is also some *direct* evidence available that points to the academic resegregation of White and racial/ethnic minority students in schools that have undergone court-ordered desegregation. The district of concern is the preceding Phoenix Union High School District (PUHSD) in Arizona.[22] The PUHSD has been under a desegregation plan via a 1985 Consent Decree and Desegregation Order (see Valencia, 1996a, for background). In the 1995–1996 school year, the PUHSD had eight comprehensive high schools (grades 9–12) and enrolled about 21,000 students at its high point. District enrollments by race/ethnicity were—in descending order—Chicano/other Latino (55 percent), White (27 percent), African American (12 percent), and other (6 percent). In 1996, Valencia was asked by plaintiffs' lawyer to prepare a consultant report on the PUHSD's desegregation plan and efforts (see Valencia, 1996a). As part of this work, Valencia also undertook an analysis of possible academic resegregation (Valencia, 1996b).

In his investigation of the PUHSD, Valencia (1996b) analyzed Fall, 1995 enrollments by race/ethnicity in mathematics, science, and English courses at the eight high schools to ascertain overrepresentation and underrepresentation patterns. Valencia performed 685 individual disparity analyses across the three types of courses at each of the eight schools. He observed a *consistent, glaring, and strong pattern*: Chicano/other Latino students (as well as African Americans) were *overrepresented*—albeit a small number of exceptions—in the non-college preparatory courses and *underrepresented* in the college preparatory courses, particularly honors courses. By sharp contrast, White students showed the converse pattern. Table 3.6 presents these racial/ethnic patterns for mathematics in one high school. The data in Table 3.6 strongly point to the existence of academic resegregation. Chicano/other Latino and African American students are overrepresented in the lower-level courses (e.g., Consumer Mathematics 1–2) and underrepresented in the higher-level courses (e.g., Integrated Mathematics 3–4, Honors). The general pattern for the White students is a mirror image.

These findings in Phoenix appear to be consistent with the observed academic resegregation in many of our urban, inner-city, racially/ethnically mixed schools across the country that have undergone desegregation (see, e.g., Mickelson, 2001; Oakes, 1995; Welner and Oakes, 1996). What is so disturbing, however, about the Phoenix situation is that the PUHSD had been subject to a court-ordered, court-monitored, multi-million dollar desegregation plan for ten years when Valencia (1996b) performed his analyses. This goes to show

Table 3.6 Racial/ethnic enrollments in mathematics at one PUHSD high school: Fall semester, 1995–1996

Course	Anglo			Hispanic			African American		
	No.	*%*	*Dis. %*	*No.*	*%*	*Dis. %*	*No.*	*%*	*Dis. %*
Math. 1–2	22	12.6	–55.8	112	64.0	19.4	27	15.4	94.4
Consumer Math. 1–2	35	17.9	–45.4	104	53.1	9.5	36	18.4	121.7
Integrated Math. 1–2	226	33.0	15.8	310	45.3	–15.5	85	12.4	57.0
Integrated Math. 1–2 Honors	50	69.4	143.5	14	19.4	–63.8	1	1.4	–82.3
Integrated Math. 3–4	161	39.7	36.4	164	40.4	–20.9	39	9.6	–12.7
Integrated Math. 3–4 Honors	60	63.8	94.5	18	19.2	–60.4	3	3.2	–61.5
Integrated Math. 5–6	122	57.8	76.2	52	24.6	–49.3	9	4.3	–48.2
Integrated Math. 5–6 Honors	63	75.9	131.4	7	8.4	–82.7	2	2.4	–71.1
Pre-Calculus 1–2 Honors	44	56.4	69.4	15	19.2	–59.3	3	3.9	–56.2
Analytic Geo. and Cal. 1–2 AP	11	78.6	136.0	2	14.3	–69.7	0	0.0	–100.0

Source: Valencia (1996b).

Note
PUHSD = Phoenix Union High School District; Dis. % = Disparity (over- or underrepresentation).

that desegregation, without true integration, is very likely to fail. As such, poorly implemented and monitored desegregation plans do little in closing the racial/ethnic achievement gap. As noted by Mickelson, "even in an ostensibly desegregated school system, Whites retain privileged access to greater opportunities to learn" (2001, p. 243).

Towards integration

Although there have been scattered attempts in recent decades to desegregate our nation's schools, very little has improved in the reduction of racial/ethnic isolation. As Orfield *et al.* (1987) commented, much of the standoff in desegregation struggles is related to opposition at the national level:

> Three of the four Administrations since 1968 were openly hostile to urban desegregation orders and the Carter Administration took few initiatives in the field. There have been no important policy initiatives supporting desegregation from any branch of government since 1971.
>
> (p. 1)

More recently, Orfield and Yun (1999) updated matters, as such:

> After 12 years of intense and focused opposition to desegregation orders under Presidents Reagan and [George H.] Bush and successful confirmation of hundreds of conservative federal judges, the law is now much closer to Reagan's vision than to that of the Warren and Burger Courts. Mandatory desegregation orders are being dissolved on a large scale and voluntary ones are being challenged in the courts. There has been no significant countervailing intellectual, political or legal force from the Clinton administration that might reverse trends.
>
> (p. 27)

As we noted, the continuous conditions that maintain school segregation are complex. What is certain, however, is that the dismantling of school desegregation started in the mid-1970s. Both Congress and the federal courts did not consider racial balance to be a remedy for *Brown*. In 1974, Congress passed the "Equal Education Opportunity Act of 1974" (EEOC Act of 1974) to redefine compliance with *Brown*. This legislation followed the successful political activism of White parents opposing school integration in general and busing in particular (Smrekar and Goldring, 1999; Solomone, 1986). Under the Act, Congress rejected racial balance as the goal of desegregation and ruled that this did not constitute denial of equal educational opportunity or equal protection, as required by *Brown*. Desegregation was redefined as the assignment of students without regard to race, color, sex or national origin—and not the assignment of students to overcome racial imbalances (Solomone, 1986). Alternative methods to busing could be used to comply with *Brown*.

In 1976 and 1977, Congress amended the Act and added stronger language to oppose any state's intent to comply with *Brown* by reaching racial balance. Congress prohibited the use of federal funds for the transportation of any student other than the school that was nearest to a student's home. The exception to this policy were magnet schools that gave parents the choice of selecting schools for their children beyond a regular attendance zone (Varady and Raffel, 1995). In the 1970s, magnet school plans became a popular vehicle to fulfill voluntary or court-ordered desegregation, particularly in areas where busing was staunchly opposed. Thus, the EEOC amendments effectively destroyed the financial basis of using busing in states and districts where racial balance was considered to be a method of alleviating school segregation.

Concurrent and complementary rulings were rendered by the federal courts. In a series of federal cases, the courts ruled that racial balance was not the only remedy for *Brown*. The most devastating case was *Milliken v. Bradley* (1977; known as *Milliken II*), where the remedy for *Milliken v. Bradley* (1974) was delineated. The federal judges ruled in *Milliken II* that alternate methods besides busing could be used to desegregate schools. Such remedies included the use of voluntary student transfer programs, magnet schools, and an enriched curriculum. The same year in *Dayton Board of Education v. Brinkman* (1977), federal judges offered a similar interpretation. The case added that local control of schools was a national tradition that needed to be upheld—thus effectively creating an infrastructure to remove school desegregation conflicts away from the courts and delegate it to communities. Though the ruling appeared to be race neutral, it retained Whites in control of the schools and gave them the opportunity to dismantle any opposition. Given that Whites constitute the majority of voters in most communities, they were able to determine educational policy through the electoral process, and select to comply with *Brown* through programs of "choice" rather than racial balance.

Desegregationists questioned the legality of *Milliken* and *Dayton*, but faced a series of defeats until 1980. Under *Brown v. Califano* (1980) the use of busing for desegregation purposes was allowed, thus reaffirming the principles enunciated in earlier desegregation busing cases (*Keyes v. Denver, Colorado, No. 1*, 1973; *Swann v. Charlotte-Mecklenburg Board of Education*, 1971). The significance of *Brown v. Califano* is that it effectively diluted the full impact of the anti-busing EEOC Act of 1974. Furthermore, this ruling could now be used to enforce *Green v. County School Board of New Kent* (1968) where the federal court ruled that racial balance could be used as a criterion in a desegregation plan after "choice programs" failed to eliminate the vestiges of school segregation.

These rulings were significant victories that could be used to desegregate students when choice plans failed because, after *Milliken* (1977), school districts throughout the country turned to magnet schools and voluntary student transfer programs to desegregate schools (Donato, 1997; Varady and Raffel, 1995; Smrekar and Goldring, 1999). The problem with magnet schools and voluntary student transfer programs, however, is that they can easily be manipulated to intensify school segregation. School districts and school boards can manipulate school policies because they have legal control over pupil assignments, the designation of which schools will be magnets, and the student selection procedure for magnet programs (e.g., priority enrollment given to neighborhood children; lottery; first-come, first-serve basis; test scores). Thus, local control allows administrators to develop the structure to determine the makeup of the schools. For example, under a magnet school district structure, where neighborhood children are given priority in student assignments, a school in a middle-class White residential area can retain its racial imbalance while in theory it is open to students beyond its regular attendance zone. In this scenario, the middle-class students are the only ones that have "choice" because they can remain in that location or attend another school. During the 1970s, this scenario was found to be widespread, for example, in the state of Missouri (Smrekar and Goldring, 1999). Conversely, magnet schools or voluntary school transfer programs do not necessarily alleviate the vestiges of school segregation in racially isolated working-class minority communities—as White or middle-class students are not mandated to attend these schools (Donato, 1997; Solomone, 1986).

Magnet school student assignments can also be manipulated to cluster White students. In Phoenix, Arizona in 1985, after a court-ordered desegregation mandate was issued to the Phoenix Union High School District (PUHSD), a magnet school desegregation plan was implemented (see Valencia, 1996a). By 1996, the magnet schools had led to the clustering of higher-income White students in nine of the 14 magnet schools (see Valencia, 1996a). This choice program was accompanied by unbalanced district school financing, overwhelmingly disadvantaging the racial/ethnic minority students because the magnet schools were better financed and disproportionately served White students. On average, per-pupil expenditures in magnet school programs were $4,288, and $2,479 in regular programs—a per-pupil expenditure difference of $1,809. Valencia (1996a)—who was commissioned by plaintiffs' attorney to prepare a report on the PUHSD's desegregation plan—zeroed in on the magnet program, which led to his recommendation to discontinue the entire program. He wrote:

> The existing magnet programs are quite costly, not cost-effective, disproportionately benefit Anglo students, have had a small effect on District-wide racial/ethnic balance, enroll only a small fraction of the District's students, and will likely have little impact on the racial/ethnic balance of the District in years to come (due to a low capture rate of Anglo students from the feeder districts and the explosive growth of the Hispanic student population).
>
> (p. 39)

In other cases where the clustering of White students has been identified was in the Northwest section of Washington, DC. The school district worked with parents to select six schools that would be converted into magnets. The outcome of this selective process was a student transfer program that allowed the concentration of upper-class students in the Six School Complex Magnet program, as 63 percent of students participating in this magnet school system were from affluent upper middle-class backgrounds (Varady and Raffel, 1995). Similar problems have been identified in Boston, Cincinnati, and Buffalo (see Varady and Raffel). Although we are critical of magnet programs, this does not mean we are against recommending them as a desegregation strategy. Magnet programs can be useful if they are implemented and monitored in ways that avoid academic resegregation and the maintenance of White privilege, and lead to a substantially positive effect on district-wide racial/ethnic balance.

During the 21st century, Chicanos and other racial/ethnic minorities that want to desegregate their schools are confronted by a governmental structure that has left the choice to local communities. The irony is that racial/ethnic minority communities that have traditionally suffered from inferior school facilities and resources have been delegated the burden of struggling, legally, against the very same systemic structure that places them at a great disadvantage with privileged Whites.

In closing, we end on an optimistic note by discussing a number of research/policy suggestions that perhaps can serve as starting points to help reverse the intensification of Chicano school segregation and to help promote integration. We offer discussions on the following ideas: (a) community case studies of historical segregation, (b) residential integration, (c) busing, (d) Chicano/African American coalitions, (e) Chicano school board membership, (f) two-way bilingual education, and (g) "critical theory" in teacher education.

Community case studies of historical segregation

To understand the origins and persistence of school segregation of Chicano students, historical community case studies can provide the methodological base to explore this long-standing practice (Álvarez, 1988; Menchaca and Valencia, 1990). Case studies may be useful in providing the background for the litigation of school segregation cases. In light of the very limited amount of current Chicano and other Latino-initiated desegregation litigation (see Orfield *et al.*, 1987), perhaps such lawsuits may be forthcoming in the 21st century as Chicano segregation further increases. A bonanza in these cases would be expert testimony, for example, on the roots of *de jure* segregation at the particular school district level. As Mexican American Legal Defense and Educational Fund (MALDEF) attorney Leticia Saucedo recently underscored: "Historical experts must continue to study and document the patterns of discrimination in education; they must create analyses that more clearly show the causal connection between current practices and past discrimination in education" (2000, p. 420).

An approach to community case studies of historical segregation includes: a collection of oral histories, analysis of residential patterns, analysis of the dates and construction of schools, and a review of available school records. Oral histories can provide data indicating if people attended segregated schools. Studying residential patterns will suggest whether the barrioization of the Mexican community was voluntary or involuntary, or both. Collection of school records may provide a documented history of the school board's intentional or unintentional plans in overall school district development, and can also be used to verify or discredit the oral histories. And, most important of all, an analysis of the dates and location of the construction of schools can possibly provide data to discern if the "Mexican" schools were constructed for the specific purpose of segregating Chicano students. For example, could the "Mexican" schools have been located in zones where both Mexican and Anglo students may have attended, rather than constructing the Mexican schools in the interior of the barrios or the Anglo school in the Anglo residential zones? And, did the construction of new schools follow a historical pattern indicating that the size of the student population did not necessitate the construction of new "Mexican" or "White" schools? Was the Chicano community included in the decision-making process in the construction and location of schools?

It is equally important to collect data on "choice plans" implemented by school districts complying with federal or state inquiries. Given that racial balance was no longer required by the government after 1974, we must examine if alternate plans failed or improved the quality of education in segregated schools. If programs fail, under *Green v. County School Board of New Kent* (1968), a Chicano community may have the legal basis to take their case to court. To determine the effectiveness of choice programs "state report cards" offer a rating system of schools. Likewise, to compare the quality of education in high-density racial/ethnic minority schools an analysis of (a) student-teacher ratio, (b) programmatic per-pupil expenditures and (c) the percentage of certified teachers, will reveal if the quality of education is better in schools serving a predominantly White population (see Valencia, Chapter 1, current volume).

A close inspection of magnet programs can also reveal if they lead to the clustering of White students or if school segregation has intensified (see Valencia, 1996a). In cities where sections have been gentrified or in rural communities where orchards and fields have been replaced by housing developments, a close analysis of where the magnet schools are located may reveal how city policymakers use magnet schools to attract high-income newcomers. In such cases, an analysis of the impact on voting patterns will be useful. That is, by attracting new residents will the voting size of the minority populations be diluted? If so, how does this impact the school boards?

Residential integration

As we have discussed earlier, a contributing source of Chicano segregated schools has histori-cally been attributed to residential segregation or ethnically isolated residential zones (Camarillo, 1984a; Montejano, 1987; Menchaca and Valencia, 1990). We agree with Gottlieb (1983) that "school and housing segregation are so deeply intertwined that much greater attention needs to be given to the interrelationships" (p. 106). As Gottlieb argues, ideally the best solution for bringing an end to school segregation is to terminate housing segrega-tion. Of course, this will not be an easy goal to obtain.

One approach to attack this problem is for public policymakers to lobby assertively for residential integration. Although it will be difficult to integrate existing neighborhoods, it can be achieved through long-term urban and suburban planning. For example, in order to attract minority families, affordable housing (i.e., single-family homes) will need to be constructed near or in White middle-class neighborhoods. Furthermore, in White neighbor-hoods that are racially/ethnically isolated, but are located adjacent to Chicano neighbor-hoods, the construction of new schools in the border zones might lead to racial/ethnic mixing in the local schools. That is, when a school is constructed in the border zone of two racially/ethnically isolated neighborhoods, a racially/ethnically mixed school community would be formed (however, see Orfield [2001] for a discussion of the instability of neighbor-hood schools that form in border zones). Although the neighborhoods would not be integrated, the students of the racially/ethnically isolated neighborhoods would attend the same school and this may lead to the formation of interracial/ethnic friendships. Possibly these friendships may encourage the students to cross the residential boundaries, and this may, in turn, lead to racial/ethnic mixing on a social basis. Although such urban planning may not lead to residential integration, per se, it can at least contribute to the formation of interracial/ethnic community bonds.

In conclusion, we strongly support efforts to achieve residential integration. Given the sharp increase in the Chicano school-age population and the growing desire for many Chicano families to buy homes, segregated municipalities have grand opportunities to realize residential integration. As Gottlieb (1983) notes, for those cities that remain silent on this issue, they reinforce their reputations as being closed communities. We recommend that scholars undertake research on housing policy and urban planning. Mexican American com-munities need information on how urban growth will impact their schools. As cities and towns expand, policy recommendations are needed to avoid segregation or resegregation. Mexican American parents need advice on whether communities should establish magnet school programs or construct new schools. Magnet school programs with racial/ethnic balance formulas can be particularly useful in gentrified cities where liberal, middle-class White families wish to live near the downtown areas (Varady and Raffel, 1995). Likewise, the construction of large schools in border zones between new and old neighborhoods can be used to avoid resegregation.

Busing

The desegregation of schools through the use of busing has created enormous controversy (Coles, 1974; Mills, 1973, 1979; Pettigrew, 1975; Varady and Raffel, 1995). Criticisms, typically from White parents, have ranged from charges that busing is dangerous to com-plaints that bus rides are much too long. Pettigrew contends that such opposition to busing reached such virulent levels in the 1970s that a national mania occurred. As discussed earlier, during the mid-1970s Congress and the federal courts opposed busing and favored less effective methods to desegregate.

It was not until 1980 that under *Brown v. Califano* the federal courts once again upheld the legality of busing. Two years later, however, though the federal courts did not overturn *Brown v. Califano* in *Crawford v. Board of Education the City of Los Angeles* (1982) and *Washington v. Seattle School District No. 1* (1982), the judges upheld the state right to pass anti-busing referendums in cases where there was no proof of intentional segregation (see Donato, 1997). These rulings were a compromise. On the one hand, busing remained a vehicle of desegregation and allowed states to use busing as a remedy in cases where intentional segregation had been proven. On the other hand, it has allowed voters to use referendums to limit busing in communities where intentional segregation has not been proven.

By the 1990s, court-ordered busing programs experienced a severe blow. The federal court under *Board of Education of Oklahoma City v. Dowell* (1991; cited in Orfield, 2001) allowed school districts that had sufficiently implemented desegregation strategies to be released from their orders and be free to resume the assignment of students to neighborhood schools. Across the nation, large school districts (e.g., St. Louis, Boston, Denver, and Oklahoma City) were released from court-ordered busing. Since then, the political slogan has been for America to return to "neighborhood schools" and "magnet school choice" programs.

Given that busing has come to an end in many locations, racial segregation has dramatically increased. As we previously discussed, Orfield and Yun (1999) noted that Latinos in Colorado were greatly more desegregated, through 1996, than their counterparts in the other Southwestern states. This, however, has dramatically changed. In the Denver Public Schools (DPS), the court released it from mandatory busing in 1995. The return to neighborhood schools began in 1996. In a recent article in the *Rocky Mountain News* (Yettick, 2001), "Dwindling diversity: Ethnic groups tend to cluster in DPS' post-busing era," recent data suggest that the racial and ethnic composition in the DPS has dramatically changed since busing ended. A major theme of the news article was how Latino school segregation has intensified. Although the growth of the Latino population in Denver has exacerbated this segregation trend, other factors add to the problem. Taking the situation as a whole, there has been an overall decrease in Anglo enrollments, Anglo parents are choosing to send their children to charter and magnet schools, and there is a problem with transportation opportunities (i.e., busing) for some groups. DPS officials argue that parents are allowed to send their children to schools of their choice. Critics maintain, however, that poor families have very little choice. For example, although "students get free school bus rides from anywhere in Denver to most of the district's magnet programs . . . to attend a charter school or a neighborhood school other than their own, students must provide transportation" (Yettick, 2001, p. 26A). In other words, White parents generally have the economic means to exercise choice. The city's poor are not in positions, however, to take advantage of the choices offered. Of the district's 127 schools, 45 are now over 56 percent Latino. Of those, 39 are 75 percent Latino, and 12 are over 90 percent Latino. There is no doubt that in the post-busing era Chicano youths are destined to become more segregated. In Denver, many Latino parents are cognizant of this problem. Latino parent, Donaciano Archuleta, for example, lamented the fact that his child attends "Valdez Elementary in north Denver, the school with the highest percentage of Hispanics in the District, 95.5 percent. Archuleta regrets that [his child] is not experiencing the diversity he and his wife knew as DPS students during court-ordered busing" (Yettick, 2001, p. 26A). With this in mind, the courts need to rethink the elimination of busing. We believe that busing is still a viable means to desegregate schools and, ultimately, to integrate them.

Chicano-African American coalitions

Even though Chicanos and African Americans have historically gained power independent of one another (Marable, 1995), we believe these groups would have greater political impact by working collaboratively. In many ways, Chicanos and African Americans share common histories, concerns, and predicaments in American schools and society. Both groups are generally segregated in schools that are less well-funded, have higher rates of teacher turnovers, suspensions, and special education placements (in some categories); are underrepresented in gifted programs; and both score—on the average—below the national norm on standardized tests (Anyon, 1997; Fine, 1991; Kozol, 1991; Valencia, Chapter 1, present volume). Given the many challenges Chicanos and African Americans face in realizing greater educational achievement, both groups might benefit from establishing a united front to lobby for their common interests. This is particularly true in the Southwest, where many Chicano and African American students attend the *same* segregated schools.

Chicano school board membership

There is a paradox in many communities across the Southwest and in other areas. The Chicano student population is tremendously increasing (Valencia, Chapter 2, present book). Yet, there is an immense underrepresentation of Chicanos on local school boards of education (Fraga *et al.*, 1988; Rios and Alonzo, 1981). While Chicano representation has improved in some areas over the past three decades, they often lack political power to promote the success of their children. In most cities, it is very difficult for Chicanos to get elected on school boards. What we have are large Chicano school enrollments, and Whites controlling the schools. We believe that Chicano school board representation needs to increase, as it is at this level where changes can be brought about. In most situations, school boards generally determine who will administer their districts and schools, who will teach in them, what reforms will be made, and which issues will be taken up for discussion—including the issue of desegregation/integration.

Two-way bilingual education

The growing number of ELLs and the limited supply of certified bilingual education teachers will inevitably exacerbate language segregation in our nation's public schools (see Valencia, Chapter 1, current book). Ovando and Collier (1985) maintain, however, that "two-way bilingual education" may be the only way to reduce the language segregation in desegregated schools. Two-way bilingual education is a model in which students of two different language backgrounds (e.g., Spanish and English speakers) are brought together in a bilingual class setting in order for both groups to become truly "bilingual" (see Guerrero, Chapter 6, current book). For example, the goal of a two-way bilingual education requires that English speakers learn Spanish and Spanish speakers learn English. But more importantly, "two-way bilingual education can be seen as an effective method of teaching a second language to English-dominant students in the United States as well as providing an integrated class for language-minority students" (Ovando and Collier, 1985, pp. 40–41).

Two-way bilingual education appears to be the only model that places and sensitizes English speakers in a second language learning environment; it also stresses linguistic integration in the classroom. There is no question that implementing two-way bilingual education programs will be difficult because of the continued resistance to bilingual education in general. The most challenging facet of two-way bilingual programs will be to convince

English-speaking parents about the value of their children learning a second language. Related to the politics and academic achievement in two-way bilingual programs, Crawford (1989) asked: "Could language-majority and language-minority children, learning side by side and assisting each other, become fluent bilinguals while making good progress, in other subjects?" (p. 165). Crawford contended that if public schools follow the criteria for effective two-way bilingual education programs, than it can be accomplished. We propose that once English-speaking parents recognize the lifelong value of bilingualism for their children, there will be more of a need to train additional bilingual teachers in the profession. Thus, both Mexican American ELLs and majority language students will benefit. In the final analysis, language integration as proposed in the two-way bilingual model should become more manageable.

Critical theory in teacher education

Given the nation's changing racial/ethnic demographic patterns, more teachers are bound to have contact with Chicano children and youths. Within this context, future teachers need to be prepared to work with this student population. We are not referring to "what teaching strategies work for Chicanos." Rather, we are talking about ways to expose preservice teachers to "critical perspectives" in teacher education programs. That is, teacher education programs can play a crucial role in preparing future teachers with critical perspectives of education that will allow them to see connections between everyday practices in schools and the larger society. If properly implemented, "critical theory" can offer preservice teachers a better understanding about school and society, new directions toward social justice, and democratic education. Landon Beyer (2001) said it best: "[critical theory] focuses on the social dimensions and consequences of educational practices, the ideological means of texts and experiences, the power relations in schools and other institutions" (p. 156). What is important about critical theory is that it allows preservice teachers to understand how curriculum favors certain forms of knowledge, affirms the dreams, desires, and values of selected groups, and how it marginalizes others (McLaren, 1989). Preservice teachers need to understand how people and events are represented in textbooks, curriculum materials, and how certain classroom practices benefit some groups and subordinate others. In short, critical theory in teacher education can allow preservice teachers to explore ways in which they may develop activities that work for social justice and toward social change (Aronowitz and Giroux, 1993; McLaren, 1989).

Conclusion

In closing, we want to leave the reader with several summary points that capture the core of this chapter. First, as history informs us, it is abundantly clear that racism is a driving force behind school segregation and Chicano school failure. Therefore, if we are to desegregate and integrate Chicano students, it is critical that we confront overt and institutional racism in the larger society, in particular within the educational system. Desegregation and integration of our schools must be viewed as important stages in the long struggle to combat and dismantle racism in the nation. Although adults are often resistant to accepting and building a culturally diverse and equitable society, our nation's children and youths are considerably more open. If Chicano and other students from racially/ethnically diverse backgrounds are properly integrated in classrooms, they should not only be exposed to a multicultural curriculum, but teachers should also have high expectations for them. Interracial/ethnic communication is important, but equally crucial are classroom environments where Chicanos and other groups have equal status. Thus, school desegregation, as a first step, can be viewed as a tremendous potential leading to integration and to the promotion of and respect for cultural diversity.

Second, there is the issue of resegregation—especially among Chicano ELLs. Notwithstanding the significant advances made by Chicano parents in their desegregative legal battles, the reality is that Chicano students continue, to a large degree, to remain segregated within desegregated settings. This is a mounting concern that certainly requires the attention of school officials, researchers, and policymakers in the years ahead. We cannot forget the changing demography and the increasing number of ELLs in our public schools. If Chicano ELLs are to receive instruction in their native language, it must be done in "linguistically integrated" settings. Moreover, Chicano ELLs need to be educated in a way that will promote their academic success. To realize this, educators and counselors need to be trained to work with ELLs. Educators, in turn, need to value their language, have high expectations, offer challenging courses, encourage Chicano parents to become involved in schools, and to share a strong commitment to empower these students (Lucas, Henze, and Donato, 1990). Anything less than this is unacceptable.

Our third point is concerned with the issue of pace. It has been well over five decades since *Méndez* and nearly five decades since *Brown*. There has been much deliberation, but very little speed in eliminating school segregation in our nation. As noted earlier, Chicano/Latino segregation has intensified to such an extent that they are now the most segregated racial/ethnic minority group in the United States. Given the projection that the Chicano/Latino population will account for a substantial portion of the increase in the country's children and youths (see Valencia, Chapter 2, this volume), it is sad to predict that the next generation of Chicano students will very likely experience more segregation than previous generations. This issue alone should stir educators, politicians, and parents of the 21st century to challenge this inauspicious trend and demand integration in our schools. Now is the time for concerted action.

How can we move ahead? How can such action be realized in the context of concrete suggestions? To answer these important questions, we refer the reader to 11 policy recommendations—a number that we have also advanced and discussed in this chapter—that are proffered by Orfield (2001), *Schools More Separate: Consequences of a Decade of Resegregation*. He suggests the following:

> We should be considering the following policy issues if we wish to offer our children and our communities more opportunity for stable interracial education:
>
> 1 Expansion of the federal magnet school program and the imposition of similar desegregation requirements for federally supported charter schools.
> 2 Active support by private foundations and community groups of efforts to continue local desegregation plans and programs, through research, advocacy and litigation.
> 3 Creation of expertise on desegregation and race relations training in state departments of education.
> 4 School district surveys documenting the value (in legal terms, the compelling interest) of interracial schooling experience in their own cities.
> 5 Creation of many two-way integrated bilingual schools in which students of each language group work with, learn with, and help each other acquire fluency in a second language.
> 6 Provision of funding for better counseling and transportation for interdistrict transfer policies.

7　Funding of teacher exchanges between city and suburban school districts and training of teachers in techniques for successful interracial classrooms.

8　Exploration of school and housing policies to avoid massive resegregation of large sections of the inner suburbs.

9　Federal and state funds and university sponsorship for the creation of integrated metropolitan-wide magnet schools.

10　Serious research to learn about the most effective approaches to effective education and race relations in schools with three or more racial groups present in significant numbers and two or more languages strongly represented.

11　Careful research and analysis documenting what happens to students in districts that restore segregated neighborhood schools.

(pp. 51–52)

Notes

1　The following four paragraphs are excerpted, with some modifications, from San Miguel and Valencia (1998, p. 357).

2　For a brief history (1848 to 1890s) of the origin and establishment of Catholic, Protestant, and public schools in the Southwest regarding the schooling of Mexican-origin students, see San Miguel and Valencia (1998, pp. 355–363).

3　Orfield (1988a) reported data for Latinos as a whole, not disaggregated by Latino subgroups (e.g., Mexican American; Puerto Rican). Given that Mexican American students comprise the strong majority of Latino students, any findings about Latinos (as a whole) in the present article can safely be generalized to Mexican Americans.

4　In his Table 19 (p. 47), Orfield (2001) lists segregation data on 12 states. We focus on the five Southwestern states in Table 3.3.

5　The following discussion of school segregation in AISD is excerpted, with minor modifications, from Valencia (2000, p. 448).

6　In Valencia (2000), there was a minor computational error. Valencia reported that there were 15 balanced and 52 imbalanced elementary schools. The correct count is 16 and 51 balanced and imbalanced schools, respectively.

7　McCurdy's (1975) references are testimonies by former Oxnard Superintendents who testified in a desegregation trial in Oxnard in the mid-1970s.

8　This paragraph is excerpted, with minor modifications, from San Miguel and Valencia (1998, pp. 371–372).

9　This and the following paragraph are excerpted, with minor modifications, from San Miguel and Valencia (1998, pp. 372–373).

10　This paragraph is excerpted, with minor modifications, from San Miguel and Valencia (1998, p. 373).

11　This note is excerpted, with minor modifications, from Valencia (2000, p. 456). Although correlational analysis does not allow us to conclude a cause–effect relation between the variables of interest, it can be very useful in generating hypotheses about particular patterns of events or behaviors that, along with other analyses, help us build conceptual models to better understand those events or behaviors. In the present case, the observed correlation of 0.87 between percent minority enrollment and percent failing TAAS indicates a robust association between the two variables. A coefficient of 0.87, once squared, equals 0.76 (called the coefficient of determination [R^2]). In the present analysis, as a statement of prediction, the correlation of 0.87 means that the variance in one variable predicts 76 percent of the variance in the other variable. This is substantial. If one assumes that school segregation is the predictor variable and TAAS performance the criterion variable, then the present analysis of AISD elementary schools suggests that school segregation is a fairly strong predictor of TAAS test scores.

12　The TASP is intended to "provide a comparison of the skill level of the individual student with the skill level necessary for a student to perform effectively in an undergraduate degree program" (Texas Education Code, §51.306 [c], 1999). Students who have accumulated 60 or more semester hours may not continue in upper-division coursework if they have not passed TASP. Students who do not pass the TASP are required to enroll in "developmental" courses to remediate skill deficits in the areas not passed, then retake TASP or pass courses approved by the state as TASP-equivalent to continue with their degree programs (Texas Higher Education Coordinating Board, 1999).

13 This section on early IQ testing and Mexican American children is excerpted, with minor modifications, from Valencia (1997a, pp. 64–65).

14 This section on curriculum differentiation is excerpted, with minor modifications, from Valencia (1997a, pp. 77 and 79).

15 The following discussion of these four early desegregation cases is excerpted, with minor modifications, from San Miguel and Valencia (1998, pp. 374–377).

16 See Section 7, Article VII of the Texas Constitution.

17 Rangel and Alcala (1972) have commented that the "other White" strategy argued in *Salvatierra* rested on the prevailing doctrine of the *Plessy v. Ferguson* (1896) case. As Weinberg (1977) has noted: "In the absence of a state law requiring segregation of Mexican Americans, they claimed equal treatment with all other 'whites.' The crucial point was to leave little leeway to be treated as blacks under both state law and U.S. Supreme Court ruling" (p. 166). The other White strategy would be used in Mexican American desegregation cases for four decades, but was finally abandoned in *Cisneros* (1970).

18 Although there were no *de jure* provisions for segregating Mexican American children under the California School Code of this era, the state did have the power to establish separate schools for "Indian," "Chinese," "Japanese," and "Mongolian" children (Álvarez, 1986).

19 Included in this cadre were attorney Gus García, Dr. Hector García, Professor George Sánchez, and the organizations LULAC, and the G.I. Forum, a newly founded Mexican American veterans advocacy group.

20 This section on post-*Brown* desegregation cases is excerpted, with minor modifications, from San Miguel and Valencia (1998, p. 385).

21 In the 1970s and early 1980s, thousands of schools across the country were closed due to declining enrollment, high inflation, and fiscal austerity. Not surprisingly, powerless working-class and racial/ethnic minority schools were pegged for closure. Some high-enrollment Chicano schools in California and Arizona were victims of this targeting, and subsequent plaintiffs in lawsuits (see Valencia, 1980, 1984a, 1984b, 1984c for coverage of these closures and litigation; also see San Miguel and Valencia, 1998, pp. 386–387, for a brief discussion).

22 This section on academic resegregation in the PUHSD is excerpted, with minor modifications, from Valencia (1997b, pp. 29–30).

References

Acuña, R. (1988). *Occupied America*. San Francisco: Canfield Press.

Allsup, C. (1979). Education is our freedom: The American G.I. Forum and the Mexican American school segregation in Texas, 1948–1957. *Aztlán, 8*, 27–50.

Álvarez v. Lemon Grove School District, Superior Court of the State of California, County of San Diego, 1931, Petition for Writ of Mandate, No. 66625.

Álvarez, R., Jr. (1986). The Lemon Grove incident: The nation's first successful desegregation court case. *Journal of San Diego History, Spring*, 116–135.

Álvarez, R., Jr. (1988). National politics and local responses: The nation's first successful desegregation court case. In H. Trueba and C. Delgado-Gaitán (Eds.), *School and society: Learning content through culture* (pp. 37–52). New York: Praeger.

Anyon, J. (1997). *Ghetto schooling: A political economy of urban educational reform*. New York: Teachers College Press.

Arias, B.M. and Bray, J.L. (1983). *Equal educational opportunity and school desegregation in triethnic districts* (Report submitted to the National Institute of Education). LEC-83–14.

Aronowitz, S. and Giroux, H. (1993). *Education still under siege*. Westport, CT: Bergin & Garvey.

Atkins, J.C. (1978). *Who will educate? The schooling question in territorial New Mexico, 1846–1911*. Unpublished doctoral dissertation, University of New Mexico, Albuquerque.

Balderrama, F.E. (1982). *In defense of La Raza*. Tucson: University of Arizona Press.

Baratz, J. (1986). *The educational progress of language-minority students: Findings from the 1983–84 NAEP reading survey*. Princeton, NJ: Educational Testing Service.

Beyer, L.E. (2001). The value of critical perspectives on teacher education. *Journal of Teacher Education, 52*, 151–163.

Bikales, G. (1989). Maximum feasible misunderstanding: Bilingual education in our schools. *Imprimis, 16*, 1–6.

Blum, J.M. (1978). *Pseudoscience and mental ability: The origins and fallacies of the IQ controversy.* New York: Monthly Review Press.

Board of Education of Oklahoma City v. Dowell, 498 U.S. 237 (1991).

Brooks, A.P. and South, J. (1995). School-choice plans worry segregation critics. *Austin American-Statesman,* April 9, pp. A1, A18–19.

Brown v. Board of Education of Topeka, 347 U.S. 483, at 494 (1954).

Brown v. Califano, 627 F. 2d 1221 (D.C. Cir. 1980).

Cadena, G. (1987). *Chicanos and the Catholic church: Liberation theology as a form of empowerment.* Unpublished doctoral dissertation, University of California, Riverside.

Calderón, C.I. (1950). *The education of Spanish-speaking children in Edcouch-Elsa, Texas.* Unpublished master's thesis, The University of Texas, Austin.

California State Constitution, Article 11, Section 1. (1849).

California State Department of Education. (1976). Assembly Bill 1329.

California State Department of Education. (1982). Assembly Bill 507.

California State Department of Education. (1983). *Desegregation and bilingual education—Partners in quality education.* Conference Proceedings. Sacramento, CA: Author.

California Superintendent of Public Instruction. (1869). *Third biennial report, 1868 and 1869.* Sacramento, CA: O.P. Fitzerald.

Camarillo, A. (1984a). *Chicanos in California: A history of Mexican Americans in California.* San Francisco: Boyd and Fraser.

Camarillo, A. (1984b). *Chicanos in a changing society.* Cambridge, MA: Harvard University Press.

Cárdenas, J. (1975). Bilingual education, desegregation and a third alternative. *Inequality in Education, 14,*19–22.

Castro et al. v. Phoenix Union High School District #210 et al., case no. CIV 82–302 PHX VAC, United States Court, District of Arizona, Phoenix, AZ (August, 1982).

Chaves, A. (1892). *Report of the Superintendent of Public Instruction.* Santa Fe, NM: New Mexican Printing Company.

Cisneros v. Corpus Christi Independent School District, 324 F. Supp. 599 (W.D. Tex. 1970), appeal docketed, No. 71–2397 (5th Cir. July 16, 1971).

Coles, R. (1974). *The buses roll.* New York: W.W. Norton.

Comas, J. (1961). Racial myths. In United Nations Educational, Scientific, and Cultural Organization (Eds.), *Race and science* (pp. 13–35). New York: Columbia University Press.

Crain, R. (1968). *The politics of school desegregation: Comparative case studies of community structure and policy-making.* Chicago: Aldine.

Crawford, J. (1989). *Bilingual education: History, politics, theory, and practice.* Trenton, NJ: Crane.

Crawford v. Board of Education of the City of Los Angeles, 458 U.S. 527 (1982).

Dayton Board of Education v. Brinkman, 433 U.S. 406 (1977).

Dayton Board of Education v. Brinkman, 443 U.S. 526 (1979) remedy; (reaffirmed Keyes and Swann).

Delgado et al. v. Bastrop Independent School District of Bastrop County et al., docketed, No. 388 (W.D. Tex. June 15, 1948).

Donato, R. (1997). *The other struggle for equal schools: Mexican Americans during the civil rights era.* Albany: State University of New York Press.

Donato, R., Menchaca, M. and Valencia, R.R. (1991). Segregation, desegregation, and integration of Chicano students: Problems and prospects. In R.R. Valencia (Ed.), *Chicano school failure and success: Research and policy agendas for the 1990s* (pp. 27–63). The Stanford Series on Education and Public Policy. London: Falmer Press.

Eby, F. (1925). *The development of education in Texas.* New York: Macmillan.

Edwards, B.T. and Wirt, F.M. (1967). *School desegregation in the North: The challenge and the experience.* San Francisco: Chandler.

Espinosa, R. and Ochoa, A. (1986). Concentration of California Hispanic students in schools with low achievement: A research note. *American Journal of Education, 95,* 77–95.

Feagin, J. (1989). *Racial and ethnic relations* (3rd ed). Englewood Cliffs, NJ: Prentice-Hall.

Ferris, D.F. (1962). *Judge Marvin and the founder of the California public school system*. Berkeley: University of California Press.

Fine, M. (1991). *Framing dropouts: Notes on the politics of an urban public high school*. Albany: State University of New York Press.

Fraga, L., Meier, K. and England, R. (1988). Hispanic Americans and educational policy: Limits to equal access. In C.F. García (Ed.), *Latinos and the political system* (pp. 385–410). Notre Dame, IN: Notre Dame University Press.

Friedman, M.S. (1978). *An appraisal of the role of the public school as an acculturating agency of Mexican Americans in Texas, 1850–1968*. Unpublished doctoral dissertation, New York University, New York.

Gaines v. Canada, 305 U.S. 337 (1938).

Gándara, P., Maxwell-Jolly, J., Garcia, E., Gutiérrez, K., Stritikus, T., Curry, J. and Asato, J. (2000, May). *The initial impact of Proposition 227 on the instruction of English learners*. University of California, Santa Barbara: UC Linguistic Minority Research Institute. Available online at: http://lmrinet.ucsb.edu

García, M. (1979). Americanization and the Mexican immigrant, 1880–1930. *Canadian Ethnic Studies, 6*, 19–34.

Garretson, O.K. (1928). Study of the causes of retardation among Mexican children. *Journal of Educational Psychology, 19*, 31–40.

Garth, T.R. (1923). A comparison of the intelligence of Mexican and full blood Indian children. *Psychological Review, 30*, 388–401.

Garth, T.R. (1925). A review of race psychology. *Psychological Bulletin, 22*, 343–364.

Garth, T.R. (1928). The intelligence of Mexican school children. *School and Society, 27*, 791–794.

Garth, T.R. (1930). A review of race psychology. *Psychological Bulletin, 27*, 329–356.

Glazer, N. and Moynihan, D. (1963). *Beyond the melting pot: The Negroes, Puerto Ricans, and Irish of New York*. Cambridge, MA: Harvard University Press.

González, G.G. (1974a). *The system of public education and its function within the Chicano communities, 1920–1930*. Unpublished doctoral dissertation, University of California, Los Angeles.

González, G.G. (1974b). Racism, education and the Mexican community in Los Angeles, 1920–1930. *Societas, 4*, 287–301.

González, G.G. (1990). *Chicano education in the era of segregation*. Philadelphia: Balch Institute Press.

Goodenough, F.L. (1926). Racial differences in the intelligence of school children. *Journal of Experimental Psychology, 9*, 388–397.

Gossett, T. (1953). *The idea of Anglo superiority in American thought, 1865–1915*. Unpublished doctoral dissertation, University of Minnesota.

Gossett, T. (1977). *Race: The history of an idea in America*. Dallas, TX: Southern Methodist University Press.

Gottlieb, H.N. (1983). The school effects of Chicago suburban housing segregation. *Integrated Education, 21*, 105–109.

Green v. County School Board of New Kent, 391 U.S. 430 (1968).

Griswold del Castillo, R. (1990). *The Treaty of Guadalupe Hidalgo: A legacy of conflict*. Norman: University of Oklahoma Press.

Gung Lum v. Rice, 275 U.S. 78 (1927).

Heizer, R. and Amquist, A. (1971). *The other Californians: Prejudice and discrimination under Spain, Mexico, and the United States*. Berkeley: University of California Press.

Hendrick, I. (1977). *The education of non-whites in California, 1848–1970*. San Francisco: R&E Associates.

Houston, R.A. (2000). *African Americans, Mexican Americans, and Anglo Americans and the desegregation of Texas, 1946–1956*. Unpublished doctoral dissertation, The University of Texas at Austin.

Hughes, L.W., Gordon, W.M. and Hillman, L.W. (1980). *Desegregating America's schools*. New York: Longman.

Hull, E. (1985). *Without justice for all: The constitutional rights of aliens*. Westport, CT: Greenwood Press.

Hyman, H.M. and Wiecek, W.M. (1982). *Equal justice under law: Constitutional development, 1835–1875*. New York: Harper & Row.

Independent School District v. Salvatierra, 33 S.W. 2d 790 (Tex. Civ. App.—San Antonio 1930), cert. denied, 284 U.S. 580 (1931).

In re Rodriguez, 81 Federal Reporter 337–356 (District Court, W.D. Texas 1897).

Jackson, A. (1986). Melville Herskovits and the search for Afro-American culture. In G. Stockings (Ed.), *Malinowski, River, Benedict, and others* (pp. 95–126). Madison: University of Wisconsin Press.

Jaeger, C. (1987). *Minority and low income high schools: Evidence of educational inequality in metro Los Angeles* (Working Paper No. 8). Chicago: Metropolitan Opportunity Project, University of Chicago.

Kansas, S. (1941). *U.S. immigration exclusion and deportation and citizenship of the U.S. of America.* New York: Matthew Bendercs.

Keyes v. School District No. 1, Denver Colorado, 380 F. Supp. 673 (D. Colo. 1973), 521 F. 2d 465 (10th Cir. 1975).

Kibbe, P. (1946). *Latin Americans in Texas.* Albuquerque: University of New Mexico Press.

Kirp, D. (1982). *Just schools: The idea of racial equality in American education.* Berkeley: University of California Press.

Koch, H.L. and Simmons, R. (1926). A study of the test performance of American, Mexican, and Negro children. *Psychological Monographs, 35,* 1–116.

Konvitz, M.R. (1946). *The alien and the Asiatic in American law.* New York: Cornell University Press.

Kozol, J. (1991). *Savage inequalities: Children in America's schools.* New York: Crown.

Lau v. Nichols, 414 U.S. 563, 566 (1974).

Leis, W. (1931). *The status of education for Mexican children in four border states.* Unpublished master's thesis, University of Southern California, Los Angeles, CA.

Lucas, T., Henze, R. and Donato, R. (1990). Promoting the success of Latino language-minority students: An explanatory study of six high schools. *Harvard Educational Review, 60,* 315–340.

Macías, R.F. (1993). Language and ethnic classification of language minorities: Chicano and Latino students in the 1990s. *Hispanic Journal of Behavioral Sciences, 15,* 230–257.

Maddux, H. (1932). *Some conditions which influence the Mexican children in Greeley, Colorado, and its vicinity.* Unpublished master's thesis, Colorado State Teachers College, Greeley, CO.

Marable, M. (1995). *Beyond Black and White: Transforming African-American politics.* New York: Verso.

McCurdy, J. (1975). School board minutes play big role in Oxnard desegregation. *Los Angeles Times* January 19, Vol. 94, Part II, pp. 1, 3.

McLaren, P. (1989). *Life in schools: Introduction to critical pedagogy in the foundations of education.* New York: Longman.

Menchaca, M. (1987). *Chicano–Mexican conflict and cohesion in San Pablo, California.* Unpublished doctoral dissertation, Stanford University.

Menchaca, M. (1989). Chicano–Mexican cultural assimilation and Anglo-Saxon cultural differences. *Hispanic Journal of Behavioral Sciences, 11,* 203–231.

Menchaca, M. (1995). *The Mexican outsiders: A community history of marginalization and discrimination in California.* Austin: University of Texas Press.

Menchaca M. (1997). Early racist discourses: Roots of deficit thinking. In R.R. Valencia (Ed.), *The evolution of deficit thinking: Educational thought and practice* (pp. 13–40). The Stanford Series on Education and Public Policy. London: Falmer Press.

Menchaca, M. (2001). *Recovering history, constructing race: The Indian, Black, and White roots of Mexican Americans.* Austin: University of Texas Press.

Menchaca, M. and Valencia, R.R. (1990). Anglo-Saxon ideologies and their impact on the segregation of Mexican students in California in the 1920s-1930s. *Anthropology and Education Quarterly, 21,* 222–249.

Méndez v. Westminister School District, 64 F. Supp 544 (S.D. Cal 1946), affirmed 161 F. 2d 774 (9th Cir. 1947).

Mickelson, R.A. (2001). Subverting Swann: First- and second-generation segregation in the Charlotte-Mecklenburg schools. *American Educational Research Journal, 38,* 215–252.

Milliken v. Bradley, 418 U.S. 717 (1974).

Milliken v. Bradley, 433 U.S. 267 (1977).

Mills, N. (Ed.). (1973). *The great school bus controversy.* New York: Teachers College Press.

Mills, N. (Ed.). (1979). *Busing USA.* New York: Teachers College Press.

Montejano, D. (1987). *Anglos and Mexicans in the making of Texas, 1836–1986.* Austin: University of Texas Press.

Moye, T. (1999). *"Sick and tired of being sick and tired": Social origins and consequences of the civil rights movement in Sunflower County, Mississippi, 1945–1986*. Unpublished doctoral dissertation, The University of Texas at Austin.

Newcombe, W. (1985). *The Indians of Texas*. Austin: University of Texas Press.

Oakes, J. (1995). Two cities' tracking and within-school segregation. *Teachers College Record*, *96*, 681–690.

Olsen, L. (1988*)*. Crossing the schoolhouse border: Immigrant students and the California public schools. Boston: California Tomorrow.

Orfield, G. (1988a). *The growth and concentration of Hispanic enrollment and the future of American education*. Paper presented at the National Council of La Raza Conference, Albuquerque, NM, July.

Orfield, G. (1988b). School desegregation in the 1980s. *Equity and Choice*, *4*, 25–28.

Orfield, G. (2001). *Schools more separate: Consequences of a decade of research*. The Civil Rights Project, Harvard University. Cambridge, MA: Harvard University. Available online at: http://www.law. harvard.edu/groups/civilrights/publications/schoolsseparate.pdf

Orfield, G., Bachmeier, M.D., James, D.R. and Eitle, T. (1997). Deepening segregation in American public schools: A special report from the Harvard Project on School Segregation. *Equity and Excellence in Education*, *30*, 5–22.

Orfield, G., Montfort, F. and George, R. (1987). *School segregation in the 1980s: Trends in the states and metropolitan areas*. National School Desegregation Project, Report to the Joint Center for Political Studies, University of Chicago. Chicago: University of Chicago.

Orfield, G. and Yun, J.T. (1999). *Resegregation in American schools*. The Civil Rights Project, Harvard University. Cambridge, MA: Harvard University. Available online at: http://www.law. harvard.edu/groups/civilrights.

Ovando, C. and Collier, V. (1985). *Bilingual and ESL classrooms: Teaching in multicultural contexts*. New York: McGraw-Hill.

Padilla, F. (1979). Early Chicano legal recognition, 1846 to 1897. *Journal of Popular Culture*, *13*, 564–574.

Paredes, A. (1978). The problem of identity in a changing culture: Popular conflict along the lower Rio Grande border. In S. Ross (Ed.), *Views across the border: The United States and Mexico* (pp. 68–94). Albuquerque: University of New Mexico Press.

Paschal, F.C. and Sullivan, L.R. (1925). Racial differences in the mental and physical development of Mexican children. *Comparative Psychology Monographs*, *3*, 1–76.

People v. De La Guerra, 40 Cal. 311 at 343 (1870).

Pettigrew, T.F. (1975). The racial integration of the schools. In T.F. Pettigrew (Ed.), *Racial discrimination in the United States* (pp. 224–239). New York: Harper & Row.

Plessy v. Ferguson, 163 U.S. 551–552 (1896).

Rangel, S.C. and Alcala, C.M. (1972). Project report: De jure segregation of Chicanos in Texas schools. *Harvard Civil Rights-Civil Liberties Law Review*, *7*, 307–391.

Reynolds, A. (1933). *The education of Spanish-speaking children in five Southwestern states* (Bulletin 1933, No. 11). Washington, DC: Government Printing Office.

Rios, R.L. and Alonzo, G.A. (1981). *Survey of Chicano representation in 361 Texas public school boards 1979/1980*. San Antonio, TX: Southwest Voter Registration Education Project.

Rist, R.C. (1979). *Desegregated schools: Appraisal of an American experiment*. New York: Academic Press.

Ross v. Eckels, 434 F 2d. 1140 (5th Cir. 1970).

Ruiz-de-Velasco, J., Fix, M. and Clewell, B.C. (2000). *Overlooked and underserved: Immigrant students in U.S. secondary schools*. Washington, DC: Urban Institute.

Salinas, G. (1971). Mexican Americans and the desegregation of schools in the Southwest. *Houston Law Review*, *8*, 929–951.

San Miguel, G., Jr. (1986). Status of the historiography of Chicano education: A preliminary analysis. *History of Education Quarterly*, *26*, 523–536.

San Miguel, G., Jr. (1987). *"Let all of them take heed": Mexican Americans and the campaign for educational equality in Texas, 1910–1981*. Austin: University of Texas Press.

San Miguel, G., Jr. and Valencia, R.R. (1988). From the Treaty of Guadalupe Hidalgo to *Hopwood*: The educational plight and struggle of Mexican Americans in the Southwest. *Harvard Educational Review*, *68*, 353–412.

Sánchez, G.I. (1932). Group differences in Spanish-speaking children: A critical review. *Journal of Applied Psychology*, *16*, 549–558.

Saucedo, L.M. (2000). The legal issues surrounding the TAAS case. *Hispanic Journal of Behavioral Sciences*, *22*, 411–422.

Sheldon, W.H. (1924). The intelligence of Mexican children. *School and Society*, *19*, 139–142.

Smrekar, C. and Goldring, E. (1999). *School choice in urban America: Magnet schools and the pursuit of equity.* New York: Teachers College Press.

Solomone, R. (1986). *Equal education under law: Legal rights and federal policy in the post-Brown era.* New York: St. Martin's Press.

Stephan, W.G. and Feagin, J.R. (1980). *School desegregation: Past, present and future.* New York: Plenum.

Surace, S. (1982). Achievement discrimination and Mexican Americans. *Society for the Comparative Studies in Society and History*, *24*, 315–339.

Swann v. Charlotte-Mecklenburg Board of Education, 402 U.S. 1 (1971).

Texas Education Agency. (2000a). *Academic Excellence Indicator System* (*AEIS*, 1998–1999). Austin, TX: Author.

Texas Education Agency. (2000b). *2000 comprehensive biennial report on Texas public schools.* Austin, TX: Author.

Texas Education Code. §51.306 (c). (1999).

Texas Higher Education Coordinating Board. (1999). *TASP policy manual* (5th ed.). Austin, TX: Author.

Texas Higher Education Coordinating Board. (2001). *Report on the performance of Texas public universities.* Austin, TX: Author.

U.S. Commission on Civil Rights. (1971). *Mexican American education study, report 1: Ethnic isolation of Mexican Americans in the public schools of the Southwest.* Washington, DC: Government Printing Office.

Valdivieso, R. (1986). Hispanics and schools: A new perspective. *Educational Horizons*, *64–65*, 190–196.

Valencia, R.R. (1980). The school closure issue and the Chicano community. *Urban Review*, *12*, 5–21.

Valencia, R.R. (1984a). *Understanding school closures: Discriminatory impact on Chicano and Black students* (Policy Monograph Series, No. 1). Stanford, CA: Stanford Center for Chicano Research, Stanford University.

Valencia, R.R. (1984b). The school closure issue and the Chicano community: A follow-up study of the *Angeles* case. *Urban Review*, *16*, 145–163.

Valencia, R.R. (1984c). *School closures and policy issues* (Policy Paper No. 84–C3). Stanford, CA: Institute for Research on Educational Finance and Governance, Stanford University.

Valencia, R.R. (1991). The plight of Chicano students: An overview of schooling conditions and outcomes. In R.R. Valencia (Ed.), *Chicano school failure and success: Research and policy agendas for the 1990s* (pp. 3–26). The Stanford Series on Education and Public Policy. London: Falmer Press.

Valencia, R.R. (1996a). *The Phoenix Union High School District desegregation plan and efforts: An analysis.* Report submitted to plaintiffs' counsel, Albert M. Flores. United States of America v. Phoenix Union High School District #210, *et al.* case number CIV 85 1249 PHX CAM, Consent Decree and Desegregation Order, United States District Court, District of Arizona, Phoenix, Arizona, May 15, 1985 for U.S. District Court of Arizona.

Valencia, R.R. (1996b). *Course enrollments by race/ethnicity in a desegregated Southwestern high school district: An analysis of access.* Unpublished report.

Valencia, R.R. (1997a). Genetic pathology model of deficit thinking. In R.R. Valencia (Ed.), *The evolution of deficit thinking: Educational thought and practice* (pp. 41–112). The Stanford Series on Education and Public Policy. London: Falmer Press.

Valencia, R.R. (1997b). Latinos and education: An overview of sociodemographic characteristics and schooling conditions. In M. Yepes-Baraya (Ed.), *ETS Invitational Conference on Latino Education Issues: Conference Proceedings* (pp. 13–37). Princeton, NJ: Educational Testing Service.

Valencia, R.R. (2000). Inequalities and the schooling of minority students in Texas: Historical and contemporary conditions. *Hispanic Journal of Behavioral Sciences*, *22*, 445–459.

Valencia, R.R. (2001). *School segregation in the Austin Independent School District: Prevalence and adverse effects on Chicano/other Latino and African American high school students.* Unpublished manuscript.

Valencia, R.R. and Black, M.S. (2002). "Mexican Americans don't value education!": On the basis of the myth, mythmaking, and debunking. *Journal of Latinos and Education, 2,* 81–103.

Varady, D.P. and Raffel, J.A. (1995). *Selling cities: Attracting homebuyers through schools and housing programs.* New York: State University of New York Press.

Washington v. Seattle School District No. 1, 458 U.S. 457 (1982).

Weinberg, M. (1977). *A chance to learn: The history of race and education in the United States.* Cambridge, England: Cambridge University Press.

Welch, F. and Light, A. (1987). *New evidence on school desegregation.* Washington, DC: U.S. Commission on Civil Rights (Clearing House Publication 92).

Welner, K.G. and Oakes, J. (1996). (Li)Ability grouping: The new susceptibility of school tracking systems to legal challenges. *Harvard Educational Review, 66,* 451–470.

Wollenberg, C. (1978). *All deliberate speed: Segregation and exclusion in California schools, 1855–1975.* Berkeley: University of California Press.

Yettick, H. (2001). Dwindling diversity: Ethnic groups tend to cluster in DPS' post-busing era. *Rocky Mountain News,* May 26, pp. 25A–27A.

Young, K. (1922). *Mental differences in certain immigrant groups: Psychological tests of South Europeans in typical California schools with bearing on the educational policy and on the problems of racial contacts in this country* (Vol. 1, No. 11). Eugene: University of Oregon Press.

Zerkel, P. (1977). Bilingual education and school desegregation: A case of uncoordinated remedies. *Bilingual Review, 4,* 180–188.

4   Chicano dropouts: an update of research and policy issues

Russell W. Rumberger and Gloria M. Rodríguez

Interest in high school dropouts among policymakers, educational practitioners, and researchers is as great today as 10 plus years ago when the original version of this chapter on Chicano dropouts was first presented (Rumberger, 1991). Attention has also continued to be focused on the Latino population, given that the proportion of Latino dropouts remains significantly higher than any other major racial/ethnic group (see Figure 4.1). In 1999, the dropout rate for White, non-Latinos was 7.3 percent, compared to 12.6 percent for Black, non-Latinos and 28.6 percent for Latinos (U.S. Department of Education, National Center for Education Statistics, 2001, Table 106). Another reason for the attention on Latinos is that this population is expected to grow faster than any other major racial/ethnic group (see Valencia, Chapter 2, present volume). For example, according to U.S. Census (1997) projections, between 2000 and 2025, the number of White youth (18–24) is expected to *decline* by 4 percent, while the number of Latino youth will *increase* by 78 percent. Thus, based on current dropout rates, the total number of young dropouts could actually increase over the next 25 years. Moreover, the number of high school age Latinos (14–17 years) is also projected to increase by 81 percent in the same time period, which could further contribute to an increase in the number of Latino dropouts in the near future.

While it is crucial to understand the disparities that exist relative to dropout incidence among the various racial/ethnic groups in the U.S., it is equally important to appreciate the within-group diversity found among U.S. Latinos. Along a variety of educational and economic indicators, the differences among Latino subgroups are actually greater than differences between Latino and non-Latino populations. For instance, in 1998, differences in dropout rates between Cuban and Mexican-origin populations were greater than differences in dropout rates between Latino and non-Latino populations (U.S. Department of Commerce, Bureau of the Census, 2000, Table 5.2).[1] Therefore, attention to subgroup differences is as warranted as attention to major racial/ethnic group differences (e.g., Chapa and Valencia, 1993).

As discussed by Valencia (Chapter 2 of present book), Mexican Americans or Chicanos represent nearly 60 percent of the total Latino population in the U.S. and an even larger proportion of the Latino population in Texas and California (also, see U.S. Department of Commerce, Bureau of the Census, 2000). Moreover, they generally have the lowest socio-economic status (SES) and the lowest level of educational attainment of all the Latino subgroups (U.S. Department of Commerce, Bureau of the Census, 2000). Thus, the circumstances of Chicano dropouts warrant particular attention by researchers and policymakers. Of course, Chicanos themselves are a diverse group who differ in such ways as language use, immigration status, and their own ethnic identities (Matute-Bianchi, 1986; Valenzuela, 1999). Our discussion of Chicano dropouts will reflect this complexity to the greatest extent possible.

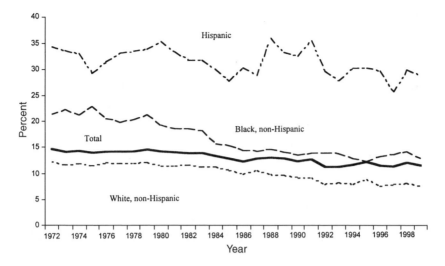

Figure 4.1 Status dropout rates of 16- to 24-year-olds, by race/ethnicity: 1972–1998.

Source: U.S. Department of Education, National Center for Education Statistics (2001, Table 106).

The purpose of this chapter is to examine the current state of knowledge and research about Chicano dropouts. Such a review requires a bringing together of several conceptual and theoretical lenses that explore more than the "snapshot" measure of school failure that dropping out represents. It is also imperative to explore and reveal the processes that help define, foster, and promote the notion of leaving school as a logical alternative to reaping the long-term benefits of graduating from high school and continuing one's education in college and beyond. Understanding the problem of dropouts also requires a sensitivity to what a formal education represents to Chicanos, Latinos, and other students of color, which can be influenced by perceptions of one's life chances, the "rules" that govern economic and social systems, and the expectations that are held both by students at risk of dropping out and the adults within and outside of the schools they attend. In fact, the immediate economic payoff of just obtaining a high school diploma may not be a sufficient motivator for Chicanos; yet as a gateway to increased life options, it may carry considerable potential.

This chapter also provides a review of the literature on Chicano (and other Latino) dropouts in the United States, with a primary focus on high school dropouts. Although the literature focuses on the high school experiences of potential and actual dropouts, one quickly discovers that this extraordinary experience has its beginnings as early as preschool age for many Chicano youths. Indeed, some of the work presented here offers insights into the long process of disengagement that can begin for some youths in their earliest encounters with school failure that serve as an unfortunate foundation for the negativity they continually experience until they leave—or are forced out—of the educational system.

Finally, this chapter reviews the programs and policies that are enacted and implemented to address the issue of Chicano dropouts in secondary schools. Such a review is difficult because each state and each school district can take a vastly different approach to identifying, preventing, and servicing dropouts. However, there are some concerns, particularly how and whether to count a student as a dropout, that are common among most states and school districts. Most recently, there is more attention to providing accurate data on dropouts and

to attending more to the question of *why* a student has left school versus creating institutional mechanisms to make sure the dropout figures appear low as evidence of sound
educational management and accountability.

The incidence of the problem: a review of the data on Chicano dropouts

The incidence of dropping out among Chicanos and other Latinos is considered to be too
high and possibly getting worse. But exactly how bad is the dropout problem for Chicanos?

Defining and measuring dropouts

The answer depends on how one defines a dropout. Because there is no universal definition
of a dropout, it is difficult to know from existing data exactly how extensive the dropout
problem is in the U.S. In general, a dropout is a person who is not currently enrolled in
school and does not have a high school diploma or equivalent certificate. A close examination of this general definition reveals a fundamental problem with the entire notion of dropping out. Dropout status, as well as enrollment status and graduation status from which it is
determined, are bivariate conditions that reveal little about the varying rate of learning and
knowledge that students acquire in school. We use the status of school enrollment and
graduation as indications of learning and knowledge when, in fact, the former may reveal
very little about the latter. Students who are enrolled in school may not be attending classes
and hence learning anything, while students who graduate from school may have acquired
very little useful knowledge.

   In other words, we use dropping out as a visible and convenient measure of academic
failure and graduation as a visible and convenient measure of academic success when neither
reveal much about how much or how little knowledge a student has acquired. Thus, in
some respects, too much attention is being placed on dropping out and graduating, when
we should be more concerned with student engagement, learning, and knowledge.

   Despite the inherent limitations of what dropout status means, there will always be continued need and interest in measuring dropouts. Unfortunately, available data on dropouts
are potentially inaccurate and incomparable because they are collected by different agencies,
using different definitions, and different sources of data. The major source of data at the
national level is provided by the U.S. Bureau of the Census, which annually collects national
information on the school enrollment and dropout status of the population from household
interviews (i.e., Current Population Survey, which is a monthly survey). Census data may
understate the extent of dropping out because school enrollment information is often
supplied by parents who may not know or accurately report the enrollment status of their
children. However, the data are the most comprehensive available and have been collected
for many years, which allows analyses of trends.

   It is useful to note that several terms are employed to describe dropouts, particularly for
educational policy purposes at the national, state, and local levels. Three of the most
commonly used terms include (Kaufman *et al.*, 2000, p. 2):

- status dropout rate—proportion of persons in an age group who have not completed
  high school and are not enrolled in school, regardless of when they dropped out;
- event (or annual) dropout rate—proportion of persons in an age group who dropout in a
  single year without completing high school, usually within specified grade levels; and

- cohort (or longitudinal) dropout rate—proportion of persons in a single age group or grade level who dropout over a specified period of time.

Dropout rates reveal how many students quit school; they do not reveal how many students actually complete it. Historically, most students have completed high school by earning a diploma, which is typically based on completing a specified number of credits in specified subject areas, similar to the system used in colleges to award degrees. In addition, some schools and districts require students to pass a competency test (Catterall, 1987). More recently, states have required students to pass a more rigorous high school exit examination often aligned to state standards (Heubert and Hauser, 1999; Valencia *et al.*, Chapter 9, this volume).

Alternatively, students can earn a high school equivalency through either a state or national examination. The most common national examination is the General Educational Development (GED) test administered by the American Council of Education (1999). The GED is a series of five subject exams in which, beginning in 1997, test takers had to exceed the performance of at least 33 percent of traditional graduating high school seniors in order to pass the test. However, states establish their own criteria for using the GED results to issue a high school equivalency certificate.

To complicate matters further, states and school districts often delineate the characteristics or conditions of leaving school for which a student would be counted as a dropout. As one example, the characteristics displayed in Table 4.1 are used in the state of Texas to distinguish between school leavers who would be counted as dropouts and those who would not. In addition to each state—in this case, Texas—employing its own system for the identification of dropouts, changes in these criteria often occur *within* each state to reflect differences in legislative priorities, thereby contributing to the difficulty of assessing how well Chicanos (or any students, for that matter) are being served in the school system. In the Texas example, the changes in the criteria for identifying school leavers as dropouts allow for districts to claim that they have "recovered" dropouts simply by identifying them according to the new criteria. As can be seen in Table 4.1, a school leaver who is a foreign student who returns to his or her home country is not considered a dropout. According to the Texas Education Agency, about 740 or 91 percent of the dropouts "recovered" in 1994–1995 under this new criterion were Latinos (Texas Education Agency, 1999). Two potential concerns therefore arise in that (a) there may be an incentive to assume that most Latino school leavers are simply returning to another country or (b) one can justify a certain percentage of Latino dropouts in this manner by considering them "recovered" using this criterion. What is important to bear in mind about this Texas example is that a "recovered" dropout is still a student who has left the school system, thereby reducing the number of dropouts that must be claimed for accountability purposes.

In light of the complexity of comparing dropout figures among states and school districts within states, it becomes obvious why researchers and policymakers rely so heavily on Census data for such analyses. The Census contains information on both status and event dropouts; status dropout rates, however, are most often compared to understand the educational condition of different age groups in the U.S. For example, the Census computes the proportion of dropouts in the population in two different ways. For persons under the age of 35 years, dropouts are persons who are not enrolled in school at the time of the Census survey and are not high school graduates; for persons 35 years of age and over, dropouts are persons who have completed less than 12 years of school or do not have a high school certificate. What do these data show?

The extent of the dropout problem

In 1998 there were more than 37 million dropouts in the United States (U.S. Department of Commerce, Bureau of the Census, 1999a, Table 1). The proportion of dropouts in the population varies by age, with the higher rates among the adult population and lower rates among the younger age groups. Among adults 55 years and over, 27 percent were dropouts in 1998, compared to 14 percent among 18- to 19-year-olds. In general, dropout rates are similar for males and females.

At virtually every age group, dropout rates are higher for Latinos than any other ethnic or racial group except American Indians. Among adults aged 25 to 29 years, for example, the dropout rate for Latinos was 37 percent in 1998 compared to only 6 percent for non-Latino Whites (U.S. Department of Commerce, Bureau of the Census, 1999a, Table 1). Mexican Americans have the highest dropout rates among all the Latino subgroups identified in the Census. In 1998, for example, the dropout rate for Mexican-origin Latino adults 25 years of age and older was 50 percent, compared to 40 percent for Cubans, 36 percent for Puerto Ricans, and 36 percent for Central and South Americans (U.S. Department of Commerce, Bureau of the Census, 2000, Table 5.2). This same pattern has also held for the 1990 U.S. Census data (Chapa and Valencia, 1993).

Although dropout rates for Latinos are indeed high, it does not mean that Latinos quit high school in the U.S. at much higher rates than other racial/ethnic groups. The reason is that more than 40 percent of all young Latinos are foreign-born and more than 40 percent

Table 4.1 Criteria for identifying dropouts in Texas: 1999

General Definition: A student is identified as a dropout if the individual is absent without an approved excuse or documented transfer and does not return to school by the fall of the following school year, or if he or she completes the school year but fails to re-enroll the following school year.

Students in the following categories are identified as dropouts:

- Students who drop out as defined above
- Students who enter the military before graduation
- Students from special education, ungraded, or alternative education programs who leave school
- Students who leave school and enter a program not qualifying as an elementary/secondary school (e.g. cosmetology school)
- Students enrolled as migrants and whose whereabouts are unknown

Students in the following categories are not included in the dropout count:

- Students who die
- Students who drop out as defined above, before the seventh grade
- Students who are out of school for temporary periods with an approved excuse
- Students showing regular attendance at a state-approved alternative program
- Students enrolled as migrants who have a subsequent school enrollment record (i.e. a Migrant Student Record Transfer System Education Record is available)
- Students known to have transferred to another public school, adult or alternative education program, or home schooling
- Students who move to another grade level
- Students who enroll in college early
- Students transferred or assigned to another public institution or state-approved educational program
- Foreign students who return to their home country

Source: Texas Education Agency (1999). Available online at: http://www.tea.state.tx.us/research/dropout95.definition.html

of foreign-born Latinos never attended school in the U.S. (McMillen *et al.*, 1997, Tables 15 and 16). In 1995, dropout rates among U.S.-born Latinos 16 to 24 years of age were 18 percent, compared to 12 percent for U.S.-born Black, non-Latinos, and 9 percent for White, non-Latinos. So while Latino dropout rates are indeed higher than other ethnic and racial groups, disparities in dropout rates from U.S. schools are not quite as great as the overall data would suggest.

Trends in dropout rates

Historically, dropout rates have declined dramatically in the U.S. In 1940, only 25 percent of the adult population had completed four years of high school; by 1998, 83 percent of the adult population had completed high school (U.S. Department of Commerce, Bureau of the Census, 1999b, Table 263). In recent years, however, improvements have slowed. In the 17-year period between 1980 and 1997, dropout rates among 18- to 21-year-olds declined from 16 percent to 13 percent, while among 22- to 24-year-olds, dropout rates declined from 15 percent to 13 percent.

Only recent trends in Latino and Chicano dropout rates can be examined because the Census did not identify Latinos until 1972 and Mexican-origin Latinos until 1979. Among Latinos 16 to 24 years of age, the proportion of male and female dropouts has remained largely unchanged between 1985 and 1999 at around 30 percent and 25 percent respectively (U.S. Department of Education, National Center for Education Statistics, 2001, Table 106). Dropout rates for White males improved in this period from 11 percent to less than 8 percent, as well as for White females, from 10 percent to less than 7 percent. Dropout rates for Black males declined from 16 percent to around 12 percent and for Black females improved slightly from 14 percent to 13 percent.

Overall, while Census data reveal general improvements in dropout rates nationally among Whites and Blacks, they show little improvement for Latino and Mexican-origin populations. Moreover, dropout rates for Latinos and Chicanos still remain almost four times as high as the rates for Whites.

Causes and explanations for Chicano dropouts

Our review turns now to an examination of the various perspectives and explanations for why Chicanos and other Latinos dropout in such high numbers, offering at times opposing views of how our educational system might either ameliorate or reproduce the conditions associated with dropouts. Without the complement of literature placing the problem of dropping out not with the students' characteristics alone, but with the schooling process itself, our review and analysis would be incomplete and unbalanced. Therefore, our review also explores the social and structural elements that surround and influence the educational lives of potential and actual dropouts. In this way, we can begin to envision policy options that offer more hope regarding factors such as persistent poverty, the undereducated status of Chicanos and most Latinos generally, and other forms of social disenfranchisement.

Much of the research on the dropout issue has focused on identifying the "causes" of the problem. This focus is part of the larger and more general effort to build models and identify the factors associated with student achievement. The major difference is that in dropout research the educational outcome of interest is dropout status, whereas in student achievement research educational achievement is most frequently measured by grades or test scores.[2]

Attempts to fully understand the causes of dropping out are hampered by the same set of factors that confronts the study of student achievement more generally. First, there are a large variety of factors that predict or influence dropout behavior, ranging from family background to school characteristics. Second, these factors tend to be highly interrelated making it difficult to assess the influence of any one factor. Third, because dropping out is often viewed as a longer- term, cumulative process of disengagement, it requires a longitudinal perspective to more fully understand how this process takes place and the factors that affect it. Finally, as is the case with any human behavior, dropping out itself is a complex phenomenon. Not all dropouts are the same, just as not all high school graduates are the same. As they themselves report, dropouts leave school for different reasons (Berktold *et al.*, 1998, Table 6).

The research literature on the causes of high school dropouts is based on a number of social science disciplines—including anthropology, psychology, and sociology—and employs a number of research techniques, ranging from ethnography to large-scale statistical studies. Each research tradition contributes to our understanding of the dropout problem. Ethnographic studies provide rich descriptions of the circumstances and experiences of students' academic and social lives (e.g., Fine, 1991; Romo and Falbo, 1996), yet they must necessarily focus on only a few, select number of students or sites. Studies based on large, nationally representative surveys can provide results that can be generalized to the national population of dropouts, but they are restricted by the populations and variables that are surveyed (e.g., Carter and Wilson, 1997).

In the discussion that follows, we present the dropout literature that is most relevant to Chicanos, though some of the work applies to other student populations, as well. Given that much of this research employs quantitative methods, it is useful to note that one problem shared by most of these dropout studies is that they can only show associations or correlations between dropout behavior and a host of other factors, such as family background or school experiences. Strictly speaking, they can never prove cause and effect. Yet, more sophisticated studies are able to more strongly suggest causal relationships by statistically controlling for a variety of spurious or intervening variables. Nonetheless, strict causality should not be inferred from even more sophisticated studies. In the discussion below, the term *influence* is used to denote association, but not causality. In more practical terms, this means that although certain characteristics (factors) might influence dropout behavior, simply possessing one of these characteristics, for example, being poor or identifying as Latino, does not *cause* one to dropout.

While all research has limitations, the cumulative findings from all existing studies are able to provide a more complete picture of the many factors that influence dropout behavior. In reviewing the research literature on actual and potential Chicano and Latino dropouts, we will address the following two questions:

1   Which personal or individual factors appear to influence dropout behavior?
2   Which institutional factors and processes appear to influence dropout behavior?

Individual factors

To address the first question, we draw on a framework developed by Rumberger (2000) for an analysis of dropouts in the U.S., which takes into account the individual level characteristics and behaviors that are associated with dropping out. Briefly, the framework is premised on viewing dropout incidence as a result of a process of educational disengagement. The framework links together three key dimensions of educational achievement, including

(a) academic achievement, as reflected in grades and test scores; (b) educational stability, which reflects whether students remain in the same school or remain in school at all; and (c) educational attainment, which is reflected in years of schooling completed and the completion of degrees or diplomas. Of course, this general framework has been developed as a lens on the dropout issue for all student populations, not exclusively for Chicano students. Nevertheless, much of the literature that produced findings that are consistent with this framework has relevancy for helping us understand further the situation of Chicano dropouts.

The first group of individual level factors has to do with the relation between dropping out and other dimensions of educational achievement. One of those dimensions is student mobility. A growing body of research suggests that both residential mobility (changing residences) and school mobility (changing schools) increase the risk of dropping out of high school (Astone and McLanahan, 1994; Haveman *et al.*, 1991; Rumberger, 1995; Rumberger and Larson, 1998; Swanson and Schneider, 1999; Teachman *et al.*, 1996). Some scholars have argued that student mobility represents a less severe form of student disengagement or withdrawal from school (Lee and Burkam, 1992; Rumberger and Larson, 1998). In fact, one study found that the majority of high school dropouts changed high schools at least once before withdrawing, while the majority of high school graduates did not (Rumberger *et al.*, 1998). Another factor is academic achievement. Numerous studies have found that poor academic achievement is a strong predictor of dropping out (Ekstrom *et al.*, 1986; Goldschmidt and Wang, 1999; Rumberger, 1995; Rumberger and Larson, 1998; Swanson and Schneider, 1999; Wehlage and Rutter, 1986).

Student engagement has also been shown to predict dropping out even after controlling for the effects of academic achievement and student background. Absenteeism, the most common indicator of overall student engagement, and student discipline problems are both associated with dropping out (Bachman *et al.*, 1971; Carbonaro, 1998; Ekstrom *et al.*, 1986; Goldschmidt and Wang, 1999; Rumberger, 1995; Rumberger and Larson, 1998; Swanson and Schneider, 1999; Wehlage and Rutter, 1986). These studies support the idea that dropping out is influenced by both the social and academic experiences of students. In other words, dropping out is not simply a result of academic failure.

Finally, a number of student background characteristics have been shown to predict withdrawal from school. Several demographic variables have been examined in the literature: gender, race and ethnicity, immigration status, and language background (Fernández *et al.*, 1989; Goldschmidt and Wang, 1999; Rumberger, 1983, 1995; Steinberg *et al.*, 1984; Velez, 1989). Other individual attributes have also been shown to predict school dropout, including low educational and occupational aspirations, and teenage parenthood (Ekstrom *et al.*, 1986; Newmann *et al.*, 1992; Rumberger, 1995; Rumberger and Larson, 1998; Swanson and Schneider, 1999; Wehlage and Rutter, 1986).

Two student background characteristics are of particular interest in understanding Hispanic and Chicano dropout behavior: immigration status and language proficiency. Most evidence suggests that both immigration status and language use influence dropout behavior only indirectly, through their effects on other measures of student achievement, such as grades and retention (Steinberg *et al.*, 1984). But two earlier studies found that more recent immigrants are more likely to drop out of school than other students, even controlling for other intervening variables (Rumberger, 1983; Velez, 1989). A more recent study that also controlled for other factors found that second-generation Hispanics had lower dropout rates than either first- or third-generation students (Rumberger, 1995), a finding consistent with the view that English proficiency and achievement tend to increase across generations, while parental optimism tends to decline (Kao and Tienda, 1995).

As mentioned earlier, the framework is based on the idea that student disengagement and withdrawal from school is a long-term process that can be influenced by students' early school experiences. Several studies, based on long-term studies of cohorts of students, have examined the predictors of dropping out from as early as first grade (Alexander *et al.*, 1997; Barrington and Hendricks, 1989; Cairns *et al.*, 1989; Ensminger and Slusacick, 1992; Garnier *et al.*, 1997; Roderick, 1993). These studies found that early academic achievement and engagement (e.g., attendance; misbehavior) in elementary and middle school predicted eventual withdrawal from high school.

One additional indicator of prior school performance has received considerable attention of late—grade retention. Historically, a large number of students are retained in school each year. Data from the National Education Longitudinal Study suggest that about one in five 8th graders in 1988 had been retained at least once since first grade (Rumberger, 1995, Table 1). As more states end social promotion and institute high school exit examination, this number will no doubt rise. As discussed in Valencia *et al.* (Chapter 9, present book) Texas' pending anti-social promotion legislation will very likely have an adverse impact on Chicano (and African American) students by increasing their already high retention rates. Furthermore, the recent discrepancies found between (under)reported dropouts and actual dropouts in Texas can be linked in part to retention in the grades prior to high school and higher-than-national-average Grade 9 retention rates (Haney, 2000). In 1998–1999 27.1 percent of Chicano and other Latino Texas 9th graders were retained—compared to 10.2 percent of White 9th graders (Texas Education Agency, 2001, Figure 3). Indeed, one of the reasons for students leaving school in Texas is being overage, a direct result of early grade retentions (Haney, 2000). Although some recent studies have suggested that retention may have some positive effects on academic achievement (Alexander *et al.*, 1994; Roderick *et al.*, 1999), virtually all the empirical studies to date suggest that retention, even in lower elementary grades, significantly increases the likelihood of dropping out (Goldschmidt and Wang, 1999; Grisson and Shepard, 1989; Jimerson, 1999; Kaufman and Bradby, 1992; Roderick, 1994; Roderick *et al.*, 2000; Rumberger, 1995; Rumberger and Larson, 1998; also, see Valencia, 2000, for a discussion of this literature in the context of Chicano retainees). For example, Rumberger (1995) found that students who were retained in grades 1 to 8 were four times more likely to drop out between grades 8 and 10 than students who were not retained, even after controlling for SES, 8th-grade school performance, and a host of background and school factors.

Institutional factors

We next address our second question by reviewing the research on Chicanos and other students of color that focuses on the various institutional factors, processes, and structures that provide the context for the educational experiences of actual and potential dropouts. This perspective is based on the growing awareness that individual attitudes and behaviors are shaped by the institutional settings of families, schools, and communities where young people live. This viewpoint was used by a recent National Research Council Panel on High-Risk Youth, who argued that too much emphasis has been placed on "high-risk" youth and their families, and not enough on the high-risk settings in which they live and go to school (National Research Council, Panel on High-Risk Youth, 1993; also, see Valencia and Solórzano, 1997, for a critique of how "at-risk" is a deficit thinking construct). Empirical research on dropouts has identified a number of factors and processes within students' families, schools, and communities that predict or otherwise illuminate dropout behavior.

We explore these studies to expand our understanding of why Chicanos persistently dropout at such high rates.

Families

As is the case with other measures of student achievement, family background exerts a powerful influence on dropout behavior. The most widely studied aspect of family background is SES, which is typically a composite measure of a series of family demographic variables such as family income and parental education (see Valencia and Suzuki, 2001, Chapter 3). Research has consistently found that SES is a powerful predictor of dropout behavior among students generally (Bryk and Thum, 1989; Ekstrom *et al.*, 1986; McNeal, 1999; Rumberger, 1983; Rumberger, 1995; Rumberger and Larson, 1998; Pong and Ju, 2000). But studies that have examined the impact of SES on dropping among racial and ethnic groups separately have found inconsistent impacts even based on the same data. For example, of the four studies that examined the relation between SES and dropping out for Hispanics based on the national High School and Beyond study of 1980 sophomores, two found that dropout rates were lower for high-SES Hispanics and higher for low-SES Hispanics (Mayer, 1991; Velez, 1989) while two other studies found no significant relation between SES and dropping out among Hispanics (Ekstrom *et al.*, 1986; Fernández *et al.*, 1989). Another early study also found no significant relation between a number of socio-economic factors (e.g., parental education and income) and dropping out among Hispanics (Rumberger, 1983), but a more recent study did (Rumberger, 1995). The reason for these inconsistent findings is unclear. It may be due to differences in the types of statistical models that were used to derive these estimates and the fact that the smaller sample sizes for Latinos makes it more difficult to establish statistical significance. In addition, Latinos generally come from lower-SES families than Whites, so the effect of SES may be less pronounced among generally low-SES populations. Finally, as suggested below, traditional measures of SES may be insufficient to capture important apects of Latino families.

Other aspects of family background also appear to influence dropout behavior, but like SES, they tend to have mostly a direct influence on the dropout behavior for Whites but not for Chicanos and Latinos. One factor is family composition. In general, research suggests that students from single-parent households are more likely to dropout of school than students from families where both parents are present even controlling for other, inter-vening factors (Astone and McLanahan, 1991; Bachman *et al.*, 1971; Ekstrom *et al.*, 1986; Fernández *et al.*, 1989; Goldschmidt and Wang, 1999; McNeal, 1999; Rumberger, 1983, 1995; Rumberger and Larson, 1998; Teachman *et al.*, 1996; Velez, 1989). One recent study, however, found that a change in dissolution of two-parent families did not increase the likelihood of dropping out apart from its effects on income loss (Pong and Ju, 2000). Interestingly, of the five studies that examined Latinos or Chicanos separately from Whites, three found no effects for Latinos or Chicanos (Fernández *et al.*, 1989; Rumberger, 1983, 1995), while the other two did (Ekstrom *et al.*, 1986; Velez, 1989).

Family size also appears to influence dropout rates: Students from larger families tend to have higher dropout rates than students from smaller families (Bachman *et al.*, 1971; Fernández *et al.*, 1989; Rumberger, 1983). But again, the direct influence of family size on dropout rates, after controlling for other factors, only holds for Whites in one study and for Latino females in another (Fernández *et al.*, 1989; Rumberger, 1983).

Altogether, to what extent do differences in family background between Chicanos and other racial/ethnic groups help explain observed differences in dropout rates among groups? First, Census data (U.S. Department of Commerce, Bureau of the Census, 1999a) reveal widespread racial/ethnic differences in several aspects of family background. In 1997, for example, about 37 percent of Black and 36 percent of Latino children were living in families with incomes below the poverty level, compared to 15 percent for White children. Furthermore, 35 percent of Latino families living below the poverty level were headed by a householder with no high school diploma, compared to 38 percent for blacks and 21 percent for Whites.

A couple of empirical studies of two different national survey data sets found that at least three-quarters of the differences in observed dropout rates between Whites and Latinos and Whites and Mexican Americans can be attributable to differences in family background (Fernández *et al.*, 1989; Rumberger, 1983). These findings suggest that much if not all of the high dropout rates for Latinos and Chicanos could be eliminated by raising their SES status to that of Whites. However, this inference may oversimplify the social position of Latinos and Chicanos relative to Whites in the U.S., or at least may point to a more serious concern with a schooling process that is so systematically biased against the poor and against students of color. Furthermore, in studies (e.g., of measured intelligence) that have attempted to equate or match Whites and people of color on SES, the literature suggests that such investigations are inherently flawed because instruments that purport to measure SES cannot untangle "class" and "caste" dimensions. As such, SES (e.g., middle class) when used to describe a White family and a Chicano family cannot, it appears, be truly isomorphic across race/ethnicity (Valencia and Suzuki, 2001, Chapter 3).

While large-scale statistical studies are able to demonstrate the importance of family background in influencing dropout behavior, generally they are unable to reveal exactly *how* this influence operates. This is because most large surveys usually ascertain *structural* characteristics of families—such as income, parental education, size, and composition—but little about family *processes* or mechanisms. Increasingly, research is now attempting to discover the various mechanisms through which families influence student achievement and dropout behavior (Coleman, 1988; Gándara, 1994; Romo and Falbo, 1996). This is where small-scale, ethnographic studies are particularly valuable because they can reveal the complex array of family mechanisms and their interrelationships (e.g., Trueba *et al.*, 1990; Valenzuela, 1999).

Existing research suggests that there are several different ways in which families influence the educational achievement of their children. One important influence is parental *academic involvement*. Regardless of racial/ethnic background, parents of high school graduates—compared to parents of dropouts—are more likely to be actively involved in their children's education through such activities as monitoring homework and attending school and teacher conferences (Carbonaro, 1998; Delgado-Gaitán, 1988, 1990; Rumberger, 1995; Rumberger *et al.*, 1990; Teachman *et al.*, 1996).

There are several possible explanations for why some parents are more involved than other parents (see Moreno and Valencia, Chapter 8, current book, for a discussion of Chicano parental involvement). In some cases, poor parents simply lack the time and resources to fully participate. In other cases, parents, especially recent immigrants, feel they lack the skill and knowledge to more fully participate and end up deferring responsibility to school officials (Delgado-Gaitán, 1988, 1990; Lareau, 1987; Moreno and Valencia, Chapter 8, current book). Yet, schools are also to blame. Sui-Chu and Willms (1996) found that almost one-quarter of the variation in school participation among U.S. eighth-grader parents was attributable to differences among schools. Supporting this conclusion, a survey found that inner-city parents are more involved with their children's schools when the schools have strong programs to encourage parental involvement (Dauber and Epstein, 1989). Gándara (1994) also found in her study of educationally ambitious Chicanos, who at one time exhibited characteristics of students at risk of dropping out, that their parents often supported the goals of the schools "without ever setting foot in them." This suggests that on-site involvement alone may not be the only way in which parents can play a positive role in the educational persistence of Chicano youth. Quantitative studies confirm that parental involvement measures that predict school dropout for White students do not always predict dropout for Hispanic students (Rumberger, 1995; McNeal, 1999)

Another way that families influence student achievement is through proper *academic encouragement*. Research has shown that extrinsic rewards and punishments reduce internal motivation, which leads individuals to explain their own behavior as the product of outside forces (Lepper and Greene, 1978). In contrast, parents who offer encouragement, praise, and other positive responses leave their children ultimately responsible for their own behavior, which helps develop internal motivation and improves academic performance (Steinberg *et al.*, 1992). This process may also operate on dropout behavior given that dropouts in all racial/ethnic groups tend to demonstrate lower levels of internal control and lower educational aspirations than other students (e.g., Ekstrom *et al.*, 1986; Rumberger, 1983, 1995).

In terms of creating an environment for achievement, Gándara (1994) found that the majority of her respondents (all of whom identified as Chicanos and all of whom managed to persist in school to very high levels of attainment) had reading materials in their homes while growing up and also had at least one parent who was an avid reader. In addition, family discussions of world politics and social issues occurred regularly for two-thirds of the respondents. It is important to note, however, that most of these families were very low income and experienced great challenges in supporting the academic development of their children. At times, supporting academic achievement among the families came at a very direct cost. That is, for those Chicano students whose families were migrant workers, the decision to "stay put" in one location and also protect their study time were done despite the economic loss to the family (Gándara, 1994).

A final way that families influence student achievement is by providing proper *social support*. Social support, in part, is shaped by parenting styles, which reflect parent–child interactions and decision-making which, in turn, can lead to differences in the amount of autonomy and psychosocial maturity in children. A parenting style that is too permissive can lead to excessive autonomy, more influence from peers, improper social attitudes and behaviors which, in turn, can hurt academic performance and increase the likelihood of dropping out (Dornbusch *et al.*, 1987; Rumberger *et al.*, 1990; Steinberg *et al.*, 1992). In contrast, students from families that stress joint decision-making are socially more mature, less influenced by their peers, have better social attitudes and behaviors and do better in school.

Some evidence suggests that Mexican American and other Latino families are less likely than non-Latino White families to foster the type of independence that tends to improve academic performance. Dornbusch *et al.* (1987) found that Latino students were less likely than White students to come from families with the authoritative parenting styles that are associated with higher grades in school. However, Gándara (1994) found that the concept of independence was discussed often by the Chicanos in her study and was reflected in references to being "hardworking," "self-reliant," and so forth. She also probed the dimension of parental support and encouragement. Interestingly, respondents' mothers at times intervened when fathers were not supportive. Other evidence of the family support for these participants included high parental aspirations, sibling support, and the reliance on "family stories" to promote a positive view of themselves and their families. Some parents in the study had higher aspirations for their sons; however, most held similar aspirations for sons and daughters. Older siblings paved the way or strongly encouraged respondents to succeed in school.

In addition, Romo and Falbo (1996) identified seven key parenting strategies employed to varying degrees by Latino (mostly Mexican origin) parents in their study of students who "defy the odds" to graduate from high school. These included:

(a) taking charge as a parent, that is, never abandoning their authority in support of their children;
(b) maintaining two-way influence, which means that parents asserted their authority in ways that were still respectful of their children;
(c) setting limits and making clear to their children what issues were "nonnegotiable" for parents;
(d) monitoring students in supportive ways;
(e) drawing the line with peers and clearly communicating their approval/disapproval of certain activities;
(f) continuing to reinforce the "stay in school" message; and
(g) staying involved in school, which included participation in school activities, as well as maintaining ongoing communications with teachers and school administrators.

Taken together, these two case studies of successful Chicano students support the general ideas that parental involvement, encouragement, and support are just as important for Chicano students to finish high school as for students from other racial/ethnic groups. Yet the specific practices may differ and it is not yet clear exactly how families do or can support Chicanos in the prevention of dropouts.

Clearly more research is needed to better understand how SES, race/ethnicity, and other family characteristics shape these various family mechanisms as well as how these family mechanisms shape student achievement. But to more fully understand how families influence student achievement and dropout behavior, one must also examine the interaction between families and schools in order to understand why certain types of attitudes and behaviors fostered and supported in the family may or may not be useful in helping students succeed in school (for a review of literature on the role home intellectual environment plays in shaping minority and White children's intellectual development, see Valencia and Suzuki, 2001, Chapter 4). This issue is also relevant to the discussion of schools.

Schools   school/dropout relation is less clear

Despite the powerful influence of family background, schools still make a difference. Of course, the kinds of schools that students attend is influenced by their place of residence and social class. Exactly *how* schools influence dropout behavior is less clear. Ethnographic studies show that dropouts report poor schooling conditions and experiences; schools either fail to engage some students or they actively try to push the difficult and problematic students out (Bowditch, 1993; Fine, 1991; Riehl, 1999; Romo and Falbo, 1996; Valenzuela, 1999).

It is widely acknowledged that schools exert powerful influences on student achievement, including dropout rates. But demonstrating the influence of schools and identifying the specific school factors that affect student achievement presents some methodological challenges. The biggest challenge is disentangling the effects of student and family background from the effects of school factors. Four types of school characteristics have been shown to influence student performance: (a) student composition, (b) school resources, (c) structural characteristics of schools, and (d) school processes and practices. The first three factors are sometimes considered as school inputs by economists and others who study schools because they refer to the "inputs" into the schooling process that are largely "given" to a school and therefore not alterable by the school itself (Hanushek, 1989). The last factor refers to practices and policies that the school does have control over and thus they are of particular interest to school practitioners and policymakers (Shavelson *et al.*, 1987).

STUDENT COMPOSITION

Student characteristics not only influence student achievement at an individual level, but also at an aggregate or social level. That is, the social composition of students in a school can influence student achievement apart from the effects of student characteristics at an individual level (Gamoran, 1992; see also Valencia *et al.*, Chapter 3, this volume, for a discussion of the relation between school segregation and Chicano student achievement). Several studies have found that the social composition of schools predicts school dropout rates even after controlling for the individual effects of student background characteristics (Bryk and Thum, 1989; McNeal, 1997a; Rumberger, 1995; Rumberger and Thomas, 2000).

SCHOOL RESOURCES *Teachers*

Currently, there is considerable debate in the research community about the extent to which school resources contribute to school effectiveness (Hanushek, 1997; Hedges *et al.*, 1994). Several studies suggest that resources influence school dropout rates. Two studies found that the pupil/teacher ratio had a positive and significant effect on high school dropout rates even after controlling for a host of individual and contextual factors that might also influence dropout rates (McNeal, 1997a; Rumberger and Thomas, 2000). One of those studies found that the higher the quality of the teachers as perceived by students, the lower the dropout rate, while the higher the quality of teachers as perceived by the principal, the higher the dropout rate (Rumberger and Thomas, 2000; see Valencia, Chapter 1 of the present book, for a discussion of the relation between techer certification and Chicano student achievement).

Perhaps what complicates the usefulness of these findings is that Chicanos and Latinos, particularly in states where they reside in large concentrations, have long histories of having less access to financial and human resources, as well as low property wealth, which still dictates the ability of local communities to adequately support needed educational services and facilities (Cárdenas, 1997; Gittell, 1998; Valencia, Chapter 1, present book). One study found that the higher the concentration of Latinos in California's unified school districts, the less access there was to teachers per pupil (Rodríguez, 1997); yet, we know that the bulk of educational dollars are used to support teacher salaries. Therefore, the inability of some Latino communities to attract and retain high quality teachers—whether employing student or administrator assessment of this quality—in turn affects their ability to prevent dropouts.

SCHOOL STRUCTURE

There is also considerable debate in the research community on the extent to which structural characteristics (e.g., size, location), particularly type of control (public; private), contribute to school performance. This issue has been most widely debated with respect to one structural feature—public and private schools (Bryk *et al.*, 1993; Chubb and Moe, 1990; Coleman and Hoffer, 1987). Although widespread achievement differences have been observed among schools based on structural characteristics, what remains unclear is whether structural characteristics themselves account for these differences or whether they are related to differences in student characteristics and school resources often associated with the structural features of schools. Most empirical studies have found that dropout rates from Catholic and other private schools are lower than dropout rates from public schools, even after controlling for differences in the background characteristics of students (Bryk and Thum, 1989; Coleman and Hoffer, 1987; Evans and Schwab, 1995; Neal, 1997; Rumberger and Thomas, 2000; Sander and Krautman, 1995). Yet, empirical studies have also found that students from private schools typically transfer to public schools instead of, or before dropping out, meaning that student turnover rates in private schools are not statistically different than turnover rates in public schools (Lee and Burkam, 1992; Rumberger and Thomas, 2000). School size also appears to influence dropout rates both directly (Rumberger and Thomas, 2000) and indirectly (Bryk and Thum, 1989), although the largest direct effect appears to be in low-SES schools (Rumberger, 1995). This latter finding is consistent with case studies of effective dropout prevention schools that suggest small schools are more likely to promote the engagement of both students and staff (Wehlage *et al.*, 1989).

SCHOOL POLICIES AND PRACTICES

Despite all the attention and controversy surrounding the previous factors associated with school effectiveness, it is the area of school processes that many people believe holds the most promise for understanding and improving school performance. Several studies found academic and social climate—as measured by school attendance rates, students taking advanced courses, and student perceptions of a fair discipline policy—predict school dropout rates, even after controlling for the background characteristics of students as well as the resource and structural characteristics of schools (Bryk and Thum, 1989; Rumberger, 1995; Rumberger and Thomas, 2000). Another study using one of the same data sets, but using different sets of variables and statistical techniques, found no effect of academic or social climate on high school dropout rates after controlling for the background characteristics of students, social composition, school resources, and school structure (McNeal, 1997a).

Current research literature on school dropouts suggests two ways that schools affect student withdrawal. One way is indirectly, through general policies and practices that are designed to promote the overall effectiveness of the school. These policies and practices, along with other characteristics of the school (student composition, size, etc.), may contribute to *voluntary* withdrawal by affecting conditions that keep students engaged in school. This perspective is consistent with several existing theories of school dropout and departure that view student disengagement as the precursor to withdrawal (Finn, 1989; Wehlage *et al.*, 1989).

Another way that schools affect turnover is directly, through explicit policies and conscious decisions that cause students to *involuntarily* withdraw from school. These rules may concern low grades, poor attendance, misbehavior, or being overage that can lead to suspensions, expulsions, or forced transfers.[3] This form of withdrawal is school-initiated and contrasts with the student-initiated form mentioned above. This perspective considers a school's own agency, rather than just that of the student, in producing dropouts and transfers. One metaphor that has been used to characterize this process is discharge: "students *drop out* of school, schools *discharge* students" (Riehl, 1999, p. 231). Several studies, mostly based on case studies, have demonstrated how schools contribute to students' involuntary departure from school by systematically excluding and discharging so-called problematic students (Bowditch, 1993; Fine, 1991; Riehl, 1999; Valenzuela, 1999). Two studies in particular help to illuminate the problems and strategies that emerge from case study documentation of the dropout problem, which are discussed next.

Michelle Fine's (1991) study of dropouts in a New York City high school, while not focused on Chicanos or Mexican Americans, provides us with a view of the processes of schooling that produce rather than prevent dropouts. Particularly challenging is the idea Fine offers about the silencing that occurs in public schools whereby the circumstances and procedures leading students to dropout are shrouded, as she suggests, to protect and maintain the school system versus the educational viability of the students. When silencing occurs, as Fine tells us, it means that one is unable to name the problem, describe its features, and therefore imagine a solution to the problem. Silencing also requires that the problem of dropouts continues to be placed entirely on the shoulders of the students at risk of dropping out and never within the parameters of scrutinizing the effectiveness and responsiveness of the school system to prevent such failures (Mehan, 1997). In order for the process of disengagement to move along within a school, it also requires a silencing that affects all of the humans in the school: students, parents, teachers, and administrators. What might be mistaken for complacency, according to Fine, is actually a very deliberate set of actions aimed at sustaining the school as a *system* rather than sustaining the individual students that are striving to learn, succeed, and build an educational foundation for the future.

Why might Fine's (1991) study be important to consider when we discuss Chicanos who dropout or are at risk of dropping out of our high schools? Consider that many Mexican American students attend school in the largest school districts in the country—and often among student populations with high concentrations of students of color (Carnegie Foundation for the Advancement of Teaching, 1988; Orfield *et al.*, 1997; Valencia *et al.*, Chapter 3, this volume). Students in this situation face many of the same obstacles experienced by the students in Fine's account, especially in terms of the bureaucratic structures that at times defy logic when they result in students leaving because there is no seemingly humane response to the tragedies and personal challenges students must overcome in order to graduate with just a high school diploma (Secada *et al.*, 1998). This discussion calls to mind the use of dropout rates as an accountability mechanism, such as in the Texas example. Such mechanisms create incentives to engage in practices to keep documented dropout figures low at the expense of meeting students' need for academic support toward graduation (Danini Supik and Johnson, 1999; Haney, 2000).

In *Subtractive Schooling: U.S.-Mexican Youth and the Politics of Caring*, Angela Valenzuela (1999) provides further evidence of how the processes of schooling can produce rather than prevent dropouts and other related school failures. Focused on a school community in Houston, Texas, Valenzuela's work offers critical insights into how Chicanos and other U.S. Mexican-origin students are affected by the structures of schooling. Valenzuela offers an important conceptualization of the challenges faced by Chicano and other Latino secondary students in their pursuit of a high school diploma. Guided by an interest in understanding further why U.S. and foreign born Latinos seem to experience differential educational success, Valenzuela conducted an ethnographic investigation of the various "friendship groups" that together comprised the Houston high school campus community in her study. She conceptualized the educational process of these groups as one of "subtractive" versus "additive" schooling. That is, rather than schools building on the richness in culture, heritage, language, and life experiences of the students, thereby engaging in an *additive* schooling process, schools tend to provide access to academic success for students at the cost of maintaining their home culture, language, and even values through a process of *subtractive* schooling.

Valenzuela (1999) further theorizes that within a framework of subtractive schooling, the perceptions that the adults at the school have of their students and vice-versa reflect two very different views of what it means to "care" about school. What Valenzuela found was that teachers' assessment of students not caring about school was often based on the way students dressed, spoke, and otherwise conducted themselves at school. On the other hand, students' assessment of their teachers not caring was in regards to the lack of concern for students, that is, teachers not caring about *them* as human beings. The study helps us understand that for many Chicanos, differential treatment and assimilationist stances (or at least the encouragement of conformity) at school might push students to disengage as a matter of self-preservation, despite the long-term personal costs of dropping out. Valenzuela's study reveals that the challenge facing Chicano and other Latino students lies in their ability to navigate successfully under these circumstances, which requires them to access and develop social capital (among their peers and their teachers) that affords them the opportunity to persist in school without necessarily having to compromise their own identities and principles (also see Stanton-Salazar, 1997).

What is perhaps most encouraging about recent research on the school effects on dropouts, particularly relative to Chicanos and other students of color, is the movement away from solely framing the discussion of dropouts as the story of misfits, troublemakers, or intellectually deficient students who cannot seem to "cut it" in regular schools. This approach to the problem of dropouts, by ignoring the contextual factors that also influence dropout behavior, has made it difficult to arrive at sound solutions because changes in personal characteristics are impossible from a policy standpoint versus changes in schooling processes via a shift in policy and educational priorities. Indeed, the literature that seeks to document how schooling experiences lead to dropouts reveals that Chicanos and others who dropout are often academically capable, politically and socially aware, and more apt to express critique of the negative elements in the world around them than are those who instead survive by conforming to the schools' rules and expectations (Fine, 1991; Mehan, 1997; Valenzuela, 1999).

Community influences

In addition to families and schools, communities and peer groups can influence students' withdrawal from school. There is at least some empirical evidence that differences in neighborhood characteristics can help explain differences in dropout rates among communities apart from the influence of families (Brooks-Gunn *et al.*, 1993; Clark, 1992; Crane, 1991). While these studies find that communities do influence dropout rates, they are unable to explain how they do so. Poor communities may influence child and adolescent development through the lack of resources (playgrounds and parks; after-school programs) or negative peer influences (Brooks-Gunn *et al.*, 1997; Hallinan and Williams, 1990; Wilson, 1987). Community residence may also influence parenting practices over and above parental education and income (Klebanov *et al.*, 1994). Students living in poor communities may also be more likely to have friends as dropouts, which increases the likelihood of dropping out of school (Carbonaro, 1998). In addition, community resources, including community-based organizations, business, and other concerned groups or individuals can greatly enhance the prospects of Chicano youth in ways that benefit the entire community (Romo and Falbo, 1996). While we may find that Chicanos reside in mostly low-income communities, the role of service and volunteerism on the part of community members is key to reinforcing the importance of educational persistence and contributing positively to one's community (Secada *et al.*, 1998).

Another way that communities can influence dropout rates is by providing employment opportunities both during or after school. Relatively favorable employment opportunities for high school dropouts, as evidenced by low neighborhood unemployment rates, appears to increase the likelihood that students will drop out, while more favorable economic returns to graduating, as evidenced by higher salaries of high school graduates to dropouts, tend to lower dropout rates (Bickel and Papagiannis, 1988; Clark, 1992; Rumberger, 1983). Research has also demonstrated that working long hours in high school can increase the likelihood of dropping out (Goldschmidt and Wang, 1999; Seltzer, 1994), although the impact of working in high school depends on the type of job held and on the student's gender (McNeal, 1997b). Perhaps a complement to these findings is also the concern raised in the Latino Dropout Project for more business support of parental involvement activities among their employees. Secada *et al.* (1998) cite instances in their research where Latino parents realized the importance of their presence in the schools, yet could not always engage in such activities due to the risk of losing their own jobs.

To summarize, research suggests that a complex myriad of factors lead to dropping out of school. In general, these factors operate similarly on all racial/ethnic groups. Thus, it is the *incidence* of these factors that explain the higher dropout rates of Latino and Chicano students. The most visible and powerful single factor is SES. Latinos and Chicanos are more likely to come from low-SES families, families where children are more likely to dropout of school regardless of race/ethnicity. The mechanisms by which families influence dropout behavior are not well understood, but they include both direct effects on students' attitudes, behaviors, and performance in school as well as indirect effects on the types of schools that students attend.

Consequences of the Chicano dropout problem

Dropping out of high school has severe economic and social consequences for both the individual and society at large. The economic consequences are well-known: Dropouts, in general, have more difficulty getting a job and receive lower wages from the jobs they do get. But there are also a host of other social consequences to dropping out, ranging from increased crime and drug use to poorer health that have not been well-documented but, nonetheless, can be considered costly (Rumberger, 1987). An important question in the current discussion is whether the economic and social consequences to dropping out of school are the same for Chicanos and Latinos as for other racial/ethnic groups.

Economic consequences

The most often discussed consequence to dropping out of school is the associated economic loss. Dropouts, in general, have higher rates of unemployment and lower earnings than high school graduates and Latino dropouts are certainly no exception (Enchautegui, 1997). For example, in 1998 the unemployment rate for dropouts was 75 percent higher than for high school graduates (U.S. Department of Education, National Center for Education Statistics, 2000, Figure 24). Even if they find a job, dropouts earn substantially less than high school graduates. A study by the U.S. Census Bureau found that more than one-third of all high school dropouts who were employed full-time and year-round in 1990 worked in "low wage" jobs that paid less than $12,195 per year—the official poverty rate for a family of four (U.S. Department of Commerce, Bureau of the Census, 1992).

In general, therefore, there appears to be a powerful economic incentive for students to finish high school. But is this economic incentive similar for Latinos and Chicanos as for Whites and other groups? Recent data suggest that the answer may be no.

Census data present a picture of unemployment during the last decade for Whites, Blacks and Latinos with no high school diploma, as well as with only a high school diploma. Clearly, there are improvements in the unemployment rates if one compares the Latino unemployment rate for individuals with a high school diploma with those who have not attained this level of education. In 1998, for example, the unemployment rate for Latinos (ages 25 to 64 years) drops by 2.8 percentage points, or 8.3 percent without a high school diploma versus 5.5 percent with only a high school diploma. Incidentally, the most dramatic difference is seen for Blacks; however, 1998 unemployment rates for Blacks with and without a high school diploma are four to five percentage points higher than the overall unemployment rates. For Whites, there is a 3.3 percentage point difference between those individuals with and without a high school diploma. These data indicate unemployment is lower among those individuals with a high school diploma versus those without one.

This "payoff" from having a diploma might be encouraging to Chicano students currently in a situation that may lead to dropping out. However, policymakers and business people would also have to consider the availability of jobs for individuals with such minimal levels of educational attainment in order to create avenues that will guarantee a payoff from having the diploma. Indeed, the logic of return on investments in education may not be so apparent, given that different levels of educational attainment by different racial/ethnic groups do not translate into comparable returns. Nonetheless, as Secada *et al.* (1998) and Fisher *et al.* (1998) have pointed out, Chicanos and other Latinos can benefit significantly from educational opportunities that exist at the postsecondary level; therefore, the high school diploma still represents an important gateway to such expanded options.

Social consequences

The social consequences to dropping out of high school include the economic consequences discussed above, given that society as a whole suffers from forgone earnings and taxes from individuals with inadequate schooling. But the social consequences of dropping out are even greater. In the first comprehensive study that had ever been done on the social consequences of dropouts, Levin (1972) identified seven social consequences of dropping out of high school, including forgone national income and tax revenues, increased demand for social services, increased crime, reduced political participation and intergenerational mobility, and poorer levels of health. He then estimated the social costs associated with the first four outcomes. For a cohort of male dropouts 25–34 years of age in 1969, forgone income over a lifetime was estimated at $237 billion and forgone government tax receipts was estimated at $71 billion (Levin, 1972, p. IX). In addition, welfare expenditures attributable to dropouts was estimated at $3 billion per year and criminal expenditures was estimated at another $3 billion dollars (Levin, 1972).

More recent investigations of the social costs associated with dropouts have been conducted using data from the states of Texas and California, which have very high concentrations of Chicanos and other Latinos (see Valencia, Chapter 2, present volume). One study of Texas dropouts estimated that over the 12 years between 1986 and 1998 the state lost a staggering $319 billion in earnings and taxes (Danini Supik and Johnson, 1999). In an investigation of Los Angeles, the estimated forgone income associated with just one cohort of dropouts in 1986 was $3.2 billion and the social costs to local government of funding criminal services, welfare, and health attributable to dropouts was $488 million (Catterall,

1987, Table 4). While these income and tax figures may be compelling enough to prompt one's attention to prevent such social costs attributable to dropouts, additional research details further how preventing students from dropping out potentially saves us from a variety of public health and safety concerns, as well.

Recent research continues to support the conclusions that dropping out leads to a range of adverse social consequences. For example, young female dropouts are 50 percent more likely to give birth to a child out of wedlock than young female graduates with similar backgrounds (Berlin and Sum, 1988), and the rate is higher among Latinas (Mahler, 1999). Dropouts are more likely to engage in criminal behavior and get arrested than graduates (Berlin and Sum, 1988; Thornberry *et al.*, 1985). Dropouts are also more likely to use both legal drugs (cigarettes and alcohol) and illegal drugs (marijuana and cocaine) than high school graduates (Mensch and Kandel, 1988). Only recently have investigations been conducted on substance abuse among Chicano and other Latino dropouts (and Latinos in good academic standing), resulting in some very troubling findings.

While it remains the case that dropouts are more likely to use legal and illegal drugs, researchers point out that the magnitude of the problem of adolescent substance abuse is often underestimated due to the reliance on in-school data in most studies (Swaim *et al.*, 1997). Swaim *et al.* found in their comparison of drug use rates (except alcohol) among Mexican American and White adolescents that rates were double for dropouts compared to current students, and American Indian dropouts had 1.8 times the current student rate of drug use. With regards to alcohol use in this study, researchers found that White dropouts reported higher rates of getting drunk than either Mexican American or American Indian dropouts, as was the case in reported use of LSD. A more recent study of White and Mexican American dropouts and students in good academic standing also confirmed that dropouts were 2.5 times more likely to report frequent alcohol use, 3.2 times more likely to classify themselves as heavy drinkers, and 3 times more likely to report frequent drunkenness compared to students in good standing (Arellano *et al.*, 1998). This study did not find significantly different results between Mexican Americans and Whites.

However, in their investigation of lifetime marijuana use, which the authors point out is the best illustration of the importance of including dropout data, Swaim *et al.* (1997) found that Mexican Americans and American Indians had significantly higher rates than Whites overall. Interestingly, without including dropouts' reported use rates, these three groups did not differ significantly in their lifetime marijuana use rates; however, because dropout rates are much higher among Mexican Americans and American Indians than for Whites, the correction for dropout incidence revealed that the two former groups faced a much greater challenge with substance abuse.

In summary, there are sizable economic and social consequences to dropping out of school for all racial/ethnic groups. Yet, there is at least some evidence to suggest that Latinos and Chicanos may have less to gain economically from finishing high school than other students. If students respond to incentives or disincentives in the labor market, as some people suggest (Bishop, 1989), then as such evidence becomes available to students it becomes harder for parents, teachers, and other persons to convince non-college-bound Chicanos to remain in school. Despite the pressures of poverty and society's need to produce more employable individuals, educators in particular face a challenge to convey to others that schools in the U.S. play a role far beyond workforce preparation alone. Indeed, the intellectual development of critical thinkers who also appreciate the complexity, diversity, and beauty of the world around them is a value of education that, while difficult to quantify, is still vital to the improvement of our society (Greene, 1995).

Addressing the problem of Chicano dropouts

How we frame the problem of Chicano dropouts will certainly determine how we frame the solutions. The problem of high school dropouts is more than an academic concern. There is widespread interest and activity both inside and outside of the education community in trying to solve the problem. Policymakers at the federal and state levels have enacted a variety of policies and programs to help solve the dropout problem for all student populations (e.g., Council of Chief State School Officers, 1987). Foundations have funded programs to address the problem. Education and community organizations have developed and implemented a wide variety of dropout prevention and recovery programs (Orr, 1987; Rumberger, 2001; Secada *et al.*, 1998). But are these efforts likely to solve the dropout problem in general, and the dropout problem among Latinos and Chicanos in particular?

The answer depends on how one views the dropout problem. If one views the dropout problem as largely a problem of educational failure that affects a relatively small proportion of students, then *programmatic approaches* might be able to effectively solve the problem. In this case, one could be quite sanguine about "solving" the dropout problem. If, however, one views the dropout problem as a larger, endemic social problem that affects the majority of students in some schools and districts, then solving the problem may require more *systemic and policy approaches*. Because such changes are more sweeping and difficult to achieve, it is harder to be as optimistic about the prospects for success. Nonetheless, a case can be made for each perspective.

Programmatic approaches

Most of the effort to address the dropout problem can be classified as programmatic solutions. Currently there are hundreds of local programs around the country that are designed to keep potential dropouts in school and help existing dropouts to get additional schooling or training. Unfortunately, there is little comprehensive information available at a national level about how much is being spent on dropout programs, how many students are being served, and whether these programs are successful.

The only recent effort to try to document dropout efforts nationally was conducted by the General Accounting Office (GAO) in the Fall of 1986. After reviewing literature and contacting a large number of national, state, and local agencies, the GAO compiled a list of more than 1,000 dropout programs (U.S. General Accounting Office, 1987, Appendix I). But a mail survey of those programs yielded useful information on a total of only 479 programs; 26 of these programs primarily served Latinos. Unfortunately, the GAO survey of dropout programs generated only 20 rigorous evaluations of the 479 programs that responded to the survey (U.S. General Accounting Office, 1987, p. 19). Evaluations that do exist nevertheless fail to demonstrate program effectiveness. For example, Dynarski and Gleason (1998) reviewed evaluations of 21 dropout prevention programs funded under the federal School Dropout Demonstration Assistance Program (SDDAP) and found only three programs improved dropout or completion rates. Similarly, Slavin and Fashola (1998) conducted a literature search of dropout prevention programs with experimental evaluations and found only two that were effective.

Although information on program effectiveness is generally lacking, there is some information on the features of successful or at least promising programs (where success is identified by program providers). For example, the majority of respondents to the GAO survey of dropout prevention and recovery programs identified five factors that had the greatest impact on program effectiveness (U.S. General Accounting Office, 1987, Table 2.3):

(a)   a caring and committed staff;
(b)   a non-threatening environment for learning;
(c)   a low student–teacher ratio;
(d)   individualized instruction; and
(e)   program flexibility.

In fact, some educators might argue that these features are also important to foster in regular school environments to improve their "holding power" relative to Chicano and Latino students (Denti and Guerin, 1999; Neumann, 1996; Romo and Falbo, 1996). Other studies of effective dropout programs have identified essentially the same set of factors (Merchant, 1987; Olsen and Edwards, 1982; Stern, 1986; Wehlage *et al.*, 1989). The Latino Dropout Project further cited the importance of counseling and adult advocacy services for Latino (potential) dropouts (Secada *et al.*, 1998). Of course, simply following this list of factors does not guarantee an effective program. Moreover, some programs may be better at serving different sorts of dropouts than others—such as those serving Latinos—which also supports the need for more comprehensive and rigorous program evaluations. The lack of evaluative information notwithstanding, we highlight one program to demonstrate the promise that exists in supporting potential Chicano and Latino dropouts in their quest to complete high school.

The Achievement for Latinos through Academic Success (ALAS) program was founded on the premise that the youth and school as well as the family and community contexts must be addressed simultaneously for dropout prevention efforts to succeed (Gándara *et al.*, 1998). ALAS was developed, implemented, and evaluated as a pilot intervention program to serve the most at-risk students in a poor, predominantly Latino middle school in the Los Angeles area from 1990 to 1995. The program specifically targeted two groups of high-risk students: special education students and other students who, because of poor academic performance, misbehavior, and low income, were at greatest risk of school failure. Most program participants were Mexican American students. The pilot program served two cohorts of special education students ($n = 77$) and one cohort of high-risk students ($n = 46$). Participating students received the intervention program in conjunction with the regular school program for all three years they remained in the target school.

Thus, ALAS consists of a series of specific intervention strategies focused on individual adolescents as well as on three contexts of influence on achievement: the family, the school, and the community (Gándara *et al.*, 1998). The intervention strategies are designed to increase the effectiveness of actors in each context as well as increase collaboration among them. ALAS provides the following specific interventions:

1   *Remediation of the student's ineffective problem-solving skills regarding social interactions and task performance* through ten weeks of problem-solving instruction and two years of follow-up problem-solving training and counseling.
2   *Personal recognition and bonding activities,* such as praise, outings, recognition ceremonies, certificates, and postive home calls to parents for meeting goals or improving behavior to increase self-esteem, affiliation, and a sense of belonging with the school organization.
3   *Intensive attendance monitoring,* including period-by-period attendance monitoring and daily follow-ups with parents, to communicate a personal interest in their attendance.
4   *Frequent teacher feedback to parents and students* regarding classroom comportment, missed assignments, and missing homework.

5   *Direct instruction and modeling for parents* on how to reduce their child's inappropriate or undesirable behavior and how to increase desirable behavior.
6   *Integration of school with home needs and community services.*

The program was evaluated using an experimental design where high-risk students were randomly assigned to the treatment or a control group and participating special education students where compared to a previous year's cohort of special education students. The evaluation examined enrollment status and credits earned in the final year of the program in 9th grade and in the remaining years of high school after the program ended. Evaluation data on mobility, attendance, failed classes, and graduation credits indicate that the ALAS program had a substantial and practical impact on students who received the intervention (Gándara *et al.*, 1998). By the end of 9th grade, students in the comparison group had twice the number of failed classes, were four times more likely to have excessive absences, and were twice as likely to be seriously behind in high school graduation credits. These results appear even more remarkable when considering that the participants in this study represent the most difficult to teach students within a pool of students generally viewed as high risk. Nonetheless, these dramatic effects were not sustained. By the end of the 12th grade, only 32 percent of the ALAS participants and 27 percent of the comparison students had completed high school. This clearly suggests that in order to increase graduation rates it is necessary to provide an ALAS-type intervention throughout the high school years.

Clearly well-designed programs aimed specifically at the difficulties Chicanos and other Latinos face is paramount to addressing the dropout problem in a proactive fashion. However, considerable attention over the years has also been paid to viable alternative routes to completing high school, and the most commonly used alternative is the General Equivalency Development exam or GED. Over the last 20 years, an increasing number of Americans have taken and completed the GED exam. In 1999, 9.2 percent of all persons 18- to 24-year-olds completed high school by taking the GED or other alternative credential, representing 11 percent of all high school completers (Kaufman *et al.*, 2000, Table 4). Among Latinos, 13.7 percent completed high school by taking the GED or other credential. Another study based on the National Educational Longitudinal Study of eighth graders in 1988 who dropped out of school found that 44 percent had received a high school diploma within six years, with one-third of those actually graduating from high school and two-thirds receiving an equivalent certificate by passing the GED exam (Rumberger and Lamb, 1998, Table 1).

Recently, some researchers and educators have become more critical of the use of the GED to circumvent the regular educational path toward a high school diploma, particularly for students of color who are in the first years of high school (Fine, 1991; Romo and Falbo, 1996). Haney (2000) found that Texas' participation in the GED is higher than national proportions, and the Census (1999b) indicates that 40 percent of GEDs issued were to students younger than 19. The key argument asserted by these researchers is: If students are experiencing difficulties, schools should be more responsive and proactive versus providing institutional incentives to students to "choose" dropping out over persisting within the regular program. Romo and Falbo found in their work on Latinos who persisted to high school graduation that some of their respondents who eventually took the GED route were actually experiencing learning disabilities in school, which largely went unaddressed. As students fall further behind the pressure of being much older than their classmates can also make the GED more attractive (Fine, 1991; Romo and Falbo, 1996). Combined with state and local policies that allow younger students to take GED training (versus reserving this option for students of adult age only), we see trends of larger proportions of students taking this option.

The reason the method of high school completion may be important is because some recent studies have questioned whether the economic payoff to a high school equivalency is comparable to a traditional high school diploma. One study compared three groups of 25- to 28-year-old males—dropouts who earned the equivalent of a high school diploma through a national examination, and high school graduates—and found that exam-certified high school graduates are statistically indistinguishable from high school dropouts in terms of wages, earnings, hours of work, and unemployment even after controlling for prior ability and other factors that differentiate the three groups (Cameron and Heckman, 1993). However, two other studies, based on a younger sample of male respondents from the same national study, found that although exam-certified graduates did not earn significantly more than dropouts immediately after completing school, their earnings did grow at a significantly faster rate over the first six years of post-school work experience, and they were more likely than dropouts to obtain postschool education and training (Murnane *et al.*, 1995, 1997). More recent studies found more varied effects of obtaining a GED—two studies found it only benefits dropouts with weak cognitive skills (Murnane *et al.*, 1999, 2000); another found it only benefits Whites but not minority dropouts (Tyler *et al.*, 2000). This research suggests that although at least some dropouts who earn the equivalent of a high school diploma through examinations such as the GED are better off than other dropouts, they are not as well off as students who complete a regular diploma.

A couple of other difficulties remain in programmatic efforts to address the dropout problem. One is that more attention needs to focused on early prevention, since many "at-risk" students are already two or more grade levels behind before they even reach high school (Denti and Guerin, 1999; Levin, 1988). Another is that more attention be focused on dropout recovery, given that only a small fraction of the more than 37 million adult dropouts are enrolled in regular schools, GED programs, or other education and training programs (Rumberger, 1990).

Systemic and policy approaches

A different approach to solving the dropout problem is necessary if one views the dropout problem as affecting a sizable number of students, as in some communities, or if one views dropping out as a social as well as an educational problem. Both of these aspects apply to many Chicanos and other minorities. However grim the picture might appear with respect to Chicano dropouts, the public school system nevertheless represents one social institution that may offer an opportunity to change the trends we see in their educational, social, and economic prospects. To pursue this agenda, however, one must tap into systemic and policy alternatives that create an *infrastructure* for educational success for potential and actual dropouts. Typically, such approaches involve more than better ways of counting dropouts or better ways of circumventing the mainstream schooling process.

Options that foster success for those students most at risk of dropping out involve a complex of community resources, including the schools, working in concert with other social service agencies, to support the students, their families, and other community members who together forge a vision for community success (Fisher *et al.*, 1998; Secada *et al.*, 1998; Verstegen, 1994). For states with large populations of Chicanos or Latinos (e.g., California and Texas), the challenge is to support local efforts with state policies that provide an appropriate mix of incentives and sanctions aimed at preventing dropouts in the first place, rather than risking the kind of silencing that can occur when the charge is simply to keep the dropout figures down.

Although such changes are difficult to achieve, some fundamental, systemic changes are currently being undertaken in the United States. Some national educational efforts have been in operation for many years to completely restructure elementary schools with predominantly poor students of color that promise to bring such students up to the achievement levels of other students, which would reduce the likelihood of dropping out in high school (Comer, 1988; Levin, 1988; Slavin and Madden, 1989). Case studies of high schools that are effective in promoting achievement and reducing dropout rates for Latino students provide further examples of what can be done (e.g., Lucas *et al.*, 1990). In addition, structural arrangements and forms of decision-making are being tried within some districts and schools to foster improved education (Hawley Miles and Darling-Hammond, 1998; Walberg *et al.*, 1989). Furthermore, we all should heed the principles of "democratic education" to bring forth an inclusive education in which the tenets, for example, of equal encouragement, optimum learning opportunities, students' rights, and useful knowledge shape the educational process (see Pearl, Chapter 11, present book).

A second reason to argue that only systemic solutions can solve the dropout problem rests on a recognition that dropping out is more of a social than an educational problem. It is a social problem in that many dropouts have a variety of other problems in their lives, such as family predicaments, substance abuse, crime, or teenage pregnancy. It also is a social problem in that the earlier discussion suggests that there are three major sources of influence on dropping out and other behaviors of young people—families, schools, and communities. If each plays a significant role in influencing the attitudes, behavior, and academic performance of young people, then each must play a role in addressing the dropout problem.

Recognition of the important role of families, schools, and communities in influencing the behavior of young people is the basis of several types of reform efforts to help potential and actual dropouts. Many educators have long-argued that parents must be centrally involved in improving the educational performance of their children. Thus, many dropout programs and effective high schools are built around parental involvement (Lucas *et al.*, 1990; Orr, 1987; Wehlage *et al.*, 1989). Other efforts to reduce the dropout problem involve strengthening the role of community, particularly community organizations and the business community (Fisher *et al.*, 1998; Secada *et al.*, 1998). In fact, some observers argue that community involvement is crucial to the successful education of youths because families and schools cannot and should not shoulder the burden alone (Heath and McLaughlin, 1987). Despite their promise, however, efforts to undertake comprehensive collaborations among community agencies and schools to reduce dropout rates have not proven successful (Wehlage *et al.*, 1992; White and Wehlage, 1995).

Ultimately, whether one believes such efforts will be successful and spread throughout the educational system depends on one's belief in the educational system as a catalyst for social change. On the one hand, there is a long-standing faith in the U.S. that education can serve to promote social change and improve the social standing of marginalized groups. On the other hand, there are critics of the status quo who point out that schools have historically tended to reinforce and perpetuate social class and racial/ethnic differences rather than eliminate them (Bowles and Gintis, 1976; Carnoy and Levin, 1985; see Pearl, Chapter 11 in this volume for a fuller treatment of the debate over various school reform efforts). Furthermore, Fine's (1991) work reminds us that the publicness of public schools is a notion that is neither unimportant nor to be neglected in the pursuit of solutions to the problem of dropouts. She cogently argues for the reclaiming of a public sphere that challenges school systems to embrace their constituents and broaden the discussion about how to ensure that young people moving through the system are left better off for having been a part of it. If we are to maintain the public sphere associated with schooling in the U.S., we certainly must foster students' ability to think critically about their social conditions and participate in efforts to improve such conditions.

The economic rationale for social intervention

No matter which category of educational approaches one believes is necessary to address the Chicano dropout problem, there is a strong economic rationale for increased social invest-ment in dropout programs and all programs designed to intervene in negative situations to support students' academic success (Levin, 1989a, 1989b). In general, the argument can be made on the basis that the benefits of increasing spending on dropout programs will far exceed the costs of funding such programs.

Unfortunately, few comprehensive studies have ever been conducted that have examined both the costs and benefits of social investment in dropout programs. Levin (1972) esti-mated that if expenditures on potential dropouts were increased by 50 percent to insure graduation from high school, then the benefits from higher earnings would exceed the costs by a ratio of 6:1. Or based simply on the increased taxes generated from those earnings, tax-payers would receive almost $2 for every dollar invested in dropout prevention. One study found that across the entire state of California, Latino dropouts (from grades 10 to 12) in just 1997 alone resulted in forgone returns of $2 billion using Levin's cost-benefit ratio of 6:1 for educational investments in dropouts (Rodríguez, 1999). Another version of Levin's approach applied to Texas also attempted to account for the additional social benefits of reduced crime, welfare, and training costs associated with dropouts and estimated that the benefits of dropout prevention would exceed the costs by a ratio of 9:1 (Ramírez and del Refugio Robledo, 1987).

In general, it appears that the benefits of social investment in dropout prevention and recovery programs would easily outweigh the costs, even if the benefits were restricted to increased tax receipts from the higher earnings associated with high school completion (Rumberger, 1990). And although Chicano high school graduates have, on average, lower earnings than non-Latino, White graduates, the social benefits of reducing the dropout rate for Chicanos would still outweigh the costs. Furthermore, as Valencia (Chapter 2, present book) has discussed, by investing in Chicano youths' education now, a stronger economic future for the good of our nation can possibly be enhanced.

Conclusions

Dropping out of high school is the unfortunate culmination of the schooling experiences of a significant number of Chicanos every year. While graduating from high school alone will not guarantee social and economic success, failure to graduate from high school will most likely deny it. Because so many Chicanos drop out of high school, the economic and social condition of the entire Chicano population is unlikely to improve until their educational status improves.

Many aspects of this problem warrant attention. First, we need to better assess the extent of the dropout problem and understand its underlying causes, and research clearly has a con-tinued role to play in trying to decipher the nature of this complex educational, indeed social, issue. Second, we need to better document the full range of individual and social con-sequences associated with dropping out, particularly given that the few estimates that have been done suggest significant returns to social investments in education (Levin, 1972;

Ramírez and del Refugio Robledo, 1987). Third, and most important, we need to get on with the development, evaluation, and implementation of programs and reforms to improve the educational outcomes and life prospects of not just Chicanos, but all students of color and marginalized populations. As is aptly pointed out by researchers at the National Council of La Raza (Fisher *et al.*, 1998), the challenge of Chicano (and other Latino) educational success is everyone's responsibility. Likewise, eliminating the myriad problems associated with Chicano dropouts is a goal to which educators, families, community members, business, government officials, and dropouts themselves must actively and positively contribute.

Notes

1 Specifically, the dropout rate among the population 25 years and older was 50.3 percent for Mexican-origin Hispanics, 29.7 percent for Cuban-origin Hispanics, and 13.8 percent for non-Hispanics. Thus, the difference in droput rates between Mexican-origin and Cuban-origin Hispanics was greater than the difference in dropout rates between Cuban-origin Hispanics and non-Hispanics (20.6 versus 15.9).

2 The extent to which general theories of student achievement can be used to explain the specific phenomenon of school dropout is rarely questioned. Yet, theories that may be useful in explaining differences in achievement outcomes such as test scores or grades may not necessarily be useful in explaining why some students drop out of school, especially to the extent that dropping out is unrelated to academic achievement as dropout theories suggest.

3 One specific example is the growth of "zero tolerance" (automatic discharge) for violations of school safety rules (Skiba and Peterson, 1999).

References

Alexander, K.L., Entwisle, D.R. and Dauber, S.L. (1994). *On the success of failure: A reassessment of the effects of retention in the early grades.* New York: Cambridge University Press.

Alexander, K.L., Entwisle, D.R. and Horsey, C. (1997). From first grade forward: Early foundations of high school dropouts. *Sociology of Education, 70,* 87–107.

American Council of Education (1999). *Who took the GED?* Washington, DC: American Council of Education.

Arellano, C.M., Chávez, E.L. and Deffenbacher, J.L. (1998). Alcohol use and academic status among Mexican American and White non-Hispanic adolescents. *Adolescence, 33,* 751–760.

Astone, N.M. and McLanahan, S.S. (1991). Family structure, parental practices and high school completion. *American Sociological Review, 56,* 309–584.

Astone, N.M. and McLanahan, S.S. (1994). Family structure, residential mobility, and school dropout: A research note. *Demography, 31,* 575–584.

Bachman, J.G., Green, S. and Wirtanen, I.D. (1971). *Dropping out: Problem or symptom?* Ann Arbor, MI: Institute for Social Research, University of Michigan.

Barrington, B.L. and Hendricks, B. (1989). Differentiating characteristics of high school graduates, dropouts, and nongraduates. *Journal of Educational Research, 82,* 309–319.

Berktold, J., Geis, S. and Kaufman, P. (1998). *Subsequent educational attainment of high school dropouts.* Washington, DC: U.S. Department of Education.

Berlin, G. and Sum, A. (1988). *Toward a more perfect union: Basic skills, poor families, and our economic future.* New York: Ford Foundation.

Bickel, R. and Papagiannis, G. (1988). Post-high school prospects and district-level dropout rates. *Youth & Society, 20,* 123–147.

Bishop, J.H. (1989). Why the apathy in American high schools? *Educational Researcher, 18,* 6–10.

Bowditch, C. (1993). Getting rid of troublemakers: High school disciplinary procedures and the production of dropouts. *Social Problems, 40,* 493–509.

Bowles, S. and Gintis, H. (1976). *Schooling in capitalist America: Education reform and the contradictions of economic life.* New York: Basic Books.

Brooks-Gunn, J., Duncan, G.J. and Aber, J.L. (1997). *Neighborhood poverty.* New York: Russell Sage Foundation.

Brooks-Gunn, J., Duncan, G.J., Klebanov, P.K. and Sealand, N. (1993). Do neighborhoods influence child and adolescent development? *American Journal of Sociology, 99,* 353–395.

Bryk, A.S., Lee, V.E. and Holland, P.B. (1993). *Catholic schools and the common good.* Cambridge, MA: Harvard University Press.

Bryk, A.S. and Thum, Y.M. (1989). *The effects of high school organization on dropping out: An exploratory investigation.* CPRE Research Report Series RR-012. New Brunswick, NJ: Center for Policy Research in Education, Rutgers.

Cairns, R.B., Cairns, B.D. and Necherman, H.J. (1989). Early school dropout: Configurations and determinants. *Child Development, 60,* 1437–1452.

Cameron, S.V. and Heckman, J.J. (1993). The nonequivalence of high school equivalents. *Journal of Labor Economics, 11,* 1–47.

Carbonaro, W.J. (1998). A little help from my friend's parents: Intergenerational closure and educational outcomes. *Sociology of Education, 71,* 295–313.

Cárdenas, J.A. (1997). *Texas school finance reform: An IDRA perspective.* San Antonio, TX: Intercultural Development Research Association.

Carnegie Foundation for the Advancement of Teaching. (1988). *An imperiled generation: Saving urban schools.* Princeton, NJ: Princeton University Press.

Carnoy, M. and Levin, H.M. (1985). *Schooling and work in the democratic state.* Stanford, CA: Stanford University Press.

Carter, D.J. and Wilson, R. (1997). *Minorities in higher education.* Washington, DC: American Council on Education.

Catterall, J.S. (1987). On the social costs of dropping out of school. *High School Journal, 71,* 19–30.

Chapa, J. and Valencia, R.R. (1993). Latino population growth, demographic characteristics, and educational stagnation: An examination of recent trends. *Hispanic Journal of Behavioral Sciences, 15,* 165–187.

Chubb, J.E. and Moe, T.M. (1990). *Politics, markets, and America's schools.* Washington, DC: Brookings Institution.

Clark, R.L. (1992). Neighborhood effects on dropping out of school. *High School Journal, 71,* 19–30.

Coleman, J.S. (1988). Social capital in the creation of human capital. *American Journal of Sociology, 94,* Supplement, S95–S120.

Coleman, J.S. and Hoffer, T. (1987). *Public and private high schools: The impact of communities.* New York: Basic Books.

Comer, J.P. (1988). Educating poor minority children. *Scientific American, 259,* 42–48.

Council of Chief State School Officers. (1987). *Children at risk: The work of the states.* Washington, DC: Council of Chief State School Officers.

Crane, J. (1991). The epidemic theory of ghettos and neighborhood effects on dropping out and teenage childbearing. *American Journal of Sociology, 96,* 1226–1259.

Danini Supik, J. and Johnson, R.L. (1999). *Missing: Texas's youth—dropout and attrition in Texas public high schools.* San Antonio, TX: Intercultural Development Research Association.

Dauber, S.L. and Epstein, J.L. (1989). *Parent attitudes and practices of parent involvement in inner-city elementary and middle schools.* Report 33. Baltimore, MD: Center for Research on Elementary and Middle Schools, Johns Hopkins University.

Delgado-Gaitán, C. (1988). The value of conformity: Learning to stay in school. *Anthropology and Education Quarterly, 19,* 354–381.

Delgado-Gaitán, C. (1990). *Literacy for empowerment: The role of parents in children's education.* New York: Falmer Press.

Denti, L.G. and Guerin, G. (1999). Dropout prevention: A case for enhanced early literacy efforts. *Clearing House, 72,* 231–235.

Dornbusch, S.M., Ritter, P.L., Leiderman, P.H., Roberts, D.F. and Fraleigh, M.J. (1987). The relation of parenting style to adolescent school performance. *Child Development, 58,* 1244–1257.

Dynrski, M. and Gleason, P. (1998). *How can we help? What we have learned from federal dropout-prevention programs.* Princeton, NJ: Mathematica Policy Research, Inc.

Ekstrom, R.B., Goertz, M.E., Pollack, J.M. and Rock, D.A. (1986). Who drops out of high school and why? Findings from a national study. *Teachers College Record, 87,* 356–373.

Enchautegui, M.E. (1997). Immigration and wage changes of high school dropouts. *Monthly Labor Review, 120,* 3–9.

Ensminger, M.E. and Slusacick, A.L. (1992). Paths to high school graduation or dropout: A longitudinal study of a first-grade cohort. *Sociology of Education, 65,* 95–113.

Evans, W.N. and Schwab, R.M. (1995). Finishing high school and starting college: Do Catholic schools make a difference? *Quarterly Journal of Economics, 110,* 941–974.

Fernández, R. M., Paulsen, R. and Hirano-Nakanishi, M. (1989). Dropping out among Hispanic youth. *Social Science Research, 18,* 21–52.

Fine, M. (1991). *Framing dropouts: Notes on the politics of an urban high school.* New York: State University of New York Press.

Finn, J.D. (1989). Withdrawing from school. *Review of Educational Research, 59,* 117–142.

Fisher, M., Pérez, S.M., González, B., Njus, J. and Kamasaki, C. (1998). *Latino education status and prospects: State of Hispanic America 1998.* Washington, DC: National Council of La Raza.

Gamoran, A. (1992). Social factors in education. In M.C. Alkin (Ed.), *Encyclopedia of Educational Research* (pp. 1222–1229). New York: Macmillan.

Gándara, P. (1994). Choosing higher education: Educationally ambitious Chicanos and the path to social mobility. *Education Policy Analysis Archives* [Online serial]. Available at: http://epaa.asu.edu/epaa/v2n8.html

Gándara, P., Larson, K., Mehan, H. and Rumberger, R. (1998). *Capturing Latino students in the academic pipeline.* Berkeley, CA: Chicano/Latino Policy Project.

Garnier, H.E., Stein, J.A. and Jacobs, J.K. (1997). The process of dropping out of high school: A 19-year perspective. *American Educational Research Journal, 34,* 395–419.

Gittell, M. (1998). *Strategies for school equity: Creating productive schools in a just society.* New Haven, CT: Yale University Press.

Goldschmidt, P. and Wang, J. (1999). When can schools affect dropout behavior? A longitudinal multilevel analysis. *American Educational Research Journal, 36,* 715–738.

Greene, M. (1995). *Releasing the imagination: Essays on education, the arts, and social change.* San Francisco: Jossey-Bass.

Grisson, J.B. and Shepard, L.A. (1989). Repeating and dropping out of school. In L.A. Shepard and M.L. Smith (Eds.), *Flunking grades: Research and policies on retention* (pp. 34–63). New York: Falmer Press.

Hallinan, M.T. and Williams, R.A. (1990). Students' characteristics and the peer-influence process. *Sociology of Education, 63,* 122–132.

Haney, W. (2000). The myth of the Texas miracle in education. *Education Policy Analysis Archives* [Online serial]. Available at: http://epaa.asu.edu/epaa/v8n41/

Hanushek, E.A. (1989). The impact of differential expenditures on school performance. *Educational Researcher, 18,* 45–51, 62.

Hanushek, E.A. (1997). Assessing the effects of school resources on student performance: An update. *Evaluation and Policy Analysis, 19,* 141–164.

Haveman, R., Wolfe, B. and Spaulding, J. (1991). Childhood events and circumstances influencing high school completion. *Demography, 28,* 133–157.

Hawley Miles, K. and Darling-Hammond, L. (1998). Rethinking the allocation of teaching resources: Some lessons from high-performing schools. *Educational Evaluation and Policy Analysis, 20,* 9–29.

Heath, S.B. and McLaughlin, M.W. (1987). A child resource policy: Moving beyond dependence on school and family. *Phi Delta Kappan, 68,* 576–580.

Hedges, L.V., Laine, R.D. and Greenwald, R. (1994). Does money matter? A meta-analysis of studies of the effects of differential school inputs on student outcomes. *Educational Researcher, 23,* 5–14.

Heubert, J.P. and Hauser, R.M. (Eds.). (1999). *High stakes: Testing for tracking, promotion, and graduation.* Committee on Appropriate Test Use, Board of Testing and Assessment, Commission on Behavioral and Social Sciences and Education, National Research Council. Washington, DC: National Academy Press.

Jimerson, S.R. (1999). On the failure of failure: Examining the association between early grade retention and education and employment outcomes during late adolescence. *Journal of School Psychology, 37,* 243–272.

Kao, G. and Tienda, M. (1995). Optimism and achievement: The educational performance of immigrant youth. *Social Science Quarterly, 76,* 1–19.

Kaufman, P. and Bradby, D. (1992). *Characteristics of at-risk students in the NELS: 1988.* Washington, DC: U.S. Government Printing Office.

Kaufman, P., Kwon, J.Y., Klein, S. and Chapman, C.D. (2000). *Dropout rates in the United States: 1999.* Washington, DC: U.S. Department of Education.

Klebanov, P.K., Brooks-Gunn, J. and Duncan, G.J. (1994). Does neighborhood and family poverty affects mother's parenting, mental health and social support. *Journal of Marriage and Family, 56*, 441–455.

Lareau, A. (1987). Social-class differences in family-school relationships: The importance of cultural capital. *Sociology of Education, 60*, 73–85.

Lee, V.T. and Burkam, D.T. (1992). Transferring high schools: An alternative to dropping out? *American Journal of Education, 100*, 420–453.

Lepper, M.R. and Greene, D. (1978). *The hidden cost of reward: New perspectives on the psychology of motivation.* Hillsdale, NJ: Erlbaum.

Levin, H.M. (1972). *The costs to the nation of inadequate education.* Study prepared for the Select Committee on Equal Educational Opportunity, U.S. Senate. Washington, DC: U.S. Government Printing Office.

Levin, H.M. (1988). Accelerating elementary education for disadvantaged students. In Council of Chief State School Officers (Eds.), *School success for students at risk* (pp. 209–226). Orlando, FL: Harcourt Brace Jovanovich.

Levin, H.M. (1989a). Economics of investment in educational disadvantaged students. *American Economic Review, 79*, 52–56.

Levin, H.M. (1989b). Financing the education of at-risk students. *Educational Evaluation and Policy Analysis, 11*, 47–60.

Lucas, T., Henze, R. and Donato, R. (1990). Promoting the success of Latino language-minority students: An exploratory study of six high schools. *Harvard Educational Review, 60*, 315–340.

Mahler, K. (1999). Dropping out of school increases chance of birth for Whites and Hispanics. *Family Planning Perspectives, 31*, 153.

Matute-Bianchi, M.E. (1986). Ethnic identities and patterns of school success and failure among Mexican-descent and Japanese-American students: An ethnographic analysis. *American Journal of Education, 95*, 233–255.

Mayer, S. (1991). How much does a high school's racial and socioeconomic mix affect graduation and teenage fertility rates? In C. Jencks and P. Peterson (Eds.), *The urban underclass* (pp. 321–341). Washington, DC: Brookings Institution.

McMillen, M.M., Kaufman, P. and Klein, S. (1997). *Dropout rates in the United States: 1995.* Washington, DC: U.S. Department of Education.

McNeal, R.B. (1997a). High school dropouts: A closer examination of school effects. *Social Science Quarterly, 78*, 209–222.

McNeal, R.B. (1997b). Are students being pulled out of high school? The effect of adolescent employment on dropping out. *Sociology of Education, 70*, 206–220.

McNeal, R.B. (1999). Parental involvement as social capital: Differential effectiveness on science achievement, truancy, and dropping out. *Social Forces, 78*, 117–144.

Mehan, H. (1997). *Contextual factors surrounding Hispanic dropouts.* Paper prepared for the Hispanic Dropout Project. Available online at: http://www.ncbe.gwu.edu/miscpubs/hdp/1

Mensch, B.S. and Kandel, D.B. (1988). Dropping out of high school and drug involvement. *Sociology of Education, 61*, 95–113.

Merchant, B. (1987). *Dropping out: A preschool through high school concern.* Policy Paper No. PP87–12–13. Berkeley, CA: Policy Analysis for California Education, School of Education, University of California, Berkeley.

Murnane, R.J., Willett, J.B. and Boudett, K.P. (1995). Do high school dropouts benefit from obtaining a GED? *Educational Evaluation and Policy Analysis, 17*, 133–147.

Murnane, R.J., Willett, J.B. and Boudett, K.P. (1997). Does acquisition of a GED lead to more training, post-secondary education, and military service for school dropouts? *Industrial and Labor Relations Review, 51*, 100–116.

Murnane, R.J., Willett, J.B. and Boudett, K.P. (1999). Do male dropouts benefit from obtaining a GED, post-secondary education, and training? *Evaluation Review, 23*, 475–502.

Murnane, R.J., Willet, J.B. and Tyler, J.H. (2000). Who benefits from obtaining a GED? Evidence from High School and Beyond. *Review of Economics and Statistics, 82*, 23–37.

National Research Council, Panel on High-Risk Youth. (1993). *Losing generations: Adolescents in high-risk settings.* Washington, DC: National Academy Press.

Neal, D. (1997). The effects of Catholic secondary schooling on educational achievement. *Journal of Labor Economics, 15*, 98–123.

Neumann, R.A. (1996). Reducing Hispanic dropout: A case of success. *Educational Policy, 10*, 22–45.

Newmann, F.M., Wehlage, G.G. and Lamborn, S.D. (1992). The significance and sources of student engagement. In F.M. Newmann (Ed.), *Student engagement and achievement in American secondary schools* (pp. 11–39). New York: Teachers College Press.

Olsen, L. and Edwards, R. (1982). *Push out, step out: A report on California's public school dropouts.* Oakland, CA: Open Road Issues Research Project, Citizens Policy Center.

Orfield, G., Bachmeier, M.D., James, D.R. and Eitle, T. (1997). Deepening segregation in American public schools: A special report from the Harvard project on school desegregation. *Equity & Excellence in Education, 30,* 5–24.

Orr, M.T. (1987). *Keeping students in school.* San Francisco: Jossey-Bass.

Pong, S. and Ju, D. (2000). The effects of change in family structure and income on dropping out of middle and high school. *Journal of Family Issues, 21,* 147–169.

Ramírez, D. and del Refugio Robledo, M. (1987). *The economic impact of the dropout problem* (IDRA Newsletter). San Antonio, TX: Intercultural Development Research Association.

Riehl, C. (1999). Labeling and letting go: An organizational analysis of how high school students are discharged as dropouts. In A.M. Pallas (Ed), *Research in sociology of education and socialization* (pp. 231–268). New York: JAI Press.

Roderick, M. (1993). *The path to dropping out.* Westport, CT: Auburn House.

Roderick, M. (1994). Grade retention and school dropout: Investigating the association. *American Educational Research Journal, 31,* 729–759.

Roderick, M., Bryk, A.S., Jacob, B.A., Easton, J.Q. and Allensworth, E. (1999). *Ending social promotion: Results from the first two years.* Chicago: Consortium on Chicago School Research.

Roderick, M., Nagaoka, J., Bacon, J. and Easton, J.Q. (2000). *Update: Ending social promotion.* Chicago: Consortium on Chicago School Research.

Rodríguez, G.M. (1997). *Getting to educational equity through school finance: The status of Latinos in California.* Unpublished doctoral dissertation, Stanford University, Stanford, CA.

Rodríguez, G.M. (1999, March). *Latino dropouts as a school finance issue: The loss of educational investment and its implications for equity.* Paper presented at the annual meeting of the American Education Finance Association, Seattle, WA.

Romo, H.D. and Falbo, T. (1996). *Latino high school graduation: Defying the odds.* Austin: University of Texas Press.

Rumberger, R.W. (1983). Dropping out of high school: The influence of race, sex, and family background. *American Educational Research Journal, 20,* 199–220.

Rumberger, R.W. (1987). High school dropouts: A review of issues and evidence. *Review of Educational Research, 57,* 101–121.

Rumberger, R.W. (1990). Second chance for high school dropouts: The costs and benefits of dropout recovery programs in the United States. In D. E. Inbar (Ed.), *The second chance in education* (pp. 227–250). New York: Falmer Press.

Rumberger, R.W. (1991). Chicano dropouts: A review of research and policy issues. In R.R.Valencia (Ed.), *Chicano school failure and success: Research and policy agendas for the 1990s* (pp. 64–89). The Stanford Series on Education and Public Policy. London: Falmer Press.

Rumberger, R.W. (1995). Dropping out of middle school: A multilevel analysis of students and schools. *American Educational Research Journal, 32,* 583–625.

Rumberger, R.W. (2000). *Who drops out of school and why.* Commissioned paper prepared for the National Academy of Sciences, Committee on Educational Excellence and Testing Equity Workshop. Paper presented at workshop on School Completion in Standards-Based Reform: Facts and Strategies, Washington, DC, July.

Rumberger, R.W. (2001). *Why students drop out and what can be done.* Paper prepared for the Conference, Dropouts in America: How Severe is the Problem? What Do We Know about Intervention and Prevention? Harvard University, January 13.

Rumberger, R.W., Ghatak, R., Poulos, G., Ritter, P.L. and Dornbusch, S.M. (1990). Family influences on dropout behavior: An exploratory study of a single high school. *Sociology of Education, 63,* 283–299.

Rumberger, R.W. and Lamb, S.P. (1998). *The early employment and further education experiences of high school dropouts: A comparative study of the United States and Australia.* Paper prepared for the Organization for Economic Co-operation and Development (OECD).

Rumberger, R.W. and Larson, K.A. (1998). Student mobility and the increased risk of high school drop out. *American Journal of Education, 107,* 1–35.

Rumberger, R.W., Larson, K.A., Palardy, G.A., Ream, R.K. and Schleicher, N.A. (1998). *The hazards of changing schools for California Latino adolescents*. Berkeley, CA: Chicano/Latino Policy Project.

Rumberger, R.W. and Thomas, S.L. (2000). The distribution of dropout and turnover rates among urban and suburban high schools. *Sociology of Education, 73,* 39–67.

Sander, W. and Krautmann, A.C. (1995). Catholic schools, dropout rates and educational attainment. *Economic Inquiry, 33,* 217–233.

Secada, W.G., Chávez-Chávez, R., García, E., Muñoz, C., Oakes, J., Santiago-Santiago, I. and Slavin, R. (1998). *No more excuses: The final report of the Hispanic dropout project*. Washington, DC: U.S. Department of Education.

Seltzer, M.H. (1994). Studying variation in program success: A multilevel modeling approach. *Evaluation Review, 18,* 342–361.

Shavelson, R., McDonnell, L., Oakes, J. and Carey, N. (1987). *Indicator systems for monitoring mathematics and science education*. Santa Monica, CA: RAND.

Skiba, R. and Peterson, R.(1999). The dark side of zero tolerance: Can punishment lead to safe schools? *Phi Delta Kappan, 80,* 372–376, 381–382.

Slavin, R.E. and Fashola, O.S. (1998). *Show me the evidence! Proven and promising programs for America's schools*. New York: Corwin Press.

Slavin, R.E. and Madden, N.A. (1989). What works for students at risk: A research synthesis. *Educational Leadership, 46,* 4–13.

Stanton-Salazar, R.D. (1997). A social capital framework for understanding the socialization of racial minority children and youths. *Harvard Educational Review, 67,* 1–40.

Steinberg, L., Lamborn, S.D., Dornbusch, S.M. and Darling, N. (1992). Impact of parenting practices on adolescent achievement: Authoritative parenting, school involvement, and encouragement to succeed. *Child Development, 63,* 1266–1281.

Steinberg, L., Blinde, P.L. and Chan, K.S. (1984). Dropping out among language minority youth. *Review of Educational Research, 54,* 113–132

Stern, D. (1986). *Dropout prevention and recovery in California*. Report prepared for the California State Department of Education. Berkeley, CA: School of Education, University of California, Berkeley.

Sui-Chu, E.H. and Willms, J.D. (1996). Effects of parental involvement on eighth-grade achievement. *Sociology of Education, 69,* 126–141.

Swaim, R.C., Beauvais, F., Chávez, E.L. and Oetting, E.R. (1997). The effect of school dropout rates on estimates of adolescent substance use among three racial/ethnic groups. *American Journal of Public Health, 87,* 51–55.

Swanson, C.B. and Schneider, B. (1999). Students on the move: Residential and educational mobility in America's schools. *Sociology of Education, 72,* 54–67.

Teachman, J.D., Paasch, K. and Carver, K. (1996). Social capital and dropping out of school early. *Journal of Marriage and the Family, 58,* 773–783.

Texas Education Agency. (1999). *Dropout definition, data collection, and methodology*. Austin, TX: Author. Available online at: http://www.tea.state.tx.us/research/dropout95.definition.html

Texas Education Agency. (2001). *Grade-level retention in Texas public schools, 1998–99* (GE01 601 07). Austin TX: Author. Available online at: http://www.tea.state.tx.us/research/pdfs/ret9899.pdf

Thornberry, T.P., Moore, M. and Christenson, R.L. (1985). The effect of dropping out of high school on subsequent criminal behavior. *Criminology, 23,* 3–18.

Trueba, H., Spindler, G. and Spindler, L. (Eds.). (1990). *What do anthropologists have to say about dropouts?* New York: Falmer Press.

Tyler, J.H., Murnane, R.J. and Willett, J.B. (2000). Estimating the labor market signaling value of the GED. *Quarterly Journal of Economics, 115,* 431–468.

U.S. Department of Commerce, Bureau of the Census. (1992). *Workers with low earnings*. Washington, DC: U.S. Government Printing Office.

U.S. Department of Commerce, Bureau of the Census. (1997). *Population projections: States, 1995–2025*. Series P-25–1131. Washington, DC: U.S. Government Printing Office.

U.S. Department of Commerce, Bureau of the Census. (1999a). *School enrollment—social and economic characteristics of students (update): October 1998*. Series P-20, No. 521. Washington, DC: U.S. Government Printing Office.

U.S. Department of Commerce, Bureau of the Census. (1999b). *Statistical abstract of the United States: 1999*. 119th edition. Washington, DC: U.S. Government Printing Office.

U.S. Department of Commerce, Bureau of the Census. (2000). *Hispanic population of the United States: March 1999.* Current Population Reports, Series P-20, No. 527. Washington, DC: U.S. Government Printing Office.

U.S. Department of Education, National Center for Education Statistics. (2000). *The condition of education 2000.* NCES 2000–062. Washington, DC: U.S. Government Printing Office.

U.S. Department of Education, National Center for Education Statistics. (2001). *Digest of Education Statistics, 2000.* Washington, DC: U.S. Government Printing Office.

U.S. General Accounting Office. (1987). *School dropouts: Survey of local programs.* GAO/HRD-87–108. Washington, DC: U.S. Government Printing Office.

Valencia, R.R. (2000). *Legislated school reform via high-stakes testing: The case of pending anti-social promotion legislation in Texas and its likely impact on racial/ethnic minority students.* Commissioned paper for the National Academy of Sciences Committee on Educational Excellence and Testing Equity. Paper presented at the National Academy of Sciences workshop on School Completion in Standards-Based Reform, Washington, DC, July.

Valencia, R.R. and Solórzano, D.G. (1997). Contemporary deficit thinking. In R.R. Valencia (Ed.), *The evolution of deficit thinking: Educational thought and practice* (pp. 160–210). The Stanford Series on Education and Public Policy. London: Falmer Press.

Valencia, R.R. and Suzuki, L.A. (2001). *Intelligence testing and minority students: Foundations, performance factors, and assessment issues.* Thousand Oaks, CA: Sage.

Valenzuela, A. (1999). *Subtractive schooling: U.S.–Mexican youth and the politics of caring.* Albany: State University of New York Press.

Velez, W. (1989). High school attrition among Hispanic and non-Hispanic White youths. *Sociology of Education, 62,* 119–133.

Verstegen, D.A. (1994). Reforming American education policy for the 21st century. *Educational Administration Quarterly, 30,* 365–390.

Walberg, H.J., Bakalis, M.J., Bast, J.L. and Baer, S. (1989). Reconstructing the nation's worst schools. *Phi Delta Kappan, 70,* 802–805.

Wehlage, G.G. and Rutter, R.A. (1986). Dropping out: How much do schools contribute to the problem? *Teachers College Record, 87,* 374–392.

Wehlage, G.G, Rutter, R.A., Smith, G.A., Lesko, N. and Fernández, R.R. (1989). *Reducing the risk: Schools as communities of support.* New York: Falmer Press.

Wehlage, G.G., Smith, G. and Lipman, P. (1992). Restructuring urban schools: The New Futures experience. *American Educational Research Journal, 29,* 51–93.

White, J.A. and Wehlage, G.G. (1995). Community collaboration: If it is such a good idea, why is it so hard to do? *Educational Evaluation and Policy Analysis, 17,* 23–38.

Wilson, W.J. (1987). *The truly disadvantaged: The inner city, the underclass, and public policy.* Chicago: The University of Chicago Press.

Part II

Language perspectives on Chicano student achievement

5 Language, public policy, and schooling: a focus on Chicano English language learners

Eugene E. García and Ann-Marie Wiese

Today, one in three children nationwide is from an ethnic or racial minority group, one in seven speaks a language other than English at home, and one in fifteen is born outside the U.S. (García, 2001). The linguistic and culture diversity of America's schools population has increased dramatically during the past decade, and is expected to increase even more in the future (see Valencia, Chapter 2 of this volume). The concept of "minority" group as a "marker" for Hispanics will become obsolete. Moreover, educating children from Chicano immigrant and non-immigrant families is a major concern of school systems across the country. For many of these children, American education is not a successful experience. While one-tenth of non-Hispanic White students leave school without a diploma, one-third of Hispanics and two-thirds of immigrant students drop out of school (National Research Council, 1997). Confronted with this dismal reality, administrators, teachers, parents, and policymakers (executive branch, legislative branches, and the courts) have urged each other to do something different—change teaching methods, adopt new curricula, allocate more funding, and hold educational institutions accountable. Such actions at the federal and state level have and will continue to affect Chicano students in general and language minority students in particular.

The present discussion is our attempt to identify and discuss federal, state, and local policy and to help further our understanding of how such declarations attempt to either disadvantage or enhance the education of Chicano students. Our emphasis is on Chicano students that may be identified as non-English speakers. We will refer to them as English language learners (ELLs). The pattern of the education for these populations in the U.S. is a continuous story of poor achievement. It need not be that way in the future. Educational institutions today must address issues of both equity and excellence. Our educational endeavor aimed at low-achieving students has been to provide equal educational opportunity. The challenge today is for those opportunities to produce excellence in academic outcomes. This is how our three-decade effort in serving these students must change: from compensatory educational "inputs" to academically successful "outputs."

Who are these students?

In contrast to racial, ethnic, and linguistic diversity among students, the vast majority of teachers and administrators are White and speak English as their native and only language. Many are experiencing the daunting personal and professional challenge in adapting in adulthood to a degree of diversity that did not exist during their childhood.

The average teacher and administrator in his 40s and 50s grew up in the 1950s and 1960s. People who were raised in the postwar period, before desegregation, were likely to have attended school with those of their own racial/ethnic group. Not until young adulthood did they encounter the civil rights movement and other expressions of racial/ethnic presence on a national level. Nor did they experience the swift increases in diversity that have occurred recently. They and their parents grew up expecting a much different world than they now face. The parents and teachers of today's teacher grew up in the 1930s and the 1940s, after the period of massive immigration from Europe to the U.S. had ended. Today's senior teacher entered school at a time when the U.S. had a much larger proportion of foreign-born persons than today. This diversity, however, was perhaps not so evident because of segregated racial/ethnic enclaves in housing and schooling, and less widespread mass communications. Over the course of their lifetime, people now in their 70s experienced decreasing diversity. The melting pot ideology matched their own observations; the children of immigrants abandoned their native language and culture as they were urged to become 100 percent Americans.

The 30-year period straddling the mid-century mark was an anomaly in U.S. history. Until the 1930s, the story of the U.S. was a tale of immigration. The grandparents of today's teacher, who grew up in the early 1900s and many of whom were immigrants themselves, experienced increasing racial/ethnic and linguistic diversity during their formative years. To these Americans, the immigration movement that brought their ancestors to the country is a closed chapter, part of their national past. But from the perspective of the entire spectrum of American history, immigration has been the norm rather than the exception. Two generations of adults have grown up in an unusually low immigration period, an environment that has shaped our perceptions of the country. The new reality is that the America of the 2000s will resemble the America of the 1900s more than the America of the 1950. Today's kindergartners will experience increasing diversity over their lifetime, as the generation of their great-grandparents did.

From 1900 to 1910, nearly 9 million immigrants entered the U.S., increasing the entire population by 10 percent. In the 1980s, about the same number of immigrants entered the U.S., but they accounted for only a 4 percent increase in a now much larger U.S. population. In the early decades of this century, and back as far as 1850, as many as one in seven people in the U.S. were foreign-born. The current rate of one in thirteen is high only in comparison to the low immigration decades of the 1950s and 1960s, when one in twenty Americans were foreign-born. By 2020, when today's kindergartners are in the work force, the foreign-born population of the U.S. is again projected to reach one in seven people (García, 2001).

Because the U.S. is so closely identified with the English language, many people assume that Anglo Americans have always formed the majority group in U.S. society. But the 1990 Census reveals that only 13 percent of Americans claim English ancestry (Waggoner, 2000). They are outnumbered by the 15 percent whose families originated in Ireland, many of whom did not speak English as a native language. An additional 5 percent identify their ancestry as "American;" many of these are Scottish Americans whose families have been in the U.S. for nine or ten generations. Thus, at most, about one-third of Americans trace their ancestry to the various cultures and languages of Great Britain.

Today, nearly one in five Americans live in households in which a language other than English is spoken (Waggoner, 2000). Half of these households are Spanish-speaking; the next most common languages are French, German, Italian, and Chinese. Educating students from immigrant families, particularly Hispanic immigrant families, may seem like an entirely new challenge, but it is not; such students have always been in American schools in large numbers. Throughout most of U.S. history, one in four or five White Americans grew up in an immigrant family.

What worked in the past may not work now

One mission of educators is to prepare young people for an occupational life. The economic environment in which today's students will seek employment has changed radically in the past few decades. Manufacturing jobs used to provide a good living for racial/ethnic minority group members and for immigrants. Most jobs in the industrial sector did not require a high level of education, or academic competence in English; however, those jobs have disappeared. The new economy will require workers who have more than basic skills; employees must be able to think critically and engage in group decision making, communicate effectively orally and in writing, and be able to adapt to changing conditions by learning new skills. A larger proportion of jobs in the future will require the kind of educational preparation that has traditionally been provided to only the top students (Tyack and Cuban, 1995).

The American economy is now intertwined with the global marketplace; workers who can interact easily with people of different cultural and linguistic backgrounds will be prized. Even the domestic workplace that today's students will enter is changing as employees and customers are becoming more diverse. Business leaders are well aware that most of their new employees will be minorities and women. Observers of American business trends comment that many companies have gone beyond debating whether they need to change; they are now actively managing diversity. If one of the purposes of education is to train young people for productive work lives, then schools will need to prepare all students for employment in a more racially, ethnically, culturally, and linguistically diverse occupational environment than in the past.

One size doesn't fit all students

Students from immigrant families are often defined by the characteristics they share—a lack of English fluency. But such a definition masks their diversity, and underestimates the challenge facing schools. Schools serve students who are new immigrants, ignorant of American life beyond what they have seen in movies, as well as Chicanos, African Americans, Asian Americans, and American Indians whose families have lived in the U.S. for generations. Students representing dozens of native languages may attend a single school; in some school districts more than 125 languages are spoken by students (Wagonner, 2000). In many schools, a majority of the students come from immigrant or racial/ethnic minority families. Some schools face a mobility problem; student turnover is high and the racial/ethnic mix shifts radically from year to year (Rumberger, 1995).

Along with linguistic diversity comes diversity in culture, religion, and academic preparation. Some students visit their home country frequently, while others lack that opportunity. Some immigrant students have had excellent schooling in their home country before arriving in the U.S. Others have had their schooling interrupted by war, and still others have never attended school. Some are illiterate in their own language, and some have languages that were only oral until recently; others come from cultures with long literary traditions. The complexity of the task for schools can be illustrated by five hypothetical students from two families. Each of these students has very different needs. The Escalonas immigrated from Colombia and the Nguyens from Vietnam. All four parents work together on an electronics assembly line. The Escalonas are both college graduates, and taught high school math in their homeland. The Nguyens were farmers in their native country, and attended school through the fourth grade:

María Escalona—8th grade:
She had excellent schooling through the 7th grade in Colombia. The math and the science curriculum in her school were more advanced than in the U.S. system. She studied English in school for three years.

Raul Escalona—5th grade:
He had good prior schooling, but had not yet begun to study English. Because he is only 10, his academic mastery of Spanish is incomplete.

Teresita Escalona—kindergarten:
She attended preschool in Colombia, and knows the Spanish alphabet as well as songs, stories, numbers, shapes, and colors.

Binh Nguyen—10th grade:
He has good schooling through the 7th grade, but has attended school only sporadically in refugee camps since then.

Tui Nguyen—3rd grade:
She has had no prior formal education. Taught by her brother, she can read and write a little Vietnamese.

Binh and Tui have had little exposure to English. They will have a few classmates who speak their native language, but many whose native language is Spanish.

The differences between these students—their age and entry into the U.S. school, the quality of their prior schooling, their own and their parents/family/community native language, and number of native language compatriots in their class, their parents' education and English language skills, and their family history and current circumstances—will affect their academic success much more than their common lack of English.

Federal policy: the Bilingual Education Act (1968)

The immediately preceding discussion has attempted to lay a foundation for understanding the demographic complexity of the Chicano ELL. This discussion turns now to educational policy: first, federal executive, legislative, and court articulations, and, second, state articulations in recent initiatives (California's Proposition 227 and Arizona's Proposition 203).

Throughout the nation's history, Americans have maintained an intense faith in education. For over 150 years, "Americans have transformed their cultural anxieties and hopes into dramatic demands for educational reform" (Tyack and Cuban, 1995, p. 1). Although most groups made some advances in the quality of schooling during the first half of the 20th century, during the 1960s certain groups called attention to the deprivation and discrimination experienced by "disadvantaged" groups. As Tyack and Cuban explained, African Americans, feminists, Hispanic Americans, and American Indians, and parents of disabled children entered the arena of educational politics, and in the process created new goals and strategies of school reform. In particular, they moved issues of equity to the forefront of educational policy, as created in the legislatures and the courts.

The U.S. Congress set a minimum standard for the education of language minority students with Title VI of the 1964 Civil Rights Act, which prohibits discrimination on the grounds of race, color, or national origin in programs or activities receiving federal financial assistance. In similar fashion, the subsequent passage of the Equal Educational Opportunities Act of 1974 (EEOA) made Title VI of the Civil Rights Act applicable to all educational institutions but did not prescribe a specific remedy. The EEOA was an effort by the U.S. Congress to define what constitutes a denial of constitutionally guaranteed equal educational opportunity. The EEOA provides:

> No state shall deny equal educational opportunities to an individual on account of his or her race, color, sex, or national origin by the failure of an educational agency to take appropriate action to overcome language barriers that impede equal participation by its students in its instructional programs.
>
> (EEOA, 1974, Sec. 1703 [f], p. 136)

Still, while Title VI of the Civil Rights Act and the EEOA focused attention on educational equity and access, they did not define "equality" for policymakers. As the Office of Education Survey of Equality of Educational Opportunity stated, the definition of equality "will be an outcome of the interplay of a variety of interests and will certainly differ from time to time as these interests differ" (Coleman, 1968, p. 27).[1]

On six occasions the U.S. Congress has passed specific legislation related to the education of language minority students (1968, 1974, 1978, 1984, 1988, 1994). The Bilingual Education Act (1968, Title VII of the Elementary and Secondary Education Act of 1965) serves as a guide for state and local policy regarding language minority students. Since its inception, the primary aim of the BEA has been "providing meaningful and equitable access for English-language learners to the curriculum, rather than serving as an instrument of language policy for the nation through the development of their native languages" (August and Hakuta, 1997, p. 16). In other words, the BEA has aimed to address equal educational opportunity for language minority students, and has not evolved as formal attention to shape language policy. The initial Title VII legislation built upon the Civil Rights Act of 1964 and originated as part of the "war on poverty" legislation. The legislation was primarily a "crisis intervention" (García and González, 1995), a political strategy to funnel poverty funds to the second largest minority group in the Southwest, Mexican Americans (Casanova, 1991). The BEA was intended as a demonstration program to meet the educational needs of low-income, limited-English-speaking children.

The "war on poverty" legislation was largely based on the cultural deprivation theory (Erickson, 1987; Riessman, 1962), or culture of poverty theory, which dominated educational psychology (see Pearl, 1997). Instead of genetic inferiority, environmental factors were viewed as the main reasons for the poor achievement of minority children. In theory, specific types of attitudes, language styles, work values, and other behaviors dampened the abilities necessary to overcome poverty. This implicitly encouraged a subtractive form of bilingual education, where the native language and culture were not viewed as resources to build on, but as barriers to overcome (Cummins, 1991). Bilingual education was a remedial effort, aimed at overcoming students' "language deficiencies," and these "compensatory efforts were considered to be a sound educational response to the call for equality of educational opportunity" (Navarro, 1990, p. 291).

No particular program of instruction was recommended. Financial assistance was to be provided to local educational agencies (LEAs) "to develop and carry out new and imaginative . . . programs" (BEA, 1968, Sec. 702).[2] Grants were awarded to local educational agencies or institutions of higher education working in collaboration with local education agencies to (a) plan and develop programs "designed to meet the special educational needs" of language minority students, (b) provide pre-service training to personnel such as teachers and teacher aides, and (c) establish, maintain, and operate programs (Sec. 704). Among the approved activities were the following programs: bilingual education, history and culture, early childhood education, and adult education for parents. Although bilingual education was mentioned as an approved activity, the legislation did not specify the role of native language instruction.

BEA reauthorization of 1974: a definition of bilingual education

In line with the legislation and litigation that provided the initial foundation for the Bilingual Education Act, the 1974 reauthorization specifically incorporated language to address equal educational opportunity and linked it to bilingual education programs: "the Congress declares it the policy of the United States to establish equal educational opportunity for all children (A) to encourage the establishment and operation . . . of education programs using bilingual education practices, techniques, and methods" (BEA, 1974, Sec. 702[a)]. For the first time, bilingual education was defined as "instruction given in, and study of, English, and, to the extent necessary to allow a child to progress effectively through the educational system, the native language" (Sec. 703 [a][4][A][i]).

The inclusion of native language instruction in the definition of bilingual education was influenced by bilingual programs in Dade County, Florida which were founded to address the needs of the first wave of professional-class Cuban immigrants.[3] The Cuban immigrants saw themselves as temporary residents of the United States who would soon return to their country, and therefore, wanted to preserve their culture and language. Thus, the bilingual programs encouraged Spanish language maintenance and English language acquisition (Casanova, 1991). At the same time, the success of the programs gave encouragement to the idea of bilingual education as a method of instruction for students from disadvantaged backgrounds (Hakuta, 1986). Native language instruction could serve as a bridge to English language acquisition, by providing equal access to the curriculum until students were English proficient. While the BEA acknowledged the role native language could play in supporting a transition to English, it did not promote bilingual education as an enrichment program where the native language was maintained.

Other changes in the legislation included eliminating poverty as a requirement, the specific mention of American Indian children as an eligible population, and a provision for English-speaking children to enroll in bilingual education programs to "acquire an understanding of the cultural heritage of the children of limited English-speaking ability" (Sec. 703 [a][4][B]). In addition to the grant categories listed in 1968, new programs were funded including a graduate fellowship program for study in the field of training teachers for bilingual education programs, a program for planning and providing technical assistance to the development of programs, and a program to develop and disseminate instructional materials.

BEA reauthorizations of 1978, 1984, and 1988: special alternative instructional programs

During the years of the next three reauthorizations, public opinion reflected a strong aversion to the use of federal funds to preserve minority languages and cultures, claiming that federal funds should focus on English language acquisition and assimilation into the mainstream (Crawford, 1999). As mentioned in the introduction to this chapter, during times of peak immigration there is a decline in the acceptance of bilingualism. Increased immigration tends to create a feeling of instability, perhaps due to the unsettling aura of change, apparent increased job competition, or fear of an inability to communicate with immigrants. This feeling of instability often leads to a fear of the unknown and an insistence on using the status quo language, English (Fitzgerald, 1993; Portes and Rumbaut, 1996). From 1981 to 1990, around 7,388,062 people immigrated to the United States; this represented a 63 percent increase in the immigrant population as compared to the previous decade (García and González, 1995). Most new immigrants were not viewed as temporary residents like the Cuban community of Dade County in the early 1970s. New immigrants were here to stay, which precipitated the danger of separatism. Preservation of minority languages could very possibly lead to the fragmentation of American society. Bilingual education programs that encouraged native language maintenance would only foster children's allegiance to minority languages and cultures, and this was not an acceptable responsibility for schools. Language maintenance should only be carried out by families, churches, and other institutions outside the school (Casanova, 1991; Crawford, 1999).

The 1978 reauthorization of the BEA added language to the 1974 definition of bilingual education that specified instruction in English should "allow a child to achieve competence in the English language" (Sec. 703 [a][4][A][i]) and when enrolling English-speaking children "the objective of the program shall be to assist children of limited English proficiency to improve their English language skills" (Sec. 703 [a][4][B]). Other changes in the legislation included the following: Parents were given a greater role in program planning and operation; personnel were required to be proficient in the language of instruction and English; and grant recipients were to demonstrate how the program would continue once federal funds were withdrawn.

The 1984 reauthorization of the BEA marked a shift from mandating only bilingual programs to the acceptance of English-only programs. Transitional bilingual education programs were defined as providing "structured English-language instruction, and, to the extent necessary to allow a child to achieve competence in the English language, instruction in the child's native language" (Sec. 703 [a][4][A]). So, the purpose of native language instruction is to support transition to English instruction, and the allocation of funding reflected a preference for this program: 60 percent of Title VII funds were allocated to the various grant categories, and 75 percent of these funds were reserved for transitional bilingual education programs. In contrast, developmental bilingual education programs were defined as providing "structured English-language instruction and instruction in a second language. Such programs shall be designed to help children achieve competence in English and a second language, while mastering subject matter skills" (Sec. 703 [a][5][A]). So, the goal of this program included native language and English language competence, yet no specific funding allocations were specified.

In addition to delineating these two bilingual education programs, the grant categories included special alternative instructional programs (SAIPS) that did not require the use of native language and 4 percent of Title VII funds were allocated to SAIPS. These programs were created in recognition "that in some school districts establishment of bilingual education programs may be administratively impractical" (Sec. 702 [a][7]). While the 1984 grant categories remained the same for the 1988 reauthorization, funds allocated to SAIPS were increased to 25 percent. Furthermore, the legislation included a three-year limit on an individual's participation in transitional bilingual education programs or SAIPS: "No student may be enrolled in a bilingual program . . . for a period of more than 3 years" (BEA, 1988, Sec. 7021 [d][3][A]).

BEA reauthorization of 1994: bilingual education, language enhancement, and systemic reform

Too often in the heat of legislation and the political process, policy development is highly centralized in the domains of various interest groups and professional policymakers. Therefore, the 1994 BEA national policy initiatives were crafted in consultation with diverse constituencies. For linguistically and culturally diverse communities, these included the National Association for Bilingual Education, the Mexican American Legal Defense and Educational Fund, which has made specific legislative recommendations of major proportion, and other educational groups, which have made recommendations related to their own interests and expertise.

Of particular significance in the reauthorization, was the work of the Stanford Working Group. This group, funded by the Carnegie Corporation of New York consulted widely with various individuals representing a broad spectrum of theoretical, practical, and policy significant expertise. In both published reports and forums, they put forward a comprehensive analysis and articulated precise recommendations for policy and legislation related to language minority students. In the final report, the Stanford Working Group set forth a series of recommendations for Title I and Title VII of the Elementary and Secondary Education Act as part of a comprehensive plan for system-wide reform. The following recommendations regarding the BEA, were among several: (a) reformulate the types of grants awarded to encourage innovation and limit fragmentation of services; (b) give priority to program applications that promote full bilingual development; (c) create a new part of the legislation to support language conservation and restoration efforts in schools and school districts serving American Indian students; and (d) enhance the BEA's "lighthouse" role in language policy, particularly in promoting and maintaining language resources. As discussed below, the 1994 reauthorization reflected the recommendations set forth by the Stanford Working Group. The 1994 reauthorization of the BEA still aimed to "to ensure equal educational opportunity for all children and youth and to promote educational excellence . . . for children and youth of limited English proficiency" (BEA, 1994, Section 7102 [c]). In particular, the reauthorization introduced new grant categories, gave preference to programs that promote bilingualism and emerged from a larger systemic reform effort.

The premise of local control

While federal educational policy provides national goals for language minority students, local education agencies are responsible for their implementation. The local education agency is the locus of control for design and implementation of programs and is eligible for the following grant categories: program development and implementation, enhancement, comprehensive school, and system-wide improvement.[4] The 25 percent cap on funding for SAIPS was retained in the 1994 legislation, but with a special provision for exceeding it if an applicant could demonstrate that developing and implementing a bilingual education program was not feasible due to the language diversity of the students or the lack of qualified instructional personnel despite documented efforts. While state education agencies must approve the grant application before submission, they play no official role in the grant's implementation. In addition, substantial efforts were made to comprehensively package funds by allowing Title VII funds to be used collaboratively with funds from Title I, Goals 2000, other ESEA programs, state education agencies, and local school districts.

While the legislation did not prescribe particular methods of instruction, each LEA should still create a program based on the general goals of the legislation. Then, it must justify particular strategies to the federal government if it is to receive funds. As the LEA articulates a program of instruction, Title VII holds the school accountable to its own goals, assessments, and evaluation procedures to determine whether language minority students are acquiring English and improving academically. Federal policy recognized both the complexity of educational responses for language minority students and the need for locally designed and implemented programs (García, 1998a). Therefore, Title VII turned to the local education agency as the locus of control in guaranteeing equal access to education for language minority students. Federal policy stands as a beacon, stating the guiding principles, providing guidance on appropriate practices, and providing assistance with developing effective programs of instruction. More specifically, the supports include the dissemination of research findings, descriptions of successful Title VII programs, and technical assistance through regional centers (García, 1998b).

Bilingualism as a priority

In considering grant applications, Title VII uses the goals delineated in the legislation as a guide. The grants authorized are to help language minority children "develop proficiency in English, and to the extent possible, their native language" (Sec. 7111 [2][A]). Furthermore, Title VII gives "priority to applications which provide for the development of bilingual proficiency both in English and another language for all participating students" (Sec. 7116 [i][1]). Overall, LEAs have the right to develop English language acquisition and academic achievement of ELLs within the context of their particular needs and resources, but priority will be given to programs that develop bilingual competencies.

Goals 2000: systemic reform and national standards

The 1994 reauthorization of Title VII reflected the guiding ideology of two major legislative initiatives, Goals 2000 and the Improving America's School Act (1994). These legislative initiatives came together to promote and support equality and quality of education for all students. As part of a larger systemic reform effort, Title VII programs would help language minority children "meet the same challenging State content standards and challenging State student performance standards expected for all children and youth" (Sec. 7111 [2][B]). In fact grant applicants must specify how the Title VII program "is coordinated with other programs under this Act, the Goals 2000: Educate America Act and other Acts as appropriate" (Sec. 7116 [g][1][B][ii]). Goals 2000 legislation provides resources for all states to develop challenging voluntary standards based on a broad consensus process for what all students need to know and be able to do.

Goals 2000 expanded upon the National Education Goals of 1990 and made them law.[5] These eight National Education Goals serve as benchmarks for state and local agendas.[6] Each state is encouraged on a voluntary basis to develop content standards, performance standards, and an action plan to help students achieve both sets of standards. In fact, Goals 2000 is "the prism" through which amendments to the ESEA were considered (Riley, 1995). The three major components of this systemic reform effort included the following: (a) curriculum frameworks which establish what children should know and provide direction for upgrading the quality of content and instruction for all schools; (b) alignment with related state educational policies; and (c) schools are given the resources, flexibility, and responsibility for preparing students to learn. This new federal policy provided a vision for reform, and at the same time, contained few prescriptions. There were no new mandates on states or localities; burdensome federal regulations were waived. This was very different from prior federal policy that focused on stringent fiscal process regulations to ensure conformity to practice.

The Improving America's Schools Act

The ESEA was reauthorized as the Improving America's Schools Act (IASA). The IASA was designed to work within the framework of Goals 2000 while focusing on student populations that demonstrate a pattern of poor academic achievement. In the past, "the remedial, 'basic skills' focus of many compensatory education programs, designed to provide additional help for poor, educationally disadvantaged students, limited-English-proficient students, and others, has often led to the use of watered-down curricula taught in uninspired, rote-oriented ways" (Smith and Scoll, 1995, p. 393). Therefore, while the IASA continued to target additional educational supports to particular students, these students were held to the same content performance standards as all other children. The intent was to help the students reach the challenging standards, and consequently, raise the level of access and achievement throughout the nation.

In the past, federal government funds created narrow categorical programs, the accumulation of which, each with separate rules, was beginning to negatively affect education (Riley, 1995). Consequently, the IASA granted schools flexibility in how they structure programs and funds. Of particular significance was the call by the Carnegie Foundation for the Advancement Teaching in its report, *The Basic School: A Community for Learning.* That work acknowledged the notion that key components of an effective school must be brought together in an integrated and cohesive manner. Good schools are effective teaching and learning communities that place a high priority on a cohesive approach to language and knowledge. *The Basic School* is based on best practice, presents a comprehensive plan for educational renewal, and has as its goal the improvement of learning for every child. This same idea was at the core of new federal education policy in 1994. For example, a school was, and still is, encouraged to integrate funds from Title I and Title VII in order to best serve all students. Allowing categorical program funds to serve all children in a school "will help erase the stigma and lower standards of many pullout programs" (Smith and Scoll, 1995, p. 398). The development of standards, the realignment of educational systems in support of those standards, and the placement of the ultimate responsibility, flexibility, and resources at the local level will take time. These are long-term challenges for every teacher, parent, and school administrator in every state and local community.

Specific issues in the proposed reauthorization

Here, we discuss particular concerns that arise from the proposed reauthorization.

Three-year goal for LEP students to reach English proficiency

The Department of Education has been articulating this three-year goal in its conceptualization of the reauthorization. The initial articulation of this three-year goal was made by the Administration as a response to Proposition 227 in California that has limited special instruction for limited-English-proficient (LEP) students to one year. The White House and the Department of Education have insisted that a goal of learning English within three years is "reasonable." The Department's current proposal has continued to stress this three-year goal throughout their ESEA reauthorization. The two most recent reiterations of this policy appeared in the FY 2000 budget and the Administration's proposed ESEA reauthorization.

FY 2000—the budget summary specifically states:

> On April 27, 1998, Secretary Riley announced a 3-year goal for preparing LEP students to transfer to all-English classroom. The Department intends to work with school districts to ensure that the English language skills of LEP students are assessed after they have participated in bilingual and English as a second language program from three years.
>
> (p. 17)

- Administration's ESEA Reauthorization Proposal—On February 3, the Department broadened from the 3-year goal as stated in the budget and embedded its goal into a larger policy of accountability for LEP students—"increase accountability for all programs so that students reach English proficiency within 3 years" (p. 19).

A 3-year goal—irrespective of how it is articulated—quickly becomes a presumption, then a requirement, and ultimately a sanction. The concerns are significant:

- A 3-year goal for English proficiency will drive curriculum in a way that focuses resources, staff, material and accountability on English language acquisition and at the expense of other content areas such as math, science, social science, etc.
- English proficiency for school-age children goes beyond conversational command of the English language. In order for LEP students to achieve comparable to their native-English speaking peers, they need academic mastery of the English language that is cognitively more demanding than merely conversational skills.
- Research indicates that LEP students may achieve, in two to three years, a significant level of fluency in conversational English but five to seven years are needed to develop the cognitive level of a native speaker. The vast majority of research indicates that the time needed to achieve proficiency in a second language can range between three to seven years. The Administration has chosen to embrace a goal that is merely at the lower extreme of such a range.

Inappropriate assessment of LEP students

During the National Voluntary Tests debate, the Administration took a position against appropriate reading assessments for LEP students. The initial proposal called for testing students' reading skills by grade 4. Yet after the debate ensued over how to test LEP students who may know how to read in their native language (other than English) the Administration narrowed the focus to "reading *in English*." In so doing, the Administration's position was that they would not support testing in any language, other than English.

As part of the proposed accountability system for ESEA reauthorization, the Administration is recommending a series of mandated assessments for LEP students in Title I and in Title VII:

- A reading diagnostic assessment would, apparently, be required for all Title I students. It is unclear if for LEP students this test could be in their native language.
- An annual test of English proficiency would be administered to LEP students served by Title I and Title VII.
- LEP students who have been in U.S. schools for three years would be required to take the state assessments *in English, without any accommodation* (*for purposes of Title I accountability*).

The proposed battery of assessments for LEP student accountability will be more harmful to these children, rather than helpful in accurately assessing their academic progress. First, in the 1994 reauthorization of Title I, policy moved away from excessive testing of students, but now the proposal apparently would excessively test only the LEP students. The disparate treatment of these students raises concerns for their civil rights. Second, under the guise of inclusion, the Administration would be imposing the inappropriate assessment of LEP students. Requiring assessments in English after attending U.S. schools for three years has no basis in sound educational practice. Assessments should be tied to the type of instruction the child is receiving, not to an arbitrary time limit. Further, prohibiting the use of necessary accommodations is inconsistent with the *Standards for Educational and Psychological Testing* (American Educational Research Association *et al.*, 1999). The National Assessment of Educational Progress currently allows for the necessary accommodations for LEP students as well as students with disabilities—another glaring inconsistency with the Administration's proposal affecting LEP students. Third, the inappropriate assessment of LEP students will generate faulty information about their academic performance. An LEP student may be reading at grade level in his/her native language but given that the reading test will be administered in English, the student's reading skills will not be tested; instead, the score will reflect the student's ability to understand English. The assessment results will go into the student's permanent record with the potential of being used for high-stakes decisions regarding the child's future educational opportunities. Fourth, under the Department's proposal the accountability for academic progress for LEP students is narrowly focused on English language, when these children need to reach academically proficient levels in math, science, and other content areas. Finally, this misdirected education goal for LEP students is not only limited to those served by Title VII but also is spreading this low expectation across all of the ESEA programs, particularly Title I.

The federal courts

The 1974 United States Supreme Court decision in *Lau v. Nichols* (1974) is the landmark statement of the rights of language minority students indicating that LEP students must be provided with language support:

> [T]here is no equality of treatment merely by providing students with English instruction. Students without the ability to understand English are effectively foreclosed from any meaningful discourse. Basic English skills are at the very core of what these public schools teach. Imposition of a requirement that, before a child can effectively participate in the education program he must already have acquired those basic skills is to make a mockery of public education. We know that those who do not understand English are certain to find their classroom experiences wholly incomprehensible and in no way meaningful.
>
> (p. 23)

This articulation of the rights of ELL students prevails today. Following is a brief discussion of the progression of this and related court action (see García, 1998a, for a more detailed review).

Lau v. Nichols

There is a clear starting point for the development of court-related policy regarding language-minority students: the 1974 United States Supreme Court decision *Lau v. Nichols* (1974). The court suit was filed on March 25, 1970, and involved 12 American-born and foreign-born Chinese students. Prior to the suit, in 1966, at the request of parents, an ESL pullout program was initiated by the district, and in a 1967 school census, the district identified 2,456 limited-English-speaking Chinese students. By 1970, the district had identified 2,856 such students. Of this number, more than half (1,790) received no special instruction. In addition, over 2,600 of these students were taught by teachers who could not themselves speak Chinese. The district had made initial attempts to serve this population. The U.S. Supreme Court's majority opinion overruled an appeals court that had ruled in favor of the district, and, instead supported the pupils and parents. The opinion relied on statutory (legislative) grounds, and avoided any reference to constitutional determination, although the plaintiffs had argued that the equal protection clause (of the Fourteenth Amendment) of the U.S. Constitution was relevant to the case. Pupils' rights to special education services flowed from the district's obligations under Title VII of the 1964 Civil Rights Act and the HEW qualifying regulation articulated in its May 25, 1970 memorandum. The plaintiffs did not request an explicit remedy, such as a bilingual or ESL program, nor did the court address this issue. Thus, *Lau* does not stand for the proposition that children must receive a particular educational service (such as bilingual/bicultural instruction or ESL), but instead that some form of effective educational programming must be available to "open the instruction" to ELL students. This explicit avoidance by the court to specify a particular remedy has plagued efforts to identify primary language instruction as an essential ingredient for instruction of Chicano students as in *Otero v. Mesa County School District No. 51* (1977), and *Guadalupe v. Tempe School District No. 3* (1978).

After *Lau*, the domain of the language-minority education lawsuits belonged almost exclusively to Hispanic litigants. Although some cases were litigated to ensure compliance with the Lau requirements of some special assistance, most subsequent cases were about the issues left unanswered in *Lau*: Who are these students? What form of additional educational services must be provided?

Aspira of New York, Inc. v. Board of Education

In *Aspira of New York, Inc. v. Board of Education* (1975), a suit was brought by a community action group on behalf of all Hispanic children in the New York School District whose English language deficiency prevented effective participation in an English schooling context and who could effectively participate in a Spanish language curriculum (Roos, 1984). The district court hearing this case adopted a language dominance procedure to identify those students eligible for non-English, Spanish-language instructional programs. The procedure called for parallel examinations to obtain language proficiency estimates on Spanish and English standardized achievement tests. All students scoring below the 20th percentile on an English language test were given the same (or a parallel) achievement test in Spanish. Students who scored higher on the Spanish achievement test and Spanish language proficiency test were to be placed in a Spanish-language program. These procedures assumed adequate reliability and validity for the language and achievement tests administered. Such an assumption was and still is highly questionable. However, the court argued that it acted in "reasonable manner," admitting that in the absence of better assessment procedures it was forced to follow previous (*Lau*) precedents.

Castañeda v. Pickard

In a key Fifth Circuit decision of *Castañeda v. Pickard* (1981), the court interpreted Section 1703(f) of the Equal Education Opportunity Act of 1974 as substantiating the holding of *Lau* that schools cannot ignore the special language needs of students. Moreover, this court then pondered whether the statutory requirement that districts take "appropriate action" suggested a more precise obligation than the Civil Rights Act requirement that districts do something. The plaintiffs predictably urged on the court a construction of "appropriate action" that would necessitate at least bilingual transitional programs. The court concluded, however, the Section 1703(f) did not embody a congressional mandate that any particular form of remedy be uniformly adopted. If Congress wished to intrude so extraordinarily on the local districts' traditional curricular discretion, it must speak more explicitly. This conclusion, the court argued, was buttressed by the congressional use of "appropriate action" in the statute, instead of "bilingual education" or any other educational terminology.

However, the court concluded that the Congress did require districts to adopt an appropriate program, and that, by creating a cause of action in federal court to enforce Section 1703(f), it left to federal judges the task of determining whether a given program is appropriate. The court noted that Congress had not provided guidance in that statute or its brief legislative history on what it intended by selecting "appropriateness" as the operative standard. Continuing with clear reluctance and hesitancy, the court described a mode of analysis for a Section 1703(f) case:

1   The court will determine whether a district's program is "informed by an educational theory recognized as sound by some experts in the field or, at least, deemed a legitimate experimental strategy." The court explicitly declined to be an arbiter among competing theorists. The appropriate question is whether some justification exists, not the relative merits of competing alternatives.
2   The court will determine whether the district is implementing its program in a reasonably effective manner (e.g., adequate funding; qualified staffing).
3   The court will determine whether the program, after operating long enough to be a legitimate trial, produces results that indicate the language barriers are being overcome. A plan that is initially appropriate may have to be revised if expectations are not met or if the district's circumstances significantly change in such a way that the original plan is no longer sufficient.

After *Castañeda* it became legally possible to substantiate a violation of Section 1703(f), following from *Lau*, on three grounds:

(a)   the program providing special language services to eligible language-minority students is not based on sound educational theory;
(b)   the program is not being implemented in an effective manner; and
(c)   the program, after a period of "reasonable implementation," does not produce results that substantiate language barriers are being overcome.

It is obvious that these criteria allow a local school district to continue to implement a program with some educational theoretical support for a "reasonable" time before it will make judgments upon its "positive" or "negative" effects. However, the *Castañeda* court, again reluctantly but firmly, spoke to the issue of program implementation. Particularly, the court indicated that the district must provide adequate resources, including trained instructional personnel, materials, and other relevant support that would insure effective program implementation. Therefore, a district that chooses a particular program model for addressing the needs of its language-minority students must demonstrate that its staffing and materials are adequate for such a program. Implicit in these standards is the requirement that districts staff their programs with language minority education specialists, typically defined by state-approved credentials or professional course work (similar to devices utilized to judge professional expertise in other areas of professional education).

Keyes v. School District No. 1, Denver

The *Keyes* (1983) court decision was originally initiated in 1969 by a class of minority parents on behalf of their minor children attending the Denver public schools, to desegregate the public schools and to provide equal educational opportunities for all children. In granting the preliminary injunction the trial court found that during the previous decade the school board had willfully undertaken to maintain and intensify racial segregation (*Keyes v. School District No. 1, Denver, Colorado*, 1969). In 1974, during the development of a desegregation plan, intervention was sought by the Congress of Hispanic Educators (CHE), on behalf of themselves as educators and on behalf of their own minor children, who attended the Denver schools. CHE was interested in ensuring that the desegregation plan ordered by the court included that educational treatment of language minority students to overcome the deficits created by numerous years of attendance in segregated and inferior schools. A sequence of additional proceedings and negotiations followed with final comprehensive court hearings commencing in May 1982. In December 1983, Judge Richard Matsch issued a 31-page opinion, which is the most lengthy and complete language-programming discussion to date in a judicial decision. Judge Matsch, applying the *Castañeda* standards, found that Denver had failed to direct adequate resources to its language program, the question of teacher skills being a major concern.

Gómez v. Illinois

The Seventh Circuit Court of Appeals, which includes Wisconsin, Illinois and Indiana, ruled in 1987 on the obligations of the states under the Equal Educational Opportunities Act of 1974 (EEOA). The court applied the tripartite test established in *Castañeda* and extended to state education agencies, as well as to local education agencies, the obligation to ensure that the needs of the students of limited-English proficiency be met. In doing so, the "Castañeda Standard" with deference to "Lau" has become the most visible legal articulation of educational rights for Chicano, language minority students in public schools.

Executive enforcement

The Office of Civil Rights (OCR) of the U.S. Department of Education is charged with monitoring school districts' compliance with the Civil Rights Act of 1964. The OCR does not prescribe a specific educational program that will provide adequate learning opportunity for language minority students. Rather, each school district is at liberty to choose any proven approach, or any approach that promises to be successful, that it considers most appropriate to its own needs, conditions, and resources. The OCR, however, requires that all programs carry out basic functions by which schools will:

- properly identify students who need language services;
- develop programs that are effective in promoting learning;
- provide adequate teachers, educational materials, and physical space;
- adequately evaluate students' progress; and
- evaluate the whole program on an ongoing basis and implement changes when and where they are found to be needed.

OCR will explore the following school districts' fundamental responsibilities:

1   To take affirmative steps and employ adequate resources to ensure that students acquire proficiency in the language of instruction.
2   To refrain from placing students in classes for the mentally retarded on the basis of criteria which essentially measure English language skills, or to deny access to college preparatory courses as a result of school's failure to impart necessary English language skills.
3   To employ no grouping or tracking systems that impede national origin students' educational development, or that operate as dead-end or permanent tracks, but to stimulate learning and the mastery of English as quickly as possible.
4   To ensure that parents with limited-English proficiency receive information about school activities in a language that they understand.

At this writing, however, OCR is exploring more specific evaluations of education equity at the district, school, and classroom level. At a national conference in San Francisco in May, 2000, educational researchers and experts from around the country joined OCR staff in generating a potential set of such indicators, based on sound education research, that could be utilized in a new wave of enforcement articulation throughout the United States (García, 1999).

State policies

Through state legislation, 12 states mandate special educational services for language minority students, 12 states permit these services and one state prohibits them. Twenty-six states have no legislation that directly addresses language minority students (García, 1999). State program policy for language minority students can be characterized as follows:

1   Implementing instructional programs that allow or require instruction in a language other than English (17 states).
2   Establishing special qualifications for the certification of professional instructional staff (15 states).
3   Providing school districts supplementary funds in support of educational programs (15 states).
4   Mandating a cultural component (15 states).
5   Requiring parental consent for enrollment of students (11 states). Eight states (Arizona, California, Colorado, Illinois, Indiana, Massachusetts, Rhode Island, and Texas) impose all of the above requirements concurrently.

Such a pattern suggests continued attention by states to issues related to language minority students (see García, 1994, for details). Of particular interest is a subset of states that when taken together are home to almost two-thirds of this nation's language minority students: California, Florida, Illinois, New York, New Jersey, and Texas. In these states, bilingual credentialing and ESL or some other related credential/endorsement is available. However, in only three of the six states is such credentialing mandated. Therefore, even in states that are highly "impacted" by language minority students, there is no direct concern for the specific mandating of professional standards. These students tend to be concentrated in a few school districts within the state, and even though their academic presence is felt strongly by these individual districts, they do not exert this same pressure statewide.

English-only state policies

Two new state initiatives in California (1998) and Arizona (2000) are the most recent efforts by states to restrict the use of a language other than English in the delivery of educational services to Chicano children. In California, the new ballot measure identified as "English for All Children" and the related state education code:

1   Requires all children be placed in English language classrooms, and that English language learners be educated through a prescribed methodology identified as "Structured English Immersion."
2   Prescribes methodology that would be provided as a temporary transition period not normally to exceed one year.
3   Allows instruction in the child's native language only in situations in which a waiver is granted, done so in writing and done so yearly by parents requiring a school visit by a parent.
4   Prohibits native language instruction only if the student already has mastered English, and is over 10 years of age and such instruction is approved by the principal and the teacher (García and Curry, 2000).

Therefore, this "English Only" policy allows native language instruction only through an exclusionary and complicated process for the 1.6 million students in the state that are identified as limited in their English-language proficiency. Moreover, teachers, administrators, and school board members can be held personally liable for fees and damages by the child's parents and guardians.

The Arizona statute, passed in November of 2000, is much like California's and requires that all public school instruction be conducted in English with some limiting provisions. Children not fluent in English are to "normally" be placed in an intensive 1-year English immersion program to teach them the language as quickly as possible while also learning academic subjects. Parents may request a waiver of these requirements for children who already know English, are 10 years or older, or have special needs best suited to a different educational approach. It is the waiver provision that becomes more restrictive than California's. Waivers for primary language use fall into three categories:

1   *Children who already know English:* The child already possesses good English language skills, as measured by oral evaluation or standardized tests of English vocabulary comprehension, reading, and writing, in which the child scores approximately at or above the state average for his grade level or at or above the 5th-grade average, whichever is lower; or,
2   *Older children:* The child is age 10 years or older, and it is the informed belief of the school principal and educational staff that an alternate course of educational study would be better suited to the child's overall educational progress and rapid acquisition of basic English language skills; or,

3   *Children with special individual needs*: The child already has been placed for a period of not less than 30 calendar days during that school year in an English language classroom. And, it is subsequently the informed belief of the school principal and educational staff that the child has such special and individual physical or psychological needs, above and beyond the child's lack of English proficiency. An alternate course of educational study would be better suited to the child's overall educational development and rapid acquisition of English. A written description of no less than 250 words documenting these special individual needs for the specific child must be provided and permanently added to the child's official school records. The waiver application must contain the original authorizing signatures of both the school principal and the local superintendent of schools. Any such decision to issue such an individual waiver is to be made subject to the examination and approval of the local school superintendent, under guidelines established by, and subject to, the review of the local governing board and ultimately the state board of education. *Teachers and local school districts may reject waiver requests without explanation or legal consequence, the existence of such special individual needs shall not compel issuance of a waiver, and the parents shall be fully informed of their right to refuse to agree to a waiver.*

In recent efforts to document the implementation of Proposition 227 in California, yet another "English Only" policy was reported to be substantially influencing the organizational environments of Chicano students. That policy is embedded in California's use of an English academic test (Stanford 9) within a newly defined Academic Performance Index designed by the state to either reward or sanction schools for measured progress or failure of such progress (García and Curry, 2000; Palmer and García, 2000). In these empirical reports, school district administrators, including principals, as well as classroom teachers indicate that Chicano students are receiving more instructional emphasis in English, even in school districts and schools that have utilized the Proposition 227 waiver process to maintain their bilingual education programs. This new accountability policy, by providing only "high stakes" assessment in English is doing more than Proposition 227 to move instruction into English for non-English speaking students (Palmer and García, 2000). (It is important to note that Texas accountability policies allow for the utilization of a Spanish language academic test.)

These California and Arizona policy provisions, taken together, are the most restrictive measures proposed yet for serving Chicano ELL students either nationally or within any state, via legislation or the courts. It is anticipated that the results of these policies will have substantive effects on the future on bilingual education and its practice within and outside the states of California and Arizona.[7]

Conclusion: preparing Chicano students for the "new" future

As the United States anticipates policies for any of its students, it is even more important to understand the seismic changes in technology, globalization, and democratization that are reflected in similar seismic changes in demography. Unfortunately, the general population is far more attuned to and comfortable with engaging in aspects of the technological, globalization, and political challenges than those challenges confronting them by demographic changes. They are almost characterized by a "blind spot" when it comes to the new demographic reality.

However, changes are all inextricably intertwined. Some 60 percent of new jobs in the near future will be in fields of information technology and communications. To those students that master and control this new technology, locally, regionally, nationally, and internationally go the spoils. They will be like those who have controlled the capital and labor in the 20th century. This link creates an obvious imperative to educate those who will either help the U.S. to prosper or serve as its growing weak link. To educate the low-achieving, but growing language minority students is a "no-brainer." These youths will serve as a foundation for national preeminence in the fields of high technology in a global workplace that promotes democratic principles and practices.

These circumstances pose a particular challenge to educators and those who look to educational agencies for help in realizing the moral imperatives of equity and social justices. These agencies are being called on to develop and implement models of culturally competent practices in treating and delivering services to growing numbers of Chicano students and families. As Wilson (1978) has noted, class has become increasingly more important than race in determining access to opportunities, power and privilege in American society. West (1993) reminds one that race is still important and García (2001) indicates that language will continue to be at the forefront of federal and state policy activity. This chapter, with its emphasis on the education of Chicano ELLs in the U.S., has attempted to further complexify understanding of the education in the U.S. through the discussion of language and culture. If one concludes that class and race counts, one also concludes that language and culture do so as well.

If one can attend to "what counts," then one could predict that as more Chicano students enter the "right" kind of schools, barriers to their academic, social and economic success, and mobility will fall. Likewise, as one becomes more attuned to the surrounding cultural diversity and the resources inherit in that diversity, cultural distinctions will blend with other features of society to create a more "equalitarian," multicultural society. This is, of course a highly optimistic scenario of the future for Chicano students and American society in general. Yet, it is most certainly a preferable prediction to one that argues that America could become another Bosnian nightmare, where racial and ethnic conflicts could escalate into major avenues of social unrest.

If the treatment of culturally and linguistically diverse students, and Chicano students in particular, in the educational institutions is like a seismic indicator of an impending earthquake, an indicator that is now sending signals of coming dangers, then options on how to respond to that signal are clear. Those signals can be ignored, but they will not go away. They can be responded to minimally, studied more, and the worst prepared for. Or the resources can be marshalled in ways that will make the inevitable an opportunity that can be benefited from. Simply put, the challenge for Chicano students is to help them help the U.S. arrive at a truly multi-racial, multi-ethnic democracy.

Notes

1 The Bilingual Education Act referred to the population of children aimed to serve, not a particular instructional program.
2 This survey was carried out under a mandate of the Civil Rights Act of 1964 to assess the "lack of educational opportunity" among racial and other groups in the United States (Coleman, 1968).
3 The bilingual programs were funded by a grant from the Ford Foundation.
4 In addition to the bilingual education grants, Title VII has set aside funds for research, professional development, and the Foreign Language Assistance Program, and the Emergency Immigrant Education Program (EIEP). By targeting immigrant children and youths, the EIEP inherently focuses on language minority children and aims "to assist eligible local education agencies that experience unexpectedly large increases in their student population due to immigration to: (a) provide high quality instruction to immigrant children and youth, and (b) help such children

and youth (1) with their transition into American society, and (2) meet the same challenging State performance standards expected of all children and youth" (BEA, 1994, Section 7301[b]). State education agencies will receive an allocation equal to the proportion of the number of immigrant children enrolled in school, and then they will distribute funds to eligible local education agencies.

5 The National Education Goals were originally adopted by the nation's governors.

6 (a) All children will arrive at school ready to learn, (b) The high school graduation rate will increase to at least 90 percent, (c) Students will master challenging subject matter, (d) Teachers will have access to training programs to improve their skills, (e) U.S. students will be first in the world in math and science, (f) All adult Americans will be literate and be able to compete in a global economy, (g) Every school will be free of drug and violence, and (h) Every school will strive to increase parental involvement and participation in their children's education (Shogren, 1994).

7 Further, prohibiting the use of necessary accommodations is inconsistent with the *Standards for Educational and Psychological Testing* (American Educational Research Association *et al.*, 1999). The National Assessment of Educational Progress currently allows for the necessary accommodations for LEP students as well as students with disabilities.

References

American Educational Research Association, American Psychological Association, and National Council on Measurement in Education. (1999). *Standards for educational and psychological testing.* Washington, DC: Author.

Aspira of New York, Inc. v. Board of Education. (1975). 65 FRD 54.

August, D. and Hakuta, K. (1997). *Improving schooling for language-minority children: Research agenda.* Washington, DC: National Council Research.

Bilingual Education Act, Pub. L. No. (90–247), 81 Stat. 816 (1968).

Bilingual Education Act, Pub. L. No. (93–380), 88 Stat. 503 (1974).

Bilingual Education Act, Pub. L. No. (95–561), 92 Stat. 2268 (1978).

Bilingual Education Act, Pub. L. No. (98–511), 98 Stat. 2370 (1984).

Bilingual Education Act, Pub. L. No. (100–297), 102 Stat. 279 (1988).

Bilingual Education Act, Pub. L. No. (103–382), (1994).

Casanova, U. (1991). Bilingual education: politics or pedagogy. In O. García (Ed.), *Bilingual education* (Vol. 1, pp. 167–182). Amsterdam: John Benjamins.

Castañeda v. Pickard. (1981). 648 F.2d 989, 1007 5th Cir. 1981; 103 S. Ct. 3321.

Civil Rights Act, Pub. L. No. (88–352), 78 Stat. (1964).

Coleman, J. (1968). The concept of equality of educational opportunity. *Harvard Educational Review, 38,* 7–22.

Crawford, J. (1999). *Bilingual education: History, politics, theory, and practice* (4th ed.). Los Angeles: Bilingual Education Services, Inc.

Cummins, J. (1991). The politics of paranoia: Reflections on the bilingual education debate. In O. García (Ed.), *Bilingual education* (Vol. 1, pp. 185–199). Amsterdam: John Benjamins.

Equal Educational Opportunities Act of 1974, Pub. L. No. (93–380), 88 Stat. 514 (1974).

Erickson, F. (1987). Transformation and school success: The politics and culture of educational achievement. *Anthropology and Education Quarterly, 18,* 146–167.

Fitzgerald, J. (1993). Views on bilingualism in the United States: A selective historical review. *Bilingual Research Journal, 17,* 35–56.

García, E.E. (1994). *Understanding the needs of LEP students.* New York: Houghton and Mifflin.

García, E.E. (1998a). Legal issues impacting educational outcomes of Hispanics in public schools. In S.H. Ochoa and A. Tashakkori (Eds.), *Education of Hispanics in the United States: Politics, policies, and outcomes* (pp. 123–147). Baton Rouge, LA: Louisiana State University Press.

García, E.E. (1998b). Promoting the contributions of multicultural students in the work force of the 21st century. In S.H. Fradd and O. Lee (Eds.), *Educational policies and practices for students learning English as a new language* (pp. VII 1–VII 13). Tallahassee: University of Florida and Florida Department of Education.

García, E.E. (1999). *Student cultural diversity: Meeting the challenges* (2nd ed.). New York: Houghton Mifflin.

García, E.E. (2001). *The education of Hispanics in the United States: Raíces y alas.* Boulder, CO: Rowen and Littlefield.

García, E. and Curry, J. (2000). The effect of California's 227: A statewide analysis. *Bilingual Research Journal, 24,* 15–36.

García, E.E. and González, R. (1995). Issues in systemic reform for culturally and linguistically diverse students. *Teachers College Record, 96,* 418–431.

Goals 2000: Educate America Act. Pub. L. No. (103–227), 108 Stat. 125. (1994).

Gómez v. Ilinois. (1987). 811 F.2d. 1030.

Guadalupe Organization, Inc. v. Tempe Elementary School District No. 3. (1978). 587 F.2d 1022 (9th Cir.).

Hakuta, K. (1986). *Mirror of language: The debate on bilingualism.* New York: Basic Books.

Keyes v. School District No. 1. (1983). 576F. Supp. 1503 (D. Colo.).

Improving America's Schools Act. Pub. L. No. (103–382), 108 Stat. 3518. (1994).

Lau v. Nichols. (1974). 414 US 563.

National Research Council. (1997). *The new American: economic, demographic, and fiscal effects of immigration.* Washington, DC: National Academy Press.

Navarro, R.A. (1990). The problems of language, education, and society: Who decides. In E.E. García and R.V. Padilla (Eds.), *Advances in bilingual education research* (pp. 289–313). Tucson: University of Arizona Press.

Otero v. Mesa County School District No. 51. (1977). 568 F.2d 1312.

Palmer, D. and García, E.E. (2000). Proposition 227: Bilingual educators speak. *Bilingual Research Journal, 24,* 169–178.

Pearl, A. (1997). Cultural and accumulated environmental deficit models. In R.R. Valencia (Ed.), *The evolution of deficit thinking: Educational thought and practice* (pp. 132–159). The Stanford Series on Education and Public Policy. London: Falmer Press.

Portes, A. and Rumbaut, R.G. (1996). *Immigrant America: A portrait* (2nd ed.). Berkeley, CA: University of California Press.

Riessman, F. (1962). *The culturally deprived child.* New York: Harper.

Riley, R.W. (1995). Reflections on Goals 2000. *Teachers College Record, 96,* 380–388.

Roos, P. (1984). *Legal guidelines for bilingual administrators.* Invited address, Society of Research in Child Development, Austin, TX, July.

Rumberger, R.W. (1995). Dropping out of middle school: A multilevel analysis of students and schools. *American Educational Research Journal, 32,* 583–625.

Shogren, L. (1994). *The education goals for 2000.* Washington, DC: U.S. Department of Education, Office of Education Research and Improvement.

Smith, M.S. and Scoll, B.W. (1995). The Clinton human capital agenda. *Teachers College Record, 96,* 389–404.

Tyack, D.B. and Cuban, L. (1995). *Tinkering toward utopia: A century of public school reform.* Cambridge, MA: Harvard University Press.

Wagonner, D. (2000). The demographics of diversity in the United States. In R.D. González and I. Melis (Eds.), *Language ideologies* (pp. 5–27). Mahwah, NJ: Lawrence Erlbaum.

West, C. (1993). Learning to talk of race. In R. Gooding-Williams (Ed.), *Reading Rodney King, reading urban uprising* (pp. 21–38). New York: Routledge.

Wilson, W.J. (1978). *The declining significance of race.* Chicago: University of Chicago Press.

6 Research in bilingual education: moving beyond the effectiveness debate

Michael D. Guerrero

The debate over the efficacy of bilingual education continues. In fact, bilingual education in the U.S. appears to be in the process of being dismantled state by state. California voters passed Proposition 227 in 1998, which dealt a serious blow to providing bilingual education programs in the state with the largest concentration of Spanish-speaking students, primarily of Mexican origin, in the U.S. In November of 2000, voters in Arizona passed Proposition 203, an even more restrictive piece of legislation aimed at eradicating bilingual education in that state.[1] In both cases, the educational approach being mandated is centered on providing English language learners (ELLs) with only one year of intensive English instruction before mainstreaming them into an all English classroom setting.[2]

Are these new educational policies evidence that bilingual education has failed to deliver its promise to ELLs, principally Spanish-speaking students of Mexican origin, to a meaningful and equitable education? Moreover, is there any research evidence to support such policies? In this chapter, a review and critique of bilingual education research conducted over the last ten years is provided. This section is followed by a discussion revolving around what this research suggests, limitations of the research, and direction for future research endeavors. This author takes the position that it is time to move beyond the narrowly focused, quantitatively-driven effectiveness debate in order to further our understanding of how to best meet the needs of ELLs. Next I will describe each of these studies. A following section offers a critique of them.

Overview of central studies in the 1990s

In the past decade, there have been five salient research studies on the effectiveness of bilingual education (chronologically, they are: Ramírez *et al.*, 1991; Rossell and Baker, 1996; Greene, 1997; Thomas and Collier, 1997; Salazar, 1998). These studies were undertaken to provide empirical research evidence to inform and guide the development of educational policies for ELLs.

Ramírez et al. (1991)

This team of researchers conducted a longitudinal research study in which they compared the effectiveness of structured English immersion and late-exit transitional bilingual education programs with early-exit transitional bilingual education programs (hereafter transitional bilingual education is abbreviated as TBE). The researchers defined a structured English immersion program as one in which specially trained teachers delivered all instruction in

English, and English was taught simultaneously with academic content (e.g., mathematics; science). The students' native language was used only to clarify instruction. Provided a student entered the program in kindergarten, the learner was expected to enter the mainstream classroom after two or three years (i.e., grade 1 or 2).

In early-exit TBE programs, students received native language instruction between 30 and 60 minutes a day, primarily to develop their initial Spanish reading skills. English was used for other areas of the curriculum and the students' primary language was used for support and clarification. The expectation was that the students receive all English instruction by grade 2. In contrast, students in late-exit TBE programs received at least 40 percent of their instruction across the curriculum in the native language from kindergarten through grade 6.

The schools in this study were selected from among those recommended by state departments of education or other educational agencies in New York, Texas, and California. Students in the participating schools were Spanish speakers born in the U.S. and most were of Mexican descent. The majority of the parents (75 percent) were not U.S. born. Generally, the students were from low-income families with yearly earnings for a family of two adults and two children being less than $15,000. Proportionately, more families from the lowest-income levels enrolled their children in late-exit programs.

Test data (i.e., language, reading, and mathematics scores from the California Test of Basic Skills in English) were collected and analyzed covering a four-year period. A statistical procedure known as Trajectory Analysis of Matched Percentiles was used to compare changes in test scores for groups of students in the three different programs. Interestingly, the growth curves for those students in late-exit TBE programs were more impressive than those of students in either the immersion or early-exit TBE program. Students who received the most native language instruction showed continued growth in grades 1 to 3 and 3 to 6; their growth did not decelerate during the later years, which is common for the general English-speaking population. That is, students in the late-exit TBE program actually accelerated in their academic growth and appeared to be gaining on English-speaking peers.

The researchers also examined whether each of the three late-exit TBE programs produced similar student achievement outcomes. Apparently, one of these programs was not adhering to its programmatic design, providing 40 percent of the instruction in Spanish through grade 6. Rather, students at this site had been abruptly transitioned into English instruction after grade 3. Consequently, the students in the other two late-exit TBE programs had significantly higher mathematics skills by the end of the 6th grade. The rate of growth for students, however, did not differ in English language and reading.

The researchers also found that there were no significant differences between the test scores of students in the structured English immersion program and the early-exit TBE program. Scores in mathematics, English language skills, and English reading skills were comparable for both groups. Ramírez *et al.* (1991) concluded:

> These findings suggest that providing LEP students with substantial amounts of instruction in their primary language does not impede their acquisition of English language skills, but that it is as effective as being provided with large amounts of English. Of equal importance is the finding that students who are provided with substantial amounts of primary language instruction are also able to learn and improve their skills in other content areas as fast as or faster than the norming population, in contrast to students who are transitioned quickly into English-only instruction.
>
> (p. 36)

Rossell and Baker (1996)

These two authors sought to determine whether bilingual education is the most effective instructional approach for ELLs. They approached their question by examining the results of 72 bilingual education program evaluations. Generally speaking, program evaluations are routinely conducted as part of the implementation of a bilingual program to fulfill a local, state, or federal accountability requirement. However, Rossell and Baker described these evaluations in the following manner:

> This is fugitive literature, most of it unpublished, and some of it available only by writing directly to school districts. It consists in large part of local evaluations that do not even come close to meeting methodologically sound research standards. This is true not only of the "in-house" evaluations performed by school district staff but of those conducted by outside consulting firms that are supposedly hired for their methodological expertise.
>
> (p. 13)

From among 300 program evaluations, Rossell and Baker (1996) identified 72 methodologically acceptable evaluations that *generally* met the following criteria:

1   They were true experiments in which students were randomly assigned to treatment and control groups;
2   They had non-random assignment that either matched students in the treatment and comparison groups on factors that influence achievement or statistically controlled for them;
3   They included a comparison group of LEP students of the same ethnicity and similar language background;
4   Outcome measures were in English using normal curve equivalents (NCEs), raw scores, scale scores, or percentiles, but not grade equivalents;
5   There were no additional educational treatments, or the studies controlled for additional treatments if they existed.

> (pp. 14–15)

The authors compared the relative effectiveness of TBE programs with that of submersion, English as a second language (ESL), and structured English immersion programs. Submersion (i.e., sink or swim) was defined as an instructional alternative in which no specific approach was used for delivering instruction; the ELLs are simply placed in the mainstream English-speaking classroom. ESL programs generally provided instruction aimed at developing the learner's English language proficiency. These programs tended to be organized on a pull-out basis (e.g., ELLs leave their home room to receive lessons approximately three times a week). The native language of the student is generally not used during ESL instruction.

Rossell and Baker (1996) define structured English immersion programs in much the same way as Ramírez *et al.* (1991). Rossell and Baker use the term transitional bilingual education programs (i.e., TBE) that is used interchangeably with early-exit TBE programs. However, Rossell and Baker, unlike Ramírez *et al.* (1991), indicate that in TBE programs children are not only taught to read in their native language, but they are also taught subject matter in the primary language. Virtually all of the evaluations involved programs in which the children spoke Spanish. No other student, family, or community data were provided.

Table 6.1 Percentage of methodologically acceptable studies demonstrating program superiority, equality, or inferiority by achievement test outcome

	Reading[a]	*Language*	*Math*
TBE v. Submersion			
TBE better	22%	7%	9%
No difference	45%	29%	56%
TBE worse	33%	64%	35%
Total *N*	60	14	34
TBE v. ESL			
TBE better	0%	0%	25%
No difference	71%	67%	50%
TBE worse	29%	33%	25%
Total *N*	7	3	4
TBE v. Structured Immersion			
TBE better	0%	0%	0%
No difference	17%	100%	63%
TBE worse	83%	0%	38%
Total *N*	12	1	8
TBE v. Maintenance Bilingual			
TBE better	100%	0%	0%
Total *N*	1	0	0

Source: Rossell and Baker (1996, p. 20, Table 1). Adapted with permission of authors.

Note
TBE = Transitional Bilingual Education; ESL = English as a Second Language; *N* = number of studies.
[a] Oral English achievement for preschool programs.

Rossell and Baker (1996) used the "voting method" to guide their analyses and findings. In this approach, each of the 72 methodologically acceptable program evaluations was reviewed to determine which of the four program alternatives it supported or did not support. In effect, the authors calculated the percentage of evaluations that *favored* TBE over submersion, ESL, and structured immersion programs in reading, language, and mathematics.[3] Table 6.1 summarizes their results. Rossell and Baker (1996) synthesized their results in the following manner:

> As Table 1 indicates, substantially more studies show harm from TBE, compared to all-English instruction, than show a benefit. This disparity widens when TBE is compared to structured immersion, an all-English program in a self-contained classroom for second language learners. Thus, the risk of academic deficiency in English is greater for TBE than for all English instruction according to the empirical comparative research.
>
> (p. 43)

Greene (1997)

Greene conducted a study drawing from the same set of program evaluations examined by Rossell and Baker (1996). He did so, "in an effort to determine the reliability of the litera-ture review conducted by Rossell and Baker" (p. 5). The principal research question in Greene's study was straight-forward: Is the use of native language instruction (as in TBE) more beneficial than being taught only in English (e.g., as in structured English immersion programs)?

In addition to the criteria for methodologically acceptable studies established by Rossell and Baker (1996), Greene (1997) added one more condition: The students had to be in the program for at least one year. Greene also approached the definition of program alternatives in a very straight-forward manner. He did not classify them by traditional program labels as Ramírez *et al.* (1991) and Rossell and Baker had done. He simply determined whether each study used the native language of the learner and included only those studies that met this and the other criteria as well. Interestingly, after reviewing the 75 methodologically acceptable studies used by Rossell and Baker, Greene found that only 11 studies met these criteria.

Greene (1997) indicated that the 11 studies included standardized test score results for 2,719 students from 13 states. The vast majority of the students appear to have been Spanish speaking. Slightly more than half of these students were enrolled in bilingual programs of some kind (e.g., early or late-exit TBE). Also, the average student in the bilingual programs received 2 years of bilingual instruction and was tested in grade 3.

With these 11 studies, Greene (1997) employed a statistical procedure referred to as meta-analysis. This statistical procedure allows the researcher to calculate the average effect size of a particular treatment from a number of different studies. In contrast to Rossell and Baker (1996), Greene found that the use of the native language of the learners had a statistically significant and moderate effect on the learners' reading achievement in English (i.e., 0.21 standard deviation). The gain on math tests measured in English, however, was not statistically significant. Greene also conducted a separate set of analyses on five of the studies that used random assignment of the learners. Bear in mind that such studies are considered more scientific or methodologically rigorous. Greene emphasizes, "The effect for reading scores measured in English, almost doubles when we focus on the random assignment studies. When we look at the higher quality research design studies we see more significantly positive benefits from native language instruction" (p. 9). Further criticism by Greene of the Rossell and Baker study will be provided later in this chapter.

Thomas and Collier (1997)

In this research effort, the authors conducted a longitudinal study in which they analyzed data spanning a 14-year period (1982–1996). The researchers compared the English reading scores of ELLs receiving instruction in six different types of programs. The Thomas and Collier study was designed to address the following two questions:

> How much time is needed for language minority students who are English language learners to reach and sustain on-grade-level achievement in their second language? Which student, program, and instructional variables strongly affect the long-term academic achievement of language minority students?
>
> (p. 16)

This study was informed by over 700,000 language minority academic student records. However, findings are based on a sample of 42,317 student cohorts that attended participating schools for at least four, but up to eight years. The student records were drawn from five moderate to large urban and suburban school systems from different parts of the U.S. Over 150 languages were represented in the student sample; however, 63 percent of the students were Spanish speakers. Almost 60 percent of the students in the programs studied were in the free or reduced lunch program. No other student data are reported.

Thomas and Collier (1997) approached their study from two vantage points. First, they examined academic achievement patterns of ELLs over the long term, from kindergarten through grade 12. Second, the two researchers included only those programs that were considered stable and well-implemented in the five school districts. As the authors state, ". . . we present a picture of the long-term potential for each program type when that program type is well-implemented and is operating at or near its 'best'" (p. 28).

The six program types consisted of: traditional ESL, content-based ESL, TBE combined with traditional ESL, TBE combined with content-based ESL, one-way developmental bilingual education combined with content-based ESL, and two-way developmental bilingual education.

Traditional ESL instruction is centered on teaching the learner discrete aspects of the English language, while content-based ESL teaches academic content and English simultaneously as in a structured immersion program. One-way developmental bilingual education programs are essentially the same as late-exit TBE programs (also referred to as maintenance bilingual programs). Two-way developmental bilingual education programs differ from one-way programs in that language majority and language minority speakers are schooled together in the same classroom. Ideally, both the one-way and two-way program models use the student's native language at least half of the time over the course of the learner's elementary school years beginning in kindergarten.

To analyze program effectiveness, Thomas and Collier (1997) utilized a methodology (i.e., blocking) that allowed them to generate general patterns of (K-12) reading achievement for students in each of the six program types. The central finding of their study is: Those programs that provided students with cognitively complex, on-grade-level academic instruction in the student's first language for as long as possible (at least through grade 5 or 6) and cognitively complex on-grade-level academic instruction through the second language (English) for part of the school day, achieved parity with native speakers of English most quickly. Only two program types produced these results: two-way developmental programs and one-way developmental (or late-exit) bilingual programs.

Parity means that students in these two program types scored at the level of the average performance of a native English-speaking student in reading. Gains were sustained, however, through middle and high school for students in both program types. In fact, the students who had received instruction through a two-way developmental program scored above the average native English-speaking student in grades 7 and beyond.

In contrast, learners in the four remaining program types never caught up to the average performance of native English speakers. Students in traditional ESL programs fared most poorly, while those in content-based ESL programs scored somewhat higher. Students in TBE combined with traditional ESL programs scored only marginally higher than those students in content-based ESL programs. Learners instructed through TBE combined with content-based ESL programs experienced the third most effective program alternative but still did not achieve academic parity with the average native English-speaking child at any point in their K-12 education.

Salazar (1998)

This study represents an effort to reexamine the findings reported by Greene (1998) and Thomas and Collier (1997). Salazar conducted what is referred to as a power analysis of Greene's meta-analysis; this statistical procedure allows the researcher to detect Type II errors or to calculate the probability of detecting a statistically significant difference.[4] Salazar maintains that the probability of making a Type II error should be no greater than 20 percent. In reexamining Greene's data, Salazar found that the probability of making a Type II error was more than two times higher (42 percent) than the recommended rate (20 percent). Salazar (1998) stated:

> The significance of the power analysis of Greene's data is that it points to one of the main reasons why we are no closer to addressing the long-term effectiveness of bilingual education programs compared with English-only programs. That is, most studies have used statistically weak designs that have failed to detect program differences. The odds (58 percent Type II Error rate) have been stacked against finding significant differences.
>
> (p. 4)

With respect to the reanalysis of the Thomas and Collier (1997) data, Salazar (1998) computed effect size differences between bilingual programs and English-only programs for English reading. This statistical procedure allows one to understand score differences associated with program types being compared. By comparing the standard deviation differences between two program types, one can calculate the differences in terms of some type of standardized test score. Salazar (1998) explained:

> In concrete terms, a difference of one-fifth to one-fourth of a standard deviation means that if a group of English language learners in a primary language program and a group in an English-only program both began the school year at the 30th percentile—and if those students in the English-only program maintained their English reading score at the 30th percentile the following school year—those students in the primary language program would now be at the 38th percentile. An effect size difference of this magnitude, therefore, translates into educationally significant gains.
>
> (p. 6)

According to Salazar, the reanalysis of the Thomas and Collier (1997) data showed an overall effect size gain of 0.26 standard deviation in favor of bilingual programs with respect to English reading. The analyses also indicate that effect sizes vary by program type and by grade. Salazar explained:

> There are little or no effect size differences between primary language programs and English-only programs in grades K-3. In fact, Thomas and Collier's data indicate that results through grade 3 actually favored the English-only comparison group when compared with two-way bilingual programs and late-exit bilingual programs. . . . The effectiveness of late-exit and two-way bilingual programs becomes evident in the middle school years and continues to widen throughout high school grades when compared with English-only programs. However, since the average bilingual education study covers a two-year period, these longitudinal effects are completely overlooked under the current short-term paradigm.
>
> (p. 7)

Summary

This handful of studies on the effectiveness of bilingual education represents the most recent efforts to provide hard evidence that would provide direction for how to best educate language minority children—primarily Spanish-speaking children of Mexican-origin. Only the Rossell and Baker (1996) study refutes the effectiveness of bilingual education. The remaining four studies each provide evidence that bilingual education is more effective in providing the kind of learning environment ELLs need in order to gradually narrow and close the academic gap between themselves and the average native English-speaking child.

The most salient point seems to be that two-way and late-exit bilingual programs, the programs that provide the greatest use of the learner's native language, generate the best results for ELLs. Their benefits, however, are not immediately evident. English-only approaches (e.g., structured English immersion) seem to provide equally good results in the early elementary grades (K-3), but these results are not sustained over the long-term (grades 4–12). Thomas and Collier (1997) explain this trend as owing to the increasing cognitive demands placed on the ELLs as they move into the upper elementary grades and on into middle and high school. ELLs receiving native language instruction through their elementary years are provided with ample opportunity to keep cognitive pace with their age- and grade-level-mates, to acquire academic English more gradually but completely, and to transfer knowledge learned in their native language as they transition into English instruction. In contrast, ELLs in all English programs begin to lose ground compared to their English-speaking peers as the curriculum and assessments become more linguistically and cognitively demanding.

It is also important to note that Thomas and Collier (1997) are the first to problematize the effectiveness debate within a long-term (K-12) and well-implemented program framework. The problem this presents is that educational policies have been informed primarily by short-term studies, essentially one- or two-year program evaluations subjected to statistical analyses. Unfortunately, short-term research efforts provide little insight into the long-term consequences of providing ELLs with a particular kind of educational program. If this assumption is valid, then it stands to reason that educational policies impacting ELLs have been based on some rather crude and primitive evidence.

Critiques of the studies

Various researchers have examined the validity of the findings of the studies discussed here, with the exception of the Salazar (1998) study that has been published only recently. It is important to bear in mind that research on the effectiveness of bilingual education is undertaken primarily to determine whether or not native language instruction facilitates English acquisition and academic achievement in turn. The surface assumption is that if this question can be definitively answered, then it would be possible to shape educational policy accordingly. The underlying assumption is that we would be able to generalize findings from a set of studies to the broader population.

Moran and Hakuta (1995) provided a succinct critique of the Ramírez *et al.* (1991) study. The most central problem with the Ramírez *et al.* investigation has to do with its design. Moran and Hakuta maintained that an inadequately designed research study has the unfortunate consequence of creating more problems as the study progresses, especially in generalizing the findings to other sites.

Moran and Hakuta (1995) also pointed out that the selection of the research sites and issues of program design represent two of the major problems with this study. The immersion and early-exit programs were selected only if they occurred in the same school district. However, the districts with late-exit programs chosen for the study did not offer the other two alternative types of programs. Consequently, no single district offered each of the three different program types, and thus such a design creates problems for comparing the effectiveness of different programs. The primary objective of the study, to compare the relative effectiveness of English immersion and late-exit programs with early-exit bilingual programs, was compromised.

Within a single district, the conditions under which programs are offered (e.g., student and teacher characteristics; resources; educational policies) are likely to be more similar than different. This shared similarity alleviates the burden for statistically controlling for factors that might influence student achievement. In short, the comparison of the effectiveness of late-exit programs to the other two program types becomes problematic.

To confound design problems even further, all of the immersion programs in two of the three school districts participated in this study. In contrast, the early-exit and late-exit programs were selected arbitrarily by school administrators. As Moran and Hakuta (1995) stated, "The potential for bias in such selection is clear, and points the way toward more design problems" (p. 453). All sites should have been selected under the same set of criteria (e.g., random; voluntary; nominated).

There were also problems related to how the programs were actually implemented. The early-exit programs studied used Spanish language instruction somewhat sparingly or to a lesser degree than is generally allowed. Consequently, there was not an ample difference between how much Spanish was used in some of the early-exit programs as compared to the structured English immersion programs. Differences in the amount of native language instruction also plagued the late-exit programs. After fourth grade, its use varied from 40 percent, to 25 percent, to 6 percent across the three sites. As was indicated earlier, there was an abrupt transition into English instruction within one of the late-exit sites. Moran and Hakuta (1995) summed up the consequences of this oversight: "Allowing programs to be compared according to their names rather than according to strict criteria that distinguish between them produces muddied results" (p. 454).

The use of the statistical method to graph projected growth curves for each program type has also been criticized in light of the design of the study. According to Moran and Hakuta (1995), the use of Trajectory Analysis of Matched Percentiles (TAMPS) was inappropriate because students were not matched by grade levels across each program type. Student cohorts for the late-exit programs were comprised of test scores in grades 3 to 6. For the other two programs, student cohort test scores were at the opposite end of the grade continuum, kindergarten to grade 3.

A further observation can also be made with reference to the effectiveness of the three late-exit programs relative to each other. There was a marked difference in student growth between two of the late exit programs—one that abruptly transitioned the students into the English language after grade 3 and another that was more faithful to the design of the model. The more effective late-exit program continued to use the native language at least 40 percent of the time from kindergarten to grade 6. Furthermore, both programs were within the same district, which helps alleviate potential confounding differences among the student population. It can be reasoned that the poorly implemented late-exit program was actually more like an early-exit TBE program, given that it withdrew native language support at the end of grade 3.

Meyer and Feinberg (1992), nonetheless, do not discard the findings of the Ramírez *et al.* (1991) study entirely. The authors led a National Academy of Sciences panel that reviewed the Ramírez *et al.* investigation at the request of the U.S. Department of Education. One of the important conclusions reached by Meyer and Feinberg is:

Taking fully into account the limitations of the study, the panel still sees the elements of positive relationships that are consistent with empirical results from other studies and that support the theory underlying native language instruction in bilingual education.

(p. 104)

The study conducted by Rossell and Baker (1996) was critiqued by Greene (1997). First, Greene indicated that there was a serious problem with the corpus of studies Rossell and Baker used to negate the effectiveness of native language instruction. Rossell and Baker had identified 75 methodologically acceptable studies to analyze; Greene, drawing from the same pool of studies and applying the same acceptability criteria established by Rossell and Baker, was only able to identify 11 studies that met these criteria. Greene did add that to be included in the analysis, the students needed to have been in the bilingual program for at least one year. This criterion, however, only omitted two studies. So what happened to the other 62 studies Greene rejected?

There were a variety of reasons why Greene (1997) eliminated studies included by Rossell and Baker (1996). Of these, 14 evaluations were rejected because there was not a marked distinction between those students who received English or Spanish language instruction. Another 25 studies were eliminated because they failed to sufficiently control for background differences between treatment and control groups. Yet, another 15 studies were dropped because they were actually duplicate studies that had already been included in the Rossell and Baker list. Five studies were rejected because they could not be found, and three studies were excluded because they were not evaluations of bilingual programs.

Second, Greene (1997) also took issue with the method Rossell and Baker (1996) used to determine whether a program evaluation supported native language instruction or English instruction. Greene (1997) stated:

Of the 38 studies that evaluate bilingual versus English only programs in Rossell and Baker's list, 21 have an average positive estimated effect and 17 have an average negative effect. Simply counting positive and negative findings, a technique known as "vote counting," is less precise than a meta-analysis because it does not consider the magnitude or confidence level of effects.

(p. 10)

According to Greene (1997), Rossell and Baker (1996) also failed to use a consistent rule for judging whether a study supported native language instruction, refuted its support, or showed no difference. In fact, Rossell and Baker classified the Ramírez *et al.* (1991) study as showing no difference between native language instruction and English language instruction. Recall, however, that Meyer and Feinberg (1992) and the National Academy of Sciences panel found positive relations between student achievement and native language instruction even as they scrutinized the Ramírez *et al.* study. Lastly, Greene also raised issues with the recency of the studies; eight of the eleven studies he (and Rossell and Baker) used were conducted prior to 1983. As Greene cautions, these older studies may have impeded capturing the effect of more current models of bilingual education.

Cummins (1999), as Greene (1997), took issue with the manner Rossell and Baker (1996) classified studies programmatically. Cummins stated:

When we look more closely at the research studies that supposedly demonstrated the superiority of "structured immersion" over "transitional bilingual education" it turns out that 90% of these studies are interpreted by their authors as supporting the effectiveness of bilingual and even trilingual education.

(p. 29)

Of course, the misclassification of a study then misrepresents which programs are considered effective or ineffective. Specifically, Rossell and Baker erroneously classify seven of the ten studies they claim support the effectiveness of structured immersion. These seven studies are actually Canadian French immersion programs that are essentially bilingual programs with the goal of developing bilingualism and biliteracy in English, French and, in some cases, Hebrew. In one instance, Rossell and Baker (1996) classified a program as an example of submersion; however, the same study was classified as Spanish–English dual immersion by Baker in 1992 and as structured English immersion in 1998.

Rossell (1998) raised some serious issues with the Thomas and Collier (1997) research study. According to Rossell, this study suffers from two serious flaws: methodological problems and the manipulation and absence of data. Related to methodology, Rossell explained:

> First, it uses a methodology—a simple descriptive cohort analysis—that is unscientific and that can produce misleading results. The method is unscientific because each grade consists of different students—11 grades are studied but most students have only four years of achievement data—and there is no statistical control for pre-treatment differences that existed before the students were in the program. Even if Thomas and Collier had followed the same students over time, this study would be unscientific because it is not possible to determine the effect of a program that a student participated in many years ago without controlling for the student's individual characteristics and the characteristics of his or her current school and program.
>
> (pp. 2–3)

Related to the issue of the treatment or program type, Rossell (1998) claimed that Thomas and Collier (1997) failed to define each of the six programs as carefully as is merited given the purpose of their study. More specifically, Thomas and Collier relied on school staff to define their program labels (e.g., traditional ESL) and did not conduct classroom observations to verify whether what was going on in the classroom matched the program type. Further, Rossell asks exactly what a "well implemented and stable program" means. Thomas and Collier offer no criteria for designating a program as such. Rossell (1998) also took issue with the fact that Thomas and Collier began with a database consisting of 700,000 student records but only used 42,317 of them. These represent only 6 percent of the broader database. According to Rossell, the two researchers picked and chose their data to construct the achievement patterns they report. Only 3 percent or 1,269 of the students were in the two-way bilingual education treatment group (i.e., the most effective). Specific student and school characteristics (e.g., socioeconomic status; ethnic background; geographic location) for this and the other groups are not reported. Rossell suggested that Thomas and Collier not only studied the best implemented programs, but also the "best" students. This would make generalizing their findings to the general population problematic.

Thomas and Collier (2000) maintained that Rossell's critique is more of an attack and far from being a scholarly product. The authors believe Rossell's critique to be a mean-spirited attempt to degrade the value of their work and one that is based only on Rossell's opinions, and not on any substantial collection and analysis of student data.

As expected, not even Greene (1998) can escape the scrutiny of researchers. Cummins (1999) questioned the methodological acceptability of the already small number (11) of studies Greene used in his meta-analysis. One study used by Greene did not actually have a control group and other studies did not describe the bilingual program in any detail. It seems that Greene included a study in his analyses that was not justifiably an example of bilingual education. In this instance, Spanish language instruction was provided but by bilingual paraprofessionals. As Cummins stated, "The apparent rigor involved in reducing the extensive corpus of bilingual education data to 11 'methodologically acceptable' studies seems destined to end up in *rigor mortis* for this approach as the credibility of even these 11 studies is whittled away." (p. 27)

Discussion

Yet another decade of research on the effectiveness of bilingual education has passed, and it seems that the controversy over the effectiveness of bilingual education is far from being settled. The impetus for the controversy, however, rests on vulnerable research designs as well as politics, a topic yet to be addressed. In this section, both factors are discussed to provide a broader and more accurate assessment of the effectiveness debate.

The case for native language instruction

What can reasonably be stated about the effectiveness of bilingual education in light of the issues that have been raised regarding the integrity of the studies? It is interesting to note that although each study falls short in one way or another, insights can be gained from each. Collectively, these insights point to the effectiveness of the use of native language instruction although questions abound as to how much native language use is necessary to produce positive program effects.

Meyer and Feinberg (1992) concluded that there is sufficient evidence to support the theory underlying native language instruction in bilingual education. They also observed that the more effective late-exit program in the Ramírez *et al.* (1991) study continued to use the native language at least 40 percent of the time through grade 6.

Evidence in support of native language instruction is also forthcoming from the Rossell and Baker (1996) study. While Rossell and Baker concluded that structured (English) immersion appeared to be a more promising program than TBE, it should be borne in mind that in a structured English immersion program, "the teacher is fluent in the student's native language" (August and Hakuta, 1997, p. 145). The point is the student's native language is still used in this approach.

More importantly, Cummins (1999) indicated that Rossell and Baker's (1996) findings actually, but unknowingly, support native language instruction. They mislabeled many of the studies that they used to demonstrate that structured English immersion was more effective than TBE. The structured immersion studies were in fact Canadian bilingual programs. Cummins (1999) explained:

> The closest equivalent to the program in the United States is dual language immersion, which has repeatedly demonstrated its effectiveness for both majority and minority students (Christian, Montone, Lindholm, and Carranza, 1997; Dolson and Lindholm, 1995; Thomas and Collier, 1997). Note that, as in the U.S. dual language programs, Canadian French Immersion programs are bilingual programs, taught by bilingual teachers, and their goal is the development of bilingualism and biliteracy.

(p. 29)

These dual language immersion programs are also known as two-way bilingual education programs. It is also interesting to note the "effectiveness" reference Cummins (1999) makes to the Thomas and Collier (1997) study in the above citation. Cummins does not take issue with the integrity of the study Rossell (1998) finds extensively flawed, though he does with the Rossell and Baker (1996) and Greene (1997) studies. In fact, no researcher other than Rossell (1998) has directly taken issue with the Thomas and Collier study. Crawford (1999), however, questions why Thomas and Collier have declined to release sufficient data and details to support their findings, why the bilingual education research circle has not pressed the researchers on this issue, and why Thomas and Collier's study has not been published in a scholarly peer-reviewed journal.

As for the Greene (1997) study, Cummins (1999) does not distinguish between the two analyses conducted. That is, it is uncertain whether the analyses Greene conducted with the randomly assigned studies—the more scientific studies—included methodologically question-able studies. Cummins critiqued some of the studies as methodologically unacceptable, but does not refer to any of the five random design studies. Recall that Greene reported a much larger effect related to native language instruction from these analyses.

In sum, findings from the Ramírez *et al.* (1991) study provide evidence of the use of the student's native language in late-exit programs; findings from the Rossell and Baker (1996) analysis do so as well, given that they were actually comparing TBE to two-way bilingual education programs. Greene's (1997) study does support native language instruction but makes no reference to program models. Is it simply a coincidence that the Thomas and Collier (1997) study, and the ensuing Salazar (1998) study, also support the effectiveness of late-exit and two-way bilingual education programs? Examined in this light, native language instruction is clearly supported by research conducted over the past decade.

The limits of research on bilingual education

An important assumption is being made with regard to the effectiveness debate between bilingual education and English-only programs. The goal in both camps has been to provide "hard evidence" that the ELLs catch up to native speakers of English more readily under their respective treatments or educational interventions. That is, there have been research efforts to show that one approach is "better" than the other and the inferior approach should be abandoned in the best interest of the children. However, this racehorse approach to the study of the efficacy of the various program models for educating ELLs may well be a research game stacked against bilingual education—a game that is unlikely to be *won* under any circumstances.

There are three general reasons that support this conclusion. First, empirical research on bilingual education entails certain methodological constraints that can plague even the best designed study. Further, there are certain problems outside of the design, but integral to the study, that can detract from the power of a well-designed study. Finally, there are broader social and political issues linked to bilingual education which clearly influence the impact educational treatments have on the academic achievement of Spanish-speaking school-age children. Each of these three constraints is discussed in turn.

Several of the research design problems have already been mentioned in the section high-lighting the critiques of Ramírez *et al.* (1991), Rossell and Baker (1996), Thomas and Collier (1997), and Greene (1998). Among the more important limitations of available research, and limitations that must be addressed by future research, are the following:

- Randomly assigning students to a control and comparison group or identifying an adequate comparison group.
- Clearly describing the central features of the educational treatment as opposed to using generic program labels (e.g., ESL; TBE; late-exit bilingual programs).
- Carefully defining and controlling for a constellation of student, teacher, program, school, community, district, and state level variables.
- Securing an adequate sample size and controlling for student mobility.
- Establishing what constitutes program effectiveness (e.g., size of the effect and in which academic areas).
- Articulating the generalizability of the findings to other school sites in sufficient detail.

In short, policy decisions cannot be driven by data from poorly designed research studies or poorly detailed program evaluations that are short term in nature. Moreover, if program evaluations are to be used, researchers must take into careful account how long the program has been in place. That is, they must determine whether or not the program is considered fully implemented and provide the evidence to support such a claim.

At a second level, one must also consider the integrity of what drives instruction and counts as learning. Consider, for example, that at the center of each study were the gains the students made in English reading on a norm-referenced or standardized test of some type. One can assume that a specified reading and language arts curriculum was used that was compatible with certain instructional approaches and a particular standardized reading test. In the state of Texas, for example, reading achievement is measured (beginning in grade 3) through the yearly administration of the Texas Assessment of Academic Skills (TAAS), which is allegedly aligned with the curriculum called the Texas Essential Knowledge and Skills (TEKS). Recent research on the integrity of the TAAS and TEKS for students, including Spanish-speaking ELLs of Mexican descent, has yielded some interesting findings.

According to Dressman (1999), the TEKS related to reading in English are based on a body of reading research that emphasizes phonemic awareness and discrete reading skills—not an entirely defensible approach to developing independent readers. Dressman pointed out:

> A close reading of these curriculum policy statements and their supporting evidence shows their propositions to be not so much research based as *research laced*. Reading them, I was unable to detect any sign of a thorough review of literacy research of the past 30 years that could be named as the foundation, or base, of the policies named in them.
>
> (1999, p. 27)

The point is that the quality of the reading curriculum in Texas, or any other state, is beyond the control of the researchers who are focused on determining whether bilingual education is more effective than English-only approaches. What use are significant research findings that are tied to a reading curriculum of questionable value?

Much the same problem arises when examining the validity of the tests used to measure academic achievement. Again, the TAAS has been the object of recent scrutiny in Texas and various researchers question the validity of the TAAS (Bernal, 2000; Haney, 2000; Hoffman *et al.*, 2001; McNeil and Valenzuela, 1998). Hoffman *et al.* (2000) found that the majority of the reading teachers they surveyed challenged the validity of the test, especially for minority students and ELLs. The authors stated:

The respondents to this survey, experts in reading and close to the classroom, are saying that the TAAS does not measure what it purports, is unfair to minority students, is affecting instruction in negative ways, is leading to teacher "drop-out", and is being used in ways that are invalid.

(p. 15)

McNeil and Valenzuela (1998) concluded that the use of the TAAS reduces the quality and quantity of the curriculum; instruction is aimed at the lowest level of skills and information and if the subject is not going to be tested, then it will not be taught. Bernal (2000, p. 503), in an examination of the psychometric properties of the TAAS, concluded, "As it stands, failing or passing the TAAS tells us little about a student's performance. . . . The TAAS exit-level test, in its present form, should not be used to deny anyone a high school diploma." To reiterate, significant research findings in bilingual education research that rest on questionable instructional practices and test scores are of little utility to bilingual education stakeholders.

There are other equally important components that underlie empirical research in bilingual education that seem to be taken at face value. English language proficiency tests are routinely used to monitor a student's progress in terms of their English language development. Scores from these measures are also used to determine when ELLs are deemed fully English proficient. Unfortunately, the validity of these kinds of tests has long been the subject of criticism (McCollum, 1983; Ulibarrí *et al.*, 1981; Valdés and Figueroa, 1994). One central problem is that a learner may score at one level on one test (e.g., limited English proficient), and at another (e.g., fully English proficient) on a different test (see Ulibarrí *et al.*, 1981). Such a discrepancy, embedded within the generalizability of research findings, could play havoc with making appropriate decisions related to transitioning the child into English instruction or exiting the child from a program.

In a like manner, the validity of Spanish proficiency tests used to endorse bilingual education teachers has recently been called into question (Guerrero, 1997). This is no trivial matter given that native language instruction is a cornerstone of bilingual education. Approximately 17 states have adopted or developed a Spanish language proficiency test for bilingual education teachers, and several states allow bilingual education but have no teacher Spanish proficiency test (Grant, 1997). Moreover, only two of these tests have been carefully reviewed for psychometric integrity (Guerrero, 2000).

Stated differently, if the bilingual teacher passes the state mandated Spanish proficiency test and obtains a bilingual education endorsement or certification, it is still difficult to ascertain what the teacher is able to do in the Spanish language. In fact, Guerrero (1999) argued that many bilingual education teachers have not been afforded the kinds of opportunity they need to be able to teach across the curriculum effectively in Spanish. In sum, when researchers state that the bilingual teachers at their research site are proficient in Spanish, research consumers would be well advised to gain a better understanding of how such a determination was made.

What does it really mean when researchers report that a bilingual education teacher is bilingually endorsed or certified? Various researchers have pointed out that bilingual education teacher training programs lack empirical support that might help justify their content (August and Hakuta, 1997). In the case of preparing bilingual education teachers to teach reading, Escamilla (2000, p. 127) pointed out,

Few universities and colleges offer specific course work in "Methods of Teaching Reading in Spanish." In many of these classes, prospective bilingual education teachers are simply told to learn best-practice strategies in English and do them in Spanish.

Similar cases have been made for science (Lee and Fradd, 1998) and math (Khisty, 1995).

In sum, if empirical research on bilingual education fails to be as effective as English-only instruction, the reasons for its ineffectiveness may not be linked to the treatment. The treatment may not be what it appears to be. That is, are students learning from a researched based curriculum? Is their learning being measured by valid achievement tests? Is the instruction being delivered by certified and Spanish-proficient bilingual education teachers? These matters may be beyond the control of the researcher, but to interpret research findings more thoroughly, they must be taken into careful account by researchers and research consumers.

Finally, one must simply recognize the limitations of empirical quantitative research as the primary tool for understanding why Spanish-speaking students achieve as they do under different instructional treatments. The fundamental ideological principle underlying the large scale empirical approach to the study of this educational dilemma is this: If we can just find the right educational program, we can remedy their educational ills. This positivistic approach conveniently discards the need to answer some very pressing questions. As Macedo (2000) put it:

> While the fields of bilingual education and ESL have produced a barrage of studies that aim primarily to demonstrate the effectiveness of English acquisition, these research studies conspicuously fail to raise other fundamental questions: Does cultural subordination affect academic achievement? What is the correlation of social segregation and school success? What role does cultural identity among subordinated students play in linguistic resistance? Does the devaluation of student's culture and language affect reading achievement? Is class a factor in bilingual education? Do material conditions that foster human misery adversely affect academic development?
>
> (p. 19)

Macedo maintains that it is academically dishonest to explain academic achievement patterns of language minority children as the simple by-product of a particular educational intervention, be it bilingual education or English-only type programs.

Thus "scientism," as Macedo (2000) calls it, is a double-edged sword for proponents of bilingual education. It is a means by which the status quo can always question the validity of the findings showing support for native language instruction because the studies can easily be dismissed as methodologically flawed. On the other hand, proponents of bilingual education, engaged in the traditional quantitative and empirical endeavors, are not allowed to explain the ineffectiveness of bilingual education as related to economic, linguistic, or cultural oppression or inequities, or as a by-product of colonialism as Macedo (2000) sees it.

In fact, none of the major studies reviewed in this chapter make reference to the marginalization or subordination of the subjects in their research. Greene (1997, p. 1), for example, interprets his findings as follows, "The conclusion of this meta-analysis is that the use of at least some native language in the instruction of LEP children tends to produce moderate improvements in standardized test scores taken in English."

From Macedo's (2000) perspective, it would seem appropriate to elaborate more fully. This could be achieved by stating that this finding is particularly significant given that it was not too long ago that students were physically punished for speaking Spanish at school (Peñalosa, 1980; also see Valencia, Chapter 1, this volume) and that English-only legislation has been passed in nearly half the states of the nation (Crawford, 1999). Relatedly, one could add that these findings are impressive given the current intensity of anti-immigration activity across the country (Suárez-Orozco, 1998) and that the parents of these successful learners categorically suffer from low-wage employment with little hope of advancement (Pérez and Salazar, 1997).

Furthermore, one must acknowledge that the overwhelming majority of Mexican–American students (both ELLS and English-speaking) attend highly segregated schools in the Southwest, and such isolation is strongly linked to low academic achievement (see Valencia *et al.*, Chapter 3, this volume). Surely, student outcomes are much more than a reflection of the instructional treatment the ELLs receive in public education. In light of these sociopolitical conditions, it seems reasonable to gauge any gain in minority student achievement as quite an accomplishment.

In this sociopolitical context, it should not come as any big surprise that there are researchers and political organizations given over to dismantling bilingual education yet purportedly advocating for ELLs. Rossell and Baker (1996) are a case in point. Greene (1997, p. 11) described them as "vocal critics of bilingual education." Crawford (1999) shares the following insight about Christine Rossell and Ron Unz, the latter of whom was responsible for the success of the anti-bilingual education Proposition 227 (California) and Proposition 203 (Arizona):

> Christine Rossell serves along with Ron Unz on the board of the Center for Educational Opportunity (CEO), an outfit headed by Linda Chávez and funded by Unz, the John D. Olin Foundation, and other conservative benefactors. All of CEO's activities are dedicated to opposing three policies: bilingual education, multiculturalism, and affirmative action. That's all it does.
>
> (p. 14)

On the other hand, a relatively objective yet critical stance has been maintained within the bilingual education research circle as Cummins (1999), Greene (1997), Moran and Hakuta (1995), and Meyer and Feinberg (1992) amply demonstrate.

It may well be that this research scenario has prompted the majority of policymakers to embrace native language instruction in a lukewarm, fence-sitting manner, or for only the short term (grades K-3). Most bilingual programs in the U.S. are in fact early-exit transitional bilingual education programs (August and Hakuta, 1997). Nonetheless, the Rossell and Baker (1996) study appears to have been enough ammunition to sway voters in California to pass Proposition 227 (Crawford, 1999), which severely limits the use of native language instruction in the state with the largest concentration of Mexican-origin, Spanish-speaking children in the country.

Future research in bilingual education

This is not a call for the abandonment of quantitative large-scale empirical research on bilingual education. It must proceed, but with some fundamental transformations, including the use of a longitudinal research framework, the examination of program features as opposed to program labels, the testing of hypotheses, and explanations of success or failure from a broader social and political perspective.

First, research must be longitudinal in nature as Thomas and Collier (1997) and Salazar (1998) advocate. While it is informative to understand the short-term impact a well implemented program has on language minority children while they are receiving the treatment, it is imperative that research examine how these students fare academically once the intervention has been discontinued. It is one achievement to catch up to the native speaker of English with educational support; it is quite another to maintain this parity without the support of instructional interventions. Guiding policy decisions without any insight into the long-term effect well implemented language minority programs have on learners is part of an outdated paradigm.

Second, these studies must abandon the practice of comparing politically loaded program labels, as recommended by August and Hakuta (1997) and Thomas and Collier (1997). As these authors suggest, what should be compared are different configurations of program features. A two-way bilingual education program that uses a skills-based approach to teaching and learning is very different from a two-way bilingual education program that utilizes critical pedagogy. Such an important distinction must not get muddled by generic and vague program labels. The presence or absence of native language instruction is critical, but its effectiveness is also contingent upon the quality of the methodologies, curriculum, materials, and assessment practices used to develop the learner's understanding of literacy, mathematics and science.

In line with specifying program attributes, new research must make a greater effort to more completely describe who the students are. To the exception of the Ramírez *et al.* (1991) study, student data reported in the remaining studies examined in this chapter are either not mentioned or sparsely provided. We must also get past grossly labeling the learners simply as Spanish-speaking. Clearly, the Mexicano or Mexican American child is different in significant ways from the Cuban and Guatemalan child. They are also viewed and treated differently by mainstream society. Similarly, first- and second-generation Mexican American ELLs respond to schooling differently and this variable must be carefully considered in research discussions.

If we wish to benefit from the generalizability of our research findings, we must also carefully delineate the local contexts in which research takes place. That is, a set of program features that might be appropriate for Spanish-speaking students from Mexico living in the Rio Grande Valley of Texas may need to be radically different for similar students whose parents are drawn to the poultry processing plants in Rogers, Arkansas, or the promise of employment in large urban communities like East Los Angeles. In short, a new research benchmark is warranted to better understand which program features best suit specific types of students (August and Hakuta, 1997) within specific contexts (Samaniego and Eubanks, 1991).

In line with this position, Cummins (1999) calls for a very different focus in conducting and using bilingual education research to inform educational policymaking. A major point Cummins argues is that it has proven virtually impossible to compare program types "due to the myriad human, administrative, and political influences that impact the implementation of programs over time" (p. 26). Consequently, research centered on the effectiveness debate in bilingual education has offered policymakers very little empirical evidence on which to base their policies.

This does not mean, however, that the studies presented in this chapter are of little use to policymakers; it simply means that they cannot answer what they were intended to answer—which program type is best. On the other hand, these studies (and many other so called "methodologically unacceptable" studies) could be used to test certain hypotheses to help construct a coherent bilingual education theory, something sorely lacking in the field. As Cummins (1999) explained, we have attempted to inform educational policy with empirical findings that are piecemeal and that are not part of a coherent theory of bilingual education tested over time:

It is the *theory* rather than the individual research findings that permits the generation of predictions about program outcomes under different conditions. Research findings themselves cannot be directly applied across contexts. For example, the fact that students in a Spanish–English bilingual program in New York City performed well academically in relation to grade norms (Beykont, 1994) tells us very little about whether a similar program might work with Mexican American students in San Diego. Yet when certain patterns are replicated across a wide range of situations, the accumulation of consistent findings suggests that some stable underlying principle is at work. This principle can then be stated as a theoretical proposition or hypothesis from which predictions can be derived and tested.

(p. 26)

Fundamentally, Cummins (1999) is arguing for a research–theory–policy paradigm and the abandonment of the predominant research–policy paradigm in which theoretical principles are not tested or part of a broader theoretical model of bilingual education under construction. This would breathe new life into the usefulness of the many bilingual education research studies that have been dismissed on methodological grounds simply because the study did not include a comparison group.

Cummins (1999) offered an illustrative example. Suppose we have 100 two-way bilingual education programs across the U.S. that show that ELLs essentially catch up, academically, to native speakers of English by the end of elementary school. A few programs are found not to have this effect but have also been found to have inappropriately implemented the program. Do the 90 or so programs showing a positive pattern tell us anything that is policy relevant? English-only advocates (e.g., Rossell and Baker, 1996) would say no because these programs are methodologically unacceptable given that they have no comparison group. Cummins believes that such a consistent and pervasive finding is very relevant to policy-making and to the development of a theoretical model of bilingual education.

In this instance, such a finding would support the validity of sustained native language instruction over a period of six or seven years and temper the hypothesis that the sooner ELLs are exposed to English the better. On the other hand, it would not necessarily disprove the effectiveness of all English approaches such as structured English immersion adopted recently in California and Arizona. However, this hypothesis testing approach would allow us to test whether all English instruction is beneficial to ELLs over the long term and not simply from one year to the next. It may well be that an all English approach is more effective than a sustained native language approach, in some cases, but more as a function of the characteristics of the learners and their respective communities than the superiority of the approach.

Proposition 227: preliminary findings

It will be especially interesting to see how pundits and researchers for and against bilingual education study the impact of Proposition 227 in California and Proposition 203 in Arizona. As one would readily expect, proponents of Proposition 227 are prematurely claiming victory in California—and the superiority of structured English immersion over bilingual education—based on only two years of data and some fuzzy math (Hakuta *et al.*, 1999). Unz claims that the test scores in English reading, as measured by the state mandated Stanford Achievement Test-9 (SAT-9), have increased by 190 percent for ELLs at one structured English immersion site. Apparently, the 190 percent increase was computed by taking the average reading score in 2000 (23 percentile points) and dividing it by the 1998 baseline score (12 percentile points). The Unz group simply, and erroneously, divided 23 by 12 to generate the increase of 190 percent. Hakuta *et al.* (1999) explained:

> The proponents' claim is probably based on making a comparison of the 1999 percentile score with the 1998 percentile score (i.e., for the increase from 12 to 23, one might divide 23 by 12, and come up with about 190%). This method, however, is incorrect. . . . As this relates to our discussion of SAT-9 scores, if increases are reported using a ratio of scores, any increase they make will seem larger than those made by non-LEP students that generally had higher initial scores. Does this mean that LEP students increased more than native English students, and therefore that we should accept the claim of a resounding success for Proposition 227? Of course not.
>
> (p. 4)

Hakuta *et al.* (1999) reported that test scores have risen for many students in California, including ELLs in bilingual education programs, in structured English immersion programs, and English-speaking students living in high poverty. According to these researchers, the state of California has been engaged in extensive school reform efforts over the last few years (e.g., class size reduction), thus it is difficult to discern exactly what impact Proposition 227 has had on ELLs. Furthermore, as Delia Pompa (2000)—Executive Director of the National Association for Bilingual Education—has recently noted "It [the analysis by pro-Proposition 227 individuals] also selectively ignored schools whose bilingual students outperformed peers on English-only campuses. In short, it made popular fact of irresponsible myth" (p. 96). It is encouraging, nevertheless, that a team of researchers has been following this balloted initiative from its inception and are in no hurry to reach a verdict. Hopefully, by the year 2010 we will be able to see the achievement patterns (K-12) of cohorts of ELLs who received instruction in structured English immersion programs and the bilingual education programs that remain intact.

Concluding remarks

It seems that proponents of bilingual education have been duped into a winner-take-all debate that cannot be won under any circumstances. To wit, there is absolutely no research evidence indicating that one year of structured English immersion is an adequate educational treatment for ELLs. Yet, this is precisely the remedy set forth in Proposition 227 in California and Proposition 203 in Arizona. Not only was the research on bilingual education disregarded, the research on structured English immersion was as well.

If English-only proponents were truly acting in the ELLs' best interests, why did they endorse an educational treatment with absolutely no theoretical or empirical substance? Even one of the longtime critics of bilingual education, Rosalie Pedalino Porter, finds Proposition 203 too extreme. The day after the passage of Proposition 203 in Arizona, González (2000, p. 1), reported Porter's reaction, "I would rather see a modification of the existing state law than a complete overthrow." Is it not abundantly clear that the debate surrounding the effectiveness of bilingual education is not really about bilingual education?

Notes

1 The reader is referred to Crawford's website for more complete information on Propositions 227 and 203: www.ourworld.compuserve.com/homepages/JWCrawford.
2 This author prefers the phrase English language learners (ELLs) to the more commonly used limited-English-proficient students (LEPs). ELLs are school-age students who are in the process of acquiring English as a second language in the U.S.
3 The total number of studies does not add up to 72 because some of the evaluations may have compared the students across reading, language, and math; others, may have reported data for only one or two of these academic areas. For example, only 14 studies compared Language scores for students in TBE and Submersion.
4 A Type II error concerns the failure to reject a null hypothesis when it is false. In this case, it is when the researcher operates from a null hypothesis (e.g., bilingual education has no significant effect on English reading achievement), and erroneously concludes that there was no significant effect from the treatment.

References

August, D. and Hakuta, K. (1997). *Improving schooling for language-minority children: A research agenda*. Washington, DC: National Academy Press.

Bernal, E.M. (2000). Psychometric inadequacies of the TAAS. *Hispanic Journal of Behavioral Sciences, 22*, 481–507.

Beykont, Z. (1994). *Academic progress of a nondominant group: A longitudinal study of Puerto Ricans in New York City's late-exit bilingual programs*. Unpublished doctoral dissertation, Harvard University, Cambridge, MA.

Crawford, J. (1999). Life in a politicized climate: What role for educational researchers? [On-line]. Available: http://ourworld.compuserve.com/homepages/jwcrawford/LMRI.htm

Christian, D., Montone, C., Lindholm, K. and Carranza, I. (1997). *Profiles in two-way immersion education*. Washington, DC: Center for Applied Linguistics and Delta Systems.

Cummins, J. (1999). Alternative paradigms in bilingual education research: Does theory have a place? *Educational Researcher, 28*, 26–32.

Dolson, D. and Lindholm, K. (1995). World class education for children in California: A comparison of the two-way bilingual immersion and European schools model. In T. Skutnabb-Kangas (Ed.), *Multilingualism for all* (pp. 69–102). Lisse, The Netherlands: Swets & Zeitlinger.

Dressman, M. (1999). On the use and misuse of research evidence: Decoding two states' reading initiatives. *Reading Research Quarterly, 34*, 258–285.

Escamilla, K. (2000). Teaching literacy in Spanish. In J. Tinajero and R. DeVillar (Eds.), *The power of two languages: Effective dual-language use across the curriculum* (pp. 126–141). New York: McGraw-Hill.

González, D. (2000). Arizona win encourages bilingual-ed opponents. [On-line]. Available: http://www.onenation.org/0011/112000a.htm

Grant, L. (1997). Testing the language proficiency of bilingual teachers: Arizona's Spanish proficiency test. *Language Testing, 14*, 23–46.

Greene, J. (1997). A meta-analysis of the Rossell and Baker review of bilingual education research. *Bilingual Research Journal* [On-line], 21. Available: http://brj.asu.edu

Guerrero, M. (1997). Spanish academic language proficiency: The case of bilingual education teachers in the U.S. *Bilingual Research Journal, 21*, 65–84.

Guerrero, M. (1999). *Spanish language proficiency of bilingual education teachers* (Center for Bilingual Education Research Monograph No. 2). Tempe, AZ: Arizona State University.

Guerrero, M. (2000). The unified validity of the Four Skills Exam: Applying Messick's framework. *Language Testing, 17*, 397–421.

Hakuta, K., Butler, Y. and Bousquet, M. (1999). What legitimate inferences can be made from the 1999 release of SAT-9 scores with respect to the impact of California's Proposition 227 on the performance of LEP students? [On-line]. Available: http://www.stanford.edu/~hakuta/SAT9/index.htm

Haney, W. (2000). The myth of the Texas miracle in education. *Education Policy Analysis Archives* [On-line serial]. Available at: http://epaa.asu.edu/epaa/v8n41

Hoffman, J., Pennington, J., Assaf, L. and Paris, S. (2001). High stakes testing in reading: Today in Texas, tomorrow? *Reading Teacher*, *54*, 482–492.

Khisty, L. (1995). Making inequality: Issues of language and meanings in mathematics teaching with Hispanic students. In W. Secada, E. Fennema, and L. Adajiian (Eds.), *New directions for equity in mathematics education* (pp. 279–297). New York: Cambridge University Press.

Lee, O. and Fradd, S. (1998). Science for all, including students from non-English language backgrounds. *Educational Researcher*, *27*, 12–21.

Macedo, D. (2000). The colonialism of the English Only movement. *Educational Researcher*, *29*, 15–24.

McCollum, P. (1983). The IDEA Oral Language Proficiency Test: A critical review. In S. Seidner (Ed.), *Issues of language assessment: Volume II Language assessment and curriculum planning* (pp. 85–94). Chicago: Illinois State Board of Education.

McNeil, L. and Valenzuela, A. (1998). *The harmful impact of the TAAS system of testing in Texas: Beneath the accountability rhetoric*. The Civil Rights Project. Cambridge, MA: Harvard University Press.

Meyer, M. and Feinberg, S. (1992). *Assessing evaluation studies: The case of bilingual education strategies*. Washington, DC: National Academy Press.

Moran, C. and Hakuta, K. (1995). Bilingual education: Broadening research perspectives. In J. Banks and C. McGee (Eds.), *Handbook of research on multicultural education* (pp. 445–462). New York: Macmillan.

Peñalosa, F. (1980). *Chicano sociolinguistics*. Rowley, MA: Newbury House.

Pérez, S. and Salazar, D. (1997). Economic, labor force, and social implications of Latino educational and population trends. In A. Darder, R. Torres, and H. Gutierrez (Eds.), *Latinos and education* (pp. 45–79). New York: Routledge.

Pompa, D. (2000) Bilingual success: Why two-language education is critical for Latinos. *Hispanic*, November, 96.

Ramírez, D., Yuen, S., Ramey, D., Pasta, D. and Billings, D. (1991). *Final Report: Longitudinal study of structured English immersion strategy, early-exit and late-exit transitional bilingual education programs for language minority children*. San Mateo, CA: Aguirre International.

Rossell, C. (1998). Mystery on the bilingual express: A critique of the Thomas and Collier study "School effectiveness for language minority students." *READ Perspectives*, *5*, 5–32.

Rossell, C. and Baker, K. (1996). The educational effectiveness of bilingual education. *Research in the Teaching of English*, *30*, 7–74.

Salazar, J. (1998). A longitudinal model for interpreting thirty years of bilingual education research. *Bilingual Research Journal* [On-line], 22. Available: http://brj.asu.edu

Samaniego, F. and Eubanks, L. (1991). *A statistical analysis of California's case study project in bilingual education*. Davis: Intercollegiate Division of Statistics, University of California, Davis.

Suárez-Orozco, M. (1998). State terrors: Immigrants and refugees in the post-national space. In Y. Zou and E. Trueba (Eds.), *Ethnic identity and power: Cultural contexts of political action in school and society* (pp. 283–330). Albany: State University of New York Press.

Thomas, W. and Collier, V. (1997). *School effectiveness for language minority students*. Washington, DC: National Clearinghouse for Bilingual Education.

Thomas, W. and Collier, V. (2000). *A response to Rossell's "Mystery on the bilingual express"*. Unpublished manuscript, George Mason University, Washington, DC.

Ulibarrí, D., Spencer, M. and Rivas, G. (1981). Language proficiency and academic achievement: A study of language proficiency tests and their relationship to school ratings as predictors of academic achievement. *NABE Journal*, *5*, 47–80.

Valdés, G. and Figueroa, R. (1994). *Bilingualism and testing: A special case of bias*. Norwood, NJ: Ablex Publishing Corporation.

Part III

Cultural and familial perspectives on Chicano student achievement

7 Chicano/Latino critical ethnography of education: cultural productions from *la frontera*

Sofia Villenas and Douglas E. Foley

Chicanas/os and Latinos/as have long challenged dominant forms of schooling and education since the beginning of European colonization some 500 years ago. Prominent educational anthropologist Enrique Trueba (1999) writes that one could say:

> the first critical ethnography was constructed in 1542 by an oppressed Indian, Francisco Tenamaztle, who had led the revolt against the Spaniards in the states of Jalisco, Michoacán, and Colima in central México. He was captured and exiled to Spain, where, assisted by Fray Cristóbal de las Casas, he defended the human rights of all the Indians.

> (p. 125)

As Trueba's words suggest, one might begin a discussion of contemporary Chicano/Latino ethnography by acknowledging its historical roots in struggles and narratives of critique and resilience that are centuries old.[1] Any account of this "ethnographic" tradition could easily be situated within a critique of education that spans across old and new forms of colonialism (Gallegos, 1998; San Miguel and Valencia, 1998), border impositions, and border crossings. There also exists a long tradition of narrating Amerindian cultural roots of survival in the intimate and communal spaces of families and communities (Trueba, 1999). Indeed, one can say that the new contributions of Chicano/Latino ethnography are a historical extension of the sentiments, experiences, and active *presence* of a people.

This review will highlight the recent developments of this borderlands or "trans-*frontera*" (Saldívar, 1997) perspective in Chicano/Latino educational ethnography. To better understand the emergence of a uniquely Latina/o sensibility, we situate these developments within the post-1960s emergence of a modern Latina/o critical ethnography. Consequently, we begin this chapter by briefly defining "critical ethnography" with particular attention to Latino/Chicano imperatives. Next, we locate Chicano/Latino ethnography within the dominant post-1960s response to the cultural deficit explanation of "minority school failure." Third, we explore the borderland epistemologies that underpin an emerging Chicano/Latino educational ethnography. We then review the more nuanced, "borderized" ethnographic portraits of Latino cultural and linguistic creativity and indictments of schools that fail Latino/Chicano children, as well as the culturally relevant pedagogies, curricula, and policies that work. Finally, the chapter closes with some reflections on how border, post-national, and diasporic perspectives might begin to alter the way we presently study Latina/o student agency and cultural production.

Chicano/Latino educational ethnography: the critical ethnography connection

It is difficult to date precisely the beginnings of 20th century Chicana/o educational ethnography. George Śanchez's (1940) *Forgotten People: A Study of New Mexicans* or Ernesto Galarza's (1971) auto-ethnographic *Barrio Boy* would surely rank as early classic educational ethnographies.[2] Given, however, the systematic exclusion of Latinas/os from academia, these classics are rarely taught as such. Moreover, there is no discernible "first generation" of Chicana/o educational ethnographers until the post-1960s civil rights era. Although this first wave of Latina/o ethnographers did not generally represent themselves as "critical ethnographers," they quickly became embroiled in the reigning educational debates over so-called "minority education." As we shall see, these 1970s and 1980s debates over "cultural deficit" explanations of ethnic minority school failure profoundly shaped their theoretical worldviews and political struggles. Before situating the work of Latina/o ethnographers in these debates, however, we would like to briefly define "critical ethnography."

Critical ethnographers generally emphasize doing prolonged, systematic fieldwork rooted in at least a year or two of participant observation, key informant work, and extensive interviews. They utilize many traditional methodological practices, but unlike traditional ethnographers, do not usually aspire to produce holistic, universalizing portraits of whole cultures. Critical ethnographers tend to be more interested in producing focused, well-theorized accounts of a particular institution or subgroup that reveal oppressive relations of power. To use critical theorist Jürgen Habermas's (1972) apt phrase, knowledge production has to have an "emancipatory intent." Or to use postmodernist Patti Lather's (1991) phraseology, critical ethnographies have to produce knowledge that has "catalytic validity," that is, that serves to change the status quo. Similarly, Enrique Trueba (1999) argues for a Freirean tradition (Freire, 1973) of critical ethnography where there is "an intimate relationship between the intellectual activity of research and the *praxis* of the daily life of researchers" (p. 128) committed to the eradication of all oppression. Put succinctly, critical ethnography is a well-theorized empirical study with a serious political intent to change people's consciousness, if not their daily lives.

To fulfill these goals, the critical ethnographer has to begin breaking with the conventional scientific ethnographic practice of being a detached, neutral observer. S/he has to openly collaborate with the oppressed. In the 1960s and 1970s, the more activist style of collaborating was to work directly for and with oppressed groups to produce the types of studies they needed and valued. If they needed a study that would help them win legal battles, rent strikes, and various political actions, then the critical ethnographer was a pen for hire. The more academic style of collaboration was to write critiques of the capitalist production system and political power structure, demonstrating the systematic, oppressive character of capitalism. Such critical academic studies were supposed to reveal the hidden, systemic, oppressive reality of capitalism, and thus raise the consciousness of the reader. Many also fall under the rubric of "cultural critiques" that expose the ideological, hegemonic character of the educational research discourse and its microinstitutional practices.

Using the aforementioned criteria, much of Chicano/Latino ethnography is a form of *critical* ethnography. It has a strong political and praxis-oriented intent rooted in historical and experiential knowledge of cultural and linguistic discrimination. Notwithstanding the first "critical ethnographies" in the context of European colonization (i.e., Francisco Tenamaztle in 1542), Latinos/as have a history of critical praxis emanating from Latin American/Chicana(o) social politics. The work of Liberation Theology with a social reading of the gospel, Freirean-inspired literacy campaigns,[3] womanist and leftist grassroots organizing, indigenous movements for self-determination, and the Chicano/a Movement have all historically informed political and practice-oriented research. Following this critical tradition, the convergence of critical ethnography and Chicano critical research in education, has been about producing knowledge that documents oppressive schooling practices for Latino children (the oppression of U.S. imperialism) and the processes of family and community empowerment (the politics of "liberation"). Our broad characterization of the recent work of Chicana(o)/Latina(o) ethnographers as "critical ethnography" perhaps will become clearer if situated in the national educational debates over explaining the achievement gap between White mainstream youths and allegedly "culturally deficient" ethnic minority youths.

The creation of "minority education" to explain the "achievement gap"

In the 1960s, White scholars created the field of "minority education" to help solve what became known as the national "achievement gap" problem. The exhaustive Coleman *et al.* (1966) report, a national survey of school achievement, reported the lagging scores of African Americans, Mexican Americans, and American Indians. The Coleman study and most subsequent studies have measured school achievement with standardized achievement tests and/or grades. During this era, liberal educational reformers blamed the "achievement gap" on the segregated, dual nature of U.S. public education. They reasoned that mixing the races would both improve the decrepit physical facilities of "colored schools" and would inspire these children to work up to the level of their White counterparts. Other liberal reformers of the 1960s championed a host of early childhood compensatory education programs like "Head Start" (see Pearl, 1997, for a discussion and critique of Head Start, which he asserts, was founded on deficit thinking). Such programs emphasized early literacy experiences and teaching good student behaviors.

Undergirding both of these liberal reform programs was a fundamental set of beliefs and assumptions about the culture of all low-achieving ethnic minority groups (Foley, 1997). In the 1960s, many liberals and conservatives subscribed to Oscar Lewis' (1965) "culture of poverty" view of the poor. According to Lewis, who conducted his fieldwork in Mexico City and New York City, the urban poor, regardless of their ethnicity, lived in disintegrating, chaotic family and community structures. Each generation passed on a way of life marked by fatalistic, violent, cynical, and unproductive attitudes and values. The liberal-minded Lewis never intended to provide grist for moralizing policymakers, but social historian Michael Katz (1989) says that is precisely what he did. He confirmed fears that the growing urban underclass needed to be re-socialized into psychologically stable, optimistic, hard-working citizens.

Lewis' sweeping negative portrayal of the poor provided the intellectual foundation for post-World War II educational researchers writing about low-income minority youths. Chicano educational psychologist Richard Valencia (1997a) and associates have reconstructed these developments in some detail in his edited volume. He contends that Social Darwinist theories of White racial superiority gradually shifted from a genetic to a cultural difference perspective (Valencia, 1997b). Post-World War educational researchers invented what Valencia calls a "cultural deficit discourse" that "blamed the victim." According to deficit thinkers, low-achieving minority youths have parents who do not teach them to be assertive problem solvers and knowledge seekers (Ginsberg, 1972). Moreover, they use a "restricted language code" that lacks elaborate grammatical, lexical, and logical functions (Bernstein, 1975). Such deficient language development was thought to stunt cognitive development. Consequently, these ethnic youths often lacked a "field-independent" style of learning and were less adept at the linear, higher-order abstract thinking. When combined with the culture of poverty thesis, deficit thinking was a sweeping portrayal of the motivational, linguistic, and cognitive deficiencies of poor ethnic minorities.

Today, 30 years later, the current "backlash" against multiculturalism has reawakened this deadly culture of poverty/deficit discourse. Urban ethnographers Michelle Fine and Lois Weis (1998) underscore the rise of moralistic, conservative policy discourse that blames what historian Michael Katz (1989) aptly dubs the "undeserving poor." Meanwhile, Herrnstein and Murray's *The Bell Curve* (1994) turns the social science clock back by exploring the failure of poor ethnic minorities as a sign of genetic inferiority (for discussion and critiques of this perspective, see Valencia and Solórzano, 1997; Valencia and Suzuki, 2001, Chapter 6). Once more, White racial superiority rears its ugly head in educational debates over affirmative action, bilingual education, Ebonics, phonics, and early childhood education, to mention only a few. The recent passage of Propositions 187, 209, and 227 in California and the *Hopwood* decision in Texas for example, will have a profound effect nationwide on Mexican American access to higher education and to good bilingual programs that meet children's linguistic needs (San Miguel and Valencia, 1998). San Miguel and Valencia argue that Mexican Americans face worsening educational conditions in an educational crisis that is unprecedented. According to these researchers, this "Latino Civil Rights Crisis," as referred to by scholars and policymakers, is a direct result of the current "backlash" and re-awakening of the culture of poverty discourse.

In general, the backlash's impact on earlier liberal reform efforts has been devastating. Gary Orfield and Susan Eaton's (1996) massive study of school segregation documents that American public schools remain a dual system based on race-class differences (also, see Valencia *et al.*, Chapter 3, present volume). The system provides relatively high quality suburban schools for the White majority and for middle-class minorities, and low quality urban schools for the predominantly ethnic minority underclasses. The difference in funding, facilities, curriculum, and instruction between these two systems of education preserves what social critic Jonathan Kozol (1991) calls a "savage inequality." So despite 50 years of educational reform, the educational achievement gap has joined death and taxes as a fundamental certainty in American life (see Valencia, Chapter 1, present book for discussion of the persistent, pervasive achievement gap between Chicano/a students and their White peers).

Three major critiques of the deficit discourse

Many progressive White scholars and a growing number of scholars of color have been shooting holes in culture of poverty/deficit thinking since the mid-1960s (Foley, 1997). Neo-Marxist scholars (Apple, 1979; Baudelot and Establet, 1971; Bourdieu and Passeron, 1977; Bowles and Gintis, 1976; Young, 1971) led the way in critiquing schooling in advanced capitalist societies like the United States, Great Britain, and France. These authors observed that while the prevailing liberal democratic rhetoric portrayed public school systems as fair and equal, the reality was quite different. Rather than transforming entrenched structures of social class inequality, schools tended to *reproduce* these structures. Scholars pinpointed various institutional mechanisms that reproduced inequality such as tracking (Oakes, 1985), cognitive tests (Lawler, 1978), teacher comportment (Apple, 1982), curricular knowledge (Anyon, 1981), and so forth. They generally agreed that public schools in the capitalist nation-state socialized students to accept their appointed places in the existing political–economic hierarchy. Despite the schools' promises of upward mobility, most members of the subordinate working class adopted the values of their parents and wound up in working-class jobs.

As many critics have pointed out (Davies, 1996; Liston, 1988), the early Marxist critique concentrated mainly on class inequality, and thus had relatively little to say about how race and gender articulate with class. Consequently, the initial Marxist critique did little to challenge the notions of culture and ethnicity underpinning deficit thinking. In addition, the early Marxist critiques of schools were too functionalist and deterministic. The schools were portrayed as little more than the instrument of powerful political and economic interests (Liston, 1988). Teachers and textbook writers appeared as guileless agents of the State or handmaidens of the ruling class. Students appeared as passive dummies, marching off to their respective fates (Connell, 1983). Much subsequent critical ethnographic research in schools sought to correct this imbalance (Levinson and Holland, 1996). In this regard, the writings of Frenchman Pierre Bourdieu (1977) and Englishman Paul Willis (1981) were particularly influential. Their work provided class theorists with a much more cultural way of looking at how schools reproduced social inequality.

Bourdieu emphasized the cultural and linguistic differences between middle and working-class youths. He generally argued that youths from privileged class backgrounds have an enormous advantage over working-class youths because they come to school already equipped with the proper etiquette, demeanor, taste, speech, and literacy styles. Bourdieu notes that possessing the "right" or preferred speech and literacy styles are a form of power or "cultural capital" that wins over teachers and leads to school success. Students from the "right classes" with the right cultural and linguistic style are expected to do better, and their speech and literary styles fit better into the school's middle-class culture.

Paul Willis' (1981) study of British working-class youths shows us the other side of the class–culture coin discussed above. He emphasizes how middle-class schools and teachers systematically devalue the linguistic and cultural practices of working-class youths. When faced with teachers and a curriculum that disrespects their aesthetics and manner of speaking and acting, working-class youths rebel against the bourgeois norms of the school. They valorize their working-class ways of speaking and acting. Unfortunately, their rebellion often consigns them to school failure. In the end, both Bourdieu and Willis demonstrate that the academic failure of poor students has more to do with institutional bias, or a mismatch between the culture of the school and the class culture of the students, than inherent cultural and linguistic deficiency. From a class–culture view, deficit/culture of poverty explanations of school achievement are nothing more than ideological, pseudoscientific theories (see Valencia, 1997c). Deficit explanations obscure the formidable institutional bias that works against working-class minorities and for middle-class students.

This new perspective became known as the "cultural production" and/or "practice" perspective in educational circles (Levinson and Holland, 1996). It generally emphasizes the multiple struggles of cultural identity groups against race, ethnic, class, *and* gender dominance (Foley and Moss, 2001). Theorists now agree that social and cultural reproduction, if and where it occurred, could not be foreordained; it had to pass through the dynamics of cultural production, and each historical setting will condition and mediate collective cultural struggles and individual actors in particular ways. The meaning of a given cultural struggle can only be discerned through a careful study of how class, race, and gender factors articulate. As we shall see, a number of Chicana(o)/Latina(o) ethnographers and progressive allies have built upon Marxist production and practice perspectives. A cultural production perspective shifts the focus from explaining school failure to understanding the complexities of cultural identity construction and language maintenance. Latino/a educational ethnographers have begun to produce a host of rich cultural and linguistic studies that explore how students use their cultural and linguistic compentencies to build school success.

A second major critique of deficit thinking based on ethnographic research emerged in the late 1960s. Sociolinguistically-oriented educational ethnographers like Heath (1983) and Philips (1983) sought to directly attack the underlying cultural deficit theory. Being good cultural relativists, they pointed out that all allegedly "deficient minority languages" were perfectly functional in their home contexts. They argued that minority youths had historically different but not deficient speech and literacy styles. The speech styles of African Americans and bilingual Mexican American and American Indian students only became "dysfunctional" when used in the middle-class culture of schools. The sociolinguistic perspective generally "explained" the school failure of minority youths as the effect of everyday miscommunications and cultural misunderstandings. Their microethnographic studies of seemingly minor speech events revealed who got to speak, who received praise, and how one was expected to succeed. More often than not, students of color who deployed a different speech style were at a distinct disadvantage. Curriculum materials that lacked cultural and linguistic sensitivity were also indicted. Here again, we see these scholars shifting the blame from the victim to the schooling institution, which is characterized as preferential towards the language of middle-class youths.

But like the Marxists, sociolinguists rarely explored how race and gender articulated with class factors. In contrast, Latino/a critical ethnographers have focused on language use in the classroom (see Gutiérrez *et al.*, 2001; Gutiérrez *et al.*, 1995) and in the family and community (see González, 1996, 2001; Mendoza-Denton, 1999; Zentella, 1997). As we shall see, they have been more attentive to racial factors. They have also produced more nuanced accounts of the creative linguistic productions of bilingual children, adolescents, and adults in Latino communities.

A third and final critique of the deficit discourse was the cultural ecological theory of Nigerian-born anthropologist John Ogbu (Ogbu, 1978, 1987; Ogbu and Simon, 1998). Unlike the Marxists and sociolinguists, he reintroduced the race factor in a serious way. Ogbu stresses that ethnic minorities are incorporated/assimilated into American society in very different ways. He makes a key distinction between immigrant people of color, such as most Asian Americans, who came to the United States freely or "voluntarily," and people of color such as African Americans, Mexican Americans, and American Indians, who were "involuntarily" or forcibly incorporated as slaves or colonized people.

Ogbu generally argues that forcibly incorporated "involuntary minorities" lack what he calls the "dual frame of reference" of voluntary minorities. Put simply, voluntary minorities see the U.S. as a land of opportunity compared to their situation "back home." They are generally optimistic and trusting of U.S. society, and work hard in school and in their jobs to succeed. Consequently, the parents of voluntary immigrants generally hold their children, not the schools, accountable for school success and failure. They see what they are learning as additive to their own cultural and linguistic traditions, not threatening or "subtractive." To use Margaret Gibson's (1988) apt phrase, voluntary immigrant minorities feel that they are "accommodating without assimilating" or losing their home culture.

By sharp contrast, Ogbu contends that many native-born "involuntary minorities" have grown up in an oppressive American racial system. Consequently, involuntary minorities compare their social and economic status to working-class White Americans, and they resent the disparities. The parents of involuntary minorities believe that their schools are worse than White suburban schools, and they often are ambivalent, critical, and distrustful of the school curriculum and teachers. Unlike the optimistic, accommodating, hard working voluntary minority, the involuntary minority develops what Ogbu calls an "oppositional" collective identity, along with anti-school peer groups. According to Ogbu, they view the requirements for school success—mastering the school curriculum and speaking and writing Standard English—as "acting white" and losing their ethnic culture. Like the rebellious working-class youths in Willis' (1981) study, they become inattentive, openly defiant and do not work hard, thus often failing in school. As we shall see, the intellectual debate surrounding John Ogbu's cultural ecological theory has been particularly intense (Erickson, 1987; Foley, 1991; Levinson, 1992; Trueba, 1988). While Ogbu reintroduced the concept of race and based his theory, in part, on studies of Latino immigrant school achievement (see Matute-Bianchi, 1991; Suárez-Orozco, 1989), Latino ethnographers have often contested Ogbu's theories (see Trueba, 1988; Valenzuela, 1999a). As we shall see, Chicana/o and Latina/o ethnographers have eschewed Ogbu's positivist dream of a universal, "scientific" explanation of ethnic school failure. Instead, they have chosen to highlight the dynamic cultural and linguistic productions of Latino family and community life, as well as schools' failed responsibilities to Latina/o students (Villenas and Deyhle, 1999). Moreover, recent studies of in-group variation among immigrants (Suárez-Orozco and Suárez-Orozco, 1995; Valenzuela, 1999a) trouble his typology of high-achieving immigrant students and low-achieving native-born students.

Since the mid-1980s, new theoretical currents have found their way into the interdisciplinary field of Chicana/o Cultural Studies. Chicana/o and Latina/o scholars have been deeply influenced by recent antifoundational postmodern, critical race, postcolonial, and feminist theories of science. The most recent wave of Chicano/a educational ethnographers has also begun to draw upon "borderland theory" that emphasizes uniquely Chicana/o epistemologies or ways of knowing. As we shall see, Latina/o ethnographers armed with this new borderlands sensibility continue to address questions raised by the original deficit theory debates. To this end, they are creating more nuanced, valorizing portraits of Latino cultural and linguistic practices in school, family, and community settings. They are also pushing mainstream educational researchers to retheorize the relationship of cultural and racial identity constructions to school and life success.

Some new (yet old) theoretical underpinnings of Latino/Chicano ethnography: *la frontera* as epistemology and methodology

Increasingly, Chicana/o and Latina/o ethnographers are embracing multiple epistemologies rooted in the sensibilities of *la frontera* and borderlands. The border, borderlands, and border crossings are a shared and collective naming of the cultural and bodily experiences under Spanish and U.S. colonialism, and U.S. and México nationalisms. This memory and experiences have been documented in anonymous *corridos* (Mexican ballad songs), *historias* (stories), and literary works to name just a few avenues. Gloria Anzaldúa (1987) has been pioneering in naming, transforming, and developing the theoretical and spiritual meanings of the lived aesthetics of the borderlands and *mestizaje* (mixed ancestry). Moreover, many Chicano/a scholars, including Emma Pérez, Angie Chabram-Dernersesian, Renato Rosaldo, José Limón, and José David Saldívar, among others, directly and indirectly describe the border and the borderlands experience as the ultimate of postmodernisms. It is the present and future way of being in the world—of juggling cultures and of embracing ambiguity, struggle, and solidarities across heterogeneities, while rejecting modernist nationalisms even as we live under modernist oppressions. These sensibilities and intellectual excavations have allowed Latinas/os to critique social reproduction theories from Chicana/o-style postmodern and poststructural perspectives. As Chicana theorist Alejandra Elenes (1997) points out:

Given the limitations of neo-Marxist theories of social reproduction, especially the limitation of race, class, gender, and sexuality analyses, postmodernism offered new avenues to interpret social conditions. While many scholars in "traditional" fields "discovered" the limitation of existing paradigms, Chicana/o scholars had already provided critiques of such scholarly research.

(p. 364)

Indeed, border and borderlands theorizing have in large part informed these critiques which have served to deconstruct essentialist notions of identity, culture, and difference (Elenes, 1997). As Emma Pérez (1999) argues, Anzaldúa's "borderlands" and the rearticulation of la *frontera* and *mestizaje* "became the keywords, the cohesive metaphoric linchpins for many late-twentieth-century writings" (p. 25). We would add that *la frontera* and borderlands are becoming the "cohesive metaphoric linchpins" (E. Pérez, 1999, p. 25) for Chicano/Latino ethnography.

Yet, these borderized epistemologies are often difficult to excavate in the aftermath of Manifest Destiny. The project of acknowledging voices unheard and unrecognized in Chicano/Latino communities through oral histories (see Leticia Garza-Falcón, 1998) is often taken for granted and silenced (E. Pérez, 1999). Emma Pérez (1999) calls this space between the colonialist and the colonized the "decolonial imaginary"—the space where activities and words of a *mestiza/o* sensibility, although "unseen, unthought, merely a shadow in the background of the colonial mind" (p. 7), persist. Although such shadowy spaces of voices and struggles are difficult to excavate, Concha Delgado-Gaitan (1987, 1990; Delgado-Gaitan and Trueba, 1991), and Enrique Trueba (1991) were pioneers in utilizing a "trans-*frontera*" sensibility (Saldívar, 1997) to excavate the many literacies, oralities, and home pedagogies of Mexican families in the U.S.

Enrique Murillo Jr. has begun to make this new epistemological foundation of Latino educational ethnography more explicit. He writes that "the value-laden ethnographer is . . . all of these things: the bodily instrument, the text-maker, and the inventor of cultures" (1999, p. 6). As bodily instruments, Latino/a ethnographers use their racialized gendered bodies (Villenas, 1996, 2000), their *mojado* (wetback) bodies (Murillo Jr., 1999), their community-centered bodies (Russel y Rodríguez, 1998), their activist bodies (Pizarro, 1998), their paradigms of *cariño* (tender caring) (Flores, 2000), and their feminist/womanist cultural knowledge and intuition (Delgado Bernal, 1998; González, 1998) to deconstruct the universalizing and objectivist foundations of the research process.

A number of young Chicana/o ethnographers have begun to evoke the metaphor of the knowing brown body, the border-crossing body marked by oppression, pain, resistance, and joy as a unique epistemological location. Delgado Bernal (1998) argues that a Chicana feminist epistemology is based on cultural intuitions born of the aforementioned unique lived cultural reality. Similarly, Nitza Hidalgo (1998) argues that "native" researchers can use culturally sensitive frameworks that center Latino family and kinship networks rather than idealized mainstream versions of "family." Francisca González (1998) adds the constructs of a braided methodological framework, *trenzas*, which is Chicana/Mexicana womanist and centers the experiences of race, language, citizenship, and gender. Marc Pizarro (1998) reconstructs the research process itself by centering Chicano/a experiences and ways of knowing in a more inclusive and culturally responsive endeavor where participants and researchers are co-constructors of emancipatory knowledge. Finally, Villenas (1996) troubles facile notions of collaborative research and native ethnographers as emancipators. Reflecting upon her fieldwork experiences, she argues that native ethnographers are susceptible to many forms of cultural dominance and cannot easily discard their previous marginalizing experiences. Nor does their new identity as university-sanctioned researchers magically bestow upon them emancipatory powers. The aforementioned are only a few of the ways that a new wave of Chicana/o and Latina/o scholars are exploring borderlands activism, cultural production, and resistance of dominance through more embodied notions of epistemology.

Perhaps Murillo Jr.'s (1999) notion of "*mojado* ethnography" best captures the image of a border ethnographer who utilizes his body and lived experience to imagine and textualize "Latina/o culture" in new ways (p. 6). Murillo Jr. describes the experiences of Chicana/o and Latina/o educational ethnographers as "peregrinating those blurred boundaries when 'other' becomes researcher, narrated becomes narrator, translated becomes translator, and native becomes anthropologist" (p. 18). Working between the spaces of narrator/narrated and translator/translated, Murillo Jr. names his intermittent identity as one of being a *mojado* ethnographer. *Mojado* is translated as "wetback" and derogatorily refers to Mexicans and Latinos/as who cross into the United States, and are legally, socially, and politically framed as "undocumented" and not belonging, or "illegal" and "alien." The origin of the word comes from the real and metaphorical crossing of the waters of the Rio Grande that separates México from the United States.

Like many other borderlands scholars, Murillo Jr. emphasizes that la *frontera* and border crossing is a real lived and often horrific experience for many diaspora Amerindians crossing *sin papeles* (without documentation) to the United States. But *la frontera* is also real for the children of the "*mojados*" who are raised in the United States and often share a collective experience of marginality and inequality of mobility in all realms—social, cultural, economic, and political. Murillo Jr. chooses to use the metaphor of *mojado* ethnographer as an "experiential and culturally-genealogical tool to make meaning of [his] cultural, racial, ethnic, discursive, political, theoretical, and even class crossings into ethnography and academia" (1999, p. 21). Given this historical condition, the mojado ethnographer learns how to search for *coyotes* (smugglers) who will secure safe passages and to move in humor and irony as no border is impenetrable. Murillo Jr. elaborates:

> In the middle of all this *desmadre* [chaos], we *Mojados* can sometimes learn to navigate cultural, intellectual and physical landscapes, *burlando la frontera* [mocking the border] every time we cross borders *a la brava* [head on] as casually as crossing the street, going unnoticed by *migra* [Immigration and Naturalization Service] and *mordelones* [corrupt smugglers or officials] (real and academic). We can "dart across the freeway of academia" and "chuckle at the turistas [tourists] who buy our artifacts buried for a few years to look like antiquities" (González-Peterson, 1997). We celebrate our biculturality and smile smugly when we say *que somos un pueblo sin fronteras* [that we are a people without borders].
>
> (1999, p. 21)

Thus, as textmaker and inventor of cultures, Murillo Jr. (1999), reinvents ethnography and border crossing cultures that resist liberal discourses of victimization. The borderized texts and cultures he invents highlight an active presence in stories, humor and irony.[4] Borderized "trickster" epistemologies and *movidas* (maneuverings), alongside Chicana feminist epistemologies and other excavations, create emergent Chicana/o and Latina/o methodological instruments, texts, and cultures.

In the sections to follow, we will highlight how borderlands scholars have excavated notions of *educación* and success, the hybrid cultural/linguistic practices of families and communities, and finally, differences in school achievement. Here again, as in the case of

Latina/o educational ethnographers' earlier engagement with critical ethnography, the authors cited do not always represent themselves as "border theorists." Nevertheless, borderlands and "trans-*frontera*" (Saldívar, 1997) sensibilities can be seen in the way they research and represent the resiliency and complexities of Latino/a lives.

Creating complex and dynamic ethnographic portraits of families and communities

Here, we focus on borderized productions of *educación* and socialization, linguistic productions in the borderlands, and borderized explorations of variation in school achievement.

Borderized productions of educación and socialization

Without a doubt, families are the starting point for teaching not simply survival, but resilience and how to live meaningful lives (Castillo, 1994). As many of the Latino/Chicano ethnographies document, Latino parents seek to instill in their children a *buena educación* (good education) as the foundation of living a good life. The Latino concept of the educated person or the broad moral notion of being *bien educado* (well-educated) subscribes to *respeto* (respect), humility, hard work, and family loyalty. Ethnographies about working-class Latino families highlight these differences particularly with respect to children's socialization as a contributing member of a family collective (Carger, 1996; Delgado-Gaitan and Trueba, 1991; Romo and Falbo, 1996; Trueba, 1999; Valdés, 1996). Guadalupe Valdés (1996) points out that a family education that involves the whole child and their place and role in the "collective" family differs significantly from the socialization patterns in White middle-class families (see also Carger, 1996). Valdés highlighted how working-class Mexicano families were household-centered rather than child-centered. Mexican children learned to fit into the family; to tolerate and share with siblings, and to avoid disrupting the family environment. In related studies, Vásquez *et al.* (1994) illustrate how elementary school children act as cultural brokers and take the responsibility of translating for family members and kin, and Romo and Falbo (1996) document how Latina/o adolescents feel responsible for the economic sustenance of the household. In these ethnographies, children were portrayed in all their multiple responsibilities and roles as family and community members. This *buena educación* of responsibility and loyalty often required a delicate balance in the midst of financial and family hardships.

Notions of success were also rooted in family loyalty and responsibility. Valdés (1996) argues "for most ordinary Mexican families, individual success and accomplishment are generally held in lesser esteem than are people's abilities to maintain ties across generations and to make an honest living" (p. 170). This notion of success was illustrated by Valdés' conversation with Rosario, the mother of a 17-year-old young man, whom she described as a "very good boy" and *respetuoso* (respectful) because he gave his summer paycheck to her to help the family. In sharp contrast, Rosario felt sorry for Valdés, whose 24-year-old son away at college did not work and send his mother money. Valdés reflected, "For Rosario, success as a mother involved teaching a young male how to be responsible . . . In her book, I was either not a great success or I had been unlucky in having a son who only cared about himself" (p. 185).

Similarly, language and literacy ethnographer Juan Guerra also excavates Mexicano notions of success that are rooted in collective responsibilities to the social network of transnational families. In Guerra's (1998) study, Jaime and Rocío Durán's home was always full of family, kin and *paisanos* (co-patriots) "recreating the vibrant communal life they had shared in their respective ranchos" (p. 65). The highly valued ritual activity of *"echar plática"* (making conversation) was essential for creating and reconstructing community. For this reason, families in Guerra's study practiced notions of success that included oral prowess. As Guerra explains, the families had:

> a distinct sense of the kinds of people whose language use they admire, of the diversity and commonality of opinion and linguistic ability in their community, and of what it takes to influence the views and actions of individuals with whom they interact on a regular basis.
>
> (p. 70)

As Octavio Pimentel (2000) has further highlighted, Mexicano definitions of success often include being a *buena gente* (good person), a person that shares his words and material possessions with those he loves and respects.

Latino/Chicano ethnographies also document the role that community and family members play as conduits of cultural and traditional knowledge (Vásquez *et al.*, 1994). Vásquez and her colleagues point out how in many communities, children have access to cultural and traditional knowledge that is reinforced during special occasions such as *cumpleaños* (birthdays), *bautismos* (baptisms), and *quinceañeras* (15th birthday for girls). While traditional folkways may be learned from *la sobadora* (masseuse) or *la curandera* (healer) and from members with specialized knowledge (i.e., farming; auto mechanics; construction), other informal sources for transmitting the "old culture" include *el paletero* (the ice cream vendor), *el panadero* (baker) and *la chismosa/el chismoso* (the gossiper) (Vásquez *et al.*, 1994). These "old cultural" ways are likewise documented by the "funds of knowledge" research that points to the valuable resources of knowledge found in Latino/Mexicano households (see González *et al.*, 1995; Vélez-Ibáñez and Greenberg, 1992).

And yet, how are these cultural bodies of knowledge taught to children? Educational ethnographers have excavated the pedagogical vehicles of *consejos* (advice-giving narratives) and *historias* (stories) as powerful sites of cultural production. Concha Delgado-Gaitan (1994), in particular, has argued for the power of *consejos* and its place in the socialization of children in Latino families. They are the means by which parents teach cultural values and morals that will guide them in good behavior and in making wise decisions. Most importantly, *consejos* are nurturing, culturally embedded and imbued with emotional empathy, compassion, and familial expectations (Delgado-Gaitan, 1994, p. 314). Marisela, a mother of four from Guatemala, narrated to Villenas (2001) how her mother taught a *buena educación* or *le aconsejaba* (gave her *consejos*) through stories. She explained,

"Nos contaba tantas historias, de la pereza, la mentira y tantas otras historias que realmente nos hacía a nosotros que nos portáramos bien (She would tell us so many stories about laziness, lying, and so many other things that really it made us all behave well)" (p. 15).

As Marisela's words illustrate, *consejos* and *historias* were important for teaching *una buena educación.* But as Villenas and Moreno (2001) explain, *consejos* and *historias* are also inclusive of *mujer*-oriented pedagogies that are often wrought with tensions and contradictions yet open with spaces of possibility. Mothers *aconsejan a sus hijas* (give advice to their daughters) to be *mujeres de hogar* (women of the home), evoking patriarchal discourses of honor and virtue. Simultaneously, mothers and daughters negotiate these with other *consejos* about knowing how to *valerse por si misma*—that is, to be self-reliant and to have self-love and respect for oneself (Villenas and Moreno, 2001). For example, Francisca González (1999) illustrates the womanist *consejos* a group of young Mexicana high schoolers learned from their mothers. Young women from *Michoacán* and *Sinaloa* remark,

Una mujer se tiene que dar su propio lugar todo el tiempo, donde esté para que la respete la gente, ¿verdad? Te tienes que dar tu lugar porque eres persona, tienes tus sentimientos, y tienes que respetarte a ti misma (A woman always has to give herself a place so that people will respect her, right? You have to give yourself your place because you are a person, because you have feelings, and you have to respect yourself).

(p. 125)

They continue by underscoring their mothers' teachings:

La mujer Mexicana es el orgullo de México [The Mexican woman is the pride of México] . . . I learn about the meaning of *la mujer Mexicana* from my mother's *consejos*. My mother tells me not to do bad things because later I am going to regret it. . . . All that I think is based on the *consejos* my mother gives me.

(pp. 145–146)

These young women with "Aztlán" and "transregional" cultures and identities, as González explains, certainly valued their mothers' *consejos* in negotiating what it meant to be a *mujer mexicana* in the United States.

In addition to teaching *una buena educación* and womanist lessons of respect and self-love, *consejos* and *historias* also serve to encourage school achievement. Romo and Falbo (1996) document how through *consejos*, parents encouraged their children to succeed in school. In their study, parent after parent gave their children *consejos* about how important it is to graduate from high school. Parents urged their own children to finish by telling them about their own lives and "what could have been" if they had studied, explaining, "If you don't study, you're going to be like us" (1996, p. 108; see Moreno and Valencia, Chapter 8 of the present book, for a coverage of literature that shows Mexican American parents do indeed value education and do indeed get involved in their children's education). The parents used themselves and the youths' older siblings who did not graduate as examples of what happens when one does not finish high school. It is not surprising then, that Latino/a and Chicano/a researchers also show how young adults carry these cultural, spiritual and community-oriented *consejos* and *historias* on to college where these serve as an impetus for achievement in higher education (see Delgado Bernal, 2001; Gándara, 1995). A *buena educación* and the teaching of cultural and traditional knowledge are cemented through relational-based pedagogies of *consejos* and *historias* that youths carry to adulthood.

Excavations of a *buena educación* that include traditional notions of success, of the role of community and family as conduits of cultural knowledge, and of *consejos* as pedagogy, are descriptions of cultural forms rooted in México or the "old country." But the symbolic and material presence of *la frontera* also marks Chicano/Latino critical ethnography with excavations of cultural/linguistic hybridity, difference, and complexity. These are ethnographies that document the everyday borderlands (postmodern) aesthetics. Vásquez *et al.* (1994), for example, argue against homogenizing portraits of Mexicano education and language socialization. Instead, they call for a "recognition perspective" that captures the "similarities in language use across various contexts, the convergence of multiple knowledge sources and the uniqueness of language use practices fostered by Mexican culture" (p. 11). They resist facile dichotomies between "cultures" as two opposing mutually exclusive systems, and instead emphasize the "dynamic interaction of exchange between two or more cultures" (p. 12). Within such complex language and cultural milieus, they make a case that "the worlds of home and school, even for language-minority children, may not always be clearly demarcated" (p. 67).

In one of their case studies, for instance, where data were collected to document the language use of two preschoolers within their working-class Mexican families and in their classrooms, Vásquez and her colleagues learned that the families of the children had very different views about learning. Jennifer's parents said she learned things because she was intelligent and learning came natural to her, while Nestor's mother emphasized that he learned because she explicitly taught him. The families also had different uses of contingent queries to extend and elaborate children's conversation. While contingent queries are often associated with White middle-class language practices, these data showed the convergence of school and home with "similarities in language use across various contexts" (1994, p. 11), indeed each sphere influencing the other. Because these data also show how children's school and home worlds interact, Vásquez and colleagues offer a powerful critique of often-discussed unidirectional views of home–school discontinuity that focus on children's reliance of home interactional patterns when at school. Rather, they ask educators and researchers to consider how schooling affects language use at home, and how children's experiences enter their conversations at home.

Vásquez *et al.* (1994) also explore the convergence of multiple knowledge sources in the home space. Again, these researchers do not treat the home space as a separate world but rather as part of a web of multiple interacting communities. A scene where Rosa and her cousin and his family have gathered to figure out how to fill out the Internal Revenue Service's SU 32 Tax Data Form illustrates how families use all of their knowledge and cultural/linguistic resources at their disposal to navigate and survive in U.S. society. Rosa used her English language skills, her personal experience about withholding allowances, as well as the experiences and knowledge of her cousin to make sense of the form together. This is just one example of the complex negotiations and the creative resourcefulness needed on the part of diaspora Latino families to cross cultural and linguistic borders. By studying language use and socialization in Mexicano communities, these authors embrace possibilities of cultural/linguistic creativity and hybridity, which reposition the teaching and learning of a *buena educación* within borderized productions of continuity and change.

Linguistic productions in the borderlands

Without a doubt, language is a critical site that best captures the borderlands' multivoiced and polyvocal aesthetics of everyday living. Rather than reformulating the concepts of "culture" or "identity," that run the risk of reifying notions of essential, unified, static, and bounded traits, linguistic anthropologist Norma González emphasizes the theory and practice of language and language ideologies (N. González, 1999). As she asserts:

> It is through and by language and discursive practices that self-hoods are constructed, identities are forged, and social processes are enacted. As a constitutive force, language shapes the shifting ethnoscapes and multiple identities that emerge from the inter-culturality of multiple knowledge bases.
>
> (p. 433)

Theorizing the relationships between linguistic/identity productions and social processes are not facile theoretical projects. The material and symbolic presence of *la frontera* and the borderlands provide Latina/o and Chicana/o scholars with an embodied understanding of the shifting ethnoscapes, multiple identities, and interculturality that González describes. For example, Chicano/a literary works written in English still take place within the borderlands context. As literary theorist Alfred Arteaga explains, "Border discourse contextualizes

Chicano poetry to such an extent that even essentially monolingual verse is read within the larger framework of a multilingual poetics" (1994, p. 11).

As we have described above, the work by Vásquez and her colleagues (1994) illustrate the multilingual poetics of everyday language use. They reveal that language is a critical site for examining the multiple and overlapping linguistic worlds of Mexican children and adults. Other ethnographic studies, however, focus specifically on the interrelationship between linguistic and identity productions, and the enactments of social processes, indeed excavating other profound and remarkable dimensions of borderized linguistic creativity (see González, 1996, 2001; Urciuoli, 1996; Zentella, 1997). Norma González (1996) asserts that continuity of traditions, change, negotiations, contestations, and the emergent nature of "culture" and identities are all constructed through language. In her study of parental narratives gathered from 12 households in Tucson, Arizona, she argues that within a borderlands context, parents are quite aware of their roles as socializers of children. They do not simply reproduce "tradition," worlds, and worldviews. Rather, they improvise, tinker with, and reproduce new social lives and cultural forms through language and discursive practices that are competing, ideological, and political.

Raquel Salazar is a good example of this complex cultural production process. She resides with her husband and three children in a "non-barrio" area of Tucson and narrated her quest for "a template on which to process her family's lives" (González, 1996, p. 59). Raquel bemoaned her perceived lack of training in financial matters and vowed that her children will be better prepared. At the same time, she also sought to redefine her consciousness and spirituality in a shift to evangelical Christianity. González explains how Raquel discursively reconstructed her identities and social life in emergent ways:

> The reproduction of the models that she and her husband were raised with is inadequate for her. They do not meet the exigencies of the life that she feels she must now face; nor does she want her children to struggle with what she considers the same formlessness. She consciously and actively assembles a framework on which to hang the practices of their everyday lives.
>
> (1996, pp. 59–60)

In yet another "constellation of borderland sociohistorical factors" (González, 1996, p. 61), Iris, who was raised in a Spanish-speaking household in Tucson, articulates normative ideologies of middle-class bliss. González describes this borderlands phenomenon by pointing out how Iris' household operates in dense relationships with immigrant and first-generation families. They often live in borderline poverty, and yet Iris' household ideology "reflects the images of a stay at home mother who bakes and sews and does crafts with her children and volunteers extensively in their schools, and a father who is the primary breadwinner and the reserved guardian of the family patrimony" (p. 62). González argues that these case studies "point to the scaffolding of new forms rising from historical antecedents. They reveal the tinkering with the intergenerational forms bequeathed to posterities that assemble inventive bridges to span the gaps between tradition and function" (p. 65).

Similarly, bridges between other borderlands of subjectivities, "cultures," power, ethnicity and gender are improvised in the linguistic production of code switching. Ana Celia Zentella's (1997) study of the language and lives of Puerto Rican families from a neighborhood she calls "*el bloque*" (the block) points to the beauty and complexity of borderlands linguistic productions. These Puerto Rican children were being raised in a transnational ghetto in America's most powerful urban center. They enjoyed Puerto Rican/U.S. American/ Nuyorican cultural identity; black/white/*trigueño/indio/jabao* racial identity; and Puerto

Rican Spanish/African American Vernacular English/ and Puerto Rican English linguistic identity. Zentella documents how code switching between all of these languages/dialects was neither about language deterioration nor language deficiency. Instead, it represented sophisticated and complex modes of language use and diverse strategic assertions of multiple and hybrid identities. As Zentella explains,

> Switches into Spanish were attempts to touch home base, a resistance to being engulfed by English. As one 16-year-old male explained it, "Sometimes I'm talking a long time in English and then I remember I'm Puerto Rican, lemme say something in Spanglish." "Spanglish" moved them to the center of their bilingual world, which they continued to create and define in every interaction. Every time they said something in one language when they might just as easily have said it in the other, they were re-connecting with people, occasions, settings, and power configurations from their history of past interactions.
>
> (p. 114)

Indeed, these children practiced an understanding of multiculturalism that was neither color-blind nor monoculture bound. Rather, their code switching was a particular way of understanding differences and recognizing the social context of culture and power "on the periphery of a prestigious English monolingual world and [that] of a stigmatized Spanish monolingual world" (Zentella, 1997, p. 114). Zentella argues, "their code switching was a way of saying that they belonged to both worlds, and should not be forced to give up one for the other" (p. 114).

Similar complexities of language and identity are further explored in the lives of gang-affiliated young women. Sociolinguistic ethnographer Norma Mendoza-Denton (1996, 1999) studied language and identity among Latina gangs in a Northern California high school she called Sor Juana Inés. She examined the linguistic patterning and social differentiation between a group of Mexicana and Chicana gang-affiliated girls who self-identified as *Sureñas* and *Norteñas*, respectively. *Sureñas* enacted their identities of *Mexicana*ness through the linguistic marker of Spanish, while *Norteñas* enacted their bilingual and bicultural Chicana ideologies through Chicano English. As symbolic markers of identity, these diverse linguistic identifications "evoked different cultural, national, and ideological orientations" (1999, p. 41). In this manner, these young women used linguistic and also cultural markers (colors; make-up; hairdo; music) to put into play identities that were both oppositional *and* about cultural integrity as they maneuvered between what Zentella (1997) names as the worlds of prestigious English and stigmatized Spanish monolingualisms. As speakers of Spanish and of Chicano English (a non-standard variety), both groups were marginalized *vis-à-vis* dominant linguistic and cultural forms espoused in the school.

Latinas/os like the Mexican American parents of Tucson (González, 1996; also see her 2001 book), the children of *el bloque* (Zentella, 1997), and the young women of Sor Juana Inés High School (Mendoza-Denton, 1996, 1999), have certainly experienced dominant linguistic and cultural forms as discursive violence. Such violence is perpetuated by an insistence on a monocultural and monolingual nation despite "trans-*frontera*" (Saldívar, 1997) and border crossing realities. And yet, ethnographic portraits of Latino youths, families, and communities as multivoiced, multilingual, and heteroglossic, challenge the monologism of the United States (Arteaga, 1994). Alfred Arteaga writes that Chicano discourse "undercuts claims of prevalence, centrality, and superiority and confirms the condition of heteroglossia. It draws the monologue into dialogue. In short, it dialogizes the authoritative discourse" (p. 14). Indeed, these portraits of linguistic sophistication, complexity, and hybridity not only challenge cultural deficit theories, but they also contribute to a deeper understanding of multiculturalisms (borderlands) and democracy (dialogization of authoritarian discourse) in the Americas. Drawing from the previous discussion of cultural and linguistic hybridity, we turn now to complex excavations of variation in youths' school achievement.

Borderized explorations of variation in school achievement

Just as children are socialized in different ways in their families and communities, participate in diverse cultural and linguistic milieus, and enact multiple identities, they also achieve differently in schools. Yet explanations for variation in school achievement defy easy dichotomizations. Educational ethnographers, Angela Valenzuela (1999a), Diego Vigil (1997), and Carola and Marcelo Suárez-Orozco (1995) are exploring Latino/Chicano variation in interesting new ways (c.f. Matute-Bianchi 1986, 1991), paying particular attention to the psychological and peer group differences between Mexican immigrants and U.S.-born Mexican students. They characterized the 1.5 generation—Latino youths born abroad but reared in the U.S.—as an intermediate case of achievers. Prior experiences in the homeland, transnational familial networks, peer relations, gender, and other factors complicate earlier studies that tend to essentialize immigrants as hard-working successful students and the native-born students as less hard-working and therefore unsuccessful.

Yet, many of the "voluntary immigrants" are only moderately successful while more middle-class Mexican Americans (Foley, 1990) and native-born Latinas/Chicanos (Valenzuela, 1999b; Mendoza-Denton, 2000), as well as other working-class Latinas/os and Chicana/os (Gándara, 1995), achieve at higher rates without abandoning their family cultures. Illustrating this point, Foley (1990), for example showed how "success" for some Mexicano students did not come at the price of one-way assimilation. Rather, middle-class Mexican American high school students in South Texas added on to their distinctly "cultural" communicative practices and performed school success as a form of ethnic resistance. Valenzuela (1999b) showed how regular-track native-born Latinas could turn romantic love and its nurturing characteristics into a pro-school ethos. Certainly many studies point to the school achievement of native-born students that do not bear out Ogbu's "involuntary minority" sentence of an anti-school ethos and/or "success" at the price of assimilation (Gándara, 1995; Romo and Falbo, 1997; Tapia, 1998; Trueba, 1999).

Valenzuela's (1999a) study at Seguín High School in Texas, further highlights the subtle and interesting in-group acculturation and achievement differences between new immigrants, the 1.5 generation, and native-born Chicanas/os. In particular, we would like to focus on her discussion of "immigrant" students. Valenzuela does indeed reaffirm that many immigrant students are models of hard-working conformity, and their pro-school peer groups provide them with considerable "social capital" to succeed in comparison to both mixed-generation and U.S.-born friendship groups. But by highlighting institutional and interactional factors, Valenzuela addresses the Suárez-Orozcos' (1995) central paradox—that new arrivals from Latin America express an eagerness to do well in school; "yet the longer they are in the United States, the less interested and motivated they become" (p. 80). At the same time, the Suárez-Orozcos (2001) argue that the stresses of immigration (i.e., culture shock; psychological losses) along with economic pressures, cultural discontinuities, and discrimination contribute to their lower high school completion rates in comparison to second- and third-generation Latina/o students.

Similarly, Valenzuela calls into question the sharp distinction that Ogbu makes between voluntary and involuntary immigrants, particularly with respect to the notion of frame of reference. Instead, Valenzuela's conversations with three Mexican "immigrant" groups—recently arrived "Urban Youth" from Monterrey, long-term-resident "English-Speaking Immigrants" and recently-arrived "Pre-Literate Youth"—illustrate a more nuanced and politicized interpretation of the dual frame of reference, or the notion of positively evaluating present circumstances in the United States through the lens of prior (less positive) experiences in México. Valenzuela argues that Ogbu's categorizations of "far superior" schooling in the U.S. and supposed better treatment merit closer examination. For instance, the youths schooled in México talked about their Mexican schools as better and more caring places despite the schools sometimes having dilapidating building structures and a lack of resources. Moreover, Amalia and other Mexican-schooled students reinterpreted the notion of "dual frame of reference" in believing that immigrants' dual frame can and should be accessible to U.S.-born youths. As Valenzuela insightfully maintains,

> [Amalia] envisions the positive and creative potential of a curriculum centered around things Mexican. She implicitly leverages a critique against Seguín's curriculum as subtractive—that is, as one that denies youths the opportunity to learn about their Mexican heritage. She believes that if others possessed her knowledge and awareness of conditions in México, they would not only cherish their present educational opportunities, they would also "get angry at poverty" and become agents of change.
>
> (1999a, p. 125)

While Amalia politicized the dual frame, other immigrant students such as recently arrived "Pre-Literate" youths, also came with *mucho empeño* (much diligence) and strong beliefs in schooling, but could not achieve academically at Seguín. Their stories will be told in the section that follows, as their "lack of success" poignantly illustrates the effects of uncaring schools. Yet more to the point, Valenzuela's insights about the relationship between immigrant students' social capital, academic achievement, and their institutional disenfranchisement complicates Ogbu's explanations of differential achievement.

In addition, there are other differences and similarities across families to consider in discussing Latino/Chicano school achievement. Javier Tapia (1998), in a study of Puerto Rican households in Philadelphia, reminds us of the issue of poverty and how in times of economic hardship, families may experience familial fragmentation, separation, and reconstruction. He explains how strategies of surviving poverty have direct and indirect influence on school achievement, but they work in complex ways exemplifying similarities and differences in Puerto Rican communities. Armed with ethnographic data collected in multiple extended households, Tapia's conclusion about school achievement reflects this complex constellation of factors while foregrounding the centrality and health of the family (also, see Vigil, 1997, 1999). Tapia argues: "Family stability, which is greatly influenced by economic stability, is the most important factor influencing poor students' school performance. However, the specific dynamics of poverty affect different households differently and different members of the same household differently" (p. 319). Tapia's attention to difference and variability in studying the effects of household poverty, again lead us away from facile dichotomies and categorizations, and point to the strength, vitality, and resilience of Puerto Rican families.

In sum, the stories and voices captured in these ethnographies about Latino school achievement emphasize the vast differences between familial ecology and orientation, household organization, transnational familial networks, peer relationships, rural and urban experiences, economic levels, prior schooling experiences, psychological experiences of loss and mourning (Ainslie, 1998),[5] and gender differences, to name a few. The youths' experiences highlight nuanced and complex accounts of Latino/a school achievement that go beyond Ogbu's categories of voluntary and involuntary immigrants and their associated cultural constructs. Moreover, guided by borderlands sensibilities, Latina/o ethnographers debunk notions about ethnic identity and school achievement on a fixed assimilation-accommodation-acculturation continuum. As Trueba (1999) insightfully maintains:

> Perhaps . . . Latinos are facing not a simple change in ethnic identity, a transition from the home culture identification to a new single identity as Americans from a specific Latino descent. Rather, it seems to be a complicated process whereby Latinos retain multiple identities, multiple interactional settings, and diverse "situated selves" at one point in time.
>
> (p. 12)

Explanations of school achievement that are dependent upon predetermined and reified categories of Chicana/o identities are doomed to miss the endless possibilities of cultural and linguistic production in the borderlands.

In this section, we have looked at how Latino/Chicano ethnographies have produced complex and dynamic portraits of families and communities. These borderized excavations of *una buena educación* and cultural/pedagogical practices are about tradition and continuity, but they are also about hybrid productions of change, variability, and difference. We have highlighted here how the symbolic and material presence of *la frontera* marks these portraits with complex understandings. Latino children are socialized differently in their families and communities; they participate in diverse cultural and linguistic worlds; they enact multiple identities in different contexts; and they achieve differently in schools. The general cultural portrait that emerges from these studies is a far cry from the cultural misrepresentations of earlier deficit-driven studies (Foley, 1997). Most importantly, they move the explanation of school failure away from the home and highlight the institutionalized schooling practices that deny Latino/Chicano youths a sound and challenging education.

Critiques of schooling

Inasmuch as *la frontera* (as borderlands aesthetics) undergirds excavations of complex, dynamic and hybrid cultural productions in Latino/Chicano communities, *la frontera* experienced also as exclusion, as oppressive nativism and as monologism, informs critical ethnographies that take aim at the oppressive, colonial nature of schooling (Bartolomé, 1994; Stanton-Salazar, 1997; Trueba, 1999). Historical and experiential knowledge of cultural and linguistic discrimination passionately motivate political and praxis-oriented ethnographic research that indicts schools for institutionalized racism. Villenas and Deyhle (1999), for example, apply the lens of critical race theory to data from recent Latino ethnographies in order to interrogate Eurocentric-based and English-only curriculum, "dumbed-down" academic programs, culturally insensitive practices, and tracking mechanisms that push out disproportionate numbers of Latino/a students before their graduation year (see Carger, 1996; Foley, 1990; Romo and Falbo, 1996; Valdés, 1996; Valenzuela, 1999a; Vásquez *et al.*, 1994; also, see Valencia, Chapter 1 of the present book for a discussion of numerous schooling conditions and outcomes that marginalize Chicano students). These scholars argue the obvious—that teachers' and administrators' enduring negative beliefs about Latino/a students and their families, their low expectations and requirement of assimilation, and the rhetoric against bilingual education (despite three decades of affirming research—see Guerrero, Chapter 6, present volume), are all racially-based constructions or racial framings.[6]

As we will see, policies and practices such as tracking and classroom misassignments are race-based outcomes that rest on the ethnocentric dismissal of Latino cultures.

The voices of Latino youths vividly illustrate their racially-based treatment in the schools. The youths in these ethnographies expressed—to researchers—their feelings of humiliation when told their families are less intelligent and worthless:

> It makes me mad; it makes me feel like they think that I'm worthless or something. "Why are you even here?" you know. It just upsets me a lot. I always figured that reverse psychology never worked on me . . . They're thinking that I'm just going to prove them wrong. But every time they tell me stuff like that it just breaks me down more than it motivates me. [Martin]
>
> (Romo and Falbo, 1996, p. 146)

> They have this image of kids, that we are just messed up in the head. That's not really true because many students here—I think their intellectual ability is just too high for them to be in regular classes, but they don't enter honor classes . . . Certain teachers say, "No, let's not read this. This is too hard for these kids. No, let's not read John Keats. No, Shakespeare's Hamlet. Let's show the movie or let's not learn about Excalibur. Let's not read it, but let's watch the film." That's something that I see, always some other kind of source that they turn to . . . something that is not on level, but a little bit more basic. [Rodrigo]
>
> (Valenzuela, 1999a, p. 98)

> Mimicking [her ESL-transition teacher], [Linda] yells, "English! English! You're in America! Go back to México!"
>
> (Valenzuela, 1999a, p. 131)

This psychological violence is part of the institutional practices that disenfranchise Latino youths, even those who come with enthusiasm and *empeño* (diligence) (Valenzuela, 1999a; Suárez-Orozco and Suárez-Orozco, 1995). The following stories of Carolina, Lupita, and Estéban—students at Seguín High School—exemplify how despite a lot of *empeño*, they could not overcome the effects of misassignments to wrong classes, lack of caring adults, and no provisions for pre-literate youths (Valenzuela, 1999a, p. 134).

Carolina explains to Valenzuela in Spanish, "School is too hard. We're always behind in our work and we don't get help . . . None of us went to school for very long in México" (Valenzuela, 1999a, p. 134). Esteban adds that he only likes P.E., because there he doesn't feel *avergonzado* (embarrassed) for not being able to read well. Lupita tells about how at the beginning of the school year she spent six weeks in a math class where she did not understand anything, and the Anglo male teacher made no effort to make the material comprehensible. As this teacher explained to Valenzuela, "When they can't even write their names, makes you wonder why they even come to school at all" (p. 135). Lupita recalls, "*A mi me tenían ahí como pendeja, como sorda y muda en esa clase*" ("They had me in there like an idiot, like a deaf mute in that class") (p. 135). Eventually, Lupita along with Carolina were placed in an English as a second language (ESL) class with a knowledgeable, skilled, and sympathetic Spanish-speaking teacher. Unfortunately, this teacher left Seguín the following semester, and Carolina and Lupita dropped out before the year's end.

Estéban was also misassigned to classes and he spent the first two months waiting to speak to the counselor. The counselor he had waited so long to see said he would not be tested, and that besides, she was not the ESL coordinator. Estéban repeated her words, "Not my job description" (p. 138). Even with Valenzuela's interventions, no schedule change resulted. But Estéban mustered his creative ingenuity and for the second semester, he had negotiated his grades and alternative evaluations with the teachers of every subject. In several classes, his teachers allowed him to take oral rather than written tests, to copy paragraphs from a textbook instead of writing essays, and to have students read aloud text-based assignments to him in the back corner of the classroom. And yet, even with a renegotiated system of evaluation, he continued to receive poor or failing grades. He hung on as long as he could but by the middle of the spring semester, he too had dropped out. As Valenzuela explains, "Despite Estéban's inventiveness and *empeño*, the cards were stacked against him, just as they were for Carolina and Lupita" (p. 139).

A school environment that made students feel *avergonzados* (embarrassed) and *humillados* (humiliated), and an uncaring system that could not appropriately place students with special literacy needs, deeply discouraged even the most motivated youths who possessed abundant amounts of *empeño*. Valenzuela indicts the schools as uncaring, culturally insensitive places that "subtract" the cultural and psychological resources of Mexican and Chicana/o youths. A schooling process filled with uncaring teachers and culturally irrelevant curriculum literally produces ethnic school failure. The recent issue of the *Harvard Educational Review* (Summer, 1998) provides a similar account of the legacy of institutionalized educational colonialism and racism toward Puerto Rican communities, families, and youths. Latina/o ethnographers thus make the link between racially-based school outcomes and larger discourses concerning the meaning of "citizen," and immigration and labor policies (Suárez-Orozco, 1998; Trueba, 1999). The call for effective schools with culturally sensitive and skillful teachers, and with curricula and programs that center Chicano/Latino youths as intelligent human beings, is embedded in the struggle of a century and a half for social justice (Moreno, 1999; San Miguel and Valencia, 1998). To this end, the work of Latino/Chicano ethnography is also about creating and promoting best practices, academically rigorous programs while excavating new spaces of resiliency for resisting and critiquing racism in the larger society.

Best practices, alternative visions of schooling and collective action

On the one hand, Chicana/o and Latina/o ethnographers are deconstructing the philosophical foundations of deficit thinking. On the other hand, they are searching for educational practices and programs that actually narrow the academic achievement gap (Ernst-Slavit and Statzner, 1994; Trueba, 1994). Accordingly, Latina/o scholars have focused both on deconstructing taken-for-granted notions about teaching and learning, unearthing pedagogical and curricular practices that really work, and centering the work and vision of parents and community.

Guided by heightened sensibilities toward epistemological racism, Chicana/o and Latina/o scholars often question the universality and neutrality of educational theories. For example, María de la Luz Reyes (1992) contends that the widely popular "whole language literacy approach" may not work as well for working-class Latino youths. Building upon the work of other African American and Chicana/o scholars (Barrera, 1992; Delpit, 1995; Valdés, 1991), Reyes characterizes the whole language approach as more attuned to the parenting and literacy styles of the liberal White middle class. Research into the insights of teachers of color lead to the contention that structured, phonics-oriented approaches to literacy is effective with children of color. Such critiques underscore the need to question whether the whole language approach or any approach is a universal, neutral theory of instruction that serves all cultural groups. Indeed, some approaches can function as forms of deficit theory that unconsciously champion White middle-class speech and literacy styles.[7]

The cultural and class universals undergirding the notion and practice of "parent involvement" are also being questioned. Valdés (1996) interrogates schools' definitions of "involvement," arguing that most often they assume a singular blueprint of how families are suppose to function, how homes are to be structured, and how parents are to interact with children (also see Moreno and Valencia, Chapter 8, present book). This blueprint of how parents are to live their lives in ways congruent with schools is based on middle-class standards and practices. Valdés argues that parent involvement programs should not be about changing the cultural practices of very able and strong families, requiring, for example, that school recitations or doing school-like activities take the place of when, how and for what reasons mothers talk to their children. Instead, Valdés asserts, any kind of parent-involvement program needs to be "based on an understanding, appreciation and respect for the internal dynamics of these families and for the legitimacy of their values and beliefs" (1996, p. 203).

Without a doubt, a focus on the strengths and knowledge of Latino families informs Latino/Chicano research that links the home to classroom practices. Anthropologists Luis Moll, Carlos Vélez-Ibañez, Norma González and others emphasize that Latino youths and their families have vast "funds of knowledge." They accumulate knowledge about farming, auto mechanics, homemaking, and indigenous medicine through complex kin and neighborhood networks (González *et al.*, 1995; Moll *et al.*, 1992; Vélez-Ibañez and Greenberg, 1992). These scholars emphasize the importance of building on such funds of knowledge through what Vygotsky calls "proximal zones of development," or culturally relevant pedagogical and curricular practices. The work of Enrique Trueba (1999) extends the Vygotskian "funds of knowledge" critique in other ways. Trueba blends the critical pedagogy of Paulo Freire in his Vygotskian critiques of how Latinos are schooled. He highlights the importance of what Vygotsky would call "scaffolding" or building "zones of proximal development" through a culturally relevant pedagogy and curriculum that is self-empowering. Trueba and various Latina/o scholars (Delgado-Gaitan, 1991, 1996; Vásquez *et al.*, 1994) demonstrate how teachers can skillfully tap into home and community funds of knowledge and also utilize the learners' bilingualism.

Unfortunately, middle-class White teachers often have little knowledge of such cultural and linguistic resources, and they tend to see communities of color and their youths negatively. Consequently, Luis Moll, Norma González and associates advocate making White teachers into ethnographers who directly experience the rich sociocultural environments of Latino families (González *et al.*, 1995). These Latina/o researchers' emphasis on directly experiencing the cultural reality of Latino families—under the careful supervision of faculty of color—is obviously a powerful pedagogical device. Such experience-based teacher education programs suggest a very effective way of producing anti-deficit thinking, anti-racist White teachers. Perhaps the only thing that will prevent the spread of such programs is the lack of political will among the professorate to commit the money and time to such labor-intensive programs.

And yet, building culturally sensitive learning environments also entails viewing the classroom as a third space—a creative space for new language and new culture that is both and neither of the home and school. Kris Gutiérrez and her colleagues advocate a classroom environment that flourishes on the hybrid language practices and the diversity of accents, dialects, and literacies to create an alternative space of intellectual, cultural, and linguistic creativity (Gutiérrez *et al.*, 2000, 2001). Gutiérrez and associates (1995) have previously used the concept of the third space to problematize both hegemonic teacher discourse as well as student resistance. They hope to promote these emergent spaces where teacher and students can meet for genuine dialogue and learning. Likewise, ethnographer Sheila Shannon (1995) argues that a new and separate culture should be developed in the classroom that does not wholly reflect the culture of dominant society (and in fact should work against society's racism) or necessarily the culture of the children's homes. Rather, this "new" culture should be based on "roles, expectations, values, and beliefs that allow children to thrive in the classroom and cope with the negative messages they receive outside school" (Shannon, 1995, p. 324). Classrooms that keep both cultural sensitivity and hybridity at the center are undoubtedly learning environments of the borderlands.

Proposing school reforms and organizational practices that honor and respect culture and language and take advantage of youths' hybrid socio-cultural and linguistic practices are an important contribution of Latino/Chicano ethnography. For example, Latina/o and Chicana/o scholars vehemently promote bilingual education and have researched effective programs for Spanish-speaking and bilingual youths. Tamara Lucas, Rosemary Henze, and Rubén Donato (1990) found that effective programs at the high school level provide native language instruction in every subject area, including upper-division and honors classes. Such programs also have culturally sensitive bilingual counselors and teachers with high expectations and rigorous standards, as well as strong connections with parents and community members. Additional promising organizational practices include collaborative governance and cooperative learning as explored by Pedro Reyes and associates (Reyes *et al.*, 1999).

Yet fundamental to the practice of bicultural education, as Antonia Darder argues, is a "commitment to a liberatory vision" that is "connected to a greater democratic political project" (1997, p. 350). Schools that nurture youths do not shy away from the political and socioeconomic forces of neighborhoods and nation-states (Ramos-Zayas, 1998). As Ana Ramos-Zayas has found in her study of a nationalist-oriented Puerto Rican high school in Chicago, an oppositional education project that is political (in this case in favor of Puerto Rican independence) can be a powerful resource for creating the context for school success. Similarly, Foley (1989, 1990) and Trujillo (1998) in their 16-year South Texas study found many activist mothers, teachers, and high-achieving Chicana/o youths in *politically active* small South Texas towns. In addition, these scholars found very large increases in the social mobility of Chicana/o students in a town transformed by the Chicano civil rights movement. Compared to their parents, 20 percent more Chicano/a youths were going on to postsecondary education. Such findings convinced Foley and his colleagues that genuine school reform must start with a strong local grassroots ethnic political movement based in families. These studies show that assimilation or acquiescence to the status quo is not necessary for school reform. Rather, restructuring schools through social activism creates a sense of hope that promotes school success.

Just as Ramos-Zayas, Foley, and Trujillo highlight the links between grassroots activism and school success, it is critical to call attention to the role of parents and community members in struggling for schools that work for their children (Delgado-Gaitan, 1996; Ramos-Zayas, 1998; Trueba, 1999; Trueba *et al.*, 1993; Vigil, 1997). Jaime Vigil's longitudinal study of city and suburban youths in Los Angeles notes the importance of a broader Mexicanization process that regenerates ethnic culture and pride. The ethno-historical study in Northern California by Trueba and his colleagues (1993) likewise captures the cultural regeneration process through the cultural and support base of such organizations as *El Comité de Beneficiencia Mexicana* (The Mexican Beneficiary Committee). Moreover, they also chronicle the emergence of a Mexican middle class and the gaining of political and economic power that shaped the context for creating effective bilingual schools. Lourdes Díaz

Soto's (1997) story is a case in point of the importance of building a political base. In her ethnography, well-educated and professional Puerto Ricans were at the forefront of the defense of a bilingual program in Pennsylvania. However, their expertise and knowledge were ignored, as they held no school board and city council positions. The school board voted to dismantle the bilingual program, and to forgo building a much-needed new school for the Puerto Rican children. Greater political and economic muscle may be necessary to create lasting educational reform.

We must not forget, however, the power of dialogue and consciousness-raising found in the intimate spaces of *el hogar* (the home space) and in friendship networks (Villenas, 2001). Delgado-Gaitan (1996) tells the story of COPLA (*Comité de Padres Latinos* or Latino Parent Committee), an organization created by Latino parents of the Carpinteria School District in California who wanted to learn how to be advocates for their children in the schools and in the wider community. COPLA successfully resolved major issues such as correspondence in Spanish to Latino parents, criteria for admitting bilingual students in the Gifted and Talented program, ESL curriculum, the hiring of bilingual personnel, and even in fighting a city ordinance that fined households with unused parked cars. In summing up the work of COPLA, Delgado-Gaitan explains that the process of dialogue was a democratic one where Latino parents together built a consciousness about oppression: "Parents changed their view of self, they changed the way they saw each other, and they acted to change conditions" (1996, p. 61). Without a doubt, school change and school reform begin with parents' visions and struggles for effective and equitable schools.

Envisioning educational practices and programs that narrow the achievement gap entails creating educational environments that center hope and possibility, that are transformative, and that begin with the students, families, and communities. Pedagogical practices, for example, must promote hybrid spaces of learning and cultural/linguistic production. Such practices must create active world citizens who not only survive racism, but also offer their own visions of the world. Indeed, the school reforms that Chicana/o and Latina/o ethnographers call for are often very different from mainstream educational reform efforts that rely on prison-like environments and strict disciplinary measures (Noguera, 1995). In sharp contrast, Noguera contends that the most fruitful way to address school violence is by creating humanizing environments full of caring relationships and social responsibility. Moreover, the sense of social responsibility created in schools must extend into the larger community and society.

Pasado, presente y nuevos caminos: past, present and new directions

We have tried to give you a flavor for the protracted struggles that Chicana(o)/Latino(a) scholars and their progressive allies have waged against racist educational explanations of Latino school failure. While educational ethnography has not produced "silver bullet" explanations of youths' school achievement, or a unified, coherent theory of why these students succeed despite the odds against them, we in fact have gained much insights and understandings of the multiple complexities involved. Educational ethnographers have documented how schools can begin from the cultural and social capital of Latino/Chicano families (Valenzuela, 1999a; Vásquez *et al.*, 1994), as well as intervene to offset the adverse effects of household poverty (Tapia, 1998; Vigil, 1999). We know that equipping students with more study and social skills helps. So does creating what Vygotsky would call "zones of proximal development" through culturally relevant curricula based on families' and communities' cultural "funds of knowledge" (Trueba, 1999) and multiple linguistic resources (Gutiérrez *et al.*, 2001; Reyes, 2001). We know that culturally and linguistically sensitive teachers, and collaborations with politically active parents and Latino communities, help empower youths. Some educational ethnographers are also aware of the philosophy and practice of "democratic education" as a valuable strategy for school reform (see Pearl, Chapter 11, present book). We are now aware of how to alter many historical, cultural, linguistic, organizational, pedagogical, curricular, and interactional factors. Finally, we are also keenly aware that collective organizing for the purpose of creating an activist base which works toward economic gains and sociopolitical power, are crucial to effecting change for social justice (Foley 1990; Trueba *et al.*, 1993; Villenas and Deyhle, 1999).

On a more theoretical level, Chicano/Latino educational ethnography consciously seeks to deconstruct or challenge the insidious notion of a culturally, racially, intellectually, and psychologically inferior "minority" group. To this end, such studies deconstruct the comfortable liberal ideology that democracies with established judicial procedures and civil rights laws have created "race neutral," egalitarian political economies. Indeed, Latina/o ethnographers link their work, if not directly but in spirit, to their LatCrit (Latino Critical Theory) colleagues from the field of law (Delgado, 1995; Hernández-Truyol, 1997; F. Valdés, 1998) who uncover the different and insidious ways in which Chicanas(os)/Latinas(os) continue to be institutionally racialized in the United States.[8] By emphasizing the continued legacy of White supremacy, Chicana/o and Latina/o scholars have accented new terms for conversations on cultural identity struggles. A host of new and renewed constructs of culture—funds of knowledge, borderlands, Vygotskian, cultural production and practice—contest the old deficit/culture of poverty view. These new formulations of culture emphasize both the survival of traditional cultural practices *and* the invention of new, hybrid, creole cultural forms. Borderlands cultural practices represent a dynamic mix of old and new forms that are constantly being invented and reinvented. This new theoretical lens helps Latina/o scholars valorize the lived realities of Latinas/os in the face of insidious new forms of racist and deficit thinking.

Moreover, borderland perspectives challenge Latina/o educational ethnographers to re-invent and re-imagine space, place, and identity in this changing geopolitical and global economic landscape. Of primary importance, Latina/o ethnographers need to continue their empirical exploration of student agency and cultural identities in the face of epic movements of Amerindian people (Latinas/os of this hemisphere), capital, technology, and consumer culture across borders. Gupta and Ferguson (1997) challenge anthropologists to link the local with "contemporary processes of cultural globalization and transnational cultural flows" (p. 5). They argue for an examination of "the complex and sometimes ironic political processes through which cultural forms are imposed, invented, reworked, and transformed" (p. 5). The experiential reality of the border and borderlands is "post-national"(Saldívar, 1997). The postnation condition, like the imagining of Aztlán, is the "vacuum that is created when social spaces are subverted, reconfigured and reconstituted" (Suárez-Orozco, 1998, p. 300). As Suárez-Orozco explains, when Latino "immigrants" feel forced to leave one nation, yet are hesitant to identity with the "cultures" of their new homes, they create new identities between and betwixt the old nation systems. Artist Guillermo Gómez-Peña asserts that the old monumental cultural and identity categories such as "*la mexicanidad* (unique, monumental, undying), and Chicanismo (with thorns and a capital C)" do not work anymore (1998, p. 133). Instead, he argues, "we are now de-nationalized, de-Mexicanized, trans-Chicanized, and pseudo-internationalized" (p. 133).

Postnation(ality), however, carries far-reaching implications because the very constructs that produce home and exile, native and immigrant, citizen and non-citizen, must also be interrogated. Native American/Chicano historian Bernardo Gallegos (1998) argues that reducing the discourse to a contest between two nations/narrations (i.e., México-U.S.;

host-home) severely limits the possibilities for reconceptualizing the subverted and reconfigured postnational spaces. Instead, Gallegos posits that in the postcolonial moment, educational scholars need to interrogate the disabling discursive categories of both "México," and the "U.S." as constructs of "nation" that erase indigenous identities and make invisible highly asymmetrical relations of power revolving around the categories of race, class, gender, language, place, and identity. Gallegos redefines "postnationality" to not only address the hybrid and reconfigured spaces of identity construction, but to expose the narrative of "nation" as oppressive to this hemisphere's people, and to highlight struggles against hegemonic productions of nation. The recent Zapatista movement in Chiapas, México, the older and continuing indigenous movement of the Quechua-speaking people in Ecuador, and the willfully imagined community of Aztlán—as Laura Elisa Pérez refers to the imagining of the Southwest—are certainly refusals and challenges to "producing the nation as usual" (L.E. Pérez, 1999, p. 20). Gallegos further argues that the reductive approach of "nation" allows for the occupation of our Amerindian bodies, discourses, territories, and conceptual spaces (1998, p. 237).

Regrettably, this hemispheric project of "postnational" hybrid visions, solidarities and new conceptual spaces is often missed by Chicana/o and Latina/o educational scholars who work under the burden of cultural and linguistic assault in the United States. Gómez-Peña (1998) explains the missed encounters between Chicanas/os and Mexicans:

> In the United States, Latino artists work in the flammable context of the multicultural wars and identity politics. We define ourselves as a culture of resistance, and in our eagerness to "resist the dominant culture" we frequently lose all sense of a continental perspective.
>
> (p. 135)

Indeed, how can a "continental" or hemispheric postnational and borderlands vision aid in reconceptualizing Latina/o student agency? What happens to our analyses of Latina/o and Chicana/o student agency when educational ethnographers remap their conceptual world through a postnational and diaspora (rather than "immigrant") lens?

Hence, *nuevas direcciones* means to expand our geospatial, political, and conceptual reach across the hemisphere, to theorize and locate new borderlands. This geopolitical "postnational" lens provides Chicana/o and Latina/o ethnographers with opportunities to expand the notion of "cultural resources" to include youths' connections to transborder real and imagined communities, and alternative narratives of the world outside of the category "nation." This lens also calls for the conceptual development of "diaspora" in order to address the integrated lives of diverse Latino groups in traditional (the Southwest; Midwest) and non-traditional receiving areas of migration (the rural South) and in relationship to other communities of color.

Finally, we must end this interpretive essay with an apology to those Chicana/o and Latina/o scholars left out of our story. This reflects our selective reading of the literature. We did not do a painstaking, formal intellectual history of the interdisciplinary field of educational ethnography. We obviously have not done justice to all the scholars and all the complexities of the field. If nothing else, we hope to leave the image of a thriving research community of scholars/activists who refuse to reify facile and singular conceptions of family, community, and youth identities. Latina(o)/Chicana(o) critical ethnographers embody the sensibilities of *la frontera* with *dignidad* (dignity) and *orgullo* (pride). They are leading the way in reinventing and producing culture, ethnography, education, and a new world that is more just.

Notes

1 Throughout this chapter, we will be using the terms Latino/a and Chicano/a most often together to be inclusive of both the political identification of Chicanos/as in the Southwest, as well as to talk about other Latino groups in the United States. In this chapter, we will also include work by other non-Latino progressive ethnographers who conduct research in Latino communities.

2 We could also look at the work of anthropologist Manuel Gamio who in 1930 published auto-biographic narratives of Mexican immigrants. He explored issues of literacy, assimilation, leadership and intellectualism, as well as race-consciousness and conflict—all themes that educational ethnographers explore today.

3 See Freire (1973).

4 Gerald Vizenor (1994), an American Indian literary scholar, brilliantly develops the ideas of survivance as an active presence, trickster ways, humor, and irony.

5 While we only briefly mention psychological aspects of immigration, the work of Carola and Marcelo Suárez-Orozco (1995, 2001) address the resilience and struggles of immigrant students from a psychological ethnographic perspective.

6 William Tate IV (1997), Gloria Ladson-Billings (1998) and Daniel Solórzano (1997) among others have been key in bringing CRT to the field of education (also, see Ladson-Billings and Tate IV, 1995; Parker *et al.*, 1999).

7 In a similar way, María de la Luz Reyes' (2001) study on emergent biliteracy goes against long-held "universals" about second language and literacy acquisition—mainly narrow interpretations of Jim Cummin's (1981) work which generally argues that children should not be exposed to second language literacy until they have mastered literacy in their first language. In sharp contrast, Reyes highlights bilingual children's experimentation with two language systems as a "natural, spontaneous, and uncomplicated approach to bilingualism and biliteracy" (p. 117).

8 See the work of Daniel Solórzano and colleagues (Solórzano, 1998; Solórzano and Delgado Bernal, 2001; Solórzano and Yosso, 2001), as well as the work of Octavio Villalpando (in press), Marc Pizarro (1998), and Francisca E. González (1998) among others, as exemplars of CRT and LatCrit scholarship in education.

References

Ainslie, R.C. (1998). Cultural mourning, immigration, and engagement: Vignettes from the Mexican experience. In M.M. Suárez-Orozco (Ed.), *Crossings: Mexican immigration in interdisciplinary perspectives* (pp. 285–300). Cambridge, MA: David Rockefeller Center for Latin American Studies, Harvard University.

Anyon, J. (1981). Social class and school knowledge. *Curriculum Inquiry, 11*, 3–42.

Anzaldúa, G. (1987). *Borderlands: La frontera*. San Francisco: Aunt Lute Books.

Apple, M.W. (1979). *Ideology and curriculum*. Boston: Routledge and Kegan Paul.

Apple, M.W. (1982). *Education and power*. Boston: Routledge and Kegan Paul.

Arteaga, A. (1994). An other tongue. In A. Arteaga (Ed.), *An other tongue: Nation and ethnicity in the linguistic borderlands* (pp. 9–33). Durham, NC: Duke University Press.

Barrera, R.B. (1992). The cultural gap in literature-based literacy instruction. *Education and Urban Society, 24*, 227–243.

Bartolomé, L.I. (1994). Beyond the methods fetish: Toward a humanizing pedagogy. *Harvard Educational Review, 64*, 173–194.

Baudelot, C. and Establet, R. (1971). *L'ecole capitaliste* [The capitalist school]. Paris: Maspero.

Bernstein, B.B. (1975). *Class, codes and control: Theoretical studies towards a sociology of language*. New York: Schocken Books.

Bourdieu, P. (1977). *Outline of a theory of practice* (Richard Nice, Trans.). Cambridge, England: Cambridge University Press.

Bourdieu, P. and Passeron, J.-C. (1977). *Reproduction: In education, society and culture*. Beverly Hills, CA: Sage.

Bowles, S. and Gintis, H. (1976). *Schooling in capitalist America: Educational reform and the contradictions of economic life*. New York: Basic Books.

Carger, C.L. (1996). *Of borders and dreams: A Mexican American experience of urban education*. New York: Teachers College Press.

Castillo, A. (1994). *Massacre of the dreamers: Essays on Xicanisma*. New York: Plume/Penguin.

Coleman, J.S., Campbell, E., Hobson, C., McPartland, J., Mood, A., Weinfeld, F. and York, R. (1966). *Equality of educational opportunity*. Washington, DC: Government Printing Office.

Connell, R.W. (1983). *Which way is up? Essays on sex, class and culture*. Sydney: George Allen and Unwin.

Cummins, J. (1981). The role of primary language development in promoting educational success for language minority students. In California State Department of Education (Ed.), *Schooling and language minority students: A theoretical framework* (pp. 3–49). Los Angeles: Evaluation, Dissemination and Assessment Center, California State University.

Darder, A. (1997). Creating the conditions for cultural democracy in the classroom. In A. Darder, R.D. Torres and H. Gutiérrez (Eds.), *Latinos and education: A critical reader* (pp. 331–350). New York: Routledge.

Davies, S. (1996). Leaps of faith: Shifting currents in critical sociology of education. *American Journal of Sociology, 100*, 1448–1478.

Delgado, R. (1995). *The Rodrigo chronicles: Conversations about America and race*. New York: New York University Press.

Delgado Bernal, D. (1998). Using a Chicana feminist epistemology in educational research. *Harvard Educational Review, 68*, 555–579.

Delgado Bernal, D. (2001). Learning and living pedagogies of the home: The mestiza consciousness of Chicana students. *International Journal of Qualitative Studies in Education, 14*, 623–639.

Delgado-Gaitan, C. (1987). Traditions and transitions in the learning process of Mexican children: An ethnographic perspective. In G. Spindler and L. Spindler (Eds.), *Interpretive ethnography of education: At home and abroad* (pp. 333–360). Hillsdale, NJ: Lawrence Erlbaum.

Delgado-Gaitan, C. (1990). *Literacy for empowerment: The role of parents in children's education*. Basingstoke, England: Falmer Press.

Delgado-Gaitan, C. (1991). Involving parents in schools: A process of empowerment. *American Journal of Education, 100*, 20–46.

Delgado-Gaitan, C. (1994). *Consejos*: The power of cultural narratives. *Anthropology and Education Quarterly, 25*, 298–316.

Delgado-Gaitan, C. (1996). *Protean literacy: Extending the discourse on empowerment*. London: Falmer Press.

Delgado-Gaitan, C. and Trueba, H. (1991). *Crossing cultural borders: Education for immigrant families in America*. London: Falmer Press.

Delpit, L. (1995). *Other people's children: Cultural conflict in the classroom*. New York: New Press.

Elenes, C.A. (1997). Reclaiming the borderlands: Chicana/o identity, difference, and critical pedagogy. *Educational Theory, 47*, 359–375.

Erickson, F. (1987). Transformation and school success: The politics and culture of educational achievement. *Anthropology and Education Quarterly, 18*, 335–356.

Ernst-Slavit, G. and Statzner, E.L. (1994). Alternative visions of schooling: An introduction. *Anthropology and Education Quarterly, 25*, 200–207.

Fine, M. and Weis, L. (1998). *The unknown city: Lives of poor and working-class young adults*. Boston: Beacon Press.

Flores, S.Y. (2000). Latino/a teachers: Paradigms of *cariño*. Unpublished manuscript.

Foley, D.E. (1989). *From peones to políticos: Class and ethnicity in a South Texas town, 1900–1989* (2nd ed.). Austin: University of Texas Press.

Foley, D.E. (1990). *Learning capitalist culture: Deep in the heart of Tejas*. Philadelphia: University of Pennsylvania Press.

Foley, D.E. (1991). Reconsidering anthropological explanations of ethnic school failure. *Anthropology and Education Quarterly, 22*, 60–85.

Foley, D.E. (1997). Deficit thinking models based on culture: The anthropological protest. In R.R. Valencia (Ed.), *The evolution of deficit thinking: Educational thought and practice* (pp. 113–131). The Stanford Series on Education and Public Policy. London: Falmer Press.

Foley, D.E. and Moss, K. (2001). Studying American cultural diversity: Some non-essentializing perspectives. In I. Susser and T.C. Patterson (Eds.), *Cultural diversity in the United States: A critical reader* (pp. 343–364). London: Blackwell Publishing.

Freire, P. (1973 [*c*. 1970]). *Pedagogy of the oppressed* (Myra Bergman Ramos, Trans.). New York: Seabury Press.

Galarza, E. (1971). *Barrio boy*. Notre Dame, IN : University of Notre Dame Press.

Gallegos, B. (1998). American Educational Studies Association 1997 Presidential Address. Remember the Alamo: Imperialism, memory, and postcolonial educational studies. *Educational Studies, 29*, 232–247.

Gamio, M. (1989 [*c.* 1930]). *The Mexican immigrant: His life-story.* North Stratford, NH: Ayer.

Gándara, P. (1995). *Over the ivy walls: The educational mobility of low-income Chicanos.* Albany: State University of New York Press.

Garza-Falcón, L.M. (1998). *Gente decente: A borderlands response to the rhetoric of dominance.* Austin: University of Texas Press.

Gibson, M.A. (1988). *Accommodation without assimilation: Sikh immigrants in an American high school.* Ithaca, NY: Cornell University Press.

Ginsberg, H. (1972). *The myth of the deprived child: Poor children's intellect and education.* Englewood Cliffs, NJ: Prentice Hall.

Gómez-Peña, G. (1998). 1995—*Terreno peligro*/Danger Zone: Cultural relations between Chicanos and Mexicans at the end of the century. In F. Bonilla, E. Meléndez, R. Morales, and M. de los Ángeles Torres (Eds.), *Borderless borders: U.S. Latinos, Latin Americans, and the paradox of interdependence* (pp. 131–137). Philadelphia: Temple University Press.

González, F.E. (1998). Formations of Mexicananess: *Trenzas de identidades múltiples.* Growing up Mexicana: Braids of multiple identities. *International Journal of Qualitative Studies in Education, 11*, 81–102.

González, F.E. (1999). Formations of Mexicananess: *Trenzas de identidades múltiples* (Growing up Mexicana: Braids of multiple identities). In L. Parker, D. Deyhle, and S. Villenas (Eds.), *Race is . . . race isn't: Critical race theory and qualitative studies in education* (pp. 125–154). Boulder, CO: Westview Press.

González, N. (1996). Contestation and accommodation in parental narratives. *Education and Urban Society, 29*, 54–70.

González, N. (1999). What will we do when culture does not exist anymore? *Anthropology and Education Quarterly, 30*, 431–435.

González, N. (2001). *I am my language: Discourses of women and children in the borderlands.* Tucson: University of Arizona Press.

González, N., Moll, L.C., Tenery, M.F., Rivera, A., Rendon, P., Gonzales, R. and Amanti, C. (1995). Funds of knowledge for teaching in Latino households. *Urban Education, 29*, 443–470.

González-Peterson, A. (1997). Border ethnographies: Problematizing the crossing. Paper presented at the annual meeting of the American Educational Studies Association, San Antonio, TX, October.

Guerra, J.C. (1998). *Close to home: Oral and literate practices in a transnational Mexicano community.* New York: Teachers College Press.

Gupta, A. and Ferguson, J. (1997). Culture, power, place: Ethnography at the end of an era. In A. Gupta and J. Ferguson (Eds.), *Culture, power, place: Explorations in critical ethnography* (pp. 1–29). Durham, NC: Duke University Press.

Gutiérrez, K., Baquedano-López, P. and Álvarez, H. (2001). Literacy as hybridity: Moving beyond bilingualism in urban classrooms. In M. de la Luz Reyes and J. Halcón (Eds.), *The best for our children: Critical perspectives on literacy for Latino students* (pp. 122–141). New York: Teachers College Press.

Gutiérrez, K., Baquedano-López, P. and Tejeda, C. (2000). Rethinking diversity: Hybridity and hybrid language practices in the third space. *Mind, Culture and Activity: An International Journal, 6*, 286–303.

Gutiérrez, K., Rymes, B. and Larson, J. (1995). Script, counterscript, and underlife in the classroom: James Brown versus *Brown v. Board of Education. Harvard Educational Review, 65*, 445–471.

Habermas, J. (1972). *Knowledge and human interests* (Jeremy J. Shapiro, Trans.). Boston: Beacon Press.

Heath, S.B. (1983). *Ways with words: Language, life and work in communities and Classrooms.* New York: Cambridge University Press.

Hernández-Truyol, B.E. (1997). Borders (en)gendered: Normativities, Latinas, and a LatCrit paradigm. *New York University Law Review, 72*, 882–927.

Herrnstein, R.J. and Murray, C.A. (1994). *The bell curve: Intelligence and class structure in American life.* New York: Free Press.

Hidalgo, N.M. (1998). Toward a definition of a Latino family research paradigm. *International Journal of Qualitative Studies in Education, 11*, 103–120.

Katz, M.B. (1989). *The undeserving poor: From the war on poverty to the war on welfare.* New York: Pantheon.

Kozol, J. (1991). *Savage inequalities: Children in America's schools.* New York: Crown.

Ladson-Billings, G. (1998). Just what is critical race theory and what's it doing in a *nice* field like education. *International Journal of Qualitative Studies in Education,* 11, 7–24.

Ladson-Billings, G. and Tate IV, W.F. (1995). Toward a critical theory of education. *Teachers College Record,* 97, 47–68.

Lather, P. (1991). *Getting smart: Feminist research and pedagogy with/in the postmodern.* New York: Routledge.

Lawler, J.M. (1978). *IQ, heritability, and racism.* New York: International Publishers.

Levinson, B.A. (1992). Ogbu's anthropology and the critical ethnography of education: A reciprocal interrogation. *International Journal of Qualitative Studies in Education,* 5, 205–225.

Levinson, B.A. and Holland, D. (1996). The cultural production of the educated person: An introduction. In B.A. Levinson, D.E. Foley, and D.C. Holland (Eds.), *The cultural production of the educated person: Critical ethnographies of schooling and local practice* (pp. 1–54). Albany: State University of New York Press.

Lewis, O. (1965 [c. 1959]). *Five families: Mexican case studies in the culture of poverty.* New York: New American Library.

Liston, D.P. (1988). *Capitalist schools: Explanation and ethics in radical studies of schooling.* New York: Routledge.

Lucas, T., Henze, R. and Donato, R. (1990). Promoting the success of Latino language-minority students: An exploratory study of six high schools. *Harvard Educational Review,* 60, 315–340.

Matute-Bianchi, M.E. (1986). Ethnic identities and patterns of school success and failure among Mexican-descent and Japanese-American students in a California high school: An ethnographic analysis. *American Journal of Education,* 95, 233–255.

Matute-Bianchi, M.E. (1991). Situational ethnicity and patterns of school performance among immigrant and non-immigrant Mexican-descent students. In M.A. Gibson and J.U. Ogbu (Eds.), *Minority status and schooling: A comparative study of immigrant and involuntary minorities* (pp. 205–247). New York: Garland Publishing.

Mendoza-Denton, N. (1996). "*Muy macha*": Gender and ideology in gang girls' discourse about makeup. *Ethnos,* 61, 47–63.

Mendoza-Denton, N. (1999). Fighting words: Latina girls, gangs, and language attitudes. In D.L. Galindo and M.D. Gonzales (Eds.), *Speaking Chicana: Voice, power, and identity* (pp. 39–56). Tucson: University of Arizona Press.

Mendoza-Denton, N. (2000). *Language and gender among U.S. Latinas/Latinos.* Paper presented at the Latinos/as in the 21st century: Mapping the research agenda, David Rockefeller Center for Latin American Studies, Cambridge, MA, Harvard University, April 7.

Moll, L.C., Amanti, C., Neff, D. and González, N. (1992). Funds of knowledge for teaching: Using a qualitative approach to connect homes and classrooms. *Theory Into Practice,* 31, 132–141.

Moreno, J.F. (Ed.) (1999). *The elusive quest for equality: 150 years of Chicano/Chicana education.* Cambridge, MA: Harvard Educational Review.

Murillo Jr., E.G. (1999). Mojado crossings along neoliberal borderlands. *Educational Foundations,* 13, 7–30.

Noguera, P.A. (1995). Preventing and producing violence: A critical analysis of responses to school violence. *Harvard Educational Review,* 65, 189–212.

Oakes, J. (1985). *Keeping track: How schools structure inequality.* New Haven, CT: Yale University Press.

Ogbu, J.U. (1978). *Minority education and caste: The American system in cross-cultural perspective.* New York: Academic Press.

Ogbu, J.U. (1987). Variability in minority school performance: A problem in search of an explanation. *Anthropology and Education Quarterly,* 18, 312–334.

Ogbu, J.U. and Simon, H.D. (1998). Voluntary and involuntary minorities: A cultural–ecological theory of school performance with some implications for education. *Anthropology and Education Quarterly,* 29, 155–188.

Orfield, G. and Eaton, S.E. (1996). *Dismantling desegregation: The quiet reversal of Brown vs. Board of Education.* New York: New Press.

Parker, L., Deyhle, D. and Villenas, S. (Eds.). (1999). *Race is . . . race isn't: Critical race theory and qualitative studies in education.* Boulder, CO: Westview Press.

Pearl, A. (1997). Cultural and accumulated environmental deficit models. In R.R. Valencia (Ed.), *The evolution of deficit thinking: Educational thought and practice* (pp.132–159). The Stanford Series on Education and Public Policy. London: Falmer Press.

Pérez, E. (1999). *The decolonial imaginary: Writing Chicanas into history.* Bloomington: Indiana University Press.

Pérez, L.E. (1999). *El desorden*, nationalism and Chicana/o aesthetics. In C. Kaplan, N. Alarcón, and M. Moallem (Eds.), *Between woman and nation: Nationalisms, transnational feminisms, and the state* (pp. 19–46). Durham, NC: Duke University Press.

Philips, S.U. (1983). *The invisible culture: Communication in classroom and community on the Warm Springs Indian Reservation.* New York: Longman.

Pimentel, O. (2000). *Buena gente and buen trabajador: Success stories in Mexicano communities.* Paper presented at the meeting of the American Educational Studies Association, Vancouver, BC, November.

Pizarro, M. (1998). "Chicana/o power!": Epistemology and methodology for social justice and empowerment in Chicana/o communities. *International Journal of Qualitative Studies in Education, 11,* 57–80.

Ramos-Zayas, A.Y. (1998). Nationalist ideologies, neighborhood-based activism, and educational spaces in Puerto Rican Chicago. *Harvard Educational Review, 68,* 164–192.

Reyes, M. de la Luz (1992). Challenging venerable assumptions: Literacy instruction for linguistically different students. *Harvard Educational Review, 62,* 427–446.

Reyes, M. de la Luz (2001). Unleashing possibilities: Biliteracy in the primary grades. In M. de la Luz Reyes and J.J. Halcón (Eds.), *The best for our children: Critical perspectives on literacy for Latino students* (pp. 96–121). New York: Teachers College Press.

Reyes, P., Scribner, J. and Scribner, A.P. (1999). *Lessons from high-performing Hispanic schools: Creating learning communities.* New York: Teachers College Record.

Romo, H. and Falbo, T. (1996). *Latino high school graduation.* Austin: University of Texas Press.

Russel y Rodríguez, M. (1998). Confronting anthropology's silencing praxis: Speaking of/from a Chicana consciousness. *Qualitative Inquiry, 4,* 15–40.

Saldívar, J.D. (1997). *Border matters: Remapping American cultural studies.* Berkeley: University of California Press.

San Miguel Jr., G. and Valencia, R.R. (1998). From the treaty of Guadalupe Hidalgo to *Hopwood*: The educational plight and struggle of Mexican Americans in the Southwest. *Harvard Educational Review, 68,* 353–412.

Sánchez, G.I. (1940). *Forgotten people: A study of New Mexicans.* Albuquerque: University of New Mexico Press.

Shannon, S.M. (1995). The culture of the classroom: Socialization in an urban bilingual classroom. *Urban Review, 27,* 321–345.

Solórzano, D.G. (1997). Images and words that wound: Critical race theory, racial stereotyping and teacher education. *Teacher Education Quarterly, 24,* 5–19.

Solórzano, D.G. (1998). Critical race theory, racial and gender microaggressions, and the experiences of Chicana and Chicano scholars. *International Journal of Qualitative Studies in Education, 11,* 121–136.

Solórzano, D.G. and Delgado Bernal, D. (2001). Critical race theory, transformational resistance, and social justice: Chicana and Chicano students in an urban context. *Urban Education.*

Solórzano, D.G. and Yosso, T.J. (2001). Critical race and LatCrit theory and method: Counterstory-telling. *International Journal of Qualitative Studies in Education, 14,* 471–495.

Soto, L.D. (1997). *Language, culture and power: Bilingual families and the struggle for quality education.* Albany: State University of New York Press.

Stanton-Salazar, R.D. (1997). A social capital framework for understanding the socialization of racial minority children and youths. *Harvard Educational Review, 67,* 1–40.

Suárez-Orozco, C. and Suárez-Orozco, M.M. (1995). *Transformations: Migration, family life, and achievement motivation among Latino adolescents.* Stanford, CA: Stanford University Press.

Suárez-Orozco, C. and Suárez-Orozco, M.M. (2001). *Children of immigration.* Cambridge, MA: Harvard University Press.

Suárez-Orozco, M.M. (1989). *Central American refugees and U.S. high schools: A psychosocial study of motivation and achievement.* Stanford, CA: Stanford University Press.

Suárez-Orozco, M.M. (1998). State terrors: Immigrants and refugees in the postnational space. In Y. Zou and E.T. Trueba (Eds.), *Ethnic identity and power: Cultural contexts of political action in school and society* (pp. 283–319). Albany: State University of New York Press.

Tapia, J. (1998). The schooling of Puerto Ricans: Philadelphia's most impoverished community. *Anthropology and Education Quarterly, 29,* 297–323.

Tate IV, W.F. (1997). Critical race theory and education: History, theory, and implications. In M.W. Apple (Ed.), *Review of research in education* (Vol. 22, pp. 195–250). Washington, DC: American Educational Research Association.

Trueba, E.T. (1999). *Latinos unidos: From cultural diversity to the politics of solidarity.* Lanham, MD: Rowman and Littlefield.

Trueba, H.T. (1988). Culturally based explanations of minority students' academic achievement. *Anthropology and Education Quarterly, 19,* 270–287.

Trueba, H.T. (1991). From failure to success: The roles of culture and cultural conflict in the academic achievement of Chicano students. In R.R. Valencia (Ed.), *Chicano school failure and success: Research and policy agendas for the 1990s* (pp. 151–163). The Stanford Series on Education and Public Policy. London: Falmer Press.

Trueba, H.T. (1994). Reflections on alternative visions of schooling. *Anthropology and Education Quarterly, 25,* 376–393.

Trueba, H.T., Rodríguez, C., Zou, Y. and Cintrón, J. (1993). *Healing multicultural America: Mexican immigrants rise to power in rural California.* Washington, DC: Falmer Press.

Trujillo, A.L. (1998). *Chicano empowerment and bilingual education: Movimiento politics in Crystal City, Texas.* New York: Garland Publishers.

Urciuoli, B. (1996). *Exposing prejudice: Puerto Rican experiences of language, race, and class.* Boulder, CO: Westview Press.

Valdes, F. (1998). Under construction: LatCrit consciousness, community, and theory. *Raza Law Journal, 10,* 3–56.

Valdés, G. (1991). *Background knowledge and minority students: Some implications for literacy.* Paper presented at the annual meeting of the American Educational Research Association, Chicago, IL, April.

Valdés, G. (1996). *Con respeto: Bridging the distance between culturally-diverse families and schools.* New York: Teachers College Press.

Valencia, R.R. (Ed.). (1997a). *The evolution of deficit thinking: Educational thought and practice.* The Stanford Series on Education and Public Policy. London: Falmer Press.

Valencia, R.R. (1997b). Genetic pathology model of deficit thinking. In R.R. Valencia (Ed.), *The evolution of deficit thinking: Educational thought and practice* (pp. 41–112). The Stanford Series on Education and Public Policy. London: Falmer Press.

Valencia, R.R. (1997c). Conceptualizing the notion of deficit thinking. In R.R. Valencia (Ed.), *The evolution of deficit thinking: Educational thought and practice* (pp. 1–12). The Stanford Series on Education and Public Policy. London: Falmer Press.

Valencia, R.R. and Solórzano, D.G. (1997). Contemporary deficit thinking. In R.R. Valencia (Ed.), *The evolution of deficit thinking: Educational thought and practice* (pp. 160–210). The Stanford Series on Education and Public Policy. London: Falmer Press.

Valencia, R.R. and Suzuki, L.A. (2001). *Intelligence testing and minority students: Foundations, performance factors, and assessment issues.* Thousand Oaks, CA: Sage.

Valenzuela, A. (1999a). "Checkin' up on my guy": Chicanas, social capital, and the culture of romance. *Frontiers: A Journal of Women Studies, 20,* 60–79.

Valenzuela, A. (1999b). *Subtractive schooling: U.S.-Mexican youth and the politics of caring.* Albany: State University of New York Press.

Vásquez, O.A., Pease-Álvarez, L. and Shannon, S.M. (1994). *Pushing boundaries: Language and culture in a Mexicano community.* Cambridge, England: Cambridge University Press.

Vélez-Ibáñez, C.G. and Greenberg, J.B. (1992). Formation and transformation of funds of knowledge among U.S. Mexican households. *Anthropology and Education Quarterly, 23,* 313–335.

Vigil, J.D. (1997). *Personas Mexicanas: Chicano high schoolers in a changing Los Angeles.* Fort Worth, TX: Harcourt Brace College.

Vigil, J.D. (1999). Streets and schools: How educators can help Chicano marginalized gang youth. *Harvard Educational Review, 69,* 270–288.

Villalpando, O. (in press). Self-segregation or self-preservation? A critical race theory and Latina/o critical theory analysis of findings from a longitudinal study of Chicana/o college students. *International Journal of Qualitative Studies in Education.*

Villenas, S. (1996). The colonizer/colonized Chicana ethnographer: Identity, marginalization, and co-optation in the field. *Harvard Educational Review, 66,* 711–731.

Villenas, S. (2000). This ethnography called my back: Writings of the exotic gaze, "othering" Latina, and recuperating Xicanisma. In E.A.S. Pierre and W.S. Pillow (Eds.), *Working the ruins: Feminist poststructural theory and methods in education* (pp. 74–95). New York: Routledge.

Villenas, S. (2001). Latina mothers and small-town racisms: Creating narratives of dignity and moral education in North Carolina. *Anthropology and Education Quarterly, 32,* 3–28.

Villenas, S. and Deyhle, D. (1999). Critical race theory and ethnographies challenging the stereotypes: Latino families, schooling, resilience and resistance. *Curriculum Inquiry, 29,* 413–445.

Villenas, S. and Moreno, M. (2001). To *valerse por si misma/*to be self-reliant between race, capitalism and patriarchy: Latina mother–daughter pedagogies in North Carolina. *International Journal of Qualitative Studies in Education, 14,* 671–687.

Vizenor, G. (1994). *Manifest manners: Postindian warriors of survivance.* Hanover, NH: University Press of New England.

Willis, P. (1981). *Learning to labor: How working class kids get working class jobs.* New York: Columbia University Press.

Young, M.F.D. (Ed.). (1971). *Knowledge and control: New directions for the sociology of education.* London: Collier-Macmillan.

Zentella, A.C. (1997). *Growing up bilingual: Puerto Rican children in New York.* Malden, MA: Blackwell.

8 Chicano families and schools: myths, knowledge, and future directions for understanding

Robert P. Moreno and Richard R. Valencia

Over the past three and a half decades parental involvement has surfaced as a major force to reduce academic failure and promote students' educational success (Booth and Dunn, 1996; Coleman *et al.*, 1966; Purkey and Smith, 1985). A variety of empirical research has demonstrated that parental involvement can improve the educational achievement of elementary and secondary school students in both White and racial/ethnic minority populations (Chavkin, 1993; Epstein, 1986; Marburger, 1990). Educational experts concur on the need to increase parental involvement, and to create a stronger home–school relationship among Mexican American families. It is believed that this stronger relationship will, in turn, increase the educational achievement of all children (Harrison *et al.*, 1990; Laosa, 1982; Slaughter-Defoe *et al.*, 1990). Unfortunately, much of the research on parental involvement fails to include families of Mexican decent. This creates a disturbing gap in our understanding of family–school relations among one of the fastest growing segments of the United States population (see Valencia, Chapter 2, present book). The purpose of this chapter is to closely examine the relationship between Chicano families and the schools with an emphasis on Mexican American parental involvement. Our discussion is organized around four sections: (a) parental involvement: a brief overview; (b) exposing the myth: Mexican Americans do not value education; (c) Chicano parental involvement: What do we know?; (d) future directions for understanding Chicano families and schools.

Parent involvement: an overview

Before we proceed, it may be useful to provide a brief overview of parental involvement research in general. Although parents have been involved in their children's education since the inception of public schooling, the 1960s sparked a particular interest in parental involvement patterns. Social and developmental scientists began to demonstrate that parents' attitudes, beliefs, and behaviors were important predictors of children's intellectual and educational achievement (Bloom, 1981), and may play a role in the existing educational inequality among Whites and certain racial/ethnic minority groups (Coleman *et al.*, 1966). In addition, early childhood education programs such as Head Start began to incorporate parental involvement in their programming (Berger, 1981; Rich, 1987).

Initially, there were two competing conceptualizations of parental involvement. Both—"parental education" and "parental control"—had important implications for the nature of family–school relationships. Those who held the "parent education" perspective viewed low-socioeconomic status (SES) parents as lacking parenting skills. It was these skills or the lack thereof, that was at the root of the problem. Much of this theorizing was based on cultural and environmental deficit models, particularly inadequate socialization of children by their parents (for a discussion, see Pearl, 1997). Parental involvement was therefore based on providing parents with the "correct" skills to interact with their children. The emphasis was to "fix" parents.

Those who viewed parental involvement as a matter of parental control took a more political perspective. They saw parental involvement as a way to develop a more inclusive educational system. Here, the push was for parents to be decisionmakers, and to change the structural conditions that perpetuated poverty (Valentine and Stark, 1979). Over time, however, the deficit-oriented parental education perspective gained in prominence and evolved as the guiding principle for developing parenting programs. A major tenant of this deficit-oriented thinking was the belief that Mexican Americans, as a case in point, do not value education. Because they do not value education, they are not involved in their children's education. However, a close examination of the evidence shows that this is simply not the case.

Exposing the myth: Mexican Americans do not value education

In recent scholarship, Valencia and Black (2002) have provided a comprehensive treatise on the deeply rooted myth that Mexican Americans do not value education. The authors discuss the basis of the myth, how it has been communicated and perpetuated, and how the myth can be debunked. Here, we draw from the Valencia and Black article in discussing the assertion that Mexican Americans devalue education.[1]

Economist Thomas Sowell wrote in his chapter on "The Mexicans" (*Ethnic America: A History*, 1981) the following: "The goals and values of Mexican Americans have never centered on education" (p. 266). Historically and contemporarily, there have been numerous assertions by individuals—in the scholarly literature and in media outlets—that Mexican American parents, particularly of low-SES background, do not value education. Thus, they fail to inculcate this value in their children via academic socialization, and seldom participate in parental involvement activities in their home or the school. As a consequence, the myth contends, Mexican American children tend to perform poorly in school (e.g., low academic achievement). These allegations cannot be taken lightly, as we have previously noted there is substantial evidence that, in general, "when parents are involved in their youths' schooling, children do better in school" (Marburger, 1990, p. 82).

The fundamental basis of the myth

Valencia and Black (2002) contend that the basis of the myth—Mexican Americans do not value education—lies in the pseudoscientific notion of "deficit thinking" (see Valencia [1997] for a comprehensive discussion of the evolution of deficit thinking in educational thought and practice from the American Colonial period to the contemporary period). Deficit thinking refers to the idea that students, particularly of low-SES background and of color, fail in school because they and their families have internal defects, or deficits that thwart the learning process.

The basis for the myth that Mexican Americans do not value education stems from the general model of deficit thinking, and from the specific variant of familial deficits. The argument goes as follows: Given that Mexican Americans (allegedly) do not hold education high in their value hierarchy, this leads to inadequate familial socialization for academic competence, which in turn, contributes to the school failure of Mexican American children and youths.

Furthermore, the myth of Mexican Americans' indifference to the value of education can be more fully understood when viewed as part of a historical tradition of deficit thinking in which Mexican Americans are described under the "Mexican American cultural model (stereotype)" in which their value orientations are presented as the root cause of their social problems (Hernández, 1970), including school failure (for overviews and critiques of the model, see, e.g., Menchaca, 2000; Romano-V, 1968). In a broader sense, the Mexican American stereotype model is grounded in the long-standing myth that behavior is equated with values (Valencia and Solórzano, 1997). As Allen (1970) has noted:

> behavior cannot be equated with values. In other words, simply because a person behaves in a certain way does not mean he desires to do so because of his beliefs or values. Another problem is that the concept is tautological: values inferred from behavior are used to explain behavior. To be useful for explaining behavior, values should be measured independently of the behavior to be explained, or no advantage can be claimed for the gratuitous labeling of the behavior.
>
> (pp. 372–373)

Mythmaking

The assertion that Mexican Americans are indifferent toward and devalue education has been communicated in various ways. These expressions are particularly seen in: (a) some very early master's theses (1920s; 1930s); (b) published scholarly literature; (c) opinions voiced in media outlets. In this subsection, we discuss examples of this mythmaking from these three categories.

Early master's theses

Taylor (1927) sought to investigate the possible reasons for "pedagogical retardation" (being overage for grade level) among young school-age Mexican American children in Albuquerque, New Mexico. The author concluded that mental retardation, lack of knowledge in English, excessive school transfers, and poor nutrition were contributing factors to pedagogical retardation among a substantial percentage of the students. Taylor also honed in on the "indifference of [the] family toward [the] value of education" (p. 173). Specifically contextualizing such "indifference" in school attendance issues, Taylor commented:

> Every possible effort is made in Albuquerque toward the enforcement of regular attendance, insofar as the administrative officers are concerned. The difficulty lies in the home. A serious lack of the realization of the importance of regular attendance is the source of the trouble in these schools. The large percentage of illiterate parents, found especially among the Mexican population, *fails to understand the full value of the opportunity offered by the public schools* [italics added].
>
> (pp. 176–177)

Other examples of these mythmakers of the past are:

• Gould (1932; southern California area study): "*As a general rule, the [Mexican] parents lack any desire for education*" [italics added] (p. 2).

- Lyon (1933; Los Angeles City School District study): "The greatest cause of [inter-cultural] conflict arises from the attitude toward education on the part of the parents and . . . Mexican girls. *The parents feel that the child is needed in the home and do not understand the necessity for education*" [italics added] (pp. 42–43).

The assertions by Taylor (1927), Gould (1932), and Lyon (1933) were not uncommon voices from the past regarding the establishment and perpetuation of the myth that Mexican Americans do not value education. Such contentions were based on deficit thinking and stereotypes. These newly credentialed individuals with their M.A. degrees failed to acknowledge the forces and conditions that likely created obstacles for Mexican American parents to fully express their appreciation for and value of education—e.g., not being welcome at schools because of racial animus, language barriers, and the need for their children to contribute economically to the household due to exploitative arrangements the parents faced in the world of work.[2]

Scholarly literature

To be sure, master's theses are considered as scholarly literature. Here, however, the focus is on literature—e.g., books, book chapters in edited volumes, journal articles—that, we assume, has gone through the rigors of peer review. We examine examples of mythmaking from three categories of scholarly literature: (a) the "culturally deprived" child literature of the 1960s; (b) the "at risk" child and family literature of the 1980s and 90s; (c) an "other" category.

"CULTURAL DEPRIVATION" LITERATURE

In the 1960s, the "culturally deprived" child (also referred to as the "culturally disadvantaged," "intellectually deprived," and "socially disadvantaged" child) was socially constructed (see Pearl, 1997, for a sustained coverage of this era). Voluminous literature spoke to the culturally deprived child and his/her (allegedly) socially pathological family and impoverished home environment (e.g., see Frost and Hawkes, 1966; Hellmuth, 1967). Mexican American children and their families (particularly of low-SES background) were, among other racial/ethnic groups, a targeted population of the 1960s mythmakers (see Marans and Lourie, 1967). Havighurst (1966), in a book chapter titled "Who are the Socially Disadvantaged?" (a discussion on the general socially disadvantaged population), presented a brief list of "family characteristics" the socially disadvantaged child lacks—compared to "modern urban" families (meaning middle-class). The characteristic most germane to our discussion is: "the socially disadvantaged child *lacks . . . Two parents who*: read a good deal; read to him; show him that they *believe in the value of education* [italics added]; reward him for good school achievement" (p. 18). Another example of mythmaking during the era of cultural deprivation is seen in Dougherty (1966) who—without the support of a single citation—commented: "*Parental indifference to the value of education is transmitted to the children* [italics added], where school careers are naturally characterized by poor attention, low achievement, and early leaving. Thus, the cycle of hopelessness and despair is repeated from generation to generation" (p. 389).

It is beyond the scope of this chapter to discuss critiques of the cultural deprivation literature. We refer the interested reader to the writings of Baratz and Baratz (1970), Labov (1970), Pearl (1997), and Valencia and Solórzano (1997). Critiques of the cultural deprivation literature model have centered, for example, on the framework's racist and classist nature, theoretical weaknesses, and methodological shortcomings of this body of research.

"AT RISK" CHILD LITERATURE

First popularized in the educational policy circles of the early 1980s, the label "at risk" is now entrenched in the educational literature as well as in the talk of educators and policy-makers (Valencia and Solórzano, 1997). Writing in 1995, Swadener and Lubeck (1995) reported that since 1989 over 2,500 articles and conference papers have dealt with the at risk construct. Given their overrepresentation among low-achieving students, and among the poor and low-SES families, Mexican Americans and other Latinos are considered by scholars of the at risk literature to be part of this group—that is, students who are at risk for school failure. Sleeter (1995) has asserted that the new term, at risk, is a resurrected metaphor of the cultural deprivation and culturally disadvantaged terms used with great frequency in the 1960s (also, see Valencia and Solórzano, 1997).

Regarding the role of the home and parents, ". . . the 'at risk' label alleges that a child suffers some environmentally induced deficiency . . . [and] by implication or design, mothers are presumed to be the *source* of the problems children experience" (Lubeck, 1995, p. 54). Furthermore, "If a child does not fare well, emotionally, socially, or academically, it is the family—but the mother specifically—who is implicated" (ibid.). Implicit in the at-risk literature is that parents of these children do not value education.

OTHER LITERATURE

Another category of scholarly literature in which mythmaking can be seen regarding the alleged indifference Mexican Americans have toward education is what Valencia and Black (2002) refer to as "other" literature. This category contains literature that does not snugly fit into either the cultural deprivation or at risk camps, although such scholarship shares the common feature of being heavily shaped by deficit thinking. Here we briefly discuss two examples of this other literature: Sowell (1981) and Dunn (1987).

This section opened with a quote by Sowell (1981), which is worth repeating: "*The goals and values of Mexican Americans have never centered on education*" [italics added] (p. 266). How does Sowell—who has written a history of racial/ethnic groups in the U.S.—support this sweeping generalization? What specific evidence does he marshal to defend such a blatant assertion? He does so by noting comparative high school completion rates across race/ethnicity: "As of 1960, only 13 percent of Hispanics in the Southwest completed high school, compared to 17 percent for blacks in the same region, 28 percent among non-Hispanic whites, and 39 percent among Japanese Americans" (p. 266). It appears that Sowell is making this argument: *Because Mexican Americans have the lowest high school completion rate of the groups he compares*,[3] *then this means that Mexican Americans do not value education*. Clearly, Sowell framed his interpretation of the racial/ethnic high school completion gap in a deficit thinking manner. Explicit in his argument is that Mexican Americans are the makers of their own educational shortcomings. Furthermore, he failed to discuss the far different interpretations of the achievement gap proffered by the authors who presented the original data Sowell describes above (Grebler *et al.*, 1970, p. 143, Table 7-1). Grebler *et al.* attributed the achievement gap, in part, to intragroup (i.e., Anglo and Mexican American) variations in ". . . rural-urban background, to immigrant status, and to poverty and other aspects of the home environment" (p. 170). Grebler *et al.* also presented a structural inequality hypothesis to explain the gap:

The extreme disparities in different locales suggests [sic] also an [sic] hypothesis concerning a strategic determinant in a larger society: the extent to which local social systems and, through these, the school systems have held the Mexican-American population in a subordinate position.[4]

Sowell's (1981) claim that Mexican Americans' goals and values have never focused on education is one of the most egregious and unfounded statements ever made about Mexican Americans and their schooling. His assertion is not only wrong (as we shall see later when we debunk the myth), but it is presented in a book on the history of racial/ethnic groups in the U.S.—a type of source that should be committed to the highest level of interpretive scholarship, not mythmaking.

A second example of mythmaking from the scholarly literature regarding the allegation that Mexican Americans do not value education is seen in Lloyd M. Dunn's (1987) research monograph, *Bilingual Hispanic Children on the U.S. Mainland: A Review of Research on Their Cognitive, Linguistic, and Scholastic Development*. While acknowledging that the schools have been implicated, in part, in not adequately serving Latino pupils (i.e., Mexican American and Puerto Rican), Dunn places the blame on parents who—he contends—do not care about education. This is a major factor, Dunn argues, as to why Latinos, as a group, have academic problems in schools. He opines: "it would be more correct to point out that these Hispanic pupils and their parents have also failed the schools and society, because *they have not been motivated and dedicated enough to make the system work for them*" [italics added] (p. 78). Furthermore, in the absence of any supportive data or sources, Dunn asserts: *It* [valuing education] *is a tradition that Hispanics in general do not appear to have*" (p. 80). Once again, we see a scholar evoke a long-standing deficit thinking tactic of shifting culpability away from structural problems in the schools (such as segregation, financial inequalities, and curriculum differentiation), to the backs and shoulders of Latino parents who are expected to carry the near exclusive burden of school success for their children. Moreover, Dunn is either unaware or chooses to disregard the available literature that Latinos do value and do get involved in their children's education.[5]

Media expressions

A third way in which the myth of Mexican Americans' indifference to the importance of education has been expressed is through individuals making such pronouncements in some forum that subsequently capture the attention of the media (particularly newspapers and television). We discuss two cases in point—Lauro Cavazos and Lino Graglia.

Lauro Cavazos, former United States Secretary of Education (and the top-ranking Latino) in President George H. Bush's administration, made some comments in early April, 1990 that set off a maelstrom of disputation. Cavazos made his comments at a press conference in San Antonio, Texas that was concerned with the first of a series of five regional hearings on Hispanic educational problems. He stated: "*Hispanics have always valued education . . . but somewhere along the line we've lost that. I really believe that, today, there is not that emphasis*" [italics added] (Snider, 1990, p. 1). There was immediate response from the media. The headlines of the *San Antonio Light* pronounced: "Cavazos Says Attitude Hurts Hispanics" (ibid.). The *New York Times'* headline of a front-page story proclaimed: "Education Secretary Criticizes the Values of Hispanic Parents" (ibid.).

Suffice it to say, Cavazos' pronouncements provoked considerable public clamor, particularly from Mexican American San Antonians. Dr. José A. Cárdenas, Executive Director of the

Intercultural Development Research Association and lifelong educational activist commented: "It's [Cavazos' assertion] a simple case of the victim being blamed for the crime" (ibid.). James A. Vásquez, Superintendent of the San Antonio Edgewood Independent School District, responded: "The terrible thing . . . is that he's denying what's happened to Mexican Americans in the history of this state, how we've been discriminated against in every way. It proves he continues to be very far removed from the community" (ibid., p. 2). Vásquez's contention of a history of widespread discrimination, including educational inequalities in Texas can be amply documented by existing scholarship (see: De León, 1983; Feagin and Booher Feagin, 1999; San Miguel, 1987; San Miguel and Valencia, 1998; Valencia, 2000).

Cavazos' unfounded and insulting statements about Hispanics' attitude toward education certainly provoked outcries. This resultant uproar paled, however, in comparison to the commotion generated by similar comments that constitutional law Professor Lino Graglia made at a news conference on September 10, 1997 at The University of Texas at Austin. At that time, Graglia was chosen as honorary co-chairman of the newly established group, Students for Equal Opportunity—a group that was "tired of hearing only from supporters of affirmative action" (Roser, 1997, p. B1). At the campus press conference, where the new student group made its debut, Graglia made the following remarks regarding affirmative action, race, and academic performance at The University of Texas School of Law:

> The central problem is that Blacks and Mexican Americans are not academically competitive [with Whites] . . . Various studies seem to show that Blacks [and] Mexican Americans spend less time in school. *They have a culture that seems not to encourage achievement* [italics added] . . . failure is not looked upon with disgrace.[6]

In an NBC *Today* interview with reporter Matt Lauer on September 12, 1997, Graglia was asked if he had any statistical backing for his cultural statements about minority students and educational achievement:

GRAGLIA: I'm not an expert on educational matters.
LAUER: But you do agree with the statement that came out of yours that says they [Blacks and Mexican Americans] have a culture that seems not to encourage achievement?
GRAGLIA: Well, I meant to say that there are some cultures, like some of the Asian cultures that insist more highly on the students going to school and achieving in school . . .

Ramiro Canales (member of the Chicano/Hispanic Law Students Association at UT) was also interviewed by Lauer, who asked Canales "how he felt about the cultural issues Graglia raised."

CANALES: Professor Graglia is not qualified to make cultural assessments. He is a law school professor and not a cultural anthropologist, and when he makes these generalizations they not only promote racial stereotypes but also distort reality as it is in Texas. I think both African American and Mexican American cultures promote success. I think that the parents of all the minority law students want their students [*sic*] to succeed.

The nefarious pronouncements from Graglia—who has a long history of speaking out against affirmative action and using busing for school desegregation (Roser and Tanamachi, 1997)—drew national and international media coverage and swift denunciations.[7] Included among the public condemnators were UT School of Law Dean Michael Sharlot, UT Interim

President Peter Flawn, UT System Chancellor William Cunningham, student organizations, professors, civil rights organizations, and racial/ethnic minority lawmakers (Martin, 1997; Roser and Tanamachi, 1997). Regarding the latter group, Hispanic state lawmakers called for Graglia's resignation. Senator Gregory Luna, head of the State Hispanic Caucus, stated: "It seems we're in an era where the Ku Klux Klan does not come in white robes but in the robes of academe" (Martin, 1997, p. 1). UT students of color were also very involved in the protest against Graglia. They staged a sit-in at the School of Law, and helped organize a political rally on campus in which Reverend Jesse Jackson, in front of 5,000 people, lambasted Graglia (Roser and Tanamachi, 1997).

The Cavazos and Graglia incidents serve as reminders that statements made about racial/ethnic groups—in which the remarks are shaped by deficit thinking, ahistoricism, ignorance of scholarly literature, and bigotry—have no value in promoting further understanding of the achievement gap between White and minority student groups. These incidents also should remind us that we need to be vigilant in responding to unfounded comments about Mexican Americans and other people of color.

In conclusion, it is quite evident that the myth of Mexican Americans not valuing education has evolved into a stereotype of epic proportions. Apparently having its roots in the 1920s master's theses, it has flourished—being promulgated in the scholarly literature of the culture of poverty, culturally deprived and at risk child, texts on racial/ethnic history and cross-cultural cognitive/academic achievement assessments, and statements by individuals that are deemed newsworthy by the media. There is no doubt that many Mexican American school-age children and youths experience, on the average, school failure. Valencia (Chapter 1, present book) discusses 15 different schooling conditions and outcomes that help to understand the nature of such school failure. To attribute, however, the persistent and pervasive achievement gap between Mexican American students and their White peers to a value orientation of Mexican American indifference to the importance of education is baseless, irresponsible, and racist. Furthermore, and very importantly, this assertion of not valuing education is a *myth*. Next, we bring forth evidence to demonstrate how this myth can be exposed.

Debunking the myth

The indiscriminate comments that we have reviewed by a number of individuals who contend that Mexican Americans have never had education as a goal, nor valued it, is far from the truth. For example, had Sowell (1981) carefully done his historical research he would have found that Mexican Americans have rallied around education for many decades (see, e.g., San Miguel and Valencia, 1998). Valencia and Black (2002) debunked the myth of Mexican American indifference to the importance of education by providing three evidentiary forms: (a) the historical/contemporary struggle for equal educational opportunity; (b) scholarly literature documenting parental involvement; (c) a case study of transgenerational parental involvement. Due to space limitations, we focus on the Chicano people's historical/contemporary struggle for educational equity. The scholarly literature documenting Chicano parental involvement is discussed later in this chapter.

The history and contemporary endeavors of the Mexican American community's quest for equal educational opportunity have been so extensive and rich that the second author (R.R. Valencia) is able to teach an undergraduate course, "Chicano Educational Struggles," at The University of Texas at Austin on this topic. The course is an analysis of how Mexican Americans have struggled for better education via five historical and contemporary processes. In brief, they are:

Litigation

Since the 1930s, Mexican Americans have brought forth lawsuits of various types in their efforts to improve the educational lot for their children and youths. Such litigation has involved, for example, *segregation* (for a discussion of key cases see San Miguel and Valencia, 1998; Valencia *et al.*, Chapter 3, current volume); *special education* (Henderson and Valencia, 1985); *school financing* (Valencia, Chapter 1, current volume); *school closures* (Valencia, 1980, 1984a, 1984b); *undocumented children* (Cárdenas and Cortez, 1986); and *high-stakes testing* (Valencia and Bernal, 2000). Notwithstanding the range of outcomes of this litigation as a whole (bittersweet ones, some losses, and some victories), taking their cases to court for over the last 70 years speaks to the reality that the Mexican American people highly value education.

Advocacy organizations

In their pursuit of improved education for their community, Mexican American parents, scholars, lawyers, and youths have founded a number of advocacy organizations. Beginning with the establishment of the League of United Latin American Citizens (LULAC) in 1929 (Márquez, 1993), many advocacy groups—in which better education is a rallying point for action—have been founded over the years. Examples of these highly visible organizations are: American GI Forum (Ramos, 1998), Mexican American Legal Defense and Educational Fund (MALDEF) (O'Connor and Epstein, 1984), and *Movimiento Estudiantil Chicano de Aztlán* (MEChA) (Muñoz, 1989). These advocacy organizations, and many others, have played critical roles in the identification of issues and in the advancement of improved educational conditions and outcomes for Mexican American students. For example, San Miguel and Valencia (1998) noted: "Over the last three decades, MALDEF has evolved into a chief source of successful education litigation for the Mexican American community, winning many lawsuits and setting highly influential case law" (p. 388).

Individual activists

Another indication that Mexican Americans value education stems from the work of scores of individuals who have championed the cause—that is, the Mexican American community's historical and contemporary resolve for the pursuit and attainment of educational equality. Historically, there have been, for example, the likes of grassroots organizer Eleuterio Escobar in San Antonio, Texas in the 1930s, 1940s, and 1950s (García, 1979); Dr. Héctor García, founder of the American GI Forum in Texas in 1948 (Ramos, 1998); Professor George I. Sánchez, scholar/civil rights activist from the 1930s to the 1970s (Romo, 1986); attorney Pete Tijerina, founder of MALDEF in San Antonio, Texas in 1968 (O'Connor and Epstein, 1984); and Professor Mari-Luci Jaramillo, pioneer of bilingual/bicultural education in New Mexico (Vásquez, 1994). To this illustrious list, we can add numerous other individual activists—university professors, lawyers, students, parents, community organizers, school-teachers, politicians, and so forth.

Political demonstrations

For decades, Mexican Americans have expressed their collective interest and action in promoting better education for children and youths by engaging in public confrontations in a display of dissatisfaction with oppression, with the goal of gaining resources. One of the more common forms of political demonstrations has been the strategy of a "blowout" (school walkout). It appears that the first such blowout occurred in 1910 in San Angelo, Texas—lasting through 1915 (De León, 1974). At the heart of the blowout was the Tejano community's demand that its children be allowed to attend the academically superior White schools. Other well-known blowouts transpired in East Los Angeles in 1968 (Rosen, 1974), and in Crystal City, Texas in 1969 (Navarro, 1995).

Legislation

A final form of struggle in which Mexican Americans have expressed their resolve in improving the educational lot for their children and youths is seen in legislative efforts. One example is the long struggle for bilingual education in Texas in which State Senator Joe Bernal and State Representative Carlos Truan persevered from 1969 to 1981 to institutionalize bilingual education (San Miguel, 1987; Vega, 1983). Another example is the "Top Ten Percent Plan," a law that went into effect in Texas in Fall, 1998. The law's intent was to increase the enrollment of minority students in public colleges, in light of the state's dismantling of affirmative action in admissions (see San Miguel and Valencia, 1998). The bill, written by State Representative Irma Rangel and State Senator Gonzalo Barrientos, allows high school students who graduate in the top 10 percent of their graduating classes to be automatically admitted to any public four-year institution of higher education in Texas, including its premier institutions (see Chapa, 1997).

In the final analysis, it is important for scholars to be steadfast in debunking the myth that Mexican Americans do not value education. Although such debunking may be deemed reactive, it is necessary. In the production of scholarship dealing with Mexican Americans, we often have to deconstruct inaccurate and unsound writings before we can construct new works. Without acknowledging this reality, it is difficult to continue the on-going proactive scholarship on the Mexican American family and its rich, varied, and positive expressions regarding the importance of the institution of education.

Chicano parental involvement: What do we know?

Throughout the mid-1960s to the present, studies examining the level of parent involvement of Mexican American and other Latino families have consistently shown these families are less involved in their children's schooling when compared to their non-Latino counterparts. For example, early studies found that Mexican American and other Latino students reported that their parents were less involved in activities such as reading to their child, and attendance at PTA meetings when compared to White and Asian American mothers (Coleman *et al.*, 1966). When asked directly, Latino parents themselves reported significantly lower levels of involvement in their children's schooling decisions as compared to African American and White populations (Lynch and Stein, 1987; Stein, 1983; Stevenson *et al.*, 1990). The discrepancy between Mexican Americans' positive view of their children's education and lower levels of involvement begs the question: What are the factors that lead to parental involvement in Chicano families? To address this question, we have taken an ecological perspective (Bronfenbrenner, 1986) to examine the various levels in which parental involvement can be impacted. We have classified the research findings in this area into three general categories: (a) personal and psychological, (b) contextual, and (c) sociocultural.

Personal and psychological

Personal and psychological variables are personal values, beliefs, or characteristics that a parent may possess that can influence his or her behavior, and thereby impact their child's development. As stated earlier, a popular position by many researchers, practitioners, and others is that low-SES and racial/ethnic minority populations (in this case, Mexican Americans) do not value parental involvement and thus do not partake in their children's schooling (for discussions, see: Hoover-Dempsey *et al.*, 1987; Lareau, 1989; Valencia and Black, 2002). Advocates of this position typically assume parents from "traditional Mexican culture" do not value educational achievement and consequently do not become involved in their children's schooling. Goldenberg (1987) has forcefully noted that this view is as "wrong-headed and, ultimately, as insidious as genetic explanations" (p. 175) because it blames Mexican Americans (and their culture) for a complex and multiply determined behavior.

Moreover, as we have previously shown, this perspective is unfounded. The available research clearly indicates that Mexican Americans place great importance on their children's education (Chavkin and Williams, 1989; Moreno and López, in press; Stevenson *et al.*, 1990; Valencia and Black, 2002). For example, Okagaki and Frensch's research (1998) showed that Latino parents hold approximately the same ideals of children's academic attainment as Whites. Similarly, in one of the most comprehensive national surveys of the public's attitudes and opinions regarding higher education ever conducted, Immerwahr and Foleno (2000) found:

> It is . . . sometimes suggested that members of these minority groups [Hispanic and African American] compared to other populations, do not place as high a value on higher education. The findings from this study seem conclusively to eliminate this . . . reason. *Higher education is important for all Americans, but it is especially important to African American and Hispanic parents, who are significantly more likely to emphasize higher education than either White parents or the population as a whole* [italics added].
>
> (p. 4)

In addition to values, there has been a great deal of work examining the relation between parental beliefs and their children's educational development (Goodknow, 1988; Marjoribanks, 1979; Miller, 1988; Segal, 1985). With respect to parental involvement, areas such as parental efficacy, educational aspirations, role definition, and school-related knowledge have all shown some promise in furthering our understanding of Chicano parents' involvement in the children's education. Parents who perceive themselves as efficacious (i.e., competent) tend to become more involved in their children's education than parents who view themselves as incompetent (Schaffer and Edgerton, 1985; Swick and McKnight, 1989). Some researchers have suggested, however, that Chicano parents may view themselves as being less competent than African American and White parents (Delgado-Gaitan, 1990; Gándara, 1995; Stevenson *et al.*, 1990). First, Chicano parents may believe that they are not qualified to help their children with their schoolwork. This is particularly the case for parents as their children get older. In part, this perceived lower competence among some may be related to the demographic reality that, as a group, Mexican Americans have a level of schooling that is significantly lower than African American and White populations (Chapa and Valencia, 1993; Hunter, 1986). Given that many Mexican American parents have not progressed far in their own schooling, they often feel that they do not have the instrumental skills to instruct their children in areas such as mathematics and reading. Second, many Mexican

American parents vary in their familiarity with their children's schools and their roles as parents within these schools (Delgado-Gaitan, 1990; Stevenson *et al.*, 1990). This, in turn, is likely to shape their efficacy beliefs regarding involvement in their children's schooling.

Another key set of beliefs is parents' educational aspirations and expectations for children's education. For both Mexican American and non-Mexican American parents, there is a clear positive relation between parents' educational aspirations and expectations for their children, and their involvement in their children's schooling (Anderson and Johnson, 1971; Henderson, 1981; Hess and Holloway, 1984; Soto, 1988). In general, Latino parents with high aspirations for their children's educational attainment are more likely to involve themselves in their schooling compared to Latino parents with low aspirations for their children's educational attainment. Similarly, Latino parents with high expectations for their children's educational attainment are more likely to involve themselves in their schooling (Keith and Lichtman, 1994; Lara-Alecio *et al.*, 1997).

In addition to parents' self-efficacy and expectations, parents must also have knowledge about school-related events. Parents' knowledge about school activities, procedures, and policies is an important factor. Simply put, parents who are more knowledgeable about school activities are more likely to be involved in these types of activities (Delgado-Gaitan, 1990; Klimes-Dougan *et al.*, 1992; Moreno and López, in press). For example, in two separate studies, Klimes-Dougan *et al.* and Moreno and López assessed Latino parents' levels of knowledge about parental involvement opportunities. Both groups of researchers found that parental knowledge about activities of the school was one of the best predictors of overall parental involvement. In other words, Latino parents with greater levels of knowledge about parental involvement activities and opportunities reported greater levels of involvement than Latino parents with lower levels of such knowledge. Similarly, Delgado-Gaitan (1990) also found that parental knowledge of school-related activities was an important factor in their level of involvement.

Finally, the way in which parents understand their responsibilities with respect to their child's education is crucial to their involvement. For example, even if parents have high educational aspirations for their children, and are competent in their ability to deal with school issues, they will be less likely to involve themselves if they do not believe that they should be responsible for the education of their children. Parents who believe that parents should be involved in their children's education are more likely to report being involved in their children's education than parents who do not accept this role definition (Meighan, 1989; Schaffer and Edgerton, 1985; Segal, 1985). Some studies have shown, however, that Mexican American and other racial/ethnic minority parents, as well as low-SES parents and those with fewer years of schooling attainment, are less likely to view themselves as playing an important role in their children's educational development. For example, in a review of parental involvement programs with limited-English-proficient populations (primarily Latino), Cárdena-Muñoz and Keesling (1981) reported that many of the parents believed that school governance decisions should be left to "professionals." Similarly, Parra and Henderson (1977), in an investigation of Mexican American perceptions of parent and teacher roles in child development, found that 98 percent of parents "did not perceive the parental role as one of deliberately promoting the intellectual development and academic achievement of their children" (p. 216). It may be that some Mexican Americans are less familiar with the family-school relationships in U.S. schools, and do not believe that they have a responsibility to be involved in their children's schooling. That is to say, however, that Latino parents may not perceive, hence include, certain types of involvement as part of their parental roles. For example, Moreno and López (in press) have shown that Latino parents tend to engage in less salient home-based parental involvement activities, as opposed to highly visible school-based activities.

Contextual

Although individual characteristics are important, parental involvement does not occur in a social vacuum: The school and neighborhood influence the nature and the ability of a parent to be involved in their children's schooling. Some educational researchers assert that schools create and maintain particular "climates," and that these climates can have a powerful effect on parents' involvement. Haynes *et al.* (1989), for example, found a positive relation between parental involvement and school climate: The more favorable the climate, the greater degree of parental involvement. Several researchers have pointed out that Chicano parents often view schools as cold and indifferent to their needs (López, 1977; Nieto, 1985, Valdés, 1996). Schools are often unprepared to deal with non-English-speaking parents, or parents who are unfamiliar with school policies and procedures.

Teachers also play a key role in establishing the school setting by influencing parental involvement on two levels. First, teachers affect parental involvement by the climate they establish for the parents. Researchers have found a relation between teacher leadership and parental involvement. That is, if parents view their child's teacher as competent, they are more likely to communicate and involve themselves with their children's teacher (Epstein, 1986, 1990; Epstein and Becker, 1982). Teachers also influence parents' school involvement practices (Becker and Epstein, 1982; Lightfoot, 1982). In general, parents are more likely to participate in their children's schooling if they perceive respect and encouragement from their children's teacher.

Armor *et al.* (1976) found that large school-to-school differences in parental involvement were consistent with the extent to which teachers actively encouraged and integrated parents into the school and its activities. More specifically, within Mexican American communities, investigators found that "there was no school wide policy on the role of parents in the classrooms: it was left up to the parent to discover whether a particular classroom teacher was receptive to his or her presence" (Armor *et al.*, p. 45). Other researchers found that teachers and school administrators discourage Latino parents' participation in their children's schooling (López, 1977; Nieto, 1985). It seems likely that parents' perceptions of teacher encouragement and the lack of established parental roles within the classroom can inhibit the involvement of Latino parents who are already unfamiliar and insecure with their role in their children's education.

Second, the extent to which a teacher believes that she or he has the capacity to produce change in student behavior has been found to be associated with school achievement, school change, and parental involvement (Armor *et al.*, 1976; Ashton, 1984; Dembo and Gibson, 1985). In a self-report survey of over 1000 participants, Epstein and Becker (1982) found that teachers who rated high on leadership abilities were more active and effective in involving parents in their children's schooling. More specifically, teachers' efficacy was associated with higher levels of four parental involvement outcomes: parent-teacher conferences, volunteering, home tutoring, and teacher perceptions of parental support (Hoover-Dempsey *et al.*, 1987). Unfortunately, many teachers report having low-efficacy beliefs about their work with their children's parents and consequently reduce their contact with parents or stop communicating with them altogether (Dembo and Gibson, 1985).

As with schools, neighborhoods also have their own unique personalities. While, some neighborhoods are perceived as warm, safe, and friendly, others are viewed as cold, dangerous, and alienating. Research studies have found significant racial/ethnic group differences in perceptions of risk from their environment, and these differences were based, in part, on their prior exposure to dangerous environmental situations (Coleman *et al.*, 1966; Furstenberg, 1993). There is, however, surprising little research that has studied the relation between neighborhood safety and parental involvement. Neighborhood safety may be especially important in Mexican American communities, as there are some communities that are more likely to experience high levels of crime and limited public transportation (Eccles *et al.*, 1993). Chicano parents' perceptions of neighborhood safety may influence their involvement in school activities and events, which are usually scheduled in the evenings.

Finally, families are also an important context. Familial and other social support systems enable parents to involve themselves in their children's schooling (Clark, 1983; Epstein, 1990). Social support systems refer to the assistance that parents receive from family members and friends regarding involvement activities. This support may take a number of forms. For example, a family member may assist a child with a homework assignment. A friend or family may aid in transportation or childcare to enable a mother or father to attend a parent–teacher conference. However, the influence of social support and parental involvement has not been well studied among Latinos. This gap is important because there is a positive relation between acculturation level/SES and levels of social support. For example, Mexican Americans with higher acculturation and schooling attainment levels report larger social support networks and more frequent contact with their network members than Mexican Americans with lower levels of acculturation and schooling attainment (Griffith and Villaviciencio, 1985). Similarly, more recent research has found that Latina mothers with greater spousal support participated in a wider array of parental involvement activities (Moreno and López, in press).

Sociocultural factors

In addition to the more malleable personal and contextual factors, sociocultural factors have been shown to be important in understanding parents' level of participation in their children's education. Sociocultural factors include characteristics such as family income, parental education, race/ethnicity, and level of acculturation. For example, race/ethnicity has shown to be an important indicator of parents' level of involvement. As mentioned before, Lynch and Stein (1987) found that Latino parents reported significantly lower levels of involvement in their children's educational planning decisions when compared to their African American and White counterparts. Similarly, Stevenson *et al.* (1990) found that Latina mothers—despite having very positive attitudes toward their children's schooling—reported being less involved in their children's schooling than African American and White parents.

Additionally, research informs us that parents from middle- and high-SES backgrounds are more likely to participate in their children's education than parents from low-SES backgrounds (Epstein, 1990; Herman and Yeh, 1983; Hoover-Dempsey *et al.*, 1987; Lareau, 1987, 1989, 2000; Moreno and López, in press; Stevenson *et al.*, 1990). More specifically, maternal schooling attainment has been singled out as a particularly important variable for understanding parental involvement activities. For example, Moreno and López (1999) found that Latina mothers who had more years of formal schooling participated in involvement activities more frequently than their less educated counterparts. One explanation is that the more educated mothers view traditional parental involvement activities as "part of their job" more than less educated mothers, particularly regarding "school-based" activities. Parents from middle-to-higher income backgrounds and with higher levels of formal schooling are thought to feel more comfortable and confident in their interactions with their children's teachers and schools. Furthermore, as a result of their educational backgrounds, these parents are more likely to believe that they have the instrumental skills to help their children with their schoolwork.

Moreno and López's (1999) findings are consistent with Lareau's (1987, 1989, 2000) analyses of family–school relationships between working-class and upper-middle class White communities. Drawing from Bourdieu's concept of "cultural capital," Lareau argues that schools are far from neutral institutions. By their selective use of particular linguistic structures, curriculum, and organization structures, schools tend to "invite" certain segments of the community and discourage others. In this case, the more educated mothers are "invited" to participate in their children's schooling as a valued partner. Whereas, less educated mothers tend to feel unqualified to help their child in an area in which they themselves were unsuccessful. Rather, the reasoning goes, they should leave the formal education of their children to the "professionals." Therefore certain parental involvement, such as classroom volunteering is not seen as part of their job. It is important to note, however, that this position is not synonymous with not caring about their child's education. It is a matter of leaving certain duties to the most qualified.

A key variable that is often ignored in this area of sociocultural factors is the families' level of acculturation. Although it is of minimal importance for the vast majority of Whites, it is crucial for understanding Mexican-origin people and other immigrant groups. Although the specific nature of the acculturation process is hotly debated, scholars understand the construct as a process that occurs when individuals are exposed to a new culture and cultural learning and behavioral adaptation takes place. Acculturation involves changes in cognition, language, and interpersonal interactions, and has been shown to be a key construct for understanding behavior across a number of psychological, social, economic, and political contexts (Marín and Marín, 1991; Rueschenberg and Buriel, 1987).

Among Mexican Americans, parents' level of acculturation seems to play an important role in their level of involvement in their children's schooling (Delgado-Gaitan, 1990; Stevenson *et al.*, 1990). Early researchers reported that "the amount of (parental) assistance that children report increases with each generation" (Anderson and Johnson, 1968, p. 11). Similarly, Reuschenberg and Buriel (1989) found a positive relation between parental acculturation status and their involvement with their children's schools. The role of acculturation, however, may not be so straightforward. Moreno and López (1999) found that Latina mothers (Mexican American, Central American, and South American) who were less acculturated, but had at least a high school education, had the greatest level of self-efficacy with respect to their involvement in their child's schooling. The less acculturated Latina mothers also had higher educational expectations of their children than their more acculturated counterparts. Although they were less acculturated with respect to the United States, these mothers possessed their own cultural attitudes and beliefs, as well as an "immigrant optimism" that served as a "resource" for their own self-efficacy and competence. Similar findings have been shown for Latina mothers' conceptualization of child development (Gutiérrez and Sameroff, 1990, Gutiérrez *et al.*, 1988).

However, Moreno and López (1999) also found that less acculturated Latina mothers had less knowledge of school activities than their more acculturated counterparts. This can be explained, in part, by the language barrier that exists in many schools. With less acculturated mothers' being limited in their English language proficiency and schools being limited in Spanish language proficiency of personnel, communication between home and school is minimal. Thus, despite the high regard for the education of their children, the ability of Latina mothers to transfer this interest to effective support for their children's learning is compromised. This problem is compounded with the finding that many Mexican American parents, particularly more recent immigrant parents, are less familiar with the school system in the United States and less knowledgeable about the involvement opportunities compared to African American and White parents (Klimes-Dougan *et al.*, 1992).

The language barrier coupled with Latina mothers' lack of familiarity with the U.S. school system creates formidable obstacles that makes it difficult for them to be involved in their children's education. Despite these obstacles, there is considerable variation in involvement patterns among Latino families. A series of investigators have contrasted the involvement practices of parents with high- and low-achieving Mexican American students, and found that high-achieving students report more involved parents (e.g., provided intellectual guidance; supported school learning at home; volunteered at school events) than low-achieving students (Henderson and Merritt, 1968; Klimes-Dougan *et al.*, 1992).[8] Similarly, Delgado-Gaitan (1990) found that parents of children in advanced reading groups tended to be more involved in their children's schooling than parents of children in the novice reading group. She noted that Mexican American parents' sociocultural background (i.e., parental schooling attainment; acculturation level), social isolation from the school community, school-related knowledge, and efficacy beliefs were related to the levels of parent involvement.

Returning to the original question: What are the factors that lead to parental involvement in Chicano families? We find that the answer is not a simple one. Our review of the literature clearly shows that parental involvement is influenced by a myriad of personal, contextual, and sociocultural factors. Thus, any effort to increase the level of parental involvement in Chicano families will require a comprehensive multilevel approach. In addition, if we are to be more inclusive in understanding family–school relationships, we will need to expand the ways in which we assess the nature and extent of parent's involvement in their children's education.

Future directions for understanding Chicano families and schools

Although past research has generally been fruitful in furthering our understanding of parental involvement, we have pointed out there are significant limitations that qualify our understanding when it comes to Chicano and other Latino families. As we have stated, much of the research has been "deficit-oriented," and as a result, many studies have employed oversimplified comparative designs that confounded race/ethnicity, social class, and acculturation level (Coleman *et al.*, 1966; Lynch and Stein, 1987; Stein, 1983; Stevenson *et al.*, 1990). By failing to adequately account for these key variables, the external validity (generalizability) of many studies are suspect. However, even well designed comparative studies are often unable to reveal the underlying processes that are at the root of group differences. Moreover, the use of a priori categories regarding the nature of parental involvement have constrained our understanding of such involvement can vary in families of different cultures within the United States.

Fortunately, more recent conceptualizations of Latino families have attempted to overcome earlier shortcomings and have taken a more in-depth approach and focused on the cultural strengths of Chicano and Latino families, rather than deficits (for a review of seven studies, see Villenas and Deyhle, 1999; also, see Villenas and Foley, Chapter 7, current volume). For example, Morrow and Young (1997) found that Mexican American children and parents enjoyed working with each other on literacy tasks, and that even though low-SES families often found it difficult to shoulder more responsibility, they were sincerely interested in their children's educational welfare. In an in-depth study of 25 Mexican American families in Arizona, Moll *et al.* (1992) noted, "[They—the families] have a very strong philosophy of childrearing that is supportive of education . . . they have goals of a university education for their children . . . all the households we visited possess similar values" (p. 137). In a related body of research examining effective instruction, Moreno (1997, 2000) and Moreno and Cisneros-Cohernour (1999) demonstrated that Mexican American mothers utilize effective teaching strategies with their preschool children that are distinct from their White counterparts.

Finally, in a four-year longitudinal study of 100 Latino students deemed at risk by their school districts. Romo and Falbo (1996) revealed that despite the youths' "at-risk" status, the families had a strong commitment to education. This commitment to education was displayed by the parents' use of *consejos* (advice-giving narratives). *Consejos* have been noted by a number of scholars as primary means in which Mexican American parents motivate and inspire their children as well as transmit values of the importance of education and work (Delgado-Gaitan, 1994; López, 2001).

What is important to note is that only by shedding the notion that appropriate family–school interactions consist of select behaviors that fit neatly into narrowly defined categories have scholars been able to uncover the important socialization processes (such as the use of *consejos*) that contribute to the well-being of Chicano children. Future researchers must continue to build on previous work, but not be confined to ideologies, methodologies, and tradition that were designed to find fault in the populations that were the focus of their inquiry.

Conclusion

In this chapter we have critically examined the relationship between Chicano families and the schools. In doing so, we have demonstrated that much of the research in this area has its foundations in deficit thinking. It is this deficit thinking that has established and perpetuated the myth that Mexican Americans do not value education. We have exposed this myth by clearly showing that Chicanos have consistently demonstrated a high value for education. Given this value for education, next we posed the question: What are the factors that lead to parental involvement in Chicano families? Although the research in this area is limited, our review of the literature shows that the frequency and nature of a parent's involvement cannot be attributed to any one factor. The degree to which a parent participates in their child's schooling is influenced by a myriad of facilitating and constraining factors that exist at various levels (i.e., personal, contextual, and sociocultural). Finally, we have provided some brief examples of recent research that transcends the foundations of deficit thinking and identifies the cultural resources that Chicano families posses and utilize to negotiate the process of their children's education. By moving beyond traditional notions of parental involvement, this research provides us with a solid foundation to gain further insight to the unique family processes of Chicano families and schools.

Notes

1 This section is excerpted, with minor modifications, from Valencia and Black (2002).
2 Not all master's theses during the early era were deficit thinking in orientation. A small number of master's theses voiced a non-deficit thinking perspective (see, e.g., Buckner, 1935; Pratt, 1938).
3 Actually, it was American Indians who had the lowest high school completion rate (11.4 percent), not Mexican Americans (see Grebler *et al.*, 1970, p. 143, Table 7–1).
4 It appears that Carter's (1970) book, *Mexican Americans in Schools: A History of Educational Neglect*, was influential in shaping this structural inequality hypothesis offered by Grebler *et al.*, who based their section "General school practices affecting Mexican Americans" (pp. 155–159) on Carter's book. This was not mentioned by Sowell (1981).

5 For a sustained critique of Dunn (1981) see the 1981 Special Issue of the *Hispanic Journal of Behavioral Sciences* (Fernández, 1988).

6 This quote by Graglia is taken from a newsclip (of the September 10, 1997 news conference at UT) shown on NBC *Today*, September 12, 1997.

7 It appears that Graglia's views on affirmative action have hurt him. According to Martin, reporter of the UT *Daily Texan*, "former President Ronald Reagan [in 1986] pulled away from appointing Graglia to the 5th U.S. Circuit Court of Appeals after complaints about his remarks regarding affirmative action" (1997, p. 2).

8 In a similar vein, Valencia and Suzuki (2001, Chapter 4) reviewed research studies involving the relation between the home intellectual environment in Mexican American families and children's cognitive performance. The consistent finding was that intellectually structuring the home environment (e.g., reading to the child) was a fairly strong predictor of children's measured intelligence.

References

Allen, V.L. (1970). The psychology of poverty: Problems and prospects. In V.L. Allen (Ed.), *Psychological factors in poverty* (pp. 367–383). Chicago: Markham Press.

Anderson, J.G. and Johnson, W.H. (1968). *Sociocultural determinants of achievement among Mexican American students*. Las Cruces, NM: ERIC Clearinghouse on Rural Education and Small Schools. (ERIC Document Reproduction Service No. ED 017 394)

Anderson, J.G. and Johnson, W.H. (1971). Stability and change among three generations of Mexican Americans: Factors affecting achievement. *American Educational Research Journal*, 8, 285–309.

Armor, D., Conry-Oseguera, P., Cox, M., King, N., McDonnell, L., Pascal, A., Pauly, E. and Zellman, G. (1976). *Analysis of the school preferred reading program in selected Los Angeles minority schools*. Santa Monica, CA: Rand.

Ashton, P. (1984). Teacher efficacy: A motivational paradigm for effective teacher education. *Journal of Teacher Education*, 35, 28–32.

Baratz, S.S. and Baratz, J.C. (1970). Early childhood intervention: The social science base of institutional racism. *Harvard Educational Review*, 40, 29–50.

Becker, H.J. and Epstein, J.L. (1982). Parent involvement: A survey of teacher practices. *Elementary School Journal*, 83, 85–102.

Berger, E.H. (1981). *Parents as partners in education: The school and home working together*. St Louis, MO: C.V. Mosby.

Bloom, B.S. (1981). *All our children learning: A primer for parents, teachers, and other educators*. New York: McGraw-Hill.

Booth, A. and Dunn, J.F. (1996). *Family-school links: How do they affect educational outcomes?* Mahwah, NJ: Lawrence Erlbaum.

Bronfenbrenner, U. (1979). *The ecology of human development*. Cambridge, MA: Harvard University Press.

Buckner, H.A. (1935). *A study of pupil elimination and failure among Mexicans*. Unpublished master's thesis, University of California, Los Angeles.

Cárdena-Muñoz, R. and Keesling, J.W. (1981). *Parents and federal education programs (Volume 4): Title VII—The study of parental involvement*. Research conducted for the U.S. Department of Education. Washington, DC: System Development Corporation.

Cárdenas, J.A. and Cortez, A. (1986). The impact of *Plyer v. Doe* upon Texas public schools. *Journal of Law & Education*, 15, 1–17.

Carter, T. (1970). *Mexican Americans in schools: A history of educational neglect*. New York: College Entrance Examination Board.

Chapa, J. (1997). *The Hopwood decision in Texas as an attack on Latino access to selective higher education programs*. Paper presented at the Harvard University Civil Rights Project, Research Conference on the Latino Civil Rights Crisis, Los Angeles, CA and Washington, DC, December.

Chapa, J. and Valencia, R.R. (1993). Latino population growth, demographic characteristics, and educational stagnation: An example of recent trends. *Hispanic Journal of Behavioral Sciences*, 15, 165–187.

Chavkin, N.F. (1993). *Families and schools in a pluralistic society*. Albany: State University of New York Press.

Chavkin, N.F. and Williams, D.L. (1989). Low-income parents' attitudes toward parent involvement in education. *Journal of Sociology and Social Welfare*, 16, 17–28.

Clark, R. (1983). *Family life and school achievement: Why poor black children succeed or fail.* Chicago: University of Chicago Press.

Coleman, J.S., Campbell, E.Q., Hobson, C.J., McPartland, J.M., Mood, A., Weinfeld, F.D. and York, R.L. (1966). *Equality of educational opportunity.* Washington, DC: Government Printing Office.

De León, A. (1974). Blowout 1910 style: A Chicano school boycott in West Texas. *Texana, 12,* 125–140.

De León, A. (1983). *They called them greasers: Anglo attitudes towards Mexicans in Texas, 1821–1900.* Austin: University of Texas Press.

Delgado-Gaitan, C. (1990). *Literacy for empowerment: The role of parents in children's education.* New York: Falmer Press.

Delgado-Gaitan, C. (1994). *Consejos:* The power of cultural narratives. *Anthropology and Education Quarterly, 25,* 298–316.

Dembo, M.H. and Gibson, S. (1985). Teachers' sense of efficacy: An important factor in school improvement. *Elementary School Journal, 86,* 173–184.

Dougherty, L.G. (1966). Working with disadvantaged parents. In J.F. Frost and G.R. Hawkes (Eds.), *The disadvantaged child: Issues and innovations* (pp. 389–394). New York: Houghton Mifflin.

Dunn, L.M. (1987). *Bilingual Hispanic children on the U.S. mainland: A review of research on their cognitive, linguistic, and scholastic development.* Circle Pines, MN: American Guidance Service.

Eccles, J.S., McCarthy, K., Lord, S. E., Furstenberg, F., Geitz, L. and Teitler, J. (1993). *How parents respond to risk and opportunity in moderate to high risk neighborhoods.* Paper presented at the biennial meeting for the Society for Research in Child Development, New Orleans, LA, March.

Epstein, J.L. (1986). Parents' reactions to teacher practices of parent involvement. *Elementary School Journal, 86,* 277–294.

Epstein, J.L. (1990). School and family connections: Theory, research, and implications for integrating sociologies of education and family. *Marriage and Family Review, 15,* 99–126.

Epstein, J.L. and Becker, H.J. (1982). Teachers' reported practices of parent involvement: Problems and possibilities. *Elementary School Journal, 83,* 103–114.

Feagin, J.R. and Booher Feagin, C. (1999). *Racial and ethnic relations* (6th ed.). Upper Saddle River, NJ: Merrill/Prentice Hall.

Fernández, R.R. (Ed.). (1988). Achievement testing: Science versus ideology [Special issue]. *Hispanic Journal of Behavioral Sciences, 10*(3).

Frost, J.F. and Hawkes, G.R. (Eds.). (1966). *The disadvantaged child: Issues and innovations.* New York: Houghton Mifflin.

Furstenberg, F. (1993). How families manage risk and opportunities in dangerous neighborhoods. In W.J. Wilson (Ed.), *Sociology and the public agenda* (pp. 231–257). Newbury Park, CA: Sage.

Gándara, P. (1995). *Over the ivy walls: The educational mobility of low-income Chicanos.* Albany: State University of New York Press.

García, M.T. (1979). *Mexican Americans: Leadership, ideology, and identity, 1930–1960.* New Haven, CT: Yale University Press.

Goldenberg, C.N. (1987). Low-income Hispanic parents' contributions to their first-grade children's word-recognition skills. *Anthropology and Education Quarterly, 18,* 149–179.

Goodnow, J.J. (1988). Parents' ideas, actions, and feelings: Models and methods from developmental and social psychology. *Child Development, 59,* 286–320.

Gould, B. (1932). *Methods of teaching Mexicans.* Unpublished master's thesis, University of Southern California, Los Angeles.

Grebler, L., Moore, J.W. and Guzmán, R.C. (1970). *The Mexican American people: The nation's second largest minority.* New York: Free Press.

Griffith, J. and Villaviciencio, S. (1985). Relationships among acculturation, sociodemographic characteristics and social supports in Mexican American adults. *Hispanic Journal of Behavioral Sciences, 7,* 75–92.

Gutiérrez, J. and Sameroff, A. (1990). Determinants of complexity in Mexican American and Anglo American mothers' conceptions of child development. *Child Development, 61,* 384–394.

Gutiérrez, J., Sameroff, A.J. and Karrer, B.M. (1988). Acculturation and SES effects on Mexican American parents' concepts of development. *Child Development, 59,* 250–255.

Harrison, A.O., Wilson, M.N., Pine, C.J., Chan, S.Q. and Buriel, R. (1990). Family ecologies of ethnic minority children. *Child Development, 61,* 347–362.

Havighurst, R.J. (1966). Who are the socially disadvantaged? In J.F. Frost and G.R. Hawkes (Eds.), *The disadvantaged child: Issues and innovations* (pp. 15–23). New York: Houghton Mifflin.

Haynes, N.M., Comer, J.P. and Hamilton-Lee, M. (1989). School climate enhancement through parent involvement. *Journal of School Psychology, 27*, 87–90.

Hellmuth, J. (Ed.). (1967). *Disadvantaged child* (Vol. 1). New York: Brunner/Mazel.

Henderson, R.W. (1981). Home environment and intellectual performance. In R.W. Henderson (Ed.), *Parent–child interaction: Theory, research, and prospects* (p. 3–32). New York: Academic Press.

Henderson, R.W. and Merritt, C. B. (1968). Environmental backgrounds of Mexican American children with different potentials for school success. *Journal of Social Psychology, 75*, 101–106.

Henderson, R.W. and Valencia, R.R. (1985). Nondiscriminatory school psychological services: Beyond nonbiased assessment. In J.R. Bergan (Ed.), *School psychology in contemporary society* (pp. 340–377). Columbus, OH: Charles E. Merrill.

Herman, J.L. and Yeh, J.P. (1983). Some effects of parent involvement in schools. *Urban Review, 15*, 11–17.

Hernández, D. (1970). *Mexican American challenge to a sacred cow* (Monograph No. 1). Los Angeles: Mexican American Cultural Center, University of California.

Hess, R.D. and Holloway, S.D. (1984). Family and school as educational institutions. In R.D. Parke (Ed.), *Review of child development research: Volume 7. The family* (pp. 179–222). Chicago: University of Chicago Press.

Hoover-Dempsey, K.V., Bassler, O.C. and Brissie, J.S. (1987). Parent involvement: Contributions of teacher efficacy, school socioeconomic status, and other school characteristics. *American Educational Research Journal, 24*, 417–435.

Hunter, C.S. (1986). *Adult illiteracy in the United States: A report to the Ford Foundation*. New York: McGraw-Hill.

Immerwahr, J. and Foleno, T. (2000). *Great expectations: How the public and parents—White, African American, and Hispanic—view higher education*. New York: Public Agenda.

Keith, P.B. and Lichtman, M.V. (1994). Does parental involvement influence the academic achievement of Mexican American eighth graders? Results from the National Education Longitudinal Study. *School Psychology Quarterly, 9*, 256–272.

Klimes-Dougan, B., López, J.A., Adelman, H.S. and Nelson, P. (1992). Two studies of low income parents' involvement in schooling. *Urban Review, 24*, 185–202.

Labov, W. (1970). The logic of nonstandard English. In F. Williams (Ed.), *Language and poverty* (pp. 153–187). Chicago: Markham Press.

Laosa, L.M. (1982). School, occupation, culture, and family: The impact of parental schooling on the parent-child relationship. *Journal of Educational Psychology, 74*, 791–827.

Lara-Alecio, R., Irby, B. and Ebener, R. (1997). Developing academically supportive behaviors among Hispanic parents: What elementary teachers and administrators can do. *Preventing School Failure, 42*, 27–32.

Lareau, A. (1987). Social class differences in family–school relationships: The importance of cultural capital. *Sociology of Education, 60*, 73–85.

Lareau, A. (1989). *Home advantage: Social class and parental intervention in elementary education*. London: Falmer Press.

Lareau, A. (2000). *Home advantage: Social class and parental intervention in elementary education* (2nd ed.). Lanham, MD: Rowman & Littlefield.

Lightfoot, S.L. (1982). Toward conflict and resolution: Relationships between families and schools. *Theory Into Practice, 13*, 97–104.

López, G.R. (2001). *On whose terms?: Understanding involvement through the eyes of migrant parents*. Paper presented at the annual meeting of the American Educational Research Association, Seattle, WA, April.

López, O. (1977). Parent participation in education: Three levels—one model. *Journal of Instructional Psychology, 3*, 45–49.

Lubeck, S. (1995). Mothers at risk. In B.B. Swadener and S. Lubeck (Eds.), *Children and families "at promise": Deconstructing the discourse of risk* (pp. 50–75). Albany: State University of New York Press.

Lynch, E.W. and Stein, R.C. (1987). Parent participation by ethnicity: A comparison of Hispanic, Black, and Anglo families. *Exceptional Children, 54*, 105–111.

Lyon, L.L. (1933). *Investigation of the program for the adjustment of Mexican girls to the high schools of the San Fernando Valley*. Unpublished master's thesis, University of Southern California, Los Angeles.

Marans, A.E. and Lourie, R. (1967). Hypotheses regarding the effects of child-rearing patterns on the disadvantaged child. In J. Hellmuth (Ed.), *Disadvantaged child* (Vol. 1, pp. 17–41). New York: Brunner/Mazel.

Marburger, C.L. (1990). The school site level: Involving parents in reform. In S.B. Bacharach (Ed.), *Education reform: Making sense of it all* (pp. 82–91). Boston: Allyn and Bacon.

Marin, G. and Marin, B.V. (1991). *Research with Hispanic populations.* Newbury Park, CA: Sage.

Marjoribanks, K. (1979). *Ethnic families and children's achievements.* Sydney, Australia: George Allen & Unwin.

Márquez, B. (1993). *LULAC: The evolution of a Mexican American political organization.* Austin: University of Texas Press.

Martin, D.H. (1997). Remarks raise lawmakers' ire. *Daily Texan,* September 12, 1–2.

Meighan, R. (1989). The parents and the schools: Alternative role definitions. *Educational Review, 41,* 105–112.

Menchaca, M. (2000). History and anthropology: Conducting Chicano research. In R. Rochín and D. Valdés (Eds.), *Toward a new Chicano history* (pp. 167–181). East Lansing: Michigan State University Press.

Miller, S.A. (1988). Parents' beliefs about children's cognitive development. *Child Development, 59,* 259–285.

Moll, L.C., Amanti, C., Neff, D. and González, N. (1992). Funds of knowledge for teaching: Using a qualitative approach to connect homes and classrooms. *Theory Into Practice, 31,* 132–141.

Moreno, R.P. (1997). Everyday instruction: A comparison of Mexican American and Anglo mothers and their preschool children. *Hispanic Journal of Behavioral Science, 19,* 527–539.

Moreno R.P. (2000). Teaching practices of Mexican American mothers with everyday and school related tasks. *Merrill-Palmer Quarterly, 15,* 613–631

Moreno, R.P. and Cisneros-Cohernour, E.J. (1999). Strategies for effective instruction: Mexican American mothers in everyday activities. *Latino Studies Journal, 10,* 56–69.

Moreno, R.P. and López, J.A. (1999). The role of acculturation and maternal education in Latina mothers' involvement in their children's schooling. *School Community Journal, 9,* 83–101.

Moreno, R.P. and López, J.A. (in press). Latino families and schools: Building community. In A.N. Valdivia and M. García (Eds.), *Geographies of Latinidad: Mapping Latina/o Studies for the 21st century.* Chapel Hill, NC: Duke University Press.

Morrow, L.M. and Young, J. (1997). A family literacy program connecting school and home: Effects on attitude, motivation, and literacy achievement. *Journal of Educational Psychology, 89,* 736–742.

Muñoz, C. (1989). *Youth, identity, power: The Chicano movement.* New York: Verso.

Navarro, A. (1995). *Mexican American Youth Organization: Avant-garde of the Chicano movement in Texas.* Austin: University of Texas Press.

Nieto, S. (1985). Who's afraid of bilingual parents? *Bilingual Review, 12,* 179–189.

O'Connor, K. and Epstein, L. (1984). A legal voice for the Chicano community: The activities of the Mexican American Legal Defense and Educational Fund, 1968–1982. *Social Science Quarterly, 65,* 245–256.

Okagaki, L. and Frensch, P.A. (1998). Parenting and children's school achievement: A multiethnic perspective. *American Educational Research Journal, 35,* 123–144.

Parra, E. and Henderson, R.W. (1977). Mexican American perceptions of parent and teacher roles in child development. *Bilingual Review, 4,* 210–217.

Pearl, A. (1997). Cultural and accumulated environmental deficit models. In R.R. Valencia (Ed.), *The evolution of deficit thinking: Educational thought and practice* (pp. 132–159). The Stanford Series on Education and Public Policy. London: Falmer Press.

Pratt, P.S. (1938). *A comparison of the school achievement and socio-economic background of Mexican and White children in a Delta Colorado elementary school.* Unpublished master's thesis, University of Southern California, Los Angeles.

Purkey, S.C. and Smith, M.S. (1985). School reform: The district policy implications of the effective schools literature. *Elementary School Journal, 85,* 353–389.

Ramos, H.A.J. (1998). *The American GI Forum: In pursuit of the dream, 1948–1983.* Houston, TX: Arte Público Press.

Rich, D. (1987). *Schools and families: Issues and actions.* Washington, DC: National Education Association.

Romano-V, O.I. (1968). The anthropology and sociology of the Mexican Americans: The distortion of Mexican American history. *El Grito, 2,* 13–26.

Romo, R. (1986). George I. Sánchez and the civil rights movement: 1940 to 1960. *La Raza Law Journal*, *1*, 342–362.

Romo, H. and Falbo, T. (1996). *Latino high school graduation*. Austin: University of Texas Press.

Rosen, G. (1974). The development of the Chicano movement in Los Angeles from 1967 to 1969. *Aztlán*, *4*, 155–183.

Roser, M.A. (1997). UT group praises Hopwood ruling. *Austin American-Statesman*, September 11, B1.

Roser, M.A. and Tanamachi, C. (1997). Jackson urges UT to fight racism. *Austin American-Statesman*, September 17, A1, A10.

Reuschenberg, E. and Buriel, R. (1989). Mexican American family functioning and acculturation: A family systems perspective. *Hispanic Journal of Behavioral Sciences*, *11*, 232–244.

San Miguel, G., Jr. (1987). *"Let all of them take heed": Mexican Americans and the campaign for educational equality in Texas, 1910–1981*. Austin: University of Texas Press.

San Miguel, G., Jr. and Valencia, R.R. (1998). From the Treaty of Guadalupe Hidalgo to *Hopwood*: The educational plight and struggle of Mexican Americans in the Southwest. *Harvard Educational Review*, *68*, 353–412.

Schaefer, E.S. and Edgerton, M. (1985). Parent and child correlates of parental modernity. In I.E. Sigel (Ed.), *Parental belief systems: The psychological consequences for children* (pp. 287–318). Hillsdale, NJ: Lawrence Erlbaum.

Segal, M. (1985). A study of maternal beliefs and values within the context of an intervention program. In I.E. Sigel (Ed.), *Parental belief systems: The psychological consequences for children* (pp. 271–286). Hillsdale, NJ: Lawrence Erlbaum.

Slaughter-Defoe, D.T., Nakagawa, K., Takanishi, R. and Johnson, D.J. (1990). Toward cultural/ecological perspectives on schooling and achievement in African- and Asian-American children. *Child Development*, *61*, 363–383.

Sleeter, C.E. (1995). Foreword. In B.B. Swadener and S. Lubeck (Eds.), *Children and families "at promise": Deconstructing the discourse of risk* (pp. ix-xi). Albany: State University of New York Press.

Snider, W. (1990, April 18). Outcry follows Cavazos comments on the values of Hispanic parents. *Education Week*, pp. 1–2.

Soto, L. D. (1988). The home environment of higher and lower achieving Puerto Rican children. *Hispanic Journal of Behavioral Sciences*, *10*, 161–167.

Sowell, T. (1981). *Ethnic America: A history*. New York: Basic Books.

Stein, R.S. (1983). Hispanic parents' perspectives and participation in their children's special education program: Comparison by program and race. *Learning Disability Quarterly*, *6*, 432–438.

Stevenson, H.W., Chen, C. and Uttal, D.H. (1990). Beliefs and achievement: A study of Black, White, and Hispanic children. *Child Development*, *61*, 508–523.

Swadener, B.B. and Lubeck, S. (1995). The social construction of children and families "at risk": An introduction. In B.B. Swadener and S. Lubeck (Eds.), *Children and families "at promise": Deconstructing the discourse of risk* (pp. 1–14). Albany: State University of New York Press.

Swick, K.J. (1987). *Perspectives on understanding and working with families*. Champaign, IL: Stipes.

Swick, K.J. and McKnight, S. (1989). Characteristics of kindergarten teachers who promote parent involvement. *Early Childhood Research Quarterly*, *4*, 19–29.

Taylor, M.C. (1927). *Retardation of Mexican children in the Albuquerque schools*. Unpublished master's thesis, Leland Stanford Junior University, Stanford, CA.

Valencia, R.R. (1980). The school closure issue and the Chicano community. *Urban Review*, *12*, 5–21.

Valencia, R.R. (1984a). *School closures and policy issues* (Policy Paper No. 84–C3). Stanford University: Institute for Research on Educational Finance and Governance, Stanford, CA.

Valencia, R.R. (1984b). The school closure issue and the Chicano community: A follow-up study of the *Angeles* case. *Urban Review*, *16*, 145–163.

Valencia, R.R. (Ed.). (1997). *The evolution of deficit thinking: Educational thought and practice*. The Stanford Series on Education and Public Policy. London: Falmer Press.

Valencia, R.R. (2000). Inequalities and the schooling of minority students in Texas: Historical and contemporary conditions. *Hispanic Journal of Behavioral Sciences*, *22*, 445–459.

Valencia, R.R. and Bernal, E.M. (Eds.). (2000). The Texas Assessment of Academic Skills (TAAS) case: Perspectives of plaintiffs' experts [Special issue]. *Hispanic Journal of Behavioral Sciences*, *22*(4).

Valencia, R.R. and Black, M.S. (2002). "Mexican Americans don't value education!": On the basis of the myth, mythmaking, and debunking. *Journal of Latinos and Education*, *1*, 81–103.

Valencia, R.R. and Solórzano, D.G. (1997). Contemporary deficit thinking: In R.R. Valencia (Ed.), *The evolution of deficit thinking: Educational thought and practice* (pp. 160–210). The Stanford Series on Education and Public Policy. London: Falmer Press.

Valencia, R.R. and Suzuki, L.A. (2001). *Intelligence testing and minority students: Foundations, performance factors, and assessment issues.* Thousand Oaks, CA: Sage.

Valdés, G. (1996). *Con respeto: Bridging the distances between culturally diverse families and schools.* New York: Teachers College Press.

Valentine, J. and Stark, E. (1979). The social context of parent involvement in Head Start. In E. Zigler and J. Valentine (Eds.), *Project Head Start: A legacy of the war on poverty* (pp. 291–313). New York: Free Press.

Vásquez, O. (1994). Mari-Luci Jaramillo. In M.S. Seller (Ed.), *Women educators in the United States, 1820–1993: A biographical sourcebook* (pp. 258–264). Westport, CT: Greenwood Press.

Vega, J.E. (1983). *Education, politics, and bilingualism in Texas.* Washington, DC: University Press of America.

Part IV

Educational testing and special education issues germane to Chicano students

9 Educational testing and Chicano students: issues, consequences, and prospects for reform

Richard R. Valencia, Bruno J. Villarreal, and Moises F. Salinas

Much has transpired in the area of educational testing since the publication of the testing chapter by Valencia and Aburto (1991) that appeared in the first edition of *Chicano School Failure and Success*. These developments in testing over the last decade have directly or indirectly affected many Chicano students, and have been positive and negative. Regarding the former, there have been, for example, the following: new scholarship on the early period of intelligence testing and its impact on Chicanos (Valencia, 1997); advances in the assessment of Chicano/Latino English language learners (Cummins, 2000; Langdon, 1992; Sandoval and Durán, 1998); insightful analyses of special education *vis-à-vis* Chicano students (Rueda *et al.*, Chapter 10, present volume); renewed interest in gifted Chicano children and youths (Valencia and Suzuki, 2001, Chapter 8); the development of new cognitive ability tests that may hold promise in promoting nondiscriminatory assessment (e.g., the Universal Nonverbal Intelligence Test; Bracken and McCallum, 1998), and the use of dynamic assessment as an alternative to standardized testing (Peña, 1996; Peña *et al.*, 2001). Another positive development has been the publication of a number of books on testing that present comprehensive coverage of testing issues and assessment advances regarding Chicanos and other groups of color (see: Armour-Thomas and Gopaul-McNicol, 1998; Geisinger, 1992; Sandoval *et al.*, 1998; Suzuki *et al.*, 1996; Valencia and Suzuki, 2001).

Unfortunately, there have also been negative developments regarding testing and Chicano students. For example, there has been a sharp decline over the last ten years in the number of cultural bias investigations of intelligence tests (Valencia and Suzuki, 2001, Chapter 5; current chapter). There has also been a resurgence of scholarship that draws upon genetic bases to explain White/Latino and White/African American group differences on cognitive ability tests (for discussions and critiques of this neohereditarianism see: Valencia and Solórzano, 1997; Valencia and Suzuki, 2001, Chapter 6). Another detrimental development—one that has swept across the terrain of U.S. public kindergarten through 12th grade (K-12) education—has been high-stakes testing and its adverse impact on Chicanos/Latinos and other students of color (Valencia, 2000a; Valencia and Bernal, 2000a).

Due to space limitations in the present chapter, we provide discussions of some, not all, of the preceding positive and negative developments. Our coverage is organized as follows: (a) functions of testing; (b) historical role of intelligence tests in the stratification of learning opportunities for Chicanos; (c) cultural bias research on intelligence tests; (d) issues in the cognitive assessment of Mexican American English language learners; (e) underrepresentation of Chicanos in gifted/talented programs; (f) adverse impact of high-stakes testing on Chicanos; (g) improvement of educational testing of Chicano students.

Functions of testing

Before an informed discussion of testing issues can proceed, it is necessary to ask a fundamental question: What functions do educational tests serve? A number of frameworks have been advanced that address this important question (e.g., Cronbach, 1984; Gronlund and Linn, 1990; Resnick, 1979; Salvia and Ysseldyke, 1988; Thorndike and Hagen, 1977; Worthen *et al.*, 1993). It must be emphasized, however, that in most cases these functions or purposes of testing are discussed in the broader context of *assessment*—that is, the process of collecting test information *as well as other forms of data* (e.g., observations and judgments) to make psychoeducational decisions about students (see Salvia and Ysseldyke, 1988).

The functions of testing framework we find most useful for the issues covered in this chapter is the structure presented by Resnick (1979),[1] who identifies three broad test functions: (a) the management of instruction, (b) public accountability, and (c) the legitimization of the schooling process.

Management of instruction

This is the rubric Resnick (1979) assigns for three purposes of testing—the *sorting, monitoring*, and *grading* functions. In the sorting function, tests are administered *before* the instructional process truly gets underway. Here, educational tests serve as mechanisms to provide information in order to assist the teacher or other school personnel in the assignment of mainstream students to instructional groups in the class, to instructional tracks, and for grade retention.[2] Also, the sorting function of tests is used, in part, to channel students into special education.

With respect to the monitoring function, tests are given *during* the course of the instruction. Here, test results are used as diagnostic feedback. Such results provide the teacher with useful information to make curriculum adjustments in order to improve teaching and student learning.[3]

The third specific function of testing within the broad management of instruction category is *grading*. In this function, tests are given *after* the instructional process and such results assist the teacher in evaluating a student's academic performance following a clearly designated period of instruction (i.e., a unit of instruction or an entire course of instruction).[4]

In the case of Chicano students, the sorting function of testing has created—by far—the most controversy in both historical and contemporary times. The use of test scores to sort students has contributed, in part, to adverse impact on Chicano children and youths as seen in curriculum differentiation in the mainstream (e.g., tracking), overrepresentation in certain special education categories, underrepresentation in gifted/talented programs, higher grade retention rates, and lower rates of college matriculation.

Public accountability

The general notion of accountability in education is that public schools should be held accountable to the public (the logic being that the public financially supports the schools). Milliken (1970) describes this idea as a collective sense "that people are increasingly demanding to know how their children are learning, what they are learning, and why they are being taught whatever they are being taught" (p. 17). Although test scores have been important elements in holding public schools accountable since the 1920s, the modern roots of the current public accountability movement go back about 20 years. What has arisen is the "standards-based school reform movement" in which state-mandated achievement tests are heavily used to hold districts, schools, teachers, and students accountable for meeting specific standards of academic performance. Later, we discuss how Chicano and other students of color have been adversely affected by the standards-based school reform movement— particularly as seen in these students' disproportionate grade retention and high school diploma denial rates (Valencia, 2000a; Valencia and Bernal, 2000a).

Legitimization of the schooling process

This is the third broad function of educational testing that Resnick (1979) discusses in her framework. The testing movement in the United States, beginning in the second decade of the 20th century, is deeply rooted in our desire for efficiency, our ideas of equality, and our need to have national standards (Resnick, 1981). The notions and values of "rational management," "scientific management," and "efficiency reform" as applied to public education at the turn of the century stem from the larger influence of the business ideology and the application of modern business methods during the Progressive period from 1890 to 1920 (Callahan, 1962). These values of rationality and efficiency were initially reactions to corruption and inefficiency in government, but because of huge problems in public schools (e.g., high rates of dropouts; overcrowding), "schools became a central target for the efficiency reformers in the decade before World War I" (Resnick, 1981, p. 625). The scientific management ethos and the use of intelligence testing in the schools took on massive proportions as seen in the creation of numerous bureaus of research and measurement from 1912 to 1922 in urban school systems. As Resnick (1981) concludes on this topic:

> The present use of testing to support decisions about ability and curriculum grouping affirms traditions of practice that have been in existence for more than 60 years . . . The American use of tests reflects our culture's interest in qualified and objective judgments, part of the rational management ethos.
>
> (p. 626)

In light of this marriage of scientific management and the intelligence testing movement (in particular), it becomes clearer why Resnick (1979) believes that intelligence testing has served a "legitimization of the schooling process" function. We assert, however, that other forms of educational testing (i.e., standardized achievement tests; mandated criterion-referenced achievement tests used for accountability purposes) also serve the legitimization function. The point is that in addition to having a practical function in schooling, tests also play symbolic roles through their aura of science and objectivity.[5] The implications here are important. If education tests are indeed objective (in content and use of results), then our highly differentiated and tracked public school system is sanctioned. Bowles and Gintis (1976), writing from a neo-Marxist perspective, have taken the legitimization function of intelligence testing a bit further. In brief, these scholars offer the following argument: (a) evidence shows that test scores (IQ) are poor predictors of individual economic success; (b) the meritocratic mechanism—test scores—are assumed to be objective; (c) because economic success, however, cannot be accounted for by cognitive scores of students, then the technocratic–meritocratic ideology is largely symbolic and is used to legitimize economic inequality.

In summary, the notion that intelligence and other forms of educational testing perform a legitimization function is a powerful idea. Its utility as an analytical tool in understanding the abusive practices of education testing with respect to Chicanos has great value.

Historical role of intelligence tests in the stratification of learning opportunities for Chicano students[6]

Several decades after the signing of the Treaty of Guadalupe Hidalgo in 1848, the testing movement—which is frequently attributed to English biologist Sir Francis Galton (Anastasi, 1988)—was launched. In his 1883 book, *Inquiries into Human Faculty and its Development*, Galton (who was Charles Darwin's cousin) discussed a number of techniques (e.g., visual discrimination and reaction time) to measure a human's psychological processes. In his 1870 book, *Hereditary Genius*, Galton was not shy about discussing his racial views in the chapter entitled, "The comparative worth of different races" (see Valencia, 1997). Undoubtedly a brilliant scientist, Galton was also a racist and a classist in his ideology and in his work (see, e.g., Galton, 1870). Galton, a firm believer in hereditarianism—the theory that individual and group differences in behavior (e.g., intelligence) can primarily be accounted for on the basis of genetics—was a key player in the eugenics movement. His pronouncements about racial differences in intelligence and societal stratification had indirect but significant influence on how American psychologists would eventually view the practice of testing Chicano children, and on how these behavioral scientists attempted to explain the differences in intellectual performance between Whites and Chicanos.

Although the testing movement was launched by Galton, it was the team of Frenchmen Alfred Binet and Théodore Simon who, in 1905, provided the fuel that ignited the movement. The Binet-Simon scale, the first cognitively based intelligence test, was subsequently imported, culturally appropriated, translated, psychometrically modified, and normed by U.S. psychologists such as Henry H. Goddard and Lewis Terman (see Valencia, 1997). By 1916, the individually administered Stanford-Binet Intelligence Scale had been developed. Terman, the test's designer, intentionally sought to obtain a standardization group that was White and middle class (Terman, 1916). His flagrant disregard of Chicanos and other children of color in creating the norm group would be an issue for decades to come.

By the time the Stanford-Binet Intelligence Scale was developed, over 200 group-administered achievement tests were available for use in the schools (Chapman, 1988), but no group-administered intelligence test had been developed. This problem would be addressed, however, with the development of the National Intelligence Tests (NIT) in 1920.[7] With respect to norming, the NIT was just as exclusive as the Stanford-Binet: No Chicano, African American, Asian American, or American Indian children were part of the standardization sample (Valencia, 1997). Soon after the publication of the NIT, "other group-administered intelligence tests were developed and ready for consumption by a very hungry and receptive public school system bent on promoting efficiency" (Valencia, 1997, p. 56). Group-administered intelligence (and achievement) tests were frequently used by the mid-1920s. In a response to differentiated intellectual abilities observed among students, some researchers and educators argued that there was a need for differentiated curriculum (see, e.g., Dickson, 1923; Terman, 1919). Intelligence tests served this sorting function very well.

Two points regarding Chicano students and intelligence tests in the 1920s are particularly noteworthy (Valencia, 1997). First, "race psychology" studies of the 1920s were unanimous and uniform in their conclusions (implicit or explicit) about Chicano–White differences in intelligence: The lower intellectual performance of Chicano students was genetically based (see: Garretson, 1928; Garth, 1923, 1928; Goodenough, 1926; Koch and Simmons, 1926; Paschal and Sullivan, 1925; Sheldon, 1924; Young, 1922).[8]

A second point regarding Chicano students and testing in the 1920s was that partially due to their typically low performance on intelligence tests, many of these children and youths were channeled into classes and programs that offered little opportunity for academic advancement and intellectual growth (see, González, 1974a, 1974b, 1990, 1999; Valencia, 1997). Let us examine Los Angeles, California as a case in point.

During the 1920s, mass intelligence testing in Los Angeles was indeed a big enterprise. By decade's end (1928–1929) a total of 328,000 tests were administered, for example, at the elementary level alone (González, 1974a). Based on IQ test results, in large part, students were placed in one of four types of elementary classes: *normal* classes, *opportunity* rooms, *adjustment* rooms, or *development* rooms. Opportunity rooms were designed for both the mentally superior (opportunity A) and slow learner (opportunity B—children whose IQs were above 70 but below the normal cut score). Adjustment rooms, on the other hand, were structured for normal children (i.e., average interval IQ) who had specific skill problems (e.g., remediation in reading; limited English proficiency; "educationally maladjusted" [most likely this was what we currently refer to as emotional and behavior disorders]). Development rooms (sometimes referred to as centers) were designed for children whose IQ was below 70; these children were typically referred to as "mentally retarded" or "mentally deficient." González (1974a) noted that the median IQ for Mexican American elementary school-age children in Los Angeles in the late 1920s was about 91.2.[9] He suggested, given the observed median IQ of 91.2, that "there was a very high probability that nearly one-half of the Mexican children would find themselves placed in slow-learner rooms and development centers" (p. 150). González' suggestion that about 50 percent of Mexican American elementary students were placed in classes for the mentally subaverage (opportunity B classes) and for the mentally retarded (development centers) translates into an astounding overrepresentational disparity of 285 percent (calculated by Valencia and Suzuki, 2001, p. 17), in that it has been estimated that Mexican American students comprised only 13 percent of the student population in 1927 in Los Angeles City and County (Taylor, 1929; cited in González, 1974a).[10]

It appears that the impact of curriculum differentiation with respect to a Mexican American student's job future was felt as early as the higher elementary grades. González (1974a) stated that some development rooms and centers (for the alleged mentally retarded) served as training grounds for manual training, and subsequently as sources for cheap labor. These development centers were run by full-time manual education, crafts, and home economics teachers. The larger centers had the services of a full-time agricultural teacher. González (1974b) reported that by 1929, there were 2,500 children in 11 development centers in Los Angeles schools. Ten of the centers were in "laboring class communities," and of the total enrollment, Mexican American children were "highly represented in five of them, constituting the entire population of one, one-third in two, and one-fourth in two others" (1974b, p. 298). The development centers were geared to training unskilled and semi-skilled workers for industry (e.g., menial occupations in restaurants, laundries, and agriculture). González (1974a) reported that 325 students graduated from the development centers in 1928–1929. Of those "65 were working in agriculture as fruit pickers, 60 sold newspapers, and the remainder scattered over a wide range of unskilled manual occupations" (p. 167). González (1974b) offered an interesting insight to the development center–business connection by quoting a school administrator who viewed the center as bonanzas to local industry:

> several employers have told us that a dull girl makes a very much better operator on a mangle than a normal girl. The job is purely routine and is irksome to persons of average intelligence, while the sub-normal seems to get actual satisfaction out of such a task. Fitting the person to the job reduces the "turn over" in an industry and is, of course, desirable from an economic point of view.
>
> (p. 298)

In addition to what occurred at the elementary school level, González (1974a, 1990) also researched the role of intelligence testing and its partial role in secondary school curriculum differentiation in Los Angeles schools. González (1990) commented: "By the mid-twenties a four-tiered tracking system, each with its specific teaching methods, curriculum, and educational objectives and consequences was in full swing" (p. 83). The Division of Psychology and Educational Research, using mass IQ testing to identify the type of course work that allegedly would be commensurate with students' mental capacity, designed four curricular tracks—very superior, normal, dull-normal, and mentally retarded. Given the widespread belief that Mexican American children were not cut out for "book study" and thus should be trained for "hand work" (see Stanley, 1920), it is not at all surprising that Los Angeles schools undertook a systematic curricular plan of "training for occupational efficiency" for Mexican Americans, a term used by González (1990). The success of the Los Angeles vocational educational program was due, in part, to the marriage between the educational system and local business. González (1990) noted that vocational education was partially shaped by modifying its curriculum based on local labor needs. It was not uncommon for the Los Angeles Chamber of Commerce and the public school system to be bedfellows. These connections were such that:

> the purpose of schooling became interwoven with, and in a number of ways, shaped by industry. The preparation of students to enter "the business and industrial world" was more than just a preparation for life. It was an education molded by business and industry.
>
> (González, 1974a, pp. 168–169)

Vocational education in Los Angeles public junior and senior high schools—which was designed to prepare students for manually oriented occupations (skilled, semiskilled, or unskilled)—hit its pace in the 1920s. By 1929, the school district offered 70 regular vocational educational courses at about half of the city's high schools (González, 1974a). Yet, these courses were not distributed evenly across the city—overwhelmingly being located in poor, working-class, "foreign-born" (e.g., Mexican; Jewish), and Black neighborhoods. Referring to the eastside sector of Los Angeles (predominantly racial/ethnic minority), González (1974a) found "Lincoln, Roosevelt, and Jefferson [high schools] combined made available for their students forty-six of the seventy regular vocational courses taught in the entire city. Roosevelt and Lincoln alone offered thirty-five vocational courses" (1974a, p. 180). In 1932, the schools were offering "class A" all-day vocational courses for the male students (about five hours for trade instruction and 1.5 for academic instruction). González (1974a) reported that three high schools (Lincoln, Roosevelt, and Fremont)—all located in working-class areas of the city—provided 26 of the total 31 class A vocational courses in the school district. None of the class A courses were offered in the westside of Los Angeles, a predominantly White, higher-socioeconomic status (SES) area.

Many Mexican American female students were not immune to having their economic and social mobility thwarted by the limitations imposed on them by vocational education. Furthermore, a case can be made that Mexican American females, compared to their male counterparts, faced more oppressive occupational outcomes as vocational training in the schools often channeled the girls into the most menial jobs (e.g., domestic servants; laundry workers; seamstresses). It appears that the schools' emphasis on very low-level vocational education for Mexican American females was partially influenced by inaccurate and disparaging images educators had of these girls. For example, Pearl Ellis in her 1929 *Americanization Through Homemaking* commented: "Mexican Americans have inherited this remarkable aptness with the needle. We should strive to foster it in them" (quoted in González, 1990, p. 49). Regarding homemaking as vocational education, it was a major course of study for many Mexican American girls. A rationale for homemaking courses appears to have been driven by observations among educators that these girls married early and had large families, and thus the role of the schools should be to prepare them for homemaking. For example, Hazel Bishop in her 1937 master's thesis (*A Case Study of the Improvement of Mexican Homes Through Instruction in Homemaking*) egregiously commented: "The Mexican woman seems to exist just to bear children" (p. 79). Bishop, quoting a fourth-grade teacher in Santa Ana, California who participated in her survey commented:

> The fact that the Mexican girl marries young and becomes the mother in the home at the age the American [White] girl is in high school means that the junior high school is trusted with her education for homemaker. For this reason, it seems to me that *all or most all of her junior high training should be directed toward making her a better wife, mother, and homemaker* [italics added].
>
> (1937, p. 91)

The geographic distribution of vocational educational courses for girls broke along similar patterns as seen in the location of vocational courses for boys—i.e., such offerings were in schools located in predominantly working-class, racial/ethnic minority neighborhoods:

> For instance homemaking was offered at only four schools: Lafayette Junior High (with an enrollment of 36 percent Black, 14 percent Mexican, and 30 percent Jewish), Belvedere Junior High (51 percent Mexican), Hollenbeck (Mexican and Jewish) and Jefferson (mixed working class). Lincoln offered dressmaking, millinery, and power-sewing. Roosevelt offered dressmaking, sewing, power-sewing, and personal hygiene. Fremont offered dressmaking and personal hygiene. What this in fact meant, was that of six vocational subjects for females Lincoln offered three, Roosevelt four, Fremont two. Only seven schools taught vocational courses for women. All of them were located in working class neighborhoods.
>
> (González, 1974a, pp. 180–181)

Historical analysis of intelligence testing and curriculum differentiation in 1920s and early 1930s Los Angeles public schools informs us that deficit thinking in relation to the schooling of Mexican American boys and girls was influential in shaping very limited educational and occupational opportunities for these students (Valencia, 1997). It appears that Mexican American students in Los Angeles public schools during the era of hereditarianism routinely faced one of two unequally attractive educational pathways—(a) dead-end "special education" for alleged slow learners, or (b) non-academic vocational education that emphasized low-level skills. For the most part, either trail led to manual occupations, typically requiring minimal or no skills. Offering a macrolevel analysis of the linkages between intelligence testing and consequences for Mexican Americans, González (1974b) tied up matters this way:

> On the basis of IQ tests administered by guidance counselors, inordinate numbers of Mexican American children were placed in coursework which prepared them for a variety of manual operations . . . This movement was a reaction of the privileged classes to the rising numbers of the working classes. Schools were redefined in the era of monopoly capitalism to be instruments through which social order could be preserved and industrialization expanded. Thus American schools were not and still are not agents of

change, but rather bolster the social stratifications and values of our society. In such an educational system, Mexican Americans were not provided with opportunities to improve their lot but instead were subjected to a socialization process that reinforced the status quo and was opposed to social change.

(1974b, p. 301)

In sum, it is not at all surprising that during the advent of the testing movement in the hereditarian, racist, and classist *Zeitgeist* of the 1920s, Chicano students were deemed to be intellectually inferior and only minimally educable. By the mid-1920s, state governments became interested in the education of Chicano students. Yet, the prevalent racial animus toward the Mexican American people and the subsequent inferior education provided them were "in part shaped by the legacy of hate engendered by the Texas Revolution and the Mexican American War" (San Miguel, 1987, p. 32). Finally, the intellectual assessment of Chicano students must be understood within the sociopolitical context of the intelligence testing movement of the 1920s. Chapman (1988) has commented that this ideological framework can be reduced to several essential components:

Intelligence could be measured by tests and expressed in a single, numerical ratio. This ability was largely constant and determined by heredity. Class and racial inequality could be explained in large part by differences in intelligence. Used in schools, intelligence tests could be used to identify ability, prescribe curricula and determine students' futures.

(p. 92)

Continuing into the 1940s and 1950s, group intelligence testing in most of our nation's public schools became a routine practice. Writing in the Fall of 1949, Benjamin Fine, columnist for the *New York Times Magazine*, commented:

Between now and June, 20,000,000 children will be subjected to tests to measure their intelligence. This figure indicates the position of influence to which IQ—Intelligence Quotient—tests have risen, in little more than a generation in American school systems. In nearly all, they are used in greater or lesser degree to determine when a child should begin to read, whether another should go to college and if a third is likely to grow up to be a dolt or an Einstein—that is, whether he is "worth worrying about" or "simply beyond help."

(Fine, 1949, p. 7)

Although group intelligence testing became entrenched in the schools, research on intelligence testing precipitously dropped during this period. Haney (1981), in a review of frequency of periodical literature on intelligence testing, observed that such writings hit a peak in the 1920s, substantially fell in the 1930s, plummeted sharply in the 1940s, and rose only very slightly in the 1950s.[11] This overall decline in research interest and inactivity in publishing on intelligence testing in the 1940s and 1950s may have been partially due to some scholars who were absent from the world of research as they served in the armed forces in World War II and the Korean War. Also, as Valencia and Aburto (1991) observed about the decline in intelligence testing research, part of this inattention was likely related to the development that group-based intelligence testing after the 1930s became widely implemented in the nation's schools and took on a life of its own, a life relatively free of controversy—until the late 1950s.

The civil rights movement of the late 1950s and early 1960s brought attention to the rights of racial and ethnic minorities as focal points of national concern. Included in this debate was the role of group-administered IQ tests in the classification of minority students within the educational mainstream and its special education tributary. Speaking of those years, Anastasi (1988) commented, "A common criticism of intelligence tests is that they encourage a rigid, inflexible, and permanent classification of pupils" (p. 67). So deep were these concerns that the use of group IQ tests was discontinued, for example, in 1964 in the New York City public schools (Gilbert, 1966).

As the allegations of discriminatory assessment mounted, three influences shaped the discourse that would eventually lead to nondiscriminatory assessment mandates: professional associations, litigation, and legislation (Henderson and Valencia, 1985). Regarding litigation, the use of the courts proved particularly valuable for Chicanos in trying to address issues of test abuse. Mexican American plaintiffs and coplaintiffs brought forth their charges in *Diana v. Board of Education* (1970), *Guadalupe v. Tempe* (1972), and *Covarrubias* (1971). This trio of cases—all settled in favor of plaintiffs—dealt with the issue of misclassification of Mexican American children as educable mentally retarded (for brief discussions of these cases, see Henderson and Valencia, 1985; Reschly, 1979). Mexican American and other minority plaintiffs were highly instrumental in raising discriminatory assessment concerns (e.g., failure to assess a child's dominant language; the use of culturally biased tests) and in promoting nondiscriminatory practices (e.g., greater use of nonverbal and performance IQ tests; due process). One of the most profound changes resulting from the antidiscriminatory assessment campaign of the late 1960s and early 1970s was the widespread ban on group-administered IQ tests, largely implemented under the auspices of local school districts.

In conclusion, historical analyses tell us that intelligence tests were instrumental, as were perceptions of Chicano students' educability, in the stratification of learning opportunities in the schools. Although group-administered intelligence tests are no longer routinely given in U.S. schools, the use of individually administered intelligence tests continue to be of concern. Issues regarding cultural bias in these tests, their utility in assessing English language learners, and their effectiveness in identifying gifted Chicano students will be addressed (along with high-stakes testing, a measure of academic achievement) in the remainder of this chapter.

Cultural bias in intelligence tests: a review of research findings with Mexican American participants

Historically, there have been charges that standardized intelligence tests penalized minority children because the content (cultural and linguistic) favored the exclusively White standardization samples (e.g., Klineberg, 1935; Sánchez, 1934; also, see Chapman, 1988; Guthrie, 1976; Thomas, 1982; Valencia, 1997).[12] Notwithstanding these allegations of cultural bias in the 1920s and 1930s, it was difficult for early critics to sustain a concerted critique against intelligence tests given the entrenchment of hereditarianism and the reification of intelligence tests by influential scholars (see Valencia, 1997, for this history).

It was not until several decades later that the issue of cultural bias reappeared. As we discussed earlier, the civil rights movement of the late 1950s and 1960s brought forward national attention to the rights of minorities. Two aspects of this debate were the role of group-administered intelligence testing in shaping curriculum differentiation (e.g., tracking) in the educational mainstream, and the role of individually administered intelligence testing in influencing the overrepresentation of minority students in special education. We also discussed that as allegations of discriminatory assessment escalated, litigation was a major influence that brought charges of cultural bias in intelligence tests to the national limelight. In addition to the issues of omission of minority students in the standardization samples, allegations of culturally biased items, and failure to appropriately assess language minority students, critics during the late 1960s and early 1970s also argued that the observed mean-level differences of performance on intelligence tests between, for example, White and African American students were due to an inherent bias in the overall structure of the test themselves. Proponents of this view argued there is no a priori reason to believe that mean mental performance should differ across racial/ethnic groups (e.g., Alley and Foster, 1978; Jackson, 1975).

It was not until the mid-1970s and through the 1980s that empirical investigations of test bias were vigorously undertaken. A number of researchers (e.g., Jensen, 1980; Reynolds, 1982a; Reynolds and Kaiser, 1990) challenged the early intelligence test critics, asserting that (a) based on the available *empirical* research, intelligence tests are *not* biased against racial/ethnic minority students; (b) the "mean difference as bias" definition is a misconception (Jensen, 1980, referred to the definition as the *egalitarian fallacy*, which is "the gratuitous assumption that all human populations are essentially identical or equal in whatever trait or ability the tests purport to measure" (p. 370); and (c) the concern of inappropriate standardization sample is a nonissue.

When research on test bias began in the 1970s, many scholars asserted that the construct of test bias can be explained in the context of validity theory and, as such, it is an empirical, testable, quantifiable, and scientific matter. Novices to the subject of test bias are typically surprised to learn that the notion of bias is derived from mathematical statistics. In this field, the term *bias* "refers to the *systematic* under- or overestimation of a population parameter by a statistic based on samples drawn from the population" (Jensen, 1980, p. 375). In traditional psychometrics, however, bias takes on a related but distinct meaning. It is typically conceived as the systematic (not random) error of some true value of test scores that are connected to group membership (see, e.g., Jensen, 1980; Reynolds, 1982a). Note that group membership is the general referent. It can refer to test bias in the contexts of race/ethnicity, sex, social class, age, and so on. Test bias in the case of race/ethnicity is often referred to as *cultural bias*, the subject of this section. Investigations of cultural bias in intelligence tests can, and sometimes do, employ empirically defined and testable hypotheses and complex statistical analyses (see, e.g., Reynolds, 1982b).

In our review of the cultural bias literature presented in this section, we focus on how the various researchers investigated cultural bias given the theories and technologies with which they had to work. In the heyday of this research (from the mid-1970s to the late 1980s), cultural bias research was typically guided by "validity theory" (i.e., looking at specific aspects of validity [e.g., predictive validity] on specific intelligence tests) and not specifically by "validation theory," as conceptualized by Cole and Moss (1989).[13] Furthermore, the advancements we now have (e.g., item response theory) were fields of statistical technology not yet fully developed during the early years of test bias research.

If test bias is conceptualized as being objective and technical, what is then meant by charges that a particular intelligence test is *unfair* towards, for example, Chicano students? Some measurement experts assert that the notions of test unfairness, and its opposite, test fairness, denote a subjective value judgment regarding how test results are used in the decision-making process (e.g., selection procedures). As such, the concepts of test fairness, and its reciprocal, test unfairness "belong more to moral philosophy than to psychometrics"

(Jensen, 1980, p. 49). Other scholars have similar, but broader, ideas about values associated with tests and how test results are used. For example, Cole and Moss (1989) place these concerns in what they refer to as the "extra-validity domain." These authors view these issues (i.e., values and validity) as connected, and not necessarily as flipsides of a coin (i.e., bias and unfairness as conceptualized by Jensen, 1980). Still, other scholars see test bias (i.e., an inherent feature of a test) and test unfairness (i.e., the use of test results) as inextricably linked—not converse constructs (see, e.g., Hilliard, 1984; Mercer, 1984).

Two final terms pertinent to the study of test bias are the "major group" and "minor group" (Jensen, 1980). Although validity coefficients are helpful in detecting test bias, they are limited in the amount of information provided. As Jensen commented, validity and bias are separate notions. Validity can apply to a single group, whereas bias always involves a comparison of two or more groups. In the case of a two-group comparison, one population is referred to as the major group, the other as the minor group. These terms are not intended to infer value judgments. More specifically, Jensen noted,

> The major group can usually be thought of as (1) the larger of the two groups in the total population, (2) the group on which the test was primarily standardized, or (3) the group with the higher mean score on the test, assuming the major and minor groups differ in means.
>
> (p. 376)

To these distinctions discussed by Jensen (1980), Valencia and Suzuki (2001) offered a fourth feature. The major group is the group that the test is believed not to be biased against. On the other hand, the minor group is the group that the test, if determined to be biased, is biased *against*. As such, test bias research can involve various groupings. For example, in the case of test bias investigations (e.g., mathematics) regarding sex, the major group is male, and the minor group is female. In investigations of cultural bias—the subject of the present section—the major group is comprised of White participants, and the minor group consists of Chicano participants.

In the remainder of this section, we present a comprehensive review of published empirical investigations that sought to examine cultural bias in intelligence tests in which Mexican American children/youths served as the minor group.[14] Our review of pertinent literature is organized and presented as follows: (a) procedures; (b) results: study characteristics; (c) results: cultural bias findings; (d) discussion, and (e) conclusions.

Procedures

This section describes the procedures used for the literature review.

Search

Studies (journal articles) to be included in this review were identified, via computerized searches, using *Current Index to Journals in Education* and *Psychological Abstracts* (ERIC and PsycINFO databases, respectively). Furthermore, studies were identified by scrutinizing the bibliographies of studies already obtained by the authors as well as those studies obtained through the computerized searches. In all, 39 investigations were identified for review (see Appendix A for a numerical listing of the studies).

Criteria for selection

The following criteria were used for selection of a germane study for review:

1   The investigation was empirical in design, in which participants were tested and the results analyzed for cultural bias. Only studies published in refereed scholarly journals were examined.
2   The measure under investigation was designed as an *individually* administered, standardized intelligence test. In some studies, more than one intelligence test was administered.
3   There was a major group (i.e., White participants) and a minor group (i.e., Mexican American participants for the purpose of this review). In a number of studies, however, there were also other minority participants.
4   The study participants were limited to children in preschool and to students in grades K-12.
5   The author(s) of the study sought to investigate, for cultural bias, one or more of the following psychometric properties of the intelligence test(s) under examination: reliability, construct validity, content validity, and predictive validity.

Results: study characteristics

In this first section of the results, we present a summary of the various study characteristics.

Year of study

Close examination of the year of publication of test bias studies reveals a discernible trend. As noted earlier in this section, research on cultural bias began in the 1970s, a period in which 16 (41 percent) of the 39 investigations were published. The decade of the 1980s also accounted for 16 (41 percent) of the publications. Finally, in the 1990s, only seven (18 percent) of the total studies were published. In the Discussion section, we offer possible explanations as to why such research waned during the past decade.

Psychometric property examined

Table 9.1 shows how the 39 investigations sorted out by psychometric properties examined for possible cultural bias.

Table 9.1 Test bias investigations by psychometric property ($N = 39$ studies)

Psychometric property	n	Grand total (%)	Study number
Reliability	6	15.4	5, 13, 22, 26, 31,34
Construct validity	11	28.2	1, 3, 8, 9, 14, 19, 24, 27, 29, 33, 37
Content validity	9	23.1	4, 6, 10, 15, 23, 25, 28, 32, 36
Predictive validity	13	33.3	2, 7, 11, 12, 16, 17, 18, 20, 21, 30, 35, 38, 39
Grand total	39	100.0	

Note
Author citations for the study numbers are listed in Appendix A.

Predictive validity was the property most frequently studied (33 percent of the 39 studies). In descending order, the other three psychometric categories examined for bias were: construct validity (28 percent), content validity (23 percent), and reliability (15 percent). In all, it appears that the observed proportions represent a fairly good psychometric mix of cultural bias studies.

Intelligence test examined

Table 9.2 contains information on the various intelligence tests that were examined for cultural bias. Eleven different intelligence measures, most of which are well known are listed (author citations are provided in Appendix B). The data in Table 9.2 show that the WISC, WISC-R, and WISC-III, by far, were the instruments of choice by researchers. Alone, the WISC-R was examined for bias in the *majority* ($n = 21$, 54 percent) of the 39 studies. When the WISC-R, its predecessor (the WISC), and its successor (the WISC-III) are combined, these three Wechsler scales were investigated in nearly two thirds (64 percent) of all studies. The Kaufman Assessment Battery for Children and the Raven Coloured Progressive Matrices were a distant second and third, respectively, in frequency of study.

Location of study

California was the leader; 41 percent of all investigations were done in this state. Arizona was second in frequency (21 percent), followed by Texas (5 percent). One study only mentioned the general region of "Southwestern United States" (No. 3). Surprisingly, 28 percent of all studies failed to mention the state in which the investigation was conducted.

Table 9.2 Intelligence tests examined for bias investigations

Intelligence test	n	Total[a] (%)	Study number
Wechsler Intelligence Scale for Children—Revised	21	53.9	1, 3, 12, 13, 14, 15, 16, 17, 18, 19, 20, 21, 22, 23, 24, 25, 26, 27, 28, 30, 37
Kaufman Assessment Battery for Children	6	15.4	17, 18, 33, 34, 35, 36
Raven Coloured Progressive Matrices	5	12.8	4, 5, 6, 7, 31
McCarthy Scales of Children's Abilities	3	7.7	9, 10, 32
Wechsler Intelligence Scale for Children	2	5.1	2, 29
Wechsler Intelligence Scale for Children—Third Edition	2	5.1	38, 39
Raven Standard Progressive Matrices	2	5.1	6, 7
Peabody Picture Vocabulary Test	2	5.1	4, 5
Differential Ability Scales	1	2.6	8
Woodcock–Johnson Psychoeducational Battery	1	2.6	17
Slosson Intelligence Test	1	2.6	11
Other measures[b]	2	5.1	7

Note
Author citations for the intelligence tests are listed, in alphabetical order, in Appendix B.
[a] Divisor for percentage of total is 39 (total number of investigations).
[b] In study no. 7, Jensen (1974b) used two additional measures of intelligence: figure copying and memory for numbers.

Number of participants

Based on the 39 investigations, our calculations show that there were 34,673 total participants.[15] Of these, 13,381 (39 percent) were major group children (i.e., White), and 21,292
(61 percent) were minor group children (i.e., racial/ethnic minority). Mexican American
participants numbered 11,614 (34 percent of the total participants; 55 percent of the racial/
ethnic minority participants).

Sex of participants

About half of the 39 investigations reported the sex of the children. Of the 19 studies that
did report the sex of the participants, four only reported such data for the total sample, and
15 provided sex data for the major and minor groups. Overall, of the 19 investigations that
reported sex of the participants, we can see a good mix of males and females for both major
and minor groups: over 6,700 were male, while over 6,600 were female.

Age of participants

The data show that the age of major and minor group participants covered a wide range,
spanning from 2 years to 17 years of age. Children ages 5 to 14 years extensively served as
participants. Compressed even further, children ages 7 to 11 years most frequently served as
participants.

Socioeconomic status (SES) of participants

Of the total 39 investigations, 28 studies (72 percent) reported data on the SES of participants. Low-SES children served (but not exclusively) in 21 (75 percent) of the 28 investigations that reported participants' SES. Low-middle and middle-SES children were participants
in 18 (64 percent) of the 28 studies. In only two studies did upper-middle SES children
serve as participants.

Language status of participants

Of the 39 reported studies, the majority ($n = 22$, 56 percent) failed to report the language
status of the participants. For the 17 (44 percent) investigations that did report language
status of the participants, the children were described as being English speaking in the
majority of the studies ($n = 11$, 65 percent). In the remaining six studies, the participants
were said to be bilingual in three studies (18 percent) and limited-English-proficient in three
studies (18 percent). We identified those investigations that actually assessed language status
with some measure. For the 17 studies that reported language status, 13 (77 percent) used
an indirect or direct measure of language status.

Educational status of participants

By far, children in regular classes were the most frequent type of participants; 30 (77 percent) of all 39 investigations exclusively utilized participants who were enrolled in regular
classes, while only three (8 percent) of the studies exclusively used participants who were
referred for possible special education placement and two investigations (5 percent) studied
both regular and referred children. Also less frequently studied were children in special
education ($n = 2$ studies, 5 percent).

Results: cultural bias findings

In this section, we provide a summary of test bias findings based on the 39 investigations. Table 9.3 lists the investigations by psychometric property, indicating the number (*n*) and percentage of studies of the grand total that resulted in a finding of "nonbias," "bias," and "mixed" finding. By mixed, we mean findings that were not unequivocally nonbiased or biased.

In sum, the data in Table 9.3 strongly suggest that the existence of cultural bias or non-bias in the 39 investigations appears to be a function of the type of psychometric property studied. In descending order, findings of *nonbias* in the various intelligence tests that comprised the corpus of the present study are observed in investigations of (a) reliability (six of six studies, 100 percent), (b) construct validity (ten of 11 studies, 91 percent), (c) content validity (four of nine studies, 44 percent), and (d) predictive validity (five of 13 studies, 39 percent).

Next, we report an even closer examination of test bias findings by describing, in detail, results for each of the four psychometric properties. For each property, we first describe the study characteristics; then, we report the cultural bias findings.

Reliability

Table 9.3 lists six investigations that examined various intelligence tests for possible bias in reliability. Reliability is a critical psychometric property of intelligence tests. In general, "Reliability refers to the *consistency* of measurement—that is, how consistent test scores or other evaluation results are from one measurement to another" (Gronlund and Linn, 1990, p. 77). In cultural bias investigations of reliability, the research question is: Is the intelligence test consistently accurate, at a comparable level, for both the major and minor groups? As seen in Table 9.3, all six investigations resulted in conclusions of nonbias.

Notwithstanding the finding of nonbias in the six reliability studies, it is important to examine each study individually because the magnitude of the reliability estimates sometimes vary across major and minor groups. Several studies (i.e., Jensen, 1974b, App. A; Oakland and Feigenbaum, 1979a, App. A; Valencia and Rankin, 1986b, App. A) reported that the reliability estimate (Cronbach's alpha) for the White group was higher compared to the Mexican American group.

Regarding how the authors of these six reliability studies concluded that the intelligence tests were equally reliable (i.e., nonbiased) for the major and minor groups, the majority of the investigations (nos 5, 13, 22, and 26) eye-balled the observed reliability coefficients and drew conclusions of equivalence. Two studies (nos 31 and 34), however, used the preferred technique of testing for a significant difference between the observed reliability coefficients.[16]

Construct validity

Table 9.3 lists 11 studies that investigated a number of different intelligence tests for possible bias in construct validity. To be sure, reliability is an important psychometric property of a test. The notion of validity, however, is "the most central concept in the whole testing enterprise. It is the main goal toward which reliability and stability are aimed" (Jensen, 1980, p. 297). From a *scientific* standpoint, construct validity is the most important type of validity (Jensen, 1980). This is so because developers of intelligence tests frequently begin with some theory of intelligence that guides their development of items and subtests. Such theoretical formulations provide us with some psychological understanding of what the test attempts to measure.

Table 9.3 Test bias findings (N = 39 studies)

Psychometric property	Total		Nonbias			Bias			Mixed		
	n	Grand total (%)	n	Grand total (%)	Study number	n	Grand total (%)	Study number	n	Grand total (%)	Study number
Reliability	6	15.4	6	15.4	5, 13, 22, 26, 31, 34	0	0.0	—	0	0.0	—
Construct validity	11	28.2	10	25.6	1, 3, 8, 9, 14, 19, 24, 27, 29, 33	0	0.0	—	1	2.6	37
Content validity	9	23.1	4	10.3	6, 10, 25, 28	2	5.1	32, 36	3	7.7	4, 15, 23
Predictive validity	13	33.3	5	12.8	7, 12, 20, 21, 39	5	12.8	2, 11, 18, 30, 35	3	7.7	16, 17, 38
Grand total	39	100.0	25	64.1		7	17.9		7	17.9	

In cultural bias investigations of construct validity, the research question is: Does the intelligence test measure similar constructs for both the major and minor groups? To investigate whether a particular intelligence test has structural similarity in constructs across populations, researchers use one of the more popular and empirically necessary approaches, factor analysis (Reynolds, 1982b). If one finds that the test has factorial similarity for the major and minor groups, then it can be concluded, to some degree, that the test is not biased in construct validity.[17]

The construct validity studies identified for review overwhelmingly had conclusions of nonbias. In all, ten of eleven studies (91 percent) concluded there was no bias, compared to only one study (9 percent) that found mixed results. It is important to note, however, that although nearly all of the studies reported nonbias, some interesting differences in factor structures for White and Mexican American subjects were found (e.g., Mishra, 1981, App. A; Reschly, 1978, App. A; Valencia and Rankin, 1986, App. A). For example, Valencia and Rankin (1986a, App. A) found that two factors on the K-ABC (Achievement and Simultaneous Processing factors) indicated factorial similarity for 200 White and Mexican American children (10.0 to 12.4 years of age). The authors reported, however, that the third factor (Sequential Processing) was substantially different across groups.

Regarding the investigation that reported mixed findings, Valencia *et al.* (1997, App. A), in a study exploring the factor structures of the WISC-R for 451 White, African American, and Mexican American children (6.8 to 14.6 years of age), reported that although a three-factor solution emerged for all groups, factors 2 and 3 (Perceptual Organization and Freedom from Distractibility, respectively) were reversed in order for the minority participants when compared to Whites.

Overall, it can be concluded that even though the overwhelming majority of the construct validity studies reported findings of nonbias, some of the results raise concerns about claiming factorial invariance across ethnic groups.

Content validity

Table 9.3 shows nine studies that investigated various intelligence tests for possible bias in content validity. In a general sense, content validity refers "to the extent that the items in the test are judged to constitute a representative sample of some clearly specified universe of knowledge or skills" (Jensen, 1980, p. 297). As noted by Berk (1982), the issue of bias in content validity is particularly important in test bias research. First, test items form the most basic level of content analysis; thus, such studies are necessary for all tests.[18] Second, it is the item level of tests that most charges of bias against minorities are directed (e.g., Hilliard, 1979; Jackson, 1975; Jensen, 1980; Koh, Abbatiello, and McLoughlin, 1984; Williams, 1971). Third, test developers, via bias investigations, can debias tests during the early stages of test construction. In cultural bias studies of content validity, the research question is: Are the items (or subtests) of the intelligence test at similar difficulty levels for both the major and minor groups?

Table 9.3 lists nine investigations of possible bias in content validity. Of this total, 44 percent ($n = 4$) resulted in a finding of nonbias, whereas the remaining 56 percent had findings of bias ($n = 2$, 22 percent) and mixed results ($n = 3$, 33 percent). Compared to the bias investigations of reliability and construct validity—which overwhelmingly resulted in findings of nonbias—the category of content validity resulted in equivocal findings.

Although four of these investigations found the various tests to be nonbiased at the item level, such a general conclusion needs to be tempered with caution. For example, Murray and Mishra (1983, App. A), found 7 percent of the total Verbal Scale items to be biased against the Mexican American participants. Likewise, Sandoval *et al.* (1983, App. A), reported that several items on the Vocabulary subtest were more difficult for African American and Mexican American children, and several items on the Information subtest were more difficult for Mexican American children.

The three investigations of possible bias in content validity that comprised the mixed set are the most complex to understand. In some instances, bias was detected on items in one subtest, but not in others, or bias was detected for one minor group, but not another. For example Jensen (1974a, App. A) reported that there were grounds for suspected cultural bias in the Peabody Picture Vocabulary Test (PPVT) (Dunn, 1959, App. B) against Mexican American boys and girls, but not against African American boys and girls.

Table 9.3 lists two studies that reported biased findings in content validity. Valencia and Rankin (1985, App. A) modified the conventional test bias investigation approach (i.e., White is the major group; racial/ethnic minority is the minor group) by using a Mexican American English-speaking and a Spanish-speaking sample as the major and minor groups, respectively. Using the item-group correlation technique and controlling for cognitive ability,[19] the authors reported that 23 (15 percent) of 157 MSCA items were biased—17 against the Spanish-speaking group and six against the English-speaking sample. The pattern of item bias for the latter group was not discernible, as the biased items cut across dissimilar subtests.[20] Of the 17 biased against the Spanish-speaking group, 12 (71 percent) clustered in two subtests: Verbal Memory I (nine biased items) and Numerical Memory I (three biased items).

The other investigation listed in Table 9.3 that found bias in content validity was by Valencia *et al.* (1995, App. A). Of the 120 items comprising the Mental Processing Scales (the intelligence test of the K-ABC battery), 17 (14 percent) were identified as biased; the same bias detection method used in Valencia and Rankin (1985, App. A) was utilized here. The strong majority, 13 (77 percent) were biased against the Mexican American group; four (24 percent) of the items were biased against the White group. Three major findings were reported. First, in the majority (75 percent) of the subtests, the number of biased items was very small (mode of one item).[21] Second, a pattern of biased items on six of eight subtests was not discernible, thus suggesting a random dispersion of bias. Third, of the 17 biased items, ten (59 percent) clustered in two subtests (Word Order and Matrix Analogies), and the vast majority (eight of ten, 80 percent) was biased against the Mexican American sample. The authors were unable to offer a cultural or psychological explanation for the observed bias. In addition to their bias examination of the K-ABC Mental Processing Scale, Valencia *et al.* (1995, App. A) also investigated possible bias in content validity of the K-ABC individually administered Achievement Scale, a totally separate scale. Although our focus in this review is on individually administered intelligence tests, we think it is important to mention that in the K-ABC Achievement Scale bias investigation by Valencia *et al.*, the authors found that an extremely high proportion (63 percent) of the items were biased—all against the Mexican American group.[22]

Predictive validity

Predictive validity is perhaps the most significant psychometric property when it comes to the actual uses of intelligence tests in education. To a certain degree, when a child's intelligence is assessed in school, the implicit or explicit purpose is to predict future performance. The question of bias in predictive validity is therefore critical, given that educational interventions (e.g., special education) for some minority students will depend on the accurate predictive validity of intelligence tests.

According to Reynolds (1982b), a test is biased with respect to predictive validity: "When the inference drawn from the test score is not made with the smallest feasible random error or if there is constant error in an inference or prediction as a function of membership in a particular group" (p. 216). In cultural bias studies of predictive validity, the research question is: Does the test predict scores on a criterion measure equally well for both the major and the minor groups?

Contrary to the cultural bias studies of reliability and construct validity reviewed in this chapter, considerably more investigations of bias in predictive validity have reported biased or mixed findings. Of the 13 predictive validity studies reviewed, five (39 percent) reported biased findings, while an additional three (23 percent) studies reported mixed findings. Yet, it is important to note that five (39 percent) of the studies failed to find any bias in predictive validity (see Table 9.3). As expected, the popular WISC-R was the most prominent test examined in these investigations of predictive validity. Regarding the criterion variable, a wide variety of achievement measures were represented, the most common one being the Metropolitan Achievement Test (MAT) in four investigations.

An example of a mixed finding investigation is Oakland and Feigenbaum (1979d, App. A). Using intercorrelation analysis, the authors reported "a number of differences in the magnitude of correlations for [the WISC-R and] Reading and Mathematics" (p. 973). Oakland and Feigenbaum concluded that the WISC-R predicted mathematics scores about equally well for all three groups, but was a much better predictor of reading achievement for the White participants.

Finally, five out of 13 investigations (39 percent) found clear evidence of bias in predictive validity. One example of a predictive validity study that found bias is Palmer *et al.* (1989, App. A). The authors focused on the issue of overidentification of minority children with learning disabilities, and reported significant predictive validity bias in the WISC-R using the K-ABC Achievement Scale as the criterion. There was evidence of bias across minority groups for the K-ABC Achievement Scale (total) and the K-ABC Achievement Scale Arithmetic subtest. Predictive validity bias was found for both referred and nonreferred participants. In addition, the authors found language-dominance related bias for the Mexican American group in both the WISC-R and the K-ABC composite scales.

Discussion

This review of research on cultural bias in intelligence tests in which Mexican American children served as minor group participants has identified a number of study characteristics, as well as a reporting of extant findings of cultural bias in four psychometric categories (reliability, construct, content, and predictive validity). In this section, we discuss—in more general terms—what has been learned. We also comment critically on this body of research.

1   Empirical research on cultural bias in intelligence tests with Mexican American and other racial/ethnic groups did not begin in earnest until 1973, and significantly diminished in the 1990s. Such abatement can likely be attributed to the rather consistent finding in the 1970s and 1980s that prominent intelligence tests (e.g., WISC; WISC-R) were concluded to be nonbiased, and thus interest in pursuing research in this area rapidly declined. Later, we offer discussion on why such a diminishment of research activity in the present is not warranted.

2   Another irony about the present findings is that although children referred for special education diagnoses and possible placement, as well as enrolled special education students, are the primary subjects of assessment using individually administered intelligence tests,

they have not been the primary participants in the 39 investigations—less than 3 percent of all participants (major and minor groups) were actually enrolled in special education. The question remains as to what degree the conclusions drawn about nonbiased/ biased/mixed findings with Mexican American children in regular classes can be generalized to Mexican American children in special education.

3   As we have found, the Wechsler scales (the WISC, WISC-R, and WISC-III) have been the dominant choice of instruments to examine for cultural bias—64 percent of all 39 investigations, compared to a number of distant followers (e.g., K-ABC). It can be concluded that what we know most about cultural bias in intelligence tests regarding Mexican American students is fairly much confined to these sister instruments—a fact that does not bode well for the study of cultural bias in intelligence tests, as a whole. Furthermore, given that the former two tests (WISC; WISC-R) are no longer used in clinical assessments—and have been replaced by the WISC-III—much of what is known about cultural bias in intelligence tests with respect to Mexican American students is based on obsolete instruments.

4   As we have described in the Results section, a substantial proportion of the investigations failed to control for the SES background, language dominance and proficiency, and sex of participants in the bias analyses. This failure to control for these important variables represents potential problems of confoundment. Regarding the failure to control for SES, although it is weakly correlated with measured intelligence, it is still an important variable to control for in test bias research (Valencia and Suzuki, 2001, Chapter 3).[23] When SES is controlled in test bias studies (e.g., Valencia, 1984, App. A; Valencia et al., 1995, App. A), the White mean/Mexican American mean difference in intellectual performance is frequently reduced, and in some cases is negligible. Regarding the failure to control for language dominance and proficiency of Mexican American participants in cultural bias studies, it has been known for decades that children from linguistically diverse backgrounds (e.g., Spanish-speaking or other language minority students) are most likely to be penalized on intelligence tests during the time of administration (e.g., Klineberg, 1935; Sánchez, 1932, 1934; Valencia, 1985a). Nonetheless, many researchers have simply ignored this issue. Finally, the failure to control for sex represents another possible confoundment in this corpus of literature (see Halpern [1997] for a discussion of how sex of participant is related to intellectual performance). In sum, given that only a handful of studies reviewed in this chapter attempted to control for SES, language status, or sex, the role of these variables in cultural bias research remains largely unknown.

5   Several studies reported predictive validity bias in a variety of intelligence tests that have been commonly used in educational placement, including the WISC-R and the K-ABC. In these studies (e.g., Palmer et al., 1989, App. A; Olivárez et al., 1992, App. A), the differences in slope and intercept between the major and minor groups' regression lines appear to lead to the possibility of unfair decisions regarding student placement into special programs. A serious consequence of this type of bias is the misidentification of minority students as learning disabled and subsequent placement in special education programs. Olivárez et al. point to the *Standards for Educational and Psychological Testing* (American Educational Research Association, American Psychological Association, and National Council on Measurement in Education, 1985) for guidance. Although the *Standards* assert that special attention should be placed on the construction and use of nonbiased instruments that are administered to culturally and racially/ethnically diverse populations, few studies of predictive validity bias are currently being conducted. Olivárez et al. go on an assert that "the large majority of the bias cases occurred with the nonreferred group, suggesting that test developers should conduct predictive bias studies

with their newly developed or revised instruments on their standardization samples"
(p. 185).

6   Our final point of discussion goes full circle to an issue raised in the introduction of this section on cultural bias in intelligence tests. Jensen, in the preface to his 1980 book, *Bias in Mental Testing*, asserted that based on the available cultural bias literature, it can be concluded that the most frequently used tests of mental ability (including intelligence measures) were "*not* biased against any of the native-born English-speaking minority groups" (p. ix). Given that Jensen's claim was made over two decades ago, does his conclusion have veracity today in light of the extant literature we have reviewed? The majority (64 percent) of the 39 investigations, as reported in the present discussion, had conclusions of nonbias (see Table 9.3). Yet, given that 36 percent of the total investigations had conclusions of mixed/biased findings, the sweeping inference of Jensen that the subject of cultural bias in intelligence is a closed issue is not accurate today. First, the identification of bias appears to be psychometric specific. Investigations of bias in reliability and construct validity demonstrated the existence of nonbias, with a few exceptions. On the other hand, about 60 percent of all content and predictive validity investigations had mixed/biased findings. Second, what we know about cultural bias in intelligence tests is confined, for the most part, to three instruments—the WISC, WISC-R, and WISC-III. Thus, to generalize about cultural bias in intelligence tests beyond these three instruments appears difficult. Third, Mexican American children overwhelmingly served as minor group participants in the 39 cultural bias investigations. As such, very little is known about cultural bias regarding other Latino groups. Regarding Puerto Rican children, for example, Valencia and Suzuki (2001, p. 122, Table 5.4) identified only two such studies (Corman and Budoff, 1974; Glutting, 1986) in their comprehensive review of the cultural bias literature.

Conclusions

By way of closure, we leave the reader with two final thoughts on the subject of cultural bias in intelligence tests. First, as we mentioned in the introduction of this section, test bias refers to an empirical, testable, quantifiable, scientific matter. Bias, a statistical notion, can be detected through empirical approaches. Any discussion of test bias is incomplete, we contend, without commenting on "test use." Test use explicitly involves decision-making. Thus, we often make judgments (e.g., identification of a student who is diagnosed as having a learning disability; using the Law School Aptitude Test to assist a selection committee to decide who gets admitted to law school; identification of a student for admission to a gifted and talented program). These decisions can lead to claims of unfairness (or its reciprocal, fairness). The point here is that test bias research only addresses one aspect of testing—the psychometric integrity of the instrument. How we use test results is the other half of the whole. This interrelatedness is particularly important in school-based interventions. Ross-Reynolds and Reschly (1983a, App. A) cogently capture this concern:

> Fairness in assessment with diverse groups depends on events prior to and following the use of formal tests. The effectiveness of special programs or other interventions that result, in part, from the use of tests with individuals is the crucial factor in fairness. *Tests that are unbiased according to the statistical criteria . . . are necessary, but not sufficient, conditions to ensure fairness* [italics added].

(p. 146)

Our second point has to do with the waning of research on cultural bias in intelligence tests. Compared to the flurry of research activity in the 1970s and 1980s, very little research has been undertaken in the 1990s in which Mexican American and other racial/ethnic minority groups have served as participants. It appears that such a precipitous decline is related to the high percentage of earlier studies that had findings of nonbias. The current state-of-the-art on cultural bias research informs us, however, that this line of research needs to be renewed with vigor. Valencia and Suzuki's (2001, Chapter 5) exhaustive review of literature on cultural bias on intelligence tests in which racial/ethnic minorities have been targets of study ($n = 62$ studies) has identified a number of shortcomings in this body of research. The authors found that members of some minority groups (e.g., Asian American) have been vastly understudied. Furthermore, we underscore what Valencia and Suzuki likewise reported: participants have overwhelmingly been students in regular classes; most of what is known about cultural bias is based on the obsolete WISC and WISC-R; and possible problems of confoundment (i.e., related to SES, language status, and sex) exist. In light of these issues, a forceful case can be made that test publishers and independent researchers have an obligation to engage in expanded research on cultural bias in intelligence tests. Furthermore, this call for research can be justified by demographic reality. Currently, the racial/ethnic makeup of the nation is dramatically changing due to the phenomenal growth of culturally/linguistically diverse school-age populations, especially Latino and Asian American (see Valencia, Chapter 2, present book). It is important that when intelligence tests are administered to racial/ethnic minority children and youths that such tests be free of cultural bias and the test results be applied fairly.

Issues in the cognitive assessment of Mexican American English language learners

In the preceding section, the focus was on Mexican American children who were believed to be, or assumed to be, English proficient. We now turn to a subgroup of the Mexican American school population – namely Mexican American English language learners (ELLs).[24] In this section, we discuss a number of cognitive assessment issues related to the Mexican American ELL school-age population. These issues include: (a) the relation between language proficiency and cognitive performance; (b) the relation between language proficiency and bilingual education; (c) issues in the construction and clinical utility of Spanish-language intelligence tests; (d) the use of interpreters in the assessment process; (e) alternatives to traditional assessment; and (f) recommendations for nondiscriminatory practices and further research.

The relation between language proficiency and cognitive performance

In assessing the cognitive abilities of Mexican American ELLs, it is necessary first to establish their language dominance and proficiency in order to determine which language is most appropriate to conduct the assessment (López, 1997). To make this determination, Holtzman and Wilkinson (1991) recommended sampling a wide range of language skills to determine language proficiency, including informal measures such as home language surveys and parental interviews, as well as formal measures such as the Language Assessment Scales (LAS) (DeAvila and Duncan, 1986). Given that Mexican American ELLs' language proficiency in English and Spanish affects their cognitive and academic achievement (Duncan and DeAvila, 1979; García-Vázquez *et al.*, 1999), conceptualizing language proficiency as a two-tiered hierarchy of language use is particularly relevant (Cummins, 1980, 1984). Cummins

(1984) posited that language use be conceptualized on two levels – *basic interpersonal conversational skills* (BICS) and *cognitive/academic language proficiency* (CALP).

BICS, Cummins theorized, reflects language that develops in everyday communicative situations, relies heavily on the context of the communication, and develops relatively quickly (two to three years) in a second language learning environment. CALP, on the other hand, emphasizes language use that is more abstract, relies heavily on the meaning and content of the language, is independent of context, and takes much longer (five to seven years) for second language learners to acquire (Cummins, 1981). It is this latter construct, CALP, that is of particular importance, as children's CALP abilities influence their performance on intelligence tests, and later academic success (Cummins, 1984). Research with ELL populations has shown that literacy (one form of CALP-level ability) in the primary and second languages appears to be the first step in promoting cognitive and academic achievement (García-Vázquez *et al.*, 1999). The manner, however, in which ELLs acquire literacy is highly dependent on the type and quality of bilingual instruction provided—an issue we turn to.

The relation between language proficiency and bilingual education

The degree to which schooling fosters CALP-level language abilities for Mexican American ELLs affects their performance on intelligence tests, as "crystallized intelligence" frequently involves established cognitive functions that are shaped by formal and informal education (Valencia and Suzuki, 2001). ELLs are placed in bilingual education programs to promote their acquisition of English. Most students, however, are placed in "transitional bilingual education" (TBE) programs (Ramírez *et al.*, 1991; see Guerrero, Chapter 6, present volume, in which the author reviews research on bilingual education, for a fuller description and discussion of bilingual programs). TBE programs typically last about two to three years, or until the student ostensibly demonstrates sufficient proficiency in English to profit from English-only instruction. In Texas, for example, ELL children in bilingual programs are reclassified as "English-proficient" when they demonstrate *oral fluency* by obtaining a score at the 40th percentile or higher on a standardized English language assessment measure (Texas Education Code, 1999). TBE programs, however, do not last long enough for bilingual children to develop CALP-level abilities (Cummins, 1981, 1984; Saville-Troike, 1984). Given that TBE programs last only about two to three years, and exit criteria typically require only BICS-level oral fluency rather than CALP-level abilities, ELL children exited from TBE programs—and who are deemed to be "English proficient"—will likely perform below the norm on verbally loaded intelligence tests (Collier, 1989; Cummins, 1984; García-Vázquez *et al.*, 1999; Zavala and Mims, 1983).

Issues in the construction and clinical utility of Spanish-language intelligence tests

Notwithstanding the complexity of the issue of Mexican American ELLs' language proficiency in relation to their performance on intelligence tests, González (1994) noted that it is difficult to ascertain if low obtained scores in ELL children are due to: "(a) a lack of valid and reliable instruments; (b) lack of appropriate norms for language-minority children; (c) use of unnatural and ambiguous stimuli such as literal translations of standardized tests in English" (p. 398). Regarding point "a" above, very little research has been conducted on the reliability and validity of these instruments with Mexican American ELLs.

From a clinical perspective, the testing of ELLs (Mexican American or other language-minority students) in English is inappropriate (American Educational Research Association,

American Psychological Association, and National Council on Measurement in Education, 1999). Thus, the findings on the reliability and validity of English-language intelligence tests in which Mexican American English-proficient children served as participants are a moot point regarding the clinical utility of such measures with Mexican American ELLs. The psychometric integrity of *Spanish*-language intelligence tests with Mexican American ELLs, however, is very salient to this discussion. We know of only two intelligence measures that are available in Spanish—the *Batería Woodcock Muñoz-Revisada* (*Batería*-R) (Woodcock and Muñoz-Sandoval, 1996), and the *Bilingual Verbal Ability Tests* (BVAT) (Muñoz-Sandoval *et al.*, 1998a).[25] There exists some research on the psychometric properties (reliability; validity) of these instruments provided by the test developers (e.g., Woodcock and Mather, 1996).[26] However, we know of no *independent* publications on the psychometric properties of these instruments that include Mexican American ELLs as participants.

An alternative to using Spanish-language intelligence tests with Mexican American ELLs is the use of test adaptations—a controversial practice. Geisinger (1994) noted that the term "test adaptation" has replaced the term "test translation" to emphasize the need to adapt a test to the culture of the examinee. This alternative, however, in clinical situations is very problematic (Damico, 1991; Geisinger, 1994, 1998; Oller, 1983). Among the problems in using test adaptations are several questionable assumptions—to wit, the content of an English-language intelligence test can be translated into the target language (in the case of Mexican American students, Spanish) with relative ease, is culturally relevant, and of similar difficulty (Geisinger, 1994). Furthermore, research on the reliability and validity of test adaptations is sorely lacking with most tests. This is not to say, however, that *no* research has been undertaken utilizing test adaptations with Mexican American ELLs. Valencia and Rankin's (1985) exploratory content bias investigation of the McCarthy Scales of Children's Abilities (MSCA) (McCarthy, 1972) is one such example (see Valencia and Rankin, 1985, App. A, in the previous section on cultural bias). After identifying the language status of the participants by means of several indirect measures, Valencia and Rankin measured 142 English- and 162 Spanish-speaking preschool Mexican American children's performance using a carefully translated version of the MSCA for the Spanish-speaking group. The authors reported that of the 23 items on the MSCA in which content bias was observed, most were biased against Spanish-speaking children, with the majority of these in subtests that measured serial-order, short-term memory. Valencia and Rankin reported no bias on the MSCA items that measured *more complex abilities* (e.g., conceptual grouping). The authors offered a linguistic hypothesis (i.e., word-length effect; acoustic similarity) to explain the Spanish-speaking children's differential performance on the simple memory items. This study by Valencia and Rankin illustrates the subtleties of test translation in examining the alleged "equivalence" of Spanish tests translated from English. The authors recommend further research in this area of test adaptation. They do not, however, recommend using their translation of the MSCA for clinical purposes.

We are not advocating that research of test adaptations as an alternative to English-language intelligence testing be abandoned. We do believe there is a right way and wrong way in the construction and clinical use of test adaptations. Adaptations that are developed by individual practitioners in an ad-hoc, informal manner *in situ* violate the standardization of the instrument being translated, have no evidence of the test's psychometric integrity, and constitute a serious violation of professional ethics, and quite possibly, the civil rights of the examinee. Such practices are clearly the wrong way to develop or use a test adaptation. Fortunately, there is right way that a test can be successfully translated for clinical use. Geisinger (1994) recommends a set of procedures for test adaptation. Some examples of these recommendations include: (a) the use of back-translations to adjust items for cultural and linguistic equivalence, (b) developing pilot testing to examine item difficulties and differential item functioning, and (c) developing representative norms for the translated test (also, see Sandoval and Durán, 1998, for a fuller discussion of these procedures). This approach is tantamount to developing a completely new test, a proposition we strongly endorse.

Related to the psychometric integrity of newly developed standardized Spanish-language intelligence tests is the issue of appropriate norms of these standardized instruments for Mexican American ELL students. Of the two Spanish-language intelligence tests previously mentioned, critics have noted that *none* of these tests were normed on bilingual or Mexican American ELLs (and other Latinos) *in the U.S.* (Sandoval and Durán, 1998). This critique is not completely accurate, as one test does include Mexican American ELLs in the norming sample—the BVAT. There are three issues, however, that must be addressed concerning the development of the BVAT. First, the test manual states that the development of the BVAT included the use of expert native speakers and back translation methods (Muñoz-Sandoval *et al.*, 1998b). No mention is made, however, of how the test developers accounted for the variety and complexity of language use in very different linguistic and cultural communities within the broader U.S. Latino population (e.g., Mexican Americans; Puerto Ricans). Second, the Spanish language norming sample of bilingual and ELL children, youths, and adults was not adequately described. The authors reported that Hispanics represent 7.7 percent of the norming sample. Hispanics represent, however, nearly 14 percent of the total U.S. population, the majority of which is Mexican American (U.S. Department of Commerce, Bureau of Census, 2000). Such undersampling constitutes a nonrepresentative sample of the target population, given that the BVAT was designed for use with bilingual and ELL populations. Third, the BVAT is described as "a standardized, wide age range, individually, administered procedure for measuring *bilingual verbal ability*" (Muñoz-Sandoval *et al.*, 1998b, p. 1). Although verbal ability is generally thought to be one facet of general intelligence, verbal ability represents only a narrow sliver of the construct. Thus, we can conclude that *the BVAT is not a measure of general intelligence*, but rather an instrument that measures several facets of cognitive ability—expressive and receptive language, and verbal reasoning.[27] These three issues illustrate a serious limitation with the use of the BVAT to estimate Mexican American (and other Latino) ELL children and youths' intellectual abilities.

The use of interpreters in the assessment process

An alternative for psychologists who do not speak Spanish when assessing the cognitive abilities of Mexican American ELLs is to use an interpreter in the assessment process. The use of interpreters, Figueroa (1990) noted, is also fraught with problems, such as dialectal differences between the child and interpreter, the interpreter's degree of proficiency across languages, and the interpreter's knowledge of cognitive and linguistic development, and experience with psychological assessment. Sandoval and Durán (1998) suggested that best practices recommend having a psychologist with proficiency in the first language (in the case of Mexican American ELLs, Spanish). We agree that a bilingual psychologist is ideal in the assessment of ELLs. However, a bilingual psychologist is a necessary, but not sufficient condition to ensure a nondiscriminatory assessment of ELLs. We will return to this later in this section. Sandoval and Durán are also careful to present potential problems with using interpreters, and note when an interpreter should not be used (see their chapter for a fuller discussion of these issues).

We agree with Sandoval and Durán's (1998) caveats, and would add that in the absence of a highly trained, psychometrically sophisticated, and culturally sensitive professional interpreter, the use of interpreters does *not* constitute best practices for assessing ELLs. Given the complexity of linguistic, cultural, educational, and cognitive variables, as well as the fact that the stakes for the Mexican American ELLs' educational future in a psychological assessment are exceptionally high, the use of interpreters for the sake of expediency is shortsighted and detrimental.

Alternatives to traditional assessment

It is clear that educational testing with Mexican American ELLs, as with any linguistically different child, is filled with challenges in obtaining valid and reliable results from standardized intelligence tests. We recognize that complications abound in the assessment of Mexican American ELLs' cognitive abilities. It is important to note, however, that such an assessment is not necessarily a daunting and ultimately futile task.

There are several prospects that suggest that Mexican American ELLs' cognitive abilities can be assessed in an appropriate, nondiscriminatory manner. First, while it is clear that language proficiency has a profound effect on Mexican Americans ELLs' performance on cognitive measures, *it is a mistake to assume that all such children cannot perform at normal levels on intelligence tests.* Valencia (1985b), in a review of research on the McCarthy Scales of Children's Abilities (MSCA), cited four different exploratory studies that examined Mexican American ELL children's performance on the MSCA (a carefully translated Spanish version of the MSCA was used; see Valencia and Rankin, 1985). Valencia (1985b) reported that Mexican American ELL children in the four investigations ($n = 302$; predominantly preschool age; low SES) performed at normative level (though depressed) on the Global Cognitive Index (GCI, an IQ analog that is additively formed from the Perceptual– Performance, Verbal, and Quantitative Scales), and at normative level (slightly above) on the Perceptual–Performance Scale of the MSCA.[28] Aggregating the data from the four studies and employing a weighted means analysis, Valencia (1985b) calculated the mean score for the Perceptual–Performance Scale and the GCI. For the Perceptual–Performance Scale, Valencia found that the Mexican American ELL children scored a mean of 51.8 (about onefifth standard deviation *above* the MSCA mean of 50). For the GCI, the children's mean was 92.7 (approximately one-half standard deviation *below* the GCI mean of 100). These results would particularly suggest that *nonverbal* measures of intelligence that are carefully adapted regarding administrative instructions offer some promise in assessing Mexican American ELLs.

The approach of assessing the cognitive abilities of Mexican American ELLs using *nonverbal* measures of intelligence must, however, include a brief discussion of three caveats. Harris *et al.* (1996) provided a comprehensive review of issues surrounding the use of nonverbal measures to estimate intelligence. First, Harris *et al.* (1996) commented that nonverbal measures limit the range of abilities sampled. Given the guidelines by professional standards to utilize a *wide range* of abilities in assessing ELL children's abilities (American Educational Research Association *et al.*, 1999), this caveat is of prime importance. Best practices suggest using *multiple data sources* to help obtain as full a picture as possible when formal verbal measures are inadvisable or unobtainable (Harris *et al.*, 1996). A second caveat is that nonverbal tests are not necessarily "language-free." Although nonverbal measures do not require verbal responses from examinees, some tasks such as sequencing pictures (e.g., K-ABC Photo Series; WISC-III Picture Arrangement) presuppose some use of language. This type of verbal mediation, called "inner speech," may allow children to utilize their native language to "talk" their way through nonverbal tasks; this language skill may not, however, be developed in children unaccustomed to using language in such a manner. A third precaution Harris *et al.* (1996) noted is that nonverbal tests are not "culture-free." One cannot assume that having access to materials and games that involve, for example, geometric figures, mazes, puzzles, or block designs are universal to all children. Children may vary considerably in their exposure to experiences with such tasks.

Recommendations for nondiscriminatory practices and further research

Despite (a) the paucity of psychometric evidence with Spanish-language intelligence tests for Mexican American ELLs, (b) the limitations of adapting intelligence tests, (c) the problems with using interpreters, and (d) caveats in using nonverbal measures, there are procedures that can help minimize bias in the assessment process. Holtzman and Wilkinson (1991) recommended using a dual language assessment model to minimize bias and inappropriate interpretation of test results. The dual language model incorporates data in both the first language and English, where appropriate, in order to determine if observed deficits in English are the result of typical delays due to the language acquisition process or indicative of true cognitive deficits. This model does not, however, obviate the need for developing Spanish-language intelligence tests that are appropriately normed, and have good evidence of psychometric integrity.

Implicit within the dual language model is the need for the assessor to demonstrate proficiency in the child's first language. As we have previously discussed, interpreters seldom provide the most equitable or reliable solution. Best practices recommend that a psychologist has knowledge of the child's cultural background and proficiency in the child's language to be qualified to assess the child's abilities. However, cultural awareness and proficiency in the first language alone may not be sufficient. Psychologists must also have training in second language acquisition and bilingual education in order to understand the complexities of the ELLs' linguistic and cognitive development, the relation between the two, and the appropriate intervention needs of the child (e.g., placement in a bilingual education classroom).

Regards to the newer nonverbal measures, such as the Universal Nonverbal Intelligence Test (UNIT; Bracken and McCallum, 1998), they may offer some promise in the assessment of Mexican American ELLs. The UNIT, which includes ELL children in its norms and utilizes pantomimed directions, measures a broad range of memory and reasoning processes, and appears to demonstrate good psychometric integrity (see Valencia and Suzuki, 2001, for a fuller review). Finally, further validity and reliability research on the most current Spanish-language intelligence tests is essential in establishing an empirically grounded knowledge base. Most importantly, research must include examining potential cultural bias on these tests with Mexican American ELL participants.

Underrepresentation of Chicanos in gifted/talented programs

In Chapter 1 of the present book, Valencia discusses 15 schooling conditions and outcomes faced by many Chicanos in the nation's public schools. In this section, we elaborate on one of those 15 conditions, namely the underrepresentation of Chicano children and youths in programs for the gifted and talented (hereafter referred to as the "gifted"). We find this a grave state of affairs, as it points to a major incongruity: *Given that Chicano students comprise a substantial portion of the school-age population, why are so few Chicanos (compared to their White peers) identified and placed in gifted programs?* Bernal (1979) noted over 20 years ago that "The juxtaposition of minority and gifted still produces cognitive dissonance in the minds of many educators" (p. 395)—that is, when a person comes across a *gifted minority* student, this reality sometimes creates psychological tension or discomfort. The existence of a *gifted minority* student challenges one's deeply held belief that such students are not supposed to exist. In the minds of many educators the idea of a *gifted minority* student seems to be an incredible, if not impossible notion, thus creating cognitive tension for the educator. At the end of this section, we offer a thought on how such mental dissonance can be rectified.

In this section, we examine three areas of concern regarding the underrepresentation of Chicanos in gifted programs. First, we discuss incidence rates of gifted Chicanos at national, state, regional, district, and school levels to illustrate the extent to which they are under-represented in gifted programs. Second, we provide a historical sketch of the research base on giftedness, focusing on how gifted Chicanos (and other racial/ethnic minorities such as African Americans and American Indians) have become to be known as the "neglected of the neglected" (Valencia and Suzuki, 2001, p. 209). Finally, we discuss research findings and best-case practices that hold promise for improving the identification and placement of Chicanos in gifted programs.

Underrepresentation of gifted Chicanos

In Chapter 1, Valencia presents underrepresentation data of gifted Chicano/Latino students for the five Southwestern states (Arizona; California; Colorado; New Mexico; Texas), based on the 1998 U.S. Department of Education, Office for Civil Rights (2001) national survey on gifted K-12 students by race/ethnicity. These disparities demonstrate a clear pattern of underrepresentation for Chicanos, and overrepresentation for White students (Valencia, Chapter 1, Table 1.4, present book). Valencia also notes that for Chicanos/Latinos, this underrepresentation pattern holds not only for the Southwest, but also for 49 of the 50 states (see Valencia, Chapter 1, present volume, for a fuller discussion; also, see Valencia and Suzuki [2001] for a comprehensive disparity analysis of gifted students by race/ethnicity for the top ten states in combined minority enrollment).

For this section, we examine incidence data from the two largest districts in each of the five Southwestern states to ascertain whether these broad national and regional underrepresentation patterns hold on a more localized level. We calculated disparities for each racial/ethnic group based on the Office for Civil Rights (OCR) data (U.S. Department of Education, Office for Civil Rights, 2001) in the same manner as Valencia did in Chapter 1, present book. Table 9.4 presents these disparities, showing discernible patterns across the ten districts for Hispanics and other racial/ethnic groups. For Hispanic students (overwhelmingly Chicanos), they are *underrepresented* in each of the ten districts, ranging from a high underrepresentation rate (77.0 percent) in Scottsdale (Arizona) Unified School District, to a low underrepresentation rate (19.3 percent) in Dallas (Texas) Independent School District. White students are *overrepresented* in all ten districts, ranging from an exceptionally high overrepresentation rate of 272.5 percent in Houston (Texas) Independent School District to a low overrepresentation rate (2.8 percent) in Jefferson County (Colorado) Public Schools.[29]

Another type of disparity analysis involves an examination at the school-by-school level within a single district. Using the 1998 OCR data (U.S. Department of Education, Office for Civil Rights, 2001), we investigated the Austin Independent School District (AISD) as a case in point. For our analysis, we compared the ten schools with the highest percentages of gifted students enrolled, to the ten schools with the lowest percentages of such students. These data are shown in Table 9.5. The pattern of percentages for gifted students is highly discernible. Students attending high-enrollment White schools (i.e., 70 percent or greater

White students) are far more likely to be identified as gifted than are students who attend high-enrollment minority schools (i.e., 70 percent or greater combined minority students). For the top ten schools (eight of which are predominantly White), 878 of the 6,644 students were identified as gifted—an incidence rate of 13.2 percent. By sharp contrast, of the 6,136 students enrolled in the bottom ten schools in percentage of gifted students (all ten were predominantly minority enrollment), only a scant 100 students were identified as gifted, a paltry 1.6 percent incidence rate. Although AISD's high-enrollment minority schools identified more gifted students in 1998 ($n = 100$) in the bottom ten schools than in 1994 ($n = 18$; see Valencia and Suzuki, 2001, p. 223, Table 8.4), students in high-enrollment minority schools are still considerably less likely to be identified as gifted. The patterns seen in our Table 9.5 are very congruent with the analysis presented in Valencia and Suzuki (2001, p. 233, Table 8.4) of AISD schools in 1994 (based on data from the U.S. Department of Education, Office for Civil Rights, 1998), indicating that these authors' concerns remain germane today:

> First, why are so few students in predominantly minority schools in the AISD identified as gifted/talented? Second, why are some predominantly minority schools in the AISD (e.g., Maplewood [in the top ten in both 1994 and 1998 in the identification of the gifted]) more successful in identifying gifted/talented students than are other very high-minority enrollment schools . . . [e.g., Norman, which was in the bottom ten in 1994 and 1998 in the identification of the gifted]? Intensive research is needed to see whether the pattern of disparities in the AISD also holds for other multiracial/ethnic districts in Texas.
>
> (p. 233)

Underrepresentation of gifted Chicanos and other minorities: a historical sketch of the research base

As the previous data demonstrate, Chicanos and other minorities are considerably underrepresented in gifted programs nationwide. Such lack of attention and efforts by school personnel in identifying a greater number of gifted minorities is also seen in the very limited attention by *researchers* in the study of gifted children and youths of color. It is important to underscore, however, that the study of the *general* gifted child and youth population has been historically an underresearched area, and furthermore this group has been educationally underserved—truly a neglected sector of our society.

Valencia and Suzuki (2001) provided a historical overview of giftedness in the U.S., with a focus on how minority students have fit in. The authors' time frame is from the early 20th century to the contemporary period. In addition to their own literature review, Valencia and Suzuki identified four reviews—Albert (1969), Ford and Harris (1990), Henry (1924), and Tannenbaum (1983)—that examined the prevalence of research on giftedness and minorities in the psychological and educational literature bases. In their synthesis of these literature reviews, Valencia and Suzuki reported a consistent historical pattern of underrepresentation of minorities in research on the gifted. This finding, however, needs to be placed within the broader context. Since the 1920s, the amount of research concerning the *general field* of giftedness has been, and continues to be, relatively small compared to the total number of citations in the psychological and educational literature. This research base, however, shrinks significantly when delimited to those citations that include racial/ethnic minority students (see Valencia and Suzuki [2001] for a fuller discussion). Given the lack of research on giftedness in general, and the persistent, minimal attention given to gifted

Table 9.4 Disparity analysis for gifted/talented in largest two districts in each of the five southwestern states (K-12): 1998

State	White			Hispanic			African American			Asian/Pacific Islander			American Indian		
	Enroll-ment[a] (%)	Gifted/talented[b] (%)	Dis-parity[c] (%)	Enroll-ment (%)	Gifted/talented (%)	Dis-parity (%)	Enroll-ment (%)	Gifted/talented (%)	Dis-parity (%)	Enroll-ment (%)	Gifted/talented (%)	Dis-parity (%)	Enroll-ment (%)	Gifted/talented (%)	Dis-parity (%)
Arizona															
Tucson USD (N = 65,599)	43.7	57.0	+30.6	43.1	30.3	−29.6	6.8	4.6	−33.0	2.4	5.4	+122.6	1.1	2.7	+155.1
Scottsdale USD (N = 26,622)	86.3	93.5	+8.4	8.3	1.9	−77.0	1.8	0.8	−54.4	2.7	3.6	+34.8	0.9	0.1	−89.1
California															
Los Angeles USD (N = 735,317)	10.7	28.7	+167.4	68.8	41.7	−39.3	14.0	9.2	−34.3	6.2	20.0	+220.7	0.3	0.5	+60.7
San Diego USD (N = 138,074)	28.2	44.7	+58.4	36.2	20.0	−44.8	16.6	8.6	−47.9	18.3	25.7	+40.5	0.6	0.9	+42.2
Colorado															
Jefferson CPS (N = 87,591)	84.7	87.1	+2.8	10.2	6.5	−36.3	1.3	0.7	−46.2	3.1	5.2	+67.7	0.8	0.5	−37.5
Denver CPS (N = 65,725)	27.5	45.0	+83.5	49.4	32.4	−34.4	21.3	16.4	−22.6	3.4	4.8	+41.2	1.4	1.1	−19.6

New Mexico														
Albuquerque PS (N = 84,467)	42.3	71.1	+68.2	47.8	21.5	−55.0	3.8	1.5	−59.5	2.0	1.9	−2.0	4.2	3.9	−6.5
Las Cruces PS (N = 21,839)	34.3	63.7	+85.7	61.1	26.0	−57.5	2.1	1.1	−47.2	1.8	8.9	+403.4	0.7	0.3	−53.5
Texas														
Houston ISD (N = 210,472)	10.3	38.4	+272.5	53.0	26.8	−49.5	33.8	25.1	−25.7	2.8	9.5	+241.7	0.1	0.1	+116.7
Dallas ISD (N = 159,732)	9.2	14.9	+62.1	49.4	39.9	−19.3	39.4	42.0	+6.8	1.6	2.7	+71.1	0.4	0.5	+4.7

Source: U.S. Department of Education, Office for Civil Rights (2001).

Note

N = Total district enrollment; USD = Unified School District; CPS = County Public Schools; PS = Public Schools; ISD = Independent School District. [a] Percentage enrollment = Percentage of racial/ethnic group in total K-12 enrollment. [b] Percentage gifted/talented = Percentage of racial/ethnic group in gifted/talented category. [c] In the percentage disparity category, a plus sign (+) indicates overrepresentation percentage and a minus sign (−) indicates underrepresentation percentage.

Table 9.5 Disparity analysis for gifted/talented in Austin Independent School District elementary schools: 1998

School	Number of students	Number of gifted/ talented students	Gifted/talented students (%)	Minority enrollment in school (%)
1. Casis	733	146	19.9	22.5
2. Barton Hills	421	81	19.2	23.8
3. Patton	849	137	16.1	26.1
4. Maplewood	359	45	12.5	73.8
5. Davis	716	85	11.9	23.7
6. Zilker	402	46	11.4	46.5
7. Kiker	1,149	125	10.9	23.1
8. Hill	802	86	10.7	19.0
9. Lee	396	42	10.6	20.7
10. Oak Hill	817	85	10.4	23.3
Total:	6,644	878	13.2	
1. Linder	602	15	2.5	85.4
2. Andrews	716	17	2.4	95.9
3. Galindo	654	14	2.1	84.3
4. Govalle	502	10	2.0	98.4
5. Houston	921	17	1.8	94.0
6. Odom	688	12	1.7	70.5
7. Brown	503	7	1.4	90.9
8. Oak Springs	323	4	1.2	98.8
9. Norman	453	2	0.4	97.4
10. Harris	774	2	0.3	95.7
Total:	6,136	100	1.6	

Source: U.S. Department of Education, Office for Civil Rights (2001).

racial/ethnic minority children—as illustrated by the reviews of Albert, Ford and Harris, Henry, Tannenbaum, and Valencia and Suzuki—it is reasonable to conclude that gifted minority children are, in the words of Valencia and Suzuki, the "neglected of the neglected" (p. 216).

Given that gifted minority students are the "neglected of the neglected," then gifted minority ELLs are the "neglected of the neglected of the neglected." To study our supposition, we investigated the scope of literature pertaining to gifted minority ELLs, by performing an electronic search similar to that undertaken by Valencia and Suzuki (2001) (their search was performed in July, 1999). Utilizing the *Current Index to Journals in Education* (*CIJE*) and *Psychological Abstracts* (*PA*) databases, we first identified all references on the gifted by using the same descriptors as Valencia and Suzuki (2001, p. 209). As of March, 2001, we found 5,137 citations in the *CIJE* database, and 2,640 citations in the *PA* database. When the search was delimited to the following descriptors: "bilingual," "limited English proficient," and "English as a Second Language," the number of citations was significantly reduced. In the *CIJE*, only 51 (1 percent) of the total 5,137 citations were identified as pertaining to gifted ELLs; in *PA*, only seven (0.3 percent) of 2,640 citations were identified.

Another way to illustrate the severe neglect of the ELL gifted population is to examine disparities between the percentage of identified ELLs, compared to their percentage in the gifted population. As examples, we investigated 1998 OCR data for two cities, El Paso, Texas and Denver, Colorado (U.S. Department of Education, Office for Civil Rights, 2001).

In 1998, 31.5 percent of the El Paso Independent School District's total enrollment was classified as ELL; the percentage of ELLs in gifted programs, however, was only 6.8 percent, a disparity of 78.4 percent underrepresentation. For Denver County Schools, ELLs accounted for 21.9 percent of the district's total enrollment, but were only 5.9 percent of the gifted population—a disparity of 73.1 percent underrepresentation. Given the large percentage of ELLs in these districts, it is important to investigate how ELLs have become the neglected of the neglected of the neglected. Although gifted Mexican American ELLs can be and are identified (as in the above discussion of EL Paso and Denver schools), it is likely that genuine efforts to identify the gifted among these children and youths are not undertaken until *after* they are deemed proficient in English. However, requiring a student to be proficient in English as a condition of giftedness is problematic, as it ignores the important point made by Barkan and Bernal (1991): "One does not have to be fluent in English to be intelligent" (p. 144).

Why is there such heavy emphasis on English proficiency in the identification of the gifted? It is likely that this near exclusive use of English in identifying giftedness is the legacy of the godfather of the giftedness and intelligence testing movements in the U.S., Lewis Madison Terman. Terman's (1925) landmark study of "genius" utilized a number of procedures to identify gifted children that are still in use to today, including *English*-language intelligence tests. Regarding gifted racial/ethnic minority students, the results of Terman's groundbreaking study were incredulous. As discussed by Valencia and Suzuki (2001), of the 168,000 children tested in California, 643 children were identified as gifted from Terman's main group. Of these, only seven (1.1 percent) minority children were identified as gifted—including one Mexican American child (see Valencia and Suzuki, 2001, pp. 213–215 for a fuller discussion).

Another Termanian legacy is the IQ model of giftedness, a paradigm that has held enormous sway in the identification of the gifted. Traditionally, giftedness has been conceptualized as superior performance on an intelligence test—typically two standard deviations or greater above the normative mean. Given the average low performance of Chicanos (and other racial/ethnic groups) on verbally loaded intelligence tests, and the exclusive use of English-language tests, it is little wonder that so few Chicano children and youths (English-speaking and ELLs alike) have been identified as gifted. This does not necessarily have to be the case, as many alternative conceptions of giftedness that emphasize inclusiveness exist (see Sternberg and Davidson [1986], *Conceptions of Giftedness*, for an excellent treatise on a number of competing models of giftedness; also, see Valencia and Suzuki, 2001, Chapter 8, for an overview of some of these models).

Identifying gifted Chicano students: some innovative strategies

Although the current condition of gifted Chicano students seems bleak, there is certainly room for optimism. Research does exist that examines innovative ways to increase the number of Chicanos (and other underrepresented racial/ethnic minorities) identified and placed in gifted programs. Even within the traditional IQ model of giftedness, research has demonstrated that some Chicanos *do* perform at *superior* levels on traditional intelligence tests. For example, Ortiz and Volloff (1987) reported that traditional intelligence tests were quite effective in identifying migrant Chicano children for gifted programs.

Research has also examined alternatives to the traditional methods of intelligence test scores and teacher nominations for identifying gifted Chicanos. These alternatives include, for example, behavioral rating scales, pluralistic assessment, parental nomination/education, and, in the case of Chicano ELLs, linking bilingual and gifted education programs (see

Valencia and Suzuki, 2001). Regarding behavioral rating scales, Elliott *et al.* (1986), as a case in point, reported that such scales offer some promise in identifying gifted Chicano students. By providing more standardized, "objective" methods for rating behaviors considered to indicate giftedness, behavioral scales might improve teachers' ability to recognize giftedness in White and minority children alike (Argulewicz and Kush, 1984).

Pluralistic assessment, such as used in the System of Multicultural Pluralistic Assessment (SOMPA; Mercer and Lewis, 1979), offers another alternative to traditional assessment procedures for giftedness. The SOMPA is a culture-bound model of assessment, in which Mexican American examinees, for example, are only compared to the Mexican American norm group. The SOMPA incorporates the WISC-R into its model, but utilizes an "Estimated Learning Potential" that is used to adjust the conventional WISC-R Full Scale IQ by taking into account a number of factors (i.e., health history, family sociocultural background, and adaptive behavior) that might affect racial/ethnic minority students' performance on the WISC-R. Although it has received heavy criticism from researchers,[30] the SOMPA has demonstrated that gifted Chicano and other minority students can be identified in greater proportions than when traditional measures are used (Matthew *et al.*, 1992; Mercer, 1977).

Parent nomination/education has also been touted as a promising tool in increasing the number of gifted and talented racial/ethnic minority students. Scott *et al.* (1992) found that parents from White, African American, and Hispanic families (Cuban American, it appears) all viewed giftedness in their children in a similar manner, but the African American and Hispanic parents were less likely to actually nominate their children. Scott *et al.* assert that an increased number of gifted minority children might be identified more readily if public school programs were more assertive in educating parents about the availability of such programs and the characteristics of gifted children.[31]

Still yet another example of ways to increase the number of gifted Chicanos are innovative programs such as seen in the San Diego (California) school system. These programs have shown that gifted Latino ELLs can be better identified and served by teachers who are certified in both bilingual *and* gifted education. The results of such dual certification have greatly increased the number of Latino students enrolled in gifted classes (see U.S. Department of Education, Office of Educational Research and Improvement [1998] for a fuller discussion; also, see Valencia and Suzuki [2001], Chapter 8, for a brief discussion).

In sum, although there are major obstacles in the identification of gifted Chicano students, we have seen some bright spots in the existing literature.[32] A number of publications have identified, through empirical findings and discourse, specific best-case practices that can lead to an increase in the number of gifted minority students. Frasier's (1989) discussion on best practices is a good example. Although her focus is on African American students, we believe that her points can be generalized to Chicanos and other students of color. Based on her extensive review of the literature on identification procedures, Frasier offered the following principles of identification that are derived from research and practice:

1   The focus should be on the diversity within gifted populations.
2   The goal should be inclusion, rather than exclusion, of students.
3   Data should be gathered from multiple sources; a single criterion of giftedness should be avoided.
4   Both objective and subjective data should be collected.
5   Professionals and nonprofessionals who represent various areas of expertise and who are knowledgeable about behavioral indicators of giftedness should be involved.

6   Identification of giftedness should occur as early as possible, should consist of a series of steps, and should be continuous.

7   Special attention should be given to the different ways in which children from different cultures manifest behavioral indicators of giftedness.

8   Decisionmaking should be delayed until all pertinent data on a student have been reviewed.

9   Data collected during the identification process should be used in determining curriculum.

(p. 214)

On a final note, we return to the "cognitive dissonance" assertion (Bernal, 1979) that we used to open this section on the underrepresentation of gifted Chicanos. We contend that this discordant frame of mind is likely the root problem of the nagging underrepresentation rates of Chicanos and other minority students in gifted programs. It appears that in order to begin the rectification of this pervasive underrepresentation, there needs to be a collective and resounding affirmation by educators that gifted students of color do exist, and they need to be vigorously identified. Embracing the "principle of affirmation" is the first step in the remediation of a long-standing problem.

Adverse impact of high-stakes testing on Chicano students

In Chapter 1 of the current volume, Valencia introduces the issue of high-stakes testing. Here, we elaborate on this major testing concern, concentrating on how some Chicano students have been, are currently being, and soon will be adversely impacted. Our focus is on high-stakes tests used to make decisions about (a) high school diploma award/denial, and (b) grade promotion/retention. Given that Texas is a leader in high-stakes testing, and in light of the large and growing Chicano public school population in the state, we examine Texas as a case in point in which high-stakes testing is adversely affecting these students. We close this section by presenting several suggestions that could lead toward a more equitable system of accountability.

The current standards-based school reform movement—in which educators and students are held accountable for reaching specific benchmarks (e.g., minimum test scores by students)—has its roots in the 1983, *A Nation at Risk* (National Commission on Excellence in Education, 1983). Standards-based school reform is sweeping across K-12 public education in the U.S., affecting millions of school children and youths. "Accountability"—the movement's mantra—is being driven by high-stakes testing, a form of testing in which test results hold important consequences for students, their parents and teachers, schools, districts, and administrators. As of 2000, there were 27 states that had, or will soon have, exit-level tests that all students must pass to graduate from high school (American Federation of Teachers, 2000).[33] Regarding the use of state-mandated tests to determine if a student should be promoted at certain grades, as of 1999 there were 16 states plus the District of Columbia that use, or will soon use tests, as promotional gatekeepers (American Federation of Teachers, 1999; Heubert and Hauser, 1999).[34]

The adverse impact of high-stakes testing on Chicano youths regarding high school diploma denial is clearly seen in Texas.[35] At center stage is the Texas Assessment of Academic Skills (TAAS) test, the cornerstone of Texas' presumptive accountability system. TAAS is administered annually to students in grades 3 to 8 and 10. Here, we primarily concern ourselves with the 10th-grade, exit-level TAAS test (consisting of reading, mathematics, and writing subtests) that high school students are required to pass (eight attempts allowed) in order to earn a diploma. Of course, students must also meet other requirements to graduate (e.g., take the required courses).

Since the 1993–1994 academic year, state data have been available on the TAAS exit-level test pass rates by a category called "economically disadvantaged" and by five categories of race/ethnicity. These data on race/ethnicity have demonstrated a pervasive and unwavering pattern: Mexican American and African American students—compared to their White peers—have significantly higher rates of failing the TAAS exit-level test. This is the case for initial, cumulative, and final test administrations (see Fassold, 2000). These profound between-racial/ethnic differences in TAAS exit-level pass rates, and the resultant dispro-portionate denial of high school diplomas to minority youths, recently prompted a group of nine Mexican American and African American students (along with two Mexican American organizations) to file a lawsuit against the State of Texas. The Mexican American Legal Defense and Educational Fund (MALDEF) filed the case.

The trial of *GI Forum et al. v. Texas Education Agency et al.* (2000) began on September 20, 1999, and ended on October 21, 1999, with closing arguments held on October 25, 1999.[36] The bench trial was held in the United States District Court for the Western Division of Texas (San Antonio Division); Judge Edward C. Prado presided. The *GI Forum* lawsuit is considered by many observers to be one of the most important legal cases in educational history involving testing (see Valencia and Bernal [2000a], for a special publica-tion devoted to the case).[37]

Witnesses and experts for the plaintiffs in *GI Forum* brought to bear rich, credible, and convincing expert reports, testimony, and analyses on the issue of adverse impact on Chicano and African American students (see: Bernal, 2000, Bernal and Valencia, 2000; Fassold, 2000; McNeil, 2000; Saucedo, 2000; Valencia, 2000b; Valencia and Bernal, 2000b; Valencia and Bernal, 2000c; Valenzuela, 2000). One aspect of the *GI Forum* case that is particularly germane to the present book is the assertion that current Chicano school failure in Texas, as well as school failure of African Americans, is strongly linked to long-standing systemic inequalities and limited opportunities to learn. The defendants and their experts in the *GI Forum* case argued, however, that historical discrimination was irrelevant to the case (see Saucedo [2000] and Valencia [2000b] for discussions of this assertion by the State). By sharp contrast, Valencia (2000b)—an expert for the plaintiffs—presented testimony that the State's position was faulty and indefensible. Linearly, Valencia's argument went as follows:

1 Many African American and Mexican American students (particularly from a low-socioeconomic status background) currently face various forms of schooling inequalities (e.g., segregation) in Texas public K-12 schools.

2 These contemporary inequalities are not vestiges of past discrimination. Rather, they are part of a historical pattern that is continually being reproduced.

3 Existing schooling inequalities lead to diminished opportunities to learn the content on TAAS.

4 The lower TAAS performance of African American and Mexican American students is primarily due to differences in opportunity to learn.

5 The TAAS exit-level test is being used unfairly because it places Mexican American and African American students in a double bind. Testing these students on what they have not been taught and then making crucial decisions (i.e., denial of a diploma) on the basis of their TAAS performance (failure in the case of the student plaintiffs) is a blatant form of discrimination.

(p. 446)

Unfortunately for the plaintiffs, the State was successful in persuading the court to issue a motion in which it clarified the court's summary judgment order regarding past discrimination. Saucedo (2000), co-counsel for MALDEF, commented that the motion effectively limited the plaintiffs' ability to introduce evidence of this history. The court ruled that plaintiffs would be allowed to produce evidence of discrimination that existed at the time of TAAS implementation, but that would have to take the form of a "snapshot" rather than of a historical narrative. On this confinement of testimony, Valencia noted: "With all due respect to Judge Prado, historical discrimination in Texas schools (even in 1990 when TAAS was implemented) cannot be viewed as a snapshot. The true picture of such discrimination would constitute numerous reels of film" (p. 446). Saucedo concluded that the court's inclination not to relate historical discrimination in Texas to contemporary racial/ethnic differences in TAAS exit-level performance strengthened the State's position that there was no connection between past discrimination and the current fact that Mexican American and African American students perform considerably lower than their White peers on the TAAS.

The ruling in the *GI Forum* trial was truly disappointing and disheartening for plaintiffs, as Judge Prado ruled in favor of the State—though he found TAAS to result in adverse impact on plaintiffs. Fassold, an expert for the plaintiffs, succinctly captured this somberness:

> At the beginning of his order, Judge Prado stated: "The test cannot be fair if it is used to punish minorities who have been victimized by state-funded unequal educations" (*GI Forum et al. v. Texas Education Agency et al.*, 2000, p. 670). By finding that the TAAS results in a disparate impact on minorities, Judge Prado found that the TAAS does indeed "punish minorities." Without relying on plaintiffs' voluminous record of educational inequality, Judge Prado cited a defense expert to support the court's finding that "Texas minority students have been, and to some extent continue to be, the victims of educational inequality" (*GI Forum et al. v. Texas Education Agency et al.*, p. 675). How does one reconcile the court's initial principle and subsequent findings? Presumably, Judge Prado did such by stating: "Implementation of the TAAS . . . helps address the effects of any prior discrimination and remaining inequities in the system" (*GI Forum et al. v. Texas Education Agency et al.*, p. 674). From the four corners of the order, support for this proposition is sparse. Nevertheless, any future challenge to a graduation exam will have to address Judge Prado's argument and substantiate counter-arguments. How does one assert that school accountability helps minorities when the above analysis demonstrates that the method of school accountability actually exacerbated the school quality educational inequity between minority and White campuses? Does a graduation exam exacerbate inequities by encouraging various ethnic groups to disproportionately dropout of school and thereby impose an inferior socioeconomic status on the children and future students of those dropouts?
>
> In the end, although Judge Prado ruled for the State, he did find that TAAS exit-level test did result in disparate impact against African American and Mexican American students. To plaintiffs, this is a mixed ruling. It acknowledges their plight, but at the same time, allows the State's inequitable accountability system to prevail.
>
> (pp. 477–478)

The second type of adverse impact of high-stakes testing on Chicano students has to do with the use of state-mandated tests to control promotion to the next grade. In Chapter 1 of the present book, Valencia introduces the long-standing and controversial practice of retaining students who are deemed to not have the requisite skills and knowledge to be promoted to the next grade. As Valencia (Chapter 1) discusses, the extant literature over-whelmingly concludes that retention is not as effective as promotion (with intervention) in improving a student's academic performance. That is, retained students—compared to their non-retained peers, often experience school failure. To understand the adverse impact of high-stakes tests used as promotional gatekeepers, we turn once again to Texas as a case in point.

Following on the heels of the first wave of standards-based school reform in Texas—that is, the TAAS exit-level exam's use as a major factor in high school diploma award or denial—is Senate Bill 4 (SB 4). The origins of SB 4 stem from Gov. George W. Bush's 1998 re-election bid in which he launched "a get-tough pledge to make it harder for public school students to advance to the next grade before mastering basic skills" (Johnston, 1998, p. 1). During his campaign, he addressed the TEA at the 1998 Midwinter Conference on his views and plans about ending social promotion:

> The defenders of the status quo are alarmed. I recently saw a headline that read: Thousands of students would fail under Bush plan. With all due respect to the headline writer, it should have read: Tens of thousands are failing today and Gov. Bush has a plan to save them. . . . Social promotion creates false hopes, fuels the dropout rate, and destroys the dreams of too many Texas children. Social promotion undermines the integrity of our entire education system, because it pushes students from grade to grade even though they are not prepared to do the work—it hides the reason for their failures: poor reading skills. . . . The voices of the status quo will say, let's continue to ignore the problem. I say, let's fix it. Let's heed the reading research that says the window of opportunity is grades K through 3. Let's put our hearts and our souls into teaching programs that work. And let's fix reading problems so every child has the building block skills to succeed. . . . My plan says a child who does not pass the reading portion of the TAAS in the third grade must receive appropriate intervention and instruction before moving to regular classes in the fourth grade.
>
> (Bush, 1998, pp. 1–3)

After sailing through the Senate and House of the Texas legislature, the anti-social pro-motion bill (SB 4) was signed into law by Gov. Bush on June 8, 1999. The new state law, described in Texas Education Code §28.0211, has promotion requirements for the kinder-garten class of 1999–2000 and later cohorts (which we focus on here). The key elements of SB 4 are as follows:

- A *reading* test (English or Spanish version) will be administered to all third graders beginning in the 2002–2003 school year.
- The phasing in of two more promotional gates for the 2002–2003 cohort will be as follows:
  —fifth grade (2004–2005), *reading and mathematics* tests (English or Spanish version);
  —eighth grade (2007–2008), *reading and mathematics* (English version).
- A student who initially fails to perform satisfactorily on the designated test will be given two additional opportunities to take the assessment instrument. If a student fails a second time, a "grade placement" committee will be formed consisting of the principal (or principal's designee), the student's parent or guardian, and the teacher of the subject of an instrument on which the student failed. If the student fails a third time, he/she will be retained at the same grade level.

- Each time a student fails the test he/she will be provided "accelerated instruction" in the applicable subject area (such instruction is decided by the grade placement committee).
- The student's parent or guardian may appeal the retention decision to the grade placement committee.
- All of the above applies to students who are limited-English proficient or are in special education.
- The law would stay in force only if there is sufficient state money to fund the program every year.

There is a growing concern among critics of high-stakes testing, experts on minority education, and civil rights organizations that SB 4 will create serious problems for Chicano/Latino and African American students in Texas public schools. Given that many of these minority students—compared to their White peers—already experience higher grade retention and dropout rates, an important question needs to be raised: *Will failing the designated achievement tests at the promotional gates (grades 3, 5, and 8) and being subsequently retained exacerbate these students' chances of acquiring a comparably successful education—particularly earning the number of required credits for the completion of high school?* In light of all the available literature pointing to the association between retaining a student and his/her diminished achievement and progress (especially the increased probability of dropping out of school; see Valencia, 2000a), and in light of all the literature showing considerable school failure of many Chicano/Latino and African American students, will the effect of SB 4 (i.e., retention in some cases) have an adverse impact on these minority students?

Based on research by Valencia (2000a) and our own analyses here, this preceding question can be soundly answered in the affirmative. Retention rates for Chicano/Latino and African American students, compared to their White peers, are consistently higher, and these racial/ethnic differences have deep historical roots (see Valencia, Chapter 1, present book). For the most recent data (Texas Education Agency, 2000, p. 48, Table 4.2), the retention rates by race/ethnicity for the promotional gates at grades 3, 5, and 8 were, in 1998–1999, as follows:

Group	Grade 3	Grade 5	Grade 8
White	1.1%	0.6%	1.5%
Chicano/Latino	3.4%	1.1%	3.3%
African American	4.0%	1.1%	2.7%

In light of these *already* higher rates of grade retention (i.e., pre-SB 4) for Chicano/Latino and African American students, *plus* their higher rates of TAAS failure at grades 3, 5, and 8 (Texas Education Agency, 2000, p. 10, Table 1.10), we project that Texas' second wave of standards-based school reform—SB 4—will result in adverse impact on retention rates for Chicano/Latino and African American students, particularly those of low-SES background attending segregated schools (also, see Valencia's [2000a] comprehensive analysis). Given the strong association between grade retention and dropping out—and assuming the educational status quo remains unchanged in Texas schools—it is inevitable that the impact of SB 4 will result in an increased rate of dropouts among these minority students. Once again, we will very likely see the perverse effects of high-stakes testing on its most vulnerable populations in Texas public schools—Chicano/Latino and African American students.

In conclusion, standards-based school reform—in which high-stakes testing plays such a critical role—is disparately impacting the educational advancement of Chicanos and other students of color. The logic of having exit-level examinations for high school graduation and using tests to control grade promotion makes sense in a perfect world in which equal educational opportunity to learn abounds. Of course, this is not so. Furthermore, as noted by Valencia *et al.* (2001, p. 319), "standards-based school reform misses the mark. It is structurally misdirected because it treats the symptoms of school failure (e.g., poor achievement) rather than the cause (i.e., inferior schools)." On a final note, it is important to emphasize that one can be critical of the notion of accountability, yet agree that it is necessary for the public school system to have a system of accountability. We agree with Valencia *et al.* (2001, p. 321) who comment:

> We argue that accountability is vital to public education. However, it must be implemented with care. We need to shape our accountability system in accordance with principles such as (1) parents' involvement in their children's schoolwork, (2) the allowance for teachers not to be fettered to rote, unchallenging, and measurement-driven instruction, (3) comprehensive diagnostic testing, and (4) multiple indicators of academic performance.[38]

Improvement of educational testing of Chicano students

In this section, we offer a number of research and policy oriented ideas how educational testing might be improved to help promote school success for Chicano students. These suggestions cover concerns related to: (a) history of educational testing, (b) research on cultural bias in intelligence tests, (c) assessment of ELLs, (d) the gifted, (e) high-stakes testing, and (f) the use of multiple data sources in assessment.

History of educational testing

Any understanding of the current issues surrounding educational testing (particularly measures of observed intelligence) is heightened by having knowledge of historical developments, trends, and issues in this area (Valencia and Suzuki, 2001). Many contemporary concerns—e.g., test bias, test norming, overrepresentation in certain special education categories, underrepresentation in gifted programs, test abuse, neohereditarianism, and the assessment of ELLs—that are germane to Chicanos and other students of color, have historical roots and thus need to be understood and analyzed in that context. It is incumbent upon researchers and applied psychologists to know the history of educational testing because a number of issues they struggle with today regarding the assessment of minority students have roots in decades past. To understand the contemporary issues in regard to educational testing and students of color, one must have a good sense of the historical context that helped to shape such concerns. Knowing this history will help researchers and applied psychologists to avoid the many problems created in the past, as well as appreciate the advancements made over the decades.

Research on cultural bias in intelligence tests

Although research on cultural bias in cognitive ability tests has considerably waned in the last decade, we strongly advocate the renewal of cultural bias research in which English-proficient Chicanos (as assessed by valid and reliable language measures) are participants.[39] Particular focus should be on current intelligence tests, both verbal and nonverbal (e.g., the Differential Ability Scales [DAS], WISC-III, Woodcock-Johnson-III, *Batería*-R, UNIT, and forthcoming revisions of the WISC [WISC-IV], DAS [DAS-2], *Batería* [*Batería*-III], and Stanford-Binet [SB-V]).

Test publishers and independent researchers have an obligation to engage in expanded research on cultural bias in intelligence tests. In such endeavors, psychometricians need to be more sensitive to the concerns of Helms (1997), who asserted that test developers need to have better informed models about the influences of race, culture, and social class on cognitive test performance. Furthermore, this call for research can be justified by demographic reality. As Valencia (Chapter 1, present volume) discusses, the racial/ethnic makeup of the nation is dramatically changing due to the phenomenal growth of culturally/linguistically diverse school-age populations, especially Latinos and Asian Americans. It is important when intelligence tests are administered to minority children and youths that such tests be free of cultural bias and that the test results be applied fairly.

Assessment of ELLs

As we have covered in the chapter, the assessment of Mexican American ELLs' cognitive abilities presents a number of significant challenges. To some scholars, these challenges are said to be insurmountable. Valdés and Figueroa (1994) have opined: "Standardized tests should not be used in any aspect of a decision-making process with bilingual populations. . . . *All such tests should be discontinued*" [italics added] (p. 203). Although we empathize with the authors' frustrations, we do not agree with their call for a moratorium. In our view, it is unwarranted. We do think that ELLs should not be administered—for the reasons we earlier discussed—standardized and translated measures of *general* intelligence, particularly tests that are heavily loaded with verbal items. We do think, however, that carefully normed measures and subscales of *nonverbal* intelligence, with sound reliability and validity, and linguistically appropriate test instructions in the mother tongue and second language, hold some promise. Of course, the caveats we previously discussed about the use of nonverbal tests should also be heeded.

Another promising area in the cognitive assessment of Mexican American ELLs is "dynamic assessment." Utilizing a test–teach–retest model, dynamic assessment "provides information regarding the amount and nature of examiner investment to produce a desired change in the learner" (Peña, 1996, p. 282). In this regard, dynamic assessment provides a much richer source of information about how the student learns, and what types of interventions might most benefit him or her. Such individualized approaches are a great advantage over standardized assessment in that the assessment and intervention processes are tailored to individual students' strengths and needs.

The gifted

We trust that we have made a convincing argument for the "principle of affirmation" in the case of underidentified gifted Chicano students—English-speaking and ELLs alike. Beginning with the work of Terman (1925) three fourths of a century ago, both researchers and educators have expressed interest about White gifted children and youths. Such attention to Chicanos and other students of color, however, has been quite sparse. This disinterest is evidenced by the persistent and pervasive patterns of underrepresentation in gifted programs as seen in various data sources, and in the limited scholarly activity by researchers. Regards to increased identification of gifted Chicano students, we suggested a number of principles, guidelines, and strategies (e.g., principle of inclusion, not exclusion; multiple indicators in the assessment process; dual teacher certification; parental involvement) that, if judiciously applied, can result in a greater percentage of Chicano students identified as gifted and placed in such programs.

High-stakes testing

The use of educational tests in which results have major consequences in students' lives— that is, high-stakes testing—is now entrenched in U.S. public schools. As discussed here and elsewhere (e.g., Valencia and Bernal, 2000a; Valencia *et al.*, 2001), high-stakes testing is having adverse impact on many Chicano students (i.e., disproportionate rates of high school diploma denial and grade retention). Given the political nature of the standard-based school reform movement (i.e., state-mandated tests are lawfully approved by legislative bodies), legal claims of adverse impact brought forth by minority plaintiffs appear difficult to win in the courts (e.g., as seen in the defeat of plaintiffs in the *GI Forum* case [see Valencia and Bernal, 2000a]). In light of this political basis of high-stakes testing, reform of such testing will likely only be attainable through the source from which high-stakes emanated—the legislative process itself. Such activities need to be pursued with vigor. Critics of high-stakes testing need to rally around assessment principles that promote (a) the use of multiple indicators to assess a student's progress, and (b) the use of test scores for diagnosis of student's strengths and weaknesses. Furthermore, critics of high-stakes testing need to make the case that the standards-based school reform movement is inherently misdirected because it treats the *symptoms* (i.e., low academic achievement) rather than the *cause* (i.e., inferior schools; unequal educational opportunity) of racial/ethnic differences in academic achievement (see Valencia *et al.*, 2001).

A final concern regarding high-stakes testing is the administration of such tests to Mexican American ELLs. Valdés and Figueroa (1994) are strong advocates of calling for a moratorium on standardized tests for "circumstantial bilinguals"—whom the authors define as: ". . . individuals whose first language does not suffice to carry out all their communicative needs. . . . Bilingual American minorities are, by definition, circumstantial bilinguals. They are forced by circumstances to acquire English" (p. 12). Specifically, Valdés and Figueroa call for a temporary suspension of "all testing of circumstantial bilingual persons when such tests are used to select, certify, or guide interventions for *individuals*" (p. 181). In their proposed ban, the authors include tests used for high school diploma award/denial and grade promotion/retention. Valdés and Figueroa assert, however, that accountability testing— in which the focus is on system effects—may have some utility in assessing circumstantial bilinguals:

> The only area wherein tests might be used carefully and responsibly is accountability testing. When system outcomes are the focus, testing bilinguals may actually lead to the identification of error variance associated with English language proficiency and may actually be of some benefit to linguistic minorities. In academic achievement testing such a practice may actually be innovative. Many states, school districts and schools exclude bilingual pupils from their testing programs. Including them may, in fact, be not only the more honest alternative; it may also be the most useful condition insofar as taxpayers may actually get a glimpse of how effective their public school systems are in providing educational programs to all pupils.
>
> (pp. 180–181)

While it is true that test scores resultant of an accountability system do reveal glaring differences in average performance between racial/ethnic groups (see Fassold's [2000] comprehensive analysis of Texas public schools), we contend that there are several issues that can be raised why Mexican American ELLs—as well as their English-proficient peers— should not be subject to the kind of accountability testing Valdés and Figueroa assert may be beneficial. We turn, once again, to Texas, as a case in point:

1 One does *not* need an expensive state-mandated system of accountability testing—such as the one in Texas—to demonstrate that White/minority differences exist in academic performance. Such data have been available for many decades (see Valencia, Chapter 1, present volume). Furthermore, the test results of these accountability systems (e.g., in Texas) are not used for diagnoses of individual students' strengths/weaknesses, but rather as "public report cards" to rate schools. Typically, high-enrollment, segregated minority schools receive the lower ratings (Fassold, 2000) and thus are subject to pernicious labeling effects.

2 TAAS, Texas' accountability test, has been empirically shown to have psychometric inadequacies (Bernal, 2000). The Spanish version of TAAS is a mere translation of the TAAS English version, with even more suspect psychometric integrity.

3 The results of the English-only version of the 10th-grade exit-level test has been observed to discourage "regular-track, Mexican American and Mexican immigrant students from completing high school or considering a college education . . . [Further-more, the test] . . . fosters alienation towards schooling through a systematic negation of these students' Mexican culture and language" (Valenzuela, 2000; also, see Valenzuela, 1999).[40]

4 As we have discussed in some detail in the section on high-stakes testing, accountability systems (e.g., TAAS) are very much misdirected (they treat the symptoms, low academic achievement—not the cause, inferior schools), needlessly drive instruction, and result in disparate, negative impact on Chicanos and other students of color (Valencia and Bernal, 2000a; Valencia *et al.*, 2001). Regarding school reform, accountability systems focus on the "output" side of schooling—test scores. Valencia *et al.* (p. 321) argue: "what is needed is an accountability model that has a tripartite structure: (1) *input* (the adequacy of resources), (2) *process* (the quality of instruction, and (3) *output* (what students have learned as measured by tests or other indicators)" (also, see Cárdenas, 1998).

In sum, we strongly disagree with Valdés and Figueroa's (1994) position that circum-stantial bilinguals may benefit from accountability tests. These authors' proposition is mis-directed and flawed in the context of psychometrics, assessment, and teaching/learning. Furthermore, it is naïve on the part of Valdés and Figueroa to presume that accountability testing as currently structured will result in, as the authors imply, school reform for Mexican American circumstantial bilinguals.

The use of multiple data sources in assessment

"In all . . . educational decisions, test scores provide just one type of information and should be supplemented by past records of achievement and other types of assessment data. *No major educational decision should ever be based on test scores alone*" (Gronlund, 1985, p. 480). This principle voiced by Gronlund is also echoed by the Board on Testing and Assessment of the National Research Council:

An educational decision that will have a major impact on a test taker should not be made solely or automatically on the basis of a single test score. Other relevant information about the student's knowledge and skills should also be taken into account.

(Heubert and Hauser, 1999, p. 3)

To this proposition advanced by Gronlund, and Heubert and Hauser, we add: When a test, whose results will have a major impact on a student's educational progress, is used with other assessment data (e.g., grade point average), *that test should not have determinative weight*. We contend that these two principles—(a) no major decision should be made on test scores alone, and (b) no test should carry the determinative weight even when other assessment data are available—should be the *sine qua non* of educational assessment. Together, these two essential principles form the basis of best-case practices of using multiple data sources in assessment. Multi-measurement efforts in the educational assessment of Chicano students are essential, a point that we have vigorously underscored throughout this chapter.

Conclusion

We wish to leave the reader with a final thought. Any discussion of improving educational testing with Chicano students in mind cannot be presented in a vacuum, as it often is. Reform efforts in educational testing need to be placed in the broader context of *school reform*. We argue that the typically lower performance of Chicano students on standardized intelligence, achievement, and state-mandated criterion-referenced tests is one manifestation of the poor schooling students receive. Given the persistent and pervasive negative schooling conditions experienced by many Chicano children and youths (e.g., segregation, language suppression, inequities in school financing, curriculum differentiation, and noncertified teachers; see Valencia, Chapter 1, present book), it is not at all surprising that their test performance is generally below that of their White peers.

One way to understand the linkage between schooling inequality and low test performance is to examine the construct of "opportunity to learn" (see Valencia, 1992). The notion of opportunity to learn is concerned with the fit—or lack of fit—between test content (those samples of behavior that are measured), and the formal curriculum (that which is taught, how effectively it is taught, and what is learned in school). For Chicanos students, the implication is clear: If Chicanos are not given the opportunity to learn the curricular material on which they later will be tested, then it is not unexpected that for many of these students their test scores will be low (Valencia, 2000b). As such, there are increasing instances in which claims like the following are being voiced: "Testing children on what they have not been taught and then stigmatizing their 'failure to learn' is a fundamental form of discrimination" (Hanson *et al.*, 1980, p. 21).

Notes

1 Resnick's (1979) framework centers on intelligence testing. Yet, we think that the functions discussed by Resnick can be generalized, in part, to other types of educational tests (e.g., standardized achievement and state-mandated competency tests).
2 In a similar vein, Gronlund and Linn (1990) refer to this function as "placement evaluation," which has also the goal of determining "the instructional sequence and the mode of instruction that is most beneficial for each pupil" (p. 12).
3 This function is often referred to as "formative evaluation," which "is used to monitor learning progress during instruction. Its purpose is to provide continuous feedback to both pupil and teacher concerning learning successes and failures" (Gronlund and Linn, 1990, p. 12).

4 This function is frequently referred to as "summative evaluation." Gronlund and Linn (1990) note: "Although the main purpose of summative evaluation is grading, or the certification of pupil achievement, it also provides information for judging the appropriateness of the course objectives and the effectiveness of the instruction" (p. 13).

5 For a riveting treatise on the symbolic validation of high-stakes testing, see Airasian (1988).

6 This section on the historical role of intelligence tests is excerpted, with minor modifications, from Valencia (1997, pp. 77–81), Valencia (1999, pp. 124–126), and Valencia and Suzuki (2001, pp. 21–22).

7 The NIT stemmed from the development of the Army Alpha and Beta mental tests used to assess the intellectual ability of recruits during World War I. As Gould (1981) noted, "These [NIT] tests are the direct result of the application of army testing methods to the school needs" (p. 178).

8 "Race psychology" (apparently coined by scholars such as Garth, 1925) was the study of racial differences (Whites and people of color), particularly in terms of intellectual performance. Of the many groups studied, African Americans were the most frequently tested, followed by American Indians, followed by Mexican Americans. Race psychologists of this era used race in a biological sense and confused race with national origin and ethnicity. Most scholars today assert that race is best understood as a social concept.

9 González (1974a) drew this median IQ data from McAnulty (1929), whose study in turn drew on a compilation of IQ test data survey in Los Angeles from 1926 through 1928. The observed median IQ of 91.2 of Mexican American children in 1920s Los Angeles was about two-thirds of a standard deviation below the typical White median (and mean) of 100. This difference of two-thirds of a standard deviation was frequently found in other race psychology studies of the time. Furthermore, Valencia (1985a), in a comprehensive review of research on intelligence testing and Chicano school-age children, estimated an aggregated mean IQ of 87.3 for these children and youths. His analysis is based on 10,739 Chicano children in 78 studies spanning six decades. Valencia noted, however, that this aggregated mean IQ of 87.3 is entirely misleading and greatly confounded by the failure of researchers to control for critical variables (e.g., English proficiency of participants).

10 There is at least one educational historian that challenges the thesis that IQ testing played a demonstrative role in curriculum differentiation in Los Angeles schools in the 1920s and early 1930s. Rafferty (1988, 1992) contended that educational historians have greatly exaggerated the role intelligence testing played in ability grouping placements of Mexican American and other minority students in Los Angeles. Rafferty's case study does shed some light on the role of IQ testing—particularly how classroom teachers may or may not have used test results for grouping purposes. However, Valencia (1997, pp. 102–103) offered this caveat:

> I think . . . that her thesis and final analysis are misleading. Rafferty criticizes other educational historians for stating that IQ tests were used *exclusively* for educational placement. My reading of the same material (see González, 1974a) leads me to believe that such historians *did* speak to *other* factors than just IQ testing. Furthermore, González notes: "placements into various curricular levels considered more than just IQs; counselors also considered nationality, parents' occupation, teacher evaluations, grades, school programs, and behavior. However, IQs provided the key to placement".
>
> (1990, p. 80)

11 Regarding intelligence testing research in which minority students served as participants, a similar trend noted by Haney (1981) has been reported. Valencia (1985a), in a literature review of Mexican Americans and intelligence testing, identified 18 journal articles published between 1920 and 1939; only one such article from the 1940–1949 period was identified.

12 This introductory material on historical issues of cultural bias, the concept of test bias, and the notions of major and minor groups is excerpted with modifications, from Valencia and Suzuki (2001, pp. 112–117).

13 Cole and Moss (1989) commented that "many definitions [e.g., Reynolds, 1982b; Shepard, 1981, 1982] of bias have been closely tied to validity theory" (p. 205). Cole and Moss asserted that this approach may be limited (e.g., too narrow a focus on specific tests, test features, or methods of investigation). As such, Cole and Moss contended that test bias—which they define as "*differential validity of a given interpretation of a test score for any definable, relevant subgroup of test takers*" (p. 205)—should be investigated, based on several major features of "validation theory," to wit:

1   The appropriate unifying concept of test validation is construct validation.

2   Evidence traditionally associated with the terms *content validity* and *criterion validity* should be considered with the construct validity notion.

3   Construct validation should be context based; it should be guided by information about test content, the nature of the examinees, and the purposes the test is intended to serve.

4   Validity evidence should include logical and empirical evidence, divergent and convergent evidence collected within a hypothesis-generating orientation that requires the examination of plausible rival hypotheses. (p. 205)

14   Portions of this section on a review of cultural bias in intelligence tests in is excerpted, with modifications, from Valencia and Suzuki (2001, Chapter 5, pp. 115–146). Valencia and Suzuki reviewed 62 investigations involving various racial/ethnic minority students. Our review here is confined *only* to the 36 studies Valencia and Suzuki identified in which Mexican Americans served as minor group participants. We also reviewed three additional studies that were not available during Valencia and Suzuki's review.

15   This N of nearly 35,000 participants (as well as the *n*s for total major and minor group participants) is inflated. That is, in some studies (e.g., Valencia and Rankin, 1986, no. 33 and 34, App. A), the researchers examined more than one psychometric property of one instrument. As such, we counted this as two separate studies. Thus, the sample sizes were counted twice.

16   Valencia (1984, no. 31, App. A) and Valencia and Rankin (1986b, no. 34, App. A) used the procedure developed by Feldt (1969), which results in a test statistic distributed as F with $N_1 - 1 df(v_1)$ and $N_2 - 1 df(v_2)$.

17   Investigators frequently use the coefficient of congruence (Harman, 1976; Levine, 1977) to determine the degree of similarity of the various factors across the major and minor groups. The coefficient of congruence is an index of factorial similarity that has interpretive aspects similar to the Pearson *r*.

18   Bias in content validity can also be investigated at the subtest level (e.g., see study no. 32 and 36). Our focus here, however, is on bias at the item level.

19   This statistical method calls for the correlation between the item and group membership with the contribution of the general ability true score partialled out. The particular item under examination is not included in the true score. The test for bias was the significance of the item-partial correlation with subgroup membership (English- and Spanish-speaking) controlling for the total score (MSCA General Cognitive Ability, an IQ analog), age, and sex.

20   The subtests are: Word Knowledge II, Verbal Memory I, Draw-a-Child, Draw-a-Design, and Opposite Analogies.

21   The subtests in which biased items were detected are: Hand Movements, Gestalt Closure, Number Recall, Triangles, Spatial Memory, and Photo Series.

22   The numbers and percentages of biased items in the respective Achievement Scale subtests are: Faces and Places (15 of 26, 58 percent); Arithmetic (10 of 16, 63 percent); Riddles (16 of 18, 89 percent); Reading/Decoding (9 of 16, 56 percent); Reading/Understanding (8 of 16, 50 percent).

23   White (1982), in a review of literature that examined the relation between SES and academic achievement (and measured intelligence), reported a mean correlation of 0.33 between SES and IQ (see Valencia and Suzuki, 2001, Chapter 3, for a fuller discussion).

24   We use the term "English language learner" (ELL) to describe children who are in the process of acquiring English. This is in contrast to the more common term "limited-English-proficient" (LEP), which defines these children in negative terms—i.e., their lack of English proficiency.

25   We have also learned that a Spanish version of the fourth edition of the Wechsler Intelligence Scale for Children (WISC-IV) is being developed (A. Prifitera, personal communication, March 7, 2001).

26   The psychometric studies presented in Woodcock and Mather (1996) actually investigate the Woodcock-Johnson Psychoeducational Battery-Revised (Woodcock and Johnson, 1990), *not* the *Batería-R*.

27   Drawing from several publications, Valencia and Solórzano (1997) presented similar criticisms of another verbal ability test—the Peabody Picture Vocabulary Test-Revised (PPVT-R)—that we believe are also applicable here. The PPVT-R has been found to correlate poorly with conventional intelligence measures (Cohen, Swerdlik, and Smith, 1992). Scores on the PPVT-R are shaped, in part, by an individual's degree of U.S. cultural assimilation and exposure to English (Anastasi, 1988). Furthermore, Sattler (1992) specifically warned that the PPVT-R "should *never*

be used to obtain an estimate of young Hispanic American children's general intelligence" (p. 586).

28 Valencia (1985b) also calculated weighted mean scores for English-speaking Mexican American participants across the four studies: GCI ($M = 99.9$); Perceptual-Performance Scale ($M = 53.2$).

29 Table 9.4 also presents data for the three other racial/ethnic groups. African Americans are *underrepresented* in all but one of the ten districts (i.e., Dallas, Texas), while Asian/Pacific Islanders are *overrepresented* in all but one district (i.e., Albuquerque, New Mexico). These patterns of under- and overrepresentation for African Americans and Asian/Pacific Islanders, respectively, are consistent with national data presented in Valencia and Suzuki (2001, p. 229, Table 8.1). Regarding American Indians, they are evenly split among the ten districts with a mixed pattern of under- and overrepresentation; however, American Indians represent a very small percentage of the total enrollments in each of the ten districts. Contrary to the mixed pattern of under- and overrepresentation reported here, Valencia and Suzuki (2001, p. 229, Table 8.1) found American Indians to be consistently underrepresented at high rates in gifted programs in the top ten states in combined minority enrollment.

30 For criticisms of the SOMPA, see Brown (1979a, 1979b), Clarizio (1979a, 1979b), Goodman (1979a, 1979b), and Oakland (1979a, 1979b). For a response to these criticisms, see Mercer (1979).

31 In a related study, Woods and Achey (1990) reported great success utilizing parent nominations and education (among a number of other procedures) as a means to increase minority enrollment in gifted programs. Although the study involved African American and White children in the Greensboro, North Carolina public schools, it is relevant to Chicanos/Latinos. The study implemented regular meetings with parents to educate them about giftedness, the school's gifted programs, and the policies and procedures for getting their children evaluated for possible placement in gifted programs. See Valencia and Suzuki (2001, pp. 237–238) for a fuller discussion of the results of this study.

32 This discussion of Frasier (1989), and the final paragraph is excerpted, with minor modifications, from Valencia and Suzuki (2001, pp. 247–248).

33 The 27 states are Alabama, Alaska, Arizona, California, Delaware, Florida, Georgia, Hawaii, Idaho, Indiana, Louisiana, Maryland, Massachusetts, Minnesota, Mississippi, Nevada, New Jersey, New Mexico, New York, North Carolina, Ohio, South Carolina, Tennessee, Texas, Utah, Virginia, and Washington. This count is up from 1984, in which 19 states had high school exit-level exams (Heubert and Hauser, 1999).

34 The 16 states are Arkansas, California, Delaware, Florida, Illinois, Louisiana, Nevada, New Mexico, New York, North Carolina, Ohio, South Carolina, Texas, Virginia, West Virginia, and Wisconsin.

35 This section on high-stakes testing and high school diploma denial and grade retention is excerpted, with minor modifications, from Valencia and Bernal (2000a, pp. 405–409, 410, 446, 477–478).

36 Plaintiffs included the GI Forum, Image de Tejas, and nine former student plaintiffs; the defendants included the Texas Education Agency, Dr. Mike Moses (then-Commissioner of Education), and the Texas State Board of Education. The case was filed as Civil Action No. SA-97–CA-1278 EP.

37 Perspectives of plaintiffs' experts in the *GI Forum* case were published in a Special Issue (November, 2000) of the *Hispanic Journal of Behavioral Sciences* (Valencia and Bernal, 2000a). Perspectives of the defendants' experts (and other individuals sympathetic to the State's case) were published in a Special Issue (November, 2000) of the *Applied Measurement in Education* (Phillips, 2000).

38 For concrete suggestions directed to test developers and policymakers regarding the improvement of high-stakes testing and accountability, see Bernal and Valencia (2000).

39 This section on cultural bias is excerpted, with minor modifications, from Valencia and Suzuki (2001, p. 146).

40 In Texas, students designated as "LEP" (limited-English proficient) are required to take the English TAAS (grades 3–8, and 10). Suffice it to say, as a group, these students' TAAS scores on reading and mathematics are lower (Texas Education Agency, 2000, p. 12, Table 1.12) than Chicano/other Latino students deemed English proficient (see Texas Education Agency, 2000, p. 10, Table 1.10). Regarding the Spanish TAAS version (reading and mathematics) grades 3–6 tests were benchmarked in 1996 and 1997. Not surprisingly, Chicanos/Latinos who take the Spanish TAAS have considerably lower scores (Texas Education Agency, 2000, p. 15, Table 1.14) than their English-proficient and LEP peers.

References

Airasian, P.W. (1988). Symbolic validation: The case of state-mandated, high stakes testing. *Evaluation and Policy Analysis, 10*, 301–313.

Albert, R.S. (1969). Genius: Present-day status of the concept and its implications for the study of creativity and giftedness. *American Psychologist, 24*, 743–753.

Alley, G. and Foster, C. (1978). Nondiscriminatory testing of minority and exceptional children. *Focus on Exceptional Children, 9*, 1–14.

American Educational Research Association, American Psychological Association, and National Council on Measurement in Education. (1985). *Standards for educational and psychological testing.* Washington, DC: Author.

American Educational Research Association, American Psychological Association, and National Council on Measurement in Education. (1999). *Standards for educational and psychological testing.* Washington, DC: Author.

American Federation of Teachers. (1999). *Making standards matter 1997: An annual fifty-state report on efforts to raise academic standards.* Washington, DC: Author.

American Federation of Teachers. (2000). *Building a profession: Strengthening teacher preparation and induction.* Report of the K-16 Teacher Education Task Force. Washington, DC: Author.

Anastasi, A. (1988). *Psychological testing* (6th ed.). New York: Macmillan.

Argulewicz, E.N. and Kush, J.C. (1984). Concurrent validity of the SRBCSS Creativity Scale for Anglo-American and Mexican American gifted students. *Educational and Psychological Research, 4*, 81–89.

Armour-Thomas, E. and Gopaul-McNicol, S. (1998). *Assessing intelligence: Applying a biocultural model.* Thousand Oaks, CA: Sage.

Barkan, J.H. and Bernal, E.M. (1991). Gifted education for bilingual and limited English proficient students. *Gifted Child Quarterly, 35*, 144–147.

Berk, R.A. (Ed.) (1982). *Handbook of methods for detecting test bias.* Baltimore, MD: Johns Hopkins University Press.

Bernal, E.M. (1979). The education of the culturally different and gifted. In H. Passow (Ed.), *The gifted and talented: Their education and development—The seventy-fifth yearbook of the National Society for the Study of Education, Part I* (pp. 395–400). Chicago: University of Chicago Press.

Bernal, E.M. (2000). Psychometric inadequacies of the TAAS. *Hispanic Journal of Behavioral Sciences, 22*, 481–507.

Bernal, E.M. and Valencia, R.R. (2000). The TAAS case: A recapitulation and beyond. *Hispanic Journal of Behavioral Sciences, 22*, 540–556.

Bishop, H.P. (1937). *A case study of the improvement of Mexican homes through instruction in home-making.* Unpublished master's thesis, University of Southern California, Los Angeles.

Bowles, S. and Gintis, H. (1976). *Schooling in capitalist America: Education reform and the contradictions of economic life.* New York: Basic Books.

Bracken, B.A. and McCallum, R.S. (1998). *Universal Nonverbal Intelligence Test.* Itasca, IL: Riverside.

Bronfenbrenner, U. (1986). Ecology of the family as a context for human development: Research perspectives. *Developmental Psychology, 22*, 723–742.

Brown, F.G. (1979a). The SOMPA: A system of measuring potential abilities. *School Psychology Digest, 8*, 37–46.

Brown, F.G. (1979b). The algebra works—but what does it mean? *School Psychology Digest, 8*, 213–218.

Bush, G.W. (1998). Remarks at TEA Midwinter Conference. Austin, TX, January 22.

Callahan, R.E. (1962). *Education and the cult of efficiency: A study of the social forces that have shaped the administration of the public schools.* Chicago: University of Chicago Press.

Cárdenas, J.A. (1998). School-student performance and accountability. *IDRA Newsletter* 25 (October), 1–2, 17–19.

Chapman, P.D. (1988). *Schools as sorters: Lewis M. Terman, applied psychology, and the intelligence testing movement, 1890–1930.* New York: New York University Press.

Clarizio, H.F. (1979a). In defense of the IQ test. *School Psychology Digest, 8*, 79–88.

Clarizio, H.F. (1979b). Commentary on Mercer's rejoinder to Clarizio. *School Psychology Digest, 8*, 207–209.

Cohen, R.J., Swerdlik, M.E. and Smith, D.K. (1992). *Psychological testing and assessment: An introduction to tests and measurement* (2nd ed.). Mountain View, CA: Mayfield.

Cole, N.S. and Moss, P.A. (1989). Bias in test use. In R.L. Linn (Ed.), *Educational measurement* (3rd ed., pp. 201–219). New York: Macmillan.

Collier, V.P. (1989). How long? A synthesis of research on academic achievement in a second language. *TESOL Quarterly, 29*, 509–531.

Corman, L. and Budoff, M. (1974). Factor structures of Spanish-speaking and non-Spanish-speaking children on Raven's Progressive Matrices. *Educational and Psychological Measurement, 34*, 977–981.

Covarrubias v. San Diego Unified School District, Civil Action No. 70-30d (S.D. Cal. 1971).

Cronbach, L.J. (1984). *Essentials of psychological testing* (4th ed.). New York: Harper and Row.

Cummins, J. (1980). Psychological assessment of immigrant children: Logic or intuition? *Journal of Multilingual and Multicultural Development, 1*, 97–111.

Cummins, J. (1981). The role of primary language development in promoting educational success for language minority students. In Office of Bilingual and Bicultural Education, California State Department of Education (Ed.), *Schooling and language minority students: A theoretical framework* (pp. 3–50). Los Angeles: California State University, Evaluation, Dissemination and Assessment Center.

Cummins, J. (1984). *Bilingualism and special education: Issues in assessment and pedagogy*. San Diego, CA: College Hill.

Cummins, J. (2000). *Language, power, and pedagogy: Bilingual children in the crossfire*. Clevedon, England: Multilingual Matters.

Damico, J.S. (1991). Descriptive assessment of communicative ability in limited English proficient students. In E.V. Hamayan and J.S. Damico (Eds.), *Limiting bias in the assessment of bilingual students* (pp. 157–218). Austin, TX: PRO-ED.

DeAvila, E. and Duncan, S. (1986). *Language Assessment Scales*. Monterey, CA: McGraw-Hill.

Diana v. State Board of Education, Civil Action No. C-70–37 (N.D. Cal. 1970).

Dickson, V.E. (1923). *Mental tests and the classroom teacher*. Yonkers-on-the-Hudson, NY: World Book.

Duncan, S. and DeAvila, E. (1979). Bilingualism and cognition: Some recent findings. *NABE Journal, 4*, 15–50.

Elliott, S.N., Argulewicz, E.N. and Turco, T.L. (1986). Predictive validity of the Scales for Rating the Behavioral Characteristics of Superior Students for gifted children from three sociocultural groups. *Journal of Experimental Education, 55*, 27–32.

Ellis, P. (1929). *Americanization through homemaking*. Los Angeles: Wetzel Publishing Co.

Fassold, M.A.J. (2000). Disparate impact analyses of TAAS scores and school quality. *Hispanic Journal of Behavioral Sciences, 22*, 460–480.

Figueroa, R.A. (1990). Assessment of linguistic minority group children. In C.R. Reynolds and R.W. Kamphaus (Eds.), *Handbook of psychological and educational assessment of children* (pp. 671–696). New York: Guilford.

Fine, B. (1949). More and more, the IQ idea is questioned. *New York Times Magazine*, September 18, 7, 72–74.

Ford, D.Y. and Harris, III, J.J. (1990). On discovering the hidden treasure of gifted and talented Black children. *Roeper Review, 13*, 27–33.

Frasier, M.M. (1989). Identification of gifted Black students: Developing new perspectives. In C.J. Maker and S.W. Schiever (Eds.), *Critical issues in gifted education: Defensible programs for cultural and ethnic minorities* (pp. 213–225). Austin TX: PRO-ED.

Galton, F. (1870). *Hereditary genius: An inquiry into its laws and consequences*. New York: D. Appleton and Co.

Galton, F. (1883). *Inquiries into human faculty and its development*. London: Macmillan.

García-Vázquez, E., Vázquez, L.A., López, I.C. and Ward, W. (1999). Language proficiency and academic success: Relationships between proficiency in two languages and achievement among Mexican American students. *Bilingual Research Journal, 21*, 395–408.

Garretson, O.K. (1928). Study of the causes of retardation among Mexican children. *Journal of Educational Psychology, 19*, 31–40.

Garth, T.R. (1923). A comparison of the intelligence of Mexican and full blood Indian children. *Psychological Review, 30*, 388–401.

Garth, T.R. (1925). A review of race psychology. *Psychological Bulletin, 22*, 343–364.

Garth, T.R. (1928). The intelligence of Mexican school children. *School and Society, 27*, 791–794.

Geisinger, K.F. (Ed.). (1992). *Psychological testing of Hispanics*. Washington, DC: American Psychological Association.

Geisinger, K.F. (1994). Cross-cultural normative assessment: Translation and adaptation issues influencing the normative interpretation of assessment instruments. *Psychological Assessment, 6,* 304–312.

Geisinger, K.F. (1998). Psychometric issues in test interpretation. In J. Sandoval, C.L. Frisby, K.F. Geisinger and J.R. Grenier (Eds.), *Test interpretation and diversity: Achieving equity in assessment* (pp. 17–30). Washington DC: American Psychological Association.

GI Forum et al. v. Texas Education Agency et al., 87 F. Supp.2d 667 (W.D. Tex. 2000).

Gilbert, H.B. (1966). On the IQ ban. *Teachers College Record, 67,* 282–285.

Glutting, J.J. (1986). Potthoff bias analyses of K-ABC MPC and Nonverbal scale IQs among Anglo, Black, and Puerto Rican kindergarten children. *Professional School Psychology, 4,* 225–234.

González, G.G. (1974a). *The system of public education and its function within the Chicano communities, 1910–1930.* Unpublished doctoral dissertation, University of California, Los Angeles.

González, G.G. (1974b). Racism, education, and the Mexican community in Los Angeles, 1920–1930. *Societas, 4,* 287–301.

González, G.G. (1990). *Chicano education in the era of segregation.* Philadelphia, PA: Balch Institute Press.

González, G.G. (1999). Segregation and the education of Mexican children, 1900–1940. In J.F. Moreno (Ed.), *The elusive quest for equality: 150 years of Chicano/Chicana education* (pp. 53–76). Cambridge, MA: Harvard Educational Review.

González, V. (1994). A model of cognitive, cultural, and linguistic variables affecting bilingual Hispanic children's development of concepts and language. *Hispanic Journal of Behavioral Sciences, 16,* 396–421.

Goodenough, F.L. (1926). *Measurement of intelligence by drawings.* Yonkers-on-the-Hudson, NY: World Book.

Goodman, J.F. (1979a). Is tissue the issue? A critique of SOMPA's models and tests. *School Psychology Digest, 8,* 47–62.

Goodman, J.F. (1979b). "Ignorance" versus "stupidity"—the basic disagreement. *School Psychology Digest, 8,* 218–223.

Gould, S.J. (1981). *The mismeasure of man.* New York: W.W. Norton.

Gronlund, N.E. (1985). *Measurement and evaluation in teaching* (5th ed.). New York: Macmillan.

Gronlund, N.E. and Linn, R.L. (1990). *Measurement and evaluation in teaching* (6th ed.). New York: Macmillan.

Guadalupe v. Tempe Elementary School District, No. 3, Civ. No. 71–435 (D. Ariz., 1972).

Guthrie, R.V. (1976). *Even the rat was white: A historical view of psychology.* New York: Harper and Row.

Halpern, D.F. (1997). Sex differences in intelligence: Implications for education. *American Psychologist, 58,* 1091–1101.

Haney, W. (1981). Validity, vaudeville, and values: A short history of social concerns over standardized testing. *American Psychologist, 36,* 1021–1034.

Hanson, R.A., Schutz, R.E. and Bailey, J.D. (1980). *What makes achievement tick: Investigation of alternative instrumentation for instructional program evaluation.* Los Alamitos, CA: Southwest Regional Laboratory for Educational Research and Development.

Harris, A.M., Reynolds, M.A. and Koegel, H.M. (1996). Nonverbal assessment: Multicultural perspectives. In L.A. Suzuki, P.J. Meller, and J.G. Ponterotto (Eds.), *Handbook of multicultural assessment* (pp. 223–252). San Francisco: Jossey-Bass.

Harman, H.H. (1976). *Modern factor analysis* (3rd ed.). Chicago: University of Chicago Press.

Helms, J.E. (1997). The triple quandary of race, culture, and social class in standardized cognitive ability testing. In D.P. Flanagan, J.L. Genshaft, and P.L. Harrison (Eds.), *Contemporary intellectual assessment: Theories, tests, and issues* (pp. 517–532). New York: Guilford.

Henderson, R.W. and Valencia, R.R. (1985). Nondiscriminatory school psychological services: Beyond nonbiased assessment. In J.R. Bergan (Ed.), *School psychology in contemporary society* (pp. 340–377). Columbus, OH: Charles E. Merrill.

Henry, T.S. (1924). Annotated bibliography on gifted children and their education. In G.M. Whipple (Ed.), *The twenty-third yearbook of the Society for the Study of Education: Part I. Report of the Society's Committee on the Education of Gifted Children* (pp. 389–443). Bloomington, IL: Public School Publishing Co.

Heubert, J.P. and Hauser, R.M. (Eds.). (1999). *High stakes: Testing for tracking, promotion, and graduation.* Committee on Appropriate Test Use, Board of Testing and Assessment, Commission on

Behavioral and Social Sciences and Education, National Research Council. Washington, DC: National Academy Press.

Hilliard, A.G., III. (1979). Standardization and cultural bias as impediments to the scientific study and validation of "intelligence." *Journal of Research and Development in Education, 12*, 47–58.

Hilliard, A.G., III. (1984). IQ testing as the emperor's new clothes: A critique of Jensen's *Bias in Mental Testing*. In C.R. Reynolds and R.T. Brown (Eds.), *Perspectives on bias in testing* (pp. 139–169). New York: Plenum.

Holtzman, Jr., W.H. and Wilkinson, C.Y. (1991). Assessment of cognitive ability. In E.V. Hamayan and J.S. Damico (Eds.), *Limiting bias in the assessment of bilingual students* (pp. 247–280). Austin, TX: PRO-ED.

Jackson, G.D. (1975). Another psychological view from the Association of Black Psychologists. *American Psychologist, 30*, 88–93.

Jensen, A.R. (1980). *Bias in mental testing*. New York: Free Press.

Johnston, R.C. (1998). The governor has social promotion in his sights. *Education Week, 17*, p. 1 (*Education Week on the Web*).

Kaufman, A.S. and Kaufman, N.L. (1983). *Kaufman Assessment Battery for Children: Interpretive manual*. Circle Pines, MN: American Guidance Services.

Klineberg, O. (1935). *Race differences*. New York: Harper.

Koch, H.L. and Simmons, R. (1926). A study of the test performance of American, Mexican, and Negro children. *Psychological Monographs, 35*, 1–116.

Koh, T., Abbatiello, A. and McLoughlin, C.S. (1984). Cultural bias in WISC subtest items: A response to Judge Grady's suggestion in relation to the PASE case. *School Psychology Review, 13*, 89–94.

Langdon, H.W. (1992). Speech and language assessment of LEP/bilingual students. In H.W. Langdon and L.L. Cheng (Eds.), *Hispanic children and adults with communication disorders: Assessment and intervention* (pp. 201–271). Gaithersburg, MD: Aspen.

Levine, M.S. (1977). *Canonical analysis and factor comparison*. (*Quantitative applications in the social sciences*, Series No 7-001). Beverly Hills CA: Sage.

López, E.C. (1997). The cognitive assessment of limited English proficient and bilingual children. In D.P. Flanagan, J.L. Genshaft, and P.L. Harrison (Eds.), *Contemporary intellectual assessment: Theories, tests, and issues* (pp. 503–516). New York: Guilford.

Matthew, J.L., Golin, A.K., Moore, M.W. and Baker, C. (1992). Use of SOMPA in identification of gifted African-American children. *Journal for the Education of the Gifted, 15*, 344–356.

McAnulty, E.A. (1929). Distribution of intelligence in the Los Angeles elementary schools. *Los Angeles Educational Research Bulletin, 8*, 6–8.

McCarthy, D. (1972). *McCarthy Scales of Children's Abilities*. New York: Psychological Corporation.

McNeil, L.M. (2000). Sameness, bureaucracy, and the myth of educational equity: The TAAS system of testing in Texas public schools. *Hispanic Journal of Behavioral Sciences, 22*, 508–523.

Mercer, J.R. (1977). Identifying the gifted Chicano child. In J.L. Martínez, Jr. (Ed.), *Chicano psychology* (pp. 155–173). New York: Academic Press.

Mercer, J.R. (1979). In defense of racially and culturally non-discriminatory assessment. *School Psychology Digest, 8*, 89–115.

Mercer, J.W. (1984). What is a racially and culturally nondiscriminatory test? A sociological and pluralistic perspective. In C.R. Reynolds and R.T. Brown (Eds.), *Perspectives on bias in testing* (pp. 293–356). New York: Plenum.

Mercer, J. and Lewis, J. (1979). *System of Multicultural and Pluralistic Assessment: Technical manual*. New York: Psychological Corporation.

Milliken, W.G. (1970). Making the school system accountable. *Compact, 4*, 17–18.

Muñoz-Sandoval, A.F., Cummins, J., Alvarado, C.G. and Ruef, M.L. (1998a). *Bilingual Verbal Ability Tests*. Itasca, IL: Riverside.

Muñoz-Sandoval, A.F., Cummins, J., Alvarado, C.G. and Ruef, M.L. (1998b). *Bilingual Verbal Ability Tests: Comprehensive manual*. Itasca, IL: Riverside.

National Commission on Excellence in Education (1983). *A nation at risk: The imperatives for educational reform*. Washington, DC: Government Printing Office.

Oakland, T. (1979a). Research on the Adaptive Behavior Inventory for Children and the Estimated Learning Potential. *School Psychology Digest, 8*, 63–70.

Oakland, T. (1979b). Research on the ABIC and the ELP: A revisit to an old topic. *School Psychology Digest, 8*, 212–213.

Oller, J.W., Jr. (1983). Testing proficiencies and diagnosing language disorders in bilingual children. In D.R. Omark and J.G. Erickson (Eds.), *The bilingual exceptional child* (pp. 78–123). San Diego, CA: College-Hill.

Ortiz, V.Z. and Volloff, W. (1987). Identification of gifted and accelerated Hispanic students. *Journal for the Education of the Gifted, 11*, 45–55.

Paschal, F.C. and Sullivan, L.R. (1925). Racial differences in the mental and physical development of Mexican children. *Comparative Psychology Monographs, 3*, 1–76.

Peña, E. (1996). Dynamic assessment: The model and language applications. In K. Cole, P. Dales, and D. Thal (Eds.), *Assessment of communication and language* (pp. 281–307). Baltimore, MD: Brookes.

Peña, E., Iglesias, A. and Lidz, C. (2001). Reducing test bias through dynamic assessment of children's word learning ability. *American Journal of Speech-Language Pathology, 10*, 138–154.

Phillips, S.E. (Ed.). (2000). Defending a high school graduation test: *GI Forum v. Texas Education Agency* [Special issue]. *Applied Measurement in Education, 13*(4).

Rafferty, J.R. (1988). Missing the mark: Intelligence testing in Los Angeles public schools. *History of Education Quarterly, 28*, 73–93.

Rafferty, J.R. (1992). *Land of fair promise: Politics and reform in Los Angeles schools, 1885–1941*. Stanford, CA: Stanford University Press.

Ramírez, J., Yuen, S., Ramey, D. and Pasta, D. (1991). *Final report: Longitudinal study of structured English immersion strategy, early-exit, and late-exit bilingual education programs for language minority children Vol. 1*. San Mateo, CA: Aguirre International.

Reschly, D. (1979). Nonbiased assessment. In G. Phye and D. Reschly (Eds.), *School psychology: Perspectives and issues* (pp. 215–250). New York: Academic Press.

Resnick, D.P. (1981). Testing in America: A supportive environment. *Phi Delta Kappan, 62*, 625–628.

Resnick, L.B. (1979). The future of IQ testing in education. *Intelligence, 3*, 241–253.

Reynolds, C.R. (1982a). The problem of bias in psychological assessment. In C.R. Reynolds and T.B. Gutkin (Eds.), *The handbook of school psychology* (pp. 178–208). New York: John Wiley.

Reynolds, C.R. (1982b). Methods for detecting construct and predictive bias. In R.A. Berk (Ed.), *Handbook of methods for detecting test bias* (pp. 199–227). Baltimore, MD: Johns Hopkins University Press.

Reynolds, C.R. and Kaiser, S.M. (1990). Bias in assessment of aptitude. In C.R. Reynolds and R.W. Kamphaus (Eds.), *Handbook of psychological and educational assessment of children: Intelligence and achievement* (pp. 611–653). New York: Guilford.

Salvia, J. and Ysseldyke, J.E. (1988). *Assessment in special and remedial education* (4th ed.). Boston: Houghton Mifflin.

San Miguel, G., Jr. (1987). *"Let them all take heed": Mexican Americans and their campaign for educational equality in Texas, 1910–1981*. Austin: University of Texas Press.

Sánchez, G.I. (1932). Group differences in Spanish-speaking children: A critical review. *Journal of Applied Psychology, 16*, 549–558.

Sánchez, G.I (1934). Bilingualism and mental measures. *Journal of Applied Psychology, 18*, 765–772.

Sandoval, J. and Durán, R.P. (1998). Language. In J. Sandoval, C.L. Frisby, K.F. Geisinger, J.D. Scheuneman, and J.R. Grenier (Eds.), *Test interpretation and diversity: Achieving equity in assessment* (pp. 181–212). Washington, DC: American Psychological Association.

Sandoval, J., Frisby, C.L., Geisinger, K.F., Scheuneman, J.D. and Grenier, J.R. (Eds.). (1998). *Test interpretation and diversity: Achieving equity in assessment*. Washington, DC: American Psychological Association.

Sattler, J.M. (1992). *Assessment of children* (3rd ed., revised and updated). San Diego, CA: Author.

Saucedo, L. (2000). The legal issues surrounding the TAAS case. *Hispanic Journal of Behavioral Sciences, 22*, 411–422.

Saville-Troike, M. (1984). What really matters in second language for academic achievement? *TESOL Quarterly, 18*, 199–217.

Scott, M.S., Perou, R., Urbano, R., Hogan, A. and Gold, S. (1992). The identification of giftedness: A comparison of White, Hispanic and Black families. *Gifted Child Quarterly, 36*, 131–139.

Sheldon, W.H. (1924). The intelligence of Mexican children. *School and Society, 19*, 139–142.

Shepard, L.A. (1981). Identifying bias in test items. in B.F. Green (Ed.), *New directions for testing measurement: Issues in testing—coaching disclosure and ethnic bias* (No. 11, pp. 79–104). San Francisco: Jossey Bass.

Shepard, L.A. (1982). Definitions of bias. In P.A. Berk (Ed.), *Handbook for methods of detecting test bias* (pp. 9–30). Baltimore, MD: Johns Hopkins University Press.

Stanley, G. (1920). Special schools for Mexicans. *The Survey, 44*, 714–715.

Sternberg, R.J. and Davidson, J.E. (Eds.) (1986). *Conceptions of giftedness.* New York: Cambridge University Press.

Suzuki, L.A., Meller, P.J. and Ponterotto, J.G. (Eds.). (1996). *Handbook of multicultural assessment.* San Francisco: Jossey-Bass.

Tannenbaum, A.J. (1983). *Gifted children: Psychological and educational perspectives.* New York: Macmillan.

Taylor, P.S. (1929). *Mexican labor in the United States: Racial school statistics.* Los Angeles: University of California Publications in Economics.

Terman, L.M. (1916). *The measurement of intelligence: An explanation of and a complete guide for the use of the Stanford revision and extension of the Binet-Simon intelligence scale.* Boston: Houghton Mifflin.

Terman, L.M. (1919). *The intelligence of school children: How children differ in ability, the use of mental tests in school grading and the proper education of exceptional children.* Boston: Houghton Mifflin.

Terman, L.M. (1925). *Genetic studies of genius: Vol 1. Mental and physical traits of a thousand gifted children.* Stanford, CA: Stanford University Press.

Texas Education Agency. (2000). *2000 comprehensive biennial report on Texas public schools.* Austin, TX: Author.

Texas Education Code. (1999). §29.065.g.2.

Thomas, W.B. (1982). Black intellectuals' critique of early mental testing: A little known saga of the 1920s. *American Journal of Education, 90*, 258–292.

Thorndike, R.L. and Hagen, E. (1977). *Measurement and evaluation in psychology and education.* New York: Wiley.

U.S. Department of Commerce, Bureau of Census. (2000). *Profile of general demographic characteristics for the United States: 2000.* Washington DC: Author. Available online at: http://www.census.gov/prod/cen2000/dp1/2kh00.pdf

U.S. Department of Education, Office for Civil Rights (1998). *Fall 1994 elementary and secondary school civil rights compliance report.* Washington, DC: Author.

U.S. Department of Education, Office for Civil Rights (2001). *Fall 1998 elementary and secondary school civil rights compliance report.* Washington, DC: Author.

U.S. Department of Education, Office of Educational Research and Improvement. (1998). *Talent and diversity: The emerging world of limited English proficient students in gifted education.* Washington, DC: Author.

Valdés, G. and Figueroa, R.A. (1994). *Bilingualism and testing: A special case of bias.* Norwood, NJ: Ablex.

Valencia, R.R. (1985a). *Chicanos and intelligence testing: A descriptive state of the art.* Unpublished manuscript.

Valencia, R.R. (1985b). The McCarthy scales and Hispanic children: A review of psychometric research. *Hispanic Journal of Behavioral Sciences, 10*, 81–104.

Valencia, R.R. (1992). Explaining cultural bias in educational tests: How important is "Opportunity to learn?". *Child Assessment News, 2*, 8–11.

Valencia, R.R. (1997). Genetic pathology model of deficit thinking. In R.R. Valencia (Ed.), *The evolution of deficit thinking: Educational thought and practice* (pp. 41–112). The Stanford Series on Education and Public Policy. London: Falmer Press.

Valencia, R.R. (1999). Educational testing and Mexican American students: Problems and prospects. In J.F. Moreno (Ed.), *The elusive quest for equality: 150 years of Chicano/Chicana education* (pp. 123–140). Cambridge, MA: Harvard Educational Review.

Valencia, R.R. (2000a, July). *Legislated school reform via high-stakes testing: The case of pending anti-social promotion legislation in Texas and its likely impact on racial/ethnic minority students.* Commissioned paper for the National Academy of Sciences Committee on Educational Excellence and Testing Equity. Paper presented at the National Academy of Sciences workshop on School Completion in Standards-Based Reform, Washington, DC.

Valencia, R.R. (2000b). Inequalities and the schooling of minority students in Texas: Historical and contemporary conditions. *Hispanic Journal of Behavioral Sciences, 22*, 445–459.

Valencia, R.R. and Aburto, S. (1991). The uses and abuses of educational testing: Chicanos as a case in point. In R.R. Valencia (Ed.), *Chicano school failure and success: Research and policy agendas for the 1990s* (pp. 203–251). The Stanford Series on Education and Public Policy. London: Falmer Press.

Valencia, R.R. and Bernal, E.M. (Eds.). (2000a). The Texas Assessment of Academic Skills (TAAS) case: Perspectives of plaintiffs' experts [Special issue]. *Hispanic Journal of Behavioral Sciences, 22*(4).

Valencia, R.R. and Bernal, E.M. (2000b). Guest editors' introduction. *Hispanic Journal of Behavioral Sciences, 22*, 405–410.

Valencia, R.R. and Bernal, E.M. (2000c). An overview of conflicting opinions in the TAAS case. *Hispanic Journal of Behavioral Sciences, 22*, 423–444.

Valencia, R.R. and Black, M.S. (2002). "Mexican Americans don't value education!": On the basis of the myth, mythmaking, and debunking. *Journal of Latinos and Education, 2*, 81–103.

Valencia, R.R. and Rankin, R.J. (1985). Evidence of content bias on the McCarthy Scales with Mexican American children: Implications for test translation and nonbiased assessment. *Journal of Educational Psychology, 77*, 197–207.

Valencia, R.R. and Solórzano, D.G. (1997). Contemporary deficit thinking. In R.R. Valencia (Ed.), *The evolution of deficit thinking: Educational thought and practice* (pp. 160–210). The Stanford Series on Education and Public Policy. London: Falmer Press.

Valencia, R.R. and Suzuki, L.A. (2001). *Intelligence testing and minority students: Foundations, performance factors, and assessment issues.* Thousand Oaks, CA: Sage.

Valencia, R.R., Valenzuela, A., Sloan, K. and Foley, D.E. (2001). At odds—Let's treat the cause, not the symptoms: Equity and accountability in Texas revisited. *Phi Delta Kappan, 83*, 318–321, 326.

Valenzuela, A. (1999). *Subtractive schooling: U.S.-Mexican youth and the politics of caring.* Albany: State University of New York Press.

Valenzuela, A. (2000). The significance of the TAAS test for Mexican immigrant and Mexican American adolescents: A case study. *Hispanic Journal of Behavioral Sciences, 22*, 524–539.

Villenas, S. and Deyhle, S. (1999). Critical race theory and ethnographies challenging the stereotypes: Latino families, schooling, resilience, and resistance. *Curriculum Inquiry, 29*, 413–445.

White, K.R. (1982). The relation between socioeconomic status and academic achievement. *Psychological Bulletin, 91*, 461–481.

Williams, R.L. (1971). Abuses and misuses in testing Black children. *Counseling Psychologist, 2*, 62–77.

Woodcock, R.W. and Johnson, M.B. (1990) *Woodcock–Johnson Psychoeducational Battery—Revised.* Itasca, IL: Riverside.

Woodcock, R.W. and Mather, N. (1990). WJ-R Tests of Cognitive Ability—Standard and supplemental batteries: Examiner's manual. In R.W. Woodcock and M.B. Johnson, *Woodcock–Johnson Psychoeducational Battery—Revised.* Itasca, IL: Riverside.

Woodcock, R.W. and Mather, N. (1996). *Examiner's manual for the Batería Woodcock–Muñoz—revisada.* Itasca IL: Riverside.

Woodcock, R.W. and Muñoz-Sandoval, A.F. (1996). *Batería Woodcock–Muñoz—Revisada.* Itasca, IL: Riverside.

Woods, S.B. and Achey, V.H. (1990). Successful identification of gifted racial/ethnic group students without changing classification requirements. *Roeper Review, 13*, 21–36.

Worthen, B.R., Borg, W.R. and White, K.R. (1993). *Measurement and evaluation in the schools.* New York: Longman.

Young, K. (1922). *Mental differences in certain immigration groups: Psychological tests of South Europeans in typical California schools with bearing on the educational policy and on the problems of racial contacts in this country, Vol.1 (no.11).* Eugene, OR: University of Oregon Press.

Zavala, J. and Mims, J. (1983). Identification of learning disabled bilingual Hispanic students. *Learning Disability Quarterly, 6*, 479–488.

Appendix A
Thirty-nine cultural bias studies examined and used in the review

1   Dean, R.S. (1980). Factor structure of the WISC-R with Anglos and Mexican Americans. *Journal of School Psychology, 18,* 234–239. **Construct Validity**

2   Goldman, R.D. and Hartig, L.K. (1976). The WISC may not be a valid predictor of school performance for primary-grade minority children. *American Journal of Mental Deficiency, 80,* 583–587. **Predictive Validity**

3   Gutkin, T.B. and Reynolds, C.R. (1981). Factorial similarity of the WISC-R for white and black children from the standardization sample. *Journal of Educational Psychology, 73,* 227–231. **Construct Validity**

4   Jensen, A.R. (1974a). How biased are culture-loaded tests? *Genetic Psychology Monographs, 90,* 185–244. **Content Validity**

5   Jensen, A.R. (1974b). Ibid. **Reliability**

6   Jensen, A.R. (1974c). Ibid. **Content Validity**

7   Jensen, A.R. (1974d). Ethnicity and scholastic achievement. *Psychological Reports, 34,* 659–668. **Predictive Validity**

8   Keith, T.Z., Quirk, K.J., Schartzer, C. and Elliott, C.D. (1999). Construct bias in the Differential Ability Scales? Confirmatory and hierarchical factor structure across three ethnic groups. *Journal of Psychoeducational Assessment, 17,* 249–268. **Construct Validity**

9   Mishra, S.P. (1981). Factor analysis of the McCarthy Scales for groups of white and Mexican American children. *Journal of School Psychology, 19,* 178–182. **Construct Validity**

10 Murray, A.M. and Mishra, S.P. (1983). Interactive effects of item content and ethnic group membership on performance on the McCarthy Scales. *Journal of School Psychology, 21,* 263–270. **Content Validity**

11 Oakland, T. (1978). Predictive validity of readiness tests for middle and lower socioeconomic status Anglo, black, and Mexican American children. *Journal of Educational Psychology, 70,* 574–582. **Predictive Validity**

12 Oakland, T. (1980). An evaluation of the ABIC, pluralistic norms, and estimated learning potential. *Journal of School Psychology, 18,* 3–11. **Predictive Validity**

13 Oakland, T. and Feigenbaum, D. (1979a). Multiple sources of test bias on the WISC-R and Bender-Gestalt test. *Journal of Consulting and Clinical Psychology, 47,* 968–974. **Reliability**

14 Oakland, T. and Feigenbaum, D. (1979b). Ibid. **Construct Validity**

15 Oakland, T. and Feigenbaum, D. (1979c). Ibid. **Content Validity**

16 Oakland, T. and Feigenbaum, D. (1979d). Ibid. **Predictive Validity**

17 Olivárez, A. Jr., Palmer, D.J. and Guillemard, L. (1992). Predictive bias with referred and nonreferred Black, Hispanic, and White pupils. *Learning Disability Quarterly, 15,* 175–187. **Predictive Validity**

18 Palmer, D.J., Olivárez, A., Wilson, V.L. and Fordyce, T. (1989). Ethnicity and language dominance-influence on the prediction of achievement based on intelligence test scores in nonreferred and referred samples. *Learning Disability Quarterly, 12,* 261–274. **Predictive Validity**

19 Reschly, D.J. (1978). WISC-R factor structures among Anglos, Blacks, Chicanos, and Native American Papagos. *Journal of Consulting and Clinical Psychology, 46,* 417–422. **Construct Validity**

20   Reschly, D.J. and Reschly, J.E. (1979). Validity of WISC-R factor scores in predicting achievement and attention for four sociocultural groups. *Journal of School Psychology*, *17*, 355–361. **Predictive Validity**

21   Reschly, D.J. and Sabers, D. (1979). Analysis of test bias in four groups with the regression definition. *Journal of Educational Measurement*, *16*, 1–9. **Predictive Validity**

22   Ross-Reynolds, J. and Reschly, D.J. (1983a). An investigation of item bias on the WISC-R with four sociocultural groups. *Journal of Consulting and Clinical Psychology*, *51*, 144–146. **Reliability**

23   Ross-Reynolds, J. and Reschly, D.J. (1983b). Ibid. **Content Validity**

24   Rousey, A. (1990). Factor structure of the WISC-R Mexicano. *Educational and Psychological Measurement*, *90*, 351–357. **Construct Validity**

25   Sandoval, J. (1979a). The WISC-R and internal evidence of test bias with minority groups. *Journal of Consulting and Clinical Psychology*, *47*, 919–927. **Content Validity**

26   Sandoval, J. (1979b). Ibid. **Reliability**

27   Sandoval, J. (1982). The WISC-R factorial validity for minority groups and Spearman's hypothesis. *Journal of School Psychology*, *20*, 198–204. **Construct Validity**

28   Sandoval, J., Zimmerman, I.L. and Woo-Sam, J.M. (1983). Cultural differences on WISC-R verbal items. *Journal of School Psychology*, *21*, 49–55. **Content Validity**

29   Silverstein, A.B. (1973). Factor structure of the Wechsler Intelligence Scale for Children for three ethnic groups. *Journal of Educational Psychology*, *65*, 408–410. **Construct Validity**

30   Valdez, R.S. and Valdez, C. (1983). Detecting predictive bias: The WISC-R versus achievement scores of Mexican American and non-minority students. *Learning Disability Quarterly*, *6*, 440–447. **Predictive Validity**

31   Valencia, R.R. (1984). Reliability of the Raven Coloured Progressive Matrices for Anglo and for Mexican American children. *Psychology in the Schools*, *21*, 49–52. **Reliability**

32   Valencia, R.R. and Rankin, R.J. (1985). Evidence of content bias on the McCarthy Scales with Mexican American children: Implications for test translation and nonbiased assessment. *Journal of Educational Psychology*, *77*, 197–207. **Content Validity**

33   Valencia, R.R. and Rankin, R.J. (1986a). Factor analysis of the K-ABC for groups of Anglo and Mexican American children. *Journal of Educational Measurement*, *23*, 209–219. **Construct Validity**

34   Valencia, R.R. and Rankin, R.J. (1986b). Ibid. **Reliability**

35   Valencia, R.R. and Rankin, R.J. (1988). Evidence of bias in predictive validity on the Kaufman Assessment Battery for Children in samples of Anglo and Mexican American children. *Psychology in the Schools*, *25*, 257–263. **Predictive Validity**

36   Valencia, R.R., Rankin, R.J. and Livingston, R. (1995). K-ABC content bias: Comparisons between Mexican American and White children. *Psychology in the Schools*, *32*, 153–169. **Content Validity**

37   Valencia, R.R., Rankin, R.J. and Oakland, T. (1997). WISC-R factor structures for White, Mexican American, and African American children: A research note. *Psychology in the Schools*, *34*, 11–16. **Construct Validity**

38   Weiss, L.G. and Prifitera, A. (1995). An evaluation of differential prediction of WIAT Achievement scores from WISC-III FSIQ across ethnic and gender groups. *Journal of School Psychology*, *33*, 297–304. **Predictive Validity**

39   Weiss, L.G., Prifitera, A. and Roid, G. (1999). The WISC-III and the fairness of predicting achievement across ethnic and gender groups. *Journal of Psychoeducational Assessment* (monograph series, Advances in Psychological Assessment, Wechsler Intelligence Scale for Children Third Edition): 35–42. **Predictive Validity**

Appendix B
Intelligence tests examined for cultural bias

1 Dunn, L.M. (1959). *Peabody Picture Vocabulary Test.* Minneapolis, MN: American Guidance Service.

2 Elliott, C.D. (1990). *The manual for the Differential Ability Scales.* San Antonio, TX: Psychological Corporation.

3 Kaufman, A.S. and Kaufman, N.L. (1983). *Kaufman Assessment Battery for Children.* Circle Pines, MN: American Guidance Service.

4 McCarthy, D. (1972). *Manual for the McCarthy Scales of Children's Abilities.* New York: Psychological Corporation.

5 Raven, J.C. (1960). *Guide to the Standard Progressive Matrices.* London: H.K. Lewis.

6 Raven, J.C. (1962). *Coloured Progressive Matrices, Sets A, A_B, B.* London: H.K. Lewis.

7 Slosson, R.L. (1963). *Slosson Intelligence Test and Slosson Reading Test.* New York: Slosson Educational Publications.

8 Wechsler, D. (1949). *Wechsler Intelligence Scale for Children.* New York: Psychological Corporation.

9 Wechsler, D. (1974). *Wechsler Intelligence Scale for Children—Revised.* New York: Psychological Corporation.

10 Wechsler, D. (1991). *Wechsler Intelligence Scale for Children—Third Edition.* New York: Psychological Corporation.

11 Woodcock, R.W. and Johnson, B.J. (1977). *Woodcock–Johnson Psychoeducational Battery.* Allen, TX: DLM Teaching Resources.

10 An analysis of special education as a response to the diminished academic achievement of Chicano/ Latino students: an update

Robert Rueda, Alfredo J. Artiles, Jesús Salazar, and Ignacio Higareda

In the first edition of this book (Valencia, 1991), an examination and analysis of the role of special education as a system was undertaken in light of significant gaps in achievement on the part of Chicano and other Latino students in the United States (Rueda, 1991). In that review, it was concluded that there were significant, systemic problems resulting in a system largely unresponsive to the educational needs of this group of students. A decade plus has passed since the publication of the initial volume. During this time there has been unprecedented and significant focus on education in the United States. Moreover, given this attention, the educational landscape is constantly shifting, and it is useful to revisit this issue at the beginning of the new millennium.

In the previous version of this chapter, the specific goals were as follows: (a) to present an historical overview of the role special education has played in the education of Chicano/ Latino students, and (b) to outline alternatives to the current system and structure and identify the challenges to be faced by the field as changes are considered and implemented. In this chapter, we will follow a similar path. We begin by recapping briefly some of the previous history as outlined in the earlier version of this chapter, in order to give the reader some orientation to the broader historical context (from the 1960s to 1989) in which the ensuing discussion is embedded. We then discuss some significant recent developments in the 1990s that have had a major impact on the issues considered in this chapter. We next discuss the current status of the special education field, using as a focus recent data from California. Finally, we discuss critical issues and challenges that remain to be addressed. In contrast to the earlier chapter, we focus for the most part on California, both because a number of other chapters in this volume take a national perspective, and because events and trends in California are having a significant impact on policy and practices in other states.

A brief historical recap from the 1960s to the 1990s

One noticeable trend in special education during this overall period was that consideration of Chicano/Latino students became much more visible in the literature. This was likely due to three interrelated developments: the civil rights movement of the late 1960s, the early work of Mercer (1973) on disproportionate identification and placement of African American and Chicano/Latino students in classes for students with mental retardation, and subsequent litigation that focused on unfair practices in assessment and other aspects of the special education process. While the civil rights movement of the 1960s initially focused on racial and ethnic issues, it was soon extended to persons with disabilities. The classic article of Dunn (1968) called attention to needlessly restrictive placements. The publication of this article sparked widespread discussion regarding the *negative* aspects of the special education service system. It was closely followed by the publication of Mercer's (1973) study that documented disproportionate representation in classes for students with mild retardation (educable mentally retarded [EMR]) and raised other issues regarding biased assessment and placement practices. These practices included, for example, inappropriate testing in English of students not proficient in the language, use of on-the-spot translations, and inappropriate norms. While Mercer later went on to develop a pluralistic assessment system that tried to take into account students' prior opportunity to learn (System of Multicultural Pluralistic Assessment [SOMPA], Mercer and Lewis, 1979), and was used in some school districts, it was never widely accepted in the psychometric community. It was believed by many to violate the standardization so prized in psychometric testing and others saw it as a way of unfairly or artificially inflating scores of minority students (for criticisms of SOMPA, see e.g., Clarizio, 1979, Goodman, 1979, and Oakland, 1979; see Mercer, 1979, for a response).

The mainstreaming debate arose in the 1960s in the midst of the civil rights era. Consistent with the premises of the social reconstructionist movement of the time, it was argued that the segregated system to serve people with disabilities (along with its knowledge base and practices) was ethically wrong, racially biased, and ineffective. As we know, the outcome of this struggle was a major victory for people with disabilities and their families in the mid 1970s. Indeed, with the passage of Public Law (P.L.) 94–142, the Education for All Handicapped Children Act (EAHCA), these individuals and families obtained constitutional rights to a free and appropriate education in the least restrictive environment, procedural safeguards, involvement in assessment and eligibility decisions, and access to due process of law. Equally important, the mainstreaming debate changed special education's structural connection with general education through the creation of a continuum of services (Skrtic, 1995).

One of the most significant developments in the period in question that distinguish it from earlier periods was the development of mandatory identification of students with learning problems. The passing of P.L. 94–142 (*Federal Register*, 1977) was equivalent to a civil rights law for students with disabilities. Key provisions were the guarantee of a free, appropriate public education for all students with disabilities, the right to due process, the right to nondiscriminatory assessment, the right to an individual education program, and an emphasis on providing services in the least restrictive environment.

This legislation had a major impact on the types and numbers of students served by the system. Federal data of 1987 (U.S. Department of Education, 1987) indicated that 4.4 million students were receiving services, slightly less than 11 percent of the school-age population nationwide. The categories of learning disabilities, mental retardation, serious emotional disturbance, and language impaired accounted for over 90 percent of all students served in special education. The category of learning disabled accounted for 4.7 percent of the total school enrollment, showing a 135 percent gain in the period from 1976 to 1986. In California, the growth was even more pronounced: The learning disabilities category grew by 185 percent (Forness and Kavale, 1989).

Although most professionals and consumers of special education services agree the EAHCA brought about positive changes in the system, litigation and criticisms continued throughout the 1970s and 1980s concerning interpretations and implementation of basic constructs included in the law (e.g., appropriate education; least restrictive environment; non-biased practices; see Skrtic, 1995; Turnbull, 1993). In the mid-1980s, a visible wave of practical criticisms gained momentum, which came to be known as the Regular Education Initiative (REI). The REI stressed the need to develop a synergistic relation between special and general education by integrating the two systems and pushing for large-scale mainstreaming, primarily of students with mild disabilities (Reynolds, 1991; Wang and Reynolds,

1985; Wang *et al.*, 1989; Will, 1986). However, advocates of students with severe disabilities also engaged in a parallel reform discourse to better serve this population. Through alternative recommendations to reconfigure the continuum of services (e.g., waivers; large-scale mainstreaming), REI advocates called for new service arrangements where general and special educators would work collaboratively. A focus on accountability and student academic performance was distinctive of the REI. For a variety of reasons (e.g., general education's interest in excellence over equity), however, the REI was largely ignored by the general education community (Fuchs and Fuchs, 1994).

Another distinguishing feature of this period was the issue of overrepresentation of special education and the resultant continuing legal challenges to placement and labeling practices. Generally, overrepresentation refers to "unequal proportions of culturally diverse students in special education programs" (Artiles and Trent, 1994, p. 514). Overrepresentation is generally calculated by contrasting the proportion of an ethnic group in general education with the proportion of the same group in a particular special education program.[1] Typically, the disability categories involved have included mild mental retardation (MMR), emotional/behavioral disorders (E/BD), and specific learning disabilities (SLD); overrepresentation generally affects African American, Chicano/Latino, American Indian, and (a few subgroups of) Asian American students (see Artiles *et al.*, in press, for an overview of overrepresentation).

California has figured prominently in concerns related to overrepresentation for the last several decades. Not surprisingly, litigation has played a major role in this struggle. Two especially noteworthy and long-standing cases will be briefly discussed here, namely *Diana* and *Larry P.* These two cases dealt with the central issues of assessment bias, disproportionate placement, and the long-term consequences of special education placement.

Diana v. State Board of Education (1970) was a class action suit filed by nine Mexican American families. The central issue in this case focused on biased testing practices due to language differences. In essence, ELLs were tested with English instruments and later placed in a class for the mildly mentally retarded or MMR (then called EMR or educable mentally retarded) based on those English test results. It was also argued in this case that both the tests and the curricula did not take into account students' culture, and that the overrepresentation of Mexican American students throughout the state's special education programs was pervasive. After lengthy legal proceedings, California settled the suit (consent decree) and agreed to do the following: Students were to be tested in their first language as well as in English; nonverbal intelligence tests could be used in the assessment process; Mexican American students were to be re-evaluated using nonverbal intelligence tests; districts were required to report on their reevaluation efforts and on plans for transitioning students from MMR programs to general education; and districts had to monitor whether Mexican American students were overrepresented in MMR programs (Figueroa and Artiles, 1999).

Despite the settlement of the *Diana* case, there has been ongoing and intense debate about the definition of "overrepresentation to a significant degree." Judge Peckham proposed a specific formula (the E-formula, a standard deviation of a proportion) that would serve as a warning sign that would allow districts to make changes as needed, but the California Department of Education argued that this amounted to a quota system.

A second highly influential case in California was *Larry P. v. Riles* (1979). While the *Diana* case primarily involved language issues, the *Larry P.* case primarily involved issues of culture. This lawsuit focused on overrepresentation of African American students and the suit argued that intelligence tests were culturally (instead of linguistically) biased. Coincidentally, this case was tried in the court of the same judge as the previous case. Unlike the earlier *Diana* case, the Department of Education refused to settle out of court and the case went to trial in 1977. After two years of proceedings, Judge Peckham ruled that IQ tests were culturally biased against African American students and placement in MMR programs constituted a "dead end" educational program. The judge also concluded that the reliance on biased assessment instruments was closely related to overrepresentation patterns. *Diana* and *Larry P.* were highly visible cases and had considerable influence on various developments in the special education field, such as features of the federal legislation and similar litigation around the country. More extensive discussion of the specifics of these and other cases and the issues they entail are found in Valdés and Figueroa (1994), and Henderson and Valencia (1985). It is sufficient to note here that these cases provided significant challenges to the prevailing assessment procedures as well as the assessment instruments themselves, especially individually administered standardized intelligence tests.

During the period of the early 1980s the National Academy of Sciences convened a panel on this issue of overrepresentation of minority students in special education. The panel's report (Heller *et al.*, 1982) reaffirmed earlier criticisms of the assessment and placement practices. As part of the panel's work, Finn (1982) reviewed the available Office for Civil Rights (OCR) data and found that minority students were overrepresented in classes for the mentally retarded (EMR and trainable mentally retarded [TMR]) as well as in classes for the emotionally disturbed. Importantly, Finn found effects for district size and size of minority enrollment, and instances of highest disproportion were found where bilingual programs were small or nonexistent. Directing attention away from individual differences in achievement in their report, the panel recommended evaluating the validity of instructional settings and doing so *before* a child is tested for special education diagnosis.

In the early 1980s, the federal government funded two Handicapped Minority Research Institutes in California and Texas. A central activity of these institutes was to examine assessment and instructional practices in special education programs with Latino enrollment. Among other findings, these researchers reported (Figueroa and Artiles, 1999; Figueroa *et al.*, 1989; Rueda, Cardoza *et al.*, 1984; Rueda, Figueroa *et al.*, 1984):

1 children of foreign-born Latino parents had a higher chance to be identified as disabled;
2 low achievement, poor reading and oral skills, articulation mistakes, limited vocabulary, and poor English comprehension were common referral and eligibility reasons;
3 testing conducted in English only, or only with an intelligence test, increased Latino students' chances to be labeled LD;
4 Latinos' IQ scores tended to decrease after receiving services in special education programs;
5 diagnostic tests in English or Spanish were not valid for Latino bilingual learners;
6 diagnostic tests given to Latino students who had never been referred to special education found 53 percent met the LD criteria; the same tests found 43 percent of MMR Latino students qualified as LD;
7 bilingual education support ended when Latino students were placed in special education; and
8 44 percent of Latinos receiving special education services had been unofficially placed as a "modification of their regular program."

During the latter part of the 1980s, there was evidence that changes were occurring in the composition of the special education population. The EMR category had begun to decrease, for example. Forness and Kavale (1989) reported that the EMR category decreased by 29 percent from 1976–1977 to 1985–1986. At the same time, there was also evidence that the number of students with specific learning disabilities (SLDs) was increasing (Ortiz and

Yates, 1983; Rueda, Figueroa *et al.*, 1984) and that overrepresentation of Latino students was evident in this category.

One distinctive feature of special education services in the late 1980s was that placements had become less restrictive from previous years; 77 percent of learning disabled students and 91 percent of language-impaired students were mainstreamed in regular classroom settings for at least part of the instructional day. In sum, the numbers of students served by the system were increasing, the largest part of the increase was comprised of students with mild disabilities, and the placements were less restrictive than in previous decades.

During the latter part of the 1980s, criticism against prevailing testing practices continued, especially the use of intelligence tests (Mercer, 1988; Miller-Jones, 1989). There was also a significant focus on alternatives and remedies for existing practices and assessments. These included more focus on pre-referral interventions (Ortiz and García, 1988; Ortiz and Maldonado-Colón, 1986), on the uses of performance-based measures (García and Pearson, 1994), use of the native language (Ortiz, 1984), and more culturally sensitive instructional models (Cummins, 1984). Furthermore, research on cultural bias in intelligence tests hit its peak in the 1980s (see Valencia and Suzuki, 2001; Valencia *et al.*, Chapter 9, this volume).

In the following section, we examine the special education context during the decade of the 1990s, the point at which the initial chapter (Rueda, 1991) left off. We focus our discussion on California because its demographic characteristics (particularly its large Chicano/Latino population; see Valencia, Chapter 2, current book), the significant recent policy developments that have occurred there, and because of the influence it often has on other parts of the country. We begin by providing a brief picture of developments both inside and outside of education that form an important part of the context in which special education is situated. We then look specifically at special education drawing on some recent data and other sources that provide a picture of current practice.

Recent developments: The decade of the 1990s

There are several recent developments that must be reviewed in order to understand the current context of special education. Although these are typically considered to be outside of the domain of special education, they do frame the environment related to the education of diverse students with disabilities. These are briefly described below.

Demographic changes

The extent of changes in the profile of the population in California has been nothing less than astounding. Children from cultures in which, collectively, more than 80 different languages are spoken enter California schools every year. The annual language census for 1999 reported a total of 1,442,692 English Language Learners (ELLs) in California, about a quarter of the total public school enrollment (California Department of Education, 1999). These students are widely dispersed among schools as well: According to these data, 904 of 1,052 school districts (86 percent) reported the enrollment of ELLs.[2] In the past decade, the ELL student population in kindergarten through grade twelve has nearly more than doubled, from 742,559 to 1.44 million students. While the number of language groups from which ELLs come is extensive, more than 90 percent of those ELLs speak one of five languages: Spanish (81.9 percent), Vietnamese (2.9 percent), Hmong (2 percent), Cantonese (1.8 percent), or Pilipino (1.3 percent). ELLs comprise about half of the Latino enrollment, and about 40 percent of the Asian enrollment in the state's public schools. Latino and Asian students represent the two largest groups from which ELLs come. There is significant variability *within* each group resulting from a variety of factors including, for example, country of origin, language background, cultural traditions, immigration status, socioeconomic level, and generation in the United States.

While the Latino ELLs is the largest group of the ELL population, it is very diverse in terms of nationality. As discussed by Valencia (Chapter 2, present volume), the 2000 U.S. Census reported that 59 percent of the 35.3 million Latinos in the U.S. are Mexican origin, about 10 percent Puerto Rican origin, approximately 4 percent are Cuban American, and about 28 percent are "Other Latino" (e.g., Central American; South American). About a third (31 percent) of the total U.S. Latino population and 41 percent of all Mexican Americans in the U.S. are concentrated in California (Guzmán, 2001). While about 200,000 migrate to the U.S. legally, it is estimated that an equal number immigrate illegally. About 90 percent of the total Latino population lives in metropolitan areas (U.S. Department of Commerce, Bureau of the Census, 1997).

Poverty continues to be an issue with the Latino population. In 1999, for example, 22.8 percent of the Latino population was estimated to be living in poverty. The median household income for this group was $30,700 compared to $44,400 for Whites (U.S. Department of Commerce, Bureau of the Census, 2000).

Taken together, these data indicate that (a) there are significant changes taking place in terms of the population profile including Latino, but other diverse groups as well; (b) there is more diversity *within* the Latino group.

Political initiatives

During the decade of the 1990s, political initiatives became an increasingly popular mechanism for deciding social policy issues including those directly affecting public schools. These initiatives were highly significant for Chicano/Latino students and their families, especially in California. In order to get a complete picture of the broader educational context, it is necessary to get a brief understanding of these policy developments developed through the initiative process (also see San Miguel and Valencia, 1998, for a discussion).

One of the more controversial measures was Proposition 187, which focused on "illegal" immigrants. Because of a significant amount of anti-immigrant sentiment in the State (see Suárez-Orozco and Suárez-Orozco, 1995), the voters of California enacted Proposition 187 in November of 1994. The specific provisions:

1   Made illegal aliens ineligible for public social services, public health care services (unless emergency under federal law), and public school education at elementary, secondary, and postsecondary levels.
2   Required various state and local agencies to report persons who are suspected illegal aliens to the California Attorney General and the United States Immigration and Naturalization Service.
3   Mandated California Attorney General to transmit reports to Immigration and Naturalization Service and maintain records of such reports.
4   Made it a felony to manufacture, distribute, sell or use false citizenship or residence documents.

The measure was described in the official ballot argument as "the first giant stride in ultimately ending the illegal alien invasion." The statute was immediately attacked as unconstitutional in several lawsuits, and its operation shackled by restraining orders. The long court fight was ended in 1998 by the federal judge who first found most of the initiative unconstitutional in 1994 (Associated Press, 1998).

Shortly after the passage of Proposition 187, in November of 1996, Proposition 209 was passed in California. Commonly known as the "Anti-Affirmative Action Proposition," among other things, it called for the state, local governments, districts, public universities, colleges, and schools, and other government instrumentalities from discriminating against or giving preferential treatment to any individual or group in public employment, public education, or public contracting on the basis of race, sex, color, ethnicity, or national origin.

Perhaps the most controversial initiative of all, and the one most directly impacting education policy, was Proposition 227, commonly known as the "Anti-Bilingual Initiative." On June 2, 1998, California voters overwhelmingly approved Proposition 227, an initiative that largely eliminates bilingual education from the state's public schools. Previously, in California the most common bilingual education model was an "early immersion" program in which students were transferred to English programs after two to three years of native language instruction. Under the new California initiative, most ELLs in that state are now placed in English-immersion programs and then shifted as quickly as possible into regular classrooms (see García and Wiese, Chapter 5, present book for further discussion of Proposition 227).

As expected, the nature of instructional program placement for ELLs has changed because of these transformations in educational policy. The impact of Proposition 227 on student program placement was reported for the first time in 1999. It was noted that 64 percent (927,473 ELLs) of the total ELL population of about 1.5 million students considered *not* to have a "reasonable" level of English proficiency were enrolled in programs of Structured English Immersion (702,592 or 75.8 percent) or Alternative Course of Study (179,334 or 19.3 percent). The remaining 32 percent or 461,894 students were placed in English language mainstream classes. ELLs enrolled in "other" instructional settings were 98,857 or 6.8 percent of the approximately 1.5 million ELLs. The numbers of students participating in programs in which they received instruction in English language development and the primary language declined from pre-Proposition 227 levels (409,879 or 29.1 percent to 169,440 or 11.7 percent) (California Department of Education, 1999). (Note: discrepancies in the total percentages reflect rounding errors in the original data base).

In a recent study on the effects of Proposition 227, Gándara *et al.* (2000) found a wide diversity of responses to the initiative in districts and schools. Districts with a history of extensive primary language programs and a significant number of staff were more likely to continue their programs than districts that did not. In addition, Gándara *et al.* found considerable confusion in the implementation of the initiative in terms of informing parents about their right to a waiver. Only 67 percent of districts in the state notified parents of this option. Finally, individual teachers implemented the new directives based on their own skill level, experience, beliefs about learning and bilingualism, and what they had done previous to the initiative. A significant number of teachers reported feeling frustrated at not being able to use their knowledge and skills to instruct their ELLs.

Instructional policy developments: reading reform

At the same time that these initiatives were being implemented, significant changes were taking place in the general education instructional context as well, especially in the area of reading. This is significant because reading-related problems tend to be prominent in the reasons for referral for students in the early grades. Publication of *Becoming a Nation of Readers* (Anderson *et al.*, 1985) focused national attention on the area of reading. In 1987,

California adopted the Language Arts Framework (California Department of Education, 1987), which provided for an integrative approach to reading and writing, with children's literature as a central feature. While it was often described as a "whole language" document, there was little or no professional development provided to teachers, and implementation was inconsistent at best.

In 1992, National Assessment of Educational Progress (NAEP) scores were broken out by state for the first time, assessing reading and writing in grades 4, 8, and 12. These scores were widely used to compare states. California scored low across the board, with 52 percent of the students scoring below the basic level of proficiency (Campbell *et al.*, 1996).

The election of a new Superintendent of Public Instruction, Delaine Eastin, in 1994, signaled a period of greater focus on reading in schools. The 1995 NAEP results further focused attention on this matter with an even poorer statewide showing. California scored second from the bottom (above Guam) in state rankings. One immediate result of dissatisfaction with test scores and state and territorial rankings was the publication in 1995 by the State Department of Education of *Every Child a Reader* (California Department of Education, 1995), developed by a state task force that advocated a "balanced" approach to reading. There was a marked shift from the whole-language flavor of the earlier state document, an emphasis that was largely blamed for low test scores, to a more skill-driven approach to reading. This document was closely followed in 1996 by the publication of *Teaching Reading* (California Department of Education, 1996) a document that promoted an explicit skills approach to reading including phonemic awareness, phonics, and decoding. The state was clearly moving away from a whole language to an explicit skills approach to reading.

This directive effort on the part of the state was assisted by the passage of Assembly Bill 1086 in summer of 1997. The bill limited the types of staff development that could be provided in schools to that which was consistent with the new approach to reading. Approved topics and providers were spelled out, in an attempt to push forward the "back to basics" direction of instruction.

While the 1998 NAEP scores showed a slight reversal of the downward trend of earlier years, there was still widespread dissatisfaction (Donahue *et al.*, 1999). Commercial reading programs thought to be consistent with the new direction of the state became increasingly popular and became the mandate in many schools and districts.

In sum, the state shifted in a relatively short period to a direction that focused on basic skills, explicit instruction, more prescriptive instructional and professional development practices, and English-only instruction. As mentioned earlier, these developments did not focus on special education specifically, but have significant implications for the achievement of Chicano/Latino students in general, and for those at-risk for special education placement in particular.

The school reform movement: accountability, standards, and "No social promotion" policy

The school reform movement sweeping the nation has heavily impacted California, like many states. The 1989 Education Summit of Governors is often cited as the point at which the movement to create standards and increase student achievement became systematically organized (McLaughlin and Shepard, 1995). From this meeting, the federal legislation known as Goals 2000: Educate America Act (P.L. 103–227) was eventually developed, and subsequently passed into law in 1994. This legislation encouraged among other features, the adoption of state standards and assessments. It also called for states to develop increased accountability for student achievement.

An additional impetus for reform was created from the Improving America's Schools Act, the reauthorization of the Elementary and Secondary Education Act in 1994 (Fowler, 1995). This legislation contained new requirements for obtaining funds under Chapter 1, the largest of the federal school programs aimed at poor, underachieving students. The overall purpose was to assist schools and students to meet content standards (P.L. 103–328). To be eligible for funds, states are required to submit plans that provide challenging content standards, state assessments, and provisions for yearly reports on progress in meeting the standards. While the federal government provided a strong push for common standards, the actual implementation and design has been carried out at the state level (McLaughlin and Rouse, 1999). Efforts toward creating national content or performance standards have been hampered by the fears of a "national curriculum" on the part of many conservatives. Not surprisingly, there are differences among the states in the ways that this reform effort has been implemented.

In California, efforts have been made to link standards to accountability, specifically in the form of standardized test scores. In 1997, the State Board required that all public school districts in California use a single yearly-standardized test for accountability purposes. Beginning in the 1997–1998 school year, the Stanford Achievement Test (an "off the shelf" standardized exam published by Harcourt Brace) became the designated assessment tool (Harcourt Educational Measurement, 1997).

More recently, the state passed the Public Schools Accountability Act of 1999. One significant aspect of the legislation was the establishment of an "Academic Performance Index," which is used to compare schools and districts in the state to each other in terms of relative rankings. The legislation further ties these test results and resultant rankings to financial incentives, thereby increasing the "high-stakes" nature of the testing context.

At the same time, the state has required that a high school exit examination be developed. Commencing with the 2003–2004 school year and each school year thereafter, each pupil completing grade 12 shall successfully pass the exit examination (High School Exit Examination) as a condition of receiving a diploma of graduation or a condition of graduation from high school.

Finally, the issue of "social promotion" has been a highly visible part of the reform movement (see Valencia *et al.*, Chapter 9, present book). In Septermber of 1998 the state passed Assembly Bill 1626, the "Pupil Promotion and Retention" measure (Pupil Promotion and Retention, 1998). This bill requires the governing board of each school district and each county board of education to approve a policy regarding the promotion and retention of pupils. The adopted policy was required to provide for the identification of pupils who should be retained or who are at risk of being retained. The legislation also requires the Superintendent of Public Instruction to recommend, and the State Board of Education to adopt, minimum levels of pupil performance on the state standardized test in reading, English language arts, and mathematics for grade level promotion. The provisions of this legislation became operative on January 1, 1999. Significantly, this legislation does not exclude special education students or students who are ELLs. While it is too early to gauge the effects of this legislation, it is predicted that significant numbers of Chicano/Latino students, especially ELLs, will be at risk for retention, hence school failure, including dropping out of school (see Bernal and Valencia, 2000; Valencia, 2000a).

Special education reforms

It should be evident that recent developments in special education, particularly as they pertain to Chicano/Latino students, have been shaped by larger demographic, economic, political, and general education reform movements. Typically, criticisms stemming from the complex confluence and interaction of the aforementioned forces have shaped the contemporary history of special education reforms. Skrtic (1995) argues there have been two types of criticism of the special education field, namely practical and theoretical. The former emphasizes special education models, strategies, and tools. Theoretical criticism focuses, in addition to the technical matters covered in the practical criticism, on the implicit theories and assumptions that guide the field's practices. Parents, special education professionals, and advocates have traditionally advanced practical criticism. In contrast, theoretical criticism has been voiced in the social sciences. Historically, Skrtic (1995) explains that the special education field has been transformed primarily as a result of practical criticisms. Two practical criticisms, in particular, have had a significant impact on the contemporary history of special education. Skrtic refers to them as episodes of criticism represented in the mainstreaming and inclusion debates. While we briefly discussed the mainstreaming development earlier, we turn to the related issue of inclusion that has been more prominent in the past decade.

The successor of the REI in the 1990s, the inclusive schools or inclusive education movement, included at least two groups of advocates with somewhat different goals and strategies, though several arguments were common to both groups. One group emphasized full inclusion, while the other emphasized merging of instructional support services and personnel. For instance, both sought to promote student social competence, social skills, attitude change, and positive peer relations in inclusive settings (Fuchs and Fuchs, 1994). More importantly, both groups agreed on the movement's rationale. Dyson (1999) identified two discourses related to the rationale for inclusive education, namely the ethics/rights and the efficacy arguments. These discourses recapitulated the criticisms of the 1960s and 1970s— specifically, that the special education system's assumptions, structures, and practices are flawed, ineffective, and unfair. The criticisms are directed at traditional assessment, classification, placement, and instructional practices that tend to oversample poor and ethnic minority students who do not show positive academic gains when placed in segregated programs. Hence, educators have the ethical imperative to transform the system to fulfill disabled students' right to an appropriate education.

One group argued for the elimination of the continuum of services by emphasizing full inclusion of students with disabilities or the merger of special and general education at the classroom level (Gartner and Lipsky, 1987; Lipsky and Gartner, 1991; Stainback and Stainback, 1992). For the most part, students with severe disabilities were the targeted beneficiaries of full inclusion, though scholars such as Lipsky and Gartner acknowledged students with the most severe and profound disabilities might need to receive services in specialized and intensive programs.

A second group of scholars included, among others, Maynard Reynolds, Margaret Wang, Marilyn Pugach, and Steve Lilly. This group targeted students with mild disabilities and although they also proposed a merger of systems, they proposed unification at the instructional support personnel level (Skrtic, 1995). Such a merger could be implemented in two steps. First, the merger would be implemented within special education by forming non-categorical programs for students with mild disabilities. This proposal is based in part on evidence about the lack of differentiation between the instructional practices carried out in these programs. The second step in the merger would be between the new non-categorical special education programs and the so-called compensatory programs that are provided to "disadvantaged, bilingual, migrant, low-English proficiency, or other children with special needs" (Reynolds and Wang, 1983, p. 206; see Skrtic, 1995 for a more detailed discussion on these two groups of inclusive education propositions).

These proposals, particularly the full inclusion recommendation, met with strong resistance from segments of the professional community and thus, debates ensued in professional journals and conferences. A major concern was that full inclusion would eventually make the field lose hard-won battles that had given recognition and entitlements to people with disabilities and it would ultimately create conditions reminiscent of the pre-EAHCA era. Furthermore, these inclusion proposals were criticized on technical (e.g., empirical support for criticisms; vagueness of reforms; general education's lack of readiness), ideological (e.g., values and beliefs about difference, development, learning, and disability), and rhetorical grounds (meaning of phrases such as "inclusion of all children") (Hallahan *et al.*, 1988; Kauffman *et al.*, 1988). Of course, such criticisms generated responses and counter-arguments from inclusion advocates (e.g., Brantlinger, 1997). The heated debates around inclusion proposals waned in recent years. Nevertheless, while calls for unification have been made (Andrews *et al.*, 2000), there remain deep philosophical and theoretical divisions within the field. Moreover, despite all the attention given to the problem, concern with overrepresentation has persisted throughout the 1980s and 1990s. This includes, for example, focused investigations of the overrepresentation problem (e.g., National Academy of Science panels in the 1980s and a current panel investigating the overrepresentation issue; see Figueroa and Artiles, 1999).

Taken together, the above developments have had major impact on the current state of education in California and in many ways have redefined the context in which special education operates for Chicano/Latino students. In the next section we review some recent data from California and consider them in the context of the above developments. We examine the implications of some of these issues more in detail in the concluding section.

Current status of special education practices: some recent data

After three decades of debate, the goal to eliminate the overrepresentation of minority students in special education programs is still elusive (Artiles and Trent, 2000; Dunn, 1968; Heller *et al.*, 1982). However, caution is necessary in examining the data. The overrepresentation is often masked if the data are not disaggregated. Early on, Finn (1982) reported that although the representation of Chicano/Latinos in MMR programs was somewhat similar to Whites, "the small Latino-nonminority difference for the nation as a whole is an average of many sizable disproportions in both directions" (p. 368). However, Finn also learned MMR overrepresentation was related to the size of the district. That is, overrepresentation was a problem in districts with large Latino enrollment (i.e., ≥ 70 percent). At the same time, he found the largest MMR overrepresentation rates were observed in small districts with large Chicano/Latino enrollment; Chicano/Latino LD overrepresentation was also associated with this group's overrepresentation in MMR. Another important factor that seemed to influence placement rates was the availability of programs to address the needs of ELLs, particularly in large school districts. Finn reported that the proportion of Chicano/Latino students in bilingual programs was inversely associated with overrepresentation levels—i.e., districts with the highest overrepresentation rates had smaller proportions of students in bilingual programs. He concluded "[i]t is possible that Latino students with poor English proficiency are misclassified as EMR when bilingual programs are not available" (p. 372).

More recently, Artiles and Trent (1994) noted that:

(1) . . . The larger the minority student population is in the school district, the greater the representation of students in special education classes

(2) The bigger the educational program, the larger the disproportion of minority students

(3) . . . Variability in overrepresentation data has been found as a function of the specific disability condition and the ethnic group under scrutiny.

(p. 414)

Recent data from the U.S. Department of Education provide a comparative look at the issue of overrepresentation for both California and the nation as a whole for three of the categories that have traditionally been problematic. The recently published *Twenty-second Annual Report to Congress on the Implementation of the Individuals with Disabilities Education Act* (U.S. Department of Education, 2000) concluded that Chicano/Latino students, ages 6 through 21 years, were generally represented among the special education population at a rate comparable to the resident population, although it noted that these relationships varied by category (U.S. Department of Education, 2000, p. II-28). For all categories combined, the report concluded that representation of Chicano/Latino students in special education (13.2 percent) was generally similar to the percentages in the general Chicano/Latino school-age population (14.2 percent). However, Chicano/Latino students exceeded the resident population percentages in three categories: specific learning disabilities (15.8 percent), hearing impairments (16.3 percent), and orthopedic impairments (14.4 percent) (U.S. Department of Education, 2000, p. II-27).

A more differentiated breakdown by categories that have traditionally been problematic in terms of overrepresentation is presented in Table 10.1 (calculated from OCR data) for both Latino students as well as for students who are ELL. Table 10.1 indicates that in California, Chicano/Latino students are overrepresented in the category of mental retardation (a 5.2 percent overrepresentation) and ELL students are overrepresented slightly higher in the same category (28.1 percent overrepresentation).[3] At the national level, Latino students are overrepresented in the category of specific learning disabilities (2.4 percent) only. There are, however, variable over- and underrepresentation patterns in the mental retardation and learning disabilities categories for Chicanos/Latinos across states (see Valencia and Suzuki, 2001, p. 202, Table 7.1, and p. 203, Table 7.2).

While the overrepresentation situation has improved from earlier decades, it appears that it has not disappeared. This is particularly the case with the persistent pattern of African American overrepresentation in the MMR category (see Valencia and Suzuki, 2001, pp. 315–316, Note 1). Although relatively more attention has been directed at understanding African

Table 10.1 Percentage of Chicanos/Latinos and ELLs in selected categories of special education placement for California and the nation

Location	Chicano/Latino				ELL			
	Enrollment[a] (%)	MR (%)	SLD (%)	ED (%)	Enrollment[a] (%)	MR (%)	SLD (%)	ED (%)
California	38.2	40.2	35.1	6.7	22.8	29.2	20.5	6.6
National	12.7	8.3	13.0	8.8	6.3	3.7	5.5	1.9

Source: U.S. Department of Education, Office for Civil Rights (1997); U.S. Department of Education (2000).

Note
ELL = English Language Learner; MR = Mentally Retarded; SLD = Specific Learning Disability; ED = Emotional Disturbance.
[a] % enrollment = percentage of group in total K-12 enrollment.

American placement in mild disability programs, we know significantly less about ELL representation in these programs, particularly as language proficiency, immigration, and legal and political issues affect this group. Many questions remain unanswered about the potential impact of English-only legislation on ELL placement in special education. For example, what will be the impact of these types of reforms on the representation of various ELL subgroups in special education at distinct grade levels? What role do socioeconomic status (SES) and English proficiency play in ELL special education placement? Recent evidence, for example, suggests that there are clear associations between factors such as gender and other sociodemographic factors such as SES and placement in special education (Oswald and Coutinho, 1999; Oswald *et al.*, 2001).

In sum, it is important to keep in mind that distinct overrepresentation patterns are evidenced depending upon how placement data are analyzed (Artiles and Trent, 1994). Overrepresentation patterns for various ethnic groups vary as the data are examined at the national, state, or district level. Such patterns also change depending on the disability category under scrutiny (e.g., some racial/ethnic groups tend to be overrepresented in SLD but not in MMR programs). In addition, the size of the school district, the availability of special education and alternative programs (e.g., bilingual education; Chapter 1 programs), and the proportion of minority students in the district can be associated with overrepresentation patterns (Artiles and Trent, 2000; Finn, 1982; Harry, 1992).

In our continuing efforts to investigate these issues, our research team has been examining the data from several large urban school districts in the state of California (southern California in particular) as a window into recent special education trends in large urban school districts with large numbers of Chicano/Latino students (Artiles, Rueda *et al.*, 2000). Although California is unique, as indicated earlier, it does play an important role as a leader in national educational and social policy, and therefore it is important to examine current trends.

We have been examining placement patterns in 11 large urban school districts in the Southern California area (varying in size from 51,905 to 77,045), and we have been able to compare data over a five-year period (1993–1994 and 1998–1999). Table 10.2 provides a summary of some of these changes.

During this relatively short time span:

1   The total elementary student population in these districts increased by 11 percent, while the Chicano/Latino population increased by 16 percent. This change in the Chicano/Latino population is consistent with the earlier discussion of widespread changes in demographic patterns.
2   There was a dramatic increase in the number of students in special education from 4,611 to 17,641, an increase of 283 percent.

In addition, other changes in the Chicano/Latino elementary school population in these districts over time included the following:

1   There was an increase of 12 percent in the ELL subgroup of Chicanos/Latinos.
2   The numbers of students receiving free/reduced lunch grew by 45 percent, an indication of increasing poverty.

In terms of the Chicano/Latino subgroup in special education, the following patterns were evident:

Table 10.2 Characteristics of students and subgroups in 11 Southwest urban school districts over a 5-year period

Group/subgroup	1993–1994	1998–1999	Increase (%)
Total elementary population			
Total students	363,050	401,961	11
Total students in special education	4,611	17,641	283
Chicano/Latino students			
Total students	251,291	291,297	16
Total ELL students	178,443	199,259	12
ELL students who receive free/reduced lunch	178,277	258,252	45
Chicanos/Latinos in special education			
Total students in special education	2,727	12,038	341
Students in special education also receiving free/reduced lunch	2,355	11,135	373
Chicano/Latino ELL students in special education	1,854	8,245	345

Source: Data provided by districts.

1   The numbers of students increased dramatically, reflecting a 341 percent increase.
2   The percentage of students in this group receiving free/reduced lunch grew by 373 percent.
3   The number of Chicano/Latino ELL students in special education increased by 345 percent.

In short, the data suggest that these districts are growing, and that the Chicano/Latino population is growing at an even faster rate. Moreover, the data suggest that poverty is a continuing and growing problem. The most dramatic increases, however, are seen in the numbers of students in special education for both the general population, but especially for the Chicano/Latino and ELL groups in the districts. Unfortunately, the state has revised its testing program, so that different assessments were administered between the two time periods being considered. Therefore, comparative data over time are not presented. However, recent achievement data are available that allow for some comparison among subgroups. These data are presented in Table 10.3, and reflect standardized scores on the SAT 9 (Stanford Achievement Test, 9th Edition) for grades 1 through 5 collected as part of the statewide accountability system.

Overall, the data suggest that students score in the lower third to lower quarter in terms of standardized scores, although there is quite a bit of variance at each grade level. Interestingly, students at almost all grade levels score lower in reading than in the other areas. In addition, there is a pattern such that all students in special education score higher than Chicano/Latino students in special education who in turn score higher than the ELL subgroup. While these differences are troublesome, academic achievement is problematic for all of the groups examined.

Next, we present a closer examination of Chicano/Latino special education placement. Table 10.4 presents special education placement data for different grade levels for the 1998–1999 school year in these same districts. When the total percentage of Chicano/Latino ELL students in special education is compared to that of all students, the figures appear to be comparable (7.2 percent versus 7.7 percent—bottom row, Table 10.3). However, when the

Table 10.3 Achievement test data (Stanford Achievement Test, SAT 9) for selected groups: 1998–1999

	Reading			Math			Language Arts		
	N	NCE	SD	N	NCE	SD	N	NCE	SD
All students in special education									
Grade 1	1,113	34.3	17.1	1,137	35.2	16.8	1,188	36.1	20.0
Grade 2	1,824	29.4	16.6	1,917	30.4	20.3	1,963	34.1	21.0
Grade 3	2,376	25.9	29.2	2,375	30.7	17.5	2,460	32.3	19.5
Grade 4	2,370	25.8	18.2	2,483	30.2	16.1	2,499	28.3	18.2
Grade 5	2,628	25.4	16.9	2,757	26.4	16.5	2,766	28.1	17.2
Chicano/Latino students in special education									
Grade 1	787	30.9	14.5	814	32.3	14.7	845	33.1	18.3
Grade 2	1,265	25.3	13.1	1,337	26.2	17.0	1,370	30.7	18.8
Grade 3	1,568	22.0	14.6	1,566	27.3	14.4	1,628	29.3	16.5
Grade 4	1,622	22.0	15.1	1,718	27.4	13.6	1,727	25.4	15.6
Grade 5	1,740	21.3	13.4	1,831	23.5	13.7	1,847	25.1	13.8
Chicano/Latino ELL students in special education									
Grade 1	583	29.6	13.3	604	30.7	13.6	627	31.1	17.4
Grade 2	983	21.0	12.0	1,043	24.9	15.3	1,061	29.6	18.2
Grade 3	1,150	19.4	12.2	1,149	25.0	12.2	1,195	27.2	15.1
Grade 4	1,121	18.8	12.0	1,184	24.3	11.1	1,190	22.9	13.5
Grade 5	1,081	17.0	10.4	1,131	20.1	11.1	1,139	21.8	11.6

Source: Data provided by districts.

Note
NCE = Normal Curve Equivalent.

Table 10.4 Special education placement number and percentage in 11 large urban school districts in California

Grade	Total students	All students in special education[a]		Total ELLs	Latino ELLs in special education	
		No.	%		No.	%
K	62,544	1,314	2.1	38,579	757	2.0
1	66,493	2,039	3.1	40,961	1,148	2.8
2	65,230	3,246	5.0	39,243	1,774	4.5
3	63,484	4,182	6.6	34,282	2,057	6.0
4	57,619	4,511	7.8	27,385	2,182	8.0
5	57,681	4,842	8.4	18,825	2,102	11.2
6	50,741	5,877	11.6	16,560	2,879	17.4
7	49,020	5,547	11.3	15,748	2,514	16.0
8	46,752	4,828	10.3	13,319	1,960	14.7
9	53,995	4,941	9.2	17,409	2,085	12.0
10	40,561	3,105	7.7	9,729	1,090	11.2
11	30,552	2,396	7.8	5,371	659	12.3
12	26,924	1,384	5.1	3,236	454	14.0
Grand total	671,596	48,212	7.2	280,647	21,661	7.7

Source: Data provided by districts.

Note
[a] These data include the categories of seriously emotionally disturbed, educable mentally retarded, language/speech impaired, moderately mentally retarded, and specific learning disability.

data are examined on a grade-by-grade basis, a different picture emerges. A trend toward higher placement rates for ELL students is evidenced beginning about grade 5, and it becomes especially pronounced in high school. We do not have data on what is driving this trend, but we hypothesize that it may be due to the decrease in support services, especially for ELLs, in high school. By grade 12, only 5.1 percent of the total student population is in special education, while 14 percent of the ELL population is in special education.

We have also been interested in tracking this population because of the recently passed English-only legislation and the other changes that have occurred in the last decade. The only data we have been able to access to date is from 1998–1999, and these data do not allow us to examine special education placements in the years before the implementation of Proposition 227. We have begun, however, to look at special education data as a function of which program students were placed in after the legislation was passed. In brief, there were three program options. Students were either put in (a) a straight English immersion program, (b) a modified English immersion program, or (c) a bilingual program (a special waiver requested by the parents had to be approved for students to receive this option). Straight immersion programs are carried out primarily in English with primary language support supplied by the paraprofessional; primary language is used for clarification when students fail to understand the instructions or content of a lesson. The modified immersion programs feature instruction primarily in English with primary language support provided by a teacher but only for concept development. Bilingual programs feature the use of primary language instruction until the student can transition into English (normally operationalized as a period between one and three years). Table 10.5 presents data on these programs for the ELL elementary school population in the 11 districts.

Table 10.5 Number and percentage of ELLs in resource specialist program by type of language program in 11 large urban school districts in California, grades 1–5: 1998–1999

Grade	Straight immersion program			Modified immersion program			Bilingual program		
	Total	RSP	%	Total	RSP	%	Total	RSP	%
K	11,113	243	2.2	20,786	349	1.7	5,487	92	1.7
1	12,478	423	3.4	21,392	514	2.4	5,954	142	2.4
2	12,718	721	5.7	20,906	805	3.9	4,513	189	4.2
3	12,453	993	8.0	17,679	818	4.6	2,867	156	5.4
4	11,921	1,200	10.1	12,760	788	6.2	1,362	94	6.9
5	8,515	1,259	14.8	8,026	653	8.1	890	73	8.2
Total	69,198	4,839	7.0	101,549	3,927	3.9	21,073	746	3.5

Source: Data provided by districts.

As the data suggest, the differences between the modified immersion program and the bilingual programs are not great. However, the data for the straight English immersion program suggest that the percentages of the ELL population who receive this program are in special education in greater numbers. In a recent examination of these data, we found a clear trend: ELLs receiving the least primary language support had greater chances to be placed in special education programs. For instance, we found that ELLs placed in English immersion classes—compared to ELLs placed in bilingual programs—were almost three times as likely to be placed in special education programs (Artiles, Rueda *et al.*, 2000). Of course, these data do not allow causal relationships to be drawn. Currently, we are working on more refined analyses of the data that currently exist, and plan to continue to monitor this pattern over time. In spite of the limitations, these data raise some serious questions about the continuing issue of overrepresentation especially in light of the current educational context as outlined in the earlier part of this chapter. Given the large increases in the special education population, how will future placements of ELL students be affected by the continued implementation of English-only policies? Will more prescriptive teaching strategies and curricula be unevenly applied to different subgroups of the student population? What will students from diverse backgrounds internalize regarding their home languages and cultural backgrounds given the political and instructional initiatives just described? These questions will take on increasing importance as the impetus of developments in California affect other urban areas around the country. Research will be needed to closely monitor developments, both in the short term and long term.

Discussion and conclusion: critical issues and challenges ahead

In the earlier version of this chapter (Rueda, 1991), overrepresentation in special education was a significant issue. Unfortunately, overrepresentation is still a problem in spite of over 30 years of attention to the issue. In our discussion of this issue, we have focused on low achievement, although the underrepresentation of gifted/talented Chicanos/Latinos is an issue as well (Figueroa and Ruiz, 1998; Ruiz, 1989; Valencia *et al.*, Chapter 9, this volume; Valencia and Suzuki, 2001). Our discussion has highlighted the importance of unpacking the data. Failure to do so runs the risk of leaving significant patterns unexposed since they are not always evident when data are aggregated.

Another significant issue in this regard is that relevant data are not routinely kept by monitoring agencies so that the significant variables of interest can be tracked easily. These include ethnic/racial group, SES, placement, type of instructional program, and language proficiency status. Oftentimes this information is not collected in the same database, requiring complex and sometimes expensive data manipulations, leaving the monitoring of these issues open only to individual investigators with substantial resources. Given the significant legal, policy, and instructional issues involved, efforts toward collecting more systematic data in these areas are needed. Unfortunately, the constellation of factors constituting the current educational context suggests that the issue of overrepresentation requires increased monitoring rather than less.

While there have been significant developments in the arena of assessment, such as the introduction of performance based assessment (García and Pearson, 1994), the current educational scene is dominated by the use of high-stakes assessment, most notable single measure norm- and criterion-referenced achievement tests (see Valencia *et al.*, Chapter 9, this volume). Furthermore, measured intelligence (e.g., IQ) remains a central element of both the definition and assessment process for eligibility in various disability categories (Valencia and Suzuki, 2001). It is interesting to note that if IQ and measured achievement are really equivalent, some of the categories that contain the largest number of students, such as learning disabilities, could not exist or at least substantial changes would be needed in its definition (Kavale and Forness, 2000). In spite of strong arguments against the use of IQ as a diagnostic tool, even apart from issues of cultural bias (Valencia *et al.*, Chapter 9, this volume) or concerns with overrepresentation issues (Fletcher *et al.*, 1998; Francis *et al.*, 1996), it is still widely used.

While overrepresentation continues to be an issue, it should be kept in mind that discovering a more accurate test that will simply sort better, or otherwise simply eliminating unbalanced placement rates is likely to do little in terms of a solution to the problem. First, a question needs to be raised about why special education placement is considered in such a negative light. If special education represented a doorway into enriched individualized educational support, high quality tutorial assistance, other forms of desirable experiences and services, and a vehicle for boosting achievement, perhaps the concern with overrepresentation would not be an issue. Unfortunately, the more common perception is that it represents loss of access to the core curriculum, low-level remedial programs, and tracking. Second, making sure that a "correct" label is applied, or that the "true" cases of "disability" have been separated from students who are only ELLs does not provide any guarantees about the quality of instruction or eventual academic outcomes.

Instruction has been a strong thread in both the regular and special education literature in the past decade, likely related to some of the factors discussed earlier in this chapter. Recent major integrative syntheses of special education interventions and instructional techniques have tried to examine the issue of "what works" in special education (Forness *et al.*, 1997; Swanson, 1999). However, language proficiency and race/ethnicity have not been disaggregated in these analyses, leaving the issue of "what works" for Chicano/Latino students in special education relatively unanswered (Artiles *et al.*, 1997). A recent attempt to conduct such an analysis for ELLs in special education (Gersten and Baker, 2000) found only nine intervention studies and 15 descriptive studies. For the small number of intervention studies, the authors concluded that they were often unclear (a) regarding how interventions were implemented, (b) what level of implementation was achieved, (c) what the language of instruction was, and (d) about relevant contextual variables that would help in interpreting or replicating the results. Clearly there remains much work to be done in this area.

One issue that deserves mention is the deficit orientation in the field that has tended to characterize issues of language and culture (Trent *et al.*, 1998; Valencia, 1997). Part of this deficit thinking paradigm may be due to the fact that some of the dominant frameworks in the field do not leave space for constructs such as culture and context (Rueda and Kim, 2001). It is also likely a function of the fact that the preferred tools of investigation in the field may not be well suited to investigating factors such as culture and context. When alternative tools are used, such as qualitative methodology they often are seen as less respectable or as unscientific. Yet, given the diverse makeup of the U.S. population, as indicated in this chapter and elsewhere in the book, culture and language need to be more central variables. It is critical that they be integrated into the research in both assessment and teaching/ learning. In short, the field needs to begin to consider sociocultural factors in research and to strike a meaningful balance between qualitative and quantitative methods.

A final note is in order. Recent evidence suggests that teacher quality is one of the most important of all of the various "inputs" that make up the educational process (Darling-Hammond, 2000; Sanders and Rivers, 1996; Valencia, Chapter 1, this volume). Unfortunately, as Darling-Hammond reports, student characteristics such as poverty, non-English status, and minority status are negatively correlated with qualifications of teachers (also, see Valencia, 2000b). Moreover, even when teachers have gone through an accredited program, it is unlikely that they will have had effective coursework and practical experience in dealing with issues of language and culture or that they will be well-prepared to do so (Artiles, Trent *et al.*, 2000).

Unfortunately, many of the factors that have been problematic in the past are still not addressed. Moreover, because of the unique set of factors that define the current educational context, the outlook for improvement in the short term is somewhat gloomy. Continued attention will be needed to monitor the progress of Chicano/Latino students in the coming years.

Authors' note

The second author acknowledges the support of the COMRISE Project at the University of Virginia under grant #H029J60006 awarded by the U.S. Department of Education, Office of Special Education Programs.

Notes

1 The calculation of overrepresentation has been a contested issue and several formulas have been proposed and used throughout the history of this problem (see Reschly, 1997, for a discussion of the strength and limitations of these formulas).
2 Update for 1999.
3 Disparities were calculated by comparing Chicano/Latino and ELL percentages in the total school enrollment to each group's percentage in the various special education categories. Specifically, the formula for disparity calculation is a follows: School enrollment percentage minus special education category percentage divided by school enrollment percentage.

References

Anderson, R.C., Hiebert, E.H., Scott, J.A. and Wilkinson, I.A. (1985). *Becoming a nation of readers: The report of the commission on reading*. Washington, DC: The National Institute of Education.

Andrews, J., Carnine, D.W., Coutinho, M.J., Edgar, E.B., Fuchs, L.S., Forness, S.R., Jordan, D.J., Kauffman, J.M., Patton, J.M., Paul, J. Rossell, J., Rueda, R., Schiller, E., Skrtic, T.M. and Wong, J. (2000). Bridging the special education divide. *Remedial and Special Education, 21*, 258–260, 267.

Artiles, A.J. and Trent, S.C. (1994). Overrepresentation of minority students in special education: A continuing debate. *Journal of Special Education, 27*, 410–437.

Artiles, A.J. and Trent, S.C. (2000). Representation of culturally/linguistically diverse students. In C.R. Reynolds and E. Fletcher-Jantzen (Eds.), *Encyclopedia of special education, Vol. 1* (2nd ed., pp. 513–517). New York: John Wiley.

Artiles, A.J., Trent, S.C. and Kuan, L.A. (1997). Learning disabilities research on ethnic minority students: An analysis of 22 years of studies published in selected refereed journals. *Learning Disabilities Research and Practice, 12*, 82–91.

Artiles, A.J., Harry, B., Reschly, D. and Chinn, P. (2002). Over-identification of students of color in special education: A critical overview. *Multicultural Perspectives, 4*, 3–10.

Artiles, A.J., Rueda, R., Salazar, J. and Higareda, J. (2000). *Factors associated with English learner representation in special education: Emerging evidence from urban school districts in California.* Paper presented at the Minority Issues in Special Education Conference, Harvard University. Cambridge, MA, November.

Artiles, A.J., Trent, S.C., Hoffman-Kipp, P. and López-Torres, L. (2000). From individual acquisition to cultural-historical practices in multicultural teacher education. *Remedial and Special Education, 21*, 79–89.

Associated Press (1998). Judge kills California immigration law. *Austin American-Statesman*, March 19, p. A3.

Bernal, E.M. and Valencia, R.R. (2000). The TAAS case: A recapitulation and beyond. *Hispanic Journal of Behavioral Sciences, 22*, 540–556.

Brantlinger, E. (1997). Using ideology: Cases of nonrecognition of the politics of research and practice in special education. *Review of Educational Research, 67*, 425–459.

California Department of Education. (1987). *English-language arts framework for California public schools, K-12.* Sacramento, CA: California Department of Education.

California Department of Education. (1995). *Every child a reader: The report of the California Reading Task Force.* Sacramento, CA: California Department of Education.

California Department of Education. (1996). *Teaching reading: A balanced, comprehensive approach to teaching reading in prekindergarten through grades three.* Sacramento, CA: Bureau of Publications.

California Department of Education. (1999). *Language census, spring 1999.* Sacramento, CA: California Department of Education.

Campbell, J., Donohue, P.L., Reese, C.M. and Phillips, G.W. (1996). *NAEP 1994 reading report card for the nation and the states: Findings from the National Assessment and Educational Progress and Trial State Assessment.* Washington, DC: Office of Educational Research and Improvement, U.S. Department of Education.

Clarizio, H.F. (1979). In defense of the IQ test. *School Psychology Digest, 8*, 79–88.

Cummins, J. (1984). *Bilingualism and special education: Issues in assessment and pedagogy.* San Diego, CA: College Hill Press.

Darling-Hammond, L. (2000). Teacher quality and student achievement: A review of state policy evidence. *Education Policy Analysis Archives, 8*, 1–67.

Diana v. State Board of Education. Civil Action No. C-70-37, (N.D. Cal.) (1970).

Donahue, P.L., Voelkl, K.E., Campbell, J.R. and Mazzeo, J. (1999). *NAEP 1998 reading report card for the nation and the states.* Washington, DC: U.S. Department of Educational Research and Improvement.

Dunn, L. M. (1968). Special education for the mildly retarded: Is much of it justifiable? *Exceptional Children, 23*, 5–21.

Dyson, A. (1999). Inclusion and inclusions: Theories and discourses in inclusive education. In H. Daniels and P. Garner (Eds.), *World yearbook of education 1999: Inclusive education* (pp. 36–53). London: Kogan Page Limited.

Education for All Handicapped Children Act of 1975, Pub. L. No. (94–142), 89 Stat. 773 (1975).

Federal Register. (1977). Education of Handicapped Children. Regulations Implementing Education for All Handicapped Children Act of 1975, August, pp. 42472–42518.

Figueroa, R.A. and Artiles, A.J. (1999). Disproportionate minority placement in special education programs: Old problem, new explanations. In A. Tashakkori and S.H. Ochoa (Eds.), *Education of Latinos in the U.S.: Politics, policies, and outcomes* (pp. 93–117). New York: AMS Press.

Figueroa, R.A., Fradd, S.H. and Correa, V.I. (1989). Bilingual special education and this special issue. *Exceptional Children, 56*, 174–178.

Figueroa, R.A. and Ruiz, N.T. (1993). Bilingual pupils and special education: A reconceptualization. In R.C. Eaves and P.J. McLaughlin (Eds.), *Recent advances in special education and rehabilitation* (pp. 73–87). New York: Andover Medical Publishers.

Finn, J.D. (1982). Patterns in special education placement as revealed by the OCR surveys. In K.A. Heller, W.H. Holtzman, and S. Messick (Eds.), *Placing children in special education: A strategy for equity* (pp. 322–381). Washington, DC: National Academy Press.

Fletcher, J.M., Francis, D.J., Shaywitz, S.E., Lyon, G.R., Foorman, B.R., Stuebing, K.K. and Shaywitz, B.A. (1998). Intelligent testing and the discrepancy model for children with learning disabilities. *Learning Disabilities Research and Practice, 13*, 186–203.

Forness, S.R. and Kavale, K.A. (1989). Identification and diagnostic issues in special education: A status report for child psychiatrists. *Child Psychiatry and Human Development, 19,* 279–301.

Forness, S.R., Kavale, K.A., Blum, I.M. and Lloyd, L.W. (1997). Mega-analysis of meta-analyses: What works in special education and related services. *Teaching Exceptional Children, 29*, 4–9.

Fowler, T. (1995). *Improving America's Schools Act of 1994: Reauthorization of the ESEA.* Washington, DC: U.S. Department of Education.

Francis, D.J., Fletcher, J.M., Shaywitz, B.A., Shaywitz, S.E. and Rourke, B. (1996). Defining learning and language disabilities: Conceptual and psychometric issues with the use of IQ tests. *Language, Speech, and Hearing Services in Schools, 27*, 132–143.

Fuchs, D. and Fuchs, L.S. (1994). Inclusive schools movement and the radicalization of special education reform. *Exceptional Children, 60*, 294–309.

Gándara, P., Maxwell-Jolly, J., García, E., Asato, J., Gutiérrez, K., Stritikus, T. and Curry, J. (2000). *The initial impact of Proposition 227 on the instruction of English learners.* Santa Barbara, CA: Linguistic Minority Research Institute.

García, G.E. and Pearson, P.D. (1994). Assessment and diversity. *Review of Research in Education, 20,* 337–391.

Gartner, A. and Lipsky, D.K. (1987). Beyond special education: Toward a quality system for all students. *Harvard Educational Review, 57*, 367–395.

Gersten, R. and Baker, S. (2000). What we know about effective instructional practices for English-language learners. *Exceptional Children, 66*, 454–470.

Goals 2000: Educate America Act. Pub. L. No. (103–227), 108 Stats. 125. (1994).

Goodman, J.F. (1979). Is tissue the issue? A critique of SOMPA's models and tests. *School Psychology Digest, 8*, 47–62.

Guzmán, B. (2001). *The Hispanic population: Census 2000 brief.* Washington, DC: U.S. Department of Commerce, Economics and Statistics Administration, U.S. Census Bureau. Available online at: http://www.census.gov/prod/2001pubs/c2kbr01–3.pdf

Hallahan, D.P., Kauffman, J.M., Lloyd, J.W. and McKinney, J.D. (1988). Introduction to the series: Questions about the regular education initiative. *Journal of Learning Disabilities, 21*, 3–5.

Harcourt Educational Measurement. (1997). *Stanford Nine Achievement Test, Ninth Edition, Stanford 9.* San Antonio, TX: Harcourt Brace and Co.

Harry, B. (1992). *Cultural diversity, families, and the special education system: Communication and empowerment.* New York: Teachers College Press.

Heller, K.A., Holtzman, W.H. and Messick, S. (Eds.). (1982). *Placing children in special education: A strategy for equity.* Washington, DC: National Academy Press.

Henderson, R.W. and Valencia, R.R. (1985). Nondiscriminatory school psychological services: Beyond nonbiased assessment. In J.R. Bergan (Ed.), *School psychology in contemporary society* (pp. 340–377). Columbus, OH: Charles E. Merrill.

Improving America's Schools Act. Pub. L. No. (103–382), 108 Stat. 3518. (1994).

Kauffman, J.M., Gerber, M.M. and Semmel, M.I. (1988). Arguable assumptions underlying the regular education initiative. *Journal of Learning Disabilities, 21*, 6–11.

Kavale, K.A. and Forness, S.R. (2000). What definitions of learning disability say and don't say: A critical analysis. *Journal of Learning Disabilities, 33*, 239–256.

Larry P. v. Riles. (1979). 343 F. Supp. 1306 (N.D. Cal. 1972) affr 502 F. 2d 963 (9th Cir. 1974); 495 F. Supp. 926 (N.D. Cal. 1979); appeal docketed, No. 80–4027 (9th Cir., Jan 17, 1980).

Lipsky, D.K. and Gartner, A. (1991). Restructuring for quality. In J.W. Lloyd, N.N. Singh, and A.C. Repp (Eds.), *The Regular Education Initiative: Alternative perspectives on concepts, issues, and models* (pp. 44–56). Sycamore, IL: Sycamore Publishing Company.

McLaughlin, M.J. and Rouse, M. (Eds.). (1999). *Special education and school reform in the United States and Britain.* New York: Routledge.

McLaughlin, M.W. and Shepard, L.A. (1995). *Improving education through standards-based reform: A report by the National Academy of Education panel on standards-based reform.* Stanford, CA: National Academy of Education.

Mercer, J. (1973). *Labeling the mentally retarded: Clinical and social systems perspectives on mental retardation.* Berkeley: University of California Press.

Mercer, J.R. (1979). In defense of racially and culturally non-discriminatory assessment. *School Psychology Digest, 8,* 89–115.

Mercer, J. (1988). Death of the IQ paradigm: Where do we go from here? In W. Lonner and V.O. Tyler (Eds.), *Cultural and ethnic factors in learning and motivation: Implications for education* (pp. 1–21). Bellingham: Western Washington University Press.

Mercer, J. and Lewis, J. (1979). *System of Multicultural and Pluralistic Assessment: Technical manual.* New York: Psychological Corporation.

Miller-Jones, D. (1989). Culture and testing. *American Psychologist, 44,* 360–366.

Oakland, T. (1979). Research on the Adaptive Behavior Inventory for Children and the Estimated Learning Potential. *School Psychology Digest, 8,* 63–70.

Ortiz, A. (1984). Choosing the language of instruction for exceptional bilingual children. *Teaching Exceptional Children, 16,* 208–212.

Ortiz, A. and García, S.B. (1988). A prereferral process for preventing inappropriate referrals of Latino students in special education. In A. Ortiz and B.A. Ramírez (Eds.), *Schools and the culturally diverse exceptional student: Promising practices and future directions* (pp. 6–18). Reston, VA: Council for Exceptional Children.

Ortiz, A. and Maldonado-Colón, E. (1986). Reducing inappropriate referrals of language minority students in special education. In A. Willig and H. Greenberg (Eds.), *Bilingualism and learning disabilities: Policy and practice for teachers and administrators* (pp. 37–52). New York: American Library Publishing.

Ortiz, A. and Yates, J.R. (1983). Incidence of exceptionality among Latinos: Implications of manpower planning. *NABE Journal, 7,* 41–53.

Oswald, D.P. and Coutinho, M.J. (1999). Ethnic representation in special education: The influence of school-related economic and demographic variables. *Journal of Special Education, 32,* 194–206.

Oswald, D.P., Coutinho, M.J., Best, A.M. and Nguyen, N. (2001). The impact of socio-demographic characteristics on the identification rates of minority students as mentally retarded. *Mental Retardation, 39,* 351–367.

Pupil Promotion and Retention. (Ed. Code Section 48070 and 60648) (California Assembly Bill 1626, Statutes of 1998).

Reschly, D.J. (1997). *Disproportionate minority representation in general and special education: Patterns, issues, and alternatives.* Des Moines: Iowa Department of Education.

Reynolds, M.C. (1991). Classification and labeling. In J.W. Lloyd, N.N. Singh, and A.C. Repp (Eds.), *The Regular Education Initiative: Alternative perspectives on concepts, issues, and models* (pp. 29–42). Sycamore, IL: Sycamore Publishing.

Reynolds, M.C. and Wang, M.C. (1983). Restructuring "special" school programs: A position paper. *Policy Studies Review, 2,* 189–212.

Rueda, R. (1991). An analysis of special education as a response to the diminished academic achievement of Latino students. In R.R. Valencia (Ed.), *Chicano school failure and success: Research and policy agendas for the 1990s* (pp. 252–270). The Stanford Series on Education and Public Policy. London: Falmer Press.

Rueda, R. and Kim, S. (2001). Cultural and linguistic diversity as a theoretical framework for understanding multicultural learners with mild disabilities. In C.A. Utley and F.E. Obiakor (Eds.), *Special education, multicultural education, and school reform: Components of quality education for learners with mild disabilities* (pp. 74–89). Springfield, IL: Charles C. Thomas.

Rueda, R., Cardoza, D., Mercer, J.R. and Carpenter, L. (1984). *An examination of special education decision making with Latino first-time referrals in large urban school districts.* Los Alamitos, CA: Southwest Regional Laboratory for Educational Research and Development.

Rueda, R., Figueroa, R.A., Mercado, P. and Cardoza, D. (1984). *Performance of Latino educable mentally retarded, learning disabled, and nonclassified students on the WISC-RM, SOMPA, and S-KABC* (Final Report-Short-Term Study One). Los Alamitos, CA: Southwest Regional Laboratory for Educational Research and Development.

Ruiz, N.T. (1989). Considerations in the education of gifted Latino students. In C.J. Maker and S.W. Schiever (Eds.), *Critical issues in gifted education: Defensible programs for cultural and ethnic minorities* (pp. 60–62). Austin, TX: PRO-ED.

San Miguel, Jr., G. and Valencia, R.R. (1998). From the Treaty of Guadalupe Hidalgo to *Hopwood*: The educational plight and struggle of Mexican Americans in the Southwest. *Harvard Educational Review*, *68*, 353–412.

Sanders, W.I. and Rivers, J.C. (1996). *Cumulative and residual effects of teachers on future student academic achievement*. Knoxville: University of Tennessee Press.

Skrtic, T.M. (1995). The special education knowledge tradition: Crisis and opportunity. In E.L. Meyen and T.M. Skrtic (Eds.), *Special education & student disability: Traditional, emerging, and alternative perspectives* (pp. 609–672). Denver, CO: Love Publishing.

Stainback, S. and Stainback, W. (1992). Schools as inclusive communities. In W. Stainback and S. Stainback (Eds.), *Controversial issues confronting special education: Divergent perspectives* (pp. 29–44). Baltimore, MD: Paul H. Brookes.

Suárez-Orozco, C. and Suárez-Orozco, M. (1995) *Transformations: Immigration, family life, and achievement motivation among Latino adolescents*. Stanford, CA: Stanford University Press.

Swanson, H.L. (1999). *Interventions for students with learning disabilities: A meta-analysis of treatment outcomes*. New York: Guilford.

Trent, S.C., Artiles, A.J. and Englert, C.S. (1998). From deficit thinking to social constructivism: A review of special education theory, research and practice. *Review of Research in Education*, *23*, 277–307.

Turnbull, H.R. (1993). *Free appropriate public education: The law and children with disabilities* (4th ed.). Denver, CO: Love Publishing.

U.S. Department of Commerce, Bureau of the Census. (1997). *The Latino population in the United States: March 1993*. Washington, DC: U.S. Government Printing Office.

U.S. Department of Commerce, Bureau of the Census. (2000). *Current population survey, March 1968–2000*. Washington, DC: U.S. Government Printing Office.

U.S. Department of Education. (1987). *Ninth annual report to Congress on implementation of Public Law 94–142: The Education for All Handicapped Children Act*. Washington, DC: U.S. Government Printing Office.

U.S. Department of Education. (2000). *Twenty-second annual report to Congress on the implementation of the Individuals with Disabilities Education Act*. Washington, DC: U.S. Government Printing Office.

Valdés, G. and Figueroa, R. (1994). *Bilingualism and testing: A special case of bias*. Norwood, NJ: Ablex.

Valencia, R.R. (Ed.). (1991). *Chicano school failure and success: Research and policy agendas for the 1990s*. The Stanford Series on Education and Public Policy. London: Falmer Press.

Valencia, R.R. (Ed.). (1997). *The evolution of deficit thinking: Educational thought and practice*. The Stanford Series on Education and Public Policy. London: Falmer Press.

Valencia, R.R. (2000a). *Legislated school reform via high-stakes testing: The case of pending anti-social promotion legislation in Texas and its likely adverse impact on racial/ethnic minority students*. Commissioned paper for the National Academy of Sciences Committee on Educational Excellence and Testing Equity. Paper presented at the workshop on School Completion in Standards-Based Reform: Facts and Strategies, Washington, DC, July.

Valencia, R.R. (2000b). Inequalities and the schooling of minority students in Texas: Historical and contemporary conditions. *Hispanic Journal of Behavioral Sciences*, *22*, 445–459.

Valencia, R.R. and Suzuki, L.A. (2001). *Intelligence testing and minority students: Foundations, performance factors, and assessment issues*. Thousand Oaks, CA: Sage.

Wang, M.C. and Reynolds, M.C. (1985). Avoiding the "catch-22" in special education reform. *Exceptional Children*, *51*, 497–502.

Wang, M.C., Reynolds, M.C. and Walberg, H.J. (1989). Who benefits from segregation and murky water? *Phi Delta Kappan*, *71*, 64–67.

Will, M. (1986). Educating children with learning problems: A shared responsibility. *Exceptional Children*, *52*, 411–416.

Part V

The big picture and Chicano school failure and success

11 The big picture: systemic and institutional factors in Chicano school failure and success

Arthur Pearl

Chicano school failure can be fully understood only when analyzed in the broadest political, economic, and cultural contexts. Macropolicies establish the boundaries of possibilities. Conceptualizing Chicano school failure from a macroperspective is no simple task, as information is scattered. What exists is uneven, and to make matters more difficult, the terrain is constantly shifting. The context within which the analysis must be made—the economic and political systems—is undergoing considerable but difficult to understand change. And yet for all the problems, the need to examine and analyze Chicano school failure in a large canvas remains.

What is presented here, like any broad-based analysis, must be perceived as tentative and provocative rather than conclusive. Particularly important in this analysis is a critique of the impact of policies that influence the configuration of work and promote equal opportunity and the extent to which these policies have hindered or helped the Chicano quest for school success. Macropolicies do not exist in a vacuum. Cultural considerations add complexity to the analysis, as do accidental events and individual efforts by teachers and students.

To make the matter even more complex is the difficulty of keeping the analysis focused on Chicanos. Most of the available information groups Chicanos with all other Latino populations, and thus disaggregation is exceedingly difficult. The history of the experiences in the United States of Mexicans, of Cubans, Puerto Ricans, and other immigrants from other Latin America countries are distinctly different and these differences are reflected in the schooling success (Moore and Pachón, 1983; Velez, 1989). Moreover, even if data were available for solely those of Mexican heritage, problems would remain. Within such a population there are many different and complex inter relationships. There are profound differences in outlook and behavior of those recently arrived and those who have been in the United States for many generations. There are important political, cultural, religious and social differences. The term "Chicano" came into existence as a political statement; it signified the call for a perspective different than immigrants who wished to assimilate into the existing political economy—Mexican Americans, and different also from those who continued to perceive themselves as strongly connected to the motherland—Mexicanos. Chicano stood for liberation from perceived political, economic, and cultural oppression within the United States. Some of the original meaning has been lost in the last third of the century but the problems for analysis remain. Just whom are we talking about? At best we can operate with rough approximations. Part of the definition is imposed from outside by institutional processes, some from individual perceptions, and some from collective movements. Trying to impose order on situations and definitions that are in flux is fraught with danger. Much more dangerous is to be overwhelmed by chaos.

There are some fairly solid places to begin. There are bits and pieces of evidence, when combined, powerfully suggest that Chicanos (here broadly defined as persons of Mexican origin) do not fare well in school, are economically disadvantaged, and have high incidences of involvement with crime.

The remainder of this chapter is organized around the following: (a) determinants of policy: systemic inequalities or individual or group deficits?; (b) establishing the context: the two worlds of work and where Chicanos fit; (c) the school experience: Chicanos continue to bring up the rear; (d) a major roadblock: the legacy of deficit thinking; (e) liberal deficit thinking: the 1960s and compensatory education; (f) modest systemic modification: the effective school; (g) the right-wing hostile takeover of education: overcoming deficits with "standards"; (h) postmodernism: confusing voice and discourse with meaningful political activity; (i) critical pedagogy: one response to conserva tive reforms; and (j) democratic education and its implications for Chicano education.

Determinants of policy: systemic inequities or individual or group deficits?

Chicano school failure can be explained either by "deficits" that place the cause of these problems on the individual, the family, or the culture (see Valencia, 1997a), *or* by systemic denial of access or equity. The argument made in this essay posits the cause of Chicanos to be societal in nature and, thus, the recommended proposals are for institutional change, with particular focus on educational policies and practices. First, however, is a brief summary of the factors considered in the analysis.

Systemic

Systemic refers to established processes whereby values, traditions, hierarchies, styles, and attitudes are deeply embedded into the political, economic, and cultural structures of any society. The systems that have emerged are the consequences of historical influences modified by current political pressures. History establishes in various, often subtle or disguised forms, the means by which people are included or excluded from positions of power and influence. Unless we fully understand the consequences of a particular history we fail to appreciate how Chicano school failure is the logical consequence of a once conquered people paying a continuous price for being displaced by victors leading to systematic exclusion from positions of authority and influence (see Moreno, 1999; San Miguel and Valencia, 1998). The legacy of that history finds current expression in denial of language, particular forms of miscarriages of justice, as well as ever-recurring stereotypes that influence decisions at every juncture and at every level of an individual's life. History establishes the basis for inclusion and exclusion in various societal institutions. Most powerfully, that historical legacy of inclusion and exclusion is increasingly infused throughout education.

Institutions

Systems function primarily through institutions. The driving force for systematic exclusion, in what has become a credential society, is education. Education has been elevated into society's principal gatekeeper and primary controller of status flow. Not only do educational institutions issue visas to the most desirable areas of work and thus access to a modicum of wealth and power, the denial of a credential for all intents and purposes destines one for poverty. Educational institutions do more than determine who will be rich and who will be poor; they also have the responsibility to prepare students for responsible citizenship. How well and fairly schools perform that duty is also treated in this chapter.

Establishing the context: the two worlds of work and where Chicanos fit

The United States is dividing itself into the rich and the poor and nothing in between. The middle is disappearing (Hacker, 1996; Hodgkinson, 1989; Pearlstein, 1995). One of the features of this rapidly changing economy is the near elimination of bridge occupations that, in the not too distant past, made upward mobility a realistic aspiration for working-class and immigrant populations. The concentration of wealth in fewer and fewer hands, the globalization of the economy characterized by industries shipped to areas of the world where labor is cheap and not bound by environmental or safety considerations, the influences of technology and the continual addition of years of education for entrance into a profession has fundamentally changed the structure of work. It is in this context that Chicano school failure is discussed.

One obvious influence on work is the economic condition of the society. During periods of economic expansion, success tends to be non zero-sum, more gain than loss. During economic recessions and depression, success is also non-zero-sum, but now more loss than gain. Increase in unemployment, a primary characteristic of an economic downturn, often has a negative impact on student aspirations—resulting not only in increased school dropouts, but also in increased violence, crime, and substance abuse. When unemployment is high, competition for scarce jobs becomes fiercer and intergroup tensions increase.

Entering the 21st century, the United States is experiencing the longest period of sustained economic growth in its history. But it is a curious "prosperity." In the 1990s a very large number of good jobs (high skill; high wage; benefits; opportunities for advancement) were created, but at the same time, a very large number of bad jobs (low skill; low wage; no benefits; very limited opportunities for advancement) also were created. Rather than following the conservative economist mantra that "a rising tide lifts all boats," in this instance "a rising tide lifted half the boats." The others remain anchored to the bottom.

Despite the major thrust of this chapter that systemic and institutional forces are stacked against Chicano access and equity, it is important to take note of the undeniable progress Chicanos have made in the last decade and a half. Chicanos increased their numbers in all of the desirable professions and occupations.[1] Latinos, and therefore Chicanos, grew significantly in good jobs, a three-fold increase in executives, administrators, and managers from 1983–1998 (300,000 to over a million) and a similar three-fold increase in all professional ranks during the same period (300,000 to over 900,000) (U.S. Department of Commerce, Bureau of the Census, 1999, Table 675).[2]

At first blush, the figures seem to indicate extraordinary achievements and progress toward equity. And while the growth is impressive and encouraging, it tells only a small part of the story. Chicanos/Latinos were as underrepresented in "good" jobs in 1998 as they were in 1983. In some critical areas this was even more so. In 1983, Chicanos/Latinos represented 5.3 percent of all people employed in the United States, or approximately 5.3 million workers. By 1998, this number had swelled to 13.3 million workers, or 10.1 percent of all employed. The distribution of Chicano/Latino workers in good and bad jobs did not change appreciably. Chicanos/Latinos continued to be under represented in good jobs. In 1998, Latinos constituted only 5.4 percent of executives, administrators, and managers (the same level of underrepresentation as in 1983). Latinos constituted only 4.6 percent of all professional occupations (a slight *increase* in underrepresentation when contrasted with 1983 figures) (U.S. Department of Commerce, Bureau of the Census, 1999, Table 675). Chicanos/ Latinos are overrepresented in bad jobs—most dramatically as farm workers, cleaners and servants, building service occupations, and as child care workers (U.S. Department of Commerce, Bureau of the Census, 1999, Table 675).

It is a strange "prosperity" in yet another important way. Median household income did not change significantly from 1985 to 1997. Table 11.1 shows that in 1997 dollars, the median annual income of White households was $37,154. In 1997, the White household median income rose by $1,818 to $38,972—nothing earthshaking there. African Americans made considerable progress during this period: from a median annual household income of $22,105 in 1985 to $25,050 in 1997. As previously indicated, Latinos gained the least by the "prosperity," from a 1985 median annual income of $26,051 (5.2 million households) to a median annual income of $26,628 in 1997 (8.6 million households). The gap between White and Latino annual income grew from $11,103 in 1985 to $12,344 in 1997.

Table 11.1 also shows that in 1997, 1.4 million or one-sixth of Latino households earned less than $10,000 and more than a quarter of Latino households earned less than $15,000 in 1997. At the other end of the scale, Latino households whose annual income exceeded $75,000 more than doubled from 370,000 to 780,000.

As seen in Table 11.2, reduction of unemployment is a prime indicator of economic good times, and unemployment fell significantly in the 1990s—but not as much for Latinos as for Whites, and slightly more than for African Americans.[3] Unemployment was negatively correlated with educational achievement for all groups.

Table 11.3 shows that Latinos continue to be overrepresented in poverty. And while poverty has been reduced somewhat during the 1990s, nearly 40 percent of Latino children under 6 years old lived in conditions of poverty in 1997, which is considerably higher than the poverty rate of 13 percent for White children.

Table 11.1 Percentage of households with median annual income for White, African American, and Latino groups: 1985 and 1997

Group/year	Median annual income in thousands of dollars							Households (in millions)
	Less than 10,000	10,000 to 14,999	15,000 to 24,999	25,000 to 34,999	35,000 to 49,000	50,000 to 74,999	More than 75,000	
White								
1985	10.7	7.8	14.8	14.1	18.4	18.8	15.5	75.6
1997	9.5	7.8	14.6	13.2	16.5	18.8	19.7	86.1
African American								
1985	25.2	11.3	18.3	13.6	14.1	11.1	5.6	9.8
1997	21.4	10.5	17.9	14.2	14.9	13.1	7.9	12.5
Latino								
1985	17.3	12.1	18.1	15.3	16.9	12.7	7.1	5.2
1997	16.8	10.7	19.7	15.0	16.6	12.2	9.1	8.6

Source: U.S. Department of Commerce, Bureau of the Census (1999, Table 742).

Note
1997 dollars are constant.

Table 11.2 Unemployment rates by educational attainment for White, African American, and Latino groups: 1992 and 1997

Group	1992			1997		
	Less than high school (%)	High school graduate (%)	College graduate (%)	Less than high school (%)	High school graduate (%)	College graduate (%)
White	12.5	6.8	2.7	7.5	4.2	1.7
African American	17.2	14.1	4.8	13.4	8.4	2.1
Latino	13.6	9.6	4.2	8.3	5.5	2.8

Source: U.S. Department of Commerce, Bureau of the Census (1999, Table 684).

At the time this chapter is being written, the prevailing view is that the economy will remain robust and will create 18 million new jobs in the decade between 1996 and 2006. Of these, over 5 million will be bad jobs with no educational prerequisite. In fact, most of the jobs in the fastest growing occupations will require no educational prerequisite, and will be low-wage, and little opportunity for advancement jobs (e.g., salespersons; cashiers; guards; custodians) (U.S. Department of Commerce, Bureau of the Census, 1999, Table 676). In occupations where growth will be steady, but not spectacular, most of the jobs will require a college education. The best guess is that more than half of the job growth in the next decade will be good jobs, but a significant proportion will be low-skill, low-paying, no benefits jobs. Given inertia and the current situation, and without significant changes in systems and institutions, Chicanos and other Latinos (and African Americans) can be expected to be underrepresented in good jobs and overrepresented in bad jobs. If the economy remains robust and unemployment remains low, more Latinos will escape poverty. However, given current political directions, an economic downturn will hit Latinos hard. This especially true if Latinos continue to lag behind in education (see Valencia, Chapter 1, present book).

Some of the underrepresentation and overrepresentation in employment categories can be explained by immigration. The huge increase is largely due to massive increases in immigration of Mexican-origin people. A recurring argument made is that concentration in bad jobs is something all immigrants go through as they work their way up the ladder to success. This thinking informs current reform efforts and underlies the campaigns for high-stakes

Table 11.3 Poverty rates for children under 6 years of age for White, African American, and Latino groups: 1977–1997

Group	Year			
	1977 (%)	1987 (%)	1992 (%)	1997 (%)
White	11	14	16	13
African American	45	50	54	40
Latino	30	42	44	38

Source: Bennett *et al.* (Eds). (1999). *Children in poverty: Statistical update, June 1999* (p. 3). Washington, DC: National Center for Children in Poverty.

testing and educational standards. However, the experience of Chicanos (as well as some notable others, e.g., African Americans and American Indians) differs significantly from the European immigrant experience. In California, native-born Latinos wages exceed immigrant Latino wages, but remain significantly below ($7,500 a year less) than non-Latinos (López *et al.*, 1999).

Education is the determining factor for eligibility for the good jobs. Good jobs go to college graduates! Clearly, Chicano future prospects will be determined by educational achievement. Furthermore, given that the competition for good jobs will be intense, improvement in educational achievement does not necessarily lead to improved economic condition. Under current and projected conditions, economic improvement is dependent on attaining the pre requisite for a credential—a college degree—and the economic gain will only be realized if the increase in college degrees earned is at least equal to that which are attained by other groups. This, however, appears unlikely. As Valencia (Chapter 1, current volume) discusses, Chicanos/Latinos are projected to demonstrate, from 1995 to 2015, the largest percentage point increase in undergraduate enrollment share, but they will continue to be greatly under represented in relation to their overall share of the college-age population.

The school experience: Chicanos continue to bring up the rear

Amidst a flurry of proclaimed reforms and a cacophony of claims and counterclaims, charges and countercharges, accusations and defenses, Chicanos continue to lose ground in school achievement (see Valencia, Chapter 1, present volume). In 1995, 83 percent of Whites 25 years or older graduated from high school. This compares with 74 percent African Americans and 46 percent of Chicanos of comparable ages. In this instance, with a disaggregated Latino classification, Chicano achievement can be compared with other Latinos, and Chicanos lag behind Puerto Rican and Cubans in attainment of high school diplomas and college degrees (see Chapa and Valencia, 1993, p. 173, Table 6; Rumberger and Rodríguez, Chapter 4, this volume; differences in immigration and social class of immigrants could account for these differences). An even greater disparity can be found in college education; whereas almost a quarter of 25-year-old and older Whites had college degrees and 13 percent of African Americans had such degrees, only 6.5 percent of Chicanos met the minimum prerequisite of a credential society (U.S. Department of Commerce, Bureau of the Census, 1999, Table 263).

Conditions have not improved for Chicanos over time. Although there has been a steady increase in the percentage of Chicanos who have high school diplomas as well as an increase in college degrees, this increase has not kept pace with either White or African American advances. Comparing accomplishments over 25 years, 1970–1995 (for persons 25 years or older), Whites increased their high school graduation rate by 28.5 percentage points (from 54.5 percent to 83.0 percent), African Americans by 42.5 percentage points (from 31.4 percent to 73.9 percent), and Chicanos by 22.3 percentage points (from 24.2 percent to 46.5 percent). When college graduation is considered, the results are somewhat similar: an increase of 12.7 percentage points (11.3 percent to 24.0 percent) increase for Whites, an increase of 8.8 percentage points (4.4 percent to 13.2 percent) for African Americans, and an increase of 4.0 percentage points (2.5 percent to 6.5 percent) for Chicanos (U.S. Department of Commerce, Bureau of the Census, 1999, Table 263).

The "good news/bad news" aspect of Chicano school achievement is further reflected in degrees earned. There was a huge increase in bachelor degrees earned by Latinos in the 1990s—over 35,000 between 1990–1996, and yet, at the same time they continued to be markedly underrepresented in degrees granted, increasingly so with the higher the degree (U.S. Department of Commerce, Bureau of the Census, 1999, Table 680). The under-representation in the minimum degree for a professional credential, the bachelor degree, approximates the previously noted underrepresentation in "good jobs."

California is not only the state with the largest number of Chicano/Latino students, it is also has the fastest growing Chicano/Latino population. Of the close to 6 million students attending public school in California in 1999–2000, 42.2 percent, or over 2.5 million were Latino. More Latinos attend public school in California than any other racial/ethnic group (see Valencia, Chapter 2, present book). Whites are a distinct minority in California public schools (constituting 2.2 million or 36.2 percent of the total enrollment) (California Department of Education, 2000). Minority representation, however, changes grade by grade. The cohort that entered high school in the Fall of 1993 was 37.1 percent Latino and 41.3 percent White; 4 years later it was 32 percent Latino and 45 percent White. Graduation widened the gap even more—31.2 percent Latinos compared with 46.2 percent Whites. When only high school graduates that met University of California and California State University requirements are considered, the minority (White) becomes the majority. Slightly more than 51 percent of that population is White, and the Latino population that represented 37.1 percent of the entering 9th grade in the Fall of 1993 had, by June of 1997, shrunk to 19.4 percent of graduates who met university requirements (California Department of Education, 2000).

Not surprisingly, admissions to the University of California (UC) are con sistent with the high school findings. The UC admission statistics are dis aggregated and specify Chicanos. When distinguished from other Latinos, the Chicano UC undergraduate enrollments in the Fall 1997 fell considerably below the number of Latinos that graduated that Spring from high school having met University requirements (UC Office of the President, 2000).

The overwhelming conclusion to be drawn from all of this is that at every level of schooling Chicanos fall behind. Things are not getting better (see Valencia, Chapter 1, current book; Valencia and Chapa, 1993).

A major roadblock: the legacy of deficit thinking

No analysis of systemic and institutional factors in Chicano school failure would be complete without taking into account the pervasive impact of deficit thinking. Deficit thinking has a long history (see Valencia, 1997a, for a comprehensive coverage of this history). The notion that the capacity to learn is rationed by race and class is deeply embedded in education. Deficit thinking gained scientific credibility in the 19th century with Francis Galton and his eugenics movement (Galton, 1884). Sir Cyril Burt gave impetus to the heritability of intelligence with his now generally recognized to be fraudulent twin studies (Burt, 1972).[4] Deficit thinking based on genetics has had its ebbs and flows (Valencia, 1997b; Valencia and Solórzano, 1997). Although seeming effectively discredited, it nevertheless makes periodic revivals (witness chronologically: Jensen 1969; Dunn, 1987; Herrnstein and Murray, 1994; see Valencia and Solórzano, 1997; Valencia and Suzuki, 2001, Chapter 6, for critiques). Deficit thinking has changed with the times and has many variations (Valencia, 1997a). If one is not satisfied with a theory based on heredity, then one can choose from cultural deprivation theories, accumulated environmental deficit theories, and flawed character development theories (Pearl, 1997). All have one thing in common: They vindicate the system and its institutions. The primary impact of deficit thinking from this author's perspective is its translation into unequal encouragement to succeed in the classroom.

Liberal deficit thinking: the 1960s and compensatory education

The 1960s were heady times for education, a period when the United States attempted to do what no society had ever attempted—eliminate poverty, restore the environment, and educate everyone equally. It was a noble ambition, marked by considerable enthusiasm and ambitious projects and programs. It was the heyday of post-World War II U.S. liberalism. Times were good. Utopia was within our grasp.

It was also a time of considerable unrest. A civil rights movement had awakened the conscience of the country leading to monumental civil rights legislation. At the same time, cities were exploding in racial rioting and campuses erupting in opposition to the Vietnam War. The liberal-based education programs began in time of turmoil and the volatility set the stage for the right-wing reaction that followed.

One defining characteristic of the period was the rejection of heredity-based deficit theories. But, it was not the end of deficit thinking. Liberal deficit theorists took over and brought forth compensatory education. The logic of the strategy is that now that the U.S. has overcome its historical injustices and has reached a point where all its citizens are treated fairly and equally, what remains is the elimination of the scars from past injustices. The education system was not to be significantly changed. Moreover, the approach is extremely circumscribed. Larger issues of unemployment and the configuration of work are ignored. As originally formulated, the emphasis was almost exclusively on early intervention. The dominant theoretical explanation for disproportionate school failure of the poor and the minority was "accumulated environmental deficit"—i.e., students entered school with a buildup of handicaps incurred in early formative years that would be irreversible unless significant action was taken when children were very young (Deutsch, 1967; Hunt, 1961; see Pearl, 1997, for a discussion and critique). If, however, intervention begins early enough, then the child can recover from the lack of intellectual stimulation at home and particularly the dearth of language (Bernstein, 1970; Englmann, 1970). The compensation for the deficits that are hypothesized to have occurred before a child enters school is supposed to level the playing field, thus equalizing everyone's life chances.

Operation head start

The key element in the early intervention strategy was Operation Head Start for low-income children, ages 3 to 5 years. The program featured a variety of early educational experiences designed to foster intellectual, social, and emotional development. Initiated in 1965 as the showcase element in President Johnson's fledgling anti-poverty program ("War on Poverty"), it, unlike many other "Great Society" projects, survived and even prospered. Since its inception, over 15.3 million children and their families have participated in Head Start (U.S. Administration for Children and Families, 1999).

There is some evidence that Head Start has been effective. As the data in Table 11.4 show, when a cohort consisting of 19-year-olds with Head Start experience is compared with a comparable same age control group, there are some impressive findings: Those with Head Start experience are more likely to be employed, graduate from high school, go on to college, and are less likely to have been arrested, or be on welfare than controls who did not have Head Start experience (Hodgkinson, 1989). The impressive findings for Head Start are not necessarily a vindication for the strategy. The Head Start cohort has, for all its accomplishments, a large percentage not graduating from high school, a substantial arrest record, and a large percentage of not being employed. The percentage of Head Start cohort college enrollees is much lower than the percentage of college admissions from advantaged back-

Table 11.4 A status comparison between Head Start and control cohort at age 19 years: Fall, 1984

Status	Head Start (%)	Control cohort (%)
Employed	59	32
High school graduate	67	49
Enrolled in college	38	21
Been arrested	31	51
On welfare	18	32

Source: Hodgkinson (1989, p. 7).

grounds. Head Start may be of particular value to Chicano children, especially those with native-born mothers. Chicano Head Start participants, when compared with siblings who were not participants, significantly closed test gap differences with White children (Currie and Thomas, 1996).

The Elementary and Secondary Education Act (ESEA)

Liberal deficit thinking informed this piece of legislation enacted in 1965. The Elementary and Secondary Education Act provided categorical aid to schools with significant numbers of impoverished students. These funds were intended to compensate for the deficits produced by poverty. Although much of the deprivations are to be found in lack of resources—e.g., limited number of books, inadequate places to study, and ramshackle buildings—that have been dramatically exposed by Kozol (1991) in *Savage Inequalities*, compensatory education also addressed alleged student deficiencies. Because local districts have used ESEA money in many different ways, it is impossible to evaluate precisely the effects it has had on student performance. Whatever impact it has had, it has not erased the educational achievement between the rich and poor or between Chicanos and Whites. ESEA, much like Operation Head Start, continues to find bipartisan support.

Bilingual education, Title VII of ESEA

Congress mandated bilingual education in 1968. The funds provided from this legislation were for categorical aid to districts with significant number of students with limited-English proficiency. The intent of the legislation was to help students overcome this "deficiency." Unlike other compensatory education programs that were designed with African Americans in mind, this program primarily focused on Chicanos and other Latinos. Bilingual education did not receive the public support afforded Head Start and other Titles of ESEA. Others in this volume treat bilingual education in depth (see García and Wiese, Chapter 5; Guerrero, Chapter 6). The concern here is with the impact that deficit thinking, especially in the design of less than optimum learning environments (described and discussed later), may have had on student achievement. Bilingual education mandated by Congress did not in any way indict edu cational practice; instead, it merely wanted to transition those with limited English into the existing school. Depending on its focus, bilingual education in its broadest sense can fit into any strategy. However, bilingual education as perceived has engendered considerable opposition and has been used as a focal point for the mobilization of political action leading to the passage of an anti bilingual initiative in California in 1998 (see García and Wiese, Chapter 5, current book; San Miguel and Valencia, 1998). Keep in mind that bilingual education was top-down mandated, met resistance from its inception, and in many ways was a program under continual siege. Adding and compounding the difficulty of effectively implementing bilingual education was the beginning and continuing shortage of qualified bilingual teachers (see Valencia, Chapter 1, present book).

Upward Bound: another 1960s program based on deficit thinking

Upward Bound was created in 1965 as part of the War on Poverty. The U.S. Government awards contracts to universities and colleges that propose to assist economically disadvantaged students prepare for postsecondary education. The typical Upward Bound program has a few activities during the school year, either at the higher education campus or at the high school, or both, and an intensive residential summer program at the university or college campus. Most students enter in 9th or 10th grade, fewer than half complete two years in the program. Upward Bound also has continued to maintain bipartisan support.

Upward Bound was in some ways a hybrid program. While there was some recognition of the inadequacy of education in schools located in economically deprived areas serving predominantly minority (e.g., African American, Chicano, and American Indian students), Upward Bound nonetheless qualifies as a deficit thinking program because its intent was to repair the students not their schools.

Affirmative action

Affirmative action also came into existence in the 1960s as a remedy for *prior* injustices resulting in *existing* underrepresentation of women and minorities in higher education and in "good" jobs. Affirmative action, according to its opponents, gave "preferential treatment" to women and underrepresented populations over "more qualified" White males. Affirmative action makes good sense from a compensatory perspective; the intervention is perceived to be a temporary adjustment to be employed only until the other compensatory catch-up efforts have been given time to be effective. If successful, Head Start students (and ESEA and Upward Bound) would take years, if not decades, to produce equity in the work place. Affirmative action brings immediate relief. However, if it continues beyond a reasonable time (whatever that might be), the compensatory justification for it is weakened. There was little initial political opposition to affirmative action. The university had plenty of room for additional students, the growth in the professions seemed limitless, and there were bridging occupations that opened up different venues for upward mobility. Over time, universities filled up, the economy bifurcated, and political opposition to affirmative action grew. The cries of "reverse discrimination" become increasingly shrill, and the responses to that cry, using a compensatory logic, were increasingly unpersuasive. Affirmative action, like bilingual education, fell victim to the initiative process in California and is beleaguered (see Valencia, Introduction, present volume; San Miguel and Valencia, 1998).

Much of the attack on affirmative action, like much of the attack on bilingual education, was based on myth and misinformation. The outcry against "quotas" and "lowering of standards" deflects attention from the reality. Affirmative action was never very much. Except for gender (an important exception) the mismatch between race/ethnicity of teachers and students has not been significantly reduced, but that has not silenced an adamant opposition far more vociferous than the limited impact of affirmative action would seem to have warranted.

The compensatory education as it has emerged over the last 35 years has become increasingly protean. By adding components at every level of schooling—whatever it may have gained in additional weaponry against inequity—it lost in theoretical clarity. Not included in the range of compen satory tactics was a serious consideration of possible institutionally imposed unequal treatments, nor was there any effort to bring into the approach activities that would take into account the rapid changes occurring outside of the school that could conceivably impact student performance. The emphasis has been on repairing damaged goods. A centrally directed political process initiated all of the compensatory efforts. The programs were designed by an intellectually elite for persons deemed to be inferior to it. Compensatory education was not created by political action. To the contrary, it was an effort to employ science for the benefit of the species. Thus, it has tried to defend itself on the basis of accomplishment rather than constituency.

Modest systemic modification: the effective school

The effective school movement rejects the deficit argument and looks for remedy in minor systemic change. The changes sought are encapsulated in the schooling process and those resources directly tied to education. The effective school movement gained steam with the conservative mood of reform that has informed public consciousness in the 1980s. The thrust of the effective school was that the compensatory approach not only failed to help the minority poor, it likely made matters worse for them. The late Ronald Edmonds, an acknowledged leader in the effective schools movement, disputed the importance of outside-of-school factors on student performance and pointed to research that clearly indicated, "school response to family background is the cause of depressed achievement for low-income and minority students" (Edmonds, 1984, p. 37). The effective school proposed: (a) strong administrative leadership; (b) high expectations from students; (c) a safe and orderly environment; (d) an emphasis on basic skills; and (e) frequent monitoring of pupil progress using measurable curriculum-based, criterion-referenced evaluation (Edmonds, 1979; 1984). The thrust of the effective school is to provide to the disadvantaged what the advantaged have. It is directed at improving delivery; it is not directed at changing the nature of schooling.

The Achievement Council, a California-based organization promoting effective school principles, has strong Chicano leadership distinguishing it from efforts that had focused almost exclusively on African Americans. The Council identifies as "roots" of "under-achievement" the following: an unchallenging curriculum with tracking for "low ability" students, fewer able and experienced teachers, ill-prepared and often culturally unaware administrators, inadequate services, and low expectations of teachers (Haycock and Navarro, 1988). The Achievement Council's prescription for success follows logically from the diagnosis of the problem—a determined principal, demanding teachers, a rich and rigorous core curriculum, parents as partners of teachers, support services for students, and teamwork between administrators, teachers, students, and parents (Haycock and Navarro, 1988).

The Achievement Council points to some significant changes among some of the California's "worst" high schools once the proposed principles were transformed into action. Sweetwater High School in San Diego County, California and Claremont Middle School in Oakland, California are two that have been "turned around." The initiation of effective school practices resulted in more Sweetwater students taking Scholastic Aptitude Tests (SATs) than any other school in the district, many of the graduating class won scholarships and grants, and for the first time in its history more than half of the graduating class went on to college (Haycock and Navarro, 1988). Similar results were obtained in Claremont Middle school, once a dumping ground for troublesome low achievers.

Robert Slavin and his colleagues have created "Success for All," a program based on effective school premises and certainly consistent with it—although giving it a different name. Success for All, its supporters insist, can be implemented "whenever and wherever," requiring nothing more than "wholehearted commitment" of district and staff. Success for All stresses: reading tutors, 90 minute reading periods of 15 students grouped by same reading level, assessment every eight weeks, a family support team, a program facilitator, teacher trainer, and an advisory committee (Slavin *et al.*, 1994).

Slavin *et al.* (1994) provide convincing evidence that Success for All is an exportable program capable of raising the academic performance of heretofore low-achieving students to the levels that nondisadvantaged students attain in places where staff and districts are committed to such achievement. But, will such achievement improve life conditions for disadvantaged students? Specifically, would it make any difference for Chicanos in the workplace? Or eliminate the gap in what really counts, college graduation?

The effective school, like the compensatory approach model is top-down and elitist. It did not come into existence as a response to a popular demand, although it can rightfully claim that there is increasing community support for its activities. The effective school is necessarily authoritarian. The student is fitted into a rigidly prescribed regimen. Like all conservative strategies, its goal is to facilitate assimilation into the society. Such assimilation requires an unexamined acceptance of existing curriculum and standardized evaluation. The effective school strives for achievement on standardized tests that may underrate what Chicanos really know.

In sum, the effective school is important and its contributions valuable. Some aspects of it—high expectations and a quality curriculum—are vital to any successful effort to reduce Chicano school failure. Its strength is its clarity of purpose, its weakness, a narrow focus. The strategy operates without consideration of broader political and economic issues.

The right-wing hostile takeover of education: overcoming deficits with "standards"

The liberal reform movement in the 1960s and 1970s tended to protect the schools and blame the students (Ryan, 1971). In 1983, the tables were turned with a vengeance. A commission appointed by President Reagan's then Secretary of Education, Terrell H. Bell, came forth with the "mother of all critiques" (Berliner and Biddle, 1995, p. 139)—the highly inflammatory *A Nation at Risk*, which is reminiscent in many ways of McCarthyism. "If an unfriendly foreign power had attempted to impose on America the mediocre educational performance that exists today, we might well have viewed it as an act of war" (National Commission on Excellence in Education, 1983, p. 1).

Indicted was the "rising tide of [educational] mediocrity" (National Commission on Excellence in Education, 1983, p. 1). The risk was not subversion, but an educational complicity in the failure to keep pace with Asians and West Europeans in the fight for dominance in the global economy. To overcome functional illiteracy, falling performance in scholastic achievement, the lack of "higher order" intellectual skills, and business and military unhappiness with the quality of performance of public school graduates, the United States required: (a) more rigorous traditional curriculum combining the old basics with the new basics of computer literacy; (b) accountability, measurable standards, and higher expectations—e.g., frequent standardized testing and grades based on performance; (c) more time on task—e.g., longer school years and school days, and mandatory homework; (d) better teaching—

e.g., higher standards for admission to the profession, professionally competitive salaries, and recognition and rewards for the best in the business; and finally (e) citizens holding educators and elected officials responsible for meeting these proposed goals (the call for increases in teacher salaries was blissfully ignored by President Reagan).

David Berliner and Bruce Biddle, in a careful and persuasive manner, expose the crisis as a manufactured fraud (Berliner and Biddle, 1995), but this exposé did not bring relief to public education. From seemingly everywhere, a torrent of criticism cascaded on the schools culminating in a phalanx of "reforms" endorsed by *both* major political parties and four presidents—Reagan, G. Bush, Clinton, and G.W. Bush. Just as every aspiring politician claimed to be "tough on crime," so too did every aspiring politician scramble to promote the right-wing agenda on schools—core curriculum, raised standards, accountability via high-stakes testing, charters or vouchers as escapes from "the failed" public schools, and the upgrading of teaching. All of which have implications for Chicano school success and failure.

Core curriculum

In *A Nation at Risk*, schools were savaged for "diluting," "homogenizing," and making a "smorgasbord" of the curriculum. Recommended for high school graduation was a required minimum in the "Five New Basics"—four years of English, three years of mathematics, three years of science, three years of social studies, half a year of computer science—plus two years of a foreign language for the college bound. Actually, because of the steady increase in college matriculating students, most schools already were moving in the direction of a core curriculum and organizing curriculum to meet university entrance requirements. The core curriculum is in itself not repressive, the vitriolic tone used in making the case for it in *A Nation at Risk*, is. Worse, the recommendations encapsulated education in an authoritarian nonnegotiable frame and set the stage for mandating precisely what was to be taught in each basic subject. The determination of important knowledge is a critical matter in the organization of schooling. In a society claiming to be democratic, conclusions about important knowledge can only be reached after a sustained and reasoned debate. No such debate has occurred. The National Commission on Excellence in Education (hereafter referred to as the "Commission")—author of *A Nation at Risk*—ordained a crisis and, in a similar capricious and arbitrary way, ordained the remedy. Already noted in critique of the effective school is the lack of relevance of the core curriculum to challenges facing Chicanos. The intent of the Commission was quite clear: "Ask not what the economy can do for Chicanos, ask what Chicanos can do for the economy." *A Nation at Risk* signaled a shift in public understanding of the purpose of public education. Ever since the inception of the comprehensive high school in the first decades of the 20th century, preparing people for work was a *part* of the educational objective. Vocational education was a partially a "public good" to meet the needs of a rapidly changing industrial society, but it was also perceived as a means to lure the recalcitrant to schools, to provide an educational benefit to those deemed unfit for challenging intellectual endeavor. The primary thrust of the high school as it was conceived was to prepare a democratic citizen. Although *A Nation at Risk* makes passing reference to democratic citizenship, what really matters is public school capacity to serve business. With such a mission, social justice issues pale to insignificance.

Standards and high-stakes testing

A Nation at Risk recommendation presages the standards-based school reform movement that has monopolized what passes for educational thinking for almost two decades. And while the Commission called for "authentic accomplishment," they meant by that the end of social promotion. The Commission promoted the use of standardized tests. The problems with standardized testing go beyond the scope of this essay and are treated elsewhere in this volume (see Valencia *et al.*, Chapter 9). Standardized tests have been advocated by presidents and have been mandated by state legislatures. In the mad rush, the tests are decreed, even before there is serious deliberation over what is meant by standards. In all of the core areas there is unresolved debate on what is to be learned. The tests are an irritant; the "high stakes" attached to them can be disastrous for Chicanos and other minority students (see Valencia, 2000; Valencia and Bernal, 2000; Valencia *et al.*, Chapter 9, this volume). Student and teacher lives can be destroyed by these test results. Little has been done to equalize resources, or to make appropriate adaptations for English language learners. But more important than all of the concern about stan dardizing student activity is the undeniable fact that testing does not alter life chances any more than measuring temperature reduces fever. In the haste to do something, there has been no serious effort to distinguish standards from obstacles.

The standards-based movement is riddled with deficit thinking that is artfully obscured. All students get the identical curriculum and are judged by identical criteria. Those that fail get left back, or are denied graduation. What could be fairer than that?

Standards as obstacles: a case in point

About two decades ago, the state of California mandated the California Basic Educational Skills Test (CBEST), an examination for all new teachers. Teacher unions supported the legislation when existing teachers were "grandfathered" in and not required to take the test. Some preliminary testing indicated the longer a teacher had been in the profession, the less successful they were on this standardized test, which measured skills at the 8th-grade English and math levels. The little pretesting of the test with existing teachers revealed no correlation between tests results and evidence of effective teaching. Tests that serve no useful purpose are obstacles. The CBEST and other such tests have been particularly difficult for prospective Chicano teachers (Valencia and Guadarrama, 1996). In this instance, delaying or preventing otherwise qualified Chicanos from entering teaching results in an even greater disparity between the proportion of the teachers and the proportion of the students. The CBEST is defended as a standard because without it, teachers who cannot read, write, or do fractions would be employed. Hogwash. Evaluating teacher competence is a problem that local districts are more than capable of handling. Placing obstacles in the path of perspective teachers and calling them standards has had ugly consequences. In times of rapidly growing teacher shortages, such as is occurring in California, standards as obstacles have compelled districts to hire teachers without credentials—most of whom are White—in districts with heavy concentrations of Chicano students. That is what insanity gets you.

Vouchers and charters

Vouchers and charters signal another shift in public understanding of education. As the conservative movement grows and evolves, everything is subsumed under deregulated capitalism and is accompanied by a steady drumbeat of denunciation of all forms of government. Paralleling the unceasing attack on public school is a dramatic shift in the intent of education—from a public good to serve society, to a private good to enhance the aspirations of the individual. Labaree (1997) has commented:

public education has increasingly come to be perceived as a private good that is harnessed to the pursuit of personal advantage; and, on the whole, the consequences of this for both school and society have been profoundly negative.

(p. 42)

Vouchers promise competitive advantage to those who wish to escape from the fatally flawed public school. As advertised, vouchers bring the virtues of capitalism to education and end the government monopoly (Chubb and Moe, 1990). With vouchers, parents use the equivalent of funds for tuition at a private school. Vouchers have been introduced in Milwaukee and Cleveland with low-income minority students, mostly African American. No consistent pattern of superiority has emerged when voucher students are compared with comparable public schools students on standardized tests scores performance (Drury, 2000). The criteria used for comparison are standardized tests, criteria applicable to education as a private good (i.e., competitive advantage). The broader concerns of society are ignored in such evaluation. Because only a small segment of the population will ever be able to use vouchers to escape a badly battered public school system, the inevitable result of a fully launched voucher system would be a two-tiered education system paralleling the two-tiered world of work. The logical consequence is a somewhat bifurcated Chicano population, with most people permanently confined to the most underfunded schools, and then consigned to the lower echelons of the work force. Vouchers, although powerfully pushed by Republican leadership, have not gained much public support. California, with its fast-growing Chicano population, overwhelmingly defeated a voucher initiative in 2000, as did voters in Michigan.

Republicans offered vouchers. Democrats, by contrast, chose charters to facilitate the escape from the "failed" education system. Charters are alternatives that allow for wide ranges of experimentation, but remain within the jurisdiction of the public school system. Charters have the potential to facilitate true democratic reforms. But with the prevailing thrust dominated by mad scrambles for competitive edge, charters are more likely to further individual aspiration than lead to generalized improvement in public schools, and thus, charters, like vouchers, reinforce a two-tiered society.

Upgrading teaching

A Nation at Risk calls for upgrading the teaching profession. No one opposes upgrading teaching. But what precisely does that mean? Does requiring every teacher to pass a test allegedly signify minimal competence in English and math, thus serving as an upgrade of the teaching profession? Does the addition of course requirements to the prerequisite for teaching upgrade teaching? Is a teacher more qualified if he/she is educated at Harvard University than at Slippery Rock Teachers College? Does raising pay produce better teaching? Are teachers more qualified with master's degrees than with bachelor's degrees? Is a teacher more qualified to teach with a straight "A" average in the university than a student with a "B" average? Is a teacher qualified to teach in affluent suburbs also qualified to teach in ghettos and barrios? Is a teacher qualified if s/he cannot speak or understand the languages the students speak? Is a teacher seeped in authoritarianism qualified to prepare students for democratic citizenship? Is a racist teacher qualified to teach anybody? Do teacher-training institutions screen applicants who are overtly racist to the same extent to which applicants are eliminated for a drug use conviction that occurred years before? Almost every proposal for improving teaching is tenuously, if at all, connected to student responsiveness. And even when there is such a connection, the measures used—performance on standardized tests— treat such a narrow segment of student activity as to be meaningful only for profoundly undemocratic goals of education. In sum, almost all proposals for "raising teacher standards" will make teaching a more exclusive club than it currently is. And it is an exclusive club.

As discussed by Valencia (Chapter 1, present book), Latino teachers in California—compared to the Latino K-12 student population—are considerably underrepresented. There is general recognition that the growing difference between the teacher population and the student population constitutes a problem (Valencia, Chapter 1). Remedy is sought by universities and colleges investing in outreach, partnership, and mentoring programs all with the dual objectives of improving Chicano (and other underrepresented populations) high school academic performance, and to interest these high school students in the teaching profession. Although most of these programs have been ongoing for at least a decade, there has been little noticeable impact—the gap is certainly not narrowing. These programs are initiated and maintained in the absence of any analysis of social and political context. They are respectable accommodations to the existing climate. Not taken into account is the bitter and ever more nasty competition for ever-shrinking numbers of slots in institutions of higher education. This is particularly true in California, where huge increases in the youth population—accompanied with very little increase in institutions of higher education—will make competition for available slots even more intense.

In conclusion, as we enter the 21st century, schools are systematically constricted by conservative philosophy. Standardized test scores define accountability, the curriculum has been top-down mandated, and efforts to improve teaching have had the unintended consequence of further limiting access to teaching of underrepresented populations.

Postmodernism: confusing voice and discourse with meaningful political activity

> The first business of educational reformers in schools and universities—multiculturalists, feminists, progressives—ought to be to sever their alliance with esoteric postmodernism; with literary metatheory (theory about theory); with fun-loving, self-annihilating hyper-skepticism. As pedagogy these intellectual practices court catastrophe. They proffer to desperate travelers trying to find their way between Scylla and Charybdis a clever little volume on Zeno's paradoxes. They give to people whose very lives depend on the right choices a lesson in the impossibility of judgment. They tell emerging citizens looking to legitimize their preferences for democracy that there is no intellectually respectable way to ground political legitimacy.
>
> (Barber, 1992, p. 125)

Systems are sustained by politics and changed by politics. Once, this was understood by virtually everybody. Politics was also commonly understood as the means by which decisions are made under conditions of conflict. Postmodernism has changed all that. Nothing is simple or understood anymore. Postmodernism emerged in architecture and in literary criticism, but it soon insinuated itself into the social sciences and thus to education. In postmodernism, simple truths are traduced and visions of a better world dismissed as hubris.

> [Postmodernism is] indifferent to consistency and continuity. . . . It self-consciously splices genes, attitudes, styles. . . . It disdains originality and fancies copies, repetition, the recombination of hand-me-down scraps. It neither embraces nor criticizes, but beholds the world blankly, with a knowingness that dissolves feeling and commitment

into irony. It pulls the rug out from under itself, displaying an acute self-consciousness about the work's constructed nature. It . . . derides the search for depth as mere nostalgia for an unmoved mover. . . . "The individual" has decomposed, as "reality" has dissolved, nothing lives but "discourses," "texts," "language games," "images," "simulations" referring to other "discourses," "texts," etc." . . . [It is] the spiritless spirit of a global class. [The experience of this class] denies the continuity of history; . . . History has ruptured, passions have been expended, belief has become difficult; heroes have died and been replaced by celebrities. The 1960s exploded our belief in progress, which underlay the classical faith in linear order and moral clarity. Old verities crumpled, but new ones have not settled in.

(Gitlin, 1990, pp. 3–4)

Education journals are supersaturated with the terms Gitlin (1990) mentions—"'discourses,' 'texts,' 'language games,' 'images,' 'simulations' referring to other 'discourses,' 'texts,' etc.," (p. 4). Differences are celebrated as each becomes the other. All of this takes place in the rarefied atmosphere of the university and is masqueraded as analysis. Much of what passes for analysis in postmodernism condemns the oppression of Chicanos in the educational system. Vignettes give "voice" to students expressing unhappiness with the ways they have been treated in school. These are voices that should be heard. But finding a voice is not in itself a political act, particularly if that is where it ends, and in postmodernism, that is where it ends. Life conditions are not changed; the system is unaltered. The net effect is a lot of Macbethian "sound and fury, signifying nothing." Because the language is arcane and the topics surreal, postmodernist discourse never finds it way to the elementary and secondary school where students and teachers are overwhelmed by conservative initiated reforms-mandated curriculum, standardized testing, grade retention, and denial of graduation. In postmodernism, real politics are eschewed, and important problems not addressed. In many ways, postmodernism in education plays into the ends of that which is sincerely opposed. Oppression by entrenched elites in imperfect democratic societies is maintained by successfully pitting one group with minimal power against another with minimal power. Postmodernism assists in this effort, not by actively promoting tension between minority groups, but by essentially withdrawing from the political process. Postmodernists transmogrify politics, insisting that by giving voice to the silenced and redefining ad infinitum oppression they are being political (e.g., Foucault, 1977). Nothing could be further from the truth. Postmodernists have excluded themselves from politics. They have removed themselves from the decision-making process. Those who go about passing laws and otherwise make policy pay no attention to their texts, discourses, etc., because they do not have to. Postmodernism may have been a reaction to the conservative onslaught (and the eclipsing if not the demise of Marxism), but whatever it does, it does not deter in the slightest the conservative onslaught. Thus, postmodernism is irrelevant to the Chicano school experience.

Critical pedagogy: one response to conservative reforms

Denouncing schools as oppressive places has a long history. Comenius did it 300 years ago. Pestalozzi and Rousseau followed not long after. In the midst of the great depression, George Counts raised the possibility that schools could be places where teachers and students learned to reconstruct society in his *Dare the School Build a New Social Order?* (1932). After World War II, a more somber mood prevailed. Schools were deemed too weak and too dependent an institution to change the social order. More powerful institutions and political forces controlled the political process (Mills, 1956). As a weak institution, all schools could do was prepare students for roles that would reproduce the existing political and economic system (Bourdieu, 1973; Bowles and Gintis, 1976). Critical pedagogy, in a sense, merges social reconstruction and social reproduction. It has gained a wide range of support in schools of education. Many speak for it: Most notable are Peter McLaren (1995, 1998) and Henry Giroux (1981, 1983, 1988, 1993).

The basic thrust of critical pedagogy is that schools are oppressive places—racist, sexist, classist, and homophobic. As such, it is important that teachers be "emancipatory intellectuals," exposing and opposing all forms of oppression. In its most recent formulations, critical pedagogy has become postmodernist. It suffers from the same thing postmodernism suffers from. It is remote from the classrooms it wants to change. Its language is inaccessible. It is elitist. It is imprecise and distorts the schooling situation. Schools *are* oppressive places, but that is not all they are. There is humor in schools that the humorless critical pedagogues do not recognize. Also, there are potentials for change that is also beyond their ken. Critical pedagogues claim to speak for democracy without specifying either what democracy is (other than the absence of oppression), or a democratic means to achieve it (Pearl and Knight, 2000). Critical pedagogy's politics is rhetoric not action. The "emancipatory intellectual" subscribes to a form of deficit thinking; the oppressed only understand their condition when someone smarter or more knowledgeable elucidates it for them.

Democratic education and its implication for Chicano education

Democratic education restores education to a public good, and is a clear alternative to the current degeneration of schooling as a means to gain competitive advantage. Democratic education is distinguished from previously described liberal and conservative efforts to shape education—not only in the rejection of deficit thinking, but also in devising policy and programs with, instead of for, Chicanos and others who have been underserved by education. And while liberals, conservatives, and critical pedagogues claim to be democratic, none substantiate that claim.

Democratic education is informed by the following principles: (a) persuasive and negotiable leadership; (b) inclusiveness; (c) knowledge made universally available and organized for important problem solving; (d) inalienable student and teacher rights; (e) informed participation in decisions that affect one's life; (f) the development of optimum learning conditions; and (g) equal encouragement. The primary goal of democratic education is an empowered and knowledgeable democratic citizen. A good education does not kowtow to business and contort curriculum to prepare workers for a mythological existing world of work. A democratic education prepares citizens to shape the work world.

Persuasive and negotiable leadership

One distinguishing feature of the democratic classroom is its leadership. The democratic authority—be it teacher, principal, coach, superintendent, or board president—persuades and negotiates. Democratic leadership can be seen in sharp contrast with democracy's two major enemies, guardianship (authoritarianism) and anarchy (Dahl, 1989). While authoritarianism is the preferred mode of school authority in many urban schools that serve the minority poor, student interests are neglected in a desperate tug-of-war between the authoritarian and the anarchistic. Teacher education should provide ample opportunity for prospective teachers to develop the requisite skills of persuasion and negotiation.

Inclusiveness

A democracy is inclusive. Democratic education is an alternative to the various forms of exclusion that have characterized schooling throughout its existence. Inclusiveness is furthered by spirited resistance to: tracking, isolation of special needs students, vouchers, and the increasingly available charter schools. Only with upgrading and valuing general public school education can inclusiveness be achieved. The democratic strength of any society is determined by quality of the education its most disadvantaged receive. Ending existing exclusionary policies and practices is not sufficient to achieve inclusiveness. An inclusive democratic culture must be created, consciously and deliberately, with a center that appeals to all. Inclusiveness cannot be imposed; a persuasive case must be made for it. Effective multiculturalism is one noncoercive means to achieve inclusiveness. Democracy must be understood as not merely the absence of repression, it is also carries with it a particular form of cohesiveness of com munity and culture. We are challenged to create such shared understanding at a time when postmodernist posturing has created a vacuum marked by an evacuation of the center and a loading up at the margins.

One form of exclusiveness can be found in the teaching profession. The growing demographic gap between the teacher population and the student population is much greater than the gap between teachers and paraprofessionals. The teacher–student gap is a logical consequence of the standards-based movement and the inability to distinguish a standard from an obstacle. In a very important sense, everything promoted as a standard is also an obstacle. The standards for entrance to the university, defended with religious intensity by opponents of affirmative action—be they SAT or ACT tests or grade point average, have a high percentage of false negatives. Roughly half of those who meet the standards (e.g., acceptable high school g.p.a.) fail to graduate within six years. There is no correlation between success in higher education and SAT scores beyond the first year in the university. What about false positives? How would people who did not meet the standard have fared if they had been admitted? Affirmative action programs could have been proposed as a test of the standard rather than as a deficit thinking program that accepted the logic of lowering the barrier and letting the "unqualified" in. If that had been done, rather than perceiving university admissions as a defense of exalted standards, admission policies might more validly be perceived as maintenance of class, race, and ethnic exclusiveness.

Standards were "lowered" after World War II and any veteran could enter any university as a GI benefit. Many of working-class origin took advantage (I being one), and did very well. The university did not suffer and few dared to criticize this affirmative action, but then the beneficiaries were almost exclusively White. African American and Chicano veterans were very effectively discouraged from taking advantage of this GI benefit.

In the 1960s, the Upward Bound Program at the University of Oregon was an experiment in democratic education. It also was a program that afforded opportunity to examine the validity of entrance standards, as 160 severely unqualified inadmissible students who had participated in the Upward Bound Program were admitted to the university. This was a very diverse group of African Americans, Chicanos, American Indians, and poor Whites. Five years later, as high a percentage of these students graduated in five years as did the qualified (Pearl and Knight, 1999). In other words, there was as high a percentage of false positives in the "unqualified" admissions as there were false negatives among the "qualified" admissions. Many went on to successful postgraduate careers as academics, teachers, principals, counselors, and lawyers (Hollins, 1991). One of these false positives was an "incorrigible delinquent," Mary Groda. She was recruited to the university from a training school for delinquent girls. She was beset with many learning difficulties and personal problems, but that did not prevent her from becoming a medical doctor. Her story is presented in the 1986 CBS film, *Love Mary*.

What distinguished the project was that it combined a rigorous traditional curriculum with a curriculum that challenged students to create the future. The workings of the university were demystified, enabling students to understand the logic and functioning of the institution that they first had to survive if they were ever to change. The students were challenged to be involved in the governance of the program and to participate in other school reform activities at the university. At the same time, they were encouraged to be excellent university students. The most important element in its success was its rejection of deficit thinking and implementation of equal encouragement (briefly described later).

New Careers is perhaps a more spectacular example of dealing with exclusiveness and exposing standards for what they are—obstacles. New Careers not only assisted minorities to graduate from the university, but also at the same time effectively recruited underrepresented minorities into teaching and other professions. In New Careers, rather than having the applicant meet the requirements of the job, a career ladder was created beginning with teacher aide, ascending through teacher assistant and teacher associate, and terminating as a professional teacher. The entry position required no prior skill or experience. New Careerists worked their way up each step of the ladder through a com bination of work experience, university courses delivered at the work site, and liberal art courses at the university (Pearl and Riessman, 1965). The largest of the New Career programs was the Career Opportunity Program (COP) of the Educational Professional Development Act (EPDA) of 1967, involving 18,000 almost exclusively poor women of color (Carter, 1977, pp. 183–184).

The COP was designed to increase the percentage of underrepresented minority teachers, demonstrate that "inadmissible" students can succeed in higher education (i.e., challenge "standards"), lift people out of poverty, better meet the needs of low-income children, improve staffing in schools, and "respond to the growing belief that the then-present designs of teacher education were inadequate, particularly in preparing teachers for the children of the poor" (Carter, 1977, p. 184). New Careers made progress on all fronts. How much progress is difficult to gauge, however, given that the program was short-lived, inconsistent within and between sites, and only superficially evaluated. COP recruited into teaching many Latinos, African Americans, and American Indians (Carter, 1977, p. 187) who successfully matriculated to the university, despite failing to meet entrance requirements (Carter, 1977, p. 204).

In the only teaching standard that should matter, meeting the needs of low-income children and improving the quality of schooling, the evidence, though uneven and necessarily incomplete and therefore inconclusive, indicates that teachers that advanced through a career ladder were at least as effective as traditionally prepared teachers (Carter, 1977).

The impact of a New Career program can be seen after two decades. The University of Minnesota, in conjunction with many social agencies, had a New Career program, including the COP; 20 years after its inception efforts, the university was made to evaluate its success. Like most other such efforts, the program participants had been poor, predominantly African American single mothers on welfare. Virtually none had completed high school. Twenty years later, of the 207 persons who had been in the program, at least one had earned a doctorate, dozens had master's degrees (one participant, the mother of Prince, the entertainer, had earned two master's degrees), and about half had graduated from the university (Amram *et al.*, 1988). Despite its successes, New Careers was dismantled.

While it is undeniable that New Careers had important democratic qualities, it also is true that the programs, as conceived and implemented, had serious flaws. The most serious problem was an unwillingness to critically examine the fundamental purposes of education.

New Careers, like the compensatory approach and the effective school model, was a top-down program. It rose when an elite supported it and it fell when that elite lost interest or power. A revitalization of education, particularly an education devoted to true equal encouragement and the full realization of the potential of Chicanos, among others, requires a political constituency powerful enough to produce such an education. The potential political constituency for a truly democratic education comes from an alliance of professionals, paraprofessionals, students and their parents and others in the community who recognize the critical need for a democratic education.

New Careers was unable to be sustained because of the unwillingness of higher education to engage in serious examination of its goals, policies, and practices. This was especially true in teacher education. Under New Careers, a totally different model for preparing teachers was being proposed, one in which most of the preparation took place away from the college campus and therefore requiring university faculty to be where the action was. If done right, every rung of the ladder would have clearly specified responsibilities and teacher education would insure that those at that rung had the knowledge and skill required to meet specific rung responsibilities. If done right, teaching would change and a fully credentialed teacher would be working with a team of paraprofessionals dispersed along every rung on the ladder. Students would, in a single day, be individually tutored, involved in small group research projects, directly instructed in a class of 25–35, and perhaps in appropriate situations assembled in groups of 150 or more. The career ladders for teacher preparation would be very different from the preparation now in existence or proposed as a reform.

The career ladder resurfaced in the 1990s. Legislation was passed in California and eventually funded. There were striking differences between the actions taken in the 1960s and those of the 1990s. The 1960s program was put into place without a constituency. The 1990s initiative began with and was made possible by the lobbying efforts of the unions representing classified workers in schools. The career ladder approach to the teacher credential has had a sizeable impact on Chicano teacher recruitment. Its impact on student performance is not yet known. Higher education is not accommodating this version of the career ladders any more than was done in the 1960s. Without a greater commitment of the other democratic principles the best that can be hoped for from the career ladders are more Mexican American teachers and some rather small gains in Mexican American student achievement on standardized tests.

Important knowledge from a democratic perspective

Students go to school ostensibly to learn important things. But what constitutes important knowledge? One way to examine democracy and important knowledge is to analyze who determines important knowledge and how the decision was made. Currently, decisions are made about knowledge that do not include the student or the parent. It matters not that students are often not in the least bit interested in learning what is being taught them.

Student opinion of important knowledge cannot be arbitrarily dismissed. If students are not convinced of the value of that which is being taught they will respond perfunctorily, if at all. Many Chicanos suspect the value of the curriculum. They study in a desperate fashion hoping that they won't be humiliated by being left back. They dream, but school has little to do with those dreams. Their desires for a better world, a fulfilling culture, an opportunity to engage in rewarding work, to live harmoniously with self and neighbors, to preserve the environment are matters treated superficially, if at all, in the curriculum.

The issue of important knowledge impacts schooling in two ways. One involves the kinds and depth of knowledge taught and the other determines which students gets how much of it. These two issues are obviously connected. Little is to be gained if equality is achieved in useless, destructive, or trivial knowledge. Nor can democracy be sustained if knowledge is rationed by race/ethnicity, class, gender, or alleged capacity to learn. All students *need* specific knowledge that can be used to solve (what are to them) important problems.

The knowledge Chicanos need is the knowledge every citizen needs. Chicanos need to be provided with what it takes to be an empowered and informed citizen. They need to possess the knowledge that permits them to participate equally and competently in debates about all aspects of social policy. A major goal of teaching is to nurture in students the understanding that in a democracy decisions are made on the basis of logic and evidence by an informed majority when everyone is equally prepared and equally involved.

It is in this context that academic subjects come alive. Language is used to communicate the important. Mathematics provides a way of thinking—a means of deciphering relationships and ordering evidence. Science is a process for accumulating evidence and determining lawfulness. History is a quest for solution. Through the arts, individuals give expression to what they perceive to be important. The classics provide perspective. The basics are not educational ends, but means to ends.

The decision process used to determine the knowledge that is important for a democratic society is democratic. It is impossible to decree such knowledge. Knowledge in a democratic society is not spinach crammed down throats of resisting children for "their own good." Not everyone may accept the importance of certain knowledge, but every student is encouraged to evaluate, to weigh, to propose, to investigate, to debate, to offer counterproposals, and to negotiate differences. In a democratic school, students do more than absorb knowledge, they develop it. They are active participants in helping design the curriculum that effectively deals with life problems (e.g., substance abuse, violence, and sexually transmitted disease).

In a democratic school, choice of career resides in the individual student and the school fulfills its responsibility by providing accurate information about the complete gamut of careers, by discouraging premature foreclosure, and by assuring every student that they have a right to consider any and all occupations. Even that would be insufficient. The encouragement of students to think about future occupations must be coupled with an in-depth study of economics to enable students to participate in economic planning and more specifically in employment development policy decisions. Education about employment must also bring into the analysis the environment to insure that economic plans do not come at the expense of livability.

Maintaining a static, lifeless, standardized curriculum not only dumbs down education it consigns Chicanos to second-class citizenship.

Rights

Individual rights are the foundation on which democracy is built. Without them, there is no place to stand. The determination of appropriate knowledge and the quality of participation depends on the rights that each individual possesses as (to use Tawney's words), "practical powers" (Tawney, 1964, p. 235). Currently, students have few rights, and even those that they have are unequally bestowed and unevenly respected. Students are often taught about rights the very moment they are denied them. The discussion here is limited to four rights, not because these are all there should be in a democratic society, or even all that have been discussed, but because these four constitute a basic foundation that have successfully withstood the test of time. The four are: (a) rights of expression; (b) rights of privacy; (c) rights to a particular form of due process; and (d) rights of movement.

Rights of expression

Freedom of expression is the right to express an unpopular opinion and to disagree with established authority. The right does not extend to slander, racial epithets, and to the disruption of others while they are exercising their rights of expression. It does not require others to listen. In fact, requiring others to pay attention is a violation of another precious right not respected in school—the right not to be a captive audience. Students must be encouraged to state opinions. It is essential that criticism of adult authority, teachers or administrators, not be suppressed. Such criticism can and should be answered by adult authority, not squelched by it. In a democratic classroom, student newspapers are not censored (although the United States Supreme Court has recently ruled that school officials can censor). Students' right to petition and to assemble are also respected in the democratic classroom.

In a democratic education, libel, slander, and "fighting words"—the use of racial epithets, sexual harassment, and verbal abuse because of sexual preference—are taken seriously. These are of particular importance to Chicanos, who are often the target of verbal abuse. Action to suppress such expression is given serious consideration and debated thoroughly.

Is conversing in a language other than English covered by rights of expression? The language a person uses does more than communicate information to others. Language also expresses identity and loyalty. All oppressed people develop secret codes that they use to communicate to those they trust and keep those they do not trust in the dark. Any school effort to suppress the language spoken at home should be seen as a violation of a student's rights of expression. To be democratic, teachers and other officials need to find persuasive reasons for students to become fluent in English. If students resist learning English, school officials should look for oppressive conditions that lessen the desire for students to learn English.

Rights of privacy

Democracy guarantees its citizens a private life. Privacy is threatened by both a lack of understanding of its importance and by increased technical capacity to pry. School authorities find many excuses to intrude into students' lives. Concern about drug use or possession of other contraband has been deemed sufficient to mandate student submission to drug testing and to searches of locker or person. Respecting rights of privacy is difficult. School authorities must act decisively if the health and safety of students are threatened. There is with privacy, as with all rights, situations that justify abrogation. Schools move in the direction of democracy when the student's right to privacy is publicly acknowledged and the unusual circumstances where violation of that right is specified and justified. Given that rights are an equity issue, schools are only democratic when there is assurance that the privacy right of every student will be equally protected. The challenge is to find ways to protect the general public without undermining rights. It will be easier to respect the rights of privacy if all students participate in the decision-making processes that lead to the establishment of rules. Rights of privacy will also be easier to be protected if students have available to them more complete knowledge of a problem to be solved and a more thorough understanding of the arguments defending the different proposed solutions to that problem.

Rights to due process

The Constitution of the United States in Amendments IV through VIII defines a system of due process. These need to be understood and practiced in schools. The due process protection in the Bill of Rights must define the parameters of school discipline policy and practice. Due process rights should be taught respectfully. Schools will make strides to becoming democratic institutions when every student, regardless of background or previous history is guaranteed the following: (a) presumption of innocence; (b) rights not to testify against oneself; (c) right to counsel to provide advice and support when accused of rule violation; (d) right to trial before an independent tribunal; and (e) protection against cruel and unusual punishment. Due process is designed for one goal—fairness. The lack of perceived fairness produces much of the alienation and anger in Chicano students.

Rights of movement

Here schools are in a quandary. Attendance in school is compulsory. Yet, fundamental to democracy and to the notion of human rights is freedom of movement. Compulsory education does not necessarily mean that student movement must be as restricted as it currently is, nor does it mean that students must be captive audiences. Rights are not easily transferred into practical powers, but schools can function efficiently while respecting rights of movement. One reasonable approach to democratizing compulsory education is to increase the number of choices that students have in school. No student should be required to remain in a situation that s/he does not find gratifying. Students should be able to exercise choice over teachers, classes, and schools. Students' charges of unfair treatment have to be taken seriously. Choice can be very difficult for schools, but the difficult is not impossible.

Participation in decisions that affect one's life

Self-government requires two kinds of knowledge; the first supplies the evidence that is applied to social and personal problems. That kind of knowledge was briefly introduced in the previous paragraphs. The second knowledge is of process—learning how to work with others to arrive at decisions. Schools concerned about democracy assume a measure of responsibility for both of these forms of knowledge. Effective participation requires the mastering of certain democratic arts or skills. All students should be involved in activities designed to accomplish the following: the ability to marshal a persuasive argument, the willingness to listen and understand the arguments of others, the capacity to negotiate, the willingness to work cooperatively with a wide range of others, the ability to assume leadership (and the willingness to relinquish it), and the capacity to establish goals and to evaluate progress to those goals. The following are necessary if a student is to become an effective and responsible citizen: (a) a revitalized school government, the most important unit of which is the classroom; (b) participation in cooperative learning; and (c) involvement with meaningful community development services.

The creation of an optimum environment for learning

If deficit thinking does not explain differences in learning outcomes, then the school environment must. Optimum learning conditions cannot be created unless first defined. The following are the characteristics of an optimum learning environment.

Encouragement to risk

For risk-taking to be encouraged, the teacher must achieve a balance between challenge and support. In existing classrooms, inequality is not based on encouragement to risk but rather on active and persistent differential *dis couragement* to risk. Very early in school life, many students learn that they should not risk because the costs of taking risks far outweigh any benefits. Teachers communicate clearly who will be punished for taking risks and who will not (Good and Brophy, 1991). Students perceive these differences in treatment and act accordingly.

Relief from unnecessary pain

For most students, school is an uncomfortable place. In school, unnecessary pain takes the form of humiliation, shame, boredom, imposed silence, and loneliness. Teachers and administrators are not the only ones who inflict unnecessary pain. Students do it to each other. Bullying, harassment, and name-calling are all part of the existing "at-risk" school culture. However, students inflicting pain on other students does not absolve the teacher from altering that situation. In the democratic classroom conscious effort is made to eliminate unnecessary pain and student suggestions to relieve pain are not only welcome but also needed.

Meaning

Meaning in school has two fundamentally different *meanings*. In one of its senses, students need to understand what is expected of them in any class activity, and in the other, students need to know that what they are learning is important. In today's classroom there is wide discrepancy in communicating both senses of meaning. Because of the way meaning is treated and because of the remote and arcane methods used to evaluate student performance, students are often so confused that they are no longer able to ascertain for themselves what they know. They have lost ownership of their intelligence and thus are unable to determine if they can or cannot read, multiply, or analyze a historical situation. In a democratic classroom all students receive equal justifications for the lesson and are equally demystified on how the lesson is to be learned (see Corbett and Wilson [1998], for students' assessment of the importance of making instructions clear and how rarely that occurs).

Sense of competence

Developing in students a sense of their own competence is a vital condition of an optimum learning environment. Currently, only a select few are encouraged to a sense of competence. Those that are not so encouraged learn quickly who they are, and in time begin to perceive themselves as teachers perceive them (Wigfield *et al.*, 1998). For an optimum learning environment, it is necessary for teachers to encourage in all a sense of competence.

Belonging

Belonging is a vital human need. Humans hunger for companionship. They are terrified by isolation. Exclusion from welcomed membership in school does not terminate a student's desire for belonging. Students demeaned, humiliated, and excluded from first-class membership in school, that is, those with attributed "deficits" will search for belonging outside of school-sanctioned activities. They will, for example, join cliques or gangs to establish identity and they will demonstrate affiliation by dress, music, language, designation of "turf," identifying behaviors (which can include violence), shared values, and other indicators of a "common culture" (Willis, 1990). These groups become references for acceptable and unacceptable behavior and, in time, rob established authority of its legitimacy. An optimum learning environment is one that welcomes every student equally and is one in which all students are encouraged to be part of the effort to make the classroom an inclusive community. Welcoming all students equally not only makes a community out of the classroom, it is an antidote to racism, ethnocentrism, sexism, and homophobia.

Usefulness

Uselessness is a dreaded condition. The *raison d'être* of current education is preparation for *future* usefulness. And that is one of the reasons students find school so deadly. They are asked to put their life on hold. In the democratic education, schools do prepare students for future challenges, but at the same time usefulness is built into day-to-day classroom activity. Usefulness is perceived as a developmental attribute—the skills, insights, and knowledge obtained in the process of being useful in school provide the basis for continual growth that open doors to a variety of valuable paid and volunteer adult usefulness. Usefulness in school is achieved when all students are given a wide range choice in providing services to others and also a wide range of choice in accepting the service of another. Usefulness in school is meaningful problem solving rather than mindless drill and alleged preparation for a murky future. In an optimum learning environment, *all* activities are organized for usefulness. The problems students solve are problems students perceive to be real and important. All students are recruited to help with the instruction and serve in many different capacities. All engage in tutoring, all share the results of research with the class, all have valuable roles to play in cooperative education projects. All engage in community development service.

Hope

If an optimum learning environment is to be achieved, a serious effort must be made to equally encourage all students to be hopeful (Freire, 1994). Inspiring hopefulness, however, cannot degenerate into cheerleading. An optimum learning environment can only be achieved when all students are provided powerful *reasons* to be hopeful. Such optimism is the result of continuous dialogue. Problems are organized with possible solutions in mind. And students are encouraged to be problem solvers, rather than be overwhelmed by their problems.

Excitement

Excitement is a legitimate and important human need. In the classroom the most important excitement is the thrill of discovery. Excitement is not a term that students usually associate with classrooms. Classrooms can be designed to be exciting only if teachers are willing to relinquish control and students are encouraged to participate in activities where they generate important knowledge, make important discoveries, and participate in important decisions.

Creativity

Humans are, by nature, a creative species. Each generation creates a new world. Creativity is the thrill of invention. There are no acceptable criteria for creativity, and often it goes unrecognized. In an optimum learning environment all students are encouraged to be constructively creative and to use creativity for community building.

Ownership

In an optimum learning environment, students own their intellectual product. They do things for themselves and for their community, and not for established authority. Students are far more motivated to achieve when they believe that they have a stake in the educational activity. There is powerful evidence in support of the extent to which students are motivated to invest in education when they "own" their schoolwork (Au, 1997).

The most plausible explanation of Chicano school failure is not "deficits," but systematic denial of access to an optimum learning environment. Such denial leads to consistency in academic performance by class and race/ethnicity across space and times (an argument supporting inherited intelligence) because the denial is systemic. The selection of teachers, the curriculum, the approaches to classroom management, the assessment of academic performance, all bring a historical consistency to the differential ways students are provided optimal learning conditions. In a credential society the systematic denial of an optimum learning environment is as much an equal rights issue as was desegregation in 1954, or voting rights in 1964.

Equality

No issue is more important to a democracy than equality and nothing is more difficult. The United States prides itself on equality. It is a term everyone uses; few define it the same. As noted by a number of authors in the present book (see, e.g., Valencia, Chapter 1; Valencia *et al.*, Chapter 3) and elsewhere (see, e.g., San Miguel, 1987; San Miguel and Valencia, 1998), equality is a burning issue with Chicanos. The term Chicano emerged as a symbol and as an organizing vehicle to combat inequality. Despite all of these efforts the world remains unequal and the gains made in the direction of equality have been painfully slow, often reversible and, too often, illusory. Equality has become ethereal; to make it operational in the classroom, equality is described here as equal encouragement to an optimum learning environment. Such definition requires no new laws or policies. Any teacher in any classroom can make an important contribution to Chicano school success by creating an optimum learning environment and taking the necessary steps to insure that all equally enjoy the benefits of such an environment.

Chicano school failure and Chicano school success are inextricably linked to larger, complexly interrelated social issues. The distribution of jobs is a function of the economy. The role of government is determined by the political mood. The condition of the global environment is at the mercy of the people's understanding of it, as is the ever-changing face of international relations and the use and misuse of technology. The lingering and at times festering conditions of race and ethnic hatred create a chronic condition that is treatable only by aroused public consciousness. The intellectual level of popular culture gravitates to the lowest common denominator of public education. All the above influences Chicano education. Chicano educational failure is the result of flawed policy and inequit able educational practice. Part of that problem stems from Chicano lack of access to power.

Deficit thinking has contaminated both liberal and conservative efforts to "reform" education. These "reforms" are exclusively catch-up activities in education and fail because there is no catch-up. The liberal and conservative reforms are top-down and elitist. Thus, the Chicano student succeeds or fails depending on what others do for them or to them.

Democratic education rejects all forms of deficit thinking, and has as its goal the empowering of everyone. Only with democratic education is it possible for Chicanos and everyone else to succeed in education. Without democratic education, Chicano success comes when others fail, especially so in an economy equally divided between good and bad jobs and when quest for competitive advantage is the dominant educational purpose.

Democracy can begin in a single classroom with an optimum learning environment. Chicano parents can demand it. No one can legitimately oppose it. Unless Chicanos and all others participate in an education that equally prepares all to solve the major problems confronting an ever-changing society, educational progress for Chicanos will be slow and uneven. Without democratic education, Chicanos will continue to try to make it in a world others control. Without democratic education, the classroom is a nightmare for Chicano children and youths who are compelled to run ever faster only to fall farther and farther behind.

Notes

1 Actually, the figures are for all Latinos (Mexican-origin, Puerto Ricans, Cubans, Guatemalans, etc.). The figures did not distinguish among Latinos, but Chicanos (Mexican descent) represent the vast majority and fastest growing segment of Latinos (see Valencia, Chapter 2, present book). These figures fairly reflect Chicano representation in the work world and the figures approximate the Chicano experience.
2 "Good jobs" are defined as those jobs requiring a credential from higher education. Not all executives, administrators, and managers require credentials, but almost all do. Furthermore, not all of the good jobs are equally good (e.g., medical doctors make much more money and have more prestige and influence than do preschool teachers). And some, very few, employed in jobs without a credential requirement do quite well. Some athletes and entertainers are extremely well paid, but these are rare exceptions.
3 The unemployment rates may have been significantly influenced by the huge growth in the prison population in the 1990s, particularly among African Americans and Latinos, and thus true unemployment among persons with less than a high school education may not have declined.
4 Valencia and Suzuki (2001) comment: "During recent years, however, the case of fraud against Burt appears to have weakened." See Valencia and Suzuki (p. 313, Note 38) for further discussion on this issue.

References

Amram, F., Flax, S., Hamermesh M. and Marty, G. (1988). *New careers: The dream that worked.* Minneapolis: University of Minnesota Press.
Au, K.H. (1997). Ownership, literacy achievement, and students of diverse cultural backgrounds. In J.T. Guthrie and A. Wigfield (Eds.), *Reading engagement: Motivating readers through integrated instruction* (pp. 168–182). Newark, DE: International Reading Association.
Barber, B.R. (1992). *An aristocracy of everyone: The politics of education and the future of America.* New York: Ballantine Books.
Bennett, N.G., Li, J., Song, Y. and Yang, K. (Eds.). (1999). *Children in poverty: Statistical update, June 1999.* Washington, DC: National Center for Children in Poverty.
Berliner, D.C. and Biddle, B.J. (1995). *The manufactured crisis: Myths, fraud, and the attack on America's public schools.* Reading, MA: Addison-Wesley.
Bernstein, B. (1970). A sociolinguistic approach to socialization with some reference to educability. In F. Williams (Ed.), *Language and poverty* (pp. 25–61). Chicago: Markham Press.
Bourdieu, P. (1973). Cultural reproduction and social reproduction. In R. Brown (Ed.), *Knowledge, education, and cultural change* (pp. 487–501). New York: Harper and Row.
Bowles, S. and Gintis, H. (1976). *Schooling in capitalist America: Educational reform and the contradictions of economic life.* New York: Basic Books.
Burt, C. (1972). The inheritance of general intelligence. *American Psychology, 27,* 175–190.
California Department of Education. (2000). *California Basic Educational Data System (CBEDS).* Sacramento, CA: Author.
Carter, W.T. (1977). The Career Opportunities Program: A summing up. In A. Gartner, F. Riessman, and V. Carter-Jackson (Eds.), *Paraprofessionals today* (pp. 183–221). New York: Human Services Press.

Chapa, J. and Valencia, R.R. (1993). Latino population growth, demographic characteristics, and educational stagnation: An examination of recent trends. *Hispanic Journal of Behavioral Sciences, 15,* 165–187.

Chubb, J.E. and Moe, T.E. (1990) *Politics, markets, & America's schools.* Washington, DC: Brookings Institute.

Corbett, H.D. and Wilson, B.L. (1998). Scaling within rather than scaling up: Implications from students' experiences in reforming urban middle schools. *Urban Review, 30,* 261–293.

Counts, G.S. (1932). *Dare the school build a new social order?* New York: John Day Co.

Currie, J. and Thomas, D. (1996). *Does Head Start help Latino children?* Rand Corporation Document No: DRU-1528-RC.

Dahl, R.A. (1989). *Democracy and its critics.* New Haven, CT: Yale University Press.

Deutsch, M. (1967). *The disadvantaged child.* New York: Basic Books.

Drury, D.W. (2000). *Vouchers and student achievement: A review of the evidence.* National School Boards Association, Policy Research Briefs [Online serial]. Available: http://www.nsba.org/research-briefs/index.htm

Dunn, L.M. (1987). *Bilingual Hispanic children on the U.S. mainland: A review of research on their cognitive, linguistic, and scholastic development.* Circle Pines, MN: American Guidance Service.

Edmonds, R. (1979). Effective schools for the urban poor. *Educational Leadership, 37,* 15–27.

Edmonds, R. (1984). School effects and teacher effects. *Social Policy, 15,* 37–40.

Englmann, S. (1970). How to construct effective language programs for the poverty child. In F. Williams (Ed.), *Language and poverty* (pp. 102–122). Chicago: Markham Press.

Foucault, M. (1977). *Discipline and punish.* New York: Vintage.

Freire, P. (1994). *Pedagogy of hope: Reliving pedagogy of the oppressed.* New York: Continuum.

Galton, F. (1884). *Hereditary genius.* New York: D. Appleton.

Giroux, H.A. (1981). *Ideology, culture and the process of schooling.* Philadelphia: Temple University Press.

Giroux, H.A. (1983). *Theories of reproduction and resistance in the new sociology of education: A critical analysis.* South Hadley, MA: Bergin and Garvey.

Giroux, H.A. (1988). *Teachers as intellectuals: Toward a critical pedagogy of learning.* Westport, CT: Bergin and Garvey.

Giroux, H.A. (1993). *Border crossings: Cultural workers and the politics of education.* New York: Routledge.

Gitlin, T. (1990). Quoted by P. Smith, *Killing the spirit* (1990). New York: Viking.

Good, T.L. and Brophy, J.E. (1991). *Looking in classrooms* (5th ed.). New York: HarperCollins.

Hacker, A. (1996). *Money: Who has how much and why.* New York: Scribner.

Haycock, K. and Navarro, S.M. (1988). *Unfinished business: Fulfilling our children's promise.* Oakland, CA: The Achievement Council.

Herrnstein, R.J. and Murray, C. (1994). *The bell curve: Intelligence and class structure in American life.* New York: Free Press.

Hodgkinson, H.L. (1989). *Reform and demographic realities.* Paper presented at the Danforth Foundation Seminar, Institute for Educational Leadership, Washington, DC, February.

Hollins, C.E. (1991). *It was fun from the beginning.* New York: Carlton Press.

Hunt, J. McV. (1961). *Intelligence and experience.* New York: Ronald Press.

Jensen, A.R. (1969). How much can we boost IQ and scholastic achievement? *Harvard Educational Review, 39,* 1–123.

Kozol, J. (1991). *Savage inequalities: Children in America's schools.* New York: Crown.

Labaree, D.F. (1997). Public goods, private goods: The American struggle over educational goals. *American Educational Research Journal, 34,* 39–81.

López, E., Ramírez, E. and Rochín, R.I. (1999). *Latinos and economic development in California.* Sacramento, CA: California Research Bureau.

McLaren, P. (1995). *Critical pedagogy and predatory culture: Oppositional politics in a postmodern age.* New York: Routledge.

McLaren, P. (1998). *Life in schools: An introduction to critical pedagogy in the foundations of education.* White Plains, NY: Longman.

Mills, C.W. (1956). *The power elite.* London: Oxford University Press.

Moore, J. and Pachón, H. (1983). *Latinos in the United States.* Englewood Cliffs; NJ: Prentice-Hall.

Moreno, J.F. (Ed.). (1999). *The elusive quest for equality: 150 years of Chicano/Chicana education.* Cambridge, MA: Harvard Educational Review.

National Commission on Excellence in Education. (1983). *A nation at risk: The imperative for educational reform.* Washington, DC: Government Printing Office.

Pearl, A. (1997). Cultural and accumulated environmental deficit models. In R.R. Valencia (Ed.), *The evolution of deficit thinking: Educational thought and practice* (pp. 132–159). The Stanford Series on Education and Public Policy. London: Falmer Press.

Pearl, A. and Knight, T. (1999). *The democratic classroom: Theory to inform practice.* Cresskill, NJ: Hampton Press.

Pearl, A. and Knight, T. (2000). Democratic education and critical pedagogy. *Urban Review, 32,* 197–226.

Pearl, A. and Riessman, F. (1965). *New careers for the poor.* New York: Macmillan.

Pearlstein, S. (1995). The winners are taking all: In the new economy more and more of us qualify as "losers." *Washington Post Weekly,* December 11–15, pp. 6–8

Ryan, W. (1971). *Blaming the victim.* New York: Random House.

San Miguel, G. Jr., (1987). *"Let them all take heed": Mexican Americans and the campaign for educational equality in Texas, 1910–1981.* Austin: University of Texas Press.

San Miguel, G. Jr. and Valencia, R.R. (1998). From the Treaty of Guadalupe Hidalgo to *Hopwood*: The educational plight and struggle of Mexican Americans in the Southwest. *Harvard Educational Review, 68,* 353–412.

Slavin, R.E., Madden, N.A., Dolan, L.J., Wasik, B.A., Ross, S.M. and Smith, L.J. (1994). Whenever and wherever we choose: The replication of "Success for All." *Phi Delta Kappan, 75,* 639–647.

Tawney, R.H. (1964 [1931]). *Equality.* London: Unwin Books.

University of California, Office of the President, Student Academic Services. (2000). *OA&SA, Student Ethnicity Report-CSS330.* Oakland, CA: Office of the President, University of California, Information Resources and Communications.

U.S. Administration for Children and Families. (1999). *Head Start: Fact sheet.* Washington, DC: Government Printing Office.

U.S. Department of Commerce, Bureau of the Census. (1999). *Statistical abstract of the United States* (119th edition). Washington, DC: Government Printing Office.

Valencia, R.R. (Ed.). (1997a). *The evolution of deficit thinking: Educational thought and practice.* The Stanford Series on Education and Public Policy. London: Falmer Press.

Valencia, R.R. (1997b). Genetic pathology model of deficit thinking. In R.R. Valencia (Ed.), *The evolution of deficit thinking: Educational thought and practice* (pp. 41–112). The Stanford Series on Education and Public Policy. London: Falmer Press.

Valencia, R.R. (2000). *Legislated school reform via high-stakes testing: The case of pending anti-social promotion legislation in Texas and its likely impact on racial/ethnic minority students.* Commissioned paper for the National Academy of Sciences Committee on Educational Excellence and Testing Equity. Paper presented at the National Academy of Sciences workshop on School Completion in Standards-Based Reform, Washington, DC, July.

Valencia, R.R. and Bernal, E.M. (Eds.). (2000). The Texas Assessment of Academic Skills (TAAS) case: Perspectives of plaintiffs' experts [Special issue]. *Hispanic Journal of Behavioral Sciences, 22*(4).

Valencia, R.R. and Chapa, J. (Eds.). (1993). Latino population growth and demographic trends: Implications for education [Special issue]. *Hispanic Journal of Behavioral Sciences, 15*(2).

Valencia, R.R. and Guadarrama, I.N. (1996). High-stakes testing and its impact on racial and ethnic minority students. In L.A. Suzuki, P.J. Meller, and J.G. Ponterotto (Eds.), *Multicultural assessment: Clinical, psychological, and educational applications* (pp. 561–610). San Francisco: Jossey-Bass.

Valencia, R.R. and Solórzano, D.G. (1997). Contemporary deficit thinking. In R.R. Valencia (Ed.), *The evolution of deficit thinking: Educational thought and practice* (pp. 160–210). The Stanford Series on Education and Public Policy. London: Falmer Press.

Valencia, R.R. and Suzuki, L.A. (2001). *Intelligence testing and minority students: Foundations, performance factors, and assessment issues.* Thousand Oaks, CA: Sage.

Velez, W. (1989). High school attrition among Hispanic and non-Hispanic white youths. *Sociology of Education, 62,* 119–133.

Wigfield, A., Eccles, J.S. and Rodríguez, D. (1998). The development of children's motivation in school contexts. In P.D. Pearson and A. Iran-Nejad (Eds.), *Review of Research in Education* (pp. 73–118). Washington, DC: American Educational Research Association.

Willis, P. (with Simon Jones, Joyce Canaan, and Geoff Hurd). (1990). *Common culture: Symbolic work at play in the everyday cultures of the young.* London: Open University Press.

12 Conclusions: towards Chicano school success

Richard R. Valencia

In this concluding chapter, I offer some final thoughts on the promotion of school success for Chicano students. Focus will be on a synthesis of ideas presented by the various contributors of this volume. Based on our discussion thus far, the task here is to address how Chicano school success might be realized. We tackle this inquiry by zeroing in on the following specific areas: (a) keeping Chicanos in school, (b) the academic and social contexts of schooling, (c) the Mexican American English language learner and bilingual education, (d) Chicano parental involvement in schooling, (e) the assessment context of schooling, and (f) democratic education.

Keeping Chicanos in school

Clearly, one of the major challenges in improving schooling for Chicano students is to keep them in school. As Rumberger and Rodríguez (Chapter 4, current volume) have underscored, the dropout problem among Chicanos is so acute that the social and economic welfare of the general Chicano population is not likely to improve until its educational status improves. In part, the "quality of life" for the next generation of Chicanos hinges on substantially lowering the scandalously high dropout rate. Although there are some effective programs that are combating the dropout issue among Chicanos (see Rumberger and Rodríguez, Chapter 4), a growing number of educational reformers are calling for deep-rooted systemic reform—necessitating changes in broad economic, political, cultural, and school curricular contexts (see Pearl, Chapter 11, present volume). In short, the Chicano dropout issue is not just an educational problem.

Furthermore, those Chicano students who drop out of secondary schools, compared to their Chicano peers who remain in school, tend to be of lower-socioeconomic status, are of immigrant background, and are more likely to be proficient in Spanish than English. Thus, one can readily identify a host of correlates to dropping out. As such, there needs to be a broad-based dropout reform agenda encompassing democratic education, universal access to high-status knowledge, bilingual education, parental involvement, economic restructuring of schools and society, and so much more.

The academic and social contexts of schooling

In Chapter 3 of the present book, authors Valencia, Menchaca, and Donato provide, in part, an overview of the problems associated with Chicano students attending segregated schools. There is no doubt that the widespread forced segregation of Chicano students in the 1920s in the Southwest cast a rigid mold for the schooling of future generations of Chicano children and youths. Furthermore, as Valencia *et al.* underscore, the current segregation of Chicano students is intensifying.

Any sustained discussion concerned with the realization of Chicano school success must have school desegregation and integration as part of its agenda. This is so because school segregation creates two major conditions that lead to adverse outcomes. First, there is the *academic* context. The isolation of Chicano students is negatively correlated with a number of academic achievement indices. As the school segregation of Chicano students in bi- or multiethnic/multiracial districts increases, achievement scores tend to decline. As well, the percentages of students enrolling in college preparatory classes and matriculating to college tend to decrease. Second there is the *social* context of school segregation. The isolation of Chicano students from their White peers—and vice versa—disallows racial/ethnic contact, which is a necessary social condition for prejudice reduction, interracial/interethnic sharing and cooperation, and appreciation of cultural diversity. In a nation that often boasts of its culturally diverse population, it is shameful that children and youths of such diverse backgrounds do not share the same schools, classrooms, and resources in an equitable fashion. As our society becomes more and more racially/ethnically diverse in the decades ahead, we have a grand opportunity to see that students of different backgrounds attend the same schools in an integrated manner. As noted by scholars at the Institute on Race & Poverty (2000):

> The goal of integrated schools goes beyond educating students in an inclusive and multicultural environment—the desired result is to integrate the minds of students, to prepare them for a pluralist society by drawing out the diversity and relationships that have always been a part of the world.
>
> (p. 4)

Although the goal of striving for school integration is a noble one, we must be cognizant that America's courts and various Presidential Administrations have turned their backs on school desegregation. In 1999, Orfield and Yun commented:

> As the century nears its end, we are a decade into the resegregation of our nation's schools. At the beginning of the twentieth century, the great black sociologist, W.E.B. DuBois, said that "The problem of the twentieth century is the problem of the color line." In the middle of this century the Supreme Court directly challenged the color line in American schools and began decades of political and legal struggle over access for minority students to integrated schools. For several decades it appeared that a permanent turning point had been reached for African American students as the South became the most desegregated region even through the Reagan Administration's efforts to end court orders, desegregation continued to increase. By the 1990s things began to turn back.
>
> As the new century approaches we have become a far more racially and ethnically mixed nation, but in our schools, the color lines of increasing racial and ethnic separation are rising. There have not been any significant political or legal initiatives to offset this trend for a quarter century. Although the Clinton Administration has seen the largest increases in segregation in the last half century, it has proposed no policies to offset the trend and has not included the issue among its priorities for education policy. Secretary Richard Riley's recent speech on the 45th anniversary of the *Brown* case praised the great decision but said nothing about the increasing turn toward segregation. Most important, the Supreme Court, which opened the possibility of desegregated

education in the 1950s has taken decisive steps to end desegregation plans in the 1990s and some lower courts are prohibiting even voluntary local plans.

(p. 5)

Yet, notwithstanding the demise of school desegregation and integration, we must push forward with efforts to demand interracial/interethnic schooling for all students. Valencia *et al.* (Chapter 3, current book) and Orfield (2001) offers a number of concrete suggestions as to how school integration can be realized (e.g., residential integration; expansion of magnet programs; two-way bilingual education). On a final point, it is important to note that racial/ethnic isolation of Chicanos and other minorities can even occur in desegregated, racially/ethnically diverse schools via "academic resegregation" (see Valencia *et al.*, Chapter 3). This form of segregation, tracking, is just as invidious as the segregation of entire schools. A number of scholars have developed suggestions as to how to "untrack" resegregated schools (see, e.g., Wheelock, 1992).

The Mexican American English language learner and bilingual education

A very important group in the Mexican American student population that is deserving of considerable attention is the English language learner (ELL) sector, the subject of two chapters in the present volume (García and Wiese, Chapter 5; Guerrero, Chapter 6). Mexican American and other Latino ELLs are greatly neglected and underserved, especially immigrant students in U.S. secondary schools (see Ruiz-de-Velasco *et al.*, 2000). Particularly painful has been the recent victimization of elementary school ELLs in California and Arizona, two Southwestern states that have dismantled their bilingual education programs via plebiscites. These pedagogically unsound, ill-informed English-only mandates are having profound, negative impact on hundreds of thousands of ELLs. Legal challenges to these oppressive and regressive propositions must continue, as bilingual education has been found, empirically, to foster school success for the Mexican American ELL. In states where bilingual education is still allowed (e.g., Texas), researchers, practitioners, and policymakers need to combine forces and work together *now* to ensure that bilingual education is safe from the anti-bilingual education ideologues, and that such programs be expanded to reach all ELLs that are eligible.

Chicano parental involvement in education

In Chapter 8 of the current book, Moreno and Valencia covered the important topic of Chicano parental involvement in the education of their children. As the authors discuss, the research evidence is clear: Parental involvement is positively associated with children's academic performance. This critical home–school connection must be recognized and advocated in any discussion of the means to realize Chicano school success. On a personal note, now that I am a father of school children (Juan and Carlos, grade 5), my wife and I truly understand and appreciate the importance of parental involvement, particularly in the supervising of, and assisting with, our children's homework.

Notwithstanding the importance of Chicano parental involvement in their children's education, we need to be aware of the personal/psychological, contextual, and sociocultural variables related to parental involvement (Moreno and Valencia, Chapter 8). Especially salient in discussions of promoting Chicano school success is the contextual level. As the literature informs us, some Chicano parents view schools as being cold and indifferent toward them. Such feelings by Chicano parents underscore the reality that parental involvement is a two-way process. Schools and teachers need to be encouraging, hospitable, and respectful toward Chicano parents, especially non-English-speaking parents who may be unfamiliar with the policies and procedures of schools.

The assessment context of schooling

Chicano students, as all students, must undergo the academic assessment of their abilities. The vast proportion of such assessment occurs in the mainstream (e.g., grading of homework assignments; state-mandated testing), and lesser so in the tributary of special education (e.g., diagnosis of a specific learning disability). In Chapter 9 of the present volume, Valencia, Villarreal, and Salinas provide comprehensive coverage of a number of testing and assessment issues germane to Chicano students (e.g., cultural bias in cognitive instruments; under-identification of gifted Chicanos). The authors also provide a number of research and policy oriented suggestions for how testing and assessment could be improved to help promote school success for Chicano students. One of these suggestions, in particular, needs to be reiterated. Two principles should constitute the *sine qua non* of educational assessment for *all* students: (a) no major decision should be made on the basis of test scores alone; and (b) no test should carry determinative weight, even when other assessment data are available. These two principles, combined, form the basis of what is known as the use of "multiple data sources" in assessment. If schools were to abide by this best-case practice, Chicano students would be partially relieved from widespread test abuse, especially in the practice of high-stakes testing.

Democratic education

Since the beginning of public education in the U.S., there has never been agreement that schools promote school success for *all* students. Hence, there has been an ongoing debate of what constitutes workable school reform. Pearl's analysis (Chapter 11, present book) points rather clearly to those strategies that have *not* shown to be successful (e.g., compensatory education). On the other hand, his ideas about "democratic education" offer us a promising vision of what it will take, in part, to achieve Chicano school success. I believe that his notions of students' rights, equal encouragement, useful knowledge, and so forth, can serve as beacons for structuring and implementing school success for Chicanos. As Pearl notes, the bottom line of workable school reform is to connect education with political action. In the years ahead, failure to pay attention to the linkages of schooling with a number of social issues, macrolevel policies, and the features of democratic education will very likely result in the continuation of Chicano schooling problems.

Although the plight of Chicano students persists, there must be optimism as we travel the road to Chicano school success. It is important to continue with a "language of critique," but also to make room for a "language of possibility." *¡Sí se puede!* It is also critical to embrace the Chicano community in order to share its views on how to attain school success for Chicano students. Community participation in school reform, if designed right, can be an emancipating democratic activity. Then, there is the curriculum. It is important to develop a perspective that curricular practices with Chicanos should incorporate aspects of equity, shared ownership, and empowerment. We also need to keep in mind that Chicano school success is intricately tied to macrolevel realities and thus any ultimate reform needs to be viewed in the context of counter-hegemonic potential. And finally, there are Chicano students themselves. We should adopt a view that the educability of Chicano students is without limits. We also need to value and guide Chicano children and youths as well as to learn from them. Most importantly, Chicano children, youths, and adults need to discuss, together, their visions and plans as to how education can help them create a better life and world.

References

Institute on Race & Poverty. (2000). *Student voices across the spectrum: The Educational Integration Initiatives Project*. Minneapolis: University of Minnesota Law School.

Orfield, G. (2001). *Schools more separate: Consequences of a decade of research*. The Civil Rights Project, Harvard University. Cambridge, MA: Harvard University. Available online at: http://www.law.harvard.edu/groups/civilrights/publications/schoolsseparate.pdf

Orfield, G. and Yun, J.T. (1999). *Resegregation in American schools*. The Civil Rights Project, Harvard University. Cambridge, MA: Harvard University. Available online at: http://www.law.harvard.edu/groups/civilrights.

Ruiz-de-Velasco, J., Fix, M. and Clewell, B.C. (2000). *Overlooked and underserved: Immigrant students in U.S. secondary schools*. Washington, DC: Urban Institute.

Wheelock, A. (1992). *Crossing the tracks: How "untracking" can save America's schools*. New York: New Press.

Index